The Survey of Kent

Documents relating to the survey of the county conducted in 1086

Colin Flight

BAR British Series 506
2010

Published in 2016 by
BAR Publishing, Oxford

BAR British Series 506

The Survey of Kent

ISBN 978 1 4073 0541 7

BAR Publishing is the trading name of British Archaeological Reports (Oxford) Ltd. British Archaeological Reports was first incorporated in 1974 to publish the BAR Series, International and British. In 1992 Hadrian Books Ltd became part of the BAR group. This volume was originally published by Archaeopress in conjunction with British Archaeological Reports (Oxford) Ltd / Hadrian Books Ltd, the Series principal publisher, in 2010. This present volume is published by BAR Publishing, 2016.

Printed in England

BAR
PUBLISHING

BAR titles are available from:

BAR Publishing
122 Banbury Rd, Oxford, OX2 7BP, UK
EMAIL info@barpublishing.com
PHONE +44 (0)1865 310431
FAX +44 (0)1865 316916
www.barpublishing.com

For Jennifer

Contents

List of tables

List of figures

Preface

We live in exciting times. Fifteen years ago, when I was thinking about Rochester bridge, I needed to get hold of a copy of William Lambard's *Perambulation of Kent* (1576). There was, back then, no easy way for me to do that. What I did was wait until I had a chance to visit Washington; and there I was able to look at two copies of the book, one in the Library of Congress and the other in the Folger Shakespeare Library. Now, in the space of a minute, I can be reading that book in the comfort of my own home, sipping at a cup of coffee meanwhile, if I feel so inclined. The first edition (two variants), the second edition, the third edition (three variants) – all are instantly available through Early English Books Online. There is nothing special about that particular book: almost every book published in England before 1700 can now be found on EEBO. Moreover, a very large number of books published between 1700 and 1800 – but regrettably not the first edition of Hasted's *History of Kent* (1778–99) – can be found through Eighteenth Century Collections Online. (But sometimes one has to keep trying: though searching for 'thorpe' will not find Thorpe (1769), searching for 'roffense' will.)

It is strange to be living in a world turned upside down. All at once, old books have become more accessible than new ones. If I want to look at the 'Laws of King Edward', the first printed edition (Lambard 1568) is only a few mouse-clicks away; if I want to see the most recent edition, I have to visit a library which owns a copy of the book – or else buy a copy for myself. This situation is absurd, and cannot possibly be endured for long. But how we are going to escape from it is not so easy to predict.

Month by month, more good things are appearing on the web. I have only just discovered, for example, that images of some selected pages from an important Rochester manuscript (Strood, Medway Archives, DRc/R1) can be found online at ttpadd.bl.uk/ttp_software/silverlight/default.html. (The selection includes five pages from the cartulary, the manuscript I call R1: 119r, 116v–7r, 176v–7r, 220v–1r. Since the contents of these last two pages are printed below (pp. 240–2), anyone who wants to develop some skill in reading twelfth-century script has an easy opportunity to do so.)

Four years ago, I expressed the hope that this book might be finished within a year or two. It has taken much longer than that. There are various excuses that I might think of offering for this delay. They sound vaguely convincing to me; but they will not be of any interest to the reader. At all events, the book is finally finished. Here it is, such as it is.

It is a pleasure for me to be able to renew my thanks to two people in particular, Caroline Thorn and Tessa Webber. Both of them gave me the benefit of their advice while I was working on the previous book (Flight 1996); both of them have helped with this book too, and I appreciate their generosity. Once again, I am grateful to David Davison, but for whom the results of ten years' work would probably have gone unpublished.

Until almost the last moment, I had been thinking that it might be useful, for readers unacquainted with Kent, if I offered some guidance as to the pronunciation of Kentish place-names, the approved spelling of which is, quite often, either ambiguous or positively misleading. There are two books which deal with this question (Hardman 1933, Glover 1976), but usage changes, and some of the pronunciations reported by those authors have an antiquated sound to me. (I remember a time when my father called Greenwich 'grinnidge', but I, to the best of my recollection, have always called it 'grennitch'.) However, since I understand that the English Place-Name Society is about to start publishing a series of volumes for Kent, beginning with a new dictionary (Cullen, to appear), I have abandoned that intention.

(Besides, I would not wish to pretend to local knowledge which I do not possess. Though I grew up in Rochester, and got to know some parts of the surrounding landscape fairly well, I have spent no part of my adult life in Kent. Large tracts of the county are as much a foreign country to me as they would be to someone from Yorkshire.)

Though I think I may claim to have worked very hard to ensure that this book is accurate, I do not imagine that it is free from error. Though I think I may claim to have made some significant progress, I do not suppose, and would not want others to suppose, that nothing remains to be done. On the contrary, I would draw the reader's attention to an item in the index, 'lost places', which includes a list of more than twenty places which have disappeared from the map, and which I have not been able to locate with adequate precision. I am sure that there are people who know exactly where some of these places were to be found: if any of those people read this, I hope that they may be willing to share their knowledge with me. To echo what I said in the preface to the previous book, corrections, additions, or comments of any kind would always be gratefully received. The e-mail address which I quoted before is defunct; my current address, which with luck will last as long as I do, is colinflight@gmail.com.

The documents printed here are published by permission of the National Archives of the United Kingdom (pp. 78–85, 97–149), the British Library (pp. 214, 218–22, 223, 236–7), Canterbury Cathedral Archives (pp. 47–54, 55–64, 208–11, 228–31), the Dean and Chapter of Rochester (pp. 65, 222–3, 240–2), Lambeth Palace Library (p. 216), and the John Rylands University Library of the University of Manchester (pp. 289–90). Figure 17 is reproduced by permission of the British Library Board.

Some readers may like to know that the PDF files for this book were made with an application called TeXShop – which is not only free (www.texshop .org) but also so good that I cannot see why anyone would think of using anything else.

Green Point, December 2009

Sigla

Manuscripts from the king's treasury

D-ExNkSk	National Archives, E 31/1
DB	—, E 31/2

Manuscript from the archbishop's treasury

T1	London, Lambeth Palace Library 1212

Manuscripts from Christ Church, Canterbury

C1	Canterbury Cathedral Library, Lit. E 28 (CCA-LitMs-E/28)
C2	—, Lit. D 4, fos. 25–32 (CCA-LitMs-D/4)
C3	the lost cartulary attested by A1, C5, T1
C4	Canterbury Cathedral Archives, Reg. K, fos. 23–72 (CCA-DCc-Register/K)
C5	—, Reg. P, fos 11–34 (CCA-DCc-Register/P)

Manuscripts from Rochester

R1	Strood, Medway Archives and Local Studies Centre, DRc/R1, fos. 119–235
R2	British Library, Cotton Domitian x, fos. 92–211
R3	—, Cotton Vespasian A. xxii
R4	Strood, Medway Archives and Local Studies Centre, DRc/R2, fos. 9–52

Manuscripts from Saint Augustine's

A1	Cambridge, Corpus Christi College 189, fos. 195–201
A2	British Library, Royal 1 B. xi, fos. 145v–7v
A3	—, Cotton Julius D. ii, fos. 84–133
A4	National Archives, E 164/27, fos. 2r–48r
A5	—, —, fos. 48r–191v

For manuscripts in Canterbury, I quote the 'RefNo' strings (which are not case-sensitive but otherwise must be exact) to be used for consulting the online catalogue at www.kentarchives.org.uk.

Chapter 1
Introduction

Like visiting Stonehenge, looking at 'Domesday Book' can be a demoralizing experience. Knowing the name but not much else, people often come to it with exaggerated expectations; and then they are disappointed. The reality does not live up to the brochure.

No book ever written said everything that one might have wished it to say; probably not even the author was satisfied with it for long. If one reads it all, one reads it for what it says; one does not waste time complaining about what it fails to say. There have always been some people who were willing to persevere with 'Domesday Book', overcoming whatever despondency they felt at first. Anyone reading a book about that book is, I suppose, likely to be in this frame of mind already. It is the right attitude, and I have no wish to say anything that sounds discouraging (or at least not quite so soon). But there is no gainsaying the fact that the record of the survey has some severe deficiencies. From time to time, for other people's benefit if not for ours, we need to remember what they are.

Anyone living in Kent – here and throughout, it is Kent that I am thinking of specifically – has not much more than an even chance of finding the place where they live recorded by name in DB-Ke. If they live in what used to be a medieval town, they are certain to find some information (but perhaps not very much); if they live in what used to be a medieval village, they are quite likely to draw a blank. Figures 1 and 2 are complementary maps of the places which existed in late thirteenth-century Kent (existed in the sense that they had their own parish churches): Figure 1 shows the places which are not described in DB, Figure 2 shows the places which are. The places shown in the first map are the places for which one would look in vain; as the reader will see, they are numerous.[1] Some of the dots are disputable, but not enough of them to make much difference to the pattern, as it shows up in small-scale maps like these.

In any other county, we should find ourselves in a quandary at once. Could it be true, we should have to wonder, that these places did not exist in the late eleventh century – that the Isle of Sheppey, for example, or most of the Weald, or much of the Marsh were still uninhabited at the time? Was there some large change in the distribution of population, over the next two centuries? In Kent, uniquely, we know the answer to that question; or at least we have a good idea of the answer. Thanks to a manuscript written at Christ Church within a few years of the survey, we have a number of lists of parish churches belonging to the diocese of Canterbury (below, pp. 228–30). Even added together, these lists are not complete;[2] but they happen to be fairly comprehensive for the areas in question (Figure 3). It can thus be proved, by independent and contemporary evidence, that many places existed at the time which are not mentioned in DB.

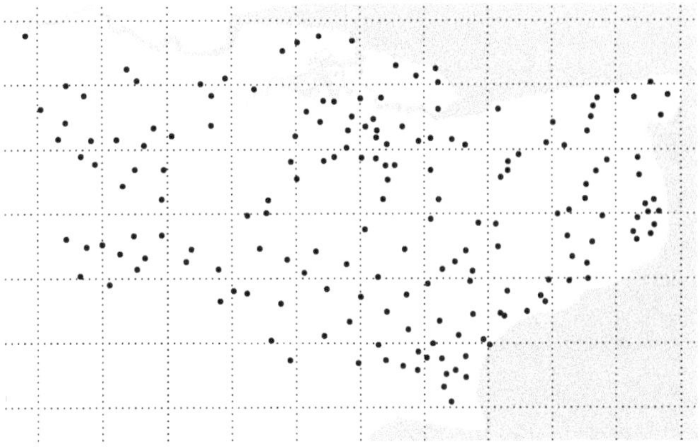

Figure 1. Places possessing a parish church in the late thirteenth century not represented by an entry in DB.

Nor is it any great mystery why they were passed over in silence. As we find it in DB, the record of the survey is organized manor by manor, not place by place. If a manor was large enough to comprise several places, all of the information was referred to a single place (the head of the manor, as it was taken to be), and the others dropped out the record.

The largest manor in Kent was the king's manor of Milton, and there are more than twenty places, demonstrably in existence at the time (including those in Sheppey), which have been tacitly absorbed into DB's description of Milton. On a smaller but still significant scale, the same thing has happened elsewhere. The archbishop's manor of Orpington, the earl's manor of Hoo, the abbot's manor of Northbourne – these and other paragraphs in DB appear to be descriptions of single places but in fact are descriptions of several places, consolidated into one.

[1] In case anyone thinks of counting them, I note that the number of dots in this map is 180.

[2] For one thing, they purposely omit most of the churches which belonged to Saint Augustine's. The surviving lists of those churches, and of the churches in the diocese of Rochester, are of rather later date; so they do not prove, beyond a shadow of doubt, that the churches existed at the time of the survey.

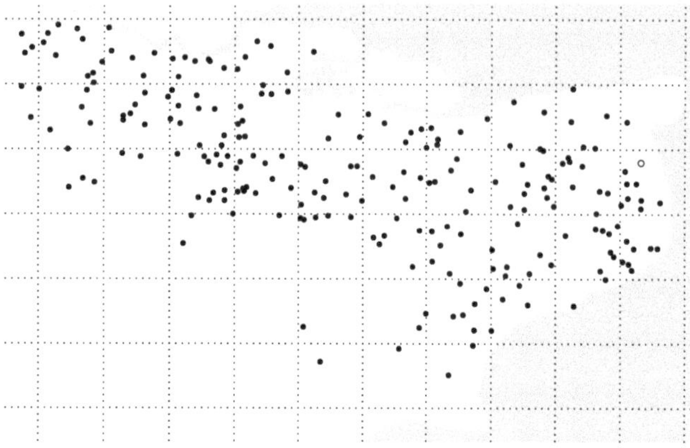

Figure 2. Places possessing a parish church in the late thirteenth century represented by one or more entries in DB.

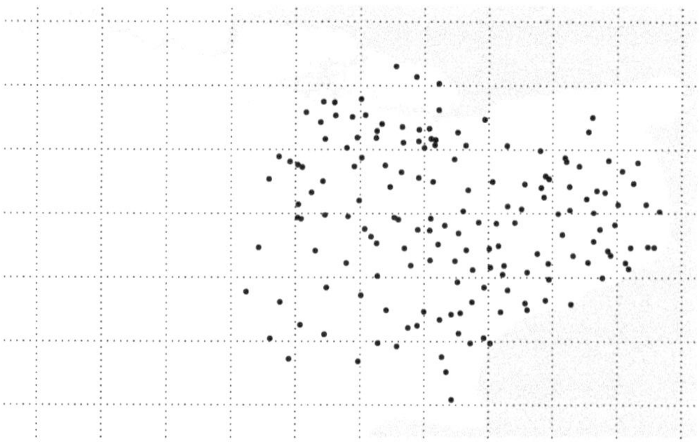

Figure 3. Places in the diocese of Canterbury known to have possessed a parish church in the late eleventh century.

In particular, we do not have to wonder whether the Weald was still an unbroken tract of forest, inhabited only seasonally by herds of pigs and the people who were there to look after them. There may have been a time when that was true; but it had ceased to be true by the late eleventh century. Though the Weald is almost blank in DB, we know for a fact that there were churches here already – and the existence of churches is proof in itself that parts of the forest had been cleared and brought under the plough, and that people were settled here permanently, in numbers sufficient to maintain a priest who would marry them, baptize their children, bury their dead. But these people were – as, by and large, their descendants continued to be – the tenants of manors located further north. Because of the way in which DB is organized, whatever information was recorded about these places was included in the paragraph about that distant manor.

Not just in the Weald but everywhere, that is the nub of the problem. The description of a single manor need not be (and often is not) the description of a single place. Some of the assets that are listed may have been in other places, perhaps a long way off. If we want to know how many mills there were on the manor of Milton, the DB scribe is happy to tell us; but he did not mean to imply that these mills all stood within fifteen minutes' walk of Milton church. And that raises the question how far it makes any sense to try plotting the data on a map, given that the only way to do this is by way of the assumption – never safe and often sure to be wrong – that the data can all be referred to the head of the manor.

1

From the late thirteenth century onwards, we are constantly being told that Kent is a peculiar place, very different, in some important respects, from any other county. Knight's service is the same here as anywhere else, but the peasantry enjoys a form of tenure which is found only in Kent. This tenure has its own name, gavelkind, and that name connotes a number of distinctive features. When a man dies, his land is divided equally between his sons, if he has more than one (or equally between his daughters, if he has no sons). If he is convicted of some felony and hanged, his heirs will still inherit. If he leaves a widow, she is to have half of his land (not one third of it) by way of dower. If the heir or heirs are under age, custody goes to some member of the family (the closest relative who has no prospect of inheriting the land himself): the lord cannot choose a guardian for them, nor can he tell them whom to marry. And so on. Broadly speaking, the effect of these peculiarities is to put the tenant in a stronger position, via-à-vis the lord from whom the land is held, than that of peasants elsewhere. By the thirteenth century, there were prominent families in Kent – the Cobhams and the Northwodes, for example – which had risen from among the ranks of the gavelkind tenantry. (They would not have been amused by being told that they were peasants.) Through the influence of men like these, the 'Customs of Kent' were finally codified in writing (in French, the language of the courts) and accepted by the king's justices as having the force of law.[3]

Anyone who looks at DB-Ke with the hope of finding evidence for the history of gavelkind tenure is – like Neilson (1932a) – sure to be disappointed. There is nothing to be found, not even the faintest hint. Nor is it surprising that this should be so. The commissioners who drew up the description of Kent had work enough on their hands without inquiring into matters not covered by their terms of reference. For the same sort of reason, the exchequer records, when they become available, are similarly unhelpful. The word 'gavelkind' does occur occasionally in twelfth-century charters, being used in a way which implies that everyone was expected to know what it meant without needing to be told. For people like us, who do need to be told, it is the records of the king's courts, surviving only from the end of the twelfth century onwards, which first

[3] The French text was first printed by Tottell (1556, ff. 147v–50v). Dissatisfied with Tottell's version, William Lambard produced a new edition (1576, pp. 416–27), with an interlined translation and a long introduction (pp. 388–415).

offer some enlightenment. (There is, for example, an interesting case which came before the court in 1223. Thomas de Nessendene (occ. 1206–14), who held Nashenden by knight's service from the king, was hanged for homicide, in 1219 or shortly before. Nashenden was promptly seized by the king and given to somebody else: there was no room for dispute about that. But Thomas had also held some land in gavelkind, from the bishop and the prior of Rochester, and his widow Alicia sued for half of this land by way of dower. By exploiting the fact that her husband had been a knight, she was able to invoke the procedure called *grand assise* (a replica of which was later developed for the benefit of gavelkind tenants), and in the end she won her case (*Curia regis rolls*, vol. 11, pp. 101–2, 193).)

Reading the records of the survey, one would not think that Kent was extraordinary. On the contrary, it seems to be a fairly typical county. Comparing its description with that of two neighbouring counties, Sussex and Surrey (contained, as it happens, in the next two booklets written by the DB scribe), one finds approximately the same categories of information, expressed by approximately the same collection of formulas. If somebody took a typical entry from DB-Ke and inserted it (changing one word) into the text of DB-Sx or DB-Sy, I doubt whether it would seem obvious at once that this entry was out of place.

As it is described in DB, the county of Kent has only two features which make it at all abnormal. First, the cadastral structure (if I may call it that) consists of two layers: a small number of large divisions on top, a large number of small divisions underneath. Most counties had only a single layer, but Kent was not alone in having two; the county of Sussex, to go no further afield than that, had a structure which was at least superficially similar. The only feature unique to Kent is the name that was given to the large divisions. As the DB scribe wrote it, the name was 'lest', and I think that he wrote it more or less correctly (see below). Second, for measuring arable land, Kent had a system of its own. Throughout the rest of southern England, land was measured in hides (and quarters of a hide, called virgates); in Kent it was measured in sulungs (and quarters of a sulung, called yokes).

The word 'sulung' was variably spelt (some scribes seem to have thought, for instance, that it should start with 'sw', not 's'), but *sulung* is a well attested form,[4] and most modern writers who have needed to use the word have chosen to spell it like this. For the DB scribe the word is *solin*; in the plural it is *solins*, and the final 's' means that he is treating it as a French word.[5] In its primitive sense, the word meant 'ploughland'. When people spoke of a sulung, they were visualizing a tract of land just large enough (as experience had taught them) to be tilled with a single plough. (Correspondingly, when they spoke of a yoke, they were assuming that a plough-team would normally consist of eight oxen, yoked together two by two.) By the eleventh century, however, the same units – hides elsewhere, sulungs in Kent – had come to be used for assessing the taxable value of every manor. Conventionally a sulung consisted of 200 acres,[6] a hide of 120 acres; when it came to the payment of geld, however, a sulung was equal to a hide. In almost every paragraph of DB, we are told how many of these units the manor has to pay geld for; so we are constantly reminded of the fact that in this respect Kent was unique.

Around more than half of the circuit, Kent was bounded by natural features – the river Thames and the sea – which left no room for discussion or disagreement.[7] The landward boundaries, with Surrey to the west and Sussex to the south, were more or less arbitrary: they were the outcome of decisions which might have been differently made. One stretch of the boundary with Surrey follows the line of a Roman road and is conspicuously straight for that reason. There may have been a time when people agreed that everything east of this road was in Kent, everything west of it in Surrey; but the line of the boundary continued to be negotiable. Somehow or other it came to be decided, for example, that Tatsfield was part of Surrey, not (as might look more logical) of Kent. We have concrete evidence for one adjustment made in the 1170s (see below). The boundary with Sussex is a sinuous line traced through the middle of the Weald. It resulted, one would guess, from a multitude of small compromises, whereby the woodland on one side of some stream or river was agreed to belong to Kent, the woodland on the other side to Sussex. But the details are all forgotten. People remembered the results, not the reasons why. Towards the east, in Hawkhurst and beyond, the boundary follows a stream which eventually falls into the Rother; and then it follows the Rother itself. Even at its widest, however, the Rother does not form the sort of boundary which people could not think of ignoring. It became the boundary, so far as it did, because people chose to let that happen.

At the time of the survey, there was a simple way of deciding whether some particular place was in Kent or not, provided it was under the plough. If the arable land was measured in sulungs and yokes, the place was in Kent; if the arable land was measured in hides and virgates, the

[4] For example, *ða seox sulung æt Wuldaham*, 'the six sulungs at Wouldham' (Campbell 1973, no. 34), *þara x sulunga boc æt Bromleage*, 'book of the ten sulungs at Bromley' (endorsement on no. 29).

[5] Masculine in French, no doubt, but neuter in a Latin context (3vb24, 5va42, 12ra22). Except once in the first paragraph of the main text (2va4), inflected forms of *solinus* or *solinum* occur only in one particular stretch of text (2rb1–48). In DB that stretch forms part of the preliminary section, where the scribe's usage is less consistent than in the main text – because here (I suppose) he was copying more closely from his source text.

[6] I do not think that there is any doubt about this. A puzzling passage in DB (2rb31–2), which seems to be saying something else, should, in my opinion, be read as a blundered attempt to say precisely this (below, p. 200).

[7] But there was, in fact, a small piece of Kent on the opposite side of the Thames. It was part of the parish of Woolwich; despite being on the Essex side of the river, it was agreed to be in Kent. Perhaps we might guess that the king had once owned some fish-traps here which belonged to the manor of Dartford.

place was not in Kent.[8] In one instance, we can actually see this criterion being applied. The manor of West Greenwich (meaning Deptford) was held by the bishop of Lisieux from the bishop of Bayeux: it was assessed at two sulungs, and (ipso facto) was in Kent (DB-Ke-6vb22). The jurors for Brixton hundred in Surrey are reported as stating that these two sulungs had formerly belonged to the king's manor of Merton; but they agreed that the land was in Kent (DB-Sy-30rb). The bishop of Lisieux held two other manors nearby. They were both assessed in hides, and (ipso facto) were in Surrey (DB-Sy-31va–b). Yet one of these manors (namely Hatcham) was – certainly later, probably then – part of the parish of West Greenwich, which was part of the diocese of Rochester.

As that remark goes to show, the outward boundaries of the two Kentish dioceses – Canterbury and Rochester – coincided very nearly but not quite perfectly with the county boundary. It was agreed that the Kent/Surrey boundary ran through the parish of West Greenwich (Rochester diocese). Where exactly it ran was not so easily settled: as late as the seventeenth century, this question was still open to discussion (Philipott 1659, p. 161). (The question did matter, because prisoners who were being transferred from the custody of the sheriff of Surrey to the custody of the sheriff of Kent were handed over here; and in theory the transfer ought to be made at just the right spot, where one jurisdiction ended and the other began.) Elsewhere a few similar discrepancies existed; but they were only small, and it is unlikely that anyone thought much about them, or found them hard to cope with.[9]

The exchequer roll for 1176 contains an entry of particular interest. It is one of a series of entries resulting from the activities of a team of itinerant justices recently sent into Kent. A second-tier baron named Hugo le Botiller (occ. 1156–79), who held West Wickham and Cooling from the heir of Warin fiz Gerold, ended up being charged with the very large sum of 48000 pence, in part for certain misdeeds which he had committed, in part 'for a boundary made between Kent and Surrey'.[10] From this it seems certain – as was pointed out by Davis (1934), who first drew attention to the significance of this entry – that Hugo was negotiating for a block of land in West Wickham, west of the Roman road, to be taken out of Surrey and put into Kent. We can go further than that. As Davis saw (and as I agree), this block of land can be identified with the unnamed hide of land in Wallington hundred which in 1086 was held from the bishop of Bayeux by Adam son of Hubert (DB-Sy-31vb), the same man who owned West Wickham at the time (DB-Ke-6va50). And we also know that half of this hide, some time later, was given to the monks of Colchester by Radulf le Botiller, Hugo's grandfather (Davis 1934, p. 154, cf. Farrer 1925, pp. 190–1). As late as the 1150s, this land was still being said to be located in Surrey, and still being called a hide. But then Hugo applied for the county boundary to be diverted around it, and the land was annexed to Kent. Whether the hide turned into a sulung in consequence is something we do not know.

The larger cadastral divisions were seven in number, and the name which the DB scribe used for them is 'lest'. Nothing is heard of these divisions before the time of the survey; in pre-conquest documents (dating from around 1000) the only high-level distinction we find referred to is that between East Kent and West Kent: *ægþer ge of East Cent ge of West Cent*, 'both from East Kent and from West Kent' (Campbell 1973, no. 37), *ealra East Cantwarena and West Cantwarena*, 'of all the East Kentishmen and West Kentishmen' (no. 34). By the 1080s, the whole of Kent was divided into seven parts.

It was not the DB scribe's way to latinize indiscriminately, and he did not latinize this word.[11] For him, 'lest' was a French spelling of the English name; I assume that we are expected to pronounce it exactly as it is written. All the way through the main text, whenever he moves from one lest to another, he inserts (in capitals, against the left margin) a heading which informs the reader of this fact. For accidental reasons, these headings are quite frequently omitted or misplaced; but the rule is clear, and the scribe is clearly doing his best to follow it. If we filter out any variation in the wording or spelling by choosing whichever variant is more common, this is what the headings look like:

IN DIMIDIO LEST DE SVDTONE.
IN LEST DE ELESFORD.
IN DIMIDIO LEST DE MIDDELTONE.
IN BOROWART LEST.
IN LEST DE WIWARLET.
IN LEST DE ESTREI.
IN LIMOWART LEST.

Two divisions have the word 'half' attached to them – consistently so, except for an occasional mistake. Nothing is

[8] The only apparent exception (DB-Ke-5ra42) is just a slip of the pen. The scribe forgot for a moment which county he was in.

[9] It was Kilburne's understanding (1659, p. 20) that the parish of Beckenham extended into Surrey, but I cannot confirm that he was right about that. Towards the south, the parish of Frant (Chichester diocese) overlapped into Kent, and the parishes of Lamberhurst (Rochester diocese) and Hawkhurst (Canterbury diocese) overlapped into Sussex. Off to the south-east, a large part of the parish of Promhill, including the church, lay beyond the boundary with Sussex, but that did not prevent Promhill from belonging to the diocese of Canterbury.

[10] *Hugo Pincerna ... ccc m' pro diss' facta mon' de Roff', et item pro alia diss' Barth' de Caisneto, et pro diuisa facta inter Kent et Surreiam* (GREx 1176:210). The first two items are fines that Hugo had incurred – for dispossessing the monks of Rochester (presumably of land near Cooling), for dispossessing Bartholomeus de Caisnet (presumably of land near West Wickham). Half of the debt was (for reasons which are not explained) forgiven in the following year (1177:205). By 1179, Hugo had reduced the balance to 3600 pence (1179:117); it was finally cleared by his son (1198:200).

[11] Except once in the preliminary section, where, uniquely, the word is in the plural: *homines de quatuor lestis*, 'the men of four lests' (DB-Ke-1rb1–2). In one other place where he might have used a plural, he preferred to repeat the word: *in lest de Sudtone et in lest de Ailesford*, 'in the lests of Sutton and Aylesford' (1va1).

said to explain what this means; but it seems to imply that some yardstick existed – some notion how big a lest ought to be – which people could use to distinguish a half-lest from a whole lest. What this notion might have been is a question I come back to later (below, p. 11).

Four of these divisions (including the two half-lests) each take their name from one specific place: Sutton (near Dartford), Aylesford, Milton, Eastry. A lest, it seems, could be thought of as having a centre, perhaps the place where a meeting of the lest would be held (if it was the case, as presumably it was, that meetings did sometimes occur).

Two divisions are named after groups of people. Though recognizable as English words, both names are oddly spelt: BOR(O)WAR(T), 'the people of the town' (meaning Canterbury),[12] LIM(O)WAR(T), 'the people of Lympne'. The O's in the middle seem to be the DB scribe's contribution: he thinks that we may need some help in pronouncing RW and MW. More significant are the unexpected T's which appear at the end.[13] Though the DB scribe normally makes two words of it (except at 3va32), apparently we ought to read BORWARTLEST, LIMWARTLEST, construing the T as part of the third syllable, BOR-WAR-TLEST, LIM-WAR-TLEST, rather than as part of the second, where it makes no sense. It seems to have been thought by somebody – not by the DB scribe, who did not quite understand what was going on, but by some previous scribe – that in this context, between R and L,[14] a special effort ought to be made to pronounce the English word correctly: he wanted us to read 'Borwar(th)lest', 'Limwar(th)lest'. That is, he wanted us to imitate the sound for which an English scribe would have used the notation 'hl'. In an English text, I gather, the word would have been spelt *hlæst*. That is a common word, and its primary meaning is 'load' or 'burden'.[15] In Kent (so I suggest) it had come to be used in a special sense, presumably denoting some share of some responsibility: 'the half-burden of Sutton', 'the burden of the people of the town', and so so.

The remaining name, WIWARLET, is particularly interesting, for reasons which will become clear in the sequel. WIWAR is another name for a group of people: it means 'the people of Wye'. To this another word has become attached. The DB scribe spells it LET, which we are to read as 'leth'; it represents the English word *læð*. That is a known word, though not a common one: it means 'meeting', 'assembly', or something of that kind.[16] (Hence the verb *laðian* or *gelaðian*, meaning 'to convene a meeting'; hence the noun *gelaðung*, 'the act of convening a meeting' (or, in a religious context, 'congregation').) So 'Wiwarleth' will mean 'the assembly of the people of Wye'.[17]

After surfacing in the records of the survey, the lests drop out of sight again. For more than a hundred years, we hear nothing about them – nothing even to prove that they still existed, though that much we can take for granted.[18] The first to reappear is the lest of Aylesford. In 1197 the manor of Aylesford was given to the count of Mortain (the king's brother Johan), the lest of Aylesford to Willelm de Caiho (three syllables, 'ca-i-o'). Because this caused a loss of income for the sheriff, the facts were recorded in the exchequer roll (GREx 1197:25): the sheriff would otherwise have been receiving a payment of 32 pounds from Aylesford, of which (as we now discover) 6 pounds was counted as the proceeds from the lest.[19]

In the thirteenth century, as the evidence increases in quantity, the lests which appear in the record are recognizably still the same entities; but we discover that some significant changes have occurred in the interim. For one thing, the word itself has been latinized: scribes by now are accustomed to writing it as *lestus* (sometimes as *lestum*, but the word is more commonly masculine than neuter, so far as it is possible to tell the difference). The two half-lests have evolved in opposite directions: Sutton has come to be regarded as a full lest, but Milton has ceased to be regarded as a lest at all.[20] (Without the evidence recorded by the

[12] That is, BORWAR is short for CANTWARBORWAR, 'the people of the town of the people of Kent'.

[13] Unlike the O's, which are found only in the main text, spellings with T occur in the preliminary section too: *Linuuartlest* (1rb3, 1rb44), *Wiuuartlest* (1rb3).

[14] With one exception (14rb40), the T occurs only in this context, after BORWAR and LIMWAR, once also in the variant heading IN WIWART LEST (13vb22).

[15] When a ship departed from the port of Chester, there was a duty to be paid of fourpence per load, *quatuor denarios de unoquoque lesth* (DB-Ch-262va). With the addition of the French suffix *-age*, duties of this kind came to be called *lestage*.

[16] It was not peculiar to Kent. A document relating to Taunton in Somerset (a manor of the bishop of Winchester's) has the compound word *motlæð* (in a plural form): on the day when king Edward was alive and dead, the tenant of land at West Bagborough, 6 miles or so from Taunton, was required to attend *threo motlæðu … on xii monþum*, 'three meetings of the assembly in every twelve months' (Toller 1898, citing Thorpe 1865, p. 433). The text – edited again by Robertson (1956, pp. 236–9) – comes from the Winchester cartulary, BL Add. 15350. Written in English and attested exclusively by Englishmen (except for the local bishop, a foreigner appointed by king Edward), it is connected with bishop Walkelin's campaign to recover full ownership of Taunton, including the right to insist on the attendance at his court of numerous distant tenants: *et ter in anno teneri placita episcopi sine ammonitione*, 'for the bishop's pleas to be held three times a year without summons' (C-So-174r, cf. DB-So-87va) – *ungeboden*, 'without being specially invited', as the English document expresses it. I ought to have cited this document in my discussion of that episode (Flight 2006, pp. 71–3); I would have done so, had I not then been ignorant of its existence.

[17] In the preliminary section, not in the main text, Limwar lest is twice referred to as 'the lest of Limwarleth' (1va13, 2rb5), i.e. the lest of the assembly of the people of Lympne. (There is, by the way, no such thing as 'Borwarleth' in DB, only Borwar lest.)

[18] A writ of archbishop Anselm for the nuns of Malling (Brett and Gribbin 2004, no. 22), addressed 'to all the men of the lest of Aylesford', cannot (in my opinion) be genuine as it stands. (The address itself is suspicious: nowhere else do we find a lest asked to act as a court of record.)

[19] In 1199, when the count became king, Willelm de Cahio was given the manor as well (GREx 1199:59), but the two deductions continued to be recorded separately for several years (till GREx 1206:23). A previous comment of mine (Flight 1997b, p. 21) should be disregarded.

[20] Milton was always a large, important hundred, more or less separately

survey, we should not have known that such a thing as a half-lest ever existed.) All of the eastern lests have changed their names, but in substance they seem to have stayed more or less the same. The reader who wishes to explore this evidence further will find the facts recounted in greater detail in chapter 10.

During the second half of the thirteenth century, the spelling *lestus* came to be replaced by *lastus*. Presumably this change reflects some shift in the pronunciation of the word *lest* itself. In spoken French, the vowel took on a different quality; in written Latin, the 'a' spelling now seemed more apt.[21]

In its specifically Kentish sense, in the form *lastus*, the word survived for as long as records continued to be written in Latin (that is, a simplified form of Latin used as a business language). The latest documents of which I can say for certain that this is true are the accounts of the tax called the 'fifteenth and tenth' collected in 1570–1. The original accounts for Kent (National Archives, E 179/126/405–15) are written in Latin, and the word that appears here is *lastus*. By this time, no doubt, bureaucratization had advanced so far that inertia was a powerful force. The headings which form the framework for this account – *Lastus de Sutton at Hone, Hundr' de Rokysley*, and so on – were, very probably, copied unthinkingly from some preceding account. Nevertheless, the fact remains that in Latin, in this sort of context, *lastus* was still the word.

Thus, for anyone who got their first knowledge of Kent by looking at government records, it was easy to discover that this county was divided into districts called by this peculiar name (there were, by now, only five of them); and it was natural to suppose that what was called a *lastus* in Latin would be called a 'last' in English. William Lambard supposed just that. In the 1560s, when he was compiling his 'Topographical dictionarie' – the raw material for a series of books which he was intending to write about individual counties – he made himself a copy of a list of the 'Lastes and Hundrethes' of Kent.[22] In the winter of 1570–1, when he wrote the first draft of the first of this series of books – 'The firste treatise of the Topographical Dictionarie, Conteyninge the Description and hystorie of the Shyre of Kent' – he was still assuming that these districts were called 'lasts'.[23] The word does not occur very often, but whenever it does occur it takes the form 'last' or 'laste'.[24] When the book was eventually published, under the title *A perambulation of Kent*, the same word appeared in all the same passages where it appeared in the manuscript; but here it was consistently spelt 'last' – perhaps because somebody thought that readers unfamiliar with the word would be liable to mispronounce it if they saw it spelt 'laste'.[25] In sixteenth-century spelling (if readers will allow me to remind them of a fact which may seem too obvious to need mentioning), final 'e' is often just a flourish:[26] it was the context, not the spelling, which determined, for instance, whether 'breathe' stood for 'breath' or 'breathe', whether 'bathe' stood for 'bath' or 'bathe'.

Once Lambard had made his home in Kent, once he had let his friends read a copy of his manuscript, it did not take long before he was told, or found out for himself, that 'last' was not the right word. In Kent the current English name for these divisions was 'lath' – often spelt 'lathe', sometimes spelt 'lath', the latter fact being the significant one. Wherever the hint came from, Lambard was quick to take it. He dropped the word 'last' and began to speak of 'laths' instead. One of the final components to be added to his book – a stretch of text which he called 'The particular of Kent' (Lambard 1576, pp. 25–47) – is an English summary of the Latin document to which I referred above, the accounts of the 'fifteenth and tenth' of 1570–1; and here he translated *lastus* as 'lath' throughout, usually (but not invariably) spelling it 'lathe'.

There is no doubt but that Lambard was right to make this change in his vocabulary. Writing in English, he had to speak of laths. The earliest official document known to me which refers explicitly to the laths of Kent is a report submitted by the commissioners of array in October 1569 (National Archives, SP 12/59, no. 1).[27] Its heading begins: 'A

administered; but it was never – or almost never (Putnam 1933, p. xlviii) – referred to as a lest. If it belonged anywhere, it belonged to the lest of Shrewinghope.

[21] A parallel change affected the word *lestage* (above, note 15). In latinized French, *lestagium* was the normal twelfth-century spelling, but later on *lastagium* became more common.

[22] Lambard's manuscript was printed in 1730; the editor's name is not known to me. I have not identified the specific source for this list (p. vi), but any Latin source would have told him that the word was *lastus*. In the printed text the English word is spelt 'laste' six times, 'last' once.

[23] The first finished version of the book is represented by two fair copies, one retained by Lambard as his working draft (Maidstone, Centre for Kentish Studies, U47/48 Z1, some pages of which are reproduced by Warnicke (1973, pls. I–III)), the other intended to circulate (British Library, Sloane 3168, dated February 1571). The first was extensively revised and augmented by Lambard himself, over the next few years; the second has only a few autograph additions, including a note on the title page, dated January 1573, warning anyone who may read this copy that it is already out of date. (A third copy, which I have not seen, belongs to Maidstone Museum. It is reported to have been made by the herald Robert Glover (d. 1588), an Ashford man by birth, and to have none of the additions which appear in Lambard's own manuscript (Livett 1938, p. 247).)

[24] To cite just one example, 'a whole laste of thirtene hundredes' (CKS, fo. 104r), 'a whole Last of thirteene Hundreds' (1576, pp. 248–9), paraphrased by Somner (1640, p. 54, as 'an whole lath of 13 hundreds'.

[25] By contrast, the word 'last' (opp. 'first') is spelt indifferently with or without final 'e'. Similarly 'paste' should be read as 'past' or 'passed' – except once, in the description of the rood of Boxley, 'wyer, paste, and paper' (1576, p. 183).

[26] For example: 'Whiche third and laste opinion, may well inough stand, eyther with the firste, or the seconde' (Lambard 1576, p. 214). Of the words which lack it here, 'third', 'may', 'inough', and 'stand' can all be found spelt with final 'e' elsewhere in the book.

[27] Calendared by Lemon (1856, p. 344). The certificate has no date; a letter which seems to have been sent with it, signed by the same commissioners, is dated Ashford, 1 Oct. 1569.

breefe certificat of all the hable men, armoure and weapon within the lathe of Saincte Augustines, Scraie, and Sheepewaie, and within a smale parte of the lathe of Aylesfoorde in the Countie of Kennt'. Though this document is only slightly earlier than Lambard's book, it suffices to prove that the word was already current.[28]

Nevertheless, it seems to me that Lambard should have stopped to think, and that we should do the same. The word 'lath' meaning 'a strip of wood' can be latinized as *latha*; so why should 'lath' not be *lathus* when it means 'a division of Kent'? There is, on the face of it, no reason why a medieval scribe, writing in Latin, should not have written *lathus*, had that been what he wanted to say. The evidence seems rather to suggest that two different words are in play here. One of them looks like an English word which was borrowed into French. It appears as *lestus* or *lastus* in latinized French; and it survives as *lastus* in bureaucratic Latin long after French had ceased to be the language of government. The second word, no more similar to the first one than 'bat' is to 'ball' (or 'county' to 'country'), does not begin to appear at all frequently till English begins to be used as a language of record; and then we find it being spelt 'lath' or 'lathe'.

The confusion between these two words (if confusion it be) goes back a very long way – as far back as the time of the survey. For the DB scribe himself, there was no confusion at all: in his understanding 'lest' and 'leth' were different words. They did not sound alike; they did not mean the same thing. But a document connected with the survey, surviving as a copy written only a few years later (chapter 2), is (as I read it) proof that the words were already sometimes mixed up. In this text, in a half-hearted sort of way, we are sometimes told which division of Kent a particular manor belongs to.[29] Just once, the expression used is exactly similar to the headings that we find in DB: *in lest de Wiwarleth* (C1-3ra23). Another phrase used just once, *in læd de Wiwarlæd* (4rb51), might be assumed to be a slip of the pen.[30] But when we come across two references to 'the half-leth of Sutton' – *in dimidio led de Sutune* (3rb22), *in medio led de Sudthune* (4vb52) – we can be certain that the person who wrote these phrases was using the word 'leth' in a context where the DB scribe always used 'lest'.

Because of the absence of documents written in English, the only evidence that we can hope to find will consist of an occasional appearance of the word in some Latin text. I am not aware of any such evidence myself, except for one thirteenth-century memorandum drawn up by a monk of Battle (Scargill-Bird 1887, pp. 125–36).[31] The author of this memorandum was trying to understand what the charters of his monastery meant when they claimed (not altogether untruthfully) that there had once been a time when twenty-two hundreds and a half were, in some sense, attached to the manor of Wye. With this aim in view, he tells us how, in his own time, Kent is organized. 'In Kent there are sixty-six hundreds, ... and these hundreds are belonging to *leth*, and there are in Kent only six *leth*', of which he then gives us a list.[32] Unlike 'hundred', the word 'leth' is not familiar to him: he does not latinize it, he is doubtful how to form its plural. Perhaps he is not a reliable witness at all – but he has done some research into the question, and 'leth' (not 'lest') is the name which he believes to be current in Kent.

Every so often, the words did become effectively synonymous: for the length of a day, a 'lest' did turn into a 'leth'. In the thirteenth century, this happened regularly twice a year (below, p. 266), when the representatives of each fraction of a hundred (each 'borough', as these fractions were called in Kent) came together for the purpose of being harangued by the sheriff. Listening to the sheriff, these men were as close as they were ever likely to come to being harangued by the king himself. The hundreds met every three weeks; the county met every four weeks; so the meetings of the lest were relatively infrequent as well as important events. It may well be that for most people – the sort of people who spoke English among themselves and only spoke French when they had to – the lest did not impinge much on their lives except on these occasions. Given the circumstances, it does not seem unlikely that people might have fallen into the habit of calling a 'lest' a 'leth'. They came to speak of 'the meeting' when what they meant was the meeting of the lest.

For the sheriff and his minions, by contrast, the lest was something which existed all year round. There was, one would imagine, a constant flow of communication, spoken (in French) and written (in French or Latin), between the sheriff and the officers in charge of the lests. ('The sheriff of Kent to the bailiff of the lest of S— greetings. I order you ....') The English word *hlæst* (if that is what it was), by becoming converted first into a French word, *lest* or *last*, and then into a quasi-Latin word, *lestus* or *lastus*, had got itself built into the language of officialdom. Through frequent repetition, it remained part of that language. Unofficially, people used a different word, *læð* or *leth* or *lath*. But

[28] If anyone can find any evidence earlier than this, I hope that they will make it known. Catch-all expressions – such as 'shyres, ryddynges, hundredes, lathes, rapes, wapentakes, townes, vyllages, and tythynges' (Pynson 1515, sig. C2r–v), 'hundredes wardes wapentakes lathes rapes or such like deuisions' (Berthelet 1543a, sig. I1r; 1546, sig. C1v) – are not what is wanted; to prove the point, the evidence should cite one or more of the laths by name, or at least explicitly connect the word with Kent.

[29] How much weight we allow to this evidence depends on how we evaluate the text as a whole. Here I quote some isolated phrases; I leave it to the reader to recontextualize them.

[30] As the reader can see, the spelling varies, but *læd* is close to the norm. The character 'æ' marks it as an English word. The C1 scribe uses 'ð' elsewhere, but not in his copy of this particular text.

[31] It is dated to c. 1230 by Cam (1933, p. 22); the passage referring to Bertram de Crioil (p. 126) suggests to me that it has to be a little later than that, say c. 1240–50.

[32] *In Cancia sunt lxvi hundredi ... et isti hundredi sunt pertinentes ad leth, et sunt in Cancia tantum sex leth, primum Sancti Augustini, Eldinge, Sipweie, ... Srewincheope, ... Gilesford, Sutthune* (Scargill-Bird 1887, p. 126). The text is slightly corrupt. *Eldinge* should be something like *Edelinge*, *Gilesford* should be *Eilesford*.

that word was hardly even borrowed into French (except perhaps in some specific context); so it had little chance of being written down anywhere, till the time arrived when officialdom began using English as a language of record.

Anyone who has some prior knowledge of the subject will, I realize, find the last few paragraphs hard to swallow. For the moment, I am asking only for one concession: I hope that the reader will understand why I have thought it best to retain the word that was used by the DB scribe. This is not an original idea. Nellie Neilson, writing an introduction for the Victoria History translation of DB-Ke (below, p. 25), made the same decision. In the first few pages her usage vacillates, presumably to give the reader time to adjust, but after that she writes the word 'lest' consistently (Neilson 1932a). A colleague of Neilson's, Bertha Putnam, in the introduction to her edition of a batch of fourteenth-century documents, uses the word 'last' throughout (Putnam 1933).[33] This decision of theirs was deprecated at the time by two contributors to *Archaeologia Cantiana*; but nothing that was said by either Knocker (1934) or Ward (1934, pp. 9–11) persuades me that it was wrong. Neilson and Putnam were both very closely acquainted with the records of central government,[34] They were reluctant to suppose that the word was misspelt by every single scribe, in every single document where it occurs; and that reluctance seems justified to me. Ward's comments in particular are mostly off the point. Nobody is going to doubt the existence of the word 'leth', nor of the word 'Wiwarleth'. The question is (to put it simply) whether the DB scribe knew what he was talking about when he spoke of 'the lest of Wiwarleth'. Like Neilson, unlike Ward, I am inclined to think that he did.

There was no special Kentish name for the smaller cadastral divisions; at the time of the survey and later, everyone seems to have been happy to call them 'hundreds', the same term that was used in the majority of English counties. For the DB scribe, the word was French by adoption, *hundret* in the singular (where 't' should be pronounced 'th'), *hundrez* in the plural (where 'z' is shorthand for 'ts'.) In the earliest booklets that he wrote, he spelt it out in full quite frequently; by the time that he came to the Kent booklet, he was abbreviating it nearly all the time,[35] writing *hund'* or *hd'* and relying on his readers to understand what that meant. Twelfth-century and later scribes treated it as a Latin word, *hundredus* or *hundredum*, but generally felt free to write it in a shortened form, *hundr'* or *hdr'*.

[33] Nellie Neilson (1873–1947) and Bertha Haven Putnam (1872–1960) worked together for many years at Mount Holyoke College in Massachusetts. An article by Hastings and Kimball (1979) gives an account of their interlocked careers, but says nothing about their personal relationship.

[34] So was Helen Cam, who also showed some slight inclination to speak of 'lests' or 'lasts' (Cam 1933, pp. 23–4).

[35] It occurs unshortened only twice (9va3, 14ra39).

Despite the name, the divisions that we find in Kent bear no resemblance to the strictly regimented hundreds, each assessed at some large round number of hides, which occur, for example, in Cambridgeshire. The hundreds of Kent varied enormously in size, and some of them were very small. Though the picture that we see may be incomplete and blurred, we can be sure that this was true in the eleventh century; it was certainly true later on. (Of the hundreds existing in the thirteenth century, one comprised more than twenty parishes, and one comprised just part of a single parish.) Because of the multitude of small and very small hundreds, the total number is much larger than might be expected, considering the size of this county. In Essex there were 22 hundreds at the time of the survey; in Kent there were more than sixty, perhaps about seventy of them. (Later on the number fluctuated slightly but never fell below sixty.)

For as long as danegeld continued to be collected (at least until the 1170s), the measure of size which mattered most, for a county as well as for a hundred, was the number of hides (sulungs in Kent) at which it was assessed. DB does not tell us how many sulungs there are in the whole of Kent. If we enjoy pain, we can try working out the answer for ourselves, from the items of data supplied by DB – but there is an easier and probably a better way. Forty or fifty years later, the exchequer knew (to within a fraction) exactly how many sulungs ought to be paying geld: rounded off to three significant figures, the answer was 1050 sulungs.[36] That total did not include the king's own manors – the same four manors that we find described in the first chapter of DB-Ke. The numbers of sulungs reported there add up to 90 or so; and that brings the total for the county to about 1140 sulungs.

At that rate, the average number of sulungs in a hundred would be somewhere between 15 and 20; but it hardly means anything to take an average when the sizes vary so much. The largest hundred is probably the one dependent on the king's manor of Milton. Here we are told that there are 80 sulungs, and another 4 sulungs which are the king's personal property (DB-Ke-2va46–7). Of the smaller hundreds we can find some examples in chapter 7 of DB, among the lands of Saint Augustine's. The hundred of Chislet includes (as far as we can tell) nothing except the manor of the same name (12rb6), which is assessed at 12 sulungs. It turns out, however, that six of these sulungs were in Thanet (below, p. 185), and possibly they were being counted in Thanet hundred. If they were, there were only 6 sulungs in Chislet hundred. The hundred of Sturry seems also to comprise just one manor (12ra41), assessed at 5 sulungs; but the manor included some land (possibly half a sulung) at Swalecliffe, and we do not know whether that land was being counted as part of Sturry hundred or not.

[36] The unrounded figure was 1051 sulungs plus five-twelfths (Flight 2005, p. 375). If the geld was levied at the rate of 24 pence per sulung, as it was in 1129/30, the fraction would be equivalent to 10 pence. The exchequer was willing to overlook an odd halfpenny, but 10 pence was not a negligible quantity.

Given the sorts of difficulties hinted at here – difficulties which, on closer inspection, become not less but more and more perplexing – it is far from easy to decide exactly how many sulungs there were in any particular hundred. Approximate answers are all that can be hoped for. If we had a good copy of some large part of the B text, as is true for Cambridgeshire, or if we had a copy of some version of the geld account, as is true for Wiltshire and the counties to the west of it, we would know how many sulungs each hundred was assessed for; and then we might be able to use that information to penetrate the ambiguities of the DB text. Lacking any help of that kind, I do not see how we can hope for any definite results.

By and large, the hundreds recorded by DB are the same hundreds which existed in the mid thirteenth century and later (chapter 10). There are some changes that we can be sure of, but they do not add up to much.[37] Three of the hundreds mentioned in DB, Reculver, Chislet and Sturry, became merged into a single hundred, called Blengate (GREx 1179:118). Some of the other hundreds changed their names. The hundred which DB calls Greenwich hundred, for instance, was called Blackheathfield hundred in the twelfth century (e.g. GREx 1166:115, 1191:147), Blackheath hundred in the thirteenth. Stursete hundred became Westgate hundred, Barham hundred became Kinghamford hundred (GREx 1179:118), and so on. Even these changes may be illusory to some extent, because hundreds could sometimes be referred to by more than one name.[38] Rather than a change of name, the evidence may just reflect a change of preference for one name over another. Similarly it is not impossible that Reculver, Chislet and Sturry, though treated as separate hundreds for the purposes of the survey, were, for some other purposes, already being treated as a single unit.

Nine of the thirteenth-century hundreds cannot be found mentioned under any name in DB. One of them, Codsheath hundred, is in a category by itself, because we find it named – and explicitly identified as a hundred – in a contemporary record (below, p. 160). In this case, therefore, the question which arises can be put something like this. Was it deliberately decided, during the fieldwork phase, that Codsheath did not have the status of a separate hundred? Or did it just happen, during the compilation phase, that the heading for this hundred (which ought to occur at DB-Ke-3ra26) dropped out of the text?

For the remaining eight – Brenchley, Marden, West Barnfield, Great Barnfield, Cranbrook, Barkley, Tenterden, Saint Martin's – we get no contemporary help; but a look at the map will tell us one obvious fact. The hundreds missing from DB are among the southernmost hundreds – Saint Martin's out in the Marsh, the others deep into the Weald. DB's failure to mention these hundreds can thus be seen as a consequence of its failure to mention many of the places here, because they were mostly dependent on places further north (above, p. 2). Cranbrook hundred, for example, as it becomes known to us later, comprises parts of the following eight parishes: Cranbrook, Frittenden, Biddenden, Benenden, Hawkhurst, Goudhurst, Staplehurst, Headcorn (Kilburne 1659, p. 336). Since none of these places was mentioned separately in DB, there was no occasion for the heading IN CRANBROOK HUNDRED to appear there. Yet we know for certain that at least six of these places did exist at the time – did not just exist but had churches (chapter 8).[39] Those places of which we do catch a glimpse – such as Tudeley in Watchlingstone hundred (7vb9), Benenden in Rolvenden hundred (11ra6), Appledore in Blackbourne hundred (5rb33) – have arable land assessed in sulungs, villains with ploughs, churches of their own. In short, they are normal manors. It does not seem much of a stretch to say that people who were numerous and settled enough to need a parish church would also need a hundred court. But that is a matter of opinion. Because nothing can be argued safely from the silence of DB, because the B text and the geld account are both lost, we are left in a state of uncertainty, and will have to learn to live with it.

Subject to some further adjustments here and there (below, p. 267), the thirteenth-century hundreds survived into the nineteenth century. From the late sixteenth century onwards, it was normal for maps of the county to include some schematized representation of the hundred boundaries (below, p. 269); but no accurately detailed maps existed until the Ordnance Survey began publishing the first generation of six-inch maps. As far as Kent is concerned, the surveying was carried out in 1853–70, and the individual sheets were published during the interval 1869–82. Archived copies of these maps (some are slightly damaged, a few are missing) have by now been made available on the web,[40] and the reader who has not discovered them already is in for an agreeable surprise. It is astonishing to see what results

[37] For some places named in DB, identifications have been proposed which, if they were right, would imply some radical change in the hundred map. It was, for example, suggested by Ward (1933, pp. 69–70), that the place which DB calls *Neuentone* should be identified as Newington near Hythe. If we want to believe that, we must also be willing to believe that this place was taken out of Bewsborough hundred and put into Folkestone hundred. For other reasons (reasons which Ward was aware of but chose to disregard), that identification does not seem tenable to me. If dubious cases like this are discounted, the weight of the evidence tells strongly in favour of stability; and I think we should make it a rule not to allow any identification which involves the assumption of a change in the hundred map unless we are given some convincing argument for it.

[38] For example, in a record dating from 1219, we find Codsheath hundred called 'the hundred of Otford', Axstone hundred called 'the hundred of Sutton' (*Book of fees*, p. 269).

[39] One other Wealden hundred, Summerden, came very close to disappearing from the record (11va21). It should also be noted, by the way, that many of the hundreds which do get mentioned in DB get mentioned only once.

[40] The separate sheets can be accessed through www.british-history.ac.uk. Another site, www.old-maps.co.uk, has the same images stitched together to make a continuous map. This site has many good features, but unfortunately only a very small viewing window.

could be achieved with nineteenth-century equipment by surveyors who knew what they were doing.

The boundaries mapped in the nineteenth century – this has often been said but may be worth saying again – are certainly not identical in every respect with the boundaries which existed in the thirteenth century, let alone the eleventh. To cite just one example, the manor of Nashenden (near Rochester) was in Larkfield hundred at the time of the survey (DB-Ke-7rb31), and was still in Larkfield hundred in the fourteenth century (*Book of fees*, p. 1344); but it was inside the boundary defined in the fifteenth century for the liberty of the city of Rochester, a somewhat larger entity than the preexisting hundred of Rochester. Nevertheless, though in the nature of the case we cannot be exactly sure, in general I see no reason to think that the hundred boundaries had shifted to any significant extent since the thirteenth century. It looks to me as if they were, even then, already firmly established in people's minds, as well as in the landscape. People were ready to argue about many things, but (as far as I know) they never argued about the location of the boundary between one hundred and the next. In a suitably tentative way, therefore, I think that we can venture to extrapolate further back. As far as the evidence allows us to verify the facts, we are not going seriously wrong if we suppose that the hundred boundaries were already in place at the time of the survey – but of course it would be foolish to imagine that every single zigzag mapped by the Ordnance Survey had a real existence in the eleventh century.

As well as the hundred boundaries, the six-inch maps trace out all the parish boundaries with the same exactitude. Small-scale maps of the hundreds and parishes, based on the six-inch maps, can be found in various places – in Lawson and Killingray (2004), for instance. To make the whole county fit onto one page, some degree of simplification is unavoidable, and the disappearance of the smaller details makes a noticeable difference to the texture of the map. This is true of the hundred map, but more conspicuously true of the parish map. There were roughly 400 parishes in Kent, some of which were very small, and many of them had detached portions, the smallest of which were very small indeed – sometimes a few acres, occasionally just a fraction of an acre. To see the full picture, to make certain that no significant facts are being overlooked, one still needs to go back to the originals.

Even at a small scale, however, one phenomenon shows up very clearly when the hundred map and the parish map are superimposed again. Over most of Kent, hundred boundaries coincide with parish boundaries, very nearly without exception;[41] in the southernmost third of Kent, hundred boundaries and parish boundaries tend to be disjunct. Cranbrook hundred contained parts of eight parishes (see above), but not one entire parish. The parish of Cranbrook itself overlapped into the hundreds of Great Barnfield and Barkley (Kilburne 1659, p. 64). The parish of Benenden (Pollard and Strouts 2005, fig. 1) was split between four hundreds, and only two short stretches of the parish boundary coincided with a hundred boundary. This is, I think, an interesting phenomenon, worth discussing further; but I do not propose to do more than mention it here. (The first step would be to ask how far the same contrast is observable in Surrey and Sussex, and by asking that I would be exceeding my remit.) One word of warning should perhaps be added: the flat pattern as we see it on the map is intrinsically ambiguous. It could be taken to mean that parishes are generally earlier than hundreds – except in the Weald, where they are later. Or it could be taken to mean that hundreds are generally earlier than parishes – except in the Weald, where they are later. Either explanation would fit the facts; to decide between them we shall need to try to find some other evidence, so as to bring some time-depth into the picture.[42]

Unlike the relationship between parishes and hundreds, which was complicated by this element of contingency, the relationship between hundreds and laths was strictly hierarchical: every hundred was contained in just one lath. The same was true for the relationship between laths and the county as a whole. It was not in the nature of the beast for a hundred to overlap from one lath into another, nor for a lath to overlap from this county into another. But that fact has no chronological implications. It tells us nothing about the order in which these different entities were created.

For what length of time the lests and hundreds had been in existence, before they suddenly spring into view in the records of the survey, is already a difficult question. In DB we can find both lests and hundreds being mentioned in contexts which relate to the time of king Edward; but much of this evidence might be regarded as dubious, if we felt inclined to be hypercritical. When the commissioners wanted to find out what incidental profits the king could expect from Kent,[43] they put the question to the men of the four eastern lests, expecting them (so it seems) to know the answer. Those men did indeed know how things stood in the time of king Edward (DB-Ke-1rb) – but there is nothing to prove that they had gained this knowledge specifically through their participation in meetings of the lests. The best evidence comes, I think, from the statement concerning

[41] Exceptions are so rare that they challenge explanation – as, for example, when we find the parish of Stanford bisected by the Stowting/Street hundred boundary. In this case the explanation is easy to find. Until the sixteenth century there were two parishes here, Stanford and Westenhanger (Frampton 1915), and the hundred boundary preserves the line of the boundary between them. (It is a point to note that the addition of one parish to another did not entail its addition to the same hundred.) Another exception is Nonington, about which I say something in the commentary (below, p. 184).

[42] In this context, I suggest, it will be necessary to give some thought to a mysterious memorandum (Sawyer 1968, no. 1564), important enough to be copied into a Christ Church gospel-book, which was put into print by Kemble (1848, p. 217, from BL Add. 14907, fos. 19v–20r, from Lambeth Palace 1370, fo. 114r). An improved text (Brooks and Kelly, to appear) is already available on the web (www.trin.cam.ac.uk/kemble).

[43] It was the second team of commissioners who had this question on their list (below, p. 194).

some disputed land at Atterton (DB-Ke-13ra37–40).[44] Four groups of people – the hundred, the townsmen of Dover, the men of the abbot of Saint Augustine's, the lest of Eastry – had all been asked to testify as to the terms on which this land was held in the time of king Edward; and that seems to imply that the jurors for the hundred and the jurors for the lest were recognized as having some knowledge of the facts, independently both from each other and from the other groups of witnesses, and as having some status for expressing an opinion. All things considered, it cannot be seriously doubted but that the lests and hundreds did exist before 1066, in more or less the same shape in which we find them recorded twenty years later; but it has to be admitted that even for this unadventurous conclusion the evidence is far from strong.

There is one point of which I think we can feel reasonably confident – as confident as we can hope to be, in the absence of any evidence which bears directly on the case. The hundreds were there first; the lests were created later.[45]

Two lines of argument seem to me to converge on this conclusion. The first starts from the general complexion of the map of lests and hundreds. Suppose it to be true that the hundreds were there first; then what happened would be something like this. For some purposes the hundreds were adequate; it was not proposed to abolish them. For other purposes the hundreds were found to be unsatisfactory: there were far too many of them. It was decided, therefore, to group the hundreds together in such a way as to create a fairly small number of larger entities. Seen as the result of some such process, the lests make good enough sense. Suppose it to be true, on the contrary, that the lests were there first: then what happened would be something like this. For some purposes the lests were adequate; it was not proposed to abolish them. For other purposes the lests were found to be unsatisfactory: there were far too few of them. It was decided, therefore, to divide up the lests in such a way as to create a fairly large number of smaller entities. Seen as the result of some such process, the hundreds rather obviously fail to make sense. The result we would expect to see is that the lests were split into some suitable number of fractions (halves, thirds, quarters, or whatever) of roughly equal size; and the hundreds are a very long way from fitting that description.

The second argument starts from the fact that pairs of hundreds could exist which shared a name. In the thirteenth century there were two such pairs: Great Barnfield and Little Barnfield, Bircholt Barony and Bircholt Franchise. Great Barnfield was part of the lest of Shrewinghope; Little Barnfield was part of the lest of Aylesford. In every respect, as far as we know, they functioned as separate hundreds: except for the name, there was no connection between them. The same applies to the two hundreds called Bircholt; and here we have the advantage of knowing that both were already in existence at the time of the survey. There was a Bircholt hundred in Wiwarleth lest (DB-Ke-13vb22), this being Bircholt Barony; there was also a Bircholt hundred in Limwar lest (4ra2), this being Bircholt Franchise.[46] Given the observable facts – two small contiguous hundreds which share a name – it does not seem a great leap to infer that there was once a time when they formed a single hundred. If we are willing to make that leap, we have to ask how this single hundred came to be split into two; and the answer to that question is written on the map. The split occurred at the moment when the lests were created: the northern half of Bircholt hundred was assigned to Wiwarleth lest, the southern half to Limwar lest.

That is as far as I feel willing to go. The lests were artificial creations of relatively recent date; whatever that date may have been, the hundreds were there before it. Beyond this point, we are in the realm of uncontrolled speculation. The distinction between East Kent and West Kent (above, p. 4) was, I take it, superseded by the division of the county into lests, though it may perhaps have retained some vestigial existence – in the assertion, for instance, made by the men of the four eastern lests that they are not obliged to travel further than to Penenden for a meeting of the county court (DB-Ke-1rb39). I would not rule out the idea that the lests were brought into existence specifically for the purpose of collecting the geld, after it had been found by experience that some new machinery was needed. Since the geld was payable in two instalments, it could be that a meeting of each lest was convened twice a year, and that those meetings continued being held until they were eventually adapted to different purposes – the purposes for which we find them being used in the thirteenth century (below, p. 266). Again, though the figures recorded in the twelfth-century exchequer rolls (above, p. 8) are somewhat smaller than this, there may once have been a time when Kent was assessed at a total of 1200 sulungs. At that rate, if each lest carried a burden of 200 sulungs and each half-lest a burden of 100 sulungs, the total would come out right. But this, if it was ever true, had ceased to be true by the time of the survey. I am not suggesting that the TRE assessments recorded in DB-Ke should be coerced into adding up to a round number, or to the same round number for each lest (or half-lest). The order of magnitude is right; I am saying no more than that.

At the time of the survey, the scope of the cadastral structure seems to have been very nearly comprehensive. Almost without exception, it could be assumed that every place would belong to some given hundred, and that every hundred would belong to some given lest. Almost but not quite.

[44] Recorded, this too, by the second team of commissioners.

[45] At around this point, some readers may be expecting me to mention two publications by J. E. A. Jolliffe – an article (1929) and a short book (1933). I cite them here only for the purpose of saying that I shall not cite them again. The article is a conjuring trick which fails to come off; the book is a work of fiction.

[46] 'Franchise' because it belonged to the archbishop. In the jargon of the time, 'barony' was the opposite of 'franchise'.

There were already some exceptions to the rule – nothing like the number which existed later (chapter 10), but some.

To begin at the bottom, the town (or ghost town) of Seasalter had a peculiar status. In DB we are told only that it lies in Borwar lest (5ra15). A contemporary document – one which gives us the archbishop's view of the facts (chapter 2) – states explicitly that 'this manor is not in any hundred' (C1-4ra4). That form of words was used deliberately: it was a way of saying, but also a way of not saying, that Seasalter was a hundred by itself. Apparently nobody wanted to call it a hundred, perhaps because it was just too small, perhaps because it did not (so it seems) pay geld. And therefore some phrase was needed which would express the fact that Seasalter belonged to a lest without belonging to a hundred – that it was (as we might choose to say) coordinate with a hundred.

The town of Sandwich was another exception, and a much more important one. Again DB does not quite make things clear. Because the relevant paragraph is put into the preliminary section of chapter 2, it can say that Sandwich 'lies in its own hundred' (3ra7) without having to say which lest (if any) it belongs to. Again the other document is plainer: Sandwich, we are told, 'is a leth and a hundred in itself' (C1-3vb50), where 'leth' is to be read as a synonym for 'lest' (above, p. 7). Nowhere else, as far as I know, is Sandwich ever called a lest. It may have been doubted whether this name was suitable; but it would (I suppose) have been agreed that the hundred of Sandwich was not part of the lest of Eastry. This hundred was, however the fact might be expressed, coordinate with a lest.

Whether the town of Dover had achieved a similar status is hard to say. Since Dover was in the king's hands and Sandwich was not, the records of the survey give us a distorted picture. Dover is described in greater detail; but, because this description was put into the preliminary section of DB (1ra), it became unnecessary to say whether Dover was or was not included in the hundred of Bewsborough, whether it was or was not included in the lest of Eastry. My guess would be that the statement made about Sandwich could also have been made about Dover – that Dover too was 'a leth and a hundred in itself'. But the only evidence that I can cite comes from the passage about Atterton (above, p. 11), where 'the townsmen of Dover' seem to have been allowed to have their say on the matter, independently from the hundred and the lest. Two other towns, Hythe and Romney, were later to become allied with Sandwich and Dover, and with Hastings in Sussex, in the confederation of the Five Ports. Both places were in existence at the time of the survey; there is no doubt about that. What is doubtful is whether the men of Hythe and the men of Romney had, by then, managed to make any progress in disengaging themselves from the cadastral structure.

As things stood in the 1080s, the most significant exception was the lowy of Tonbridge – that is, the approximately circular territory surrounding the castle built at Tonbridge by Ricard son of count Gislebert (Ricard de Tonebrige, as he was also called).[47] Ricard held two manors from the king – Yalding in Twyford hundred, East Barming in Maidstone hundred – which are described in the normal way in a chapter of DB-Ke (14rb2–15), but nothing is said there about Tonbridge. Because of the disruption which the creation of the lowy had caused, incidental references to Ricard's territory occur quite frequently in other chapters of DB, but nowhere do we find a description of Tonbridge itself.

Though this fact has caused some puzzlement, the explanation is really rather simple. The lowy of Tonbridge was not part of Kent: it was, in a manner of speaking, a county by itself. If it was surveyed at all, it would have had to be surveyed separately. By the time of the survey (this much we do discover) the lowy had already contracted somewhat. Two preexisting manors, Hadlow and Tudeley, had been taken out of the lowy and put back into Kent. Ricard had conceded that he held these two manors from the bishop of Bayeux (DB-Ke-7vb2, 7vb10). More to the point, he had conceded that Hadlow was part of Littlefield hundred and that Tudeley was part of Watchlingstone hundred; therefore they were both in Aylesford lest, and therefore they were both in Kent.

It is the other side of the story which DB does not report: we are not told what Ricard had gained for himself in return for these concessions. In the light of later evidence, however, the answer seems clear enough. He had gained recognition of the claim that he held the lowy of Tonbridge (in its redefined shape) directly from the king on very special terms – not on the same terms as a manor like Yalding or East Barming, with which the sheriff of Kent might interfere, but on terms which meant that he was answerable to no one except the king. Was a team of commissioners, specially appointed for the purpose, sent to survey the lowy? If it was, why was their report not copied into DB? These are sensible questions in themselves, but there is little point in asking them, given that they only arise because of the absence of evidence.

Whatever it was intended to achieve, the survey was not intended to cover eveything. There certainly did exist a castle at Dover – but there is not one word in the records of the survey which informs us of this fact. Why should there be? If the king had questions he wanted answered, he wrote to the keeper of the castle and demanded an immediate reply. He was not going to wait for the survey to find out the answers.

2

The decision to proceed with a survey of the whole of England, officially known (in Latin) as the *descriptio totius Angliae*, was made at a meeting of the king's court in Glouces-

[47] The word 'lowy' is a stab at an English spelling of French *lieuee*, [lyœ'eə], represented in Latin as *leucata*.

ter at Christmas 1085 (ch. 10).[48] Over the next few months, in every county, a small team of commissioners – trustworthy men, qualified for this task by their knowledge of the county – carried out the investigations which they had been ordered to conduct; and the results were set down in writing (in Latin) in what I call the B text. For one county alone, Cambridgeshire, a large part of the B text survives – not in the original, but in the form of a copy made at Ely in the late twelfth century. If this copy had not been made, or if it had all been lost (as part of it has been), we should know almost nothing about the earliest stage of the survey.

For each county, the B text was organized cadastrally – hundred by hundred, village by village (ch. 8). The unit of inquiry was the manor, but the manors were located inside the cadastral frame. In outline, therefore, the text takes on this shape:

In Cambridgeshire.
– In Staploe hundred.
– – In this hundred Burwell defended itself for 15 hides in the time of king Edward.
– – – Of these 15 hides the abbot of Ramsey holds 10.25 hides . . .

Having descended down the hierarchy to this level, it then reports, for each individual manor, the items of information which form the factual content of the survey:

Who holds it? If not from the king, from whom?
How many hides?
How many ploughs does the land suffice for?
How many ploughs on the domain? How many for the villains?
How many hides of domain?
If there are fewer ploughs than the land suffices for, how many more might be made on the domain? How many more for the villains?
How many villains, bordars, slaves?
How many mills? What are they worth?
How much meadow?
How much pasture?
How much livestock – cows, sheep, pigs, horses – on the domain?
Altogether how much is the manor worth?
How much was it worth when the man who holds it got possession?
How much was it worth in the time of king Edward?
Who held it in the time of king Edward?

Having answered all relevant questions for this manor, it moves on to the next manor; in due course it moves on to the next village; in due course it moves on to the next hundred. Eventually it comes to the end of the last manor in the last village in the last hundred; and then it terminates.

[48] The next few paragraphs are a summary of the conclusions presented in a previous publication (Flight 2006); I cite the chapters where the reader will find a fuller account of the facts. Though I omit much, I mention all the identifiable elements in the parchment trail which recorded the survey's progress.

As soon as it had been completed, the B text was delivered to the king's treasury in Winchester. (Probably the deadline was Lady Day, 25 March.) The next step was for one of the treasury officials – the man whom I call scribe alpha – to collate the B text with the account of the payments of geld which the treasury had received. (The second instalment fell due at about this time.) Hundred by hundred, scribe alpha checked the entries in the geld account with the paragraphs in the B text, making sure that all the proper payments had been made, and that only the proper deductions had been claimed. If he found some discrepancy, as very often he did, he made a note of the fact; and the resulting text survives in the original for Dorset, Devon, Cornwall and Somerset (ch. 6).

During the summer months of 1086, every county was visited by a second team of commissioners (four of them in Worcestershire, probably the same elsewhere). Unlike the first team, this team was made up of men who had no vested interest in the county. That was a deliberate policy, as a contemporary observer tells us (ch. 10); it seems also to have been the policy for this second team, unlike the first one, to be headed by a bishop. A team of scribes (probably three of them) arrived from Winchester to meet up with the commissioners: they brought with them the B text for this county and the memorandum containing the treasury's queries. In the course of the formal proceedings, representatives of every hundred were brought before the commissioners. Their names were written down; the section of the B text describing their hundred was read out to them (in French); and they were required to swear that all the facts which the king had demanded to know were correctly reported there. If the hundred contained a manor of the king's, the commissioners expected to be told of any encroachments; if there were problems with the geld account, they insisted on some explanation. If the ownership of any manor was in dispute, the claimant was given the opportunity – now or never – to speak up, and some statement of the facts was put on record. And lastly, from representatives of the county as a whole, the commissioners demanded some statement of any facts, outside the scope of the B text as it stood, of which these men thought the king should be informed.

After that, the modified version of the B text was taken back to Winchester – together with a memorandum replying to scribe alpha's queries, such as survives in the original for Wiltshire – and the fieldwork phase of the survey was at an end, as far as this county was concerned. (Or so, at least, it should have been. But it is not unlikely that questions came up which the second team of commissioners did not have time to deal with on the spot. In that event, I suppose, somebody would have to be appointed – perhaps a third team of commissioners, perhaps a government official – with instructions to look into some particular problem, reporting back when they had got to the bottom of it.)

The B text was the end of one phase of the survey; it was also the beginning of another. Once the finalized reports began arriving back in the treasury, work could begin on the construction of a new version of the survey text, reorganized on feodal lines. From this new version, it would be possible to find out straight away, county by county, which manors belonged to the king himself, and which belonged to each of the his barons. (In this context the expression *baro regis* took on a special sense: any person who held a manor directly from the king was the 'king's baron' with respect to that manor. Quite possibly this person might be somebody else's baron with respect to some other manor, in the same or some other county. But in this county, with respect to this manor, he or she was to be counted as one of the king's barons.)[49]

That was the intention; and someone had worked out in advance a plan for its realization. The first step was the compilation of the C text. For each county, the C text consisted of a collection of booklets – one for the king, one for each of his barons – into which were copied the relevant extracts taken from the B text.

To fit the extracts into this new frame, some adjustment to the wording was needed at the start of each paragraph. The C text for Cambridgeshire, for instance, would include a booklet with the title 'Land of the abbot of Ramsey in Cambridgeshire', and the first paragraph would need to start something like this:

In Staploe hundred the abbot of Ramsey has a manor which is called Burwell. It defended itself for 10.25 hides, ...

After that, the rest of the paragraph could be copied word from word. The next paragraph would start 'The same abbot has a manor which is called ...', and the scribe could write that much straight away, even before he resumed his scan through the source text, in search of the next paragraph to copy.

Portions of the C text survive in the original for five counties – Wiltshire, Dorset, Devon, Cornwall, and Somerset (ch. 4). These were the last C booklets to be compiled, and by that time it had been decided to simplify the procedure by dropping the cadastral indications (which is why there are no hundred headings in DB, as far as these counties are concerned).[50] In all other respects, however, the surviving C booklets can be assumed to be representative. The most striking fact about them is the large number of scribes who participated in the writing of them. There are three scribes – I call them mu, alpha and beta – who worked on the C text for all five counties (and who also worked on the contemporary geld accounts); these men, it seems clear, were permanently employed in the treasury. The scribes who collaborate with them were men who had been hired to help in the work of the survey. They seem to have been organized in teams of three; for part of the time they were out in the field; during intervals when they were back at headquarters they might help with the writing of the C booklets. Even so, it was two of the treasury's men, alpha and beta, who did most of the work. In principle, the compilation of the C text is a perfectly straightforward business; the difficulty lies in devising some arrangement which will make it possible for five or six scribes to share the task, without constantly getting in one another's way. But it is not impossible for that number of scribes to collaborate, in a reasonably efficient fashion; and it is clear from the result that some suitable arrangement had indeed been devised.

Almost all of the information from the B text found its way into the C text; except that they were organized differently, the contents were nearly the same. Some information was lost, however, because there was no place for it in the C text. In the case of a village, like Burwell, which comprised two or more manors, the individual assessments were reported in C (such as 10.25 hides for the abbot's manor) but the total assessment (15 hides) was not. Nor did C have a place for one of the crucial elements in the finalized B text, the lists of names, hundred by hundred, of the men who had sworn to its accuracy. That information, if anyone needed it, was only to be found in B – which was, after all, the place where it properly belonged.

One after another, the collections of C booklets were handed over to a different team of scribes, the scribes responsible for the production of the D text. Their task was a simple one. For each county, they sorted the C booklets into some suitable order (there were no strict rules about this, though of course the king was put first) and recopied the contents as a continuous text.[51] The start of each booklet of C became the start of a chapter in D. Essentially the D text – which survives in the original as three complete booklets, for Essex, Norfolk and Suffolk – was just a fair copy of the C text. Its only original ingredients were the numbers assigned to the chapters and the index of chapters supplied at the beginning. Unless by accident, nothing was omitted. Nothing was added, because there was nothing to add – unless perhaps some report arrived, resulting from further inquiries in the field, which was thought to be worth recopying as an appendix to the D text.

The D booklets, amounting to roughly 6000 pages (3000 leaves) altogether, comprised the full record of the survey,

[49] The reader should be wary of the expression 'tenant in chief', which is meaningless by itself, but is often used as a shortened equivalent for 'tenant in chief of the king'. The phrase *en chief* denotes the fact that the relationship between this lord and this tenant, with respect to this particular tenement, is immediate, *sans moien*, not mediated by any third party. Everyone who owned any land (or any rents and services deriving from land) was 'tenant in chief' of someone; only rarely was that someone the king. In any case, this is the jargon of thirteenth-century lawyers, and I doubt the wisdom of borrowing their language to talk about the survey.

[50] The decision was made while work was in progress on the C text for Oxfordshire. Up to and including Staffordshire, the C scribes made a point of including cadastral indications (as is proved by the appearance of hundred headings in DB), despite the time and trouble this cost, even though these indications were inessential.

[51] If some division of labour seems desirable, that is easy to arrange. One scribe takes the upper half of the stack of C booklets; he starts from the beginning of the D text. Another scribe takes the lower half; he starts from a point in the middle. Each of them makes a booklet. Once the booklets are complete, the addition of the chapter numbers will be enough to transform them into a single booklet.

in this feodally organized version of the text (ch. 2). But that was still not the end of the story. One after another, the D booklets were passed on to another scribe, who (as far as the evidence goes) was not involved in the production of C or D. His job was to create a shortened version of the text, such as could be contained in a single volume. By employing larger leaves and a two-column format, by omitting some categories of information, by developing an assortment of abbreviated formulas for the information that he meant to keep, this scribe was able to compress the contents of several pages of D onto one page of his own manuscript. By the systematic use of capital letters and red ink, he made it as easy as he could for readers to navigate the text. (He also took it upon himself to change the order of the chapters, in line with some stricter notion of etiquette.) The manuscript which he created is a a very fine piece of work; but it is, essentially, only an edited version of the D text, rearranged, condensed and reworded.

This short version of the survey text, DB, survives in the original for every county (ch. 1), apart from those three for which the D text survives instead. (That is the fact of the matter: DB as it exists and D as it exists are complementary. How that came to be so is another question.) For one county, we have a copy of a portion of the B text which can be collated with DB; for five counties, we have portions of the C text which offer the same opportunity. For the majority of counties, DB stands alone, or very nearly so.

There is evidence from Kent which illuminates some aspects of this process. From Christ Church – that is, from the monastery attached to the cathedral church in Canterbury – copies survive of two versions of a text which seems to be connected with the fieldwork phase of the survey. Both versions are edited below (chapter 2); the first version has been cited occasionally but not printed before. (Unhappily, the only known copy of this version fell into the hands of correctors who thought that they were doing the right thing by making it agree with the second version; but they did not succeed in eliminating all the discrepancies.) In its longer version this text – which I call α – consists of three segments, covering respectively the lands in Kent of (i) the archbishop, (ii) the archbishop's monks, and (iii) the bishop of Rochester. (The restriction 'in Kent' applies to all three segments.) Though every other English bishop held his lands directly from the king, the bishop of Rochester held his from the archbishop (he was the archbishop's baron, not the king's); so it is not a surprise to find a description of the church of Rochester's manors appended to this text. But there are some features of α which (not for lack of trying) I fail to understand. In spite of these difficulties, I still think that it has to be read as the archbishop's reply to a letter from the first team of commissioners, who wanted to be supplied with some basic information about each of the archbishop's manors in Kent. (How many sulungs was the manor assessed for in the time of king Edward? How many now? Altogether how much is it worth?) Because only a few basic questions were being asked, it seems clear that this correspondence took place at a very early stage in the commissioners' proceedings – which means, I suppose, in early 1086.

From Saint Augustine's – the ancient abbey situated in the eastern suburb of Canterbury – there survives a single copy of a sequence of excerpts from the finalized B text for Kent. The text was printed by Ballard (1920); I edit it again below (chapter 3). The copy is late and somewhat inaccurate; some passages included in the text as it survives were certainly inserted into it at Saint Augustine's. Despite the errors, despite the interpolations, the origin of this text – which I call B / xAug – is not in any doubt. Somebody worked through the B text, looking for the paragraphs of interest to Saint Augustine. Having found such a paragraph, sometimes he just made a note of it (a single sentence giving the basic facts), sometimes he copied it in full. The cadastral indications were mostly omitted, but we can supply them for ourselves, with the help of DB; once we do that, it becomes clear that the source text was cadastrally organized, which is the proof that it must have been B. Luckily for us, Saint Augustine owned at least one manor in every lest; so these excerpts give us the full sequence for them. Of the hundreds only a minority are represented, and only a partial sequence can be recovered.

Here, in outline, is the shape of the B text for Kent, so far as we find it reflected in B / xAug:

In Kent.
– In the half-lest of Sutton.
– – In the hundred of Littleleigh.
– In the lest of Aylesford.
– – In the hundred of Eyhorne.
– In the half-lest of Milton.
– – In the hundred of Milton.
– In the lest of Wiwarleth.
– – In the hundred of Faversham.
– – In the hundred of Wye.
– – In the hundred of Felborough.
– – In the hundred of Chart.
– – In the hundred of Boughton.
– – In the hundred of Calehill.
– – In the hundred of Longbridge.
– In the lest of Borwar.
– – In the hundred of Canterbury.
– – In the hundred of Bridge.
– – In the hundred of Downhamford.
– – In the hundred of Chislet.
– – In the hundred of Sturry.
– – In the hundred of Fordwich.
– – In the hundred of Whitstable.
– – In the hundred of Thanet.
– In the lest of Eastry.[52]
– – In the hundred of Preston.
– – In the hundred of Sandwich.
– – In the hundred of Cornilo.
– – In the hundred of Bewsborough.

[52] The placement of this line is doubtful (below, p. 187).

– In the lest of Limwar.
– – In the hundred of Stowting.
– – In the hundred of Blackbourne.

For eastern Kent, where the abbey's manors mostly lay, this gives us a fairly good picture. More than that we cannot expect.

These are the treasures; other archives are less productive. From Rochester, despite the existence of an excellent cartulary compiled in the 1120s, the only relevant document known is an edited version of the third segment of text α (below, p. 65). The manor of Lewisham had belonged since the time of king Edward to the ancient abbey of Saint Peter of Gent (DB-Ke, chapter 8); the manor of Wye had been granted to the king's own foundation, the abbey of Saint Martin of the Battle (chapter 6); from neither quarter do we get any help at all. The biggest disappointment is the absence of any documents from the church of Saint Martin's of Dover – an ancient church, and one whose possessions came in for some special investigation in the course of the survey (below, pp. 196–200). There are no surviving records of any kind. The sad fact seems to be that the monks of Christ Church, when they got possession of Saint Martin's church (as they succeeded in doing in 1139), did not get possession of its archive.

From the evidence of DB-Ke itself, it is possible to draw some conjectural conclusions regarding previous versions of the text. Since we are trying to extrapolate backwards in time, the logical order runs in reverse, from DB to D, from D to C, and finally from C to B. But the few suggestions which I have to make are not dependent on one another; so I propose to reverse the logical order and follow what I take to have been the sequence of events. The evidence which I shall be using comes from the cadastral headings – not just from the ones which occur in just the right place (as the majority do), but also from the ones which are either misplaced or omitted altogether. Table 1 gives a list of the adjustments which I believe should be made to DB's lest and headings, for the facts to be described correctly: on the left (col. 1) are the headings as they appear in DB; on the right (col. 2) are the headings as I think they ought to be. Some of the entries (not just the ones marked with a query) are certainly open to debate, and I explain my reasons for including them (and for not including some others) at a later stage. For present purposes, this table is (in my opinion) sufficiently reliable.

Though it may take a little practice, the reader who studies this table should soon start to recognize some patterning. It sometimes happens, for instance, that a hundred heading occurs a little later than it should. In that case the same hundred will be noted in two successive lines, in col. 2 in one line, in col. 1 in the next. Two lines which pair off like this, such as the ones which mention Chatham hundred, convey the suggestion (which no one is going to dispute) that the heading IN CHATHAM HUNDRED is out of place: to put things right, this heading should be moved back from 8va2 to 8rb48. The lest headings too are sometimes delayed, and pairs of lines in this table reflect that fact as well. There is a pair, for example, which conveys the suggestion that the heading IN LIMWAR LEST should be moved back from 5rb32, where it goes with the heading for Blackbourne hundred, to 5rb28, so that it goes instead with the heading for Ham hundred. (It should be noted that lest headings do not occur in isolation: in DB they are invariably prefixed to a hundred heading.) Small dislocations of this kind could occur at any stage in the compilation process, and it is probably not worth asking at which particular stage some particular heading got put in the wrong place. Similarly, there is some tendency for the lest heading to go missing from the start of a chapter, but that is something which could have happened at any stage, in C or D or DB. Nevertheless, I do see a few indications, in DB and Table 1, which seem to point towards some specific conclusion.

It is an odd feature, possibly a significant feature, of DB that the lest headings are sometimes repeated for no apparent reason. (This happens first at 6vb21, where the heading IN SUTTON HALF-LEST occurs in connection with the heading for Greenwich hundred, though in fact it is redundant: this hundred is already covered by the lest heading at 6ra2.) For obvious reasons, there is no chance for this to happen except in a long stretch of text comprising more than one hundred in a single lest; for reasons which will shortly emerge, there is little chance for it to happen with the eastern lests (but it does happen once, with Eastry lest, at 11rb22). In effect this means that we are unlikely to find lest headings repeated except in the first half of chapter 5 – that is, the very long chapter (representing just over half of the whole text) which describes the lands of the bishop of Bayeux.[53] Where there is some likelihood of it happening, it does happen. Most notably, the heading IN AYLESFORD LEST, which occurs – as it should – at 7ra27 (in connection with Larkfield hundred), is repeated at 7vb9 (in connection with Watchlingstone hundred) and then repeated again, three columns later, at 8va9 (in connection with Rochester hundred).

We can, I think, rule out the idea that these redundant headings originated with the DB scribe. True, he might have thought that it would be helpful for his readers if he repeated the lest headings from time to time; but anyone acting on that thought would repeat the headings more often, and not in the places where we actually find them repeated.[54] We may assume that he found these headings in his source text (i.e. in D-Ke) and copied them by inertia – because he saw no particular reason for omitting them. If we agree to look for some other explanation, we may think it a promising idea that the headings mark the start of quires of D. This idea, as it seems to me, can also be ruled out.

[53] To be precise, this chapter accounts for 52 per cent of the text, excluding the preliminary section.

[54] The logical plan would be to repeat the lest heading in connection with the first hundred heading on each verso page – at 6va15, 7va1, 8va2, 9va3, and so on. That is not at all what we find.

(1) Headings as they exist in DB			(2) Headings as they ought to exist	
	Axstone	3ra18	Sutton	Axstone
		3ra26		? Codsheath
	Reculver	3va11	Borwar	Reculver
Borwar	Petham	3va32		Petham
	Boughton	3vb15	Wiwarleth	Boughton
	Longbridge	3vb46	Limwar ?	Longbridge
Limwar	Bircholt	4ra2		Bircholt
		[4ra10–18]		
	Axstone	4rb1	Sutton	Axstone
		4rb16		Helmstree
		4rb22		Westerham
		4rb29	Aylesford	Eyhorne
	Eyhorne	4rb36		
	Faversham	4rb42	Wiwarleth	Faversham
	Eastry	4va10	Eastry	Eastry
	Heane	4va17	Limwar	Heane
	Helmstree	4vb1	Sutton	Helmstree
		5rb17		? Adisham
	Ham	5rb28	Limwar	Ham
Limwar	Blackbourne	5rb32		Blackbourne
	Wye	5rb38	Wiwarleth	Wye
	Romney Marsh	5rb43	Limwar	? Worth
		5va1	Sutton	Axstone
		5va30	Aylesford	Larkfield
Sutton	Greenwich	6vb21		Greenwich
Aylesford	Watchlingstone	7vb9		Watchlingstone
		8rb48		Chatham
	Chatham	8va2		
Aylesford	Rochester	8va9		Rochester
		8vb41		Wrotham
		8vb49		Shamell
	Shamell	9ra24		
		9vb26		Bewsborough
	Bewsborough	9vb32		
	Barham	9vb35	Borwar	Barham
Eastry	Eastry	11rb22		Eastry
		[11va22–5]		
	Eastry	11va40		
		11vb15		Bewsborough
	Bewsborough	11vb17		
	Loningborough	11vb23	Limwar	Loningborough
	Bircholt	11vb29	Wiwarleth	Bircholt
		11vb39	Wiwarleth	Wye
		12ra21		Canterbury
		12rb24		Canterbury
	Romney Marsh	12vb32	Limwar	Worth
	Greenwich	12vb40	Sutton	Greenwich
		13ra2	Wiwarleth	Wye
Wiwarleth	Longbridge	13ra12		Longbridge
		[13ra37–41]		
	Blackbourne	13vb32	Limwar	Blackbourne
Limwar	Street	13vb35		Street
	Bircholt	14ra15	Wiwarleth	Bircholt
	Twyford	14rb1	Aylesford	Twyford

Table 1. Anomalies affecting the cadastral headings of DB-Ke. (Square brackets distinguish three paragraphs which have fallen so far out of the frame that they can hardly be put back in.)

The quantity of text contained between the two repetitions of the Aylesford heading occupies 1.5 pages of DB. By my estimate (Flight 2006, pp. 26–9), it would have occupied roughly six times that number of pages in D, which is 8–9 pages, not much more than half a quire. (My estimates are crude, but I see no reason to think that they are grossly wrong.) The same applies to C – but it does not apply to B. Of the contents of each quire of B, roughly half would have found its way into the C booklet corresponding with DB's chapter 5; and the other half, chopped up into pieces, would have been distributed among the other C booklets.

That gives us, at last, a plausible explanation. In the B text, it seems, there was some indication of the current lest at or near the beginning of each quire. For the rest, inertia prevailed. Because nobody saw why he should be the one to omit them, these indications were copied from B into C, from C into D, and lastly from D into DB. But how much is that suggestion worth? The argument is tenuous; the conclusion is of little interest, even if it is right. I mention it partly to make the point that we cannot hope to infer very much about B, however hard we try, when all we have to infer from is DB.

lest	hundred	D / DB
Sutton	Helmstree	4vb1
Aylesford	Littlefield	8
	Eyhorne	18
	Toltingtrough	24
	Maidstone	31
	Shamell	41
Borwar	Thanet	46
	Downhamford	5ra3
	Canterbury	9
Wiwarleth	Faversham	20
	Felborough	26
	Chart	37
	Calehill	42
Eastry	Eastry	5rb7
	? Adisham	17
Limwarlet	Ham	28
	Blackbourne	32
Wiwarleth	Wye	38

Table 2. Cadastral headings for the section of the D text represented by chapter 3 in DB. The headings absent from DB (which may or may not have been present in D) are supplied from Table 1.

A second suggestion which I have to make seems more convincing to me, as well as being of rather more significance. It is a striking fact that the eastern lests, as we find them represented in DB, are in a disorganized state. This is true, it should be noted, whether or not we make the adjustments recommended in Table 1. The headings, that is, are mostly correct as they stand: but sometimes they send us back to a lest which we thought had already been dealt with. To some extent, the disruption seems to result from sporadic dislocations affecting single paragraphs. Several chapters (3, 5, 7, 9) have one or two stray paragraphs at the end which look as if they may have been (at some stage) deliberately left till last because they were problematic.[55] But disruption on a much larger scale occurs in the longest chapter, chapter 5. On the face of it, this chapter ought to be a straightforward reproduction of the B text, lest by lest and hundred by hundred, minus those manors which did not belong to the bishop of Bayeux. But that is not what we find. The western lests (Sutton, Aylesford, Milton) are in good shape; the eastern lests are fragmented, and the headings tend to alternate (Borwar, Limwar, Eastry, Borwar, Wiwarleth, Limwar, Eastry, Limwar, Eastry).[56] Something similar has happened in chapter 9, where only three lests are represented, but where again the headings tend to alternate (Wiwarleth, Limwar, Eastry, Wiwarleth, Limwar).[57] Furthermore, in every chapter where they are both represented,[58] DB puts Borwar before Wiwarleth, though not just geography but also B / xAug would lead us to expect that Wiwarleth ought to come first.

These facts, I think, can only mean that the quires which made up the second half of the B text got themselves disarranged, before the C text began to be compiled.[59] To work this out in detail would mean arriving at some reconstruction of the B text, detailed enough to show where each quire began, such that some transposition of these hypothetical quires would produce results approximating to the results observable in DB. I doubt whether that is feasible; certainly I have not been able to do it. But something happened to bring about this fragmentation of the eastern lests; a transposition of the quires of B would cause that kind of disruption; and no other process that I can think of would have a similar effect.

If this explanation is right, there is one corollary which follows. At the time when some excerpts were made from it for Saint Augustine's, the B text was properly organized. Since it is not to be thought that B was made available to outsiders till after the C scribes had finished with it, we have to infer, not only that B was kept for some length of time, but also that somebody went to the trouble of putting the quires back into the right order.[60]

[55] The two paragraphs relating to Hastingleigh, for instance, one at the end of chapter 5 (11vb29) and the other almost at the end of chapter 9 (14ra15), look as if they may both have been postponed because it seemed doubtful at first how much of this place belonged to the bishop of Bayeux, how much to Hugo de Montfort.

[56] The second Borwar heading is the one which needs to be supplied at 9vb35. I disregard the two paragraphs at the end.

[57] The first and last of these headings need to be moved (from 13ra12 to 2, from 13vb35 to 32) but with that adjustment are correct. Again I disregard some stray paragraphs at the end.

[58] Except for chapter 12, where a sporadic dislocation has put Wiwarleth at the very beginning, even before Sutton.

[59] This would seem to suggest that the treasury officials had used the B text for some other purpose – a final check of the geld account, perhaps – before they got round to using it for this one.

[60] Whether this means that B was about to be bound is a question that I leave for the reader.

lest	hundred	D/DB
Sutton	Axstone	3ra18
	? Codsheath	26
	Helmstree	42
	Littleleigh	48
Aylesford	Larkfield	3rb5
	Toltingtrough	11
	Wrotham	19
	Maidstone	35
	Chatham	3va1
Borwarleth	Reculver	11
	Petham	32
	Stursete	43
	Barham	3vb9
Wiwarleth	Boughton	15
	Calehill	22
Eastry	Wingham	34
Limwar	Longbridge	46
	Bircholt	4ra2
	Loningborough	31
	Selbrittenden	42
Sutton	Axstone	5va2
	Bromley	25
Aylesford	Larkfield	31
	Shamell	5vb1
	Rochester	19
	Hoo	28
Sutton	Axstone	4rb2
	Helmstree	17
	Westerham	23
Aylesford	Eyhorne	37
Wiwarleth	Faversham	43
	Boughton	46
	Calehill	4va2
	Teynham	7
Eastry	Eastry	10
Limwar	Heane	17
	Street	25
	Langport	30

Table 3. Cadastral headings for the sections of the D text represented by chapters 2 and 4 in DB.

Third and last, there is something to be said about the D text. The cadastral headings as we find them in DB are, in two places, conspicuously more defective than elsewhere: in the subchapter covering the lands of the archbishop's knights (4rb–va) and in the chapter covering the lands of the bishop of Rochester (5va–b). This fact, I think, should be explained along the following lines. The C scribes, in dealing with the lands of the archbishopric, decided to make two booklets: one for the manors which (to the extent that the B text made this clear) were earmarked for the maintenance of the monks (the archbishop's monks, as DB calls them, i.e. the monks of Christ Church), and another for everything else. The contents of the former booklet were then treated in the regular way – first copied into D, then recopied in an edited form as chapter 3 of DB – and the cadastral headings came through that process as well as they usually did (not perfectly but fairly well). The contents of the latter booklet were treated differently. One of the D scribes decided (or was told) to distribute the contents into three separate sections.[61] Section (i) was to include all the manors which (to the extent that the C text made this clear) were held at least partly in domain; section (ii) all the manors held from the archbishop by the bishop of Rochester; section (iii) all the manors held by the archbishop's knights.[62]

In principle, that is not a difficult task. The scribe just needs to make three passes through the C booklet: for each section in turn, he selects and copies the paragraphs he wants, skipping over the rest. Nothing is likely to go wrong – unless some paragraph gets copied twice, or does not get copied at all.

When the text is reorganized in this way, however, many of the paragraphs will become separated from the cadastral headings by which they were previously governed; so the question arises whether to supply new headings where they are needed. Reorganizing the B text, the C scribes did make a point of doing that. Reorganizing the C text, the D scribe did not. Perhaps the question never occurred to him (unlike the C scribes, the D scribes were not required to exercise much creativity); if it did, he decided to spare himself the trouble. He copied the cadastral indications which were staring him in the face, but did not supply the indications which he would have had to work out for himself (Tables 2–3).

Why do we find a cadastral heading prefixed to the Bromley paragraph in DB (5va25)? Because Bromley was the only manor in Bromley hundred belonging to the archbishop. The C text would have said something like this:

In the hundred of Bromley the same archbishop has a manor which is called Bromley and the bishop of Rochester holds from him ...

In section (ii) of the D text, that turned into something like this:

In the hundred of Bromley the same bishop holds a manor which is called Bromley ...

and in DB that turned into this:

IN BROMLEY HUNDRED. The same bishop holds BROMLEY ...

Why do we not find cadastral headings prefixed to the following paragraph (5va31)? Because Wouldham was not the only manor in Larkfield hundred belonging to the archbishop. The C text would have said something like this:

[61] It seems best not to call them chapters. Whether they were to be counted as separate chapters or not would only be decided later, when the numbering was added.

[62] I see no textual evidence to prove that the sections were placed in this order, but courtesy would put the archbishop first and the bishop next after him. (In later lists of the archbishop's knights, the bishop of Rochester comes first.)

In the lest of Aylesford in the hundred of Larkfield the same archbishop has a manor which is called (East) Malling ... The same archbishop has a manor which is called Wouldham and the bishop of Rochester holds from him ...

In D the first of these paragraphs went into section (i), carrying with it the cadastral indications, which turn up as they should in DB (3rb5); but the second paragraph went into section (ii), where it was no longer governed by any headings.

This explanation fits the facts about as well as can be expected (not perfectly but fairly well), and I think that it is sure to be right. It also has one incidental advantage, in that it allows us to make sense of a puzzling feature of DB. It seems that the D scribe who wrote section (ii) did not consider it necessary to keep repeating the phrase 'from the same archbishop'. No doubt he thought that it was obvious enough, from the arrangement of the text, that the bishop of Rochester – like the rest of the archbishop's knights, like the archbishop's monks – was one of the archbishop's tenants. But the DB scribe did not understand that. Looking through the D text, deciding (as he normally did) what changes he should make to the order of the chapters, he fell into the mistake of supposing that the bishop of Rochester was one of the king's barons; so he turned section (ii) into a separate chapter, putting it where (by his rules) it ought to be put.[63] The upshot is that anyone reading DB would think that the bishop of Rochester held his lands directly from the king – which is obviously what the DB scribe thought himself. Perhaps we may find it surprising that he was ignorant of the bishop's peculiar status; but ignorant is what he was, and he displayed his ignorance by treating section (ii) as he did. We should see this, I suppose, as one more sign (below, p. 162) that Kent was not a part of the country with which the DB scribe was personally acquainted.

In view of the complexity of the process which resulted in DB-Ke, it is hardly surprising that some paragraphs got lost, somewhere along the way. In DB itself, we see the proof that this could happen: on checking what he had written, the scribe discovered that he had dropped a paragraph (he had jumped ahead, from a point near the end of one entry, to the corresponding point in the next), and so added it in the margin (9rb). If he had failed to make a sufficiently careful check, that paragraph would have been lost. The same sort of risk existed at every stage, and a number of paragraphs – three at least – did indeed go astray. In DB's chapter 2, 'Land of the archbishop of Canterbury', there ought to exist a paragraph for Teynham (a version of which survives in α). In chapter 7, 'Land of the church of Saint Augustine', there ought to exist a paragraph for Ripple (a version of which survives in B / xAug). The third case is not quite so certain, but I think we can be fairly sure that there were two manors called Chalk, only one of which is to be found described in DB (8vb49). These are the only omissions that I have been able to detect; perhaps there may be others.

[63] By his rules (Flight 2006, p. 137), an English bishop (chapter 4) should come after an archbishop (chapters 2–3) but before a foreign bishop (chapter 5).

3

By around 1200, the records resulting from the survey had mostly been discarded or dispersed. They had ceased to serve any useful purpose; sooner or later a new broom swept them away. The thirteenth-century Exchequer had only two of the old books still in its custody: DB itself, and the volume of D which covered the three counties not covered by DB. In spite of the disparities between them, they had come to be thought of as a single book; they shared the nickname 'Domesday'. At first that name was used only by government officials, in informal memoranda. By around 1300, however, it was being used in official records, and many people outside the Exchequer were aware of the existence of the book, and of the legal significance that was attached to it, even if they had no clear understanding what the book contained. Until the mid eighteenth century (see below), 'Domesday Book' was kept in a triple-locked strongbox, not to be opened except with the concurrence of three different officials, each of whom held one of the keys. From Arthur Agard (d. 1615) onwards, several Exchequer employees are known to have taken some serious interest in the book.[64] Even for them, access to the original was not exactly easy. For outsiders, it could be difficult. A letter of introduction was only the first step. There was a not inconsiderable fee to be paid before the book could even come out of its box;[65] on top of that, transcripts were charged for at the rate of fourpence a line.

Before 1700, historians writing about Kent – Lambard (1576), Somner (1640), Philipott (1659) – made very little use of DB-Ke. They were aware of its existence, of course, but only vaguely aware of its contents. It seems to have been known, for instance, that DB had some interesting things to say about Dover, and anyone investigating the history of the Cinque Ports, by asking among his friends, would probably have been able to obtain a copy of someone else's copy of the relevant excerpts. But nobody got closely acquainted with DB-Ke itself.

William Lambard (1536–1601) has one passage mentioning 'Domesday Book' which seems to imply that he had seen the original (whether one or both volumes is not clear): it is notable, he says, that 'Saxon' letters – i.e. the special characters which English scribes had developed for writing English (or English words in a Latin text) – are almost absent here (1576, p. 210). Probably that counts as the first published comment on the palaeography of DB. In writing his book about Kent, however, Lambard seems to have been relying on excerpts made by someone else: 'that copie of Domesdaye booke, whiche I haue seene, concerning the description of this Shyre' (p. 327). A single sentence which

[64] One product of that interest worth noting here is a collection of excerpts from DB-Ke (BL Harley 1905) made by one of the deputy chamberlains, John Lowe (d. 1708).

[65] 'Until of late years it has been kept under three different locks and keys, one in the custody of the treasurer, and the others of the two chamberlains of the Exchequer, and was not to be opened but on paying a fee of 6s. 8d.' (Webb 1756, p. 7).

he quotes – *De adulterio Rex habebit hominem, Archiepiscopus mulierem* (p. 180, from 1rb30–1) – is, I imagine, the first passage from DB ever to be put into print.

William Somner (1598–1669), born and brought up in Canterbury, found employment and made his home there. Within a short walk, he had access to important archives, especially that of the cathedral church, previously almost untouched; and he found in them more than enough material to keep him busy, during the time that he could spare from his official duties. One of his discoveries – the only one which is immediately relevant here – was the manuscript I call C1. From it he printed (1640, pp. 425–40) the first two segments of text α (above, p. 15), omitting the Rochester segment.[66] From internal evidence, he could see that this text was connected with the survey of the whole of England. Beyond that, he could only guess – and his guess was that it consisted of excerpts from 'Domesday Book'. In his later publications, the source cited by that name is often α as he had printed it, not DB itself.[67]

Thomas Philipott (d. 1682), living in Greenwich, had access to many of the records of central government, but shows no sign of having consulted DB. Nearly always, his allusions to 'Dooms-day Book' turn out to be references to Somner's edition of α. The rest are too vague or too garbled to be worth citing.

An important collection of excerpts from DB was published by Thomas Gale (d. 1702), as an appendix to his edition (1691) of a batch of medieval chronicles. Gale's source was a transcript of 'Domesday Book' (both volumes) loaned to him by Sir John Trevor (d. 1717), who, at the time, was speaker of the House of Commons.[68] From this copy of DB-Ke, Gale printed much of the preliminary section (1ra–va, 2ra),[69] and also the Sandwich paragraph from the start of chapter 3 (3ra). Anyone who thought of comparing the paragraph from DB as it was printed by Gale (1691, p. 761) with the paragraph printed from C1 by Somner (1640, p. 433) could have seen that they were, though certainly connected, by no means as simply connected as Somner had supposed.

If good intentions were all it took, John Harris (d. 1719) would be the man whom we should have to thank for putting us in full possession of the evidence. Harris became one of the prebendaries of Rochester Cathedral in 1708; a few years after that, he issued a prospectus for a 'History of Kent' that he was planning to write.[70] The book grew into two volumes: but Harris died while volume I was in the press, and volume II never appeared.[71] Even the volume which did get published falls very far short of the promises which Harris had made for it; in particular it failed to include, as he had said that it would, 'a Transcript of Doomesday Book as far as relates to KENT, with many Corrections and Additions from several Manuscripts and Charters' (quoted by Rawlinson 1720, p. 89). It seems that Harris did follow through with his plan to the extent of procuring a transcript of the DB-Ke text, presumably in its entirety (Webb 1756, p. 13). Some efforts were made later to track it down, but they did not succeed.[72] The transcript made for Harris, if it existed, was never seen again.

By the mid eighteenth century, 'Domesday Book' had at last become more easily accessible. It was kept in the chapter house at Westminster, in the sole custody of Richard Morley, appointed keeper of the records in 1741.[73] A paper read to the Society of Antiquaries in December 1755 and published as a pamphlet soon afterwards – *A short account of some particulars concerning Domes-day Book, with a view to promote its being published* (Webb 1756) – includes a grateful compliment for Morley, 'whose readiness to oblige the members of this society with the inspection of this, and other records in his office, without fee or reward, it would be want of candour not to mention' (p. 7). One of Morley's subordinates was Abraham Farley (1712–1791), whose name will occur repeatedly in the next few paragraphs. (He was, as it happens, a Kentishman by birth; but he moved up to London in his twenties and stayed there for the rest of his life.)

During the 1760s, down in Kent, work was beginning on what would become the first comprehensive history of the county. Edward Hasted (1732–1812) was its author – in the end its only author.[74] There was, briefly, some thought that he might assist Charles Whitworth (d. 1778) in producing a new edition of Philipott's book, revised and brought up to date. Happily that plan fell through. Meanwhile Hasted had made contact with another potential collaborator, Thomas Astle (1735–1803). For a short period, between about 1762

[66] Though Somner is vague about his source, I take it to be certain that the text came from C1. Elsewhere, in speaking of prior Alan (1640, p. 280), he mentions the Palm Sunday incident (below, p. 39), recorded, as far as I know, in this manuscript alone. (The passage which he quotes here is from C1-7va8–10.)

[67] Not always so. Some genuine excerpts from DB are quoted in his book about gavelkind (1660, pp. 122–3), and in an essay about 'The Roman ports and forts in Kent' which was found among his papers (Somner ed. Brome 1693, pp. 35, 47).

[68] The transcript used by Gale was still in existence in the 1750s (Webb 1756, p. 8); it is not heard of again after that.

[69] Everything, that is, apart from the two stretches of text relating to Saint Martin's of Dover.

[70] An edited version of Harris's prospectus was printed by Rawlinson (1720, pp. 88–92), who says that Harris had been at work for 'above eight years' before volume I was published.

[71] The intended contents are listed in the preface to the first volume (Harris 1719, pp. iii–iv).

[72] 'Dr. Harris's papers, on his dying insolvent, came into the hands of Edward Goddard, esq; of Clyffe Pypard, c. Wilts, who had them 1761; but Mr. Hasted has not been able to recover them' (Gough 1780, p. 445).

[73] His predecessor, John Lawton, appointed in 1727, had already obtained possession of all three keys.

[74] Throughout this paragraph I am relying heavily on the biography of Hasted by Black (2001), and on a letter of hers replying to some questions of mine. I thank her for her help.

and 1767, Hasted and Astle were very close friends. Between them they came up with the plan that Astle should marry a Kentish wife (he already had his eye on a suitable young lady), find himself a house in the county, and join forces with Hasted in writing a new 'History of Kent'. None of that came about. Astle married someone else, the friendship cooled,[75] and Hasted was left to write the book by himself.

It was during that period, I think, the period when Hasted and Astle thought of themselves as collaborators, that Abraham Farley was asked to make a transcript of DB-Ke – the transcript which survives as BL Stowe 851, fos. 13–119.[76] Apparently it was Astle, not Hasted, who handled the negotiations.[77] The transcript, once made, was (so I suppose) loaned by Astle to Hasted, and remained in the latter's possession for several years it was certainly in his hands in 1769, when he had occasion to draw up a catalogue of his manuscripts (Black 2001, pp. 187–8). At some uncertain date it was returned to Astle;[78] and from that point onwards it followed the same trajectory as the rest of Astle's manuscripts,[79] finally arriving in the British Museum.

The book which began to take shape was organized topographically – lath by lath, hundred by hundred, parish by parish. (In that respect, and also in starting from the west, its structure bore some resemblance to the B version of the survey text.) Unlike Harris, Hasted did not intend to publish DB-Ke as a connected text: he dissected it into its constituent paragraphs and distributed them among the parishes to which they belonged. For this to be possible, he had to identify the place-names; and that, very largely, he managed to do successfully. With almost no help from previous writers, with little help from anyone else, Hasted was able to identify all of the easy names, and many of the difficult ones (including some which look easy but are not). To say that there are a few mistakes is not to detract from the magnitude of Hasted's achievement. Thanks to him, DB-Ke became reconnected with the landscape of Kent.

Like most books, Hasted's book grew in the writing and took much longer to complete than had been expected. The first volume appeared in 1778, the second in 1783, the third in 1790, the fourth and final volume in 1799. By the time that the book was complete, very nearly the entire text of DB-Ke had been put into print, piece by piece – a paragraph taken from the transcript made by Farley, followed by an English translation. Before the last folio volume came out, a revised edition, in a smaller, more affordable format, had already begun to appear. It was completed in twelve volumes within four years (1797–1801). Except for one specimen paragraph (vol. 1, p. 392), the excerpts from the Latin text were dropped from this edition, on the assumption that very few people would be capable of understanding them (p. 423); the translations alone were kept.[80]

Well before that, the entire text of 'Domesday Book' had been made available in print. After much discussion and more than one false start, it had been decided to publish an edition of both volumes, primarily for the use of members of the houses of parliament.[81] By 1774, a plan had been devised which was not prohibitively expensive, and the people had been found who were competent enough to put the plan into execution. The text was printed under the supervision of John Nichols (1745–1826), from transcripts of the originals supplied by Abraham Farley. The copy of DB-Ke which Farley had made in the 1760s is a fairly loose transcript, reproducing the substance but not the appearance of the original; the copies which he made for the parliamentary edition – unfortunately none of them survive – were as tight as he could make them. It was Farley's job also to check and recheck the proofs, as they were printed off. He did his share of the work very well.

The type that was used was designed by Nichols, manufactured by Joseph Jackson (1733–1792), and set by a nameless compositor who is the true hero of the story. It was intended to be capable of reproducing most of the special characters appearing in the manuscript; but of course there had to be some limits. Comparing the printed text with a facsimile, one does not need to look very hard before starting to see its defects. Some characters were not available. The compositor had **p(ro)** but not **P(ro)**; while working on the text for Kent, apparently he had no ampersand. Some characters which he did have were redundant: the **ct** and **sl** ligatures used by him were not used by the DB scribe. In this and some other respects, eighteenth-century conventions were too strong to be resisted. Thus **æ** was substituted for tailed 'e', **j** for consonantal 'i',[82] round **s** for long 's' at the end of a word. Nevertheless, within its limitations,

[75] In 1767, with Hasted's unwitting help, Astle stole a batch of Anglo-Saxon charters from the library at Surrenden Dering – borrowed them with no intention of returning them. More than forty years later, Hasted was still bitter about that (Black 2001, pp. 126, 351).

[76] The date suggested by Hallam (1986, p. 214), 'c.1775', is certainly a little too late.

[77] Which would explain why Astle knew and Hasted did not know how much this transcript cost. Hasted was under the impresion that it had been charged for at the standard rate, fourpence per line (which would mean, by my reckoning, upwards of 42 guineas). Astle knew that Farley had only charged 16 guineas for it (BL Stowe 851, fo. 1r).

[78] Black (2001, p. 303) suggests that the manuscript was bought by Astle in 1796, when Hasted (in prison for debt) was reduced to selling off much of his library. Astle did certainly buy one manuscript then (BL Stowe 855); but we only know that because he wrote a note on the flyleaf to say so. There is no similar note in the transcript of DB-Ke – nothing to suggest that Astle did not regard it as his own property.

[79] Including the Anglo-Saxon charters stolen from Surrenden Dering (above, note 75), now BL Stowe Charters 1–42. Speaking of one of these charters (Sawyer 1968, no. 111), Hasted says that it 'is in the Surrenden library' (1797–1801, vol. 8, p. 425); he means that it is not but ought to be.

[80] The folio edition (1778–99) of Hasted's *History* remains hard to get hold of; for my part, I have only ever once seen a copy. The 12-volume octavo edition (1797–1801) was reprinted in facsimile in 1972, and (minus the maps) can now be accessed through ECCO.

[81] The prehistory of this edition is recounted by Condon and Hallam (1984), more briefly by Hallam (1986).

[82] In printed Latin **j** denotes [y] (as in 'yet') – except at the start of a word, where it can optionally be read as [dzh] (as in 'jet'), the same as in printed English.

despite its anachronistic features, the parliamentary edition is a splendid piece of typography, almost unbelievably accurate.[83]

To the extent that it was completed – it had no title page or other preliminaries; nor did it have any index – the parliamentary edition was complete by 1783.[84] Since the 1970s, it has taken on a new lease of life, because it was used to provide a ready-made Latin text for the Phillimore edition of 'Domesday Book' (see below). As far as DB-Ke is concerned, I give a list of errata elsewhere (below, p. 150), in case readers who own copies of the Phillimore volume for Kent may like to emend them accordingly.

By the 1850s, the Rev. Lambert Larking was working on an edition of the DB-Ke booklet which, had it been completed, would have advanced the whole question far beyond the point which Hasted had reached.[85] By 1861 he was letting it be known that the edition was under way: there is a paragraph in the *Gentleman's Magazine* for December 1861 which speaks of Larking's book, announcing that it is expected to appear 'early in the ensuing year'.[86] But his health was failing by then, and the edition had still not been published, nor even nearly finished, when Larking died in 1868.

After his death, as much of his draft as was in a fit state for publication was put together to make a book (Larking 1869), edited by his younger brother, J. W. Larking;[87] but that is no more than a shadow of the book which had originally been intended. What ought to have been the most important part of it, the commentary on the text (pp. 149–90), extends no further than the first three pages of DB-Ke (1r–2r), ending with the index of tenants. It is a sad fact that Larking's vast knowledge of medieval Kentish history was never brought to bear on the main text of DB. It is another sad fact that Larking's edition, incomplete but far from useless, has generally been ignored.

[83] The actual type used for the parliamentary edition was destroyed in 1808, by a fire at Nichols's printing house, but a font of similar design was used for the publications of the Record Commission. The Pipe Roll Society, when they began printing the twelfth-century exchequer rolls which had not been published previously, used 'Record type' at first; but in 1903 they decided to abandon that policy. It would, no doubt, be feasible now to design an electronic font far better than the one designed by Nichols; perhaps someone has already done it.

[84] The rest of the story is told by Hallam (1986, pp. 147–8). It seems worth adding, by the way, that one page from DB – the first page of the Surrey booklet (30r) – was engraved by James Basire and published by the Record Commission (Basire 1800).

[85] Lambert Blackwell Larking (1797–1868), vicar of Ryarsh and Burham. The Kent Archaeological Society owes its existence very largely to him; he served as its first honorary secretary (1857–61) and edited the first three volumes of *Archaeologia Cantiana* (1858–60). There is an obituary by T. D. Hardy in *Archaeologia Cantiana*, vol. 7 (1868), 323–8.

[86] *Gentleman's Magazine*, vol. 211, p. 606 (Dec. 1861).

[87] John Wingfield Larking (1801–1891). There is a note of his death in *The Times*, 20 May 1891, 7d; it speaks only of his career in the consular service.

One component of Larking's book – as intended and also as published – was a lithographed facsimile of the original manuscript. It was the work of Frederick Netherclift.[88] The plates are superb; but they are not, and cannot be expected to be, accurate in every detail. For each page, the image had to be traced from the original by hand, before being transferred to the surface of the stone from which it would eventually be printed. (In fact, two images were needed for every page, one for the main text and another for the rubrication.) In making this facsimile, Netherclift did not just have to copy every letter; he had to reproduce every single stroke of the scribe's pen. He must have looked at the manuscript more closely and more thoroughly than anyone else has ever done. His accuracy is impressive, but of course it is not quite perfect.

From the 1820s onwards, lithography had been widely used as a means of producing illustrations for scholarly books. It was relatively cheap. It had the advantage over other techniques that corrections were easy to make. It was not just good enough (as long as one did not expect to print more than a few hundred copies); in skilled hands it achieved a subtlety of effect which engraving on metal could not even approach.

By the 1860s, however, hand-drawn lithography was (for this sort of purpose) already obsolescent. A crude technique of photographic reproduction, given the name photozincography, had been invented by the Ordnance Survey in 1859, and the Survey's superintendent, Colonel Sir Henry James (1803–1877), was looking for ways to demonstrate its usefulness. It had recently been decided that 'Domesday Book' should be given a new binding. Knowing that, James came up with the idea of producing a cheap facsimile of DB and D-ExNkSk, county by county, while the sheets were unbound. For anyone who understood the process, it was obvious that photozincography was not really very suitable for making facsimiles of ancient documents. It worked well for reproducing maps, or anything that consisted of black shapes on a white background; but it was not sensitive enough to reproduce a text written in variably dark ink on variably pale parchment. Nevertheless, James made the proposal, and got government approval for it in 1860.[89]

Behind the scenes, Larking tried to prevent the pages relating to Kent from being photozincographed. He had some success; it was agreed that Kent should be put at the end of the queue. But James was not the sort of man who could easily be deflected from his purpose. By April 1863, every other DB county had been dealt with, and Larking meanwhile had made no progress with his book. He withdrew

[88] Frederick George Netherclift (1817–1892), lithographic artist and publisher. The plates commissioned by Larking appear to have been made in about 1857, 'at least two years' before the invention of photozincography (Larking 1869, p. viii).

[89] The first results – for the pages relating to Cornwall – were exhibited at the Archaeological Institute in April 1861; there is a report of the meeting in *Gentleman's Magazine*, vol. 210, pp. 652–3 (June 1861). The Cornwall facsimile was published soon afterwards, priced at 4s. 6d. Hallam (1986, pp. 154–7) has the whole story.

his objection, and the Ordnance Survey facsimile for Kent came rolling off the press while Netherclift's plates continued gathering dust.

Thirty years afterwards, it was still possible to buy a complete set of parts of the Ordnance Survey facsimile. (Most were priced at 8 shillings, but the larger counties cost more.) As late as 1893 every fascicle was still available. Kent was one of two counties – Shropshire the other – which had gone out of print by 1896. Gloucestershire and Yorkshire were gone by 1897, Somerset, Staffordshire and Warwickshire by 1910.[90] But the other fascicles were still being advertised for sale in 1913. (I have not tried to trace the story further than that.)

For a long time (much longer than I had realized),[91] the Ordnance Survey facsimile was the image which people had in mind, when they thought about DB. Until the 1970s, it seems to have been fairly generally assumed that one could establish the text well enough by checking the parliamentary edition against the Ordnance Survey facsimile, without ever (or hardly ever) needing to consult the original. This assumption is safe only up to a point. There are many features of the manuscript which could not possibly have been reproduced typographically which also fail to show up in the facsimile. In effect it was being assumed that nothing significant was photozincographically invisible; and that was a risky proposition.[92]

There is a sequel to the story of Larking's edition. One of the sources which Larking had used was the text which I call xAug (above, p. 15). The only surviving copy occurs in a register from Saint Augustine's which had somehow found its way into the collection of 'miscellaneous books' belonging to the Exchequer official called the King's Remembrancer.[93] Larking knew of that copy: from it he transcribed a long stretch of text relating to the city of Canterbury, containing much more information than the corresponding section of DB. When his unfinished book was published, that transcript was included in it (Larking 1869, pp. 34*–5*).

Years later, it caught the eye of Adolphus Ballard (1867–1915). Though Ballard had no particular interest in Kent, he could see that this text might help to elucidate the workings of the survey; so he went back to the original register and made a transcript (not a very accurate one) of the whole of the xAug text. He went on to prepare an edition of it, with the paragraphs of xAug set alongside the parallel passages appearing in DB and C1. (For C1 he consulted the original in Canterbury, not Somner's edition.) The edition was complete by 1910 – that is the date given at the end of the introduction (p. xxvii) – but publication was much delayed. The book did not finally appear until 1920, by which time Ballard was dead.

After 'various vicissitudes' (Page 1932, p. xv), the Victoria History volume containing a translation of DB-Ke came out in 1932.[94] The translation was originally made by the Rev. F. W. Ragg,[95] who also drew the accompanying map; but it was afterwards revised to an unknown extent by the editor, William Page (1861–1934), and some of the place-names came to be identified differently. In consequence of that, the translation is, in difficult cases, quite often in contradiction with the map.[96] Apparently nobody had looked at Hasted, nor at Larking's edition. The changes made by Page were based on some desultory research by L. F. Salzman (1878–1971), who checked through a few manuscripts – all of them late, all of them in London – which were thought to be possibly relevant. Only one of them was really worth consulting, the register from Saint Augustine's in the PRO;[97] Page and his associates seem not to have realized that the most important stretch of text had already been put into print. To be blunt, none of the people principally involved had any special knowledge of Kent, and there are places where their ignorance becomes rather painfully obvious.

An introduction was provided by Nellie Neilson, who was apparently required to take the translation as given;[98] none

[90] These statements are based on the catalogues of current publications which were sometimes bound in at the back of the PRO calendars.

[91] My previous remarks on the subject (Flight 2006, p. 10) were made in ignorance, and the reader should disregard them.

[92] It might have been helpful to know, for instance, that the scribe changed his mind, while he was writing a particular sentence about Sandwich, with the result that two words had to be written over an erasure (3ra13). In order to know that, one has to be able to see that the parchment is not quite as pale or as smooth as it should be, and that the script is not quite as dark or as sharp around the edges as it should be. Photozincography could not capture nuances like these.

[93] It was certainly there by the mid seventeenth century. William Somner cited the manuscript and quoted one sentence from xAug (Somner 1660, p. 122, from A4-19v3–4).

[94] Page images of the whole of this volume can be found online at the Kent Archaeological Society's web site, www.kentarchaeology.org.uk.

[95] Frederick William Ragg (1845–1929), curate of Nonington 1877–80, vicar of Masworth in Buckinghamshire 1880–1906. He translated three other portions of DB for the Victoria History, but these were all published much earlier: Hertfordshire (1902), Bedfordshire (1904), Berkshire (1906). Those were the days when the Victoria History had some impetus behind it.

[96] For example, *Stepedone* (9rb) is marked on Ragg's map (with a query) as a place in Sheppey (which happens to be correct); but the translation has a footnote proposing to identify it as 'a manor in Norton', i.e. as Stuppington TQ 9659, which is not even in the right hundred.

[97] This is the manuscript cited in the footnotes as 'A'. 'B' is a fourteenth-century cartulary from Dover priory (Lambeth Palace 241). As for 'C', this is a late copy of α/C1; these references ought all to have been replaced with references to Neilson's translation of the latter manuscript. (There are also a few footnotes citing BL Stowe 924, a fair copy of the excerpts from Kentish cartularies made by Sir Edward Dering (1598–1644).) The footnote 'Since edited by Mr. Turner for the British Academy' (Page 1932, p. 201) confuses the 'White Book', the register consulted by Salzman, with the 'Black Book', edited in its entirety by Turner and Salter (1915–24).

[98] I notice, for instance, that she makes a point of saying, more than once, that *homines de Walt* (2vb3) means 'men of the weald' (Neilson 1932a, pp. 180, 182, 187); the translation has 'Walter's men' (p. 209). The intro-

of the footnotes attached to the text are credited to her. Unlike Page and his colleagues, she was aware of Larking's edition, and cited it here and there; she also knew that the manuscript which Salzman had consulted in the PRO contained the text which had been edited by Ballard. (It had, by chance, been published in tandem with a text from Lincolnshire edited by her.)

Probably not even Neilson herself thought highly of this introduction. Reading between the lines, one gets the sense that she wrote it because somebody had to, not because she really wanted to. The fact is that DB-Ke does not say much about the questions of legal history which were of interest to her. It is clear that she did a great deal of work, counting and tabulating the data along lines which in other counties had been productive; but here they did not seem to lead towards any definite conclusions. She began by warning her readers that they might find DB 'disappointing' (p. 177); as she approached the end she was still conscious that they might be left feeling 'disappointment' (p. 200).

Probably it was Neilson's suggestion that a translation of the Canterbury manuscript, C1, should also be included in this volume; certainly that is what happened. Since Somner's time, C1 had largely been lost sight of again. A description of it appeared in one of the reports of the Historical Manuscripts Commission (Sheppard 1881, pp. 315–16); but it was Ballard (1920), by quoting extracts from it in his edition of xAug, who finally brought the manuscript back into prominence. Working from photographs, Neilson produced a translation of almost the whole text,[99] most of which had never been published before. The commentary is inadequate; the place-name identifications are only haphazardly successful;[100] no effort was made to coordinate Neilson's translation of C1 with the translation of DB-Ke, except that they were indexed together.

Whatever its merits or demerits, that translation was soon superseded. Prompted by David Douglas (1898–1982), the Royal Historical Society committed itself to publishing a facsimile edition of the manuscript. The edition came out in 1944: it contained not just a reduced, monochrome facsimile of every page, but also a careful transcription of the entire text, and a long but not altogether apposite introduction (Douglas 1944).

After that, for anyone having access to a good library, it was possible to get hold of all the principal documents relating to the survey of Kent, in one form or another: Douglas's edition of C1, Ballard's edition of B / xAug, the parliamentary edition of DB and the Ordnance Survey facsimile.

The aim which inspired the Phillimore edition of 'Domesday Book' (1975–86) was to make 'a cheap text and uniform translation' easily available to everyone.[101] I cannot imagine that anyone would fail to approve of that objective, or fail to admire the efficiency with which the enterprise was carried through. As for me, the work which I have done would not have been practicable without the Phillimore edition: I have said that before (Flight 2006, pp. 10–11) and am glad to have this opportunity to say it once again. For each county, the Phillimore edition consists basically of two components: on the left-hand pages a reproduction of the parliamentary edition, dissected into pieces of suitable size; on the right-hand pages a parallel translation into English. At the end of each volume there are notes, indexes and a map of the county.[102]

It would, I think, be fair to say that the Phillimore translations are not universally liked; their uniformity was achieved by imposing a set of rules which, perhaps, were not all well-advised. They are also more prone to error than one would wish. In passages which consist of something more than a string of formulas, the meaning is sometimes simply misunderstood. Theoretically the 'draft translations' were 'the work of a team', and each of them was 'checked by several people'. But that is only going to work if there is at least one person involved who can recognize Latin idioms when he or she sees them.[103] In any case, I take leave to doubt whether the translation of DB-Ke was checked as thoroughly as that.[104]

The volume for Kent, edited by Philip Morgan, was published in 1983. Some errors in the parliamentary edition were noted and corrected; a few doubtful readings were checked against the original. As far as the place-names are concerned, the Phillimore edition does not advance much beyond the Victoria History; the identifications which were new were mostly wrong.[105]

A new facsimile of DB was published in 1986 (Alecto Historical Editions 1986); the history of the whole project is recounted by Pearson (2001). As in 1861–3, the production of a facsimile was coordinated with a rebinding of the

duction was written before 1929 (p. 183, note 30a) and (so it seems) only slightly revised in the run-up to publication.

99 Except for some late twelfth-century documents added at the end, of which she thought, reasonably enough, that a précis would suffice.

100 Identifications marked with an asterisk are not to be trusted far; those marked with a dagger are at least worth thinking about. The latter are Gordon Ward's suggestions; he published a commentary of his own (Ward 1933) on C1's lists of parish churches.

101 The quotations in this and the following paragraph come from the 'Introduction', which appears (with variations) in every volume.

102 It has annoyed me occasionally that the pages are not numbered. If there is information in the notes which one needs to cite, there is no easy way to do it.

103 Without wishing to be cruel, I suppose that I have to justify this statement by citing a few examples. Here are some from DB-Ke: *si plus opus esset* (1ra15) does not mean 'If there was more labour'; *si abierit domum* (1rb8) does not mean 'If he has gone away from home'; *sin autem* (1rb12) does not mean 'But if'.

104 For example, nobody noticed that the phrases *et super homines ipsorum* (1rb16) and *in ciuitate* (3va48) are missing from the translation.

105 Again I suppose that I have to cite an example. There is a list of three places which paid rents to the canons of Saint Martin's – *Nordeuuode, Ripe, Brandet* (2rb17, 34–5) – and the Phillimore edition is wrong about every one. Two of them were successfully identified by Larking (1869); the one which Larking got wrong (Ripple) can be identified by means of the text printed by Ballard (1920).

manuscript. While they were unbound, the sheets were all photographed in colour – the man who took these photographs was Miki Slingsby – and the photographs were reproduced, by way of a process called continuous-tone lithography, to make the facsimile itself. They were printed on sheets and half-sheets which replicated the construction of the original; the gatherings were stitched together but not bound.

Despite the hyperbolic claims that were made for it at the time, the Alecto facsimile is not very good. The reproduction has a muddy look; it failed to do justice to the photographs, or to the manuscript itself. Scanned images of all the photographs taken in 1985 (of D-ExNkSk as well as DB) were made available for sale through the National Archives in 2006;[106] the resolution is mediocre (the PDF files are roughly half a megabyte each), but anyone who looks at these images will see at once how much detail was lost from the facsimile.

It was decided at an early stage (unwisely in my opinion) that the facsimile would need to be accompanied by a translation into English. That meant, straight away, that a huge investment of time and effort was required, beyond what was needed for producing the facsimile itself. Like the facsimile, the resulting translation was printed in gatherings which replicated the construction of the manuscript; and the text was laid out – column by column, paragraph by paragraph – in the same way as the Latin. The smallest marks in the margin (erasures, mysterious dots, and so on) were all meticulously recorded (this was Caroline Thorn's contribution); but no notice was taken of alterations in the main text, which, one might think, are more likely to be significant.[107]

The 'Alecto County Edition' of DB-Ke came out six years later (Williams and Martin 1992). There is nothing specific to be said about the facsimile; the translation was based on the Victoria History version, but extensively revised throughout. By and large, the changes made in the language were changes for the better, but some errors were introduced. (One formula is consistently mistranslated. *Silua x porc'* does not mean 'woodland for 10 pigs'; it means what Ragg took it to mean, 'woodland (to render) 10 swine', i.e. as much woodland as yields 10 pigs by way of rent.) The place-names, with only a very few exceptions (Williams and Martin 1992, p. 67), are identified exactly as they were by Morgan (1983).[108]

[106] www.nationalarchives.gov.uk/documentsonline/domesday.asp.

[107] To bring the story up to date, I should note that the entire Alecto translation, of D-ExNkSk as well as DB, has been reformated (unintelligently) and reprinted as a separate book (Williams and Martin 2002); I leave it to the reader to decide whether the book is worth buying. As far as Kent is concerned, I notice (without looking hard) that a comment added by Agard at the foot of fo. 1v has attached itself to a paragraph with which it has no connection (p. 5) and that the marginal entry on fo. 9r has been dropped (p. 22).

[108] Two places correctly identified by Morgan are misidentified here, for no reason that I can guess at. *Lerham* (4va2) is not 'Lenham (?Heath)'; *Bermelie* (8vb30) is not 'East Barming'.

A long introductory essay by Richard Eales was written especially for the 'County Edition' (Eales 1992). There is no original research in it. It takes the text and translation as given; it cites all the published documents, in their published form, but does not cite any others. It is almost entirely retrospective: it focuses primarily on the period before 1066, secondarily on the interval between 1066 and 1086; the final paragraphs carry the story forward as far as 1088. Within those limitations, it is a thorough, thoughtful review of the evidence, and of the uses which historians have tried to make of it.

For most people, unfortunately, this essay and the others like it are hard to get hold of, because libraries which could afford to buy even one volume of the Alecto edition are few and far between. I had thought that this problem would have resolved itself by now, with the publication of the 'Digital Domesday County Edition'. But that project seems to have ground to a halt, and I cannot discover when, if ever, the disc for Kent is going to be released.

To give the reader some sense of the differences between them, I print two sample passages as they appear in each of these three versions (Table 4). The first is the opening paragraph, part of the description of Dover (1ra4–28), where the Latin text was reporting facts peculiar to this one place; the second is a short paragraph, chosen at random from the middle of the text (7va21–4), where the standard formulas sufficed for what had to be said.

As the reader may have perceived, I am not enthusiastic about any of these translations, but that does not mean that I am planning to produce a version of my own. In the commentary (chapter 5), some passages will be found put into English, with explanatory remarks where they seem to be needed. But these piecemeal translations are not intended to be uniform: sometimes they are tight, sometimes they are loose, whatever the immediate context seems to call for.

Anyone who tries translating DB had to decide on some policy for the treatment of proper names. For my part, I dislike the trend towards spelling the English personal names in a tenth-century West-Saxon manner (so that 'Ulstan', 'Sired', 'Brixi', become 'Wulfstan', 'Sigeræd', 'Beorhtsige'). By the late eleventh century, even English-born scribes would have thought such spellings old-fashioned. (The historian Edmer, who invariably wrote his name *Edmerus*, would have been surprised to find himself turned into someone called 'Eadmær'.) More to the point, it is characteristic of the Latin text (see below) that simplified spellings are preferred, and a translation ought to be faithful in this respect. If the translator thinks it desirable to note that 'Brixi' is the DB scribe's idea of a phonetic spelling for 'Beorhtsige', that can be done, and done just once, somewhere in the apparatus.

The tendency to archaize the English names seems all the more objectionable when it collides with the convention that French names should be spelt in the modern English manner. As it happens, I dislike that convention too. There is, as far as I can see, nothing to be gained by replacing 'Willelm' with 'William', 'Rannulf' with 'Ranulph', 'Goisfrid' with 'Geoffrey'. Any editor who thinks it necessary to state that 'Willelm' is an eleventh-century spelling for 'William' can find some place to do it: a footnote, a table of equivalences, a parenthesized remark in the index. With only some slight exceptions, the DB scribe is consistent in the spelling of these names, and it is not the translator's job to overrule him. The same considerations apply to French place-names used as surnames. It is, for instance, a well-established fact that Radulf de Curbespine took his name from a village near Bernay which is now called Courbépine; but again that fact belongs in the apparatus, not in the translation itself.

4

Transcriptions, translations, and other derivative versions have their uses; but the reader who has access to a facsimile – of DB itself, or of C1 or R1 – should not pass up the chance of approaching that much closer to the original. The men who wrote these manuscripts were good scribes, doing their best to write legibly. They had their quirks, of course, but who does not? It always takes a little effort at first to get used to somebody else's handwriting. Though some medieval scripts are very difficult to read, the sort of script that these scribes were using is not. The alphabet has few surprises; the letter-shapes are mostly familiar enough. Long 's' can be disconcerting at first – but anyone who has looked at a printed book more than two hundred years old will have had to learn to distinguish long 's' from 'f'. It just requires a little practice. The same is true here. Using a transcription as a crib, anyone who tries will soon find that they have taught themselves to read DB, or C1 or R1, at least to the extent of being able to decipher the writing.

Not everyone, I know, was taught Latin at school (as I was, for seven years, by an excellent teacher). But again I would urge the reader not to boggle. This is not literary Latin, intended to be recited aloud before a sophisticated audience. There are no rhetorical tricks, no figures of speech, no jokes. This is business Latin, deliberately kept simple, intended only for making statements of fact. The vocabulary is restricted; the syntax is straightforward. Especially in DB, much of the text consists of short formulas, repeated in one paragraph after another. Using a translation as a crib, the reader who comes across one of these formulas for the first time can discover what it means – and can rest assured that it will mean the same thing the second or the third or the hundredth time, as often as it recurs.

It has often been said that DB is hard to read because the Latin is so heavily abbreviated. I am not even sure that this is true: it rather depends on the reader. The scribe, no doubt, thought that he was making things easier, not harder, by cutting words short as he did. By using a formula like *T'ra e' .. car'*, he was letting his readers know that they were not expected to care about details of spelling and grammar: they should simply take note of the facts. As for me, when I see the notation *TRE*, I do not stop to think that this means *tempore regis Edwardi*, which means 'in the time of king Edward', which means 'before 1066'. I read it as 'tee ar ee'. There must once have been a time, I suppose, when I did not know what that meant, but I know well enough by now. Similarly, when I see a sentence like *ual' iiii sol'*, I do not stop to think that this means *valet quatuor solidos*, which means 'it is worth four shillings', which is 48 pence. I read it as 'val four sol', and I know what that means straight away, without needing to turn it into a well-formed English sentence.

By talking to myself like this, in a mixture of English words and truncated Latin words, I am not doing anything that I think I should be ashamed of. On the contrary, I take it that the DB scribe was expecting his readers to do something similar to this – though the readers whom he expected to have were people who would think, not in English like me, but in French. Abbreviated Latin resembles abbreviated French; the more drastic the abbreviation, the closer the resemblance. The sentence *ual' iiii sol'* is perfect French, if one chooses to read it as such. Subject to the same condition, *iiii* is perfect English. Anyone who writes a numeral – '48 pence' rather than 'forty-eight pence' - is giving his or her readers the option of using the language that they are most comfortable with.

Because the language was dead and the orthography was fossilized, it is always hard to know how a medieval scribe was pronouncing his Latin, or expecting his readers to pronounce it. Spelling mistakes are the only clue that one can look for; and a well-taught scribe, like the DB scribe, does not make mistakes of that kind.[109] The pronunciation current in Rome was of course regarded as the norm; but the church of Rome has (so it is said) traditionally been tolerant of some variation. If an abbot from Normandy, for instance, visited Rome, he would be expected to have a command of Latin grammar; but he would not be expected to pronounce the words in precisely the same way as an Italian abbot. Tolerance, however, is bound to have its limits. It may be that a Norman abbot would have been well-advised to have a few elocution lessons, if he did not want to be sneered at behind his back.[110]

[109] Of the manuscripts mentioned in this book, only C5 has numerous wrong spellings (below, p. 280).

[110] A biography of archbishop Lanfranc, written at Le Bec in about 1140, includes an interesting passage (ed. Gibson 1993, pp. 671–2) which might seem to be relevant here. The author is trying to imagine what it would have been like, a hundred years earlier, for a highly-educated Italian (such as Lanfranc) to enter a primitive Norman monastery (such as Le Bec then was); this Italian, he thinks, would have had to be careful how he spoke his Latin, if he were not to seem to be showing off. But the thought in this author's mind turns out to be, not that the monks of Le Bec might have been pronouncing their Latin differently, but that they might have been pronouncing it wrongly – that they might have been so ignorant of the language that they could not distinguish between long vowels and short

Victoria History (1932)	Phillimore (1983)	Alecto (1992)
DOVERE [Dover] in the time of King Edward used to pay 18 pounds, of which money (*denariis*) King Edward had two-thirds (*partes*) and Earl Godwin the (other) third. [This was one moiety]. And tallying with this (*contra hoc*) the canons of St. Martin had another moiety. The burgesses supplied to the king once in the year 20 ships for 15 days, and in each ship were 21 men. This (service) they did because he had remitted (*perdonaverat*) to them the sac and soc. Whenever the king's messengers came there they paid 3 pence for the passage of a horse in the winter and 2 pence in the summer, the burgesses finding a steersman and one other helper; and if more help was needed it was obtained out of (the steersman's) pay (*de pecunia ejus*). In the interval between (*a*) the feast of St. Michael and (*usque ad*) that of St. Andrew the town was under the king's peace (*trewa* regis erat in villa*). If any one broke it the king's reeve took for the breach a fine from all in common. A permanent settler (*manens assiduus*) in the town paid customary dues to the king (and) was exempted from toll throughout England. All these customs were in force there at the time when King William came into England. Just after he came (*in ipso primo adventu ejus*) into England the town was burnt down, and therefore a right valuation could not be made of what it was worth when the Bishop of Bayeux received it. It is now valued at 40 pounds, and yet the reeve pays therefrom 54 pounds, to the king 24 pounds of pence at 20 to the ore; to the Earl 30 pounds by tale (*ad numerum*). * *Vel pax* is interlined here.	DOVER before 1066 paid £18, of which pence King Edward had two parts and Earl Godwin the third. Against this, the Canons of St. Martin's had the other half. The burgesses gave 20 ships to the King once a year for 15 days. In each ship were 21 men. They did this because he had given over to them full jurisdiction. When the King's messengers came there, they gave 3d in winter and 2d in summer for horse passage. The burgesses found a steersman and 1 other assistant. If there was more labour, it was hired with his own money. From the Feast of St. Michael until the Feast of St. Andrew the King's truce, that is peace, was in the town. If anyone broke it, the king's reeve received the common fine for it. Whoever lived permanently in the town and paid customary dues to the King was exempt from toll throughout the whole of England. All these customs were there when King William came to England. At his first arrival in England the town was burnt. Its valuation could not therefore be reckoned, what its value was when the Bishop of Bayeux acquired it. Now it is assessed at £40; however, the reeve pays £54, that is £24 of pence, which are 20 to the ora, to the King and £30 at face value to the Earl.	DOVER in the time of King EDWARD rendered £18, of which money King Edward had two parts and Earl Godwine the third. Besides this the canons of St Martin had the other half. The burgesses gave to the king once in the year 20 ships for 15 days, and in each ship were 21 men. They did this for him because he had remitted to them the sake and soke. Whenever the king's messengers came there they gave 3d. for the passage of a horse in the winter and 2[d.] in the summer. The burgesses found a steersman and one other helper; and if more help were needed it was hired out of his pay. From Michaelmas up to the feast of St Andrew there was a truce of the king, that is peace, in the town. If anyone broke it the king's reeve took a common fine for it. Whoever dwelt permanently in the vill rendered a customary due to the king [and] was quit of toll throughout England. All these customs were there when King William came into England. On his very first arrival in England the vill itself was burned down, and therefore a valuation could not be made of what it was worth when the Bishop of Bayeux received it. It is now valued at £40, and yet the reeve pays from it £54: to the king £24 of pence at 20 to the ora, to the earl £30 by tale.
Wadard holds NOTESTEDE [Nursted] of the bishop. It is assessed at 2 sulungs. There is land for 2 ploughs. On the demesne is 1; and there are 4 bordars and a church and 4 serfs, and woodland (to render) 3 swine. T.R.E. it was worth 4 pounds, and when received 3 pounds. Now (it is worth) 5 pounds. Ulstan held it of King E(dward).	Wadard holds NURSTEAD from the Bishop. It answers for 2 sulungs. Land for 2 ploughs. In lordship 1. 4 smallholders. A church; 4 slaves; woodland, 3 pigs. Value before 1066 £4; when acquired £3; now £5. Wulfstan held it from King Edward.	Wadard holds NURSTEAD of the bishop. It is assessed at 2 sulungs. There is land for 2 ploughs. In demesne is 1 [plough], and there are 4 bordars, and a church, and 4 slaves. [There is] woodland for 3 pigs. TRE it was worth £4; when received, £3; now £5. Wulfstan held it of King Edward.

Table 4. Three translations of two passages from DB-Ke.

By and large, the spelling of Latin is transparent. Every character has just one value: the sound which it denotes is always the same, and is always to be pronounced. There are two large exceptions, **i** and **u**, which each represent both a consonant and a vowel; and then there are some particular exceptions which offer additional scope for variation. As far as I can catch any hint, the rules which the DB scribe was following would look something like this:

c before **e** or **i** is [tsh] (as in the English word 'cheap')

ch is [k] (only in Greek words)

g before **e** or **i** is [dzh] (as in 'gem')

gn is [ny] (as in 'onion')

vowels. What would Lanfranc have done if he had been ordered to mispronounce a Latin word? He would have remembered his vows and obeyed.

h is silent (as in 'honest')

i as a consonant is [y] (as in 'yet')

sc before **e** or **i** is [ts] (as in 'tsar')

u as a consonant is [v] (as in 'vain')

At the start of a word, Latin [y] had evolved into French [dzh] (i.e. the same sound as soft **g**), and this shift tended to feed back into the pronunciation of Latin, among people who had grown up speaking French. A word like *iugum*, for example, could turn from ['yugum] into ['dzhugum], under the influence of the everyday language. My feeling is that the DB scribe would have regarded that as a vulgar habit, not to be encouraged; but I cannot say that I have any solid grounds for this suspicion. On the other hand, there is good evidence to suggest that he was, rather oddly, pronouncing

sc as [ts] in a word like *scilicet*.[111] (In a word like *scira*, an English word treated as a Latin word, this [ts] is an approximation to English [sh] – a sound for which the DB scribe had no better spelling, because for him it did not exist in either Latin or French.)

The letter **k** is a puzzle by itself. For some reason which I do not understand, this scribe made a point of using it in the word *marka*, where one might have thought, as many scribes did think, that **c** would serve the purpose. Otherwise he did not use **k** at all.

The DB scribe wrote in Latin because he was conscious of writing for posterity; but the posterity which he had in mind was one inhabited by people who – like himself and his friends and colleagues – thought and conversed in French. To put oneself into the place of one of the readers whom he imagined having, it might seem like a good idea to gain some acquaintance with eleventh-century French, as it was put into writing by an eleventh-century scribe.

It *would* be a good idea, if only it were possible. For anyone aware that there survives a great quantity of written English dating from before 1066, it may come as a shock to discover that there is very little written French earlier than the twelfth century. Ker's *Catalogue of manuscripts containing Anglo-Saxon* (1957) is a big book: concisely worded and closely printed, it runs to more than 600 pages. A catalogue of manuscripts containing Old French, designed on a similar scale and restricted to the period before 1100, would (at a guess) not exceed a dozen pages. As far as I can gather, there is not a single piece of eleventh-century French prose or verse surviving in an eleventh-century manuscript.[112]

That French verse was composed in the eleventh century, and was sometimes put into writing, is not in any doubt. But the very fact that it was written in French branded it as ephemeral. A poet who wanted his work to survive had no choice but to write in Latin. If he wrote a poem in French, he might show it to his friends; if they liked it, they might make a copy; but the chances of any copy finding its way into a library were vanishingly small.

The closest one can get to eleventh-century French is to find a twelfth-century manuscript which looks as if it was copied from an earlier exemplar. There survives, for instance, a manuscript written at Saint Alban's, probably in the 1130s, which includes a copy of a French poem, more than 600 lines long, recounting the legend of Saint Alexis.[113] The scribe, it seems, had no poetic ambitions of his own: he was simply making a copy of the exemplar that he had in front of him. Because this is verse, it can be said for certain that the copy is a rather bad one. Numerous lines do not scan or assonate correctly;[114] a few stanzas have lost a line or two. Most important, it seems clear that there were some grammatical features which this scribe failed to comprehend, because, by his time, they had already dropped out of the language. It is from evidence like this, fitted into some general understanding of the way in which the language evolved, that eleventh-century French can, after a fashion, be reconstructed.

In fact, if I am not mistaken, the French words and phrases that one finds embedded in the Latin text of DB form the largest single contemporary record of the eleventh-century language. By itself, the DB-Ke booklet does not produce much of a crop (Table 5); but in DB as a whole some hundreds of words occur which are either unadorned French, or French only very thinly disguised as Latin. The morsels of French contained in DB were extracted and listed, long ago, in an article by Hildebrand (1884). Via that article, some of them have found their way into dictionaries and manuals of Old French. Perhaps they are too small to be of much linguistic interest: there are none that consist of more than three consecutive words. Even so, it would seem to me that the time is overdue for someone to take another look at the evidence.[115] Hildebrand was working from the printed text; his extracts came from the C text and the D text as well as from DB itself; and of course it never occurred to him to think that DB was all the work of a single scribe – a man with ideas of his own. A closer study, focusing on this one man's work, might turn out to be a worthwhile undertaking.[116]

From this point of view, the value of DB derives largely from one of the innovations which the DB scribe was aiming to make. Most other scribes, when they came to a French surname or place-name, turned it into Latin as a matter of course. The DB scribe (so it seems) regarded this as a foolish affectation, allowable perhaps in a work of literature but not appropriate here. If the word was French, that was how he wrote it. There was a baron who went by

[111] Chiefly from his experiments in spelling *cotsets*, an English word treated as a French word, which occurs very frequently in some booklets (but never in DB-Ke). Both in the middle and at the end, **ts** can be replaced with **z**, which is normal for written French; in the middle only (where it is followed by **e**), **ts** can be replaced with **sc**.

[112] On the other hand, if anyone would like to see a specimen of tenth-century French, I can tell them where to look. The manuscript in question (Valenciennes, Bibliothèque municipale 150), which came from the abbey of Saint-Amand, is (so the catalogue tells me) a ninth-century copy of the sermons of Saint Gregory of Nazianzus translated (from Greek into Latin) by Rufinus of Aquileia. Three blank leaves at the back (fos. 141–3) were used by later scribes for an assortment of additions, and one of these additions (fo. 141v1–15) is a piece of French verse in praise of the Spanish martyr Saint Eulalia. Images and text can be found at bookline-03.valenciennes.fr/bib/decouverte/histoire/cantilene/141v.htm.

[113] The manuscript is now in Hildesheim. It was described in detail, and all the artwork was reproduced, by Pächt, Dodwell and Wormald (1960). An online edition can be accessed through www.abdn.ac.uk/stalbanspsalter/index.shtml.

[114] By assonance is meant that in each stanza the last stressed syllable in every line has to have the same vowel.

[115] It might be worth noting, for instance, that this scribe writes *l'asne* (meaning 'the ass') without regard for the case. If he had been writing poetry, no doubt he would have used the nominative form *li asnes* where the context required it; but here he does not bother.

[116] An article by Clark (1992), though well worth reading, falls short of what is needed.

appevile 9va
barbes 11rb
labatailge 11vb
braibove 8vb
columbels 1ra bis, 2ra, . . . , columbers 11vb
curbespine 1ra, 2ra, 2rb, . . . , curbespin(a) 11vb, 12va
dowai 6vb
(h)erbag(ium) 3vb, 4rb, 9vb
folet 4va
gand 12vb bis
girunde 10va
hesding 6rb, 6va, 9ra
maminot 7ra
mannevile 13va
maresc 10vb, 11ra, 13ra, . . . , maresch 13rb ter
marsuin 5va
molin 6va, molins (plural) 3va
montfort 1ra, 4va, 9vb, . . . , monfort 9rb
ow 4ra, 4rb, 7vb, . . .
paisforere 9vb, paisfor' 10vb, pastforeire 6rb
parag(ium) 7rb, 11rb
pasnag(ium) 9vb, 11vb, 12ra, . . .
pevrel 9ra
port 2va, 2vb, 6ra, . . . , porth 6ra, 10ra, 10rb, . . .
ros 6ra, 6rb, 6vb, . . .
tahum 8va, taum 10vb
tenut (error for *tenuit*) 13vb
tinel 11rb
valbadon 11vb, 12va

Table 5. French words in DB-Ke. (No more than three instances of any spelling are cited; the dots denote that there are more. In Latinized words the Latin elements are bracketed.)

the nickname 'goat'. The C scribes wrote that as Latin and called him Willelm *capra*; the DB scribe wrote it as French and called him Willelm *chievre*.[117] Similarly he made it a rule to write *de curbespine*, not *de curva spina*, *de dowai*, not *de duaco*, *de montfort*, not *de monte forti*, *de valbadon*, not *de valle badonis*. By and large, later scribes came to follow his example.

The spelling which had been developed for French was based, of course, on the spelling used for Latin; but it was not yet as rigidly fixed. In some respects, the DB scribe can be seen experimenting with different spellings, as he goes along (Flight 2006, p. 141); but this does not happen to any large extent. As with Latin, the reader is expected to know that certain characters vary in value, according to the context. In French, however, the demands being made on the reader are very much greater. (One had to know, for instance, that **a** and **e** should be pronounced through the nose if they were followed by **m** or **n**.)

As far as the consonants are concerned, the rules which the DB scribe was following (and expecting us to follow) would look something like this:

c before **a** is [k]

c before **e** or **i** is [tsh] (as in 'church')

ch is [k] where **c** would be [tsh]

d between vowels is [dh] (as in 'mother')[118]

g before **a** is [g]

g before **e** or **i** is [dzh] (as in 'gem')

gl or **lg** is equivalent to **ll**

gn or **ng** is equivalent to **nn**

h is [h] (only in non-Latin words)

i as a consonant is [dzh] (as in 'judge')

ll is [ly] (as in 'million')

nn is [ny] (as in 'minion')

qu is [kw][119]

rr is [rr], the only double consonant that persisted in spoken French (other doublings, **ll**, **nn**, **ss**, **uu**, are merely tricks of spelling)

s between vowels is [z][120]

ss is [s] where **s** would be [z]

t following a vowel at the end of a word is [th] (as in 'thick')

u as a consonant is [v]

uu is [w] (only in non-Latin words)

z is shorthand for **ts**, normally used only at the end of a word

One negative feature should also be taken note of. In words which in Latin began with [sk], [sp] or [st], the tendency in French was to turn the [s] into a separate syllable by starting the word with a vowel (a 'prothetic *e*', as the jargon has it). Thus *spina* 'thorn' would become *espine* [əs'pinə], *scutum* 'shield' would become *escut* [əs'kuth]. The DB scribe did not approve of this tendency. He spelt such words without an **e**, and presumably pronounced them accordingly.

If the DB scribe had been transported forward into the nineteenth century, he could have found people in France who – if they were patient enough to make the effort – would probably have been able to understand something of what he was saying: as far as I can judge, his best hope would have been to try talking to an old lady whose idea of a long

[117] Linguists may think it worth noting this as proof that Latin [ka] had (if the syllable was open) shifted to [kie] or [kye] in the sort of French that the DB scribe was speaking.

[118] 'Between vowels' is a simplification. The same thing happens if **d** is followed by **r** and then by a vowel. Thus *pedre* 'father' is ['pedhrə]. In his spelling of English, to countermand this rule, the DB scribe wrote **dd** for [d] between vowels.

[119] Normally so, though possibly [k] in some particular words. That the DB scribe was pronouncing it [kw] is clear from his spelling of English names like *Queníntone* (DB-Gl-167vb), *Querendone* (DB-Bu-149va), *Quintone* (DB-Nn-228va).

[120] Again a simplification: **s** becomes [z] before some consonants too. Thus *masle* is ['mazlə], *asne* is ['aznə]. (It is possible, however, that in this sort of context the [z] had already ceased to be pronounced.)

journey was an outing to the market in Valenciennes.[121] I rely on the reader's good sense to treat this experiment in time-travel with a suitable degree of disdain. It is not to be thought that the DB scribe was attempting to transcribe the sort of French which was spoken in the particular town or village where he had chanced to be born. He was aiming to construct a written form of French which would be more or less easily understood by all his expected readers; and those readers might come from any part of northern France, from Flanders to Brittany, which had contributed some of the manpower for the invasion and settlement of England.

The third ingredient of the DB text consists of those words which are neither Latin nor French. Most importantly, that means the place-names. The challenge facing the DB scribe was to devise some system of spelling for these foreign words (foreign to him and his anticipated readers) which could be used consistently throughout the book that he was writing. Nothing like this had ever been attempted on such a scale before. The system had to work for the whole of England; it had to be able to cope with Breton personal names, and with Welsh and Cornish place-names; it had to allow for the fact that English was pronounced rather differently in the north from in the south. But the nub of the problem was how to spell the English place-names, pronounced as they were, at the time of the survey, in the southern part of the country. He had no intention of using the conventional orthography which English scribes had developed for writing English. His readers would not understand it, and would not want to have to learn it. What he planned to construct in its place was some system of phonetic spelling, based on his spelling of French, which would allow his readers (if they were familiar with written French, as he took it for granted that they would be) to pronounce these strange names, without much hesitation, in a tolerably accurate way.

There were, we might guess, some parts of the country of which the DB scribe had personal knowledge. (But it seems fairly clear, by the way, that Kent was not one of those parts.) Some cities and towns were important enough that he had surely heard of them, even if he had not visited them. Most of the time, however, he had nothing to guide him beyond the name of the village as he found it spelt in his source-text – as it had been written down by one of the B scribes, as it had been copied by one of the C scribes, as it had been copied again by one of the D scribes. From that spelling, he had to guess what the English name would sound like; and then he could respell the name, according to his own rules. Sometimes D's spelling misled him into making a wrong guess; that was the risk that he was taking. Sometimes it made no sense to him; and in that case he could only copy it as he found it, hoping at any rate not to make things worse. But in general it was good enough that he could guess correctly at the English name – correctly enough, at least, for us to be able to identify the place in question, from the DB scribe's respelling of its name.

In some respects, the spelling that he used was too simple to be fully adequate. For instance, he had no way of writing [th] (as in 'thick'). In French that sound only occurred at the end of a word: it was written with a **t**, and the reader was expected to know how to pronounce it. In English the sound could occur at the beginning of a word. Having given the matter some thought (as I take it for granted that he did), the DB scribe decided that **t** would be good enough: if his readers said [t] instead of [th], as in *Turneham* (8rb38) for Thurnham, they would still be understood (and not giggled at too much) by the natives. On the other hand, there were some peculiar sounds which they would have to be given some help with. How, for instance, could they be induced to say [kn] (as in Knowlton)? An English scribe would have written **cn**, not expecting his readers to have any trouble with that. The DB scribe decided to turn the [k] into a separate syllable by inserting an **e** between the **c** and the **n**; but that meant that he also had to insert an **h** between the **c** and the **e** (because **cen** would be read as [tshen]); so Knowlton became *Chenoltone* (11rb33), to be read as [kənol'tonə].

The orthography developed by the DB scribe was long-lastingly influential, but not all of his suggestions were accepted by later scribes. One which lapsed was his use of **ch** for [k]. The twelfth-century exchequer rolls (surviving continuously from 1156 onwards) do largely retain this usage at first (*Chent*, *Chemesinges*, *Chingeswude*, for Kent, Kemsing, Kingswood); but sometimes they use **ch** to mean [tsh] (*Chiselherst*, *Chert*, *Cherringes*, for Chislehurst, Chart, Charing), which had already become its value in the approved spelling of literary French.[122] The ambiguity persists for more than thirty years. Each time we meet the notation **ch**, we have to stop and think: are we supposed to read it as [k] or [tsh]? The roll for 1194 (which, without having seen it, I would guess to be the work of a newly appointed scribe) is the first one where we can see a new system at work. In this and the subsequent rolls, except for an occasional hiccup, **ch** is always [tsh]; and words which the DB scribe would have written with **ch** are, to make doubly sure, written with **k** instead of **c**.

For the most part, however, the DB scribe's innovations stood the test of time. Adopted and (in some respects) augmented by later generations of scribes, they became so thoroughly integrated into the spelling of English that it is hard for us to realize that somebody had to think them up and

[121] The sort of French which was spoken in the region called Hainaut – partly in France, partly in Belgium – did not quite fit into the conventional classification of French dialects. Approached from the Belgian side, it seemed too much like Picard to be counted as a form of Wallon; approached from the French side, it seemed too much like Wallon to be counted as a form of Picard. But it was, whatever it was called, decidedly different from Parisian French. The people who spoke it were not only aware of the differences: they made a point of exaggerating them – to the extent, for instance, of dropping the *e* from the front of a word like *eglise*, on the assumption that this was a Parisian affectation (another objectionable prothetic *e*) which they should take care not to imitate.

[122] As fas as Kent is concerned, the first use of **ch** for [tsh] occurs in the roll for 1158: *Cheritun'* (GREx 1158:181) is certainly Cheriton. (But of course one cannot rely on single instances, which might be the result of some momentary misunderstanding. The pattern is what counts.)

put them to work in the first place. But if we stop to wonder why 'know' is written with 'k' instead of 'c', or why 'quick' is written with 'qu' instead of 'cw', a large part of the answer is to be found in DB.

5

So, finally, to business. In chapters 2–4, the reader will find transcriptions of the three surviving texts – α, B / xAug, DB-Ke – which were generated by the survey of Kent carried out in the spring and summer of 1086. These are the primary sources. Chapter 5 is a commentary, to be read in parallel with the DB-Ke text. Without aiming to say everything that might be said, I have done my best to embed the text into the landscape – not just to identify the named places, but also to indicate, as far as possible, which paragraphs are likely to cover some places not mentioned by name. Beyond that, I have used my discretion, commenting only on those passages which seem to me to require some explanation, to the extent that I think I have something useful to say.

Chapter 6 contains a derivative text, essentially just an epitome of DB-Ke, which has some (but not very many) points of interest; I would not have thought it worth printing if it did not survive in a very early copy. The other chapters are not directly connected with the survey, but will, I hope, prove useful. Chapter 7 is a collection of documents (a few of which have not been printed before) which help to illuminate some aspects of the feodal landscape as it existed at around the time of the survey. Chapter 8 consists of lists of parish churches (one not previously printed), the earliest of which do certainly date from the late eleventh century. More distant still, chapters 9 and 10 are a cursory review of some of the thirteenth-century (and later) evidence which, I suggest, the reader will need to take account of. Without some awareness of this evidence, the records of the survey risk being misunderstood, or not understood as exactly as they might be – or so I think the reader who makes the experiment will discover.

Throughout this book, I have concentrated on the prospective side of the question, rather than the retrospective. I have tried to trace connections forward in time, from the late eleventh century as far as the mid thirteenth; I have made little effort to trace them backwards, into the pre-conquest past. Of course that needs to be done as well; but it is not the first thing to be done.

Chapter 2
The archbishop's response to the commissioners' questionnaire

The text with which we have to start – text α, as I propose to call it – might not be the place where we would choose to start, if we had any choice. It is not an easy beginning. There are three segments – the lands of the archbishop himself, the lands of the archbishop's monks, the lands of the bishop of Rochester – which (as the sequel proves) were not all of equal interest to every copyist. There are several surviving copies – but happily only three of them have textual value, and the rest can be ignored. Of these three copies, each has a different version of the text, for as much of the text as it contains. Only one copy has the entire text; but each segment exists in two versions. There is, in short, a broken landscape ahead of us, through which we have to try to find our way. Table 6 is a map which I hope will help the reader to navigate this chapter.

segment	α1 / C4	α2 / C1	α3 / R1
1	70rb–1va	2va–3va	—
2	71va–2va	3vb–5ra	—
3	—	5ra–c	209r–10r

Table 6. Versions and copies of the segments of text α.

I begin by giving some description of the manuscripts in question. Then I look at the differences between one version and another. And lastly I try to work out how this text is connected with the conduct of the survey.

C4 = Canterbury Cathedral Archives, Reg. K, fos. 23–52, 190, 53–72

The bound volume which is now called Register K – it was known to Somner as the *liber tuberosus*, 'book with knobs on' (Urry 1967, p. 375) – is a bewildering agglomeration of miscellaneous material, much of which seems to have been assembled in the time of prior Henric of Eastry (1285–1331). But it includes one booklet of much earlier date than that, and this is the only part of the volume which has any interest for us. The booklet was described by Urry (1967, pp. 17–19) and proved by him to date from about 1215 – i.e. to the period just after the monks' return from exile, when they were busy reasserting their control over the church's property.

Though I cannot be certain how the booklet is constructed, I am satisfied that fo. 23 is the beginning of one quire and fo. 72 the end of another.[1] There are about 40 lines per page; the number of columns is allowed to vary – one, two or three – depending on the nature of the text. The headings have been added in red; the coloured initials, alternately red and blue,[2] are all in place; there is an illuminated 'R' at the beginning. In its pristine form this was a rather pretty manuscript, all (I think) the work of a single scribe. But some stretches of text have been very heavily amended by later hands, and the appearance of the manuscript is marred by many additions, often carelessly written. On top of that, the whole register has suffered some damage around the edges, supposed to have been caused by the fire of 1670.

For more than two-thirds of its length, as far as fo. 60v, the contents of C4 run parallel with those of a slightly earlier booklet (Reg. H, fos. 1–24), dated by Urry to *c.* 1205 (1967, pp. 10–14). From fo. 61r onwards, these are the contents:

(i) A note of the quantities of goods required by way of farm for different numbers of weeks (61r).

(ii) A list of payments due from parish churches (61v). This is an updated version of one of the lists of churches in C1 (see below); I print it in chapter 8 (pp. 230–1).

(iii) A list of incidental payments due from the monks' manors (62r–6r).

(iv) A list of rents arising from property in London (66v–9r).

(v) A list of the farms to be paid from the monks' manors (69v–70r). The title and a few of the entries were printed by Urry (1967, p. 26).[3]

(vi) A manor-by-manor description of the lands in Kent belonging to the archbishop and the monks (70r–2v).

This last article is the copy of α1. Apart from Urry, the first person to study it closely was F. F. Kreisler; the results of a

[1] The medieval foliation runs from 'i' to 'lii': fo. xi is missing (or else the number was omitted); fo. xxxii is the stray singleton, numbered 190, which has now been put back where it belongs.

[2] Except for a single green initial, at 70va27.

[3] This document purports to be describing the arrangements put in place by Lanfranc, but is obviously not contemporary. In this version at least, it seems to date from about the beginning of the thirteenth century: the only tenant mentioned by name, Herebert Deu enemi, is a man who occurs in the exchequer rolls for 1201–4 (because he held a quarter of a knight's fee in Ospringe from the king). Another copy of this text is to be found in manuscript T1 (below, p. 285).

collation of C1 and C4 are presented in an appendix to his thesis (Kreisler 1967, pp. 297–309).

As it appears here, text α consists of two segments, each with its own title. Segment 1 is headed *De maneriis archiepiscopatus in Kantia, et de sullinges que sunt in eis* (70rb); segment 2, similarly, *De maneriis prioratus in Kantia, et de sullinges que sunt in eis* (71va). As in C1, the second segment concludes with a paragraph relating to Burston (7rva27–9), and the scribe stops at this point.[4] Whether he really regarded this as the end, or whether he was intending to make himself a new quire and then continue, as in C1, with a segment covering the bishop of Rochester's manors, it is simply impossible to say.

After the text had been completed, at least two other scribes were involved in making corrections to it.[5] Because their interventions never collide, it is not clear which of them was active first; from the style of the script, neither seems to be very much later than the main scribe. Hand X (to call it that) is the hand which, as well as making corrections, wrote some additions at the end – the word *Summa* at the foot of col. 72va (which would seem to have been, in his opinion, all that was needed to complete the copy of text α), and a short list of one-line entries in col. 72vb.[6] This is a rounder, rougher hand than the main scribe's, usually not very difficult to distinguish. Hand Y is conspicuously different: the script is small and cursive, and has a spidery look to it.[7]

The indications are that both scribes were altering this version of the text to bring it into line with the version represented by C1. Hand X, repairing an omission in the entry for Sandling, added the following words, just as they appear there: *ab ep'o baioc' et defendebat se in tempore E regis pro i sull'* (71rb16 = 4vb47). Hand Y, altering the entry for Sandwich, cancelled the word *postea* and replaced it with *in preterito anno reddidit*, as in C1 (71vb6 = 3vc4); and this shows that the scribe was revising the text, not just correcting mistakes.

One stretch of text in particular has been extensively reconstructed (71va31–40). There are three subparagraphs following the paragraph for Eastry, and this is what they looked like at first:

Tilemanestune est de terra monachorum, et in tempore E regis se defendebat pro i sull', et nunc facit similiter, et ualet xxx solid'.

... (erasure) ... *apud fenglesham dimid' sull' quod tenuit lieuenoth tempore E regis ab archiep'o, et ualet xx sol'.*

... (erasure) ... *dimid' sull' stepenberghe, quod Godwinus tenuit de archiep'o Aðzi tempore E regis, et tunc se defendebat pro dimid' sull', sicut et nunc, et ualet xxx sol'.*

But hand X has dealt violently with these entries, making additions between the lines and over erasures,

quod Will' folet tenet ab arch'ep'o

Idem Will' folet h't de predicta terra ab arch'ep'o

Id' W' h't de predicta terra ab arch'p'o

the effect of which is to force this stretch of text, not quite into verbal agreement, but into substantive agreement with C1 (3vb24–44).

From our point of view, these changes are changes for the worse. This copy in C4 is only of interest to the extent that it differs from the copy in C1; and corrections which were aimed at effacing that difference diminish its value for us. In dealing with this manuscript, therefore, I look only at what was written by the original scribe, ignoring any alterations that were made by other hands.

By the end of the thirteenth century, this booklet had been brought together with the other quires that constitute Reg. K, and the copy of $\alpha 1$ thus came to be juxtaposed with a sequence of excerpts from D and DB relating to the monks' manors in Essex, Suffolk, Oxfordshire, Buckinghamshire, Surrey and Sussex (Reg. K, fos. 73r–v). That juxtaposition makes it easy to prove that the other surviving copies of $\alpha 1$ are derived from Reg. K, and therefore of no textual value.

These other copies are of segment 2 only, the segment of special interest to the monks. It turns up again first in a late thirteenth-century manuscript, a single quire (so it seems) which eventually became part of another composite register (Canterbury Cathedral Archives, Reg. P, fos. 42–9). This book was damaged around the edges, presumably in the fire of 1670;[8] for the most part, however, the text is perfectly legible, though here and there a few letters have been lost. The main scribe filled the first nine pages (42r–6r); he supplied the headings, in bright red ink, but not the coloured initials with which each paragraph was intended to begin. Under the title *De maneriis prioratus in Kancia, et de sullingis que sunt in eis* (42r1), he copied segment 2

[4] We might expect him at least to announce that he has reached the end of a segment by writing *Summa* here, as he did at the end of segment 1 (71va18). He did not do that. The word *Summa* does appear at the foot of this column, but it was added by another hand (see below).

[5] A few corrections may be the work of a third hand, rounder than the main scribe's, neater than hand X. I have not been able to make up my mind about this.

[6] I print this list, for what little it is worth, because it occurs only here. *Berkesore, i sull'. Leisdune, i sull'. In essexia. Suthcherche, iii hidas et dim'. Middeltune, ii hid' et dim'. Lellinge, xvii hid'. Bockinge, iiii hid' et dim'. In Suthfolchia. Illege, ii hid'. Hedlege, i hid'.* The two places in Kent are Barksore (in Lower Halstow) and Leysdown, given to the church by Henric II, in 1178 and 1173 respectively. (But the monks had a previous claim on Barksore, by virtue of a charter of king Stephan.)

[7] This is the hand which added a gloss *eadwardi* in the very first line (70rb3). The hand which added a similar gloss in C1, at 3va4, is probably the same. (If so, that would tend to prove that these correctors were consulting C1 itself, not some copy of it.)

[8] Another component of Reg. P (fos. 11–34) is the booklet which I call C5 (below, p. 280). That booklet suffered much more severely than the quire in question here.

word for word as it appears in Reg. K. Then (omitting the little list added at this point by hand X) he continued with the excerpts from D and DB, as they appear in the following quire of Reg. K. Except for the heading *De Coggeshale* (44v15), there is nothing to warn us that we are starting on another county. As far as the survey of the manors in Kent is concerned (42r1–4v14), it is obvious at once that this copy derives from Reg. K,[9] because it incorporates all the corrections made by hands X and Y. The evidence could not be clearer.

Though the Reg. P scribe does not give the impression of writing carefully, his copy is a very accurate one. But there are a few small mistakes – fortunately so, because they mean that the rest of the story can be dealt with in a few words. From Reg. P, the same stretch of text was copied into a third, slightly later register, now BL Cotton Galba E. iv (fos. 30r–2v);[10] and from there it was printed by Bandinel (1813, pp. 100–3). There is only one statement here which stands in need of proof, that Galba was copied from Reg. P; and that is implied by the fact that any significant variants which occur in Reg. P recur in Bandinel's edition.[11] Besides these, the printed text has numerous other errors.[12] Presumably some are the fault of the Galba scribe, some of Bandinel's copyist, some again of his compositor; but I cannot say how the blame should be apportioned. Since I do not see that the question is of any interest, I have spared myself the trouble of working out the answer.

C1 = Canterbury Cathedral Library, Lit. E 28

This is a manuscript comprising just eight single leaves – eight leaves, however, of quite extraordinary size. Vertically they measure more than 540 mm, horizontally more than 390 mm. Even folded in half, they would be the size of an unusually large book; unfolded, they are about as large of the largest books that medieval scribes could make.[13]

It is a good question why anyone would think of creating a manuscript which looks more like a portfolio than a book. The question was put by Cheney (1983) – who, many years before, had helped with the production of the facsimile edition – and the answer which he suggested seems sure to be right. These leaves were not intended to stand alone. They were meant to be inserted into a textus – a gospel-book or something similar – from which they would imbibe an odour of sanctity. Not a single leaf has been discovered which might be part of this hypothetical textus; so we cannot say to what degree the design of these new leaves was modelled on that of the pre-existing book. Nevertheless, I think we can be sure that the receptacle intended for C1 was a book of which the Christ Church monks were especially proud, and that the scribe who created C1 was aiming to produce a piece of work which would stand comparison with it. So far I agree with Cheney; I differ only in thinking it unlikely that the intention was ever achieved.[14] In my opinion, the leaves remained unbound.[15]

The leaves are ruled for three columns, with 54 lines in each. Proportionally the lines are rather close together (the spacing is about 7.5 mm), and the script is not inordinately large. The quantity of text which the scribe had to copy could easily have been fitted into six leaves of this size; even after leaving spaces here and there (including one whole column), the scribe had only ten lines remaining when he started on the recto of the seventh leaf. Thus almost two whole leaves were surplus to his requirements. Since the eighth leaf was not discarded, it was evidently not thought unwelcome for some space to be available here, in case it might be found useful by subsequent scribes (as in fact it was). For this scribe, however, reaching this point (7ra10) meant that he had reached the end.

After that he went back to the beginning and started inserted brightly coloured initials in the spaces which he had left for them. (This is the sort of feature which may perhaps have been imitated from the book into which C1 was expected to be inserted.) Four colours were used; there are a few omissions and numerous irregularities, but the normal rota is red, blue, green, purple.[16] Some sections of the text are lists of short items, and here every line or almost every line begins with a coloured initial; elsewhere every paragraph does.

Once the initials were finished, the final step would have been to insert the headings in the spaces that had been reserved for them. In this respect the scribe's intentions are not always precisely clear. Sometimes he seems to be using blank spaces simply to separate one paragraph from another, without any thought of using these spaces for headings (e.g. in columns 1rc–va and 5va–c). Where the space

[9] As was recognized by Kreisler (1967, p. 224).

[10] So cited by Kreisler (1967, p. 14); I have not seen this manuscript myself.

[11] For instance, in the Orpington paragraph, where C4 has *quidam liber homo* (72va2), Reg. P has *quidem homo liber* (44r18); and the latter reading is the one which turns up again in Bandinel (1813, p. 102).

[12] The sub-paragraphs for Finglesham and Statenborough (Bandinel 1813, p. 101) are especially corrupt.

[13] C1 was published in facsimile by Douglas (1944) – not in colour, nor at full size. Though Douglas omitted to say so, the facsimile is only two-thirds the size of the original. The measurements reported by Cheney (1983, p. 11) are 542 × 395 mm.

[14] If these leaves were indeed bound into a textus, it becomes a question how they and they alone could survive. One has to be willing to suppose, for instance, that they were 'saved by some antiquary' (Cheney 1983, p. 13) when the textus was taken apart – and that having been saved they were donated to the Dean and Chapter.

[15] I explain the reason below; but there is a consequential point which ought to be mentioned at once. If it is true that the leaves did not get bound, it will follow that they did not get trimmed around the edges; so the hypothetical textus would not have been quite as large as C1.

[16] In a few places, where the rota had started going wrong, the scribe wrote small coloured letters in the margin to get things under control. At 6ra45, for example, a small green letter is the cue for a blue initial. It is these small letters – not the capitals, which are too plain to offer much scope for individuality – which satisfy me that the initials are the work of the main scribe.

happens to come at the top of a column, however, the intention is unambiguous, and that happens seven times. (One line was left blank at the top of columns 1vb, 2rb, 3rc and 5rc, two lines at the top of columns 2rc, 2va and 3vb.) For one reason or another, the original scribe failed to supply the headings (my guess would be that he was waiting to be provided with some gold foil);[17] and that failure created a quandary. Because these leaves were not quite finished, it became a question whether they were finished enough – finished to the point that they were ready to be inserted into the hypothetical textus. It seems to me (as I have said) that in fact they remained unbound, at least for the time being.

As far as I know, the scribe has not been identified in any other manuscript.[18] He writes a heavy, laboured sort of script, easy to read but not very pleasant to look at. (Perhaps it is worth wondering why a rather mediocre scribe was entrusted with a task of such importance.) One foible which occurs throughout is a failure to get the spacing right where *s* is followed by an ascender: thus *Ans fridus mas leclerc* (6rb53) or *Os bertus pais forire* (6rc11) look like four words each, not two. The scribe can cope with English place-names, even when they are spelt in an English manner. He is not disconcerted by insular characters (ash,[19] eth, thorn, wyn), when he comes across them; *k* and *y* are part of his repertoire.[20]

One feature of this scribe's work which has attracted comment before, from Ward (1933), Douglas (1944), and others, is his proclivity for making mistakes – small mistakes, affecting just one or two letters – which are so very obviously wrong that it looks like an act of perversity to make them. Since many of these errors occur in the place-names, we might think of explaining them on the assumption that the scribe was ignorant of English. For example, the *m* in *Fremgaham* (6vb1) looks to us like an obvious mistake. (On the previous page the name is *Frenigeham* (6rc9); further down the same column it is *Frenigaham* (6vb46); the place in question is Farningham.) No English-speaking scribe would have thought that *Fremgaham* was a well-formed name; to a foreigner it might have seemed no odder than all the other odd names which he was having to copy. Though there may be some truth in it, this explanation does not meet the case. It does not account for errors like the *m* in *Gmðhyrste* (1va24). One does not need any knowledge of eleventh-century English to know that this cannot be right: whatever the language may be, this sequence of letters is impossible to pronounce. And yet, deliberately, distinctly, an *m* is what this scribe wrote.

The answer is, I think, that the scribe was under instructions to copy the text exactly as he found it. He was not to exercise even the slightest discretion; he was to copy what he saw, or thought he saw, regardless of whether it seemed to him to make sense. And that is what he did. Though put into a format which is entirely new, the text itself is a letter-by-letter reproduction, as mechanically accurate as the scribe can make it,[21] of the text which he had in front of him. If the exemplar was carelessly written, so that sometimes *u* looked more like *n* or *I* looked more like *l*, the apparent reading is the one which this scribe felt himself obliged to copy; and some of the documents in front of him were indeed quite carelessly written.

This last remark prepares the way for the observation that the contents of the manuscript are something of an anticlimax. What this scribe had been given to copy was a batch of mundane business records, not intended and hardly suitable for the reverential treatment that they were accorded here.

The contents consist (as I count them) of ten separate documents:

(i) A list of cash payments due to the archbishop at Easter from priests and churches (1ra–b).

(ii) A note of certain payments due to Christ Church from the abbey of Saint Augustine (1rc).

(iii) A list of churches with their subordinate churches (1rc–va).

(iv) A list of the payments from churches which used to be due before archbishop Lanfranc changed things (1vb).

The first four articles are all printed in chapter 8 (below, pp. 228–30).

(v) A list of incoming payments of Peter's pence (1vc).

(vi) A synopsis of $\alpha 2$, giving just the names of the manors and their TRE assessments (2rb–c). Printed below (p. 66).

(vii) The copy of $\alpha 2$ (2va–5rc), first printed (minus the Rochester segment) by Somner (1640).

(viii) Some excerpts from the preliminary section of the DB booklet for Kent (5va).[22]

[17] The red headings which appear in these spaces were inserted by somebody else; I discuss them further on. (The same scribe added a little red *Æ* against the blue *Ę* which begins the Sandling paragraph (4vb44). He was protesting (I suppose) that the Latin character ought not to have been used as a substitute for English *Æ*.)

[18] I withdraw the suggestion (Flight 2006, p. 111) that he may have been a professional employed for the purpose. At the time I was doubtful whether his script could be said to have a Christ Church look to it; but Tessa Webber assures me that it does, and I am happy to defer to her opinion.

[19] It is another of his foibles, however, that sometimes, by inadvertently adding an extra stroke, he turns an *æ* into an ampersand.

[20] But the insular form of *r* did catch him out (unless, what is possible, the error existed already in his exemplar). As Ward (1933, p. 61) pointed out, the strange name *Aqus* (1rc52) is sure to be *Acris* misread. Squinting at this word, one can see how the *r* splits apart, the first element joining with *c* to make *q*, the second with *i* to make *u*. Probably the *p* in *Norðcip'* (1va1) is also an *r* misread.

[21] The errors in this manuscript are reminiscent of the errors that occur in a piece of printed text which has been put through a scanner. Anyone who has surfed the web will have come across examples of that.

[22] The excerpts are these: *Per totam ciuitatem* ... from 2ra32–3, *Archiepiscopus calumniatur* ... from 2ra42–3, *De adulterio* ... from 1rb30–3,

(ix) A list of the payments due to the archbishop from his domain manors (5va–c). This document alone is not confined to Kent: it includes the archbishop's manors in Surrey, Middlesex and Sussex (in that order).

(x) An epitome of DB-Ke, not including chapters 2–4 or 13, incorporating a few extraneous facts (5vc–7ra). Printed below as chapter 6.

One of these articles (vii) accounts for slightly more than half of the total quantity of text, a second (x) for almost a quarter. The other eight documents are all fairly short: fitted into this format, the shortest (ii) runs to 13 lines, the longest (ix) to 94 lines. Presumably we should visualize these shorter documents as slips or sheets of parchment of various sizes. The two longer documents, however, would probably consist of booklets – possibly of more than one quire in the case of article (vii).

It looks as if this collection of documents was put together in the archbishop's household, not inside the monastery: the clearest sign of this is the presence of a list of the archbishop's domain manors (ix), taken together with the absence of a similar list for the manors belonging to the monks. Three of the documents (vi–viii) cannot be earlier than 1086; another (x) cannot be earlier than 1088 (below, p. 206). At the end of article (iv) we find a sentence saying that the arrangements in question had been discontinued by archbishop Lanfranc, and the phrase 'of blessed memory' attached to Lanfranc's name is proof that he was dead. This sentence reads like the sort of explanatory remark which might have been added to an existing document, perhaps only just before it was handed to this scribe. But in any case it goes to prove that C1 cannot have been written till after Lanfranc's death in May 1089.

When Lanfranc died, perhaps even before he died, people must have started wondering who the next archbishop would be. They were left in suspense for a very long time. Months went by, years went by, and still the king made no move towards choosing a new archbishop. Finally, almost four years later, it was decided (God knows why) that Anselm abbot of Le Bec was the right man for the job. Even then it took until September 1093, four years and four months after Lanfranc's death, before the archbishop elect was ready to come to Canterbury,[23] another three months before he was willing to let himself be consecrated.

Except in vague terms, we are not told what was happening in Canterbury during this lapse of time. Up to a point, we know without needing to be told, because the rules were plain enough. As soon as the archbishop died, his domain manors – that is, the manors listed in article (ix) – would be taken into the king's hands; and there they would stay, managed by the king's agents, for the king's profit, for as long as the vacancy lasted. The archbishop's knights (a category which included the bishop of Rochester) would remain in possession of the manors that they held in feod: for the time being, any services normally owed to the archbishop would be paid to the king instead, but otherwise nothing would change. It was the archbishop's monks who would find themselves in a difficult position – not just the monks, but also (though no one cared much about them) the numerous servants who depended on the monks for their livelihood.

A contemporary witness (as I take him to have been) tells us that Christ Church – meaning the monks – did indeed 'suffer many hardships'.[24] But the new archbishop was already in office by the time that these words were written. Having allowed himself this backward glance, this shudder at the thought how bad things had been, the writer preferred to look hopefully ahead. There is a passage in Edmer's *Historia Novorum* (ed. Rule 1884, p. 26) which tells us more; but Edmer, though he had lived through these events, did not write his account of them till much later (not before 1109), and many things had happened in the interim which might have affected his judgment.

The nub of the matter was the king's refusal to allow any special treatment for the manors which, while Lanfranc was alive, had been assigned to the maintenance of the monks. Perhaps it was pointed out to the king that the monks' manors were (mostly) listed separately in the records of the survey of 1086; if the point was put at all, it was put in vain. The agents who arrived to take charge of the archbishopric put themselves in possession of the monks' manors, together with the archbishop's domain manors. They 'estimated what was needed for the bare subsistence of the monks' and paid them no more than that. Out of this allowance the monks had to find their food and drink and their clothing; they also had to find their servant's wages. However generous this allowance was (it was probably not very generous), it would, of course, have seemed inadequate to the monks. According to Edmer, the situation became so desperate that it was necessary for some of the monks to be sent to other monasteries;[25] possibly (though Edmer does not mention it) some of the servants had to be retrenched as well.

It was, arguably, Lanfranc's fault that the monks found themselves in this predicament. We do not know whether they took this view themselves; possibly some of them did and some did not. The hard fact is, however, that Lanfranc had failed to provide the monks with the sort of writ-

Quidam prepositus ... from 2ra43–8. The last excerpt can be found printed in parallel with the passage from DB in Flight (2006, p. 35).

[23] We are told, by someone who thought that a word of apology was needed, that there were 'many reasonable causes' for this delay.

[24] Cambridge, Corpus Christi College 173, fo. 32v, published in facsimile by Flower and Smith (1941). The passage is quoted in Flight (2006, p. 111).

[25] Edmer does not say which monasteries he has in mind; the obvious places would seem to be Rochester and Saint Alban's, perhaps Saint Augustine's, perhaps even Caen and Le Bec. Vague though it is, this remark of Edmer's may be of some significance – in relation to the spread of the Christ Church style of script, for example.

ten documents which might have afforded them some protection after he was gone. Nor was it just the monks of Christ Church who were left in this exposed condition. The priests of Saint Gregory's church,[26] the inmates of the two hospitals founded by Lanfranc – they too might have been more secure if they had been provided with some documents which the king's agents would have no choice but to respect. It seems (to me) astonishing that no such documents were issued. Perhaps they would have made no difference. Perhaps the most explicit document that one can imagine – a diploma approved by the king, witnessed by numerous bishops and barons, endowing the monks with certain named manors and safeguarding their right to these assets during a vacancy – would still have been disregarded by Willelm II. Yet there were some among Lanfranc's contemporaries who would have thought that a diploma such as this was something worth having: it could not do any harm, and conceivably it might do some good. Apparently Lanfranc thought otherwise.

This is the context, so I suggest, for the production of manuscript C1. By some means, the monks had got hold of the records of Lanfranc's administration.[27] There was nothing here which would deter the king from the course on which he was set; but it was not unreasonable to hope that the next archbishop might make it his policy to restore everything to the state which had existed on the day when archbishop Lanfranc was alive and dead. As their hardships increased, the monks held onto this hope; and sooner or later the decision was made that any documents which might be useful for that purpose should be put in order and preserved for posterity, in a suitably awe-inspiring form. In short, I think it likely that the manuscript dates from 1089×94 – perhaps from near the end of that interval, when there was already some light at the end of the tunnel.[28] So far as C1 can be said to have had an author (somebody had to choose the documents, or at least to put them in order), prior Henric would have been the man.

The manuscript's subsequent history need only be briefly described. At some uncertain date, red headings were supplied for articles (vi) and (vii), where spaces had been left for headings by the original scribe. The hand has been identified by Gullick as that of a scribe who rubricated several manuscripts which had been written at Christ Church at the end of the eleventh or beginning of the twelfth century, but which had not been rubricated by the scribes who wrote them (Gullick and Pfaff 2001, p. 291). It looks (to me) as if he was, at some precise moment, in or not long after

C4	C1
De maneriis prioratus in kantia, et de sullinges que sunt in eis.	INCIPIVNT MANERIA MONACHORVM IN CENT.
De northewde.	—
De Estreia, et de geddinges.	DE EASTREGE.
De Tilemanestune.	DE TILEMANNESTVNE.
De fenglesham.	—
De Stepenberghe.	—
De Bocland.	—
De Sandwich'.	DE SANDWIC.

Table 7. Rubrics for the first few paragraphs in segment 2 of text α.

the 1120s, instructed to check through the monks' book-collection, adding rubrics in any books where they were missing, so that the books could be bound.[29]

For some manuscripts, this scribe would have had to retrieve the exemplar (or another copy of the same text) if he was going to get the wording right. In C1, however, there is nothing which he could not easily have invented for himself, on the spur of the moment. By and large, the rubrics write themselves:[30] so we cannot read much into the fact that the headings in C1 are mostly the same as the headings in C4. On the contrary, it is more likely to be significant that sometimes they fail to agree. To the extent that there is room for them to do so, the rubrics do tend to vary between C4 and C1. Table 7 gives the headings from the beginning of segment 2, as they appear in those manuscripts, and the reader will see that they differ at many points. Apparently it must be true, for at least one set of headings, that the rubricator was making them up as he went along. The point to hold onto is this. In C4 the headings are properly part of the text, as it was designed and executed by the original scribe; in those circumstances, I can see no justification for omitting them. The C1 headings are in a different case. It is a matter of judgment whether to include them or not, and I have preferred to drop them.

One small fact is more important than it looks. On fo. 2r this scribe inserted three headings, the last of them at the top of column 2rc: *HĘC SVNT MANERIA MONACHORVM IN CĘNT*. The end of this heading, *CHORVM IN CĘNT*, is offset on the opposite page, at the top of column 1va. That simply means that the second leaf was turned over and placed on the first leaf before the ink was dry. The significant point is that the second leaf was skewed with respect to the first one, by an angle of about 4 degrees, at the moment when

[26] It is, I hope, no longer necessary to say that the 'foundation charter' for Saint Gregory's (Brett and Gribbin 2004, no. 1) is a forgery.

[27] I see it said – by Brett and Gribbin (2004, p. xxxi), for example – that Lanfranc died at Canterbury. He was certainly buried there; I am not sure if it is known for a fact that he died there.

[28] The vacancy is said to have lasted for 'four years, nine months and nine days'. That seems to imply that things did not return to normal, from the monks' point of view, till March 1094.

[29] In this paragraph I am relying on the facts reported by Gullick; but the interpretation which he placed on them does not seem convincing to me. In particular, the manuscript from Durham, cited by Gullick as proof that this scribe was at work before 1096, does not, to me, prove anything of the kind. On the contrary, the evidence suggests that this manuscript was still at Christ Church in the 1120s, and did not migrate to Durham till after that. The doubts which I expressed about it before (Flight 1997a, p. 188) have strengthened, not weakened, since then.

[30] Anyone who doubts this should make up their own set of headings, and then compare them with the headings in C1.

they came into contact; and that makes it virtually certain that the leaves were unbound at the time.[31]

In the course of time, the blank pages at the end were mostly filled up by two later scribes. One of them added article (xi), a list of the archbishop's knights (7rb–c),[32] which forms a suitable appendix to the original contents. A further batch of documents (xii–xvii) was added by another scribe again (7va–8vb). They all date from the time of prior Alan (1179–1186); the hand could be, and presumably is, contemporary.[33] So far as they tell a story, prior Alan is the hero of it. (In the first document, for instance, we are told how he had no choice but to embarrass the archbishop publicly, in his own cathedral, on Palm Sunday in 1181.) After making himself obnoxious once too often, Alan was removed from the scene by being made abbot of Tewkesbury (where he seems to have come to lead a quieter and happier life). Just before he left Christ Church (so I suppose), he made sure that the monks whom he was being forced to abandon would have some permanent record of his achievements; and this is the place that was chosen for the purpose.

By the 1180s, then, the manuscript had reached its present form. There was still some space remaining at the end, including one whole column (8vc), but nobody ever made use of it. At some moment in the thirteenth century,[34] articles (i–xi) were copied from C1 into another manuscript, the lost cartulary which I call C3. (Whether articles (xii-xvii) were copied as well is a question which cannot be answered.) From C3, this whole stretch of text, except for article (x), was copied into manuscript T1, a booklet produced in the archbishop's treasury in the time of archbishop Kilwardby (1272–1278). These facts are discussed in greater detail in Appendix I (below, pp. 285–7). I mention them here only to make the point that the copies found in T1 are of no textual value: they derive (at second hand) from the copies in C1.

Did anything ever come of the plan to insert C1 into a textus? When the rubrics were added, the leaves were still loose; and it is probably fair to infer that they were being kept (like the other books which were rubricated by the same man) in one of the cupboards in the cloister which constituted the library, while their intended receptacle was doubtless kept (with the other textuses) in the church. Yet it would, I suppose, have been obvious to a twelfth-century monk (as it was to Cheney) what thought had existed in the mind of their creator. At any moment, therefore, if the will had existed, the original plan could still have been carried out. I see no reason to believe that it ever was; what happened, I think, was something rather different. Perhaps towards the end of the twelfth century,[35] somebody implemented his own version of the plan. Inspired by the idea behind C1, but not much impressed with its workmanship, he produced a new set of leaves (more elegantly written, more sumptuously decorated, as we may imagine them to have been) containing the same or a similar collection of documents; and these were the leaves which were finally bound into the textus – the 'great textus' mentioned in a charter of archbishop Hubert's (Cheney and John 1986, no. 389).[36]

Once that had been done, there could no longer be any thought of binding C1. Even so, the leaves seemed worth keeping and were kept. They were, I suppose, rolled up together (the natural thing to do with a batch of sheets of this size) and put on a shelf in the library. Once in a while, it seems, they were taken down – on one occasion to be collated with C4, on another occasion to be copied into the cartulary. But after that they remained on the shelf, untouched and more or less forgotten, until they were discovered by William Somner.

R1 = Strood, Medway Archives and Local Studies Centre, DRc/R1, fos. 119–235

This is a another famous manuscript, a handsome cartulary compiled in the 1120s by one of the best and best-known Rochester scribes. The title which he provided for it is *Privilegia aecclesiae sancti Andreae hrofensis concessa* (fo. 119r), 'Privileges granted to the church of Saint Andrew of Rochester', and that is the title by which I refer to

[31] It is not absolutely impossible for two bound leaves to be brought into contact in this way. In order to make it happen, however, one has to form a triangular pleat down the middle of the second leaf (while the ink is still wet) before letting it touch the first leaf; and anyone perverse enough to do this would need at least three hands.

[32] Douglas's (1944) discussion of this list – which should be read alongside Colvin's (1964) discussion of a later list (*c.* 1170) – is not altogether satisfactory. Most of the names appearing here are (so far as we know) the names which would be expected to occur in a list drawn up in the 1090s; but there are some anachronisms – most obviously the name 'Biset' (7rb32), appearing where one would expect to find the name of Ansgot de Rovecestre. In the form in which we have it, I do not think that this list can be earlier than *c.* 1160.

[33] Very briefly, these are the contents: (xii) a narrative account of an incident which took place at Christ Church on 29 March 1181 (7va); (xiii) a narrative account of the sequence of events which began with the death of Walter bishop of Rochester on 27 July 1182 and ended with the humiliation of his successor (7vb–8ra); (xiv) a charter of archbishop Ricard (Cheney and Jones 1986, no. 85) relating to Eynsford church, with three lines of narrative by way of introduction and five lines by way of conclusion (8ra–c); (xv) a charter of Willelm de Einesford, recounting the history of the dispute over Eynsford church and saying that he is happy with the outcome (8rc–va); (xvi) a charter of prior Alan and the convent of Christ Church, making Willelm de Einesford an honorary member of their community (8va–b); (xvii) a charter of Willelm de Einesford, saying that he has been fully indemnified for the hundred marks which he lost through standing surety for archbishop Thomas (8vb). Throughout this stretch of text, the coloured initials are missing.

[34] Not until after the gloss *s. ædwardi* had been added to the Ulcombe paragraph (3va4). This insertion is important for tracking the transmission of the text.

[35] Not, I suspect, till after prior Alan's time. Alan, it seems, was still under the impression that sooner or later C1 was going to be bound.

[36] There are only two things known about this book: before 1203 it contained a survey of the monks' lands; after 1203 it also contained a copy of this charter. (The wording is explicit: the convent has put its seal to the original 'and has caused a copy of it to be entered in the great textus where there is also a survey of their lands', *et eius rescriptum in textu magno ubi et terrarum suarum descriptio annotari fecit.*) Cheney was hoping to find some trace of this textus. He thought that he had failed. If I am connecting the dots correctly, he came closer than he realized.

it.[37] (For some reason which escapes me, historians prefer to call it by a name which is neither authentic nor apt.) An excellent facsimile edition is available (Sawyer 1962).

In its pristine form, the manuscript consisted of four booklets, and documents dating from (or referring to) the period which interests us – the reigns of Willelm I and Willelm II - were contained in booklet 2. This booklet comprised two quires (numbered VII–VIII by the scribe himself): the first survives intact (fos. 168–75), but the second has been very badly cut about. As I reconstruct it (Flight 1997a, fig. 4), booklet 2 would originally have looked like this:

fos. 168–76; one or two leaves missing;[38] fos. 209–10; one leaf missing; fos. 211–12; one leaf missing (replaced with fo. 213); fo. 214; one leaf missing (replaced with fo. 181); fo. 182

Cutting out or replacing whole leaves was not enough to achieve the desired result. Some of the original leaves that were allowed to survive had to pay for their survival by being partially erased. Though the details are hidden from us, it seems clear enough what was happening. A fairly large number of documents, thought to be worth copying in the 1120s, became so much of an embarrassment later that they had to be suppressed. The originals were (we may assume) destroyed or purposely mislaid; the cartulary was expurgated. Whatever the motives for it, the treatment was brutally effective. We are never going to know what it was that the monks decided, on second thoughts, not to let us know.

Among the surviving documents, only one is directly relevant,[39] a survey of the bishop's manors (fos. 209r–10r). By and large, it runs parallel with segment 3 of $\alpha2$ / C1, but it differs from that version in many points of detail, and on one point of substance. I call this Rochester version $\alpha3$.

The document or documents preceding this one was or were suppressed: counting backwards from the start of $\alpha3$, we find four erased lines (209r1–4), one or two missing leaves, and another eight erased lines (176v17–24).[40] It is a tantalizing thought that some important evidence may have been lost here; but (unless someone can decipher some of the erased text) that is not a thought which I see any point in pursuing. The document following $\alpha3$ was not suppressed: it is a record of the benefactions of Willelm I, drawn up, no doubt, very shortly after his death (210r–v).

There is no other copy of $\alpha3$ known to me; but there does exist a derivative text, which likewise survives only as a single copy,[41] in an early thirteenth-century register (R3, fo. 66v). The text has been drastically shortened, to the extent that from our point of view it ceases to have any value, but not to the extent that its ancestry is doubtful. The entry relating to Bromley, for instance, has been reduced from this:

Brunlega se defendebat in tempore eaduuardi regis pro vi solinis, et nunc pro iii, et est appreciatum xviii lib', et tamen ep's habet inde de firma sua xx libras et xviii solid', et hoc idem manerium est ipse hundredus.

to this:

Brumlega defendit se pro tribus suling', et hoc idem manerium est ipse hundredus.

What little interest this text possesses derives from a few interpolated passages which tell us something about the holdings on the monks' manors belonging to the bishop's knights. (We are told, for example, that the assessment of three sulungs for Wouldham includes 'the sulung of Little Wouldham and the half sulung of Robert le Neveu'.)[42] But this is early thirteenth-century information, too late to be relevant for us.

Before looking more closely at the differences between $\alpha1$ / C4 and $\alpha2$ / C1, we can simplify matters by making two preliminary observations. First, without looking very hard, we can see that six whole paragraphs are differently placed: all six are in segment 1 in C4, in segment 2 in C1. It is not obvious which ordering is more authentic than the other. Because of this uncertainty, and because the difference in placement is bound to entail some difference in the wording, it seems safest, for present purposes, to disregard these paragraphs.

Second, in dealing with C4, some allowance has to be made for the relative lateness of the manuscript. Without looking at all, we can feel fairly sure that the scribe will have modernized the spelling, to some degree. There is at least one feature of the text, as it appears in C4, which seems certain to have originated in C4 itself. Halfway through, the scribe starts using the perfect tense – *habuit* not *habet*, *tenuit* not *tenet* – in passages which refer to anyone other than the archbishop or the monks. This happens first in the paragraph relating to Eynsford, in the sentence concerning

[37] I have one correction and one addition to make to my description of the manuscript (Flight 1997a, ch. 2). (i) The suggestion made there (p. 23) that some of the entries on fo. 202r were written by the main scribe is wrong. None of them were. (ii) The extra line which has been added at the foot of fo. 192v, presumably when the following leaf was removed, *was* written by the main scribe. Rather sadly, this tends to prove that he himself began the work of mutilating the manuscript.

[38] Quire VIII has been damaged so badly that we cannot be sure how many leaves it had originally. It may have been a quire of 12; it may have been a quire of 10 with an extra singleton tucked in towards the back.

[39] Three others, all from this same booklet, are printed in chapter 7 (below, pp. 222-3). The list of parish churches (below, pp. 240–2) comes from booklet 4.

[40] At which point we arrive at the end of a long document (175v–6v) recounting the dispute between bishop Gundulf and sheriff Picot with regard to some land in Cambridgeshire.

[41] It was printed, not very accurately, by Thorpe (1788, p. 2).

[42] *Wldeham defend' se pro iii sullin' cum sullino de parua Wldeham et dimid' sull' Rob' nepot'.* This is one of the entries added at the end by a second scribe (Flight 1997a, p. 82), who had to do some work on this copy to knock it into shape.

the portion of the manor swallowed up by the lowy of Tonbridge. The scribe writes *et ex eo h't* – and then he stops, changes his mind, obliterates *'t* with an oversized *a*, and completes the word as *habuit* (71rb26): 'And from it Ricard of Tonbridge holds ... or, rather, used to hold as much as is worth three pounds.' From this point onwards, in this sort of context, he uses the perfect tense nearly all the time.[43] Towards the end, the word *reddit* gets the same treatment, and again we can actually see the scribe changing his mind. In the Farningham entry he writes *reddit* – and then he alters the *t* into a large *d'* (72va10), so that the word becomes *reddid'* (for *reddidit*, 'used to pay'). I suppose that he found it absurd to continue using the present tense in statements which were so manifestly out of date, but in any case the fact itself seems plain: it was this scribe, writing this copy, who decided to change the tense of some of the verbs. Discrepancies of this sort are a surface phenomenon, therefore, and we can cheerfully ignore them.[44]

Subject to these limitations, all variants which look as if they might be significant are listed in Table 8.[45] In view of the number and nature of the discrepancies, the conclusion to be drawn from this table seems clear enough. We are dealing with two different versions of the text, rather than with two copies of a single version. Each version contains some information (proved to be authentic by the fact that it appears in DB) which is absent from the other. This is obviously true for $\alpha 2$; not quite so obviously, it is true for $\alpha 1$ as well (71vb38, 72ra33, 72rb30). That is why I have felt compelled to print both copies. If the choice had been left to me, I should have preferred to conclude that C4 was just a defective copy of C1, perhaps with a few unimportant interpolations; and then I should have written it off. But the facts are too recalcitrant for that.

Even so, the differences do not cut very deep. Almost everywhere, the two versions are as nearly identical as can be expected, given that some allowance has to be made for variations introduced by the copyists concerned (especially on the part of the C4 scribe, who allowed himself some latitude for editing the text). They report the same facts; they use the same formulas. If one version has an explanatory remark – such as *quia archiepiscopus habet aliud ad suam propriam carucam* (70vb23 = 3ra13) – or an abnormal turn of phrase – such as *et nunc pro totidem* (71ra30 = 3rb46) – the other version is, very nearly, certain to have it too.

They also share many defects, large and small. Among their larger flaws, both versions fail to report the current assessment for certain manors (Reculver, Gillingham, Maidstone, Wrotham); both omit to tell us how much Lyminge or Maidstone is worth. At the other end of the scale, both versions twice have the present tense *habet* where the context requires a past tense (70va38 = 2vc36, 70vb25 = 3ra16). The examples quoted are all from segment 1, but (as the reader may wish to verify) similar comments apply to segment 2 as well. Thus, to a large extent, either copy can serve as a check on the other.

For segment 3, instead of comparing C1 with C4, we have to compare it with a copy from Rochester, $\alpha 3$ / R1, from which, conversely, segments 1–2 are missing. To all appearances, $\alpha 3$ is just an edited version of this segment of $\alpha 2$. Collating the copies that survive, we find only two large discrepancies. The first is that one whole entry is differently placed: in C1 the Frindsbury paragraph comes right at the beginning (5ra16), which means that it seems to be covered by the statement 'These manors are in Axstone hundred' (5rb2); in R1 it keeps company – as it should – with the other paragraphs relating to Shamell hundred.

The other large difference affects the opening sentences of every paragraph. The wording used here in C1 (consistent with that used for segments 1–2) runs something like this:

Sutfliote est manerium ep'i rofensis et in tempore E regis se defendebat pro vi sull' ...

In R1 the wording has been simplified, and the order of the constituent phrases has become highly unstable. In his first paragraph, the compiler of $\alpha 3$ simplifies only slightly, retaining the phrase *manerium epi' hrofensis*,[46] but putting it in apposition to the place-name:

Suthfleta manerium ep'i hrofensis se defendebat in tempore eaduuardi regis pro vi solinis ...

But after that he simplifies more drastically, letting it be taken for granted that all these manors belong to the bishop of Rochester, and giving only the place-name:

Stanes se defendebat pro vi solinis in tempore eaduuardi regis ...

For the rest, the wording is mostly word for word the same as C1. The only exception to this rule is the Trottiscliffe paragraph, both versions of which are anomalous; since they also disagree as to the facts, their divergence appears to reflect some difference of opinion regarding the manor's assessment (below, p. 70).

Whatever their significance may be, the differences between one version and another are not large – in particular, not large enough to alter the fact that text α should be read as the response to a questionnaire (Flight 2006, p. 113). The paragraphs of α were framed as replies to a set sequence of

[43] But a corrector has put some of these verbs back into the present tense. The last alteration of this kind occurs in the Mersham entry (72ra29); after that the corrector gave up.

[44] This applies to some other discrepancies too, such as C4's use of *dominicum* in preference to *dominium*. Some numerals which are oddly expressed in C1 (such as *c lib' et vii*, *lx sol' et x*) are normally formed in C4 (*c et vii lib'*, *lxx sol'*); no doubt they were regularized by the C4 scribe.

[45] The erasures in C4 were made for the purpose of assimilating the text to C1 (above, p. 34). Though we do not know what C4 said originally, we can be sure that it said something different from C1: otherwise there would have been no need for the erasure.

[46] The *hr* spelling is probably the R1 scribe's; he seems to have insisted on it (below, p. 290), where he felt he could.

	$\alpha 1$ / c4		$\alpha 2$ / C1
70rb8	ø	2va12	tenitune
23	vii de stursete tantum	44	unum iugum uuic et est de terra monachorum sc'ę trinitatis
25	ø	48	In fordwic habet archiep's vii mansuras terrę quę modo non faciunt seruitium ad mare ut in tempore E regis
30	tenet inde i sull' ab archiep'o in feodo	2vb5	habet i sull'
31	et wibertus et arnoldus suus filius habent inde	6	wibertus et arnoldus habent
37	Ad berham est hundredus	16	et est in hundret de berham
70va1	ø	25	id est suurtling
71ra11	reddit	3rb9	ille qui tenet reddit inde
23	ø	33	i sull' et d'
25	postea tenuit	37	nunc tenet illud
25	a lanfranco	37	ab isto lanfranco
26	ø	39	et dimidio
36	lanfrancus	3rc5	iste lanfrancus
40	ipsum reddit	11	illud reddit inde
71rb5	ø	20	de firma
20	ø	40	pro ii sull'
25	ø	51	et nunc tenet radulfus filius hospaci ab archiep'o
29	ø	3va6	tenet comes de o' de archiep'o et
71va12	In hundredo de cornhille habet archiep's i sull' de prebenda sc'i martini	14	ø
18	Summa ... (*blank*) ...	36	Tota summa clxxx et vii sull' et dimidium
26	ø	3vb11	Hoc manerium est de hundret de cantuarberia
31	Tilemanestune	24	willelm' folet tenet i manerium tilesmannestune ab archiep'o et hoc
34	... (*erasure*) ... apud fenglesham dimid' sull'	31	Iste idem will' habet de predicta terra dimidium sull' ab archiep'o in fenglesham
37	... (*erasure*) ... dimid' sull' stepenberghe quod godwinus tenuit de archiep'o aðzi tempore E regis et tunc se defendebat pro dimid' sull' sicut et nunc	37	Iste idem will' habet adhuc ab eodem archiep'o et de prędicta terra monachorum stepenberga quod se defendebat tempore E regis pro dimidio sull' et nunc facit et godwinus tenuit illud in tempore E regis ab archiep'o ædzi
71vb2	monachorum ... eorum	48	sc'ę trinitatis ... monachorum
6	postea	3vc4	in pręterito anno reddidit
7	ø	5	et in isto anno debet reddere lx et x lib' et allecia sicut prius
8	... (*erasure*) ...	10	lx et xvi plus
12	In leth de estreie est hundr' de edesham quod est in eodem manerio	19	ø
19	ø	34	Hoc manerium habet hundret in se ipso et in læd est de æstraie
24	Hic finit leth de burwarleth	50	ø
38	et tamen reddit xxvii lib'	4ra26	ø
72ra18	set postquam illud tenuit	4rb12	per gablum et postquam ep's habuit hoc dimidium sull'
33	et se defendit pro i sull'	41	ø
36	ø	48	i sull'
72rb15	in feodo	4va38	ø
17	monachorum ... eorum	43	sc'ę trinitatis ... monachorum
18	ø	45	similiter fuit et
30	et nunc pro vii	4vb11	ø
72va11	ø	4vc7	et nunc similiter
39	ø	5ra11	Tota summa cxxx et iii sull' et dimidium

Table 8. Variants for segments 1–2 of text α.

questions; and therefore they conform to a regular pattern. In its simplest expression, the pattern looks like this:

Northfleet is the archbishop's manor, and in the time of king Eadward it defended itself for six sulungs, and now for five, and it is appraised at 27 pounds (71ra9 = 3rb6).

The same pattern applies throughout, except that the first clause is modified appropriately, from one segment to the next: 'Reculver is the archbishop's manor', or 'Eastry is the monks' manor', or 'Southfleet is the bishop of Rochester's manor'. (An extra clause appears in segment 2, telling us how the income from the manor is assigned: 'for the monks' food', or 'for their clothing', as the case may be.)

Though all of the paragraphs in segment 3 fit into that simple pattern, in segments 1 and 2 there is more variety. Some of the larger manors include subordinate holdings. If that is the case, the paragraph continues with a number of sub-paragraphs giving some basic information for each holding: the name of the tenant, the number of sulungs, the value. Some of the smaller manors belong in their entirety to one of the archbishop's tenants. If that is the case, the paragraph begins differently, with a statement of the pertinent facts, TRE and now. For example:

Brasted (is a manor which) Wlnod cild held from the archbishop in the time of king Eadward, and now Haimo holds it from archbishop Lanfranc, and then it defended itself ... (71ra24 = 3rb35).

It seems to have been doubtful, in some instances, whether a manor should be described in a sub-paragraph or in a paragraph by itself. If that doubt was not resolved, a manor could end up by being described twice. Graveney, for example, is described in a sub-paragraph (70va40 = 2vc42) appended to the paragraph for Boughton under Blean; but it is also described in a separate paragraph (72va13 = 4vc12), at the end of segment 2. It was held 'in feod from the archbishop' by one of the archbishop's men; but it was recognized as 'the monks' manor' none the less, and the tenant accordingly paid a farm to them.

The last five paragraphs in segment 2 (Graveney among them) are all repetitious. In three cases it is stated explicitly that the sulungs mentioned here are included in the assessments previously reported: Loose and Hunton are to be counted with the monks' manor of East Farleigh, Burston with the archbishop's manor of Maidstone. But the details tend to differ. That is most obviously true for the holding called Burston. In a sub-paragraph appended to the Maidstone paragraph (71ra1 = 3ra46) we have been told that there are two men who have one sulung of this manor, and that they pay 192 pence to the altar of the Holy Trinity (i.e. to the monks), though the sulung is worth more than that. In this paragraph at the end (72va27 = 4vc43) we are given some additional information (that the place in question is Burston, that the two men who own it are named Wulfric and Cole), but also some information which does not square with what we were told before (there is half a sulung there, not a whole sulung, and the owners pay 100 pence, not 192 pence). In short, we are being given a different account of the facts, only partly compatible with the first one. Perhaps we might imagine that one account came from the monks of Holy Trinity, the other from the men of Maidstone. At all events, the upshot seems to have been that the compiler of text α had two discordant statements in front of him, and – not being in a position to decide between them – included them both as they stood.[47]

It was obviously intended to provide information regarding the hundred to which each manor belongs; but some lack of coherence is evident in this respect too. The normal policy (the policy followed more frequently than not in segments 1–2, invariably in segment 3) is for the information to be given at the end of the paragraph. In the case of Gillingham, for instance, we are given the usual facts; and then we are told that 'this manor is in the hundred of Chatham' (70vb39 = 3ra43).[48] If, however, the next manor belongs to the same hundred, the statement is postponed to the end of that paragraph – and then postponed again, if need be, until the end of the hundred in question is reached. Thus we are not immediately informed which hundred Otford belongs to. To find that out, we have to scan ahead until we find a statement which covers Otford; and this comes at the end of the Sundridge paragraph, where we are told that 'these manors are in the hundred of Codsheath' (71rb1 = 3rc13). Conversely, if we want to know what is meant by 'these manors', we have to scan backwards until we run up against a contradictory statement – in this case the statement 'This manor is is the hundred of Westerham', at the end of the Brasted paragraph (71ra27 = 3rb41). There are some hiccups,[49] but this policy works well enough, most of the time, as far as the hundreds are concerned. (The lest indications, though a few do occur, are miserably inadequate.) The odd thing is that a minority of the paragraphs in segments 1–2 are very differently treated. Right at the beginning, we are told explicitly which lest and which hundred we are in. The Lyminge paragraph, for example, starts like this: 'In Limwarleth, in the hundred of Loningborough, the archbishop has in his domain a manor (called) Lyminge which in the time of king Eadward ...' (70va14 = 2vb46) – after which the rest of the paragraph conforms to the usual pattern (barring the fact that in this particular paragraph the values are all unreported). I do not understand the reason for this variation.

As I commented before (Flight 2006, pp. 111–12), the provenance of this text seems clear from the fact that the ordering of the paragraphs in segment 1 coincides with

[47] The sulung called 'Almsland' is also described twice: under Lyminge in segment 1 (70va19 = 2vb54), separately in segment 2 (72ra32 = 4rb39). Here again the details do not tally.

[48] Some of these statements make use of a formula which seems rather awkwardly constructed: *Hec maneria habet archiep's in hundredo de Calehelle*. The sentence would read more easily back to front: *In hundredo de Calehelle habet archiep's hec maneria* .... And in that form it looks line a line from a cadastrally organized list: 'In the hundred of ... the archbishop (monks, bishop) has (have) the manor(s) of ... .'

[49] For instance, we are not told that Darenth and Eynsford are in Axstone hundred, or that Ulcombe is in Eyhorne hundred.

that used in another text – article (ix) in manuscript C1 (above, p. 37) – which can only have been produced in the archbishop's household, and which (except in this respect) seems to have no connection with the survey of 1086. On that topic I have nothing to add. But there is some other evidence which tends towards the same conclusion. Now and then, text α seems to be giving us a view of the facts different from that which was accepted and put on record by the commissioners. The manor of Sandling is listed here among the lands of the archbishopric (71rb15 = 4vb44), but the commissioners found (as DB reports) that it belonged to the bishop of Bayeux. The manor of Stowting is stated here to belong to Willelm de Arcis (70va6 = 2vb34), but the commissioners found that it was held by the count of Eu. The existence of Codsheath hundred, taken for granted here (71rb1 = 3rc13), appears not to have been admitted by the commissioners. Because our ignorance of the circumstances allows us so much freedom to guess at the reasons for them, discrepancies like these are easily explained away. Nevertheless, taken all together, they suggest to me that we are seeing things from somebody else's point of view – specifically from the archbishop's.

To this extent, I think we can feel sure of our ground. Text α is the archbishop's response to a questionnaire which came from the commissioners – the commissioners responsible for carrying out the investigations which were needed to construct the B text. In a sense, therefore, α is a joint production. Some of the decisions which gave this text its shape were made by the commissioners. Its scope was determined by them: it should confine itself to Kent. Its content was dictated by them: these were the questions to which they wanted answers, at this stage in their proceedings. Beyond that point, text α is the work of the people who knew the answers – the officials engaged in the management of the archbishop's estates.

Having come this far, I think we can go a little further. Sooner or later, we shall have to ask ourselves why α exists in two versions; perhaps this is the right moment for that. A plausible answer might be that the shorter version, $\alpha 1$, is a preliminary draft, and that the longer version, $\alpha 2$, is the finished product. But we cannot say that without considering the consequences. On this view of the case, the fact that $\alpha 2$ survived would imply that it was returned to the archbishop, after the commissioners had finished with it; and it would then become conceivable that some or all of the additions appearing in this version were made by the commissioners' scribes, while they had the original in their hands.

With that thought in mind, we need to look more closely at the variants listed in Table 8. The passages appearing in the right-hand column are not all to be regarded as additions in $\alpha 2$: some share of them, no doubt, should be diagnosed as omissions from our copy of $\alpha 1$.[50] The majority, however, seem sure to be genuine additions – corrections or clarifications inserted in this version of the text.

If we listen carefully enough to what these additions are saying, I think we can hear voices speaking which do not emanate from the archbishop's household. One sentence especially,

> In Fordwich the archbishop has seven measures of land which now do not do service at sea as they did in the time of king Eadward,

sounds discordant to me: it sounds like a complaint from the men of Fordwich. 'The archbishop's tenants have stopped paying their share, and therefore the rest of us have to pay something extra.'[51] Reading the added passages in the description of Sandwich, I think I can hear the men of Sandwich speaking. 'Well, yes, that used to be true. Last year we did indeed pay the archbishop fifty pounds. But this year we are supposed to be paying him seventy pounds – plus, of course, the usual number of herrings.' In these passages, unless my ears are deceiving me, we overhear some snatches of the conversation which went on, while the B text was being put together, between the commissioners and the spokesmen for the hundreds.

The additions which distinguish $\alpha 2$ from $\alpha 1$ were, I suspect, mostly made by the scribes who accompanied the commissioners. These scribes had the original of $\alpha 2$ in their possession; once in a while (by no means systematically) they inserted some annotation of their own. The same explanation might apply to one omission too: the sentence referring to the prebend in Saint Martin's church (71va2) could have been cancelled by these scribes, on the grounds that this and the other prebends were held from the church's patron, not directly from the king. And it could have been their decision as well that certain paragraphs should be transferred from segment 1 to segment 2.[52] Nevertheless, even on the most generous assessment, their contribution would not have amounted to much. To a very much larger extent, $\alpha 2$ is still the work of the archbishop's scribes. In reading text α, especially in version $\alpha 1$, we can be confident, nearly all the time, that we are reading a text which was put together in the archbishop's household, in the early months of 1086.

Even so, there are some aspects of the evidence – three in particular – which look as if they ought to be significant, but for which I can find no adequate explanation. I should not be dealing fairly with the reader if I were to leave this unsaid.

First, I do not understand why some of the paragraphs in segments 1–2 depart from the normal pattern by starting

[50] One large omission from C4, sure to be accidental, occurs in the Sandling paragraph (71rb16 = 4vb47). This variant is not listed in Table 8, because Sandling is one of the paragraphs which got transposed.

[51] The corresponding passage in DB is attached to the description of Fordwich, which (because the town belonged to Saint Augustine's) is included in chapter 7 (DB-Ke-12rb22).

[52] But perhaps we might prefer to make an exception for the Sandling paragraph.

with a sentence which locates the manor in the cadastral frame (above, p. 43). (This is true for both versions, by and large. There are some discrepancies between $\alpha 1$ and $\alpha 2$ – most notably in the paragraphs for Adisham and Newenden – but I do not see that they help us to crack the puzzle.) Looking at the Pluckley paragraph (70vb29 = 3ra23), I can imagine that it may have originally conformed to the normal pattern (as the paragraphs before and after it do), before being reconstructed with a different beginning. But I see no similar signs elsewhere. Besides, even if this were the right explanation for Pluckley, I should still be at a loss to explain why only only some paragraphs, or why these particular paragraphs, were rewritten in this way.

Second, I do not understand why six paragraphs are differently placed, all included in segment 1 by C4, in segment 2 by C1. It is conceivable that they were moved into segment 1 by the C4 scribe himself, who certainly did allow himself some scope for editing the text, and may perhaps have taken the liberty of reorganizing it as well. (A variation on this theory would be that these paragraphs had been marked for transposition in the exemplar from which he was copying, and that he was just following instructions.) The manors in question are all places which, by the thirteenth century, had ceased to be of any interest to the monks; so perhaps it might have seemed more rational to transfer them to segment 1. As far as the textual evidence is concerned, we cannot hope to find any clue unless the transposition was botched to some extent – i.e. unless the damage done to the text by extracting a paragraph from one segment and inserting it into the other was not fully made good. The paragraph for Sandling, as it appears in C4, has a blundered sentence at the end (71rb17); since that sentence makes perfect sense in C1, where it refers to Orpington as well as Sandling (4vb44), we may take this as a sign that the paragraph was originally part of segment 2. On the other hand, the sentence at the end of the Preston paragraph, which is redundant in C1 (4va6) but not in C4, is a hint that the paragraph for Leaveland was moved in the opposite direction, from segment 1 into segment 2; and in that case the transposition would have to have been made early on, before C1 was written. In short, the indications are slight; such as they are, they are also contradictory. Given that (given too that Sandling was a special case), I find it impossible to arrive at any firm conclusion.[53]

Third, I do not understand why the order of the paragraphs in segment 3 is, very nearly, the same as in DB-Ke. In most respects, this segment runs parallel with segments 1–2. The same categories of information are reported; the same wording is used. C1 gives a total at the end of this segment, just as it does at the end of the others; it even has the strange word *rubitoniensis*, which appears once here (5ra17), once near the end of segment 2 (4vc3), never (to my knowledge) in any other text. And yet, in this respect, there is divergence. Segments 1–2 have an ordering of their own, quite different from DB's; segment 3 has (almost) the same ordering as DB. Since that ordering was only brought into existence when the B text was compiled, we have a problem.

Less obviously, there is another feature which sets segment 3 apart. In all probability, a more detailed description of these manors would have revealed a pattern of tenure resembling that which is recorded in segments 1–2. Just like the archbishop, the bishop of Rochester had to make provision for his monks. Somehow or other, he also had to find ten knights for the archbishop – his share of the sixty knights which the archbishop had to find for the king. (If he chose, he could pay for them out of his own pocket; but sooner or later, just like the archbishop, he created tenancies charged with some proportion of the load.) It is, however, very difficult to say how far this sort of pattern would have taken shape by the time of the survey. If Rochester's early thirteenth-century annals can be trusted – and probably they can be – the monks arrived in 1083 (R3, fo. 27v); so they were already there when the survey took place. It is clear that some allocation of lands had been made to them well before 1089, because archbishop Lanfranc (who died in that year) had already approved one change in that allocation (R1, fo. 172r–v).[54] The allocation of lands to the bishop's knights is a matter about which we are very poorly informed. Several holdings were certainly or probably created by bishop Gundulf, some of them on his domain manors, some of them on the monks' manors; but Gundulf survived until 1108, and – to be brief – it is impossible to decide how many of these holdings existed in 1086.

That difficulty arises from the fact that we get no help from either α or DB. As far as DB is concerned (though the DB scribe himself did not understand this), the absence of more detailed information is unsurprising. It is in keeping with the policy followed throughout the survey. From the king's point of view, the bishop of Rochester was a subtenant, and it was not necessary to inquire into the arrangements that he had made for his monks and knights and other sub-sub-tenants. That information was not worth collecting (at the price of a vast amount of extra effort), because it was not relevant.[55] From the archbishop's point of view, by contrast, the bishop of Rochester was a tenant,[56] and the information would be needed every time that a bishop died. Thus, in a description drawn up by one of the archbishop's officials, we might expect to find some interest being shown

[53] One question arises which I need to note but will not try to answer. Was the reorganization of the text connected with a pseudo-historical theory which the monks had developed by this time, to the effect that they had, voluntarily, surrendered a share of their land to archbishop Lanfranc, to help him make provision for his knights – 'which is why to this day there is not one knight on all the land of the monks, but only on the land of the archbishop'?

[54] The monks acquired the nearby manor of Wouldham in exchange for a manor in Suffolk which had proved to be inconveniently remote.

[55] More precisely, it would only become relevant if the bishop died while the archbishopric was in the king's hands – and that, though it might possibly happen, would happen only very rarely. (In fact it did happen twice in the twelfth century, in 1137 and 1184.)

[56] In other words, the bishop was *tenant en chief* with respect to the archbishop, just as the archbishop was *tenant en chief* with respect to the king.

in the assignment of lands to the bishop's sub-tenants. But that is not the case. Unlike segments 1 and 2, segment 3 has no depth: it is as flat as the description that we find in DB (even flatter, in fact, because at one point DB goes deeper and α does not).

These two DB-like features of segment 3 – the ordering of the paragraphs and the absence of tenurial depth – distinguish it so clearly from segments 1–2 that we are, I think, permitted to suppose that it had a different ontogeny. Taking advantage of the doubt which exists as to whether this segment was included in $\alpha 1$, we can construct an explanation for it without feeling obliged to force the same explanation onto the rest of the text – in a word, without letting the Rochester tail wag the Canterbury dog. One theory which would fit the facts might look something like this. The man who had written segments 1–2 decided, some time later, to write a similar description of the bishop of Rochester's manors. He used the same format and language that he had used before (even allowing himself, just once, to repeat the word *rubitoniensis*); but he took the ordering of the paragraphs and all the items of factual information from some version of the survey text (a version, we should have to think, which unlike DB had the hundred headings all in place). I am satisfied that this is a viable explanation (as the reader can confirm by making the experiment);[57] whether it is the right one, or something close to the right one, I hardly feel able to say.

Some of these problematic features are discussed in greater detail in the comments at the end of this chapter (below, pp. 66–70). The reader may find those comments helpful, as far as they go – or else may prefer to ignore them, so as to be able to take an unprejudiced view of the evidence. Sooner or later, I have no doubt, fresh eyes will see further, and see more clearly, than mine.

I print all three versions line for line, as they appear in the manuscripts. For the reasons already indicated, I ignore the alterations made by other hands in manuscripts C4 and C1 – the numerous corrections added to C4, the red headings added to C1. The reader, I hope, will take my word for it that these additions do nothing but distract attention from the evidence which really counts.

The transcription aims to be tight, but there are some scribal tricks which I have not thought it necessary to imitate. The C1 scribe, after leaving space for a coloured initial, writes the next letter or the next few letters as small capitals. (At 2va3, for example, he leaves a space for the initial and writes *TVRsæte*.) This looks well enough when written by hand, but in print it becomes unsightly, and I have disallowed it. The R1 scribe, admirable in every other respect, has one annoying mannerism: whenever the start of a new sentence happens to fall at the start of a new line, he pushes the beginning of the first word out into the margin – which makes it look as if he is starting a new paragraph when in fact he is just acting out of habit. So I have disallowed this trick as well. All the scribes concerned felt free to shorten some words – especially recurrent words, like 'saint' or 'archbishop' or 'shilling', which no one could possibly misread. In dealing with these abbreviations, I have followed the same sort of rules that I use for DB-Ke (below, pp. 95–6).

The pages or columns are labelled, and every fifth line is numbered. I use these numbers for reference, and suggest that the reader should adopt the same policy. Blank lines are marked with colons at the beginning, so that they too can be counted. (But a colon at the end of a word denotes the punctuation mark called *punctus elevatus*.) Brackets enclose any particles of text (including the coloured initials) which show any sign of having been altered or added; brackets surrounding empty space represent erasures. Where some explanation is needed, an asterisk refers to the notes which appear at the end of each text.

[57] But it is not a complete solution: for example, it does not tell us how the Frindsbury paragraph got itself misplaced in $\alpha 2$/C1.

α1 / C4-70rb

(De maneriis archiep'atus in kantia, et de sullinges que sunt) (in eis.) (De Sturset e.)

(S) tursete est manerium archiep'i, et in tempore E regis se defendebat pro vii sullinges, et nunc similiter, et est appreciatum *hoc est in dominico xl lib'. Et nunc habet archiep's xxv burgenses, qui reddunt x sol' de gablo. Et ex hiis supradictis *viii sulling' habet Godefr' dapifer unum sulling' de archiep'o et est appreciatum c sol'. Adhuc autem et uitalis habet inde unum iugum terre de archiep'o, et est appreciatum xx sol'. Haimo uero similiter tenet inde dimidium sulling', quod tenuit alric bigge a priore arch' in tempore E regis, et est appreciatum c sol'. Robertus de hardres tenet inde i iugum terre ex hiisdem sull', et est appreciatum xxx sol', et ex hiis vii sull' habet ar'ep's i sull' apud sc'm martinum, et de eodem sull' habet Rad' camerarius in feodo medietatem de ar'ep'o, et ualet iiii lib'. Et d'nicum ualet vii lib'. Et in Cantuar' sunt vii burgenses, qui redd' huic manerio viii sol' et iiii *de gablo. Et item sunt ibi xxxii mansure, et unum molendinum, que tenent clerici sc'i Gregorii ad eorum eccl'iam. Ibique manent xii burgenses qui redd' eis xxxv sol', et molendinum redd' v sol'. Adhuc etiam tenet ailwardus iii iuga in natindon', unde redd' tempore E regis et adhuc redd' altari sc'e trinitatis xii sol', et est appreciatum xl solid'. Albold uero tenet de supradictis sull' vii de stursete tantum quod est appreciatum xxx sol'. Hic finitur hundredus de Stursete. (De Wingeham.)

(W) ingeham est proprium manerium archiep'i, et in tempore E regis se defendebat pro xl sull', et nunc pro xxxv, et ualet c lib' hoc quod archiep's inde habet. Et ex hisdem sull' habet Will's de archis unum sull' fleotes ab archiep'o in feodo, et ualet vi lib'. Et uitalis tenet inde i sull' ab archiep'o in feodo et ualet xlv sol'. Et Wibertus et Arnoldus suus filius: habent inde iii sull', et ualent xii lib'. Et heringod habet inde i sull' decem agros minus, et ualet xl sol'. Et Godefridus archibalistarius habet inde i sull' et dimid', et ualet c sol'. (De B[urn]e.)

(B) urne est proprium manerium archiep'i, et in tempore E regis se defendebat pro vi sull', et nunc similiter, et est appreciatum xxx lib'. Ad berham est hundredus. (De P[etham.])

(P) etham est proprium manerium archiep'i, et in tempore E regis se defendebat pro vii sull', et nunc similiter, et est appreciatum xx lib'. Et ex istis sull' habet Godefridus dapifer dimid'

α1 / C4-70va

sull', quod pertinet ad uestimenta monachorum. Et Nigellus habet i sull' et i iugum terre, que est appreciata lx sol'. Hoc est in hundredo de petham. (De Aldintune.)

(I) n hundredo de bilichold: habet archiep's i manerium Aldintune, et in tempore E regis se defendebat pro xxi sull', et nunc pro xx, et ualet c et vii lib'. Et ex hiis habet Will's de archis i manerium Stutinges, quod alfere tenuit de archiep'o, et tunc defendebat se pro i sull' et dimid', et nunc pro i, et ualet x lib'. Item ex supradictis sull' de aldintune habet archiep's dimid' iugum et dimid' uirgam in limenes, et ualet xii lib', et tamen qui tenet redd' xv lib' de firma. In Rumene sunt xxv burgenses qui pertinent ad aldintune. (De Limminges.)

(I) n limuuarlet in hundr' de noniberghe habet archiep's

in suo d'nico i manerium limminges, quod tempore E regis se defendebat pro vii sull', et nunc similiter. Robertus filius Watsoni habet ex hiis ii sull' in feodo. Et Robertus de hardes dimid' sull'. Et osbertus peisforera dimid' iugum. Et in marisco de Rumene i sull' elmesland, de elemosina monachorum sc'e trinitatis, et non est de supradictis sull'. Et de isto sull' habet Will's folet i iugum, id est Sturtune. Et de eodem sull' habet supradictus Rob' tria iuga, i. Odgareswike et Castwisle et Eaddruneland. (Racl'.)

(R) aculf est manerium archiep'i, et in tempore E regis se defendebat pro viii sullinges, et est appreciatum xlii lib' v sol'. Tres minutes minus. (De Northwde.)

(N) *o(r)thwde est manerium archiep'i, et in tempore E regis se defendebat pro xiii sull', et nunc similiter, et est appreciatum li lib' v sol'. Ex hiis sullinges habet Vitalis de Cantuar' i sull' et i iugum, et in tanet i sull' et dimid'. Et etiam in macebroc habet xii agros et dimid' sull' ab archiep'o, Et ezi lamerch, et tota hec terra est appreciata xiiii lib' vi sol' vi d'. Hec maneria habet archiep's in hundredo de ipso Raculf. (De Boctune.)

(B) octune est manerium archiep'i, et in tempore E regis se defendebat pro v sull' et dimid', et nunc similiter, et fuit appreciatum in tempore E regis x libr', et archiep's habet inde c et xv sol' iii d' de gablo. Nunc autem ualet xx lib', set tamen redd' xxv lib' de firma, et archiep's habet suum gablum sicut prius. Ric' constabu-

α1 / C4-70vb

larius habet inde i manerium grauenai in feodo ab archiep'o, quod in tempore E regis se defendebat pro i sull', et nunc similiter, et ualet vi lib'. Hanc terram habet archiep's in hundredo de boctune. (De Leuelande.)

(L) euelande est terra archiep'i, quam ricardus constabularius tenet in feodo ab archiep'o. Et Decanus Cantuar' habuit et tenuit eandem terram, et in tempore E regis se defendebat pro i sull', et nunc similiter, et ualet xx sol'. Hec terra est in hundredo de feueresham. (De Tenham.)

(T) enham est manerium archiep'i, et in tempore E regis se defendebat pro v sull' et dimid', et nunc similiter, et est appreciatum l lib'. Dimidium sull' terre tenet Godefridus de malling' in Scapaie ab archiep'o, quod ualet iiii lib', et tamen reddit c sol'. Oswardus uero tenuit hoc idem sull' ab archiep'o cantuar' in tempore E regis. Hanc *predictam habet archiep's in hundredo de tenham. (De Lenham.)

(L) enham est manerium archiep'i, quod Godefridus de mallinges tenet de eo in feodo, et in tempore E regis se defendebat pro ii sull', et nunc similiter, et ualet viii lib'. Et tamen redd' xii lib' x sol' de firma. (De Cerring'.)

(C) erringes est manerium archiep'i, et in tempore E regis se defendebat pro viii sull', et nunc pro vii. Quia archiep's habet aliud ad suam propriam carucam. Et ualebat in tempore E regis xx lib'. Et habet inde archiep's iiii lib' vii sol' de gablo. Nunc uero ualet xxx lib', set tamen reddit xl lib' de firma, et archiep's habet inde gablum sicut prius. (De Plukele.)

(I) n hundredo eodem et in lest de wiwarlet habet archiep's i manerium Plukele in d'nico, quod in tempore E regis se defendebat pro i sull', et nunc similiter, et ualet vi lib', et tamen reddit xx lib' de firma. Hec maneria habet archiep's in hundredo de Calehelle. (De Gillingeham.)

(G) illingeham est manerium proprium archiepiscopi, et in tempore E regis se defendebat pro vi sull'. Et est appreciatum hoc quod archiep's habet inde in d'nico xviii lib'. Et hoc quod Asketillus de ros et Robertus brutinus habent xl sol'. Et tamen reddit archiep'o de firma xxv lib' xix sol'. Hoc manerium est in hundredo de chetteham. (De Meidestane.)

α1 / C4-71ra

(M) eidestane est proprium manerium archiep'i, et in tempore E regis se defendebat pro x sull'. Ex hiis tenet Radulfus i sull' quod est appreciatum l sol'. Et Will's frater Gundulfi ep'i ii sull' et sunt appreciata x lib'. Et ansketillus de Ros i sull' quod est appreciatum lx sol'. Et duo homines habent inde i sull', qui reddunt altari sc'e trinitatis xvi sol', et tamen ualet illud sulling' xx sol'. Hoc manerium habet hundredum in se ipso. (De Northflete.)

(N) orthflete est manerium archiep'i, et in tempore E regis se defendebat pro vi sulling', et nunc pro v. Et est appreciatum xxvii lib'. Set tamen redd' xxxvii lib' de firma. Et infra leugam de Tunebrege est inde tantum, quod est appreciatum xxx sol'. Hoc manerium et mepeham iacent in hundredo de toltentrui. (De Bixle.)

(B) ixle est manerium archiep'i, et in tempore E regis se defendebat pro iii sulling', et nunc pro ii. Et est appreciatum xx lib', et reddit xxx lib' et viii sol'. Et est in hundr' de almes tre. Et in dimid' led de Sutune *iiii sull'. (De Earhethe.)

(E) arhethe est manerium archiep'i, et in tempore E regis se defendebat pro iiii sull', et nunc similiter. Et osuuardus tenuit illud ab archiep'o in tempore E regis, et est appreciatum xvi li'. Et tamen reddit xxi lib'. Hoc manerium habet archiep's in hundredo de litelet. (De Bradestede.)

(B) radestede tenuit Wlnod child ab archiep'o tempore E regis. Et postea tenuit haimo a Lanfranco archiep'o, et tunc se defendebat pro i sull' et nunc similiter, et est appreciatum xvii lib'. Istud manerium est in hundr' de hostreham. (De Otteford.)

(O) teford est manerium archiep'i, et in tempore E regis se defendebat pro viii sull', et nunc pro totidem. Et est appreciatum lx lib'. Et hoc quod haimo inde tenet est appreciatum lxx sol'. Et hoc quod robertus interpres et *Godefridus de ros inde tenent viii lib' x sol'. Et hoc quod *Rob' de tunebreg' inde tenet x lib' et xxiii porcos. (De Sunderh'.)

(S) underherste est manerium archiep'i, quod Godwinus tenuit tempore E regis iniuste, et archiep's Lanfrancus explacitauit illud contra ep'm baiocensem iuste per concessum regis. Et in tempore E regis se defendebat pro i sull' et dimid', et nunc similiter, et est appreciatum xviii li', et tamen qui tenet ipsum reddit xxiiii lib' et unum equitem

α1 / C4-71rb

de firma archiep'o. Hec maneria sunt in hundredo de codesede. (De Wrotham.)

(W) rotham est man' ar'ep'i, et in tempore E regis se defendebat pro viii sulling', et est appreciatum xxiiii lib', et tamen ille qui tenet redd' inde xxxv lib'. Et de hiis predictis viii sulling' tenet Will's dispensator i sull' quod est appreciatum iii lib'. Et gosfridus de ros aliud quod est appreciatum iii lib'. Et faremannus i sull' et dimid', et est appreciatum c sol'. Et hoc quod ricardus habet: xv lib'. Hic finit hundredus de Wrotham. (De Mallinges.)

(M) allinges est man' arch'i, et in tempore E regis se defendebat pro ii sull', et nunc similiter, et est appreciatum ix lib'. Et tamen reddit de firma arch'o xv lib'. Hoc manerium habet archiep's in hundr' de Lauerkefeld. (De Sendlinge.)

(W) luiet tenuit sendlinge ab archiep'o in tempore E regis, et nunc tenet hugo nepos herberti *( ) et dimid', et nunc similiter, et est appreciatum viii lib'. Hoc manerium *sunt in hundr' de elmestrie, et *sunt in medio Leth de *suthtu( ) (De Derente.)

(D) erente est man' arch'i, et defendebat se in tempore E regis, et nunc similiter, et est appreciatum xv lib'. Et x sol' habet inde ricardus infra castellum suum, et tamen archiep's habet in firma sua xviii lib'. (De Eineford.)

(E) ineford est man' arch'i, et in tempore E regis defendebat se pro vi sull', et nunc similiter, et est appreciatum xx lib', et ex eo *habuit ricardus de tunebrig' tantum quod est appreciatum iii libr'. (De Hulecumbe.)

(H) ulecumbe tenuit ælferus in tempore E regis de archiep'o, et defendebat se pro ii sull' et dimid', et nunc defendit se pro ii sull', et est appreciatum xi lib'. (De Niwindenne.)

(N) iwindenne est man' arch' quod in tempore E regis tenuit Leofric de arch'o, et pro i sull' se defendebat et subiacebat *saluude, et nunc est appreciatum viii lib' *x sol' de Gersuma. Hoc man' est in limwarlet in hundredo de silebrichtindene. (De Saltwde et Hedhe.)

(I) n limwarlet in hundredo de hede tenuit hugo de muntfort i manerium Saltwde de archiep'o, et comes Godwinus tenuit illud. Et tunc se defendebat pro vii sull', et nunc sunt v, et tamen non scottent nisi pro iii. Et in burgo de hede sunt cc et xxv burgenses qui pertinent huic manerio

α1 / C4-71va

de quibus non habet hugo nisi iii forisfacta, et est appreciatum xxviii lib' vi sol' iiii d'. (De Langeport.)

(I) n langeport *ten[uit] robertus de rumene i sull' et dimid' de archiep'o, quod archiep's *( ) diraciocinauit contra ep'm baiocensem, et Godwinus comes tenuit illud, ibique pertinebant ac pertinent xxi burgenses, de quibus rex in mare habet seruitium. Ideoque quieti sunt per totam angliam, exceptis tribus forisfactis que habet robertus in rumene. Adhuc uero pertinet ibi i iugum terre, et hec omnia ualent xvi lib'.

(A) rchiep's habet iiii prebendas apud niwentune, et sunt appreciate vi lib'.

(I) n hundredo de Cornhille habet archiep's i sull' de prebenda sc'i martini.

:

:

:

:

Summa,

:

(De maneriis prioratus in kantia, et de sullinges que) (sunt in eis.) (De northewde.)

(N) orthewde est manerium monachorum sc'e trinitatis, et est de cibo eorum, et est de hundredo de cantuaria, et in tempore Edwardi regis se defendebat pro uno sull', et ei subiacent c burgenses iii minus, qui reddunt viii lib' vi d' de gablo, et est appreciatum xvii lib'.

(De Estreia, et) (de geddinges.) (E) streia est man' monachorum, et de cibo eorum, et in tempore E regis se defendebat pro vii sull', et nunc similiter. Et in alia parte sunt dimid' sull' et i iugum et v acre Gedinges, et ualet xxxvii lib' x sol' iiii d' inter totum.

(T) ilemanestune est de terra (De Tilemanestune.) monachorum, et in tempore E regis se defendebat pro i sull', et nunc facit similiter, et ualet xxx solid'.

(I) *( ) apud fenglesham (De fenglesham.) dimid' sull' quod tenuit lieuenoth tempore E regis ab archiep'o, et ualet xx sol'. (De Stepenberghe.)

(I) *( ) dimid' sull' stepenberghe, quod Godwinus tenuit de archiep'o Aðzi tempore E regis, et tunc se defendebat pro dimid' sull', sicut et nunc, et ualet xxx sol'. (De Bocland.)

α1 / C4-71vb

(B) oclande se defend' pro i iugo. Hic finit hundredus de Estreia.

(S) andwiz est man' monachorum, et est de (De Sandwich'.) uestitu eorum, et est leth et hundredus in se ipso et reddit regi seruicium in mari sicut douoria. Et homines illius uille antequam rex eis dedisset suas consuetudines, reddebant xv lib'. Quando autem archiep'c recuperauit, reddebant xl lib' et xl milia de allecibus, et postea l lib' et allecia sicut prius. In tempore E regis erant ibi ccc *(et) vii mansure. Nunc autem *( )

(M) oneketune est *monachorum manerium, et de cibo eorum, et in tempore E regis se defendebat pro xx sull', et nunc se defendit pro xviii, et est appreciatum xl lib'. Hoc manerium est in hundr' de tanet.

(I) n leth de estreie est hundr' de edesham, quod est in eodem manerio.

(E) desham est man' monachorum, (De Edesham.) et de cibo eorum, et in tempore E regis se defendebat pro xvii sull', et nunc similiter, et de gablo redd' xvi lib' et xvi sol' iiii d', et ualet xxx lib' de firma et c sol' de gersuma, et ex hiis sull' habet robertus filius watsoni ii, id est egethorn, qui ualent vii lib', et tamen qui tenet redd' ix lib'. Et rogerus *ten[uit] ex hiis i sull' ad bereham, quod ualet iiii lib'. (De Iecham.)

(I) echam est man' monachorum et de cibo eorum, et in tempore E regis se defendebat pro iiii sull', et nunc similiter, et est appreciatum xxxii lib'. Et hoc quod will's de hedesham *hab[uit] scilicet i sull' ad rokinges, ualet vii lib'. Hoc manerium est in hundr' de dunhamford. Hic finit leth de burwarleth. (De Sesaltre.)

(S) esaltre est burgus monachorum, et de cibo, et proprie de coquina eorum, et Blittere tenuit illud de monachis, ibique est terra ii carucarum, et est appreciatum c sol'. Hoc manerium in nullo hundredo est. (De Chertham.)

(C) *her(t)ham est man' monachorum, et de uestitu eorum, et in tempore E regis se defendebat pro iiii sull', et nunc similiter, et est appreciatum xxv lib', et tamen reddit xxx lib'. (De Godmeresham.)

(G) odmeresham est man' monachorum, et de uestitu eorum, et in tempore E regis se defendebat pro viii sull', et est appreciatum xx lib', et tamen reddit xxx lib'. Hic finitur hundredus de Feleberghe. (De Chert.)

(C) hert est man' monachorum, et de uestitu eorum, et in tempore E regis se defendebat pro iii sull', et nunc similiter, et est appreciatum xx lib', et tamen reddit xxvii lib'. Ipsum chert est hundredus. (De litlechert, et de pette.)

(L) itlechert est man' monachorum, et de cibo eorum,

α1 / C4-72ra

quod in tempore E regis se defendebat pro iii sull', et nunc pro ii et dimid', et ualet viii lib'. Ex hiis sull' *hab[ui]t Will's hermefridi dimid' sull' i. pette ab archiep'o in feodo, et redd' inde altari sc'e trinitatis xxv d' pro omnibus consuetudinibus, et ualet xl sol'. (De Apeldre.)

(I) n leth de limware iacet hundredus de blaketune, in quo robertus de rumene *ten[u]it ad firmam i manerium *apedre, et est de cibo monachorum sc'e trinitatis, et in tempore E regis defendebat pro ii sull', et nunc pro i, et ualet xii lib'. Set tamen redd' xvi lib' xvii sol' vii d'. (De Welles.)

(W) elles est man' monachorum, et est de cibo eorum, et in tempore E regis se defendebat pro vii sull', et nunc pro v, et ualet xx iiii lib' et iiii d', et tamen reddit xl lib' de firma. *Ho(c) manerium et litlecherth, sunt in hundr' de calehille. (De Holingeburne.)

(H) olingeburne est man' monachorum, et de cibo eorum, et in tempore E regis se defendebat pro vi sull', et nunc similiter. Et de isto manerio tenet ep's baiocensis dimid' sull' de archiep'o. Set postquam illud tenuit, nunquam redd' inde scottum, et est appreciatum hoc manerium inter totum xxx lib'. (De Boctune.)

(R) atel tenuit boctune de archiep'o, et defendebat se in tempore E regis pro dimid' sull', et istud dimid' sull' est et fuit de vi sull' de holingeburn'. Postea autem tenuit illud radulfus fil' thoroldi ab archiep'o, et est appreciatum xl sol'. Hec maneria sunt in hundredo de heihorne. (De merseham.)

(M) erseham est man' monachorum, et de cibo eorum, quod tempore E regis se defendebat pro vi sull', et quando archiep's eum recepit: pro v et dimid', et modo pro iii. Et Hugo de mundford *hab[ui]t ex hiis unius medietatem, et ualet xviii lib'. Hoc manerium iacet in limwarlet in hundredo de langebrege. (De Elmesland.)

(R) odbertus fil' watsonis tenuit de priore cantuar', elmesland ad firmam, et se defendit pro i sull', et precepto eiusdem prioris redd' firmam sacriste eiusdem eccl'ie. (Werthorn'.)

(I) n limwarlet et in hundr' de hamme habent monachi i man' werehorne, de uestitu eorum, et est appreciatum lx sol'.

(De Broke.) (I) n leth de wiwarlet et est hundredus, tenuit Robertus de rumene i manerium *bro( ) ad firmam, de cibo monachorum, et pro i sull' se defendebat, et nunc pro dimidio, et ualet iiii lib'. (De Berewiche.)

α1 / C4-72rb

(I) n limwarlet in hundr' de strate habuit Will's de edesham de terra monachorum i man' berewich de archiep'o, quod tenuit Godricus decanus, et pro dimid' sull' se defendebat, et nunc similiter, et est appreciatum xi libr'. (De prestune) (i. coptune.)

(P) restune est manerium monachorum, et est de uictu eorum, et in tempore E regis se defendebat pro i sull', et nunc similiter, et est appreciatum xv lib'. Hoc manerium est in hundredo de fauersham. (De Farnleghe.)

(F) arnleghe est manerium monachorum, et est de cibo eorum, et in tempore E regis se defendebat pro vi sull', et est appreciatum xxii lib'. Hoc quod abel monacus inde tenuit per iussum archiep'i, fuit appreciatum vi lib'. Et hoc quod ricardus inde habuit infra leugam suam: iiii lib'. Et de istis vi sull' tenuit Godefridus dapifer dimid' sull' in feodo, quod appreciatum est ix lib'. Hoc manerium habent monachi in hundr' de meidestane. (De Peccham.)

(P) eccham est man' monachorum, et de cibo eorum, et in tempore E regis se defendebat pro vi sull'. Et ex istis tenuit ricardus de tunebrege ii sull' et i iugum, et ex istis ii sull' et iugo isto: nunquam scottauit ricardus postquam habuit ea, et in tempore E regis fuit hoc manerium appreciatum xii lib', et nunc viii lib'. Et prefata pars ricardi ualet iiii lib'. Et in stutingeberga quod tenuit edricus de E rege est dimid' sull'. Vnde ipse edricus dabat scottum ad peccham spontanee, non quod pertineret ad sc'am trinitatem nec ad monachos. Hoc manerium est de hundr' de litlefeld. (Mepeham.)

(M) epeham est man' monachorum, et de cibo eorum, et in tempore E regis se defendebat pro x sull', et nunc pro vii, et est appreciatum xxvi lib', et infra leugam ricardi habetur tantum quod est appreciatum xviii sol' et viii d'. Hoc manerium habent monachi in hundredo de tolnetre. (De Cliue.)

(C) liue est man' monachorum, et de uestitu eorum, et in tempore E regis se defendebat pro iii sull' et dimid', et est appreciatum xvi lib'. Hoc manerium est in hundredo de samele. (De Orpintune.)

(O) rpintona est man' monachorum, et de uestitu eorum, et in tempore E regis se defendebat pro iii sull', et nunc pro ii sull' et dimid', et est appreciatum xxv lib'.

α1 / C4-72va

Et tamen reddit de firma xxviii lib', et in hoc eodem manerio tenuit malgerus ab archiep'o iii iuga terre que quidam liber homo tenuit in tempore E regis. Et hec iii iuga non scottabant cum hoc manerio, et sunt de explacitatione quam fecit archiep's contra ep'm baiocensem, per concessum regis, et illa iii iuga sunt appreciata l sol'. Et ex hiis eisdem sull' habet dirmannus dimid' sull' ad kestane. (De freningeham.)

(F) reningeham est manerium monachorum et de uestitu eorum, quod ansgodus rubitoniensis tenuit ab archiep'o, et tamen *reddid' firmam monachis. Et in tempore E regis se defendebat pro i sull', et est appreciatum xi lib'. Hoc manerium est in hundr' de clakestane. (De Grauene.)

(G) rauene est manerium monachorum et de uestitu eorum, Quod Ricardus constabularius tenuit in feodo ab arch'po, et tamen reddidit firmam monachis, et pro i sull' se defend', et iacet in hundredo de boctune. (De hlose.)

(H) lose est manerium monach', et de uestitu eorum, et pro i sull' se defend', quod *monachus tenuit et redd' firmam monachis. Hoc sulling' iacet in vi sull' de fernleghe.

(I) n swirdlinge est dimid' sull' (De Swerlinge.) et pertinet ad uestitum monachorum, quod Godefridus dapifer tenuit, et firmam redd'. (De huntintune.)

(H) untintune est man' monach', et de uestitu eorum, et defend' se pro dimid' sull', quod Godefridus dapifer tenuit et firmam redd'. Istud dimid' sull' est de vi sull' de fernleghe. (De Burrichestune.)

(B) urrichestune tenuerunt Wluricus et Cole, et est ibi dimid' sull', et reddiderunt inde c den' altari sc'e trinitatis. Hoc dimid' sull' est de x sull' de meidestane.

Notes

70rb5 hoc] *read* hoc quod 70rb7 viii] *read* vii 70rb17 de] *read* d' de 70va27 ( )orthwde] *with* r *inserted* 70vb16 predictam] *should be* predictam terram 71ra18 iiii sull'] *interpolated here by error* 71ra32 Godefridus] *should be* Gosfridus 71ra33 Rob'] *should be* Ric' 71rb16] *erasure, perhaps* i sull' 71rb18 sunt] *should be* est 71rb18 sunt] *should be* est 71rb19] *the end of this word erased* 71rb26 habuit] *with* a *written over* 't 71rb33 saluude] *should be* Saltwde 71rb33 x] *should be* et x 71va3 tenuit] *altered* 71va4] *erasure* 71va34] *some words erased* 71va37] *some words erased* 71vb7 et] *partly erased* 71vb8] *some words erased* 71vb9 monachorum manerium] *marked for transposition* 71vb18 tenuit] *altered* 71vb22 habuit] *altered* 71vb29 ( )hertham] *with* t *inserted* 72ra2 habuit] *altered* 72ra7 tenuit] *altered* 72ra7 apedre] *should be* apeldre 72ra13 Hoc] *with* c *inserted* 72ra29 habuit] *altered* 72ra38] *the end of this word erased* 72va10 reddid'] *with* d' *written over* t 18 monachus] *should be* Abel monachus α2 / C1-2va

:

:

(S) tursæte est manerium archiep'i, et in tempore eadwardi regis se defendebat pro vii sullinges, et nunc similiter, et est apretiatum hoc quod est in dominio xl lib'. Et nunc habet archiep's xx et v burgenses, qui reddunt x sol' de gablo, et ex his supra dictis vii sullinc habet Godefridus dapifer unum sullinc *de archiep'o, tenitune, et est apretiatum c sol'. Adhuc autem et uitalis habet inde unum iugum terrę de archiep'o, et est apretiatum xx sol'. Hamo uero tenet inde similiter dimidium sulling, quod tenuit alric bigge a priore archiep'i in tempore E regis, et est apretiatum c sol'.

(R) odbertus de hardes tenet inde unum iugum terrę ex isdem sull', et est apretiatum xxx sol', et ex his septem sull' habet archiep's unum sull' apud sc'm martinum, et de eodem *sull'ino habet Radulfus camerarius in feodo medietatem de archiep'o, et ualet iiii lib', et dominium ualet vii lib'.

(E) t in canturberia sunt vii burgenses, qui reddunt huic manerio viii sol' et iiii denarios de gablo.

(E) t iterum sunt inibi xxx et ii mansurę et unum molendinum, quę tenent clerici sc'i gregorii ad eorum ęccl'am. (I) bique manent xii burgenses qui reddunt eis xxxv sol', et molendinum reddit v sol'.

(A) dhuc etiam tenet ægelwardus iii iuga in natinduna, unde reddidit tempore E regis et adhuc reddit altari sc'ę trinitatis xii sol', et est apretiatum xl sol'.

(A) lbold uero tenet de supradictis sull' unum iugum, uuic, et est de terra monachorum sc'ę trinitatis, quod est apretiatum xxx sol'.

(H) ic finitur hundretus de sturstæte. In fordwic habet archiep's vii mansuras terrę quę modo non faciunt seruitium ad mare ut in tempore E regis.

(W) ingeham est proprium manerium archiep'i, et in tempore E regis se defendebat pro xl sull', et nunc

α2 / C1-2vb

pro xxx et v, et ualet c lib' hoc quod archiep's *habet inde.

(*) t ex isdem sull' habet Will' de archis unum sull' fleotes ab archiep'o in feodo, et ualet vi lib'. Et uital' habet i sull' et ualet xl v sol'. Wibertus et arnoldus habent iii sull', quę ualent xii lib'. Et heringod habet inde i sull' decem agros minus, et ualet xl sol', et Godefridus archibalistarius habet inde i sull' et dimidium, et ualet c sol'.

:

(B) urnes est proprium manerium archiep'i, et in tempore E regis se defendebat pro vi sull', et nunc similiter, et est apretiatum xxx lib', et est in hundret de berham.

:

(P) eteham est proprium manerium archiep'i, et in tempore e regis se defendebat pro vii sull' et nunc similiter, et est apretiatum xx lib', et ex istis sull' habet Godefridus dapifer dimidium sull' quod pertinet ad uestimenta monachorum, id est Suurtling. Et nigellus habet unum sull' et unum iugum terrę quę est apretiata xl sol', hoc est in hundredo de peteham.

:

(I) n hundredo de bilicholt: habet archiep's unum manerium, Aldintune, et in tempore E regis se defendebat pro xx et *un(o) sull', et nunc pro xx, et ualet c lib' et vii. Et ex his habet Will' de archis unum manerium stutinges, quod ælfere tenuit de archiep'o, et tunc defendebat se pro unum sull' et dimidium, et nunc pro uno, et ualet x lib'. Item ex supradictis sull' de aldintune habet archiep's dimidium iugum et dimidiam uirgam in limines, et ualet xii lib', et tamen qui tenet reddit xv lib' de firma. In rumene sunt xxv burgenses, qui pertinent ad aldintune.

:

(I) n limiuuarlethe in hundret de noniberge habet archiep's in suo dominio unum manerium liminges, quod tempore E regis se defendebat pro vii sull', et nunc similiter. Rodbertus filius *Watson(is) habet ex his ii sull' in feodo. Et rodbertus de hardes dimidium sull'. Et osbertus pasforera dimidium iugum. Et in maresco

α2 / C1-2vc

de rumene iacet unum sull', ælmesland, de elemosina monachorum sc'ę trinitatis, et non est de supradictis sull'. Et de isto sull' habet Will' folet unum iugum, id est Sturtune. Et de eodem sull' habet supradictus Rodbertus tria iuga, id est ordgares uuice, et cassetuisle, et eadruneland.

:

(R) aculf est manerium archiep'i, et in tempore E regis se defendebat pro viii sull', et est apretiatum xl et ii lib' et v sol', tres minutes minus.

:

(N) ordeuuode est manerium archiep'i, et in tempore E regis se defendebat pro xiii sull', et nunc similiter, et est apretiatum l et i lib' et v sol'. Ex iis sull' habet Vital' de canturberie unum sull' et unum iugum, et in tanet sull' et dimidium, et etiam in macebroc habet xii agros et dimidium sull' ab archiep'o, Et ezilamerth, et tota *terra est apretiata xiiii lib' et vi *sol et vi denarios. Hęc maneria habet archiep's in hundret de ipso raculf.

:

(B) octuna est manerium archiep'i, et in tempore E regis se defendebat pro v sull' et *dimidi(o), et nunc similiter, et fuit apretiatum in tempore E regis x lib', et archiep's habet inde c sol' et xv et iii denarios de gablo. Nunc autem ualet xx lib', sed tamen reddit xx et v lib' de firma, et archiep's habet suum gablum sicut prius. Ricardus constabularius habet inde unum manerium grauenai in feodo ab archiep'o quod in tempore E regis se defendebat pro uno sull', et nunc similiter, et ualet vi lib'. Hanc terram habet archiep's in hundret de boctune.

:

(T) eneham est manerium archiep'i, et in tempore E regis se defendebat pro v sull' et dimidio, et nunc similiter, et est apretiatum l lib'.

α2 / C1-3ra

Dimidium sull' terrę tenet Godefridus de melling in scapac ab archiep'o, quod ualet iiii lib', et tamen reddit c sol'. Osuuardus uero tenuit hoc idem sull' ab archiep'o cantuarberię in tempore E regis. Hanc prędictam terram habet archiep's in hundret de tenham.

:

(C) erringis est proprium manerium archiep'i, et in tempore E regis se defendebat pro viii sull', et nunc pro vii, Quia archiep's habet aliud ad suam propriam carrucam, et ualebat in tempore E regis xx lib', et habet inde archiep's iiii lib' et vii sol' de gablo. Nunc uero ualet xxx lib', sed tamen reddit xl lib' de firma. Et archiep's habet inde gablum sicut prius.

:

(I) n eodem hundredo et in lest de wiwarleth habet archiep's unum manerium plukelai in dominio quod in tempore E regis se defendebat pro uno sull' et nunc similiter, et ualet xv lib', et tamen reddit xx lib' de firma. Hęc maneria habet archiep's in hundret de calehela.

:

(G) elingeham est proprium manerium archiep'i, et in tempore E regis se defendebat pro vi sull', et est apretiatum hoc quod archiep's habet inde in dominio x et viii lib'. Et hoc quod anscetillus de ros et rodbertus brutinus habent xl sol'. Et tamen reddit archiep'o de firma xx et v lib' et xviiii sol'. Hoc manerium est in hundredo de certaham.

:

(M) æidestane est proprium manerium archiep'i, et in tempore E regis se defendebat pro x sull'. Et ex iis tenet Radulfus unum sull', quod est apretiatum l sol', et Will' frater ep'i Gundulfi ii sull', et sunt *appretiat(a) x lib'. Et anscetillus de ros unum sull', quod est appretiatum lx sol'. Et duo ho-

α2 / C1-3rb

mines habent inde i sull', qui reddunt altari sc'ę trinitatis xvi sol'. Et tamen ualet illud sull' xx sol'. Hoc manerium habet hundret in se ipso.

(N) ordflita est manerium archiep'i, et in tempore E regis se defendebat pro sex sull', et nunc pro v, et est appretiatum xx et vii lib'. Sed tamen ille qui tenet reddit inde de firma xxx et vii lib'. Et infra leugam de tonebrig est inde tantum quod est appretiatum xxx sol'. Hoc manerium, et meppaham, iacent in hundredo de toltentrui.

:

(B) ixle est manerium archiep'i, et in tempore E regis se defendebat pro iii sull', et nunc pro ii. Et est appretiatum xx lib'. Et reddit xxx lib' et viii sol'. Et est in hundredo de ælmestrou, et in dimidio led de sutune, *iiii sull'.

:

(E) arhede est manerium *est archiep'i, et in tempore E regis se defendebat pro iiii sull', et nunc similiter. Et osuuardus tenuit illud ab archiep'o in tempore E regis, et est appretiatum xvi lib'. Et tamen reddit xx et i lib'. Hoc manerium habet archiep's in hundredo de litelet, *i sull' et d'.

:

(B) radestede tenuit Wlnod cild ab archiep'o tempore E regis. Et nunc tenet illud haimo ab isto lanfranco archiep'o, et tunc defendebat se pro uno sull' et dimidio, et nunc similiter, et est appretiatum xvii lib'. Istud manerium est in hundredo de hostreham.

:

(O) tteford est manerium archiep'i, et in tempore E regis se defendebat pro viii sull', et nunc pro totidem. Et est appretiatum lx lib'. Et hoc quod haimo inde tenet est appretiatum lx sol' et x. Et hoc quod rodbertus interpres et Gosfridus de ros inde tenent viii lib' et x sol'. Et hoc quod Ricardus de tonobrig inde tenet x lib' et xx et iii porcos.

α2 / C1-3rc

:

(S) underhersce est manerium archiep'i, quod Goduuinus tenuit tempore E regis iniuste, et archiep's iste lanfrancus explacitauit illud contra ep'm baiocensem iuste per concessum regis, et in tempore E regis se defendebat pro *(uno) sull' et dimid', et nunc similiter. Et est appretiatum xviii lib', et tamen qui tenet illud reddit inde xx et iiii lib' et unum equitem de firma archiep'o. Hęc maneria sunt in hundredo de codesede.

:

(W) roteham est manerium archiep'i, et in tempore E regis se defendebat pro viii sull', et est appretiatum xx et iiii lib', et tamen ille qui tenet reddit inde de firma xxx et v lib'. Et de iis prędictis viii sull' tenet Will' dispensator i sull' quod est appretiatum iii lib'. Et Gosfridus de ros aliud quod est appretiatum iii lib'. Et faremanus unum sull' et dimidium, et est appretiatum c sol'. Et hoc quod Ricardus habet xv lib'. Hic finit hundredus de uurotaham.

:

(M) ellingettes est manerium archiep'i, et in tempore E regis se defendebat pro *i(i) sull' et nunc similiter, et est appretiatum *(i)x lib', et tamen reddit de firma archiep'o xv lib'. Hoc manerium habet archiep's in hundredo de lauercefeld.

:

(D) ærente est manerium archiep'i, pro ii sull' se defendebat in tempore E regis, et nunc similiter, et est appretiatum xv lib'. Et x sol' habet inde ricardus infra castellum suum, et tamen archiep's habet in firma sua xviii lib'.

:

(E) *ine(s)ford est manerium archiep'i, et in tempore E regis defendebat se pro vi sull', et nunc similiter, et nunc tenet Radulfus filius hospaci ab archiep'o, et est appretiatum xx lib', et ex eo habet Ricardus de tonobrig

α2 / C1-3va

tantum quod est appretiatum iii lib'.

:

(H) ulecumbe tenuit ælferus in tempore *E regis de archiep'o, et defendebat se pro ii sull' et dimid', et nunc tenet comes de o' de archiep'o, et defendit se pro ii sull', et est appretiatum xi lib'.

:

(A) rchiep's habet iiii prebendas ad niuuentune, et sunt appretiatę vi lib'.

:
:
:
:
:
:
:
:
:
:
:
:
:
:
:
:
:
:
:
:
:
:
:

Tota summa, c lxxx et vii sull' et dimidium. :

:
:
:
:

:
:
:
:
:
:
:
:
:
:
:
:

α2 / C1-3vb

:
:

(N) ordwda est manerium monachorum sc'ę trinitatis, et est de cibo eorum et est de hundred de cantuarberia, et in tempore E regis se defendebat pro uno sull', et ei subiacent c burgenses iii minus, qui reddunt viii lib' et vi denarios de gablo, et est appretiatum x et vii lib'. Hoc manerium est de hundret de cantuarberia.

:

(E) strege est manerium monachorum et de cibo eorum, et in tempore E regis se defendebat pro vii sull', et nunc similiter. Et in alia parte est dimidium sull' et unum ioc et v *( ) æceres, gedinges, et ualet xxx et vii lib' et x sol' et *iii denarios inter totum.

:

(W) illelm' folet tenet i manerium, tilesmannestune ab archiep'o, et hoc est de terra monachorum, et in tempore E regis se defendebat pro i sull', et nunc facit similiter, et ualet xxx sol'.

(I) ste idem Will' habet de predicta terra dimidium sull' ab archiep'o in fenglesham, quod tenuit liuenot in tempore E regis ab archiep'o, et ualet xx sol'.

:

(I) ste idem Will' habet adhuc ab eodem archiep'o, et de prędicta terra monachorum stepenberga, quod se defendebat tempore E regis pro dimidio sull', et nunc facit. Et godwinus tenuit illud in tempore E regis ab archiep'o ædzi, et ualet xxx sol'.

(B) ocland se defendit pro i iugo. Hic finit hundret de æstrege.

:

(S) andwic est manerium sc'ę trinitatis, et de uestitu monachorum et est læth et hundretus in se ipso, et reddit regi seruitium in mare sicut douera, et homines illius uillę antequam rex eis dedisset suas consuetudines, reddebant

α2 / C1-3vc

xv lib'. Quando archiep's *archiep's recuperauit, reddebat xl lib' et xl milia de allecibus. Et in prętérito anno reddidit l lib' et allecia sicut prius. Et in isto anno debet reddere lx et x lib' et allecia sicut prius. In tempore E regis erant ibi ccc et vii mansurę. Nunc autem lx et xvi plus.

:

(M) unechetun est manerium monachorum et de cibo eorum et in tempore E regis se defendebat pro xx sull', et nunc se defendit pro x et viii, et est appretiatum xl lib'. Hoc prędictum manerium est in hundred de tenet.

(E) desham est manerium monachorum sc'ę trinitatis et de cibo eorum, et in tempore E regis se defendebat pro xvii sull' et nunc similiter et de gablo reddit xvi lib' et xvi sol' et iiii denarios, et ualet xxx lib' de firma, et c sol' de gersuma, et ex iis sull' habet rodbertus filius watsonis ii id est egedorn qui ualent vii lib'. Et tamen qui tenet reddit inde viiii lib'. Et Rogerius tenet ex his i sull' ad beraham, qui ualet iiii lib'. Hoc manerium habet hundret *(   ) in se ipso, et in læd est de æstraie.

:

:

:

:

(I) echam est manerium monachorum et de cibo eorum, et in tempore E regis se defendebat pro iiii sull', et nunc similiter, et est appretiatum xxx et ii lib', et hoc quod will' de hedesham habet inde uidelicet i sull' ad rocinges, ualet vii lib'. Hoc manerium est in hundret de dunahamford.

:

(S) æsealtre est burgus monachorum et de cibo et proprie de coquina eorum, et *blitt&re

α2 / C1-4ra

tenet illud de monachis, ibique est terra duarum carrucarum et est appretiatum c sol'. Hoc manerium in nullo hundret est.

:

(C) ertaham est manerium monachorum et de uestitu eorum, et in tempore E regis se defendebat pro iiii sull', et nunc similiter, et est appretiatum xx et v lib', et tamen reddit xxx lib'.

(G) odmæresham est manerium monachorum et de uestitu eorum, et in tempore E regis se defendebat pro viii sull', et est appretiatum xx lib', sed tamen reddit xxx. Hic finitur hundretus de feleberga.

:

(C) ert est manerium monachorum et de uestitu eorum et in tempore E regis se defendebat pro iii sull', et nunc similiter, et est appretiatum xx lib'. Ipsum cert est hundret.

:

(L) itelcert iterum est manerium monachorum et de cibo eorum quod in tempore E regis se defendebat pro iii sull', et nunc pro ii et dimidium, et ualet viii lib', et ex iis habet Will' filius hermenfridi dimidium sull', id est pette, ab archiep'o in feodo, et reddit inde altari sc'ę trinitatis xxv denarios pro omnibus consuetudinibus, *et ualet xl sol'.

:

(I) n *letd de limuuare iacet hundret de blacetune, in quo *Rodbertus de rumenæ tenet ad firmam i manerium apeldre, et est de cibo monachorum sc'ę trinitatis, et in tempore E regis se defendebat pro ii sull' et nunc pro i, et ualet xii lib'. Sed tamen reddit xvi lib' et *xvi sol' et vii denarios.

(W) ælle uero est manerium monachorum sc'ę trinitatis, et est de cibo eorum, et in tempore E regis se defendebat pro vii

α2 / C1-4rb

sull', et nunc pro v, et ualet xxiiii lib' et iiii denarios, et tamen reddit *xi lib' de firma. Hoc manerium et litelcert sunt in hundret de calehele.

:

(H) olingeburne est manerium monachorum et de cibo eorum, et in tempore E regis se defendebat pro vi sull' et nunc similiter, et de isto *m(a)n(e)rio tenet ep's baiocensis dimidium sull' ab archiep'o per gablum et postquam ep's habuit hoc dimidium sull' nunquam reddit inde scottum et est appretiatum inter totum hoc manerium xxx lib'.

:

(R) atel tenuit boctune de archiep'o cantuarberię et defendebat se in tempore E regis pro dimidio sull' et istud dimidium sull' est et fuit de vi sull' de holingeburne. Nunc autem tenet illud Radulfus filius toroldi ab archiep'o et est appretiatum xl sol'. Hęc maneria sunt in hundret de haihorna.

:

(M) erseham est manerium monachorum sc'ę trinitatis, et de cibo eorum, quod tempore E regis se defendebat pro vi sull' et quando archiep's eum recepit pro v et *dimidi(o) et modo pro iii. Et hugo de mundford habet ex iis unius medietatem, et ualet xviii lib'. Hoc manerium iacet in limuuar led in hundret de langebrige.

:

(R) odbertus filius watsonis tenet de priore cantuarberię ælmes land ad firmam, et pręcepto eiusdem prioris reddit firmam secrestano eiusdem ęccl'ę.

:

(I) n limuuarlæd et in hundret de *hamine habent monachi sc'e trinitatis de uestitu eorum i manerium, Werehorne, i sull', et est appretiatum lx sol'.

:

(I) n læd de Wiuuarlæd *et est hundret in quo tenet Rodbertus de rumenæ i manerium broc ad firmam de cibo monachorum, et

α2 / C1-4rc

pro i sull' defendebat se, et nunc pro dimidio, et ualet iiii lib'.

:

(I) dem rodbertus habet in lange port de terra monachorum i sull' et dimidium de archiep'o quod idem archiep's diratiocinauit contra ep'm baiocensem, et Godwinus comes tenuit illud, ibique pertinebant ac pertinent xx et i burgenses de quibus rex in mare habet seruitium, ideoque quieti sunt per totam angliam exceptis tribus forisfactis quę habet Rodbertus in rumene. Adhuc uero pertinet ibi i iugum terrę, et hęc omnia ualent xvi lib'.

:

(I) n limuuarlæd et hundred de selebrichtindæne habet archiep's de terra monachorum i manerium niuuendene in dominio quod in tempore E regis tenuit leofric de pręterito archiep'o, et pro i sull' se defendebat, et subiacebat *saltwnde, nunc est appretiatum viii lib' et x sol' garsumę.

:

(I) n *limwarl&d in *hund(r)ed de strate habet Will' de edesham de terra monachorum i manerium de archiep'o, Bereuuic quod tenuit Godricus decanus et pro dimidio sull' se defendebat, et nunc similiter, et est appretiatum xi lib'.

:

(I) n *limwarl&d in hundred de hede habet hugo de munford de terra monachorum i manerium saltwode de archiep'o, et comes Godwinus tenuit illud, et tunc se defendebat pro vii sull', et nunc sunt v, et tamen non scottent nisi pro iii, et in burgo de hedȩ sunt cc et xxv burgenses qui pertinent huic manerio de quibus non habet hugo nisi iii forisfacta, et est appretiatum xxviii lib' et vi sol' et iiii *denari(i)s.

:

α2 / C1-4va

(P) restetune est manerium monachorum et est de uictu eorum, et in tempore E regis se defendebat pro i sull', et nunc similiter, et est appretiatum xv lib'. Hoc manerium est in hundred de *fe( )ue(r)sham.

:

(L) iueland est terra monachorum quam Ricardus constabularius tenet in feodo ab archiep'o, et decanus cantuarberiȩ habuit et tenuit eandem terram, et in tempore E regis se defendebat pro i sull', et nunc similiter, et ualet xx sol'. Hȩc maneria habent monachi in hundred de *fe( )ue(r)sham.

:

(L) enham est manerium monachorum quod Godefridus de mellinges tenet ab archiep'o in feodo, et in tempore E regis se defendebat pro ii sull', et nunc similiter, et ualet viii lib', et tamen reddit xii lib' et x sol' de firma.

:

(F) ernlege est manerium monachorum et est de cibo eorum et in tempore E regis se defendebat pro vi sull', et est appretiatum xxii lib', et hoc quod abel monachus inde tenet per iussum archiep'i est appretiatum vi lib', et hoc quod Ricardus inde habet infra leugam suam iiii lib', et de istis vi sull' tenet Godefridus dapifer dimidium sull' quod est appretiatum ix lib'. Hoc manerium habent monachi in hundred de mædestane.

:

(P) echam est manerium sc'ȩ trinitatis de cibo monachorum, et in tempore E regis similiter fuit, et se defendebat pro vi sull', et ex istis habet nunc Ricardus de tunebrige ii sull' et i iugum, et ex istis ii sull' et ioco isto nunquam scottauit Ricardus post quam habuit ea. Et in tempore E regis fuit hoc manerium appretiatum xii lib', et nunc viii lib'. Et prȩfata pars Ricardi ualet

α2 / C1-4vb

iiii lib'. Et in stotingeberga quod tenuit edricus de E rege est dimidium sull' unde ipse edricus dabat scottum ad pecham spontaneȩ non quod pertineret ad sc'am trinitatem, nec ad monachos. Hoc manerium est de hundred de litelfeld.

:

(M) epaham est manerium monachorum et de cibo eorum et in tempore E regis se defendebat pro x sull', et est appretiatum xxvi lib', et infra leugam Ricardi habetur tantum, quod est appretiatum xviii sol' et viii denarios. Hoc manerium habent monachi in hundred de toltetriu.

:

(C) liva est manerium monachorum et de uestitu eorum, et in tempore E regis se defendebat pro *ii sull' et *dimidi(o), et est appretiatum xvi lib'. Hoc manerium est in hundred de scamele.

:

(O) rpintuna est manerium monachorum et de uestitu eorum et in tempore E regis se defendebat pro iii sull', et nunc pro ii sull' et dimidio, et est appretiatum xxv lib'. Et tamen reddit de firma xx et viii lib'. Et in hoc eodem manerio tenet malgerus ab archiep'o iii iuga terrę quę quidam liber homo tenuit in tempore E regis. Et hęc iii iuga non scottabant cum hoc manerio, et sunt de explacitatione quam fecit archiep's contra *(ep'm) baiocensem per concessum regis. Et illa iii iuga sunt appretiata l sol'. Et *(ex) iis eisdem sull' habet dirmannus dimidium sull' ad kestane.

:

(*Ę) lfgæt tenuit Sændlinge ab archiep'o in tempore E regis, et nunc tenet hugo nepos herberti ab ep'o baiocensi, et defendebat se in tempore E regis pro i sull' et dimidio, et nunc similiter et est appretiatum viii lib'. Hęc maneria sunt de hundred de ælmestriu, et sunt in medio led de sudthune.

:

α2 / C1-4vc

(F) reningeham est manerium monachorum, et de uestitu eorum quod *an(s)godus rubitoniensis tenet ab archiep'o, et tamen reddit firmam monachis, et in tempore E regis se defendebat pro i sull' et nunc similiter, et est appretiatum xi lib'. Hoc manerium est in hundred de clacstane.

:

(G) rauene est manerium monachorum et de uestitu eorum quod Ricardus constabularius tenet in feodo *( ) ab archiep'o, et tamen reddit firmam monachis, et pro i sull' se defendit, et iacet in hundred de boctune.

:

(H) lose est manerium monachorum et de uestitu eorum, et pro i sull' se defendit, quod abel monachus tenet, et firmam monachis reddit. Hoc sull' iacet in vi sull' de fernlege.

:

(I) n surling est dimidium sull' et pertinet ad uestitum monachorum quod Godefridus dapifer tenet et firmam reddit.

:

(*H) untindune est manerium monachorum et de uestitu eorum, et defendit se pro dimidio sull', quod Godefridus dapifer tenet et firmam reddit. Istud dimidium sull' est de vi sull' de fernlege.

:

(B) urgericestune tenent Wlfricus et cole, et est ibi dimidium sull', et reddunt inde c denarios altari sc'ę trinitatis. Hoc dimidium sull' est de x sull' de meidestane.

:

:

:

:

:

:

α2 / C1-5ra

:

:

:

:

:

:

:

:

:

:

Tota summa, c xxx et iii sull' et dimidium.

:

:

:

(F) rendesberi est manerium ep'i rubitoniensis, et in tempore E regis se defendebat pro x sull', et nunc pro vii, et est appretiatum xxv lib', et infra leugam de tunebrige est inde tantum quod ualet x sol', et etiam de hallinges est tantum infra leugam eandem quod est appretiatum vii sol'.

:

(S) utfliote est manerium ep'i rofensis, et in *tempor(e) e regis se defendebat pro vi sull' et nunc pro v, et est appretiatum xx et i lib', et Ricardus habet inde infra suam leugam ualens xx sol', et tamen hoc idem manerium reddit ep'o xx et iiii lib', et *( ) unam unciam auri de firma.

:

(S) tanes est manerium ep'i rofensis et in tempore E regis se defendebat pro vi sull' et nunc pro iii, et est appretiatum xvi lib', tamen habet ep's inde in firma sua xx lib', et i unciam auri, et i marsuinum.

:

(F) alceham est manerium ep'i rofensis, et in tempore E regis se defendebat pro ii sull', et nunc similiter, et est appretiatum viii lib'.

:

(L) angefeld est manerium ep'i rofensis, et in tempore E regis

α2 / C1-5rb

se defendebat pro i sull', et nunc similiter, et est appretiatum c sol'. Hęc maneria sunt in hundred clacestane.

:

(B) runlege est manerium ep'i rofensis, et in tempore E regis se defendebat pro vi sull' et nunc pro iii, et est appretiatum x et viii lib', et tamen ep's habet de firma xx lib' et x et viii sol'. Hoc idem manerium *est hundredus.

:

(W) oldeham est manerium ep'i rofensis, et in tempore E regis se defendebat pro vi sull', et nunc pro iii, et est appretiatum xiii lib'.

:

(M) ellingetes est manerium ep'i rofensis, et in tempore E regis se defendebat pro iii sull', et nunc pro sull' et *dimidi(o), et est appretiatum iiii lib'.

:

(T) rotescliue est manerium ep'i rofensis et defendit se pro iii sull', et est appretiatum vii lib'.

:

(S) noelande est manerium ep'i rofensis, et in tempore E regis se defendebat pro vi sull', et nunc similiter, et est appretiatum ix lib'. Hęc prędicta maneria habet archiep's in hundredo de lauercefeld.

:

(H) allinges est manerium ep'i rofensis, et in tempore E regis se defendebat pro vi sull', et nunc pro ii et dimidio, et est appretiatum xvi lib'.

(C) ukelestane est manerium ep'i rofensis, et in tempore E regis se defendebat pro ii sull' et *dimidi(o), et nunc pro ii, et est appretiatum x lib'.

:

(D) anitune est manerium ep'i rofensis, et in tempore E regis se defendebat pro ii sull', et nunc pro dimidio, et est appretiatum vi lib' et x sol'. Hęc maneria sunt in hundred de scamele.

α2 / C1-5rc

:

(B) ordestele est manerium ep'i rofensis, et in tempore E regis se defendebat pro ii sull', et nunc pro i et dimid', et est appretiatum x lib', et iiii xx domus subiacebant ibi in tempore E regis, una pars illarum est apud supra dictam bordestellam, et alia pars in frendesberia, et sunt appretiatę viii lib', sed tamen ille qui tenet reddit inde xi lib' et xiii sol' et iii denarios. Hoc manerium habet ep's in hundred de rouecestre.

:

(S) tocces est manerium ep'i rofensis, quod Godwinus comes tenuit contra uoluntatem seruientium sc'i andreę, et archiep's Lanfrancus diratiocinauit illum contra ep'm baiocensem iuste, et in tempore E regis se defendebat pro v sull', et nunc pro iii, et est appretiatum viii lib', sed tamen ille qui tenet reddit inde xiii lib' et xx denar'. Hoc manerium est in hundred de ho'.

:
:
:
:
:
:
:
:
:
:
:
:
:
:
:
:

Tota summa, lx et vi sull' et dimidium.

Notes

2va11 de] *with* d *written over an unfinished letter* 2va25 sull'ino] *so written* 2vb2 habet inde] *marked for transposition* 2vb3 *initial not supplied* 2vb33 uno] *with* o *above* um 2vb51 Watsonis] *with* is *over an erasure* 2vc26] hęc *added before* terra *by another hand* 2vc27 sol] *should be* sol' 2vc34 dimidio] *with* o *above* um 3ra52 appretiata] *with the final* a *above* i 3rb23 iiii sull'] *interpolated here by error* 3rb25 est] *repeated by error* 3rb33 i sull' et d'] *interpolated here by error* 3rc9 uno] *over an erasure* 3rc31 ii] *with the second minim inserted* 3rc33 ix] *with the minim inserted* 3rc48 ( )inesford] *with* s *inserted* 3va4] E] *glossed* s. Ædwardi *by another hand* 3vb20] *small erasure* 3vb21 iii] *perhaps should be* iiii 3vc1 archiep's] *cancelled* 3vc35] in de *erased* 3vc54 blitt&re] *with* & *for* æ 4ra39 et] & *started twice* 4ra41 letd] *so written, perhaps with* et *for* & *for* æ 4ra42 Rodbertus] *with* d *written over* b 4ra49 xvi] *perhaps should be* xvii 4rb3 xi] *should be* xl 4rb11 manerio] *with* a *altered from* o *and* e *altered from* a 4rb32 dimidio] *with* o *above* um 4rb45 hamine] *so written* 4rb51 et est] *so written* 4rc27 saltwnde] *so written* 4rc31 limwarl&d] *with* & *for* æ 4rc31 hundred] *with* r *inserted* 4rc40 limwarl&d] *with* & *for* æ 4rc53 denariis] *with the second* i *above* o 4va7 fe( )uersham] *with an* r *erased and* r *inserted* 4va17 fe( )uersham] *with an* r *erased and* r *inserted* 4vb21 ii] *should be* iii 4vb22 dimidio] *with* o *above* um 4vb38 ep'm] *added at the end of the line* 4vb41 ex] *inserted* 4vb44] *a red* Æ *added between the columns by the rubricator* 4vc3 ansgodus] *with* s *inserted* 4vc15] *small erasure* 4vc35] *a red* h *in the margin; the initial itself is green* 5ra28 tempore] *with the final* e *inserted* 5ra35] i *erased* 5rb12 est] *with* e *written over an unfinished letter, perhaps* h 5rb22 dimidio] *with* o *above* um 5rb45 dimidio] *with* o *above* um α3 / R1-209r

(S) uthfleta manerium ep'i hrofensis se defendebat in tempore eaduuardi regis pro vi solinis, et nunc pro v, et est appretiatum xxi lib', et ricardus habet inde infra leugam suam ualens xx solid', et tamen hoc idem manerium reddit ep'o xxiiii libras, et i unciam auri de firma. Stanes se defendebat pro vi solinis in tempore eaduuardi regis, et nunc pro iiii, et est appretiatum xvi lib', et tamen ep's habet inde in firma sua xx lib', et i unciam auri, et i *marsuin. Falcheham defendebat se in tempore eaduuardi regis pro ii solinis, et nunc similiter, et est appretiatum viii lib'. Langefelda defendebat se in tempore eaduuardi regis pro i solino, et nunc similiter, et est appretiatum c solid'. Hęc maneria predicta ad hundredum de clacestane pertinent. Brunlega se defendebat in tempore eaduuardi regis pro vi solinis, et nunc pro iii, et est appreciatum xviii lib', et tamen ep's habet inde de firma sua xx libras et xviii solid',

α3 / R1-209v

et hoc idem manerium est ipse hundredus. Wldeham se defendebat in tempore eaduuardi regis pro vi solinis, et nunc pro iii, et est appretiatum xiii lib'. Melingetes se defendebat in tempore eaduuardi regis pro iii solinis, et nunc pro solino et dimidio, et est appreciatum iiii lib'. Trotescliua defendebat se pro i solino, et adhuc facit, et est appretiatum vii lib'. Snoilanda defendebat se in tempore eaduuardi regis pro iii solinis, et nunc similiter, et est appretiatum ix lib'. Hęc predicta maneria habet *(archi)ep's in hundredo de lauorcesfelda. Hellingas defendebat se in tempore eaduuardi regis pro vi solinis, et nunc pro *duo et dimidio, et est appretiatum xvi libras. Frandesberia defendebat se in tempore eaduuardi regis pro x solinis, et nunc pro vii, et est appretiatum xxv lib', et infra leugam de tonebrigge est inde *tantum x solidos, et etiam de hallingis est tantum infra eandem leugam quod est appretiatum vii solidos. Cuclestana in tempore eaduuardi regis defendebat se pro ii solinis et dimidio, et nunc pro *duo, et est appreciatum x libras. Denituna defendebat se tempore eaduuardi regis pro i solino, et nunc pro di-

α3 / R1-210r

midio, et est appretiatum vi libras et x solid'. Hęc maneria sunt in hundredo de scamela. Borgestealla defendebat se tempore eaduuardi regis pro ii solinis, et nunc pro solino et dimidio, et est appretiatum x libras. Et *quattuor uiginti domus subiacebant ibi in tempore eaduuardi regis, et una pars illarum est apud supradictam borgestellam, et alia pars in frandesberia, et sunt appretiatę viii lib', sed tamen ille qui tenet reddit inde xi libras et xiii solidos et iii denarios. Hoc manerium habet ep's in hundredo de hrouecestra. Stoches quod goduuinus comes tenuit contra uoluntatem seruientium sc'i andreę, et archiep's lanfrancus disrationauit *eum contra ep'm baiocensem iuste, tempore regis eaduuardi se defendebat pro v solinis, et nunc pro iii, et est appretiatum viii libras, sed tamen ille qui tenet reddit xiii libras et xx denarios. Hoc manerium est in hundredo de hou.

Notes

209r15 marsuin] *distinctly so written* 209v11 archiep's] *with* archi *erased* 209v14 duo] *should be* duobus 209v18 tantum] *should be* tantum quod ualet 209v22 duo] *should be* duobus 210r5 quattuor] *should be* quater 210r15 eum] *should be* id *or* illud

Comments

Because C1 is the only complete copy (not to speak of its being the earliest and best copy), these comments follow the order of the paragraphs as they appear there. The reader will find a concordance at the end (below, p. 71) which should make it easy to navigate between the different versions of α, or between them and DB.

At the end of each segment, C1 has a sentence reporting the total number of sulungs. These totals, which relate to the TRE assessments, seem to have been calculated from a synopsis of $\alpha 2$ which was also copied into C1 (2rb–c), perhaps with the idea that it would serve as an index to the copy of $\alpha 2$ itself. For reference, I print this synopsis here (Table 9), but the reader who is willing to take my advice will not spend much time on it. It is helpful up to a point; beyond that point it starts to become a distraction. (There is, for example, as far as I can see, nothing to be gained by asking why segment 3 is appended to segment 1. Probably the answer is that the C1 scribe was imitating the layout of his exemplar – but anyway how can it matter?) The information contained in these lists was all taken from $\alpha 2$; the totals calculated from these lists were then inserted into $\alpha 2$. Taken as they stand, they add up to a grand total of 387.5 sulungs. But the totals for segments 1 and 2 both seem to err on the low side (see below), and in Rochester the total for segment 3 would have been thought to err on the high side.

Whether these numbers have any authority is doubtful; they are probably just one man's attempt to add up the figures in front of him. The numbers which counted were the totals decided by the treasury officials, after they had had a chance to collate the survey text with the most recent geld accounts. An official list dating from c. 1120 (but surviving, unfortunately, only in one late copy) gives a grand total of 392.5 sulungs for the archbishop and bishop of Rochester, 56.75 sulungs in domain plus 335.75 sulungs paying geld (Flight 2005, p. 374).

2va3) Stursete. C1 adds two facts: that Godefrid's sulung is at Thanington, and that Albold's holding consists of a yoke called Wyke.

2va48) C1 adds this: 'In Fordwich the archbishop has seven measures of land which at present are not doing service at sea as (they did) in the time of king Eadward.' The corresponding passage in DB is in chapter 7, because the men making this complaint were tenants of the abbot of Saint Augustine's.

2vb19) Petham. C1 identifies Godefrid's holding as Swarling; it is mentioned again in one of the redundant paragraphs (4vc29) at the end of segment 2. Its value is not reported. The value of Nigel's holding is given as '60 shillings' in C4, '40 shillings' in C1; it is doubtful which reading – *lx* or *xl* – is the right one.

2vb30) Aldington. Both copies of α say that Stowting belongs to Willelm de Arcis; DB says that it is held by the count of Eu. (It is the count's descendants, not Willelm's, who are found in possession later.)

Stursæte	vii	Nordewede	i
Wingaham	xl	Muncetun	x( )
Burne	vi	Eastrege	vii
Petham	vii	Sandwic	
Ealdintune	xxi	Eadesham	xvii
Limminges	vii	Ieacham	iiii
Raculue	viii	Sæsealtre	
Nordewode	xiii	Certeham	iiii
Boctune	v et d'	Godmeresham	viii
Tenham	v et d'	Cert	iii
Cerringes	viii	Litelcert	iii
Plucele	i	Apeldre	ii
Gellingeham	vi	Welle	vii
Medestane	x	Holingeburne, Boctune,	vi
Nordflicte	vi	Mersham	( )
Bixle	iii	Elmesland	i
Erhide	iiii	Werehorne	i
Ottoford	viii	Broc	i
Sunderhersce	i et d'	Langeport	i et d'
Wroteham	viii	Niuuende	i
Mellinges	ii	Bertune	d'
Derente	ii	Hethe, Sealtuuode	vii
Ęmesford	vi	Prestetune	i
Vlecumbe	ii	Liofeland	i
		Leanham	ii
Frendesberi	x	Fearnlege, Hloso,	vi
Sudfliote	vi	Pecham	vi
Stanes	vi	Meapham	x
Falceham	ii	Cliue	iii
Langefeld	i	Orpintune, Sendlinge, Kestane	
Brunlege	vi	Frenigeham	i
Woldeham	vi	Grauene	
Meallingettes	iii		
Trottescliue	iii		
Snoclande	vi		
Hallinges	vi		
Cuclestane	ii et d'		
Danitune	ii		
Bordestele	ii		
Stocces	v		

Table 9. The synopsis of $\alpha 2$ (C1-2rb–c) used for calculating the TRE assessment totals.

2va46) Lyminge. Both copies of α are defective here: no values are reported, either for the domain or for any of the tenancies. The sulung called 'Almsland' is described again at the end of segment 2 (4rb39).

70va35) Boughton under Blean. Ricard's holding, Graveney, is described again at the end of segment 2 (4vc12).

2vc51) Teynham. Text α is especially valuable here, because the manor of Teynham went missing from the survey text, somewhere along the line. Only Godefrid's holding (half a sulung in Sheppey) is reported in DB (4va7); the main entry (which probably ought to follow the one for Pluckley) is omitted.

3ra23) Pluckley. This paragraph looks as it has been reconstructed at the beginning. By analogy with the surrounding

paragraphs, we would expect it to start like this:
Plukelai est proprium manerium archiep'i et ...
But in fact it starts like this:
In eodem hundredo et in lest de wiwarleth habet archiep's unum manerium Plukelai in dominio quod ...
The phrase 'In the same hundred' is true but odd – true because Pluckley was indeed in the same hundred as Charing, odd because we have not yet been told which hundred Charing belongs to. To find that out, we have to wait for the end of the Pluckley paragraph, where a sentence of the normal kind occurs: 'These (are the) manors (which) the archbishop owns in the hundred of Calehill.'

Both copies have the phrase *in lest de wiwarleth.* Except that C4 lacks the final *h*, the spelling is the same.

Pluckley's value is given as 'six pounds' in C4, 'fifteen pounds' in C1 and DB. Probably this means that the value was misreported in $\alpha 1$.

3ra33) Gillingham. 'This manor is in the hundred of Chatham.' C1 seems to be confusing Chatham with Chartham (4ra7).

3ra46) Maidstone. The sulung mentioned at the end of this paragraph is Burston, described again (but said to comprise only half a sulung) in one of the redundant paragraphs at the end of segment 2 (4vc43).

3rb6) Northfleet. 'This manor and Meopham lie in the hundred of Toltingtrough.' Meopham is one of the monks' manors, described in segment 2 (4vb9). Why is it mentioned here?

3rb23) 'four sulungs'. This seems to be a marginal note, properly referring to the next paragraph, which in both copies got attached to the end of this paragraph. In C1 alone a similar note – 'one sulung and a half' – has attached itself to the end of the Crayford paragraph (3rb33).

3rb35) Brasted. The assessment is 'one sulung' in C4, 'one sulung and a half' in C1 and DB.

3rc39) Darenth. There is some confusion affecting the assessment clause. In both copies the word-order is abnormal, and only C1 has the phrase 'for two sulungs'.

3rc48) Eynsford. C1 and DB give the name of the current tenant, Radulf son of Hospac. At the end of this paragraph we ought to be told that these manors (Darenth and Eynsford) are in Axstone hundred.

3va3) Ulcombe. C1 and DB give the name of the current tenant, the count of Eu. At the end of this paragraph we ought to be told that this manor is in Eyhorne hundred.

3va10) Newington church. The archbishop's share is mentioned only incidentally in chapter 13 of DB.

In C4 alone (71va12), there is also a note of the archbishop's share of Saint Martin's church in Dover.

3va36) For segment 1, the total given is 187.5 sulungs (Table 10). But that figure seems to have been arrived at by counting 2 sulungs for Ulcombe, as in the synopsis (Table 9); and the synopsis is sure to be wrong here. Following

Stursete	7	
Wingham	40	
Bishopsbourne	6	
Petham	7	
Aldington	21	
Lyminge	7	
Reculver	8	
Northwood	13	
Boughton under Blean	5.5	
Teynham	5.5	
Charing	8	
Pluckley	1	
Gillingham	6	
Maidstone	10	
Northfleet	6	
Bexley	3	
Crayford	4	
Otford	8	
Sundridge	1.5	
Wrotham	8	
East Malling	2	
Darenth	2	
Eynsford	6	
Ulcombe	2	so C1-2rb25
	187.5	

Table 10. Sum of TRE assessments for segment 1.

α and DB, we need to count 2.5 sulungs for Ulcombe, and that will raise the total to 188 sulungs. Furthermore, the synopsis lacks an entry for Brasted (it ought to occur between Crayford and Otford), and this manor, as C1 and DB agree, was assessed at 1.5 sulungs. Counting that in, we get an adjusted total of 189.5 sulungs for segment 1.

In C4, the word 'Total' occurs, but it is followed by a blank. There is probably no point in asking what this means. (The first question would be: what did the C4 scribe find in his exemplar? A blank? A cancelled number? A number which he chose not to copy because he knew that it was wrong?)

3vb3) Northwood. C1 has a redundant sentence at the end. Perhaps it was added by someone who did not realize that (abnormally) the hundred was named in the body of the paragraph.

3vb15) Eastry. The two versions differed greatly (until C4 was altered) in their descriptions of the first three subordinate manors: Tilmanstone, Finglesham, Statenborough. The version represented by C4 did not give the name of the current tenant, Willelm Folet; C1 and DB do that. For Buckland, neither version gives us the name of the tenant: only DB does that.

The synopsis seems to assume (correctly, I think) that the assessments for all these manors are counted in the seven sulungs of Eastry.

3vb48) Sandwich. Here again, the two versions differed greatly (or did, until C4 was altered). The farm being paid to the archbishop is one point on which they diverge. According to C4, Sandwich pays him fifty pounds. According to C1, which seems to reflect some statement from the men of the town, Sandwich was paying fifty pounds up until 'last year' (the financial year which ended in September 1085), but is due to pay seventy pounds 'this year'. (The word *debet* means 'is supposed to', 'is about to', or something of the sort.) The increase in the number of built-up plots is given as 76 in C1, and that is the number reported in B / xAug, as well as in DB. Originally C4 had some different number here; but the number was erased, when C4 was being made to agree with C1.

4ra22) Great Chart. C4 has a clause which is absent from C1, 'and yet it pays 27 pounds'. This is one of the places where C4 agrees with DB against C1, and the question arises how these agreements should be accounted for. The obvious answer is that they result from errors on the part of the C1 scribe. Thus here we might think that he omitted these words accidentally, his eye having jumped from the *lib'* at the end of the previous clause to the *lib'* at the end of this one. Mistakes of this type are easily made by scribes who are copying hurriedly, phrase by phrase; but I doubt whether that description applies to the C1 scribe. On the contrary, it looks to me as if he was working very slowly, copying letter by letter. If we are reluctant to put the blame on the C1 scribe, there are two alternative explanations: (a) that he was copying, not from $\alpha 2$ itself, but from a copy of $\alpha 2$ which already had some defects; (b) that this information was omitted accidentally from $\alpha 2$, but nevertheless became known to the commissioners later, through some other channel. I would vote for (b).

4ra41) Appledore. The hundred is called 'Blackton' in both versions of α, 'Blackbourne' in B / xAug and DB, as in all later records. Probably this was just a slip of the pen in $\alpha 1$: the $\alpha 2$ scribe reproduced the error, perhaps without realizing that it was one, but the commissioners' scribes were in a position to know better.

4ra51) Westwell. The farm being paid is 'forty pounds' in C4 and DB, 'eleven pounds' in C1. The numeral in C1 is certainly *xi* (and was so read by C3 / T1); but there is a small smudge above the *i*. It looks to me as if *xi* was altered to *xl* but then altered back to *xi*. However that may be, it seems certain that *xi* is an error, and that *xl* is the correct reading.

4rb12) Hollingbourne. In the passage relating to the bishop of Bayeux's half sulung, C4 lacks the phrase *per gablum* which is present in C1 and DB.

4rb39) Almsland. C1 lacks the clause 'and it defends itself for one sulung'. Since the synopsis counts one sulung here, the omission appears to be the fault of the C1 scribe. But there may be some confusion at work between this and the following paragraph. DB has the same information as C4. The same sulung is also described under Lyminge in segment 1 (2vb54).

4rb45) Warehorne. C4 lacks the words 'one sulung'. DB agrees with C1.

4rc5) Langport. In C4 this paragraph is part of segment 1 (71va3). Neither version reports, what we find reported elsewhere, that this manor had been recovered from the bishop of Bayeux.

Northwood	1	
Eastry	7	
Sandwich		
Monkton	20	α and DB
Adisham	17	
Ickham	4	
Seasalter		
Chartham	4	
Godmersham	8	
Great Chart	3	
Little Chart	3	
Appledore	2	
Westwell	7	
Hollingbourne	6	
Mersham	6	α and DB
Almsland	1	$\alpha 1$ and DB
Warehorne	1	$\alpha 2$ and DB
Brook	1	
Langport	1.5	
Newenden	1	
Westenhanger	0.5	
Saltwood	7	
Preston	1	
Leaveland	1	
East Lenham	2	
East Farleigh	6	
East Peckham	6	
Meopham	10	
Cliffe	2.5	so $\alpha 2$
Orpington	3	α and DB
Farningham	1	
	133.5	

Table 11. Sum of TRE assessments for segment 2.

4rc20) Newenden. In C4 this paragraph is part of segment 1 (71rb31).

4rc40) Saltwood. In C4 this paragraph is part of segment 1 (71rb36).

4va9) Leaveland. In C4 this paragraph is part of segment 1 (70vb5), and that is where it seems to be more at home. The sentence at the end, 'This land is in Faversham hundred', refers to Leaveland alone. In C1 the sentence at the end is differently worded – 'These (are the) manors (which) the monks own in Faversham hundred' – because here it refers to Preston (4va1) as well as Leaveland. But the Preston paragraph ends with a sentence of the same type – 'This manor is in Faversham hundred' – which is redundant as things stand. Apparently this sentence became redundant when the Leaveland paragraph was inserted into this segment, but survives because nobody took the trouble to cancel it.

4va19) East Lenham. In C4 this paragraph is part of segment 1 (70vb18), and that is where it seems more likely to belong. C1 fails to tell us which hundred East Lenham is in;

it fails to mention the fact that East Lenham is in the same hundred as Westwell (4ra51) and Little Chart (4ra29).

4vb9) Meopham. C1 lacks the phrase 'and now for seven'. DB has the same information as C4.

4vb19) Cliffe. The TRE assessment is given as 3.5 sulungs in C4 and DB, as 2.5 sulungs in C1. The synopsis is defective.

4vb44) Sandling. Because of the difference in the coloured initial, the TRE tenant's name is differently reported – as *Wluiet* (= Wulfgeat) in C4, as Ælfgeat in C1. Either way, this report is contradicted by DB, which says that the manor was held by a man named Bonde. But a man named *Uluiet* does appear in DB as Hugo's predecessor at two other manors (8rb11, 8rb17); so probably we should give C4 the benefit of the doubt.

In C4 a string of eleven words has gone missing from this paragraph. This is the only large defect occurring in that copy for which, apparently, the C4 scribe is to blame. Perhaps he skipped a line of his exemplar.

The Sandling paragraph seems to be more at home in segment 2, which is where we find it in C1. The sentence at the end, 'These manors are of Helmstree hundred', covers the Orpington paragraph (4vb26) as well as this one. In C4 this paragraph is part of segment 1 (71rb15). The logical place for it would be after Bexley (71ra15), which was in the same hundred, but that is not where we find it. Also the final sentence is oddly worded – 'This manor (singular) are (plural) in Helmstree hundred' – as though somebody started altering it (from singular to plural or vice versa) but did not finish the job. And the Orpington paragraph in segment 2 lacks a sentence to say that this manor is in Helmstree hundred.

It should not be forgotten, however, that Sandling was in a category by itself. The archbishop was not in possession of this manor at the time; he was arguing that he should be. (DB puts Sandling in chapter 5, 'Land of the bishop of Bayeux', but accepts that the manor was held from the archbishop in the time of king Eadward.) Even if we knew for certain how this paragraph came to be moved, it might be unwise to assume that the same was true for other paragraphs.

4vc1) Farningham. Here both versions have the nonce-word *rubitoniensis*, which somebody thought (but nobody agreed) was a clever way to say 'of Rochester'. In C1 the word recurs at the start of segment 3.

4vc12) Graveney, Loose, Swarling, Hunton, Burston. In both versions, segment 2 ends with this string of seemingly redundant paragraphs. The holdings in question have all been described before, Loose and Hunton in segment 2, the others in segment 1. In detail, however, the facts reported here are sometimes rather different.

5ra11) The total given by C1 for segment 2 is 133.5 sulungs (Table 11). It is not quite as easy to see how this total was arrived at as it for segments 1 and 3. Two of the entries in C1's synopsis were later rubbed out and rewritten, but

Southfleet	6	
Stone	6	
Fawkham	2	
Longfield	1	
Bromley	6	
Wouldham	6	
West Malling	3	
Trottiscliffe	3	C1 and DB
Snodland	6	
Halling	6	
Frindsbury	10	
Cuxton	2.5	
Denton	2	
Borstal	2	
Stoke	5	
	66.5	

Table 12. Sum of TRE assessments for segment 3.

that does not cause us much trouble. From α and DB, we can be sure what the original readings ought to have been: 20 (not 18) sulungs for Monkton (2rc4) and 6 (not 2.5) sulungs for Mersham (2rc17). More seriously, something had gone wrong near the end of the list: apparently the figure for Orpington (3 sulungs) was pushed up into the previous line, and the figure which ought to appear in that line dropped out (2rc31–2). To get the arithmetic right, it seems that we need to count 2.5 sulungs for Cliffe, as in C1 (4vb19). Making these corrections, and counting one sulung each for Almsland and Warehorne as in the synopsis, we arrive at the total reported by C1. For Cliffe, however, the figure reported by C4 and DB is 3.5 (not 2.5) sulungs: if that is right, as it presumably is, the total will come to 134.5 sulungs.

5ra16) Frindsbury. This paragraph is out of place in C1. Frindsbury belongs in Shamell hundred, with Halling, Cuxton and Denton, and that is where R1 puts it. Possibly this error reflects the existence of some lost version of segment 3 which began with Frindsbury (and the other Shamell hundred manors), not with Southfleet (and the other Axstone hundred manors), as in DB and R1.

5ra38) Stone. The current assessment is 3 sulungs in C1, 4 sulungs in R1 and DB. This discrepancy might be due to a scribal error in C1; but other numerical differences occur which cannot be explained away so easily.

Wherever there is some disagreement between C1 and R1, DB has the same TRE assessment as C1, the same current assessment as R1. In some sense, therefore, DB is textually intermediate between C1 and R1. But there are various ways in which that might have come about,[58] and I cannot decide what the best explanation might be.

5rb25) Trottiscliffe. The assessment of this manor was evidently the subject of some dispute. Neither C1 nor R1 uses the standard formula, *et in tempore E regis se defendebat pro .. sull', et nunc ....* C1 says only *et defendit se pro iii*

[58] Not to leave it vague, there are four ways: C1 $\leftarrow$ DB $\rightarrow$ R1, C1 $\leftarrow$ DB $\leftarrow$ R1, C1 $\rightarrow$ DB $\rightarrow$ R1, C1 $\rightarrow$ DB $\leftarrow$ R1.

sull', leaving it doubtful whether this is supposed to be the TRE figure or the current figure (the verb is ambiguous as to tense), or whether we are meant to assume that the figure has stayed the same. (The synopsis counts it as the TRE assessment.) R1 says something different, and says it both unambiguously and emphatically: this manor 'used to defend itself for one sulung, and it still does' (*defendebat se pro i solino, et adhuc facit*). (This is the voice of the bishop of Rochester's spokesman: he sounds somewhat annoyed.) DB's understanding of the facts is different again: 'TRE for three sulungs, now for one sulung' (5va41).

5rb29) Snodland. C1 says that the assessment was and still is 6 sulungs; R1 says that it was and still is 3 sulungs. Both use the standard formula: only the numeral differs.

5rb48) Denton. The TRE assessment is 2 sulungs in C1, 1 sulung in R1 (*pro i solino*).

5rc45) For segment 3, the total reported by C1 is 66.5 sulungs (Table 12). The arithmetic is straightforward – but some of the items would have been disputed in Rochester.

Concordance

segment 1

C4	C1	R1		DB-Ke
70rb3	2va3		Stursete	3va44, 4ra10
—	48		mansurae in Fordwich	12rb22
26	52		Wingham	3vb35
35	2vb13		Bishopsbourne	3vb10
38	19		Petham	3va33
70va4	30		Aldington	4ra3
14	46		Lyminge	4ra32
24	2vc11		Reculver	3va12
27	17		Northwood	3va20
35	32		Boughton under Blean	3vb16, 4rb46
70vb5			Leaveland	4rb43
10	51		Teynham	4va7
18			East Lenham	4va2
22	3ra10		Charing	3vb23
29	23		Pluckley	3vb29
34	33		Gillingham	3va2
71ra1	46		Maidstone	3rb36
9	3rb6		Northfleet	3rb12
15	17		Bexley	3ra43
19	25		Crayford	3ra49
24	35		Brasted	4rb23
29	44		Otford	3ra26
35	3rc2		Sundridge	3ra36
71rb3	16		Wrotham	3rb20
11	30		East Malling	3rb36
15			Sandling	7ra17
20	39		Darenth	3ra19
24	48		Eynsford	4rb9
28	3va3		Ulcombe	4rb30
31			Newenden	4ra43
36			Saltwood	4va17
71va3			Langport	4va30
10	10		prebends in Newington	14va22
12	—		prebend in Dover	1vb11

segment 2

C4	C1	R1		DB-Ke
22	3vb3		Northwood	5ra9
27	15		Eastry	4va10, 5rb8
71vb2	48		Sandwich	3ra7,5rb47
9	3vc12		Monkton	4vb47
13	20		Adisham	5rb18
20	41		Ickham	5ra3
25	52		Seasalter	5ra15
29	4ra7		Chartham	5ra26
32	14		Godmersham	5ra32
36	22		Great Chart	5ra37
40	29		Little Chart	5ra42
72ra6	41		Appledore	5rb33
11	51		Westwell	5rb1
15	4rb7		Hollingbourne	4vb19
20	18		Boughton Monchelsea	4rb37
26	28		Mersham	3vb47
32	39		almsland	5rb43
35	45		Warehorne	5rb28
37	51		Brook	5rb38
	4rc5		Langport	4va30
	20		Newenden	4ra43
72rb1	31		Westenhanger	4va25
	40		Saltwood	4va17
5	4va1		Preston	5ra21
	9		Leaveland	4rb43
	19		East Lenham	4va2
9	28		East Farleigh	4vb31
17	43		East Peckham	4vb9
28	4vb9		Meopham	4vb25
34	19		Cliffe	4vb42
38	26		Orpington	4rb17, 4vb2
	44		Sandling	7ra17
72va8	4vc1		Farningham	4rb2
13	12		Graveney (Boughton under Blean)	
17	21		Loose (East Farleigh)	
20	29		Swarling (Petham)	
23	35		Hunton (East Farleigh)	
27	43		Burston (Maidstone)	

segment 3

C4	C1	R1		DB-Ke
	5ra16		Frindsbury	5vb14
	27	209r5	Southfleet	5va2
	38	11	Stone	5va9
	47	15	Fawkham	5va17
	53	17	Longfield	5va22
	5rb6	21	Bromley	5va25
	14	209v2	Wouldham	5va31
	19	4	West Malling	5va36
	25	6	Trottiscliffe	5va41
	29	8	Snodland	5va46
	37	12	Halling	5vb10
		15	Frindsbury	5vb14
	42	20	Cuxton	5vb1
	48	23	Denton	5vb6
	5rc2	210r3	Borstal	5vb19
	17	13	Stoke	5vb28

Chapter 3
Extracts from B-Ke made for Saint Augustine's

The register known as the 'White Book of Saint Augustine's' (National Archives, E 164/27) is a rather untidily written manuscript, measuring roughly 215 × 145 mm, which was approaching its final form in about 1320.[1] After the dissolution, it became one of a haphazard collection of cartularies which passed into the keeping of the exchequer official called the King's Remembrancer. It is known to have been there in the middle of the seventeenth century (above, p. 24).

The manuscript is mostly made up of quires of 12. There is a quire of 4 at the end (fos. 230–3), and there seems once to have been a matching quire of 4 at the beginning, though only the last leaf of it survives (fo. 1, numbered '4' by the hand which added the medieval foliation). Not counting these outermost quires, the manuscript consists of two booklets:

(1) documents relating to the abbey's endowment (fos. 2–192, sixteen quires, lacking one leaf at the end);

(2) annals till 1331 (fos. 194–228, three quires, lacking one leaf at the end).

Several scribes contributed, and their hands are rather hard to distinguish (or at least I find them so). As a first approximation, I suggest that it is possible to recognize the following stints:

2r1-27r9	scribe 1
27r10-48r16	scribe 2
48r16-58r14	scribe 3
58v1-97v21	scribe 4
98r1-103r13	scribe 3
103r13-17	scribe 5
103r17-110v4	scribe 4
110v5-7	scribe 5
110v7-91v11	scribe 4
191v12-2r10	-
194r1-223v10	scribe 3
223v10-7v20	-

As can be seen from this list, the bulk of the manuscript, from 48r onwards, was written by just two men, scribes 3 and 4, and most of it was written by the latter.[2] Both were demonstrably at work in the 1320s. Scribe 3 was responsible for the annals: the last entry in his hand is the one for 1325.[3] A different hand, which seems to occur only here, added a few more sentences to the annal for 1325 and continued as far as 1331; there is space for more entries after that, but none were ever supplied. As for scribe 4, the last and latest documents copied by him date from 1323–4; but there are some fairly pronounced changes of appearance in this final stretch of text (185r1, 189r9), and the preceding stretch (as far as 184v) may perhaps be slightly earlier – not earlier, however, than 1316–17. The two scribes were working together; at one point there was some misunderstanding between them and the same stretch of text was copied twice (58v1–8, by scribe 4; 58r15–22, an addition by scribe 3). From the inclusion of a series of form letters,[4] it seems likely that the manuscript was intended to form a manual for the abbot; and the abbot at the time was Radulf de Burne (1310–1334). The scribes who created it were, I suppose, clerks employed in the abbot's household, not members of the monastic community.

It is clear enough that the manuscript was completed in the 1320s. Nevertheless, the first four quires (fos. 2–49) may perhaps be significantly earlier than that.[5] There seem to me to be two hands represented here, though the general appearance of the script is similar for both. Neither hand reappears further on; as far as the contents are concerned, there is nothing later than the mid thirteenth century. From the look of the script, I suppose that it might be a generation earlier than that used in the rest of the book; but I would doubt whether it could be earlier than the end of the thirteenth century. Though I do not see how we can hope to arrive at any definite conclusion, I am inclined to think that the first four quires result from some earlier project, begun but left unfinished, which was taken up again and carried

[1] There are also a 'Red Book' (BL Cotton Claudius D. x) and a 'Black Book' (BL Cotton Faustina A. i). How far these names are authentic I cannot say; I have not found them used in any of the manuscripts that I have seen.

[2] Only two short passages were contributed by scribe 5, who barely did enough to deserve a number. His writing is conspicuously bad; the sign for *et* is shaped like *2*, not as usual like *7* or *Z*.

[3] The change of hand on 223v was noted by Holtzmann (1930, p. 44).

[4] Though most have been reduced to formulas – the person concerned is *A de B*, the church in question is *talis ecclesia* – there are some which retain a date; the latest of these is dated 5 April 1317 (183v–4r). (As I noted elsewhere (Flight 2000, p. 290), this is a letter of collation to the vicarage of Plumstead.)

[5] Scribe 2 ends his stint at 48r in the middle of a sentence (*Hoc nimirum intuitu* ...), a few lines into the text of a papal privilege dating from 1144 (Jaffé 1885–8, no. 8582). Scribe 3 began his first stint by copying the rest of this letter; but it would not have been hard for him to recognize which document this was, even if some length of time had elapsed.

through to completion in the time of abbot Radulf. Perhaps we might think of associating the original project with Radulf's predecessor, Thomas de Findone (1283–1310); but this is just a guess.

Whether the difference in date is significant or not, it will be convenient to make a distinction between the earlier and the later parts of the book. I refer to the initial section (fos. 2r–48r) as A4, to the rest of the book as A5. Since all the documents of any interest to us were copied either by scribe 1 or by scribe 4, in effect the sigla refer respectively to them.

Scribe 1 wrote what is, from our point of view, by far the most important stretch of text. (It fills the first two quires and overlaps into the third.) As a scribe he was competent enough; but he was not writing carefully, and it is often hard to be sure exactly what he meant. His minims are generally ambiguous: no distinction is made (that I can see) between *n* and *u*, or between *m* and *in* and *ui* – unless he remembers to accent the *i*, as he usually does. His *c* is the same as his *t*, and only the slightest hairline diferentiates *e* from *c*. In English words the same sign that is used for *y* is used for *th* as well. In short, this scribe made some heavy demands on his readers – perhaps because he was hardly expecting to have any readers, other than himself. (In fairness perhaps it ought also to be said that his writing is easier to read than scribe 2's.)

Since this scribe was certainly at work before 1320, perhaps before 1310, it may be worth noting the fact that he seems to be more comfortable with arabic than roman numerals. Copying ancient documents like these, he understands that roman numerals are appropriate; but every so often, in an absent-minded moment, he writes an arabic numeral. Usually he notices his error at once and corrects it;[6] occasionally he fails to see it.

The contents of this stretch of text can be summarized as follows.

(i) A list of charters and other documents (2r–8r), ranging in date from the seventh to the late twelfth century. Partly printed by Kelly (1995, pp. 189–94).[7] The compiler of this list, presumably scribe 1 himself, seems to have been working from an collection of documents which were tied up in bundles of several items each, but otherwise not kept in order.[8]

(ii) A letter of pope Alexander III (8r–v = Jaffé 1885–8, no. 13120); extracts from two letters of pope Urbanus III (8v–9r = no. 15607, 9r = no. 15602).[9]

(iii) A narrative account of the negotiations involved in the settlement of a dispute between the monastery and archbishop Theobald in 1143–4 (9r–11v). This is a very strange piece of work, veering between forgery and fiction; but it drops all pretence at the end.[10]

(iv) A survey of the abbey's lands, *Noticia terrarum sancti Augustini in comitatu de Kent in quo lasto et in quo hundredo*, followed by various memoranda relating to its possessions in Milton hundred (11v–14r). The *Noticia* was apparently compiled in the time of abbot Hugo II (1126–51).[11] A note added by a fifteenth-century hand tells us that this copy was taken from the 'textus of Saint Adrian', *extractum de textu sancti Adriani* (11v): that was the name which came to be used for the book which the monks considered to be their most important register.

(v) A further sequence of lists and memoranda (14r–17r), running parallel with an earlier manuscript, the one which I call A2 (below, p. 218). The first item to appear in both manuscripts is a list of the abbot's knights, the title of which, in A2 as well as in A4, refers back to article (iv), *Isti sunt milites feofati in suprascripta terra*; so it seems clear enough, not only that both manuscripts were copied from a common exemplar, but also that this was the same exemplar used for the preceding article by A4, i.e. the 'textus of Saint Adrian'.

(vi) *Excepta de compoto solingorum comitatus Cancie secundum cartam regis* (17r–25r). These are the excerpts from B-Ke, printed by Ballard (1920), and printed again below.

(vii) Charters of king Offa (25r–v = Kelly 1995, no. 15) and king Wictred (25v–6r = no. 10). The same two charters, in the same order, in the same shortened form, are also to be

[6] In one place, for example, he writes a *3* and then changes it to *t*, so that he can replace the numeral with the word *tres* (19v18).

[7] Though Kelly does not say so, the numbers that appear in the printed text are her contribution; neither these nor any other numbers appear in the manuscript itself.

[8] This is the interpretation suggested by Kelly (1995, pp. xlvi–vii); I agree with it. Very briefly, the suggestion goes like this. If these hypothetical bundles had been numbered, and if the top of each bundle had been marked, the ordering of the documents would have been approximately the same as in a lost twelfth-century cartulary, partly reconstructable from two surviving copies (below, p. 218) – the reason being, either that the organization of the cartulary was dictated by that of the archive, or that the archive was reorganized, to make it match up with the cartulary. Because the bundles were not numbered, the compiler of this list put them in a random order; because they were not marked on the top, he put some of them upside down. The upshot is that the ordering of the items is globally very different from the order in the cartulary but locally very close to it; and the correlation may be either positive or negative, depending on whether the compiler was starting from the top or the bottom of this particular bundle.

[9] These two letters of Urbanus III were subsequently copied in full by scribe 4 (64v, 67v).

[10] There is a better copy in BL Cotton Claudius D. x, fos. 20r–1r, and part of the text – the part which manages to sound vaguely authentic – was printed from that manuscript by Brett and Brooke (1981, pp. 808–10). Two genuine documents are embedded in the narrative: a letter of Henric bishop of Winchester (Franklin 1993, no. 32, where the last sentence is part of the surrounding narrative, mistakenly printed as if it were part of this text) and a letter of pope Lucius II (Jaffé 1885–8, no. 8581). The entire narrative was incorporated into Sprott's chronicle; from there it was copied into Thorne's.

[11] Parts of it derive from B-Ke, by way of the excerpts copied separately into A4 (17r–25r); parts of it derive from chapter 7 of DB-Ke, by way of some meagre excerpts copied separately into A5 (143r–4v). Its date is fixed by a sentence near the end which mentions Robert de Ver, in connection with the payment of a mark of silver from Horton (13r): Robert de Ver (occ. 1127–51) was the third husband of Hugo de Montfort's daughter Adelina.

found in the manuscript I call A3 (fos. 105v–6r), in a stretch of text which seems to have been copied from a twelfth-century cartulary, perhaps contained in the 'textus of Saint Adrian' (below, p. 218). Apparently this stretch of A4 was copied from the same exemplar as A3.[12]

(viii) *De primatu super Eboracensem quam Cantuariensis ecclesia habere debet* (26r–7r), a copy of version 2 of the primacy agreement of 1072 (Bates 1998, no. 68), shortened towards the end.[13]

For the rest, the book does not contain much of any significance for us. Two stretches of text in A5, both written by scribe 4, are of some incidental interest. One is a sequence of documents (76v-87r) copied, so it seems, from a lost twelfth-century cartulary (the same source which I take to have been used for article (vii) above). The other is a series of excerpts from chapter 7 of DB-Ke (143r–4v).[14]

From here onwards I focus on article (vi), the text which carries the title *Excepta de compoto solingorum*,[15] 'Excerpts from the reckoning of sulungs'. I refer to it as xAug. It is possible (perhaps we may think it probable) that this text was copied from the same exemplar that had been used for articles (iv) and (v), the 'textus of Saint Adrian'; but there is no way to prove it. A more significant conclusion can be proved – proved beyond doubt, I think. As the following paragraphs set out to show, this is the only surviving copy of the only known set of excerpts from the earliest version of the survey text for Kent.

There is, I take it, no need to argue that the source-text from which these excerpts were taken was some version of the survey text. Despite the abbreviation to which they have been subjected, despite the abbreviation which the corresponding entries in DB-Ke have also undergone, numerous passages can still be found which are manifestly in verbal agreement. This was demonstrated by Ballard (1920); I am not aware that anyone since then has ever thought of doubting it.

If that is agreed, the question becomes: which version of the survey text was it? The answer to that question is easily arrived at, because it can be shown that the source-text was organized cadastrally. That being true, it can only have been the B text.[16]

It is not instantly obvious that the source-text for xAug was organized in this way, because, in xAug itself, many of the cadastral headings have gone missing. Nevertheless, with the help of DB-Ke we can supply the omitted headings without much trouble; and as soon as we do that, the conclusion falls out straight away (Table 13).[17] From our point of view, it is a great stroke of luck that the abbey owned some land in every lest. Thanks to that, we can state it to be true, for all seven lests, that the entries belonging to any one lest form a single block. A similar statement is true for the hundreds as well, with one small exception (21r11–12). For any hundred which comprises more than one entry, those entries also form a single block.

This pattern of evidence would prove nothing whatever if the entries were all contained in a single chapter of DB (derived from a single chapter of D, derived from a single C booklet). In that case we would expect them to be cadastrally organized, to the extent that the original order had been preserved, regardless of which version of the survey text they came from. But here again we profit from a stroke of luck, because the man who made these excerpts did not confine himself to the entries which eventually came to be included in DB-Ke's chapter 7, the chapter describing the abbey's own possessions. He interested himself in many other entries as well; and therefore we have the evidence which makes the proof complete.

Because these excerpts were made, because this copy survives, we are in a position to demonstrate the existence of B-Ke – to demonstrate, that is, that there did exist a version of the survey text for Kent which was organized cadastrally, lest by lest and hundred by hundred. The actual order is known for every lest, but only for 24 hundreds, not much more than a third of the total number. Even with that limitation, this is an important result.

In Kent, and in many other counties, the traces of a cadastral order inherited from the B text can be recognized in the organization of individual chapters, as they appear in DB. How distinctly these traces can be seen, how far the latent order can be reconstructed, varies from county to county. To put it crudely, the larger the number of chapters and the smaller the number of hundreds, the easier we can hope that it will be to piece together the ordering that existed in the B text.

In Kent the odds are against us: the number of chapters is rather small and the number of hundreds is uncommonly

[12] It is almost possible that A4 was copied from A3; but there are a few variants which, on that view, would have to be regarded as the result of some rather intelligent emendation on the part of the A4 scribe, and it is hard to think that he was paying that much attention.

[13] This last article was not of any special interest to Saint Augustine's; but I think that we are expected to read it from a prejudiced point of view, as proof that a simple-minded archbishop of York had let himself be bamboozled by an unscrupulous archbishop of Canterbury. The following item (28r–32r) – the first to be added by scribe 2 – is a piece of late twelfth-century pseudo-history which expressly sets out to show how a simple-minded abbot of Saint Augustine's was bamboozled by the same unscrupulous archbishop.

[14] The excerpts used by the compiler of the *Noticia terrarum* (above, note 11).

[15] The first word has often been emended to *Excerpta*, but for that there is no necessity (Flight 2006, p. 123), and therefore no justification.

[16] Here I am applying the rule which I worked out in dealing with the excerpts made for the monks of Ely (Flight 2006, pp. 99–103). But the present case is very much simpler than that one, and the conclusion is much clearer.

[17] There is only one doubtful point – where to mark the beginning of Eastry lest – and it cannot affect the conclusion.

lest	hundred	B / xAug / A4	A4	DB-Ke	ch. 7
Sutton	Littleleigh	East Wickham	17r9–11	6va28	
		Plumstead	17r11–13	12ra3	1
Aylesford	Eyhorne	Leeds	17r13–19	7vb30	
		Lenham	17r20–4	12ra10	2
Milton	Milton	Milton	17r24–v14	2va46	
		Newington	17v14–21	14va3	
Wiwarleth	Faversham	Wilderton	17v24–18r1	12rb30	12
		Badlesmere	18r2–5	10rb11	
	Wye	Dernedale	18r5–7	12rb37	14
		Ashenfield	18r7–9	12rb34	13
	Felborough	Shillingheld	18r9–11	12va1	18
	Chart	Repton	18r11–14	12rb46	17
	Boughton	Selling	18r14–15	12rb39	15
	Calehill	Rooting	18r16–18	12rb43	16
	Longbridge	Kennington	18r18–21	12vb25	28
Borwar	Canterbury	city of Canterbury	18r22–19v6	2ra1	
		Longport	19v6–13	12ra22	4
		half sulung	19v13–15	12rb24	11
		Northgate	19v15–19	5ra9	
		Westgate	19v19–20r6	3va44	
		Nackington	20r6–8	9va6	
		Saint Martin	20r8–13	4ra10	
		32 mansurae	20r13–15	3ra3	
	Bridge	Bridge	20r15–17	12ra17	3
		Bekesbourne	20r17–19	9rb30	
	Downhamford	Wickhambreaux	20r19–v1	9rb43	
		Littlebourne	20v1–3	12ra30	5
		Garrington	20v3–7	12ra36	6
	Chislet	Chislet	20v7–11	12rb6	9
	Sturry	Sturry	20v11-12	12ra41	7
	Fordwich	town of Fordwich	20v13–20	12rb13	10
	Whitstable	Blean	20v21–3	14rb41	
		Swalecliffe	20v23–1r1	10ra1	
	Thanet	Minster	21r1–4	12ra48	8
Eastry	Preston	Elmstone	21r4–10	12vb5	24
(three rods of land in Eastry hundred)			21r11–12	12vb13	25
		Preston	21r12–16	12va48	23
	Sandwich	town of Sandwich	21r16–v2	3ra7	
	Cornilo	Northbourne	21v2–13	12va5	19
		Little Mongeham	21v13–17	12va27	20
		Great Mongeham	21v22		
		Walmer	21v22		
		Ripple	21v23–2r2	—	
	Bewsborough	Sibertswold	22r3–5	12va38	21
			—	12va43	22
		town of Dover	22r6–v15	1ra4	
		prebends of Saint Martin's	22v15–4r10	1va11	
Limwar	Stowting	Bodsham	24r11–12	12vb17	26
		Elmsted and Horton	24r13–14	12vb20	27
	Blackbourne	?			
	?	Burmarsh	24r15–17	12vb33	29
(customs of four eastern lests)			24r17–5r11	1rb1	
(sac and soc in two western lests)			25r12–17	1va1	

Table 13. Extracts from B-Ke made for Saint Augustine's.

large. But here there are lests as well as hundreds, and the lests are few in number. For them at least the order is fairly easy to reconstruct. Though chopped and changed to some considerable extent, especially towards the end, the latent order is SAMBWEL – Sutton, Aylesford, Milton, Borwar, Wiwar, Eastry, Limwar. That is the same as the order in xAug, except for one dislocation: in xAug Borwar comes after Wiwar, but here it tends to come before it. This dislocation is interesting in itself, because it suggests that the B text consisted of some number of separate components which were, for some length of time, at risk of becoming transposed (above, p. 18).

As far as I can see, there is little hope of our reconstructing the order of the hundreds, beyond the partial sequence that is given by xAug. Some individual facts are clear enough and important enough to be worth noting. It seems fairly certain, for instance, that the survey of Wiwar lest began with Faversham hundred – which, after all, is rather what we might expect, Faversham being the only hundred where the king himself owned land, once Wye had been donated to the monks of Battle. Yet even in Wiwar, where xAug gives us a very good start, the indications that we get from DB are so inadequate, and so self-contradictory, that I doubt whether the hundred order can be worked out in full, in a way which would carry conviction.

Some significant features of the organization of the B text show up very clearly in xAug. The descriptions of all the towns that are represented here – Canterbury, Fordwich, Sandwich, Dover – are set into the cadastral frame. By the time that these passages turn up in DB, all but one have been extracted from that frame. The paragraphs relating to Dover and Canterbury (the latter heavily abridged) have come to be included in DB's preliminary section (1ra–b, 2ra); and DB's chapter 2 has a preliminary section of its own (3ra), which consists of one passage relating to Canterbury and the whole of the Sandwich paragraph. Only the Fordwich paragraph (12rb13) has not been moved. Similarly, the description of the prebends of the canons of Saint Martin's is inside the cadastral frame here, but in DB has been taken out of it (1va–b). In fact, there are only two passages in B / xAug which fall outside the frame. In DB the corresponding paragraphs are, again, included in the preliminary section (1rb, 1va); but here they come right at the end, forming a kind of appendix. From their placement in B, and from their content, I think we can conclude, with a fair degree of confidence, that these passages were added to the B text by the second team of commissioners.

How much time elapsed, after the completion of the B text, before these excerpts were taken from it is not easy to say. If xAug consisted of nothing but excerpts from B, its date would be impossible to fix. Whenever the excerpts were made – just after B had been completed, just before it ceased to exist, or somewhere in between – there would be no difference that we could hope to see. It is fortunate, therefore, from this point of view, that the text as we have it includes a number of interpolations, one of which, as Ballard (1920) observed, seems to be approximately datable. The paragraphs relating to Northbourne and Little Mongeham (21v2–17) are followed by an added sentence (21v17–21) recounting the story of a successful law-suit which took place, as we happen to know, in May 1110;[18] and the gist of it is that 'abbot Hugo' had proved his case 'in the court of king Henric'. As far as the dating is concerned, the significance of this sentence lies not so much in what it says as in what it fails to say. Anyone writing after 1154, after the accession of a second king of the same name, would (very probably) have thought it necessary to call this king 'Henric I'.[19] So the interpolation is likely to be earlier than 1154. Anyone writing after 1126, when this abbot was succeeded by a second abbot of the same name, would (probably) have thought it necessary to call him 'Hugo I' – especially so because either Hugo could have fought a case in the court of Henric I, and because the second Hugo would still have been alive (or just recently dead) at the time when this sentence was written. So the interpolation is likely to be earlier than 1126. This argument is thin, to be sure, but I am inclined to trust it. If it is indeed safe to conclude that additions were being made to xAug in the time of abbot Hugo I (1107–26), it will follow that the excerpts themselves are at least as early as that. Essentially this was all said by Ballard (1920, p. xii), and I do not see that there is anything much to add.[20]

The rest is a matter of judgment. It seems quite likely to me that the excerpts were made at the instigation of abbot Hugo, soon after his arrival in 1107. Before that, for a period of fourteen years, the abbacy had been left vacant – deliberately and scandalously left vacant, so that the abbey's income (minus whatever was thought sufficient for the monks' subsistence) could be diverted into the hands of the king.[21] We know for a fact that the new abbot was quick to exert himself in recovering control over the abbey's possessions, and xAug might have been needed for that purpose. In order for that to be true, we should have to be willing to think that the B text was still in existence, and still thought important enough to be worth making excerpts from,[22] more than twenty years after the completion of the survey. I have no trouble believing that myself; but anyone who finds it incredible is free to imagine an earlier date for xAug. It is possible that the excerpts were made in the time of abbot Wido (1089–93); it is even possible that they

[18] The resulting writ is Johnson and Cronne 1956, no. 944.

[19] Just as Willelm I is called *Willelmus primus* in two other interpolated passages (17v11, 17v24).

[20] But it is a point worth noting that extracts from xAug were incorporated into a composite text (above, note 11) which seems to date from the time of abbot Hugo II (1126–51).

[21] Later vacancies show up in the exchequer rolls. In 1173, after the abbot-elect had been deposed, the king took the abbey into his hands and put it out to farm for 180 pounds a year, pending the election of a new abbot (GREx 1174:1–2, 1175:221, 1176:209). The next time around, the monks were willing to pay huge sums to get custody of the abbey for themselves (GREx 1212:15).

[22] Why the excerpts were taken from B, rather than from D or DB, is not a question which I would want to ask. How could we hope to answer it?

were made in the time of abbot Scotland, the abbot in office at the time of the survey (he died in September 1087). Perhaps the reader can discover some way of deciding between these possibilities; for my part, I cannot.

If, from one point of view, we have to be glad that the text has been interpolated, from another point of view we have to regret the fact. Some of the passages inserted in the text are easy enough to recognize. Some are obviously anachronistic: a passage mentioning *rex Willelmus primus*, or *abbas Hugo*, or *rex Henricus* cannot have come from B-Ke. (There is also one sentence (21v7) which cannot have been added until the mid thirteenth century.) Some are so blatantly partisan that they must have been written by somebody at Saint Augustine's. The problem is that there may be other interpolations which are less self-evident than these. We value this text, among other reasons, because it contains much factual information derived from B-Ke which is not to be found in DB; but we have no means of making a sharp distinction between what came from B and what was added later. If we choose to disregard that problem, we take a risk. Though the danger does not seem serious to me, I would not wish to let the reader think that there is no danger at all.

The text is not in good shape. There are numerous mistakes, numerous places where something has obviously gone missing. (Conversely a small unwanted word has crept in here and there.) Some of these errors may have been inherited from the exemplar; but many of them are visibly the fault of the scribe who made this copy. Besides, it had better be repeated that in some respects his writing is hard to read.[23] Slips of the pen occur frequently. Sometimes the scribe stumbles over a word – *canonicus*, for example, trips him up three times (22r8, 22v16, 23v21) – and his attempts at correction tend rather to make things worse. As a general rule, I let the scribe have the benefit of any doubt; and this means, in the last resort, that I print what I think he was intending to write, even if he did not quite succeed in writing it.

Given that the text is so defective,[24] I have taken some liberties with it that I would never think of taking with a text that survived in the original, or in an accurate copy. By and large I retain the spelling used in the manuscript. Though I tolerate the *p* in words like *dampnum*, *calumpnia*, I draw the line at some late medieval spellings (such as *yems* for *hiems*) which would look painfully incongruous. All changes involving more than one letter are noted; the rest are too trivial to mention. The punctuation and capital letters are largely my contribution, and the scribe is not answerable for them. Errors so slight that they hardly affect the sense (such as *in mare* for *in mari*) are left uncorrected; more serious mistakes are treated in one of two ways. If the sense can be restored by changing a few letters, or by adding or omitting one small word, I make the emendation; otherwise I insert an ellipsis. The uncorrected readings are given in the notes at the end, in case anyone should want to look at them.

Those passages which seem to me to be interpolations (many of them were seen in the same light by Ballard) are printed in grey type.[25] It is conceivable that some of these interpolations were made by the compiler of xAug himself: I do not mean to say that they are all significantly later than the main text, only that they are (in my opinion) unlikely to have been copied from B-Ke. In the manuscript these passages are not differentiated in any way; but the reader will find it helpful, I hope, to have them discreetly marked off.

Not just here but throughout the book, there is some marginal annotation by later hands; but the additions made alongside xAug are not of any interest (except as proof that this particular text was still being looked at from time to time). Like Ballard, I have made it my policy to print everything that was written by the main scribe, nothing that was not.

[23] To cite just one example, the name which ought to be *Ansfridus* seems to me to be spelt *Aufridus*, like *Gaufridus*; but Ballard preferred to read it as *Anfridus*, and I cannot say with confidence that he was wrong.

[24] The second-hand excerpts included in the *Noticia terrarum* (above, note 11) were so much reworked that it would only complicate the issue to cite them here. Of the emendations which I have made, just one – 17r17 *cambiam* – reflects a reading found in the *Noticia*.

[25] I have also used grey type for two words (17v5, 19v6) which seem sure to be corrupt, but which I do not see how to emend.

B-Ke / xAug / A4-17r

Excepta de compoto solingorum comitatus Cancie secundum cartam regis, uidelicet ea que ad eccl'iam sc'i Augustini pertinent, et est in regis domesday.
Plumstede quod tenuit Brixi cild, tempore regis Edwardi se defendit pro ii solin' et uno iugo, modo tenet illud abbas de sc'o August' de feodo ep'i baiocensis, et est apreciatum x lib', sed tamen reddit xii *lib'. Alia pars de Plumstede quam tenuit Serag, tempore regis Edwardi se defendit pro ii solin' et uno iugo, et est appreciatum xii li', sed tamen reddit xiiii li'. Ledes tenuit comes Lifwinus de rege Edwardo, et defendit se pro tribus solin', et modo defendit se pro ii solin'. Et Etheloldus tenebat illud de ep'o baiocensi, sed nunc habet rex Will's illud in manu sua, et est apreciatum xx lib', sed tamen reddit xxv lib'. De isto manerio habet abbas sc'i Augustini dimid' solinum propter *cambiam de parco de Wicham, et reddebat tempore regis Edwardi x sol'. Item de eodem manerio *tenet comes Robertus de Eu iiii dennas siluarum in Suthsexa, que *appreciate sunt xx sol'. Lenham manerium est de cibo monachorum sc'i Augustini, tempore regis Edwardi se defendit pro v solin' et dimid', et est appreciatum xxviii li'. Et in supradicto manerio ... quod uocatur Bromfeld. Ibi habet adhuc sc's Augustinus dimidium iugum terre quod iacet ad istud manerium, et est appreciatum v sol'. Middeltune manerium

B-Ke / xAug / A4-17v

est de dominio regis, et defendit se tempore regis Edwardi pro quater viginti solin', et est apreciatum illo tempore cc li', et quando Hamo dapifer illud recepit, tunc se defendebat pro lxxii solin' unum iugum minus, et est apreciatum cc li' xx li' minus. Ex hiis quater uiginti solinis tenet Hugo de Port viii sol' et unum iugum de ep'o baiocensi, qui omnes consuetudines reddebant in isto manerio, hec *ergo tenuit Edwardus. Et adhuc ex lxxii solin' supradictis unum iugum minus dantur xi libre et x sol' in Newentone de gablo, et xxviii pense caseorum, et de istis predictis lxxii solin' unum iugum minus sunt ix solini qui reddunt in Newentone socam et saccam et gablum et omnes consuetudines extra *aueriam.
Ex hiis solin' habet sc's Augustinus partem suam que fuit diracionata in hundredo de Middeltone et in comitatu Kancie tempore regis Will'i primi.
Tamen Hamo qui nunc tenet Middelton regi sepcies uiginti libras cum incensione *et pensa et xv lib' et vi s' *ii d' minus reddit cum numero, et xii lib' quas uicecomes habet ad suum opus. Newentune manerium tenuit Suidgar de regina Eaditha, tempore regis Edwardi se defendit pro vii solin' et dim', et modo tenet illud Albertus, et est apreciatum xxxvii lib'. Et hoc quod archiep's habet est apreciatum vi li', et quod ep's baiocensis habet ualet lx solid', et Godefridus habet unum iugum terre de ep'o baiocensi et ualet x solid', et Adam filius Huberti habet tantum silue *quod ualet xl den'. Et due mansiones sunt in Roucestre quas ep's baiocens' tenuit, que reddunt huic manerio duos solid'. De isto manerio diracionauit sc's Augustinus et abbas Scotlandus viii prebendas et eccl'iam cum omnibus terris et consuetudinibus ad illas pertinentibus tempore regis Will'i primi. Wilrintun manerium est de cibo monachorum sc'i Aug',

B-Ke / xAug / A4-18r

tempore regis Edwardi defendit se pro uno solino, et est appreciatum iiii li'. Badlesmere manerium tenuit Godrich wisce de rege Edwardo, et defendit se pro uno solino, et modo tenet illud Aufridus de ep'o *baiocensi, et est appreciatum iiii libras. Hoc idem manerium reclamant monachi sc'i Augustini per cartam et sigillum regis Edwardi. *Dernedale manerium sc'i Augustini tempore regis Edwardi *defendit se pro dim' solin', et modo tenet illud Adam de abb'e ad gablum, et ualet xx sol'. *Echemersfelde manerium sc'i Augustini tempore regis Edwardi defendit se pro uno solino, modo tenet illud Ascetillus marescallus de abb'e, et ualet xl solid'. Schellingehelde *manerium sc'i Augustini tempore regis Edwardi se defendit pro dimid' solin', et modo tenet illud Auufredus masculus clericus de abb'e, et ualet xxx sol'. Rapetune manerium sc'i Augustini tempore regis Edwardi se defendit pro uno solino, et modo tenet illud Ansierus de abb'e, et abbas dedit sibi adhuc tres uillanos cum ii iug' terre, et est apreciatum iiii li' et v s'. Sellinge manerium sc'i Augustini tempore regis Edwardi se defendebat pro vii solin', et ualet xv li'. Rotinge manerium sc'i Augustini tempore regis Edwardi se defendebat pro dimidio iug', et modo tenet illud quidam uillanus de abb'e, et est apreciatum xl solid'. Keningtune ... sc'i Augustini tempore regis Edwardi se defendebat pro iiii solin', et cum hiis solin' habet adhuc sc's Augustinus unum iugum in dominio quod nunquam scotauit, et est apreciatum inter totum x li', sed tamen habet abbas quinquaginta solid' plus. Hic incipit Burewarelest. *De ciuitate Canterburia ... rex Edwardus in d'nio li burgens' qui reddebant iii lib' et xvii solid' et v d' de gablo. Et in eadem ciuitate fuerunt cc et xii homines

B-Ke / xAug / A4-18v

de quibus rex *habebat sacam et socam, et tria molendina que reddebant regi xlii s' de gablo, et viii agri prati unde pascebantur equi regis, euntes et redeuntes, et mille ag' minute silue unde homines patrie et burgenses ciuitatis reddebant preposito regis xx solid', et teloneus panis reddebat xx solid'. Et si extranei mercatores ueniebant in ciuitate et accipiebant hospicium in terra sc'e trinitatis uel sc'i Augustini, tunc habebant ... sui prepositi. Sed fuit *quidam prepositus nomine Brimannus qui per totam terram ciuitatis accepit omnes consuetudines et teloneum iniuste, de quo fecerunt monachi clamorem regi Will'o, qui precepit ut inde fuisset ... ante ep'm baiocens' et ante Hugonem de Mundfort et comitem Ow et Ricardum filium *Gisleberti, qui eum iurare fecerunt ut de hac re uerum diceret, quibus post iusiurandum dixit quod *uero toloneum habebat acceptum per totam ciuitatem, sed iniuste de terra sc'e trinitatis uel sc'i Augustini. De molendinis uero que sunt infra muros ciuitatis, si ex utrisque partibus aque ambe ripe sunt unius senioris, tunc exclusam et molendinum potest mutare quo ... uoluerit, ita tamen ut alterius ... molendino non noceat, et de rota molendini in spacio duarum *perticarum potest deliberare *uiam in antea uel retro propter emendacionem molendini, et ut dictum est alterius senioris molendino non noceat. Et si ex una parte aque est ripa unius senioris, et alterius ex altera, tunc non potest ... ulla *edificacio uel mutacio excluse sine licencia illius cuius est altera pars ripe, et ex spacio duarum *perticarum in antea est aqua in dominio regis. Et si panis aut *ceruisia esset facta alio modo quam constitutum est in antiquo tempore, uolebant inde *monachi habere forisfacturam, sed Brimannus supradictus prepositus accepit hanc forisfacturam sicut *tholoneum.

B-Ke / xAug / A4-19r

loneum. Et omnes *uie ciuitatis que habent duas portas, hoc est introitum et exitum, ille sunt de consuetudine regis. Et si aliquis facit forisfacturam aliquam ... unam leucam et in spacio trium perticarum et trium pedum, illam habebunt prepositi regis de ciuitate. Et si aliquis in hoc supradicto spacio fossam fecerit uel sudem miserit uel callem regis *cinxerit sine licencia prepositi regis, quocumque ierit ille qui hoc fecerit secuturus erit, donec rex habeat inde forisfacturam suam. Regina E et Alnoth cild et *Osbern bigga et Sired de Chileham, isti habuerunt in ciuitate consuetudines suas de suis hominibus. Tholoneus panis reddebat lx s'. Et quando Haimo recepit ministerium huius ciuitatis erant omnes consuetudines regis sicut prius, sed modo sunt xxxii burgenses minus propter escambium castelli, qui reddebant regi xl s' et ii d'. Ex hiis habet modo archiep's vii, et abbas sc'i August' xiiii, et xi sunt perditi infra fossatum castelli. Et adhuc sunt cc et xii liberi homines de quibus habet rex sacam et socam. Sutores et draparii reddunt xxx s' et portarius v s'. Molendinum lxv s'. Tholoneus panis reddit viii sol' plus solito. Et de minutis debitis x s'. In tempore regis Edwardi est appreciatum ministerium li li', et quando Haimo recepit similiter, sed tamen qui nunc tenet reddit xxx li' cum incensione et pensa. Extra portam ciuitatis in *calle regis erant due domus, una foris et alia intus, de quibus monachi sc'e trinitatis unam destruxerunt et aliam prohibuerunt ne *fuisset facta, que reddebant regi xvi d' de gablo. Et in alio loco tantum terre que reddebat iii d'. Item demonstrant burgenses *ciuitatis xlv mansiones terre unde habebant liii s' de gablo tempore regis Edwardi, et ipse rex habebat *inde sacam et socam. Hec omnia nunc *tenent Ranulfus de Columbeles et Vitalis de Canterbire de *feodo ep'i baiocensis,

B-Ke / xAug / A4-19v

sed illi non cognoscunt nisi de xxvi. Adhuc tenet idem Ranulfus v agros terre cum una eccl'ia que pertinent ad monasterium sc'i Augustini. Item dicunt burgenses quod idem Ranulfus tenet quater uiginti agros de allodiis eorum, et ipse dicit se eos tenere de ep'o baioc'. Adhuc idem Ranulfus tenet xxxiii agros terre quos burgenses semper habuerunt in gilda eorum de donis *omnium regum. Langeport manerium sc'i August' est i solin' in d'nio, et iacet in hundredo de Canterbir', et semper fuit et est quietum, ibique fuerunt burgenses lxx qui reddebant de gablo iiii li' et x s'. Et uillani et bordarii qui manent extra ciuitatem reddunt vii li' et x s' et viii d' de gablo et unum sextarium mellis. Et quatuor molendini qui reddunt xxix sol' et iiii d'. Et in alio hundredo est unum iugum terre quod subiacet huic solino et ualet iiii sol'. Hoc manerium totum appreciatum est xxxv li'. Adhuc habet sc's Augustin' extra ciuitatem in dominio dimidium solin' et iiii agros terre, et est de elemosina monachorum, et est appreciatum iiii lib' et ii s' et unum sextar' farine. In hundredo de Canterbiria habet archiep's unum manerium Norgate, et est de cibo monachorum sc'e trinitatis, tempore regis Edwardi se defendit pro uno solino, cui nunc subiacent c burgenses *tres minus qui reddunt ix lib' et vi d' de gablo, et est appreciatum xvii li'. Item habet archiep's unum *manerium in dominio nomine Stursete, tempore regis Edwardi se defendit pro vii solin', et sunt ibi xxv burgenses qui reddunt x sol' de gablo, et est appreciatum dominium archiep'i xl li'. Ex hiis vii sol' habet Godefridus dapifer unum solinum de archiep'o et est appreciatum

B-Ke / xAug / A4-20r

c solid', similiter et Vitalis tenet unum iugum terre et est appreciatum *xxx s', sed et Hamo tenet dimidium solinum liberaliter ... et est apreciatum xxx sol'. Alboldus uero tenet inde unum iugum terre et est appreciatum xxx s'. *( ) Adhuc eciam tenet Elwardus liberaliter tria iuga terre in Natindune que dant altari sc'e trinitatis xii sol' et sunt appreciata xl sol'. Natingdune tenet Hamo dapifer de ep'o baiocensi, tempore regis Edwardi se defendit pro dimidio solino, et est appreciatum iii li'. ... Hoc dimidium solinum clamant burgenses ciuitatis sicut aliam supradictam terram. Ad

Sc'm Martinum habet archiep's in d'nio unum solinum et iacet in viii sol' de Sursete et ualet d'nium vii li'. De isto solino habet Radulfus camerarius medietatem in *feodo de archiep'o et ualet iiii li'. Infra muros ciuitatis sunt ... burgenses qui reddunt huic manerio viii solid' et iii den' de gablo. Adhuc sunt xxxii mansure et unum molendinum que tenent clerici ciuitatis ad gildam, ibique manent xii burgenses qui reddunt eis xxxv sol', et molendinum reddit v sol'. In hundredo de Brugges Burn' manerium sc'i Augustini tempore regis Edwardi se defendit pro uno solino, et est appreciatum c sol'. Aliud manerium Burnes tenuit *Liuinges de rege Edwardo et defendit se pro ii solin', et modo tenet illud *baiocens' ep's in dominio, et est appreciatum xii li', sed reddit xviii li'. Wicham manerium tenuit Elured bigge de rege Edwardo, et defendit se *pro iiii sol', et modo tenet illud ep's baiocens' in d'nio, et est appreciatum xxx li'. Huic manerio subiacet dimidium ... quod est liberum, et tenuit illud Siredus de Eluredo bigge, et modo tenet illud Godefridus filius Rogeri mala terra

B-Ke / xAug / A4-20v

de ep'o baiocensi. Littelbourne manerium est de d'nico allodio sc'i August', et pro septem solin' se defendit, et est appreciatum xxxii li'. De isto manerio habet ep's baiocens' in suo parco tantum quod est *appreciatum iii li'. Et pro hac terra dedit idem ep's aliam terram nomine Garwynton' sc'o August' et fratribus propter escambium terre parci sui, et modo tenet eam Randulfus de Sc'o Wandrigesilo de abb'e, et defendit *se pro dimid' solin' et pro xlii agris terre, et est appreciatum iiii li'. In hundredo *de Blengate Chistelet manerium sc'i August' tempore regis Edwardi se defendit pro xii solin', de hiis solin' sunt sex ad Margate, et est ... illud manerium inter totum *lxxviii li'. De isto manerio *habent iiii milites tantum quod est appreciatum xii li', et adhuc sunt in isto manerio tres arpenne uinee sine precio. Stureye manerium sc'i August' se defendit pro v solin' quietis, et est appreciatum lvi li'. Ad Fordwik habet sc's Augustinus unum paruum burgum qui tempore regis Edwardi se defendebat pro uno iugo, et ipse rex Edwardus dedit sc'o August' duas partes huius burgi, et terciam partem dedit postea ep's baioc' qui erat comes Kancie ex concessione regis Will'i. Adhuc *subiacent huic burgo xxxiii agri terre, et erant in isto burgo tempore regis Edwardi c mansure terre iiii minus, et modo sunt lxxiii, et est appreciatum inter totum xi li'. Ibique habet archiep's vii mansuras terre que in mari debent seruire cum aliis burgensibus, sed archiep's modo eis aufert inde seruicium. In hundredo *de witstaple Blean tenuit Normannus de rege Edwardo, et defendit se pro uno solino, et modo tenet illud Hamo de rege Will'o, et est appreciatum vi *li'. Swalcliue tenuit Edwardus snoch de rege Edwardo, et defendit se pro dimid' solin', et modo tenet illud

B-Ke / xAug / A4-21r

Vitalis de ep'o baioc', et est appreciatum xxx s'. In hundredo de Thanet Thanet terra sc'e Mildrethe est manerium sc'i August', regis Edwardi tempore se defendit pro xlviii solin', et est appreciatum c li'. De isto manerio habent tres milites tantum quod est appreciatum ix li'. Elfgethetun manerium dedit Godehose sc'o Augustino et reddebat inde per annum xxv d' super altare sc'i August', tempore regis Edwardi defendit se pro dimid' solino et uno iugo et xx agris terre, modo tenet illud Aufridus masculus clericus de abb'e. Item tenet idem Aufridus dimidium solin' in eodem manerio et reddit sc'o August' per annum c d', et ualet inter totum lx s'.

In hundredo de Estrie habet sc's August' tria iuga terre, et ualent xx sol'. Prestune manerium sc'i Aug' est in se ipso *hundred, et pertinet ad cameram monachorum sc'i Augustini, tempore regis Edwardi se defendit pro v solinis. Ex hiis solin' habet Vitalis unum solinum et dimid' iugum in *feodo de abb'e, et est appreciatum d'nium abb'is xiiii li' et hoc quod tenet Vitalis c sol'. Sandwich burgum sc'e trinitatis est de uestura monachorum, et est hundred in se ipso, et reddit regi seruicium in mare sicut illi de Doura, et homines illius uille, antequam eis rex dedisset suas consuetudines, reddebant xv li'. Et quando archiep's recuperauit, reddebant xl li' et xl mil' de allecibus, ... modo uero debent reddere lxx li' et alleces sicut *prius. Tempore regis Edwardi erant ibi ccc et vii mansure, modo sunt lxxvi plus. In isto burgo habet sc's August' unum agrum, et ibi sunt xxx mansure que reddunt monachis iiii mil' de allecibus uel x s',

B-Ke / xAug / A4-21v

et regi faciunt seruicium in mare *sicut alii. In isto agro habet eciam sc's August' unam eccl'iam. In hundredo de Cornilo Norbourne manerium sc'i Augustini tempore regis Edwardi defendit se pro xxx solinis. De hiis solinis habet Odelardus dapifer unum solinum, Gilbertus habet ii solin' xxv agros minus, Wadardus tres solinos lx agros minus, Marcherus ... Letardi dimid' solin', Ranulfus ... de Walbadun unum iugum et reddit unum denar'. Hec est terra quam tenet Simon de Holte. Item Odelardus unum solinum de Bawesfeld, Odelinus unum solinum. Et est apreciatum dominium quater uiginti libras, et hoc quod Odelardus habet inde c solid', et quod Gilbertus vi li', et quod Wadardus ix li', et quod Marcherus viii s', et quod Osbernus xxv solid', et quod Acardus xx s', et quod Ranulfus de Columbeles iiii s' et ii d', et quod alius Ranulfus l d', et quod Odelinus iiii li'. Moningham manerium sc'i Augustini tempore regis Edwardi se defendit pro ii solin' et *dimidio, de isto manerio tenuit Wadardus totam terram uillanorum que *semper fuit et esse debet de propria firma monachorum, et modo est appreciatum hoc quod monachi habent xvi li', et quod Wadardus tenuit x li'. Totam istam terram et illam de Northbourn' diracionauit abbas Hugo in curia regis Henr' cum *concessu eiusdem regis, presentibus multis optimatibus, ep'is, abbatibus, comitibus, uicecomitibus, aliisque quamplurimis, eamque cum sigillo regio confirmatam sc'o Augustino hereditario iure restituit. Estmoningham. Walemere. Ripple manerium tenuit Wlmerus de abb'e sc'i August' tempore regis Edwardi, et defendit se pro uno solino et dimid', et modo tenet

B-Ke / xAug / A4-22r

illud Aufridus masculus clericus de abb'e Scotlando, et reddit per annum sc'o Augustino c d' et sc'o Martino c d', et est appreciatum totum manerium *viii li'. Hundredum de Cornilo est de Estrileast. In hundredo de Beauuesberga Siberdeswelde manerium sc'i August' est de uestitu monachorum, tempore regis Edwardi se defendit pro ii solin', et est appreciatum viii li'. Estrielest. Doura est burgum regis, tempore regis Edwardi reddebat prepositus de Doura xviii li', ex quibus rex habebat xii li' et comes Godwynus vi li', et contra hoc habebant *canonici de sc'o Martino aliam medietatem. Et quando rex dedit burgensibus illorum sacam et socam, tunc burgenses econtra dederunt regi xx naues *semel in anno per xv dies ad custodiendum mare. Et in unaquaque naui xxi homo. Et quando legati regis ueniebant illuc, dabant tres d' in *hieme pro equo *transfretando, et in estate dabant ii d'. Et burgenses inueniebant eis stirmannum et unum alium hominem, si uero plus necesse fuisset de peccunia eorum *conducebatur. Et a festiuitate sc'i Michaelis usque ad festiuitatem sc'i Andree *erat triwa regis in illa uilla. Si uero aliquis in hoc termino fecisset aliquam forfacturam, . . . uicecomitis communiter accipiebant illam. Et omnes burgenses qui ibi manebant non dabant tholoneum in tota Anglia. Et hii sunt qui tenent mansuras terre in Doura ex quibus rex habet suas consuetudines perditas. Robertus de Romenal habet duas mansuras, Radulfus de Curbaspina iii, Will's filius Theoldi et *Robertus niger vi, . . . Will's filius Ogeri . . . Hugo de Mundfort i, Durandus i, Rog' de Oistresham i, Wadardus vii, Gosfridus

B-Ke / xAug / A4-22v

filius Modberti i, Hunfridus loripes i de qua medietas est forfacta regi. Will's filius Gauufridi habet unam gidhallam quam burgenses habent perditam, hec erat elemosina regis et ibi sunt tres domus. Item Rog' de Oistresham habet unam domum factam in aqua et in terra regis sine licencia alicuius hominis, unde iste habet gablum et rex nichil. Omnes isti reuocant ep'm baioc' ad guarant et datorem. Ranulfus de Columbeles habet xv agros terre de quodam uthlago, de qua rex habet dimidium gablum et medietatem terre, sicut omnes dicunt. Sed et Herbertus filius *Iuonis fecit unum molendinum in introitu portus, ubi confringuntur naues omnes per conturbacionem fluctuum maris. Et Hugo *nepos Herberti dicit quod ep's baioc' hoc concessit *fieri auunculo suo, sed econtra dicunt burgenses hoc esse regi dampnum et suis. Nunc autem apreciata est firma huius burgi xl li'. Sed tamen qui tenet reddit liiii li', uiginti et quatuor libre dantur regi de xx d' in ora, cum incensione et pensa, et xxx libre dantur ep'o baioc' cum numero. De prebendis *canonicorum sc'i Martini de Doura. In least de Estrie sunt duo hundreda, scilicet Beauuesberga et Cornila, in quibus iacent xxi solin', et in lasto de Limwarlest iacent iii solini, unus ex hiis iacet in hundredo de Strete, et alius in hundredo de Brichholt, et tercius in hundredo de Blakebourne. Tempore regis E erant omnes prebende communes et ualebant lxi li', et quando ep's baiocens' uenit, diuisit eas inter canonicos eccl'ie ut sibi placuit. Radulfus de Sc'o Samsone habet in Cherletune unum solinum terre

B-Ke / xAug / A4-23r

de prebenda sc'i Martini, istam tenuit Lifwynus tempore regis Edwardi et ualebat c sol', et est de hundredo de Beauuesberga, et ualet modo iii li' et x sol'. Item in eadem Cerletune habet Will's filius Ogerii unum solinum de prebenda quam Siredus tenuit tempore regis Edwardi, et ualebat tunc xii li' et modo vi *li'. Adhuc habet ipse Will's extra prebendam unam eccl'iam in burgo de Doura que reddit xii s', sed canonici *calumpniantur eam. In hundredo de Beauuesberge habet *Alfwinus in Bokelande unum solinum de prebenda quam ipsemet tenuit tempore regis E, et ualebat tunc c s' et modo iiii li'. In eodem hundredo habet Wlricus in Gusistune unum iugum terre de prebenda quam tenuit Alricus tempore regis E, adhuc habet xxv agros terre qui iacent in hundredo de Cornilo, et ualet inter totum xx s'. Siredus de Sc'a Margareta tenet in hundredo de Beausberge unum solinum de prebenda quam pater suus tenuit tempore regis E, et ualet c s'. In hundredo de Beauuesberge habet Radulfus canonicus unum solinum ad Sc'am Margaretam de prebenda quam tenuit Aluricus de rege E, et ualebat tunc iiii li' et modo iii li' et x s' et ii d'. In hundredo de Beauuesberge tenet Alericus de prebenda unum solinum terre apud Sc'am Margaretam, et ualet lx s'. In eodem hundredo habet Robertus niger apud Sc'am Margaretam unum solinum terre de prebenda quam Smet capellanus tenuit de rege E, et ualet lx s'. Item in eodem hundredo habet Walt's de Cambremer ad Sc'am Margaretam unum solinum terre de prebenda quam tenuit Swytgar de

B-Ke / xAug / A4-23v

rege E, et ualebat tunc iii li' et x sol', et modo ualet lx s'. In hundredo de Beauuesberge et Cornila habet Rob' trublet unum solinum de prebenda quam tenuerunt duo homines Suithgar et Goldstan tempore regis E, et ualet lx s'. In hundredo de Beauuesberge tenet Edwynus canonicus dimid' solinum et xxv agros ad Sc'am Margaretam et quater uiginti agros in hundredo de Cornila de prebenda quam ipsemet tenuit tempore regis E, et ualebat tunc xii li' et modo lx s'. De prebenda istius accepit ep's baioc' viii agros terre et dedit Alano, qui et ipse dedit Vlrico. In hundredo de Beauuesberge habet Will's pictauensis dimid' solinum et xii agros et dimid' ad Siberdeswelde et in hundredo de Cornila dimid' solinum et xi agros et dimid', et ualebat tempore regis E iiii li' et modo lx s'. In hundredo de Cornila habet archiep's cant' unum solinum terre de prebenda sc'i Martini, et ualet vi li' *et x s'. In eodem hundredo iacent l agri terre quos ep's baioc' dedit Ascetillo archidiacono cant', et ualent xx s'. Item in hundredo de Beauuesberge dedit ep's baiocensis Ascetillo archidiacono l agros terre, et ualent xxx s'. In hundredo de Cornila tenet Athelolldus iii iuga terre ad Dale de prebenda quam ipse habuit tempore regis E, et ualent iii li'. In hundredo de *Beauuesberge et Cornila habet sc's Augustinus unum solinum terre *de prebenda ad Dale et Guthistun, tempore regis E *ualebat xl s' et modo xxx s'. In hundredo de Cornila habet Will's filius Theoldi dimid' solinum et dimid' iugum ad Dale de prebenda quam tenuit Diryngus *canonicus tempore regis Edwardi, et ualet lx s'. In hundredo de Beauuesberge habet Nigellus unum iugum terre ad Sc'am Margaretam ... tempore regis Edwardi et ualebat *tunc *xxv s' et modo

B-Ke / xAug / A4-24r

xx *s'. In hundredo de Beauuesberge habet Sigar unum iugum et dimidium ad Siberdeswelde de prebenda ... tempore regis E, et ualebat *tunc xxx s' et modo xxv s'. In eodem hundredo habet Will's Godefridi filius unum solinum terre ad *( ) Feruengela de prebenda quam tenuit Siredus tempore regis Edwardi, et ualebat tunc vi li' et modo iiii li'. Item in eodem hundredo habet Baldewynus unum solinum terre ad Hucham de prebenda quam frater eius tenuit tempore regis Edwardi, et ualebat tunc c solid' et modo iiii li'. In hundredo de Beauuesberge habet Godricus latimarius unum solinum terre in Bokelande de prebenda quam Wlwynus siluagius presbiter tenuit tempore regis E, et ualebat tunc viii li' et modo vi li'. Finis de prebendis sc'i Martini de Doura.
In hundredo de Stutinge tenet Godefridus de abb'e sc'i Aug' unum manerium *Bodesham, et defendit se tempore regis E pro i solino, et ualet iiii li'. In eodem hundredo habet sc's August' unum manerium Elmestede et Hortune, et defendit se tempore regis E pro ii solinis et uno iugo, et *ualet viii li'. In hundredo de Blakebourne ... habet sc's Augustinus unum manerium Burewaremarais, tempore regis E se defendit pro ii solin' et iii iug' terre, et ualet xxx li'. In hoc concordant homines de quatuor lestis, scilicet de Burewareleast et de Estrieleast et de Wiwarelest et de Limwarelest. Si aliquis homo

fecerit sepem uel fossatum unde stringatur callis regis, uel foueam in illo calle fecerit, uel palum fixerit, aut arborem stantem infra callem inciderit, uel si arborem stantem extra callem cedendo intra ceciderit et postea ramum uel frondem aut ipsam arborem sine licencia portauerit, pro unaquaque harum *forfacturarum soluet regi c solid', et licet abierit inde domum non calumpniatus nec

B-Ke / xAug / A4-24v

diuadiatus, tamen sequetur illum prepositus regis ubicumque fuerit, et regi c s' emendabit. De grithbreche uero, si quis eam fecerit et calumpniatus aut diuadiatus in calle *fuerit, viii li' regi emendabit. Sin autem, quietus erit erga regem, non erga dominum cuius homo fuerit. Item concordant hoc, quod rex habet has supradictas forfacturas super omnes allodarios tocius *comitatus de Kent et super ipsorum homines, excepta terra sc'e trinitatis et sc'i Augustini et sc'i Martini, et excepta terra Godrici de Burnes et Godrici Karlessune et Alnothchild et Osbern bigge et Sired de Chileham et Turgis et Norman et Atsur, super eos habet rex tantummodo forfacturam de capitibus eorum. Et quando moritur allodarius, rex habet releuamen de terris suis qui *habebant suam sacam et socam. Et de aliis terris, scilicet Oslaces ... Bocland et tercium Bocland, Herst, unum iugum de Ore et unum iugum Hertei, Scheldrisham, *Machehauue, Ernulwyntun, Oslacintun, Piria, altera Piria, Thruliga, Ospringes, Hortune, de hiis terris habet rex has forfacturas, hamsocne, grithbriche, forestal. Et de adulterio tantummodo hominem per totum Kent et archiep's mulierem, excepta *terra sc'e trinitatis et sc'i Augustini et sc'i Martini, de quibus rex nichil habet. Et de latrone qui iudicatur ad mortem habet rex medietatem peccunie sue. Et de huthlago qui uthlagatus fuerit, qui postea illum recipit sine licencia, rex habet inde forfacturam. Et de terris *supranominatis, scilicet Alnothchild, Sired de Chileham, Godrich de Burnes eorumque similium, habet rex ... diebus custo-

B-Ke / xAug / A4-25r

diam apud Canterb' et apud Sandwich si ibi fuerit cum corredio suo. Et si non *habuerint regis corredium, sine forfactura recedent. Et si submoniti fuerint ad schiram, *ibunt usque Pinnendone ... longius, et si non uenerint, rex habebit de istis *forfacturis c s', excepta grithbreche que viii lib' emendatur, et de callibus sicut superius. Item in Limwarelest in Brissegueia habet rex hanc consuetudinem, scilicet duas carectas et duas sticcas anguillarum pro uno inwardo. Et in terra Sophis habet xii d' pro uno inwardo, et de uno iugo in Northbroche xii d' aut unum *inwardum, ... hee terre iacent in Wy, et hee terre custodiebant regem apud Canterbiriam uel apud Sandwich per tres dies si rex illuc uenisset, et si aliquis inde forfecisset de custodia, regi emendasset per c s'. In leasto de Suttune et in least de Agelesford habuerunt isti sacam et socam, Brixichild, *Athellod de Helteham, ... Athsur de Liesenes, Alfwyn horn, Wrnold lewite, Ordinge de Hortune, Osbern de Chilesfeld, Leuenoth de Suttune, Edward de Terstane, Wlstan et Lieuric *de Otringebire, Osward de Northtune, Edgeth de Eselholte, Elred de Eldynge.

Notes

17r11 lib'] *missing* 17r17 cambiam] camiam 17r18 tenet comes Robertus] tenescome Roberto 17r19 appreciate] appreciata 17v5 ergo] *seems corrupt* 17v9 aueriam] auiam 17v13 et pensa] expensa 17v13 ii] et ii 17v19 quod] que 18r3 baiocensi] baiocense 18r5 Dernedale] *with* l *altered from* n 18r5 defendit] et defendit 18r7 Echemersfelde] Echemesrsfelde 18r9 manerium] est manerium 18r22 De] *with* D *written large* 18v1 habebat] habelat 18v6 quidam] quidem 18v10 Gisleberti] Giseiberti 18v11 uero] uerum 18v16 perticarum] particularum 18v17 uiam in antea] vi animantes 18v20 edificacio] edificio 18v21 perticarum] particularum 18v22 ceruisia] seruicia 18v23 monachi habere] mo'ihre 18v24 tholoneum] ptholoneum 19r1 uie] *with* e *inserted* 19r5 cinxerit] cinxncerit 19r7 Osbern] Osbenrn *with the first* n *dotted out* 19r18 calle] calde 19r20 fuisset] fusset 19r22 ciuitatis] cuitatis 19r23 inde] in 19r24 tenent] tenet 19r24 feodo] feuodo 19v6 omnium] *seems corrupt* 19v18 tres] *with* t *written over a* 3 19v19 manerium] manium 20r1 xxx] 30 xxx *with* 30 *dotted out* 20r3–4] Sed et hamo tenet / dimidium solinum *dotted out* 20r11 feodo] feuodo 20r17 Liuinges] Liinges 20r18 baiocens'] baiocenc' 20r20 pro iiii sol'] per 4 sol' 20v3 appreciatum] *blundered* 20v6 se] *missing* 20v7 de] de de 20v9 lxxviii] *with* l *inserted* 20v10 habent] habet 20v16 subiacent] subiacet 20v21 de witstaple] dwitstaple 20v23 li'] *missing* 21r12 hundred] hundredo 21r15 feodo] feuodo 21r21 prius] *blundered* 21v1 sicut] si 21v14 dimidio] dimidii 21v15 semper fuit] superfuit 21v18 concessu] concensu 22r2 viii] 8 22r8 canonici] *blundered* 22r10 semel] simul 22r12 hieme] yeme 22r12 transfretando] tranfretando 22r14 conducebatur] conducebantur 22r15 erat] erit 22r22 Robertus] Roberter 22v9 Iuonis] luonis 22v10 nepos] nopos 22v11 fieri] *missing* 22v16 canonicorum] *blundered* 23r5 li'] *missing* 23r7 calumpniantur] calumpniant 23r7 Alfwinus] Asfwinus 23v12 et] *missing* 23v18 Beauuesberge] Beauuesberege 23v18 de] *missing* 23v19 ualebat] ualet 23v21 canonicus] *blundered* 23v23 tunc] *missing* 23v23 xxv] *with* v *inserted* 24r1 s'] *missing* 24r2 tunc] *missing* 24r3] Feuer *cancelled* 24r12 Bodesham] de Bodesham 24r14 ualet] ualent 24r22 forfacturarum] forfactura 24v3 fuerit] fecerit 24v6 comitatus] coiuitatis *with* o *inserted* 24v11 habebant] habebat 24v17 terra] *missing* 24v21 supranominatis] super nominatis 25r2 habuerint] huerint 25r3 ibunt] ibunt ibi 25r4 forfacturis] forfactis 25r8–9 inwardum] in / inwardum 25r13 Athellod] Athellodlod 25r16 de] *missing*

Comments

17r7–8) 'Excerpts from the reckoning of sulungs of the county of Kent according to the king's record, namely those which belong to the church of Saint Augustine.' But this title understates the scope of the text; and the word 'sulung', which seems to be *solingum* here (the pronouns 'those which' are neuter), is *solinus* in the main text. Probably, therefore, the title was not added till later – perhaps when xAug was copied into the 'textus of Saint Adrian', if we think that it was so copied. The phrases *compotus solingorum* and *carta regis* are notable in any event: they show that the B text of the survey could be thought of (could, when the title was added, still be thought of) as a *carta* containing a *compotus* – a *compotus solingorum* for Kent, a *compotus hidarum* for the other southern counties.

17r8) *et est in regis domesday.* Apparently a garbled gloss on *secundum cartam regis*, inserted by someone who thought (mistakenly) that these excerpts came from DB. I suppose that it ought to read *id est in domesday regis.* At the end of the title the words *W. conquestoris* were added by a different hand. (Ballard omitted them, no doubt because he saw that they were not by the main scribe; I omit them for the same reason.) This is the hand of a fifteenth-century annotator whose marginal comments occur throughout the book. There are places where he has something useful to tell us – he reports that one stretch of text came from the 'textus of Saint Adrian' (11v); he supplies some words omitted from a charter of Henric I (82r); he identifies the source of the excerpts from DB-Ke, *Extracta de domesdæy R. W. conquestoris* (143r) – but here he has nothing to say that we cannot see for ourselves.

17v2) *et est apreciatum illo tempore.* The verb has to be read as a past tense, 'and was appraised at that time'. Possibly *est* should be emended to *erat*; but I refrain from making this change because the usage is repeated below (19r16).

17v5) Possibly *hec ergo* ought to be *hec omnia*, as at 19r23. But *omnia*, however it is written, is not easily misread as *ergo*.

17v6) *Edwardus* should be *Oswardus*, but I refrain from making the correction (because, for all we know, the error may go back to the original).

18r15) The word 'defended', usually *defendit*, is *defendebat* in this and the next two paragraphs.

18r22–19v6) This whole stretch of text was first put into print by Larking (1869, pp. 34*–5*). Much of the information given here is missing from DB, probably because the DB scribe did not think it worth reproducing, but it does have some points of interest. Perhaps the most valuable fact is one which emerges incidentally: we discover that the city of Canterbury was already divided into districts – later on there were six of them, usually called wards (Somner 1640, p. 96) – each of which had its own *senior*, 'elder' or 'alderman'. Some of the mills inside the city were located upstream from somebody else's mill, or on the boundary between one ward and the next, and dissension could arise when the mill or its sluice needed to be repaired.

18v11–12) *quod uerum toloneum habebat acceptum*, 'that he had indeed taken the toll'. The use of an auxiliary verb to form a perfect tense marks the B text as being written in a relatively relaxed style. It is common in colloquial Latin (and in French); but the DB scribe prefers some more dignified expression. (Here he might have said *acceperat*; but in fact he went a notch higher still and used the infinitive *accepisse* (2ra46).) Other instances occur below: *habet suas consuetudines perditas* (22r19–20, *perdidit* in DB), *quam burgenses habent perditam* (22v2–3), *habet unam domum factam* (22v4, *fecit* in DB).

18v17) The manuscript has *vi animantes*, which makes no sense at all; I emend this to *uiam in antea*, 'a roadway at the front'. The expression *in antea* is a colloquialism which the scribe seems not to grasp (but he gets it right four lines later). It means 'in front, towards the front'; it can also mean 'forward in time', as in *ab hac die in antea*, 'from this day forward' (pseudo-Lanfranc, ed. Knowles rev. Brooke 2002, p. 162).

19r5) For *cinxerit* the manuscript has *cinxncerit*, quite distinctly so written. This is one of several places where the scribe seems to offer us a choice of readings. Here, for example, he allows us to read the word as either *cinxerit* or *cincerit*. Similarly *feuodo* (19r24, 20r11, 21r15) can be read as either *feodo* or *feudo*, *Osbenrn* (19r7) as either *Osben* or *Osbern*. Sometimes the scribe makes his own choice (as he does with *Osbenrn*, putting a dot under the first *n* to cancel it); sometimes he leaves the choice to us. I take it that the exemplar displayed some corrections, and that the A4 scribe, not wanting to ignore them but doubting whether they had authority, kept his options open by packing the alternative reading into the word.

19r16) As at 17v2, *est appreciatum* has to be a past tense: 'in the time of king Edward was appraised'.

19v6) I cannot think that *omnium regum* is right. Perhaps *omnium* is the mangled remains of a word like [*pri*]*orum*. Or perhaps the phrase is a mutilated fragment of something like *de elemosina regis Edwardi et omnium regum antecessorum suorum* (DB-Ht-142ra).

20r3–4) Distracted by the recurrence of the phrase *et est apreciatum xxx sol'*, the scribe lost his place and started copying the previous sentence again, *Sed et hamo tenet dimidium solinum*. Having got that far, he noticed his mistake and cancelled what he had written.

20r9) *et iacet in viii sol' de Stursete*. Probably the numeral ought to be *vii*, as at 19v21 (and as in DB-3va44). A scribe who writes *sol'* for 'sulung' is inviting his readers to confuse this word with 'shilling'. The A4 scribe falls into that trap himself (20r20).

20r20) The manuscripts has *per 4 sol'*, which would seem to mean 'by four shillings'. (This '4' is one of the arabic numerals which the scribe did not suppress.) But of course it ought to be *pro iiii solin'*, 'for four sulungs'.

20v7) *In hundredo de de Blengate*. The text seems to have been tampered with here (which perhaps explains why *de* is written twice). As far as we can gather, Blengate hundred did not exist at the time of the survey: the manor of Chislet was in Chislet hundred (DB-Ke-12ra6).

21r11) *In hundredo de Estrie habet sanctus Augustinus tria iuga terre*. 'Three yokes' should be three rods, as is clear from DB, and from an independent list of the abbey's lands (below, doc. 11). This paragraph is the only one which does not fit quite correctly into the cadastral frame (Table 13), and there is obviously something peculiar about it. In A4 the scribe makes a point of starting this entry on a new line, even though this means that almost the whole of the preceding line is left blank. In DB the corresponding paragraph (12vb13) reads like an afterthought. I think we can be sure that this entry was added to the B text by the second team of commissioners, but not properly integrated into it.

21v7) 'This is the land which Simon de Holte holds.' An interpolation dating from the mid thirteenth century: it seems to be the latest ingredient of all, not just in the text of xAug, but in the whole stretch of text written by scribe 1. Simon de Holte (occ. 1236–58) acquired his lands by marrying the daughter of Stephan de Denintone.

21v18) It is one of the A4 scribe's foibles that he tends to confuse *concessus* and *consensus*. Here he writes *cum concensu*, which I take to mean *cum concessu* (as in doc. 10, p. 221); but *concessu* or *per concessum* would sound better.

21v22) 'East' (i.e. Great) Mongeham and Walmer are represented only by their names. Apparently the B text had nothing to say about these places – except perhaps that Great Mongeham was appraised with Adisham, and that Walmer was appraised with Folkestone.

21v23) This paragraph relating to Ripple has no counterpart in DB. We would expect to find the manor listed there between Little Mongeham and Sibertswold, at 12va37–8: I discuss the case in the commentary at that point (below, p. 187).

22r5) Here or near here, there ought to be an entry for the manor called *Wlatenholt* (DB-12va43). Perhaps the entry was overlooked by the compiler of xAug; perhaps it was omitted accidentally, by somebody copying xAug.

22r17) There is something wrong with this sentence. I take it that a word such as *ministri* has been omitted before *uicecomitis*; so the meaning will be that the sheriff's officers take receipt of the money. From here onwards, the spelling *forfactura* is preferred to *forisfactura*. That is a change for the worse; but eight new asterisks would be needed to countermand it, and I am not willing to pay so high a price.

22v14–15) The formula *cum incensione et pensa* seems to have been borrowed from some other paragraph (17v12–13 or 19r17–18) and inserted here as a gloss on 'twenty pence to the ora'. But the meaning was not quite the same. The 'twenty pence' formula meant a surcharge of 25 per cent. The 'fire and weight' formula, if it were taken literally, would imply that a sample of the money was refined and tested for weight (as was supposed to be the practice in the twelfth-century exchequer). Conventionally, however, it seems to have meant a surcharge of 30 per cent: to discharge a debt of 50 pounds, one had to pay 65 pounds (DB-Sx-16rb).

22v15–4r10) The description of the prebends belonging to the canons of Saint Martin's agrees very closely in substance (not in wording) with the corresponding section of DB (1va–b). Some information given in xAug is missing from DB, presumably because it was omitted by the DB scribe; some information given in DB is missing from xAug, presumably because it was omitted by xAug's compiler. Those passages in DB which I take to have resulted from some supplementary investigation – the added paragraph at the foot of column 1vb, the assorted memoranda in column 2rb – are not represented in xAug. They were, it seems, not properly part of the B text.

24r8–9) This man (Ballard misread the name) is the same Wulwy – known as 'the wild one' – who is mentioned in DB in connection with some land at Atterton claimed by the canons of Saint Martin's from Hugo de Montfort (13ra37).

24r15–16 'In the hundred of Blackbourne Saint Augustine has a manor (called) Burmarsh.' That is what the manuscript says, but I do not see how it can be right. Burmarsh, later, was in Worth hundred, a long way from Blackbourne hundred. It is not inconceivable that the situation was different in the late eleventh century; but I think it would be rash to entertain that thought, given that our copy of xAug is far from perfectly reliable. It seems safer to suppose that something has gone wrong with the text.

Concordance

DB-Ke		B / xAug
1ra4	town of Dover	22r6
1rb1	customs of eastern lests	24r17
1va1	sac and soc in western lests	25r12
11	prebends of Saint Martin's	22v15
2ra1	city of Canterbury	18r22
2va46	Milton	17r24
3ra3	32 mansurae in Canterbury	20r13
7	town of Sandwich	21r16
3va44	Westgate	19v19
4ra10	Saint Martin	20r8
5ra9	Northgate	19v15
6va28	East Wickham	17r9
7vb30	Leeds	17r13
9rb30	Bekesbourne	20r17
43	Wickhambreaux	20r19
9va6	Nackington	20r6
10ra1	Swalecliffe	20v23
10rb11	Badlesmere	18r2
12ra3	Plumstead (chapter 7 begins)	17r11
10	Lenham	17r20
17	Bridge	20r15
22	Longport	19v6
30	Littlebourne	20v1
36	Garrington	20v3
41	Sturry	20v11
48	Minster	21r1
12rb6	Chislet	20v7
13	town of Fordwich	20v13
24	half sulung next to Canterbury	19v13
30	Wilderton	17v24
34	Ashenfield	18r7
37	Dernedale	18r5
39	Selling	18r14
43	Rooting	18r16
46	Repton	18r11
12va1	Shillingheld	18r9
5	Northbourne	21v2
27	Little Mongeham	21v13
38	Sibertswold	22r3
43	*Wlatenholt*	—
48	Preston	21r12
12vb5	Elmstone	21r4
13	three rods of land in Eastry hundred	21r11
17	Bodsham	24r11
20	Elmsted and Horton	24r13
25	Kennington	18r18
33	Burmarsh (chapter 7 ends)	24r15
14rb41	Blean	20v21
14va3	Newington	17v14

Chapter 4
The shortened version of the final report

The DB version of the survey of Kent occupies a booklet by itself, beginning and ending with a leaf left entirely blank (National Archives, E 31/2/1, fos. 0–15). Of the 25 surviving booklets (Table 14), DB-Ke was the ninth to be written. The scribe, long since, had settled into his task, and there are no very striking differences between this booklet and the ones which were written either just before or just after it.[1] But the scribe was continually adjusting his procedure, making changes in the format or in the organization and wording of the text (which is what makes it possible to seriate the booklets), and some significant changes of this kind can be found to occur in DB-Ke, on closer inspection. Though we can see such changes taking place, we can only guess at the scribe's reasons for making them. Sometimes one can understand why the scribe might have thought that some change in the wording, for instance, would be a good idea. Sometimes, perhaps, the only motive was boredom: the scribe had become so weary of writing out exactly the same formula, over and over again, that he decided to try something different. (It is worth remembering, I think, that not every fact has an interesting explanation.)

One change which took effect when the scribe started work on this booklet was a change in the procedure followed for ruling the pattern of guidelines onto the parchment. The booklet comprises two gatherings of eight leaves each. These gatherings differ from one another with respect to the ruling. The first (fos. 0–7) is a regular quire – four sheets folded together to make eight leaves – and the ruling here consists of seven vertical lines (two on either side and three down the middle) plus fifty horizontal lines (Gullick 1987, fig. 14.6, 'Ruling pattern 2'). This pattern makes its first appearance in DB-Ke. It continues to be used for the other aspect 3 booklets (DB-Sx, DB-Sy, DB-Ha, DB-Be), and for the first quire in aspect 4 (DB-GlWo, fos. 162–9); a left-over sheet of the same type turns up in one of the aspect 5 booklets (DB-Le, fos. 233–4).

The second gathering (fos. 8–15) consists of three whole sheets (fos. 8 + 15, 9 + 14, 11 + 12) plus a pair of half-sheets (fos. 10 and 13). There are variations in detail, but as a first approximation it is true to say that the pattern of ruling is the same that the scribe had used for the aspect 1–2 booklets: eight vertical lines (two on either side of either column) and 44 horizontal lines (Gullick 1987, fig. 14.6, 'Ruling pattern 1'). This gathering, it seems clear, was assembled from some left-over sheets that the scribe did not want to waste. He took this opportunity to use them up – not in the first quire, which had to be as neat as he could make it, but here, where neatness was not quite so necessary. The details are as follows.

Sheet 8 + 15. The outermost sheet was originally ruled according to pattern 1. When the scribe decided to make use of it here, he spun it around, so that the top edge became the bottom edge, and then reruled it with 50 horizontal lines, closer together than the old lines, according to pattern 2. On this sheet alone, there are two systems of horizontal lines. Mostly they overlap, but (because the sheet had been inverted) two of the old lines protrude at the bottom, four of the new lines at the top.[2] (This meant that the scribe could get off to a good start, at the beginning of each column, before he had to worry about distinguishing the new lines from the old ones. Presumably that was his reason for turning the leaf around before reruling it.)

Sheet 9 + 14. This sheet has normal pattern 1 ruling; there is nothing peculiar about it.

Half-sheet 10. This is a mule: the vertical ruling is of pattern 1, the horizontal ruling of pattern 2. Apparently the scribe had started ruling this sheet, some time previously, but then decided not to finish the job. Now he changed his mind again. Half of the sheet looked as if it ought to be worth keeping; so he cut away the portion that he did not want, and ruled the half-sheet that remained with 50 horizontal lines, across the eight vertical lines that were there already.

Sheet 11 + 12. Normal pattern 1 ruling.

Half-sheet 13. Another mule, exactly matching the other half-sheet.

These facts are proof (if anyone is still asking for it) that pattern 1 is earlier than pattern 2, and that DB-Ke is earlier than the other booklets which use pattern 2.

If the scribe was doubtful at first whether these sheets were acceptable, as apparently he was, the reason may have been that he thought the parchment too thin. On the whole, there is much more show-through in this second quire than there is in the first one. For example, the three lines of text added

[1] It remains uncertain which booklet was written immediately before DB-Ke, but the choice seems to lie between DB-Ht and DB-Bu (though DB-Ca should perhaps still be considered a third alternative). The booklet written next after DB-Ke was, without doubt, DB-Sx.

[2] Some of this was clear to me from the facsimile (Flight 2006, p. 17), but I did not understand exactly what had happened till after seeing the photographs.

aspect	counties	binding sequence	17th-century foliation	alternative foliation
1	Yorkshire–Lincolnshire	26	297–372	1–76
1	Nottinghamshire–Derbyshire	25, 24	280–96, 272–9	77–101
1	Huntingdonshire	17	203–8	102–7
2	Middlesex	10	126–31	108–13
2	Bedfordshire	18	209–18	114–23
2	Cambridgeshire	16	189–202	124–137
2	? Hertfordshire	11	132–42	
2	? Buckinghamshire	12	143–53	
3	Kent	1	0–15	160–75
3	Sussex	2	16–29	176–89
3	Surrey	3	30–6	190–6
3	Hampshire	4	37–55	197–215
3	Berkshire	5	56–63	216–23
4	Gloucestershire–Worcestershire	14	162–78	224–40
4	Herefordshire	15	179–88	241–50
4	Shropshire-Cheshire	23	252–71	251–70
4	Staffordshire	22	246–51	271–6
4	Warwickshire	21	238–45	277–84
5	Northamptonshire	19	219–29	285–95
5	Leicestershire	20	230–7	296–303
5	Oxfordshire	13	154–61	304–11
5	Wiltshire	6	64–74	312–22
5	Dorset	7	75–85	323–33
6	Somerset	8	86–99	334–47
6	Devon–Cornwall	9	100–25	348–73

Table 14. Seriation of the DB booklets (Flight 2006, table 41).

at the foot of column 10vb are almost perfectly legible, back to front, on the other side of the leaf; and most of the text on page 14r can be read quite easily from a reversed image of the verso page. In places there is so much show-through that the text is difficult to decipher.[3]

In the first gathering, almost everywhere, the written lines conform to the ruling; the only divergences occur in the preliminary section, near the foot of column 2ra (2ra43–8) and in column 2rb (2rb2–48). The second gathering, because of its improvised construction, was something of an obstacle course. When the scribe started writing on these leaves, he was aiming to make 50 lines per column, the same as in the first quire. With two leaves, that was straightforward: the newly-ruled half-sheets (fos. 10 and 13). Elsewhere it was not so easy. On one leaf he had to pick his way through two overlapping systems of horizontal lines (fo. 8); elsewhere he had to ignore the ruled lines and judge the spacing by eye (fos. 9, 11–12, 14). Mostly he managed quite well, but the number of written lines does tend to creep up beyond 50. On page 11r in particular he lost control of the spacing, ending up with 57 lines in the first column, 54 in the second. Towards the end, by contrast, where he was dealing with a sequence of short chapters (14r–v), he was less resolute in his disregard for the pattern 1 ruling, and the number of written lines drops below 50 in consequence.

It is not clear to me whether the preliminary section (1r–2r) was written before or after the main text (2v–14v). In the D booklet (to judge from the three which survive) the material contained in this section would have been placed at the back, not at the front. It is possible that the DB scribe (after calculating how many pages to leave blank) dealt with the main text first and then came back to add the preliminary section. I suspect that this is what he did; but I do not see how the question can be decided.

At least from 2v onwards, the text appears to have been written in order throughout. In some of the DB booklets, there are chapters which were obviously inserted afterwards, in spaces which had been left for them.[4] In this booklet, there are very few places – perhaps only one (4va17–18) – where the scribe shows any sign of hesitation. By and large, it seems, his source text caused him no trouble. He could finish one paragraph, finish one chapter, before moving on to the next.

[3] The problem is most acute with fo. 10, especially in the lower half of the outer column. Perhaps someone who has the technology might like to try enhancing the images, by gradually subtracting a reversed copy of 10v from a copy of 10r and vice versa. Though I can vaguely imagine how this might be done, I am quite incapable of doing it myself.

[4] If there are differences in the wording, added chapters can be made to show up in diagrams of the type which I used in working out the seriation (Flight 2006, chapter 2). The next editor of DB-Yo, for instance, might like to bear this point in mind.

There is some tendency for the script to become less formal as the work proceeds.[5] Probably in every DB booklet this happens to some extent; here it is accentuated by the relatively careless spacing of the lines in parts of the second gathering. Furthermore, there are some sudden changes of appearance.[6] The script, which has been growing larger, all at once becomes smaller. (In other words, the scribe resharpens his pen.) Despite the variation in manner, despite these observable discontinuities, I do not think it can be doubted but that the main text was written throughout by a single hand. A few small additions, probably or possibly by other hands, will be found listed below; but they are so few and so small that even all together they carry little weight. Within the last twenty years, as far as I am aware, everyone who has expressed an opinion on the subject (an opinion founded on some study of the manuscript) has agreed with the conclusion first arrived at by A. J. Fairbank in 1952–3.[7] As nearly as makes no significant difference, DB is all the work of one man.

In chapters 1–2, the scribe is making no special effort to save space. As he works on, he becomes more economical, and the text becomes denser accordingly. In particular, if he reaches the end of a paragraph with only a few more words to go, he prefers not to start a new line for them: instead he turns these words up or down – i.e. writes them at the end of the preceding line, if there is room for them there, or, if not, at the end of the following line. When there is also a heading to be included (which happens for the first time at 4rb46), a single line can consist of three sub-lines, the first of which should not be read till last. For a modern reader, this trick may seem perplexing at first – which is why I mention it here.

Furthermore, some elements of the text are, quite deliberately, written between the lines, in the way that medieval scribes often worked when they wanted to add glosses to elucidate difficult words. By putting them there, the DB scribe gives his readers the option of ignoring them. For example, the word *uicec'* is often (not always) placed above the name of the sheriff in question; the word *com'* is treated similarly. At 11ra1, where he turns up the end of a sentence and does not lack for space, he still makes a point of writing *com'* above *Goduino*. But the spaces between the lines are also used for making corrections, and – from our point of view – the distinction between glosses and corrections cannot be sharply drawn.

The rubrication of the DB-Ke booklet followed the usual scheme, and there is nothing much that needs to be said about it. When he had completed the main text (or thought that he had), the scribe went back to the beginning, supplied himself with some bright red ink, and worked through the booklet again to add the finishing touches. The elements written entirely in red, in the spaces which had been left for them, are these:

at the top of each page, the name of the county;[8]

at the start of each chapter, a title and a number;

in the index, a number against each item matching the number of the chapter in the main text;

a few important initials.[9]

Red ink was also used to accentuate some features of the existing text. Two things were done consistently:

a red line was drawn horizontally through any element written in capital letters (place-names, cadastral headings, the word *TRINITATIS*);

a red shadow was added to the initial letter at the start of each paragraph.

Less consistently, flicks of red ink were added to some other capitals – sometimes for a reason, sometimes perhaps just because they happened to catch the scribe's eye. Taken all together, the rubrication makes a great difference to the appearance of the manuscript, and the effect which the scribe was aiming for was very successfully achieved.

There are a few deficiencies. The running head is missing from one page (11r); some place-names and hundred headings lack the horizontal line which ought to have been drawn through them.[10] Most of these omissions occur in the second quire, where, in this as in other respects, the scribe tended to become less careful. Apart from that, their incidence seems to be haphazard, and I have not thought it necessary to note them individually.[11]

Though rubrication was intended to be the end of the story, in the event it was not. As in many of the other booklets, some corrections were made in DB-Ke at a later stage, after the scribe had put away his pot of red ink. Four short paragraphs, all of them obviously added, are distinguished further by the absence of rubrication. They were inserted respectively (i) in blank space at the end of column 1vb, (ii) in blank space at the end of column 4va, (iii) in the outer margin alongside column 9rb, and (iv) in the lower margin beneath column 10vb. Neither the initial letters nor the capitalized place-names show any touch of red. The second of these additions is of particular interest, because it includes a formula – *Olim xx sol'. Modo ual' xxx solid'* (4va42) –

[5] One symptom of the scribe's more formal manner is the use of the ampersand character & alongside the usual 7-shaped sign for et. By this token, the most formal part of DB-Ke is the beginning of the very first column, where ampersand is used four times out of four (1ra4–11).

[6] Several such changes are noted in the comments (below, pp. 151–6); 6va23 is a good example, if the reader would like to look at one straight away.

[7] I commented before on the significance of this discovery (Flight 2006, pp. 14–15).

[8] In this booklet the running head is *CHENTH* (except for 14v, where the name is spelt *CHENT*), except for 11r, where it is omitted.

[9] In this booklet there are three of them (1ra4, 2ra2, 3ra3).

[10] For example, on the same page which lacks its running head, four red lines are missing (11ra6, 9, 13, 54). I do not see that anything can be argued from this, except that the scribe was losing concentration.

[11] But I do have a list on file, if anyone would like to see it.

which the scribe did not start using until he was approaching the end of the DB-So booklet (Flight 2006, p. 21). It seems to follow from this that the scribe was revising the text of DB-Ke some weeks or months after he had first written it. If it was discovered (somehow or other) that a paragraph had gone missing, he was still prepared to go back and make the omission good. It also seems to follow that the rubrication of DB-Ke had been finished before the main text of DB-So was begun.

As well as these four whole paragraphs, there are numerous small alterations and additions distributed throughout the booklet. It is clear that some of these corrections had been made instantly, while the text was being written: the scribe stopped, fetched back to the point where he had gone wrong, and started again from there. But mostly it is impossible to say exactly when a particular correction was made. It may be that most of the changes, large and small, resulted from a single operation. Here and there, small erasures in the margin (or between the columns) coincide with alterations in the text; and these suggest that a fairly thorough check was under way. I take it that the scribe was collating his version of the text with the source text that he had used for it – in other words, that he was doing no more than correcting his own mistakes. As far as I can see, there is nothing that would justify a deeper explanation than that.

A small number of corrections appear to have been made by somebody else, not by the DB scribe himself. Most of them may be the work of a single hand – the corrector called 'scribe B' by Caroline Thorn (Thorn and Thorn 2001) – but I am not sure that all of them are; on the evidence of DB-Ke alone I would not wish to commit myself to any definite identifications.[12] In any case they do not amount to much. Mostly they consist of just one or two words; the longest consists of a whole sentence (10rb39), but that is still only five words. For the history of the text, however, these additions are important, because at least twice it seems likely that the corrector had gone to the trouble of searching through the B text, to retrieve some item of information accidentally omitted from the D text (10rb39, 13vb3). The DB scribe may occasionally have thought of doing this (as at 1vb1), but I see no reason to think that he ever actually did it.

Over time, numerous extracts came to be made from DB, for one reason or another. Because the original survives, almost as legible now as it was when it was created, these extracts are seldom of any textual interest; unless something is known of the circumstances in which they were made, they are hardly of any interest at all.[13]

As far as Kent is concerned, the earliest extracts by far are the ones which turn up in manuscript C1 (above, pp. 36–7). If the dating which I have suggested for this manuscript is right, they prove that the DB version of the survey text was in existence before May 1089. The same manuscript also contains a copy (the earliest of three that survive) of an abridged version of DB-Ke, which I call ε for short. But I reserve all discussion of that for the following chapter.

At some later date, the monks of Christ Church obtained a verbatim transcript of all the passages in DB which were of interest to the archbishop or to them: extracts from the preliminary section (DB-Ke-2ra) and a complete copy of chapters 2–4. What survives is a single quire (C2 = Canterbury Cathedral Library Lit. D 4, fos. 25–32), written in a rather untidy form of Christ Church script.[14] I would guess that it dates from the second quarter of the twelfth century; but this is just my opinion, and the reader should not trust it very far. In any case, the date when this manuscript was written may not be the significant date. As we find it here, the text is decidely corrupt; in particular it is marred by some strange repetitive errors (such as *Will's* for *uill's*, 'Willelm' for 'villain') which suggest to me that it is not a first-hand copy. I suspect (but cannot prove) that a transcript was originally made by an exchequer clerk, at the monks' request, and that the whole thing was subsequently copied out again (because it was not very easy to read) by a Canterbury scribe.

Errors aside, C2 comprises only two original elements: the title, written in red,[15] and some marginal annotation, also written in red (Table 15). From the beginning of chapter 2 onwards, this annotation repeats the place-names which appear in the main text, spelling them differently, and introducing each of them with the preposition *De*: 'Concerning Darenth', 'Concerning Otford', and so on. It also repeats, for each manor, the number of sulungs for which it is stated to be liable; where there is a choice to be made, the numbers chosen are the *Modo* assessments, not the TRE assessments.

Originating here, this marginal subtext, from 'Concerning Darenth' onwards, took on a life of its own. In an edited form (some entries were rearranged and some expanded), it was copied into the lost cartulary which I call C3, and from there it was copied into two surviving manuscripts, C5 and T1. (These manuscripts and the relationships between

[12] Caroline Thorn has been kind enough to let me see a list of the corrections in DB-Ke which she proposes to attribute to 'scribe B'. There are nine of them altogether: 4rb31, 7rb46, 9ra19, 9rb8, 9vb6, 10rb39, 11vb23, 13va38 (*sol'* altered to *lib'*), 13vb3.

[13] There exists, for example, a shortened version of the DB-Ke text, written (so I suppose) by an exchequer scribe in the second half of the twelfth century. (In its original form it was a roll; but the strips have been cut up into pieces of suitable length and mounted on the leaves of a book (BL Cotton Vitellius C. viii, fos. 143–56).) Having collated this version with DB, I find that I have nothing to say about it, except that it exists.

[14] It was catalogued by Woodruff (1911, p. 13) and mentioned by Urry (1967, pp. 7–8) but has not been taken much notice of. The text breaks off at a point corresponding with DB-Ke-3vb49. (We discover, by the way, that the correction from *vii* to *vi*, two lines higher up in DB, had already been made.)

[15] The original title does not use the name 'Domesday'. A reference to 'the lord king's Domesday' appears at the top of this page, but that is a much later (perhaps fourteenth-century) addition.

DB-Ke	C2	C2 margin	C3 / T1 (ed. Hoyt 1962)	Notes
		De terris et maneriis que pertinent ad d'nm ar'ep'm et ad monachos ęccl'ię xp'i cant[uarię]		
2ra2–31	25r1–v20			
2ra32–43	26r2–14	De saca et socnæ quas r[ex] habet in ciuitate cantuarię		
2ra43–8	26r16–v5	De quibusdam consuetudin[ibus] pertinentibus ad eccl'[am xp'i] et ad eccl'am sc'i augus[tini]		
3ra2–5	26v6–9	Burgenses ar'ep'i		
3ra7–16	26v11–7r4	De Sandwicc		
2ra49–50	27r6–8	De ciuitate rouecestrię		
3ra18–25	27r9–v7	De Derenta ii sull[']	De Derenta ii sull'	(1)
3ra26–35	27v9–8r1	[De] Otteford [vii]i sull'	De Otteford viii sull'	
3ra36–41	28r2–9			(2)
3ra42–7	28r10–16	De Bixle ii sull[']	De Bixle ii sull'	
3ra48–b4	28r17–v5	De Earhetha iiii sull'	De Earhetha iiii sull'	
3rb5–11	28v6–13	De Meallinges ii sull'	De Mallinges ii sull'	
3rb11–18	28v14–9r3	De Norhfleate v sull'	De Northflete v sull'	
3rb19–34	29r4–20	De Wroteham viii sull'	De Wroteham viii sull'	
3rb35–49	29v1–17	[De] Meidestana x sull'	De Medestane x sull'	
3va1–10	29v18–30r9	[D]e Gellingeham [ ] sull'	De Gilingham v sull'	(3)
3va11–19	30r10–19	De Ræ[cu]lfe viii [su]ll'	De Raculfe viii sull'	
3va20–31	30r20–v12	De Norhthewude iii sull'	De Northwude iii sull'	(4)
3va32–42	30v14–1r6	[De] Petham [vii] sull'	De Petham vii sull'	
3va43–b8	31r7–v5	De Sturs æte vii sull'	De Stursete vii sull'	
3vb9–14	31v6–13	[De] Burne [vi] sull'	De Burne vi sull'	
3vb15–21	31v14–2r2	De Boctuna v sull' et dim'	De Boctune v sull' et demi	
3vb22–28	32r3–12	De Cerringe[s] viii sull'	De Cerringes viii sull'	
3vb29–33	32r13–19	De Plukele i sull'	De Plukele i sull'	
3vb34–46	32v1–16	[De Wi]ngeham [xxx]v sull'	De Wingeham xxxv sull'	
3vb46–4ra1	32v17–20	[De] Mer[seham iii su]ll'		(5)
4ra2–9			De Aldingtune xv sull'	
4ra10–18			De Sc'o Martino i sull' et di'	
.			.	
.			.	
.			.	
5vb28–38			De Stokes iii sull'	

Table 15. Title and marginal annotations in manuscript C2. Notes: (1) Two versions of the Darenth paragraph appear in the main text: a blundered version (27r9–17), followed by a correct version (27r19–v7); the marginal note is attached to the blundered version. (2) The Sundridge paragraph lacks a marginal note; C3 lacks an entry for Sundridge. (3) The assessment is wrongly reported in C3 (five sulungs instead of six); the marginal note has been partly cut away, and it is doubtful whether the numeral here was given correctly (as it is in the main text) or not. (4) The marginal note, followed by C3, gives the correct place-name ('Northwood' instead of 'Norton'); the wrong assessment (three sulungs instead of thirteen) appears in the main text, and the marginal note, followed by C3, reproduces the error. (5) In C3 the entry for Mersham occurs further down the list, among the monks' manors.

them are discussed in Appendix I.) From T1 this version of the text was printed by Hoyt (1962), who, unaware of its relationship with C2, misunderstood it rather thoroughly.[16] It is, in fact, of very little interest – except incidentally, as proof that Christ Church's copy of DB extended as far as the end of chapter 4. (Some easy arithmetic will show that the copy originally occupied three quires – the one which survives and two which have been lost.) But it exemplifies a fact worth remembering, that information derived from DB can often be found percolating through late medieval manuscripts, sometimes in an attenuated and more or less garbled form.

The original, meanwhile, remained in the exchequer's custody, locked up in a strongbox except when it was being consulted. Once it had become a legal fiction that DB was infallible, the rule established itself that nobody should alter the text in any way. Even notes in the margin were prohibited, with only the rarest of exceptions. For a book which is known to have been consulted on numerous occasions, it remains remarkably clean.

The first person to break the taboo was Arthur Agard; later on, some other exchequer officials followed Agard's lead. In DB-Ke there are three of these early modern additions to be noted. (1) A remark by Agard, dated 1583, written at the foot of fo. 1v, commenting on a passage which appears on the opposite page (2rb31–2). (2) Two excerpts from the *Dialogus de scaccario*, copied by John Bradshaw in 1627 onto the blank page at the beginning (fo. 0r).[17] (3) The numbering of the leaves, done by Edward Fauconberge in 1660, with a note to that effect added on the first page, underneath Bradshaw's excerpts. Only the first of these additions relates specifically to Kent. It is the earliest recorded comment on a passage which has attracted much attention since then; in due course I shall divulge my own thoughts on the subject (below, p. 200).

There is an unintentional eighteenth-century addition which takes the form of a matching pair of blots, on fos. 10v and 11r. What happened, it seems clear, is that someone who had the book open at this point accidentally deposited a drop of ink on fo. 11r and then, without realizing what he had done, closed the book on top of it. As the leaves came together, the drop was flattened, and half of the ink transferred itself onto the previous page. Some time later, somebody discovered these blots and attempted to remove them, using water or some other solvent and a brush. He succeeded in dispersing some of the ink, but the blots were not removable. When he realized that he was doing more harm than good, he gave up; and the blots still exist, each surrounded by a penumbra of diluted ink.

In the 1770s, when one of the deputy chamberlains of the exchequer, Abraham Farley, made the transcript which was used for printing the parliamentary edition of DB (above, pp. 22–3), these blots were already there. In the printed text the illegible words are marked by spaced-out dots, and the boundaries between what Farley could and could not read coincide exactly with the edges of the blots, as they appear today.[18]

In the 1760s, the blots were not there. We know this because there is a surviving transcript of the pages relating to Kent made by Farley at that time (BL Stowe 851). The history of this transcript is not altogether clear (above, p. 22), but I think that it was commissioned by Thomas Astle and loaned by him to Edward Hasted. In any case, it seems likely that the transcript was made in about 1763–4 (certainly it is earlier than 1769); and the words which were illegible in the 1770s were not illegible then. There are two consequential points. First, a shadow of suspicion has to fall on Farley. The circumstances are such as to suggest that it was Farley who did the damage, while he was copying the DB-Ke text for Astle and Hasted, and that it was Farley again who tried vainly to undo the damage, when he came to make the complete transcript for the parliamentary edition. But there is no proof against him, and in any case it is too late now to think of pressing charges. Second, the existence of this transcript makes it possible to restore the missing words. I have done that. And thus it would be true to say – if the reader will allow me to crow for a moment – that the edition below is the first and only edition of DB-Ke which offers a complete text.[19]

In working out the design of this edition, I have relied on two assumptions: first, that anyone who wants a translation into English will be able to find one; second, that anyone who wants to make absolutely certain what the manuscript says will be able to get hold of a facsimile. In a word, I have taken it for granted that my edition ought to serve as a crib, not as a substitute for the original.

From the beginning, I was always intending to print the text line for line. If we want to be able to move freely between the edition and the manuscript, there is no alternative to that. But I have simplified the layout in one respect. In the manuscript, frequently, words were written between the lines. Some are glosses, explanatory notes such as 'sheriff' above the name Haimo, placed there as a matter of policy (which is not to say but that some of them were added

[16] Even in the form in which it was known to Hoyt, this list is quite plainly derived from DB; there should never have been the slightest doubt about that. As for Hoyt's claim that he had discovered the stretch of text which is missing from all known copies of ε, this was just a guess, and obviously not a good guess. As was noted by Eales (1992, pp. 5–6), the assessments reported in ε are the TRE numbers; Hoyt's list gives the *Modo* numbers.

[17] This page is reproduced by Hallam (1987, fig. 7).

[18] And as they appeared when two facsimiles were made, in the 1850s and 1860s respectively (above, pp. 23–4). After 1790, the illegible words on fo. 10v could have been restored at any time, by anyone who thought of looking at Hasted's book. But I am not aware that anyone ever did so.

[19] In fairness, however, I ought to add that some of the blotted words were deciphered correctly by Samuel Henshall (d. 1807), with Henry Ellis's help (Henshall and Wilkinson 1799, pp. 75, 83).

weeks later, while the scribe was checking what he had written). Some of them are corrections, inserted later wherever space could be found for them (which is not to say but that some of them were added almost instantly, within a matter of seconds). There is no sharp distinction to be made; glosses, corrections and ambiguous instances have to be treated alike. I have thought it best to put them all into the text, marking them off with brackets – a device unknown to the DB scribe but familiar to modern readers.

With regard to the scribe's alphabet, only a few comments are needed. The characters are all still current, with two exceptions: **ę**, which occurs very frequently, and **æ**, which occurs very rarely (just twice, to be exact). A few letters – most obviously **d** – come in more than one form, but I have not attempted to reproduce distinctions of this kind.[20] One characteristic feature of the script is the use of some special ligatures: **NT** and **NS** for *-nt* and *-ns*, **TR** in *TRINITAS*. These I have resolved without comment.

Capitalization is almost exactly as in the manuscript. A very large capital is used to mark the beginning of each chapter, a fairly large capital to mark the beginning of each paragraph; I have not attempted to reproduce gradations like these. Sometimes, but not very often, the scribe resorts to the trick of capitalizing the second word of a sentence which starts with the sign for *et*; in such cases I suppress the capital. With some letters, the form of the capital is just an enlargement of the small form, and at times it is hard – especially with round **d** and **h** – to be sure of the scribe's intention. In doubtful cases I have used my best judgment, inclining towards a capital if the word is a proper name, in the opposite direction if not.

There is a distinctive sign – a slanting line with a triangular pennon at the top – used by the scribe to mark the beginning of a sub-paragraph. It is normally placed in the margin; but it does sometimes occur in the body of the text (where the scribe wants to make it clear that he is starting a new topic but does not want to start a new line). This sign is represented below as a double slash. The same or a similar sign (with a 2-shaped tick added to the foot of it) is also used to separate words turned up or down into one line from the end of another line. Space permitting, I have added these overrun words to the end of the line where they belong: I mark the line break with a single slash, which usually (but not quite always) corresponds with a sign in the manuscript.

Punctuation poses few problems for the editor. The scribe uses only two signs, a general-purpose dot and a mark resembling an upside-down semicolon. This second sign, called *punctus elevatus*, invites the reader to inflect the voice upwards and make a moment's pause – like so: – before continuing the sentence. I have transcribed it exactly as it occurs in the manuscript. With the dot I have taken some liberties. In general I transcribe it as either a full stop or a comma, depending on whether it marks the end of a sentence or not. (This is usually easy to decide.) But I have occasionally omitted a comma, in places where there is no break in the sense to justify it. I have also omitted the dots which the scribe uses for distinguishing numerals, because (to my eye) the text looks better without them. For the same reason, I have transcribed *T. R. E.* as *TRE*, *. e'* (meaning *est*) as *e'*.

The main difficulty comes in deciding how to deal with the abbreviations. Writing in a shortened form of business Latin, the scribe makes use of a large assemblage of conventional signs, expecting his readers to be familiar with them (which modern readers, by and large, are not). For anyone editing DB – or any administrative record written in a similar style – this immediately creates a quandary. One solution is to do what Nichols did, design a special font which can reproduce all (or nearly all) of the abbreviations appearing in the manuscript. But I have not even thought of trying that. If readers have to learn what all the special characters mean before they can read the text, they may as well look at a facsimile.

On the other hand, it seems to me a bad idea to jump to the opposite extreme and print the text *in extenso*, i.e. with (almost) every word spelt out in full.[21] It forces the editor, over and over again, to make decisions which the original scribe allowed himself not to make; it gives the reader no sense of the appearance of the original. I do not see it as the editor's duty to transform a piece of business Latin into a literary text. Both extremes, I think, should be avoided.

The only special character which I have used is an approximation to the symbol used (and apparently invented) by the DB scribe as a shorthand notation for the word *manerium* (for any form of this word, in fact, regardless of case and number). This symbol is the scribe's signature, so to speak, and some effort has to be made to reproduce it.[22]

For the rest, I have aimed at finding a happy medium, extending some of the abbreviations but letting the others stand. I doubt whether anyone would thank me for explaining this in detail, but at least I should indicate some of the rules which I have set for myself. The abbreviations which I have chosen to extend are mostly covered by this list:

r denoted by a superscript vowel, as in *p(r)ati*, and similarly *u* after *q*, as in *q(u)ia*;

m denoted by a stroke over a vowel, as in *isde(m)*, *unu(m)*;

[20] The parliamentary edition distinguishes between long **s** and round **s**, but in this it is following the eighteenth-century convention (round **s** at the end of a word, long **s** everywhere else), not the scribe's actual usage. Similarly it uses **j** for i-consonant. It is an admirable piece of typography, but recognizably a product of its time.

[21] For instance, how should we deal with the formula *T'ra e' x car'*? Is the word for 'plough' to be spelt with single *r*, as at 2va5, or with double *r*, as at 13ra36? Is it to be put into the genitive case, as at 7rb38, or into the dative case, as is suggested by the occasional appearance of the preposition *ad*, e.g. at 3va34? Any policy which obliges us to answer (or even ask) questions like these is sure to be a bad policy.

[22] I have experimented with a special character for *et* (Flight 2006, p. 78), but – because the word occurs so frequently – the text immediately takes on a look which I think the majority of readers would find forbidding.

um denoted by an oblique stroke through the tail of a 2-shaped *r*, as in *eor(um)*, *legator(um)*;

en denoted by a stroke over an *m*, as in *em(en)dabit*, *tam(en)*;[23]

on denoted by a stroke over a *c*, as in *c(on)cordant*;

p(ro), *p(er)*, and *p(re)*, each denoted by adding one extra stroke to a *p*;

et denoted by a 7-shaped sign, or occasionally by an ampersand;[24]

some special signs, usually or always occurring at the end of a word, the meaning of which is constant, such as *(us)*, *(ur)*, *-b(us)*, and *-q(ue)*;

some short words with set abbreviations, such as *h(oc)* and *h(ęc)*, *q(uo)d* and *q(uam)*, *s(ed)*, *e(ss)e*, *sic(ut)*, *m(od)o*, *u(er)o*, *(er)go*.

Abbreviations marked with a sign whose meaning can only be determined from the context – including a zigzag sign which often means *er* but in general can mean almost anything – are left unextended. Finally, if more than two letters are missing from a word of more than four letters – *lib(ras)*, *sol(idos)*, *den(arios)*, *def(en)d(it)*, *ep(iscopu)s* – I make it a rule to leave things as they are.

Here is a single sentence, chosen at random (from 2ra15–16), printed as it would appear if the abbreviations were all extended:

Sup(er) h(ęc) om(ni)a h(abe)t uicecom(es) c(entum) (et) (decem) sol(idos).[25]

And this is how I propose to deal with it:

Super hęc omnia h't uicecom' c et x sol'.

Anyone who wants to know how often the word *hęc* is abbreviated, how often spelt out in full, will need to look at a facsimile; this edition is not going to provide an answer to that question.

My aim throughout has been to produce a text which will be easy to read (easier, at least, than the manuscript) and easy to correlate with the original, whenever something needs to be checked. (It goes without saying that I have also tried my hardest to make sure that the text is accurate.) No edition can answer every conceivable purpose. For most purposes, I hope, the present edition will prove adequate.

[23] Or as in *Am(en)*; but that is not a word one would expect to find in DB.

[24] Some scribes use these signs to abbreviate words like *(et)iam*, *hab(et)*; the DB scribe does not do that.

[25] 'Over and above all these things the sheriff gets a hundred and ten shillings.'

DB-Ke-1ra

:

:

:

(D) OVERE Tempore regis EDWARDI reddebat xviii libras, de quibus denariis habebat rex E duas partes, et comes Goduinus terciam. Contra hoc habebant canonici de sc'o Martino medietatem aliam. Burgenses deder' xx^{ti} naues (regi) una uice in anno ad xv dies, et in una quaque naui erant ho'es xx^{ti} et unus. Hoc faciebant pro eo quod eis perdonauerat saccam et socam. Quando missatici regis ueniebant ibi: dabant pro caballo transducendo iii^{es} denarios in hieme, et ii^{os} in estate. Burgenses uero inueniebant stiremannum et unum alium adiutorem. Et si plus opus esset: de pecunia eius conducebatur. // A festiuitate S' Michaelis usque ad festum Sc'i Andreę: treuua (i. pax) regis erat in uilla. Siquis eam infregisset: inde prepositus regis accipiebat communem emendationem. // Quicunque manens in uilla assiduus, reddebat regi consuetudinem: quietus erat de theloneo per totam Angliam. Omnes hę consuetudines erant ibi, quando Will's rex in angliam uenit. In ipso primo aduentu eius in angliam, fuit ipsa uilla combusta, et ideo precium eius non potuit computari, quantum ualebat quando ep's baiocensis eam recepit. Modo appreciatur xl lib', et tamen prepositus inde reddit liiii^{or} lib'. Regi quidem $xx^{ti}iiii^{or}$ lib' de denar' qui sunt xx^{ti} in ora: comiti uero xxx^{ta} lib' ad numerum. In Douere sunt xxix mansurę, de quibus rex per(di)dit consuetudinem. De his habet Robertus de romenel duas, Radulfus de curbespine iii, Will's filius Tedaldi i, Will's filius Ogeri i, Will's filius Tedoldi et Robertus niger vi, Will's filius Goisfridi iii in quibus erat gihalla burgensium. Hugo de montfort i domum, Durandus i, Rannulfus de columbels i, Wadardus vi, Filius Modberti unam. Et hi omnes de his domibus reuocant ep'm baiocensem ad protectorem et liberatorem (uel datorem).

// De illa masura quam tenet Rannulfus de columbels quę fuit cuiusdam exulis (i. utlage): concordant quod dimidia terra est regis, et Rannulfus ipse habet utrunque. Hunfridus (loripes) tenet i masuram, de qua erat forisfactura dimidia regis. Rogerus de Ostreham fecit quandam domum super aquam regis, et tenuit hucusque consuetudinem regis. Nec domus fuit ibi TRE. // In introitu portus de Douere est unum molendin', quod omnes pene naues confringit per magnam turbationem maris, et maximum damnum facit regi et hominibus, et non fuit ibi TRE. De hoc dicit nepos Herberti, quod ep's baiocensis concessit illum fieri auunculo suo Herberto filio Iuonis.

:

DB-Ke-1rb

Has infra scriptas leges regis concordant ho'es

de iiii^{or} lestis, hoc est Boruuar lest, et Estrelest, et Linuuartlest, et Wiuuartlest. Siquis fecerit sepem uel fossatum pro quo strictior fiat publica uia regis, aut arborem stantem extra uiam intra prostrauerit, et inde ramum uel frondem portauerit: pro una quaque harum forisfactur' soluet regi c sol'. Et si abierit domum non apprehensus uel diuadiatus: tamen minister regis eum sequetur, et c solid' emendabit. De gribrige uero siquis eam fecerit et calumniatus (in calle) aut diuadiatus fuerit: viii lib' regi emendabit. Sin autem: quietus erit erga regem, non erga d'nm cuius homo fuerit, de aliis forisfacturis sicuti de gribrige, sed per c sol' emendabit. Has forisfacturas h't rex super omnes alodiarios totius comitatus de chent, et super ho'es ipsorum. Et quando moritur alodiarius: rex inde habet releuationem terrę, excepta terra S' TRINITATIS et S' Augustini, et S' martini. Et exceptis his, Godric de Burnes, et Godric carlesone, et Alnod cilt, et Esber biga, et Siret de cilleham, et Turgis et Norman, et Azor. Super istos h't rex forisfacturam, de capitibus eorum tantummodo. Et de terris eorum h't releuamen, qui h'nt suam sacam et socam. Et de his terris scilicet Goslaches, et Bocheland, et alium Bocheland, et tercium Bocheland, et Herste, i iugum de ora, et i iugum de Herte, Schildricheham, Macheheue, Ernulfitone, Oslachintone, Piria, et alia Piria, Brulege, Ospringes, Hortone, h't rex has forisfacturas, Handsocam, Gribrige, Foristel. De adulterio uero per totum chent h't rex hominem, et archiep's mulierem, excepta terra S' TRINITATIS, et S' Augustini, et S' Martini, de quibus rex nichil h't. De latrone qui iudicatus est ad mortem, h't rex medietatem pecunię eius. Et qui exulem receperit sine licentia regis: inde h't rex forisfacturam. De terris (su)pra nominatis Alnodi (cild) et similium eius: h't rex custodiam vi diebus apud cantuariam, uel apud sanuuic: et ibi h'nt de rege cibum et potum. Si non habuerint: sine forisfactura recedunt. Si fuerint premoniti ut conueniant ad sciram: ibunt usque ad pinnedennam, non longius. Et si non uenerint: de hac forisfactura et de aliis omnibus rex c sol' habebit, excepta Gribrige quę viii lib' emendatur, et de callibus sicut superius scriptum est.

// In Linuuartlest in briseuuei h't rex consuetudinem, scilicet ii caretas et ii sticas anguillar' pro uno ineuuardo, et in terra sophis h't xii den' pro uno ineuuardo, et de uno iugo de northburg xii den' aut unum ineuuard', et de dena xviii den', et de Gara unum ineuuard'. He terrę iacent in Wi: et ho'es de his terris custodiebant regem apud cantuariam uel apud Sanuuic per iii dies, si rex illuc uenisset.

DB-Ke-1va

In Lest de Sudtone et in Lest de Ailesford habuer' isti sacham et socam, Brixi cilt, Adelold de Elteham, Anschil de Becheham, Azor de Lesneis, Aluuinus (hor), Wluuard wit, Ordinc de hortone, Esbern de cillesfelle, Leuenot de Sudtone, Eduuard de Estan, Vlestan et Leuric de Otrinberge, Osuuard de Nordtone, Edid de Aisiholte, Alret de Ellinges.

:

:

(TERRA CANONICORVM S' MARTINI DE DOVRE.)

IN LEST de Estrede habebant canonici de sc'o Martino TRE xxi solin in hund' de Cornely et in hund' de Beusberge. In Lest de Linuuarlet habebant iii solins, unum in Estret hund', alium in Belissolt hund', et tercium in Blacheborn hund'. TRE erant prebendę communes, et reddeb' lxi lib' int' totum. Modo sunt diuisę per singulos, per ep'm Baioc'.

IN BEVSBERG HD'.

Radulfus de S' Sansone ten' i M' in prebenda. *Cerlentone uocatur, et defd' se pro i^{o} solin. Ibi h't iii uill'os et iiii bord' cum i car'. Int' tot' ual' lxx sol', TRE: c sol'. Leuuinus tenuit in prebenda.

In ead' uilla ten' Will's filius Ogerii i solin, et ibi h't i uill' et vii bord' cum dim' car', et i molin' de xl sol'. Ibi quidam francig' h't i car'. Isd' Will's ten' i monast' in Dovere de ep'o, et redd' ei xi sol'. Canonici calumn'. Hoc tot' ual' vi lib', TRE: xii lib'. Sired tenuit.

In Bochelande ten' Aluui i solin, et ibi h't vi uill' et x bord' cum i car' et dimid'. Int' tot' ual' iiii lib', TRE: c sol'. Iste idem tenuit in prebenda.

In Gocistone ten' Vlric i iug', et ibi h't ii uill'os et i bord' cum i car'. Ad hanc terram pertin' xxv ac' terrę in Corneli hund', et ibi sunt v bord' cum dim' car'. Int' tot' ual' xx sol', TRE: x sol'. Elric tenuit in / prebenda.

IN HOC EOD' HVND' IACET S' MARGARITA.

Ibi h't *Sired i solin, et i car' in d'nio, et vi bord' cum iiii seruis. Val' c sol', TRE: iiii lib'. Pat' eiusd' Sired tenuit in prebenda.

Ibidem ten' Radulfus i solin, et h't i car' in d'nio, et vii bord'. Val' lx et ix sol' et ii den', TRE: iiii lib'. Alric tenuit in prebenda similit'.

Ibidem ten' Alred i solin, et h't in d'nio i car', et ii uill' et ii bord' cum dim' car'. Val' lx sol', TRE: xx sol'. Pat' huius tenuit in prebenda.

Ibid' ten' Robertus niger i solin, et h't ibi iii uill'os et vi bord' cum i car'. Val' xxx sol', TRE: xx sol'. Esmellt tenuit capellanus RE.

Ibid' ten' Walterus i solin, et ibi h't iii uill' et v bord', cum i car' et dim'. Val' lx sol', TRE: lxx solid'. Sigar tenuit in prebenda.

DB-Ke-1vb

* Ibid' ten' Turbatus dimid' solin, et ibi h't ii uill'os et i bord' cum dimid' car'. Et isdem Robertus hab' dimid' solin in CORNILAI HD', et ibi dimid' car' in d'nio, et v bord'. Int' tot' ual' iii lib', TRE: iiii lib'. Goldstan tenuit.

Ibidem ten' Eduuine dimid' solin, et adhuc xxv acras terrę. In d'nio h't dimid' car', et i uill'm cum dimid' car'. In CORNILAI HD' h't isd' Eduinus quat' xx et v acras, et ibi i uill'm cum i car'.

Val' iii lib', TRE: iiii lib'. Ipsemet tenuit TRE. De hac prebenda sumpsit ep's Baioc' viii acras, et dedit Alan clerico suo. Modo h't Vlric de Oxeneford. IN CORNELAI HVND'.

In Addelam ten' Anschitil (archidiac') i solin, et ibi h't in d'nio ii car', cum vi bord'. Hanc terram tenuit Stigandus archiep's. Huic eid' Anschitillo ded' ep's baioc' l acras terrę ad delam, et alias l acras apud sc'am Margaritam, ubi h't i uill'm et dim' car'. Hę c acrę erant de prebendis ut testificantur. Int' totum ualet viii lib', TRE: vii lib'. IN BEVSBERG HD'.

In Sibertesuualt ten' Will's pictau' dimid' solin et xii acras, et in Addelam dimid' solin xii acras minus, et ibi h't ii uill'os et iii bord', cum i car' et dim'. Totum hoc ualet lv sol', TRE: iiii lib'. IN CORNELAI HVND'.

In Addelam ten' Adeloldus iii uirg', et ibi h't iii uill'os et viii bord' cum i car'. Val' et ualuit semper lx sol'. Istemet tenuit TRE. IN BEVSBERG HD' ET IN CORNELAI HD'.

In Addelam ten' abb' S' Augustini i solin, et ibi h't iii uill'os et vii bord' cum i car' et dimid'. Val' xxx sol', TRE: xl sol'. Antecessor eius tenuit in prebenda similit'.

In Addelam ten' Will's filius Tedaldi dimid' solin et dimid' iugum, et ibi h't in d'nio i car', et ii uill'os et ii bord'. Val' lx sol', TRE: xl sol'. Derinc (filius Sired) tenuit.

In Sibertesuualt ten' Sigar i iugum et dimid', et ibi h't in d'nio dimid' car', et ii uill'os et i bord'. Val' xxv sol', TRE: xxxv sol'. Pat' ipsius tenuit in prebenda.

Nigellus medicus apud sc'am Margaritam ten' i iugum et dimid', et ibi h't *(i uill'm) cum ii bobus. Val' xx sol', TRE: xxv sol'. Spirites tenuit in prebenda. IN BEVSBERG HD'.

In Ferlingelai ten' Will's filius Gaufridi i solin, et ibi h't in d'nio i car', et iiii uill'os cum i car'. Val' iiii lib', TRE: vi lib'. Sired tenuit in prebenda.

In Huham ten' Balduinus i solin, et ibi h't iiii uill'os et v bord' cum ii car'. Val' iiii lib', TRE: c sol'. Eduinus tenuit.

In Bocheland ten' Godricus i solin, et ibi h't ii car' in d'nio, et iii uill'os et iiii bord' cum i car', et una ęccl'a. Val' vi lib', TRE: viii lib'.

* (In Sibertesuuald ten' Vlstan f. Vluuin i solin, *et ibi h't dimid' car', et iii uill'os et ix bord' cum i car'. TRE ualb' c sol'. Modo lx sol'. Pat' eius tenuit.)

:

:

:

:

DB-Ke-2ra

:

(I) N CIVITATE CANTVARIA habuit Rex EDWARDVS l et i burgens', reddentes gablum, et alios cc et xii super quos habebat sacam et socam, et iii molend' de xl sol'. Modo burgens' gablum reddentes sunt xix. De xxxii^{obus} aliis qui fuerant: sunt uastati xi in fossato ciuitatis, et archiep's h't ex eis vii, et abb' S' Augustini alios xiiii, pro excambio castelli, et adhuc sunt cc et xii burgens', super quos h't rex sacam et socam, et (iii) molend' redd't c et viii sol', et theloneum redd' lxviii sol'. Ibi viii acrę prati quę solebant esse legatorum regis, modo redd't de censu xv sol', et mille acrę siluę infructuosę, de qua exeunt xxiiii^{or} solidi. Int' totum TRE ualuit li lib', et t'ntd' quando (Haimo) uicec' recep', et modo l lib' appreciatur. Tamen qui ten' nunc reddit xxx lib' arsas et pensatas, et xxiiii lib' ad numerum. Super hęc omnia h't uicecom' c et x sol'.

Duas domos duorum burgensium, unam foris aliam intra ciuitatem, quidam monachus ęccl'ę cantuar' abstulit. Hę erant positę in calle / regis.

// Burgenses habuer' xlv mansur' extra ciuitatem, de quibus ipsi habeb' gablum et consuetud': rex autem hab' sacam et socam.

Ipsi quoque burgenses habebant de rege xxxiii acras terrę in gildam suam. Has domos et hanc terram ten' Rannulfus de Columbels. Habet etiam quat' xx acras terrę super hęc, quas tenebant burgens' in alodia de rege. Tenet quoque v acras terrę, quę iuste pertinent uni ęccl'ę. De his omnibus reuocat isdem Rannulfus ad protectorem ep'm Baiocensem.

// Radulfus de Curbespine h't iiii mansuras in ciuitate, quas tenuit quędam concubina heraldi, de quibus est saca et soca regis, sed usque nunc non habuit.

Isdem Radulfus ten' alias xi masuras de ep'o (baioc') in ipsa ciuitate, que fuer' Sbern biga, et redd't xi solid' et ii den' et i obolum.

Per totam ciuitatem cantuarię h't rex sacam et socam, excepta terra ęccl'ę S' TRIN', et S' Augustini, et Eddeuę reginę, et Alnod cild, et Esber biga, et Siret de Cilleham.

Concordatum est de rectis callibus quę habent per ciuitatem introitum et exitum, quicunque in illis forisfecerit: regi emendabit. Similit' de callibus rectis extra ciuitatem: usque ad unam leugam, et iii perticas, et iii pedes. Siquis ergo infra has publicas uias intus ciuitatem uel extra foderit uel palum fixerit: *sequitur illum prepositus regis ubicunque abierit, et emendam accipiet ad opus regis.

Archiep's calumniatur forisfacturam in uiis extra ciuitatem ex utraque parte, ubi terra sua est. // Quidam prepositus Brumannus no'e TRE cepit consuetudines de extraneis mercatoribus in terra S' TRINITATIS et S' Augustini. Qui postea TRW ante archiep'm Lanfranc' et ep'm baiocensem recognouit se iniuste accepisse, et sacramento facto iurauit quod ipsę ęccl'ę suas consuetudines quietas habuer' RE tempore. Et exinde utreque ęccl'ę in sua terra habuer' consuetud' suas, iudicio baronum regis qui placitum tenuer'.

Ciuitas ROVECESTRE TRE ualebat c solid'. Quando (ep's) recep': similit'. Modo: ual' xx lib', tamen ille qui ten' reddit xl lib'.

:

DB-Ke-2rb

(ITEM POSSESSIO S' MARTINI.)

De communitate Sc'i MARTINI h'nt simul iii canonici unum solin et xvi acras, idest Sired, Godric et Seuuen. In hac terra sunt iiii^{or} uill'i et ix bord' cum una car'. Reddunt xxii solid'. // De Lest LIMWARLET, unum solin' in Blacheburne hund', et ibi sunt ix uill'i cum ii car'. Redd't xvi sol' et viii den'. // In STRET hund' iacet un' solin de Stanetdeste. Ibi vii uill'i h'nt ii car' et dimid', et vii bord', et un' pratum, redd't xvi sol' et viii^{to} den'. // In BILESOLD hund' un' solin' de Stanestede, ibi sunt vii uill'i et vii bord' et h'nt iiii car'. Et redd't xx sol' ii den' minus. Ad ista iii^{a} solina sunt v denę, et vi uill'i et v bord', et redd't ix sol' iii denar' minus, h'nt iii car' et dimid'. In Brensete paululum terrȩ sunt ii uill'i et iii bord' et h'nt dim' car'. Reddunt l denar'. Illa iiii^{or} solina supradicta h'nt canonici S' Martini in communitate int' nemus et planum. TRE ualb' x lib', modo similit'. Terra Nordeuuode et terra Ripe et terra Brandet redd't xx sol' et vi den' ad S' Martin' in elemosina. In inland S' Martini manent vii bord', cum dimid' car'. Redd' lx solid' ad calciamenta canonicorum. S' Margarita redd' viii lib'. (Ibi est unus rusticus.) Theloneum de doure TRE ualb' viii lib', modo: xxii lib'. Tres ȩccl'ȩ apud Doueram redd't xxxvi solid' et viii denar'. De pastura Medrecliue et de hortis douere exeunt ix sol' et iiii denar'. Vna pastura in Sibertesuualt: xvi den' redd'. Sc's Martinus h't x molend' et dimid', redd't vii lib', TRE tantd' reddider'. Modo appreciantur xii lib', sed non ad proficuum canonicorum. Sub illis molinis manent viii ho'es. Apud scortebroc una pastura redd' ii solid'. De hac communitate h't archiep's singulis annis lv sol'. Ibi sunt vi ho'es cum i car' et dimid'. In communi terra S' Martini sunt cccc^{te} acrȩ et dimid', quȩ fiunt ii solinos et dimid'. Hȩc terra nunquam reddid' aliquid consuetudinis uel scoti, quia xxiiii solini hȩc omnia adquietant. Apud Ripam sunt c acrȩ, quȩ se adquieta(n)t ubi TRE se adquietaba(n)t. Apud Nordeude sunt l acrȩ, et c apud Brand, que adquietant se ubi et superiora. In hac terra sunt iii uill'i et ix bord', h'nt i car' et dimid'. Hȩc omnia si canonici haberent sicuti ius esset: ualere(n)t illis lx lib' singulis annis, modo non h'nt nisi xlvii lib' et vi sol' et iiii denar'.

// Rannulfus de Columbels aufert eis un' pratum. Rotbertus de romenel aufert eis singulis annis xx denar', et unam salinam et unam piscariam. Herbertus filius Iuonis ded' ep'o baiocensi mark' auri pro uno molino eorum, nolentibus illis. Lanbertus un' (molin'). Wadard un' (molin'). Radulfus de curbespine un'.

// Alnod (cild) per uiolentiam Heraldi abstulit S' Martino Merclesham, et Hauochesten, pro quibus ded' canonicis iniquam commutationem. Modo ten' Robertus de Romenel, quod ei canonici calumniantur semper.

:

HIC ANNOTANTVR TENENTES TERRAS IN CHENT.

(I) REX WILLELMVS.
(II) Archiep's Cantuar'.
(III) Et monachi et ho'es eius.
(IIII) Ep's Rofecestrens'.
(V) Ep's Baiocensis.
(VI) Abbatia de Batailge.
(VII) Abbatia S' Augustini.
(VIII) Abbatia de Gand.
(IX) Hugo de montford.
(X) Comes Eustachius.
(XI) Ricardus de Tonebrige.
(XII) Haimo uicecomes.
(XIII) Albertus capellanus.

DB-Ke-2va

(I) (TERRA REGIS.)

IN DIMIDIO LEST DE SVDTONE. IN ACHESTAN HD'.

Rex WILLELMVS ten' TARENTEFORT.

Pro uno solino et dimidio se defd'. T'ra e' xl caruc'. In d'nio sunt ii car', et cxlii uill'i *cum x bord' h'nt liii car'. Ibi sunt iii serui, et i mold'. Prati xxii acrȩ. Pasturæ xl ac'. De silua viii denȩ paruȩ, et iii magnȩ. Ibi ii hedȩ, idest ii^{o} portus.

TRE: ualuit lx lib', et t'ntd' quando haimo (uicec') recepit. Modo appreciatur ab anglis lx lib'. Prepositus uero francig' qui ten' ad firmam, dicit quia ual' quat' xx^{ti} lib' et x lib'. Ipse tamen reddit de isto M̄ lxx lib' pensatas, et cxi solid' de den' xx^{ti} in ora, et vii lib' et xxvi den' ad numer'. Super hęc reddit uicec' c sol'.

Homines de hund' testificantur, quod de isto M̄ regis ablatum est unum pratum, et un' alnetum, et un' mold', et xx^{ti} acrę terrę, et adhuc tant' prati quantum pertin' ad x acras terrę, quę omnia erant in firma regis E dum uiueret. Hęc ual' xx^{ti} sol'. Dicunt autem quod Osuuard tunc uicecom' pręstitit ea
* Alestan preposito Lundon', et modo ten' heltus dapifer et nepos / eius. Testantur quoque quod HAGELEI de isto M̄ ablata est, quę se defd' pro dim' solin. Hanc terram tenebat uicecom', et quando uicecomitatum amittebat: in firma regis remaneb'. Ita permansit et post mortem RE. Modo ten' Hugo de port, cum liiii acris terrę plus. Totum hoc ual' xv lib'.

// De eod' M̄ regis adhuc sunt ablatę vi acrę terrę, et quędam silua quam isd' Osuuardus (uicec') posuit extra M̄, per quoddam uadimon' xl solidorum.

// Ęccl'am huius M̄ ten' ep's de Rouecestre, et ual' lx sol'. Extra hanc sunt adhuc ibi iii ęcclesiolę.

:

:

IN LEST DE ELESFORD. IN LAVROCHESFEL HVND'.

Rex W ten' ELESFORD. Pro uno solin se defd'. T'ra e' xv car'. In d'nio sunt iii car', et xl uill'i cum v bord' h'nt xv car'. Ibi viii serui, et i mold' xl den', et xliii ac' prati. Silua lxx porc'. Int' tot' ualeb' TRE xv lib', et t'ntd' quando Haimo (uicec') recep', modo ual' xx lib'. Tamen redd' xxxi lib', et uicec' inde h't iii lib'. De hoc M̄ ten' Ansgotus iuxta rouecestre tantum terrę, quod appreciatur vii lib'. Ep's etiam de Rouecest' pro excambio terre in qua castellum sedet, tantum de hac terra ten', quod *xvii^{tem} sol' et iiii^{or} den' ual'.

:

IN (DIMIDIO) LEST DE MIDDELTVNE. IN MIDDELTVN HVND'.

Rex W ten' MIDDELTVNE. *Pro quat' xx^{ti} solins se defd'. Extra hos: sunt in d'nio iiii solins, et ibi iii car' in d'nio. In hoc M̄ ccc^{ti} et ix uill'i cum lxxiiii bord', h'nt clxvii car'. Ibi sunt vi mold' de xxx solid', et xviii^{to} ac' prati. Ibi xxvii salinę de xxvii solidis.

DB-Ke-2vb

Ibi xxxii piscarię de xxii sol' et viii den'. De theloneo xl sol'. De pastura xiii sol' et iiii den'. Silua cc xx porc', et ho'es de Walt reddunt l sol' pro Ineuuard' et Aueris. In hoc M̄ sunt x serui. Int' totum TRE ualeb' cc lib' ad numerum, et t'ntd' quando Haimo (uicecom') recep', et modo similiter.

// De hoc M̄ ten' Hugo de port viii solins et unum iugum, qui TRE erant cum aliis solins in consuetudine. Ibi h't iii car' in d'nio. Hęc terra quam ten' Hugo de port, *( ) ual' xx lib', quę computantur in cc^{tis} lib' totius M̄ MIDDELTVN, qui ten' reddit cxl lib' ad ignem et ad pensam, et insuper xv lib' et vi sol' ii denar' minus ad numerum. Haimoni (uicec') dat prepositus xii lib'.

// De silua regis h't Wadardus tant' quod redd' xvi den' per ann', et dimidiam denam tenet quam TRE quidam uillanus tenuit, et Alnod cild duas partes cuidam uill'o per uim abstulit.

// Ęccl'as et decimas huius M̄ ten' abb' S' Augustini, et xl sol' de iiii solins regis exeunt ei.

:

:

IN LEST DE WIWARLET. IN FAVRESHANT HVND'.

Rex W ten' FAVRESHANT. Pro vii solins se defd'. T'ra e' xvii car'. In d'nio sunt ii^{e}. Ibi xxx uill'i cum xl bord' h'nt *(xxiiii) car'. Ibi v serui, et i molin' de xx sol', et ii^{e} ac' prati. Silua c porc', et de pastura siluę *xxxi sol' et ii den'. Mercatum *(de iiii) lib', et ii^{e} salinę de iii solid' et ii den'. Et in cantuar' ciuitate, iii^{es} hagę (de xx denar') ad hoc M̄ pertin'. In totis ualent' TRE ualeb' lx lib' v solid' minus, et post: lx lib'. Modo ual' quater xx^{ti} lib'.

:

:

:

:

:

:

:

:

:

:

:

:

:

:

:

:

:

:

:

:

:

:

DB-Ke-3ra

(II) (TERRA ARCHIEP'I CANTVARIENSIS.)

:

(I) N CIVITATE CANTVARIA habet archiep's xii burgenses, et xxxii mansuras quas tenent clerici de uilla in gildam suam, et reddunt xxxv sol', et un' mold' de v sol'.

:

SANDWICE iacet in suo proprio HVND'. Hoc burgum ten' archiep's, et est de uestitu monachorum, et reddit simile seruitium regi sicut DOVERE. Et hoc testificantur homines de isto burgo, quod antequam rex EDW' dedisset illum S' TRIN', reddeb' regi xv lib'. Tempore (mortis) RE: non erat ad firmam. Quando recep' archiep's: reddeb' xl lib' de firma, et xl milia (de) allecibus ad uictum monachorum. In anno *(quo facta) est hęc descriptio: reddidit (sanuuic) l lib' de firma, et alleces sicut prius. TRE: erant ibi ccc et vii mansurę hospitatę, modo sunt plus lxxvi, idest simul ccc lxxx (octog') iii.

:

IN ACHESTAN HVND'.

Archiep's cantuar' ten' in d'nio TARENT. Pro ii solins se defd'. T'ra e' In d'nio e' una car', et xxii uill'i cum vii cot' h'nt vii car'. Ibi vi serui, et ii mold' de l sol'. Ad hoc M̄ pertin' v burgenses in rouecest', redd' vi sol' et viii den'. Ibi viii ac' prati. Silua xx porc'. In totis ualent' TRE ualuit xiiii lib'. Quando recep': x lib', modo xv lib' et x sol'. Tamen qui tenet M̄ redd' xviii lib'.

Ipse archiep's ten' OTEFORT in d'nio. Pro viii (solins) se defd'. T'ra e' xlii car'. In d'nio sunt vi car'. Ibi c et unus uill's cum xviii bord' h'nt xlv car'. Ibi viii serui, et *(vi) molini de lxxii solid', et l ac' *pra(ti). Silua cl porc'. De hoc M̄ ten' iii teigni i solin et dimid', et ibi h'nt in d'nio iii car', et xvi uill'os cum xi bord' h'ntes iiii car'. Ibi v serui et ii mold' de xxiiii sol', et xxviii acras prati. Silua xxx porc'. In totis ualent' TRE et post ualeb' Modo appreciatur d'nium arch' lx lib'. Teignorum: xii lib'. Ricardus de Tonebrige quod in sua leuga ten': appreciatur x lib'.

Ipse archiep's ten' SONDRESSE. Pro uno solin et dim' se defd'. T'ra e' In d'nio sunt iii car', et xxvii uill'i cum ix bord' h'nt viii car'. Ibi viii serui, et iii mold' et dim' de xiii solid' et dim' (i. vi d'). Ibi viii ac' prati. Silua lx porc'. Ibi ęccl'a. In totis ualent' TRE ual' xii lib'. Quando recep': xvi lib', et modo xviii lib'. Tamen reddit xxiii lib', et unum militem in seruitio arch'.

IN HELMESTREI HVND'.

Ipse archiep's ten' BIX. Pro iii^{bus} solins se defd' TRE, et modo pro ii^{obus}. T'ra e' In d'nio sunt ii car', et xli uill' cum xv bord' h'nt x car'. Ibi ęccl'a, et iii mold' dc xlviii solid', et viii ac' prati. Silua c porc'. In totis ualent' TRE et post ual' xii lib', et modo xx lib', et tamen reddit xxx lib' et viii sol'.

IN LITELAI HVND'.

Ipse archiep's ten' ERHEDE. Pro iiii solins se defd'. T'ra e' viii car'. In d'nio sunt ii^{e}, et xxvii uill'i cum ii bord' h'nt viii car'.

DB-Ke-3rb

Ibi ęccl'a, et iii mold' de l solid' et vi den'. Ibi v serui, et x ac' prati. Silua xl porc'. In totis ualent' TRE ual' xii lib', et t'ntd' quando recep'. Modo xvi lib', et tamen redd' xxi lib'.

IN LEST DE ELESFORT. IN LAVROCHESFEL HVND'.

Ipse archiep's ten' in d'nio *METLINGES( ). Pro ii solins se defd'. T'ra e' vii car'. In d'nio sunt iii car', et xxxviii uill'i cum xii bord' h'nt v car'. Ibi ęccl'a et *v serui, et ii mold' de x sol', et xxi acra prati. Silua lx porc'. In totis ualent' TRE ual' ix lib'. Similit' quando recep', et modo t'ntd', et tamen redd' xv lib'. IN TOLLENTREV HVND'.

Ipse archiep's ten' *(in d'nio) NORFLVET. Pro vi solins defd' se TRE, et modo pro v. T'ra e' xiiii car'. In d'nio sunt ii^{e}, et xxxvi uill'i h'nt x car'. Ibi ęccl'a et vii serui, et i molin' de x sol' cum una piscar', et xx ac' prati. Silua xx porc'. In totis ualent' TRE ual' x lib'. Quando recep': xii lib', et modo xxvii lib', et tamen redd' xxxvii lib' et x sol'.

Ricardus de tonebrige quod ten' in sua leuga de hoc M̄, ual' / xxx sol'.

IN BROTEHAM HVND'.

Ipse archiep's ten' BROTEHAM. Pro viii solins se defd'. T'ra e' xx car'. In d'nio sunt iii car', et lxxvi uill'i cum xviii bord' h'nt xiiii car'. Ibi ęccl'a et x serui, et iii mold' de xv solid', et ix^{uem} ac' prati. Silua quando fructific': quingent' porc'.

De hoc M̄ ten' Will's dispensat' i solin, et ibi h't i car' in d'nio et ii uill'os cum dim' car'.

De eod' M̄ ten' Goisfr' de archiep'o i solin, et ibi h't i car', et vi uill'os cum i bord' h'ntes ii car'.

De ipso M̄ ten' Farman i iug' et dim' de archiep'o, et ibi h't iii car', et vi uill'os cum xii cot' h'ntes ii car'. Ibi x serui.

In totis ualent' TRE ual' hoc M̄ xv lib', et post xvi lib'. Modo appreciatur d'nium arch': xxiiii lib', et tamen redd' xxxv lib'. Militum: *xi lib'. Ricardus de Tonebrige quod ten' in sua leuga: appreciatur xv lib'.

IN MEDDESTAN HVND'.

Ipse archiep's ten' MEDDESTANE. Pro x solins se defd'. T'ra e' xxx car'. In d'nio sunt iii car', et xxv uill'i cum xxi bord' h'nt *xxv car'. Ibi ęccl'a et x serui, et v molin' de xxxvi solid' et viii den'. Ibi ii piscarię de cc lxx anguill'. Ibi x ac' prati. Silua xxx porc'.

De hoc M̄ ten' de archiep'o iii milit' iiii solins, et ibi h'nt iii car' et dim' in d'nio, et xxxii uill'os cum x bord' h'ntes vi car', et x seru', et h'nt i molin' de v solid', et xiii acras prati, et ii piscar' et dimid' de clxxx anguill' et ii salin'. Silua xxiii porc'.

In totis ualent' TRE ual' hoc M̄ xiiii lib'. Quando recep': xii lib', et modo d'nium archiep'i ual' xx lib'. Militum xv lib' et x sol'. Monachi cantuar' h'nt omni anno de duobus ho'ibus huius M̄: xx sol'.

:

DB-Ke-3va

IN CETEHAM HVND'.

Ipse archiep's ten' GELINGEHAM. Pro vi solins se defd'. T'ra e' xv car'. In d'nio sunt ii car', et xlii uill'i cum xvi bord' h'nt xv car'. Ibi ęccl'a, et iii serui, et iii piscarię de xlii solid' et viii den', et i molin' de xvi solid' et viii den', et xiiii ac' prati. Silua xx porc'.

De hoc M̄ ten' quidam francig' terram ad i car', et ibi h't ii bord'. In totis ualent' TRE ual' hoc M̄ xv lib'. Quando recep': xii lib', et modo xxiii lib', et tamen redd' xxvi lib' xii den' minus. *Quod ten' francig': xl sol'.

IN ROCVLF HVND'.

Ipse archiep's ten' ROCVLF. Pro viii solins se defd'. T'ra e' xxx car'. In d'nio sunt iii car', et quat' xx^{ti} et x uill'i cum xxv bord' h'nt xxvii car'. Ibi ęccl'a et i molin' de xxv den', et xxxiii ac' prati. Silua xx porc', et v salinę de *(l)xiiii den', et una piscaria. In totis ualent' TRE ualuit hoc M̄ xiiii lib'. Quando recep': similit', et modo xxxv lib'. Super hęc h't archiep's vii lib' et vii solid'.

Ipse archiep's ten' NORTONE in d'nio. Pro xiii solins se defd'. T'ra e' xxvi car'. In d'nio sunt ii^{e} car', et quat' xx^{ti} et xii uill'i cum xl bord' h'nt lix car' et dimid'. Ibi ęccl'a, et x ac' prati. Silua l porc'.

In totis ualent' TRE ualuit hoc M̄ xxiiii lib' et v sol', et post t'ntd', et modo redd' archiep'o l lib' et xiiii sol' et ii den', et archidiacono xx sol'.

De hoc M̄ ten' Vitalis de archiep'o iii solins et un' iug' et xii acras terrę, et ibi h't v car' et *(xxix) bord' et v seruos, et vii salinas de xxv sol' et iiii den'. Ibi est ęccl'a et una parua dena siluę. Int' totum ual' xiiii lib' et vi sol' et vi den'. *( )

IN BOROWARTLEST. IN PITEHAM HVND'.

Ipse archiep's ten' PITEHAM. Pro vii solins se defd'. T'ra e' ad xx car'. In d'nio sunt iii car', et xxxii uill'i cum xxi bord' h'nt xix car'. Ibi ii ęccl'ę. Ibi ii^{o} serui, et xiii ac' prati. Silua xx porc'.

In totis ualent' TRE ualuit hoc M̄ xvii lib' et vi sol' et iii den', et post t'ntd', et modo ual' xx lib'.

De hoc M̄ ten' Godefridus et Nigellus de archiep'o un' solin et dim' et *( ) iugum, et ibi h'nt iiii car', et iiii uill'os cum viii bord' h'ntes iii car'. Int' tot' ual' ix lib'. De his h'nt monachi viii sol' per ann'.

IN ESTVRSETE HVND'.

Ipse archiep's ten' ESTVRSETE in d'nio. Pro vii solins se defd'. T'ra e' xx car'. In d'nio sunt iiii car', et xvii uill'i cum quat' xx^{ti} et iii bord' h'nt xvi car'. Ibi (Ęccl'a, et) xii molins de iiii lib' et v sol', et c ac' prati. Silua l porc'. Ad hoc M̄ pertinuer' TRE in ciuitate lii masurę, et modo non sunt nisi xxv, quia alię sunt destructę *i(n) noua hospitatione archiep'i.

DB-Ke-3vb

In totis ualent' TRE et post ualeb' xxiiii lib' et xii sol' et vi den'. Modo ual' xl lib'.

De hoc M̄ h'nt v ho'es archiep'i unum solin et vi iuga, et ibi h'nt v car' et dimid' in d'nio, et viii uill'os cum xxvi bord' h'ntes ii car', et iii mold' et xxxiiii acras prati. Silua x porc'. Int' totum ual' ix lib'.

De ipso M̄ ten' Haimo uicec' dimid' solin de arch', et ibi h't ii car' cum v bord' et uno seruo, et ii mold' de xv sol'. Val' / c solid'.

IN BERHAM HVND'.

Ipse archiep's ten' in d'nio BVRNES. Pro vi solins se defd'. T'ra e' l car'. In d'nio sunt v car', et lxiiii uill'i cum liii^{bus} bord' h'nt xxx car' et dim'. Ibi ęccl'a et ii mold' de viii sol' et vi den', et xx ac' prati. Silua xv porc'. De herbagio xxvii den'. In totis ualent' TRE et post ualeb' xx^{ti} lib', modo xxx lib'.

IN BOLTVN HVND'.

Ipse archiep's ten' in d'nio BOLTVNE. Pro v solins et dim' se defd'. T'ra e' In d'nio sunt ii car', et xxxi uill's cum xxxi bord' h'ntes xv car'. Ibi iiii ac' prati, et piscaria de x den'. Salina de xvi den'. Silua xlv porc'. In totis ualent' TRE et post ualeb' xv lib' et xvi sol' et iii den' et i obolum. Modo ual' xxx lib' et xvi sol' et iii den' et i obolum.

IN CALE HELLE HVND'.

Ipse archiep's ten' in d'nio CHERINGES. Pro viii sol' se defd'.

T'ra e' *xl car'. In d'nio e' un' solin et ibi iiii car' et dim'. Ibi xxvi uill'i cum xxvii bord' h'nt xxvii car'. Ibi xii serui, et un' molin' de xl den'. Ibi xxv ac' prati. Silua xxvi porc'.
In totis ualent' TRE ualeb' xxiiii lib'. Quando recep': t'ntd'.
Modo appreciatur xxxiiii lib', et tamen reddit lx lib'.

Ipse archiep's ten' in d'nio PLVCHELEI. Pro uno solin se defd'. T'ra e' xii car'. In d'nio ii car' et dim', et xvi uill'i cum vii bord' h'nt xi car'. Ibi viii serui, et xii ac' prati et dim'. Silua cxl porc'. Int' tot' TRE ualeb' xii lib'. Quando recep': viii lib', et modo xv lib', et tamen redd' xx lib'.
IN LEST DE ESTREI. IN WINGEHAM HVND'.

Ipse archiep's ten' WINGHEHAM in d'nio. Pro xl solins se defd' TRE, et modo pro xxxv. T'ra e' In d'nio sunt viii car', et quater xx^{ti} et v uill'i cum xx bord', h'ntes lvii car'. Ibi viii serui, et ii mold' de xxxiiii sol'. Silua v porc', et ii^{ę} siluulę ad clausuram. In totis ualent' TRE ual' lxxvii lib'. Quando recep': similit', et modo c lib'.
De hoc M̄ ten' Will's de arcis i solin in Fletes, et ibi h't in d'nio i car', et iiii uill'os et un' militem cum i car', et unam piscar' cum salina de xxx den'. Tot' ual' xl sol'.
De ipso M̄ ten' v ho'es archiep'i v solins et dim', et iii^{a} iuga, et ibi h'nt in d'nio viii car', et xxii bord' et viii seru'. Int' tot' ual' xxi lib'. IN LANGEBRIGE HVND'.

Ipse archiep's ten' in d'nio MERSEHAM. Pro *vi( ) solins se defd' TRE, et modo pro iii. T'ra e' xii car'. In d'nio sunt iii car', et xxxix uill'i cum ix bord' h'ntes xvi car'. Ibi ęccl'a, et ii mold' de v sol', et ii salinę de v sol', et xiii ac' prati. Silua xxx porc'.

DB-Ke-4ra

In totis ualent' TRE ual' et post x lib'. Modo xx lib'.
IN LIMO WART LEST. IN BELICOLT HVND'.

Ipse archiep's ten' ALDINTONE in d'nio. Pro xxi solin se defd' TRE, et modo pro xv solins. T'ra c car'. In d'nio sunt xiii car', et ducenti uill'i x minus cum l bord' h'nt lxx car'. Ibi ęccl'a, et xiii serui, et iii mold' de xvi sol', et iii piscar' de xxi den'. Ibi clxx ac' prati. Silua lx porc'.
In totis ualent' TRE ualeb' lxii lib', et t'ntd' quando recep'.
Modo redd' c lib' et xx sol'.

Ipse archiep's ten' uillam quę uocatur S' Martinus et pertin' ad Estursete, et iacet in ipso hund', et defd' (se) pro uno solin et dim'. T'ra e' In d'nio sunt ii car', et xxxvi bord'.
Ad hanc terram pertin' vii burgenses in cantuaria, redd'tes viii sol' et iiii den'. Ibi v mold' de xx sol', et parua silua.
In hac uilla ten' Radulfus dim' solin de archiep'o, et ibi h't ii car' in d'nio, et v uill'os cum iii bord' h'ntes ii car' et dimid'. TRE ualeb' vii lib' dim' solin S' Mart', et aliud dim' solin ual' semper iiii lib'.

In ROMENEL sunt quat' xx et v burgenses qui pertin' ad ALDINT' M̄ archiep'i, et ualuer' et modo ualent d'no vi lib'.
De ipso M̄ Aldinton iacet in Limes dimid' iugum et dimid' uirga. Archiep's ten' in d'nio, et ibi h't i car' et un' uill'm cum xviii bord' h'ntes i car' et dimid'. Ibi sunt vii pb'ri qui reddunt vii lib' et v sol'. T'ra e' ii car'. Val' et ualuit xii lib', et tamen reddit xv lib'.
De eod' M̄ ten' comes de OW Estotinghes pro i M̄.

Pro uno solin et dim' se defd' TRE, et modo pro uno solin tantum. T'ra e' viii car'. In d'nio sunt ii^{e}, et xxvii uill'i cum xiii bord', h'ntes vii car', et i molin' de xxv den'. Ibi ęccl'a, et xx ac' prati. Silua x porc', et viii serui. TRE: et post: ual' viii lib'. Modo: x lib'.

IN MONIBERGE HVND'.

Ipse archiep's ten' in d'nio LEMINGES. Pro vii solins se defd'. T'ra e' lx car'. In d'nio sunt iiii, et c et unus uill's cum xvi bord' h'ntes lv car'. Ibi ęccl'a et x serui, et i molin' de xxx den', et i piscar' de xl anguill', et xxx ac' prati. Silua c porc'. Ibi pertin' vi burgens' in HEDE. TRE ualeb' xxiiii lib', et postea xl lib', et modo similit', et tamen reddit lx lib'. De hoc M̄ ten' iii ho'es archiep'i ii solins et dim', et dimid' iugum, et ibi h'nt v car' in d'nio, et xx uill'os cum xvi bord', h'ntes v car' et dimid', et i seruum, et ii molin' de vii sol' et vi den', et xl acras prati. Silua xi porc'. Ibi ii ęccl'ę. Int' tot' ual' xi lib'.

IN SELEBRIST HVND'.

Ipse archiep's ten' NEWEDENE. Pro uno solin se defd'. T'ra e' Ibi sunt xxv uill'i cum iiii bord', h'ntes v car'. Ibi est mer-catum de xl sol' v den' minus. Silua xl porc'. Int' totum TRE ualeb' c sol'. Quando recep': xii lib', et modo x lib', et tamen prepositus redd' xviii lib' et x solid'.

:

:

:

DB-Ke-4rb

(TERRA MILITVM EIVS.)   IN ACHESTAN HVND'.

Ansgotus ten' de archiep'o FORNINGEHAM. Pro uno solino se defd'. T'ra e'   In d'nio sunt ii^{e} car', et xiii uill'i cum v bord' h'ntes iii car' et dim'. Ibi vi ac' prati. Silua xx porc', et Ricardus de Tonebrige de ead' silua tntd' h't in sua leuua. TRE ualebat hoc M̄ vii lib', et modo xi lib'. De his h'nt monachi cantuar' iiii lib' ad uestitum suum, et

Radulfus filius Vnspac ten' Elesford de archiep'o. Pro vi solins se defd'. T'ra e'   In d'nio sunt v car', et xxix uill'i cum ix bord' h'nt xv car'. Ibi ii ęccl'ę, et ix serui, et ii mold' de xliii sol', et xxix ac' prati. Silua xx porc'. TRE: ualeb' xvi lib', et modo ual' xx lib'. De hoc M̄ ten' Ricardus de Tonebrige tantum siluę unde exire poss' xx porc', et i molin' de v solid', et unam piscariam in sua leuua.

Malgerius ten' de archiep'o *( ) iii iuga in Orpinton, et pro tanto se defd' extra Orpinton TRE. Modo sunt ii *iug(a) intus Orpint', et tercium extra. T'ra e'   In d'nio i car', et iiii uill'i cum i bord', et iiii seru', et dimid' car', et iii ac' prati, et silua *x(i) porc'. TRE ualeb' xl sol'. Quando recep': xx sol', et modo l sol'.

Haimo uicec' ten' de archiep'o BRIESTEDE. Pro uno solin et dimid' se defd'. T'ra e' x car'. In d'nio sunt ii^{e}, et xxiiii uill'i cum xvi bord' h'nt xii car'. Ibi ęccl'a et xv serui, et ii mold' de xxiiii sol'. Silua quat' xx porc', et de herbagio ix solid' et vi den'. Int' tot' TRE ualebat x lib', et t'ntd' quando recep', et modo xvii lib'. Hoc M̄ tenuit Alnod abb' de archiep'o cantuar'.

Comes de OW ten' de archiep'o OLECVMBE. Pro ii solins *((et dimidio)) se defd' TRE, et modo pro ii tant'. T'ra e' *ix car'. In d'nio sunt ii car', et xxiii uill'i cum viii bord' h'nt vii car'. Ibi ęccl'a et un' mold' de iiii sol', et viii ac' prati. Silua *(quat' xx^{ti}) porc'. Int' tot' TRE ualeb' x lib'. Quando recep': viii lib'. Modo xi lib'. Hoc M̄ tenuit Alfer de arch'.

IN HAIBORNE HVND'.

Radulfus filius turaldi ten' BOLTONE de archiep'o. Pro dimid' solin se defd', et iacet in vi solins de Holinge-borne. *(T'ra e' i car' et dim'. In) d'nio e' una car', et iii uill'i cum ii bord' h'nt i car'. Ibi ęccl'a, et ii ac' prati, et silua xvi porc'. Int' totum ual' et ualuit semper xl solid'.

IN FAVERSHAM HVND'.

Ricardus h'o archiep'i ten' de eo LEVELANT. Pro uno solin se defd'. T'ra e' In d'nio i car', et ii uill'i cum i bord' h'nt i car'. Silua v porc'. TRE et post ual' xxx sol', / modo xx sol'.

Isdem Ricardus ten' de arch' IN BOLTONE HVND'. GRAVENEL. Pro uno solin se defd'. T'ra e' In d'nio e' i car', et viii uill'i cum x bord', h'nt ii car'. Ibi v serui, et x ac' prati, et iiii salinę de iiii sol'. TRE et post: ualuit c sol', modo vi lib'. De his h'nt monachi cant' / xx sol'.

DB-Ke-4va

IN CALEHELLE HVND'.

Godefridus dapifer ten' de archiep'o LERHAM. Pro ii *solin se defd'. T'ra e' In d'nio sunt ii car', et xv uill'i cum ii bord', h'nt iiii car'. Ibi iiii serui, et vi ac' prati, et i molin' de vii sol', et silua de x porc'. Int' tot' ual' viii lib', et tamen reddit xii lib' et x sol'. IN THERHAM HVND'.

Isdem Godefridus ten' de archiep'o in SCAPE dimid' solin. T'ra e' In d'nio i car' cum ii bord', et iiii serui. TRE et post: ualuit xxx sol'. Modo: iiii lib', et tamen reddit c sol'.

Osbernus filius Letard ten' i iugum IN ESTREI HVND'. de archiep'o in BOCOLAND, et ibi h't in d'nio i car', et ual' x sol'.

Will's folet ten' de archiep'o FLENGVESSAM. Pro dim' solin se defd'. Ibi h't vi uill', cum i car' et dim'.

Isd' Will's ten' Estenberge de archiep'o, et pro dim' solin se defd' et ibi h't xii uill'os cum i car' et dimid'.

He terrę ualeb' TRE xl sol'. Quando arch' recep': x sol'. Modo / xxx sol'.

Hugo de Montfort ten' de archiep'o IN HEN HVND'. SALTEODE. Pro vii solins se defd' TRE, et modo pro iii solins. T'ra e' xv car'. In d'nio sunt ii car', et xxxiii uill'i cum xii bord' h'ntes ix car' et dimid'. Ibi ęccl'a et ii serui, et ix mold' de xx solid', et xxxiii ac' prati. Silua quat' xx^{ti} porc'.

Ad hoc M̄ pertin' cc xxv burgenses in Burgo hedę

Int' burgum et M̄ ual' TRE xvi lib'. Quando recep': viii lib', modo int' totum xxix lib' et vi sol' et iiii den'. IN ESTRAITES HD'.

Will's de Eddesham ten' de archiep'o BEREWIC pro uno M̄. Pro dimid' solin se defd'. T'ra e' iii car'. In d'nio sunt ii, et ix uill'i cum ix bord' h'nt i car' et dim'. Ibi xviii ac' prati. Et silua xx porc'. TRE: ualeb' lx sol', et post: xx sol'. Modo vii lib', et tamen redd' xi lib'. IN LAMPORT HVND'.

Robertus de Romenel ten' de archiep'o LAMPORT. Pro uno solin et dim' se defd'. T'ra e' vi car'. In d'nio sunt ii^{e}, et xxix uill'i cum ix bord', h'nt ix car'. Ibi vii salinę de viii sol' et ix den'.

Ad hoc M̄ pertin' xxi *burg's, qui sunt in Romenel, de quibus h't archiep's iii forisfacturas, Latrocinium, pacem fractam, foristellum. Rex uero h't omne seruitium ab eis, et ipsi h'nt omnes consuetudines et alias forisfacturas pro seruitio maris, et sunt in manu regis. TRE et post ualuit x lib', et modo xvi lib'.

* (Will's ten' de archiep'o TILEMANESTONE. Pro uno solin se se defend'. In d'nio s't ii car', et v bord'. Olim xx sol'. Modo ual' xxx solid'.)

:
:
:
:
:
:
:
:

DB-Ke-4vb

(III) (TERRA MONACHORVM ARCHIEP'I.) IN HELMESTREI HVND'.

Archiep's cantuar' ten' ORPINTVN. Pro iii solins se defd' TRE, et modo pro ii solins et dim'. T'ra e' In d'nio sunt ii^{e} car', et xlvi uill'i cum xxv bord' h'ntes xxiii car'. Ibi iii mold' de xvi solid' et iiii den', et x ac' prati, et v^{e} denę siluę de l porc'. *In totis ualent' TRE ualeb' xv lib'. Quando recep': viii lib', et modo xxv lib', et tamen reddit xxviii lib'. Ibi sunt ii^{e} ęccl'ę.

IN LEST DE ELESFORD. IN LITEFELLE HVND'.

Ipse archiep's ten' PECHEHAM. Pro vi solins se defd' TRE, et modo pro v solins et uno iugo. T'ra e' x car'. In d'nio sunt ii^{e}, et xvi uill'i cum xiiii bord' h'nt iiii car' et dim'. Ibi (ęccl'a et) x serui, et i mold', et vi ac' prati. Silua x porc'.

De terra huius M̄ ten' unus h'o archiep'i dimid' solin, et cum his vi solins geldabat TRE, quamuis non pertineret M̄ nisi de scoto, quia libera terra erat.

De *eod' M̄ ten' Ricardus de Tonebrige ii solins et un' iugum, et ibi h't xxvii uill'os h'ntes vii car', et siluam x porc', et tot' ual' iiii lib'.

TRE ualeb' M̄ xii lib'. Quando recep' archiep's: vii lib', et modo quod habet ualet viii lib'. IN AIHORDE HVND'.

Ipse archiep's ten' HOILINGEBORDE. Pro vi solins se defd'. T'ra e' xxiiii car'. In d'nio sunt ii^{e}, et lxi uill's cum xvi bord' h'nt xxiii car'. Ibi ęccl'a et xii serui, et ii mold', et viii ac' prati. Silua xl porc'. Int' tot' TRE et post, ualeb' xx lib', et modo ual' xxx lib'.

Huic M̄ adiacet dimid' solin, *quod nunquam *reddid' scot. Hunc ten' ep's baioc' de archiep'o ad gablum. IN TOLLENTREV HD'.

Ipse archiep's ten' MEPEHAM. Pro x solins se defd' TRE, modo pro vii. T'ra e' xxx car'. In d'nio sunt iiii, et xxv uill'i cum lxxi bord' h'nt xxv car'. Ibi ęccl'a et xvii serui, et xvi ac' prati. Silua x porc'. In totis ualent' TRE ualeb' xv lib' et x sol'. Quando recep': xv lib'. Modo: xxvi lib'. Ricardus de Tonebrige h't in sua leuga quod ual' xviii sol' et vi den'. Siluam xx porc'.

Ipse archiep's ten' FERLAGA. IN MEDESTAN HVND'.

Pro vi solins se defd'. T'ra e' xxvi car'. In d'nio sunt iiii, et xxx^{ta}v uill'i cum lvi bord' h'nt xxx car'. Ibi ęccl'a, et iii mold' de xxvii solid' et viii den'. Ibi viii serui, et vi piscarie de mille cc anguill'. Ibi xii ac' prati. Silua cxv porc'.

De terra huius M̄ ten' Godefridus in feuo dimid' solin, et ibi h't ii car', et vii uill'os cum x bord' h'ntes iii car', et iiii seruos, et i mold' de xx den', et iiii acras prati. Et siluam xxx porc'.
Totum M̄ TRE ualeb' xvi lib', et post t'ntd', et modo: xxii lib'.
*Quod Abel modo ten': vi lib'. *Quod Godefridus: ix lib'. Quod Ricardus in sua leuga: iiii lib'. IN ESSAMELE HVND'.

Ipse archiep's ten' CLIVE. Pro iii solins et dimid' se defd'. T'ra e' vi car'. In d'nio e' una car' et dim', et xx uill'i cum xviii bord' h'nt v car' et dim'. Ibi ęccl'a, et ii serui, et xxxvi ac' prati. Silua de xii den'. TRE ualeb' tot' M̄ vi lib', et post: vii lib', / et modo xvi lib'.
IN BOROWART LEST. IN TANET HVND'.

Ipse archiep's ten' MONOCSTVNE. TRE pro xx solins se defd', et modo pro xviii. T'ra e' xxxi car'. In d'nio sunt iiii, et quat' xx^{ti} et ix uill'i cum xxi bord' h'nt xxvii car'. Ibi ii ęccl'ę, et unum mold' de x solid'. Ibi noua piscaria, et una

DB-Ke-5ra

salina de xv denar'. Silua x porc'.
In totis ualent' ualeb' TRE et post: xx lib', et modo xl lib'.

Ipse archiep's ten' GECHAM. IN DVNEHAMFORT HD'.
Pro iiii solins se defd'. T'ra e' xii car'. In d'nio sunt iii, et xxix uill'i cum lx cot' h'nt xvi car' et dim'. Ibi ęccl'a, et iiii mold' de c solid', et xxxv ac' prati. Et silua xxx porc'.
Tot' M̄ ualeb' TRE et post: xxii lib'. Modo: xxxii lib'.
De terra huius M̄ ten' Will's h'o suus tantum quod ual' vii lib'.

Ipse archiep's ten' NORDEVDE. IN CANTVARIE HVND'.
Pro uno solin se defd'. T'ra e'   In d'nio i car' et dim', et vii uill'i cum xxvi bord' h'nt ii car'. *Huic M̄ pertinent in ciuitate cantuaria c burgenses iii minus, reddentes viii lib' et iiii sol'. Ibi viii mold' de lxxi sol', et xxiiii ac' prati. Silua xxx porc'. Int' tot' ual' et ualuit xvii lib'.

In eod' BOROWART LEST iacet paruum burgum no'e SESELTRE quod proprie pertin' coquinę archiep'i. Quidam no'e Blize ten' de monachis. In d'nio e' una car', et xlviii bord' cum i car'. Ibi ęccl'a, et viii piscarię (cum gablo) de xxv sol'. Silua x porc'. TRE et post: ualuit xxv sol', / et modo c sol'.
IN WIWARLET LEST. IN FAVRESHANT HD'.

Ipse archiep's ten' PRESTETONE. Pro uno solin se defd'. T'ra e' vi car'. In d'nio sunt iii, et xiii uill'i cum xiiii bord' h'nt iii car'. Ibi ęccl'a et i seruus, et i mold' sine censu, et una piscaria de cc l *anguillis. Ibi ii ac' prati. Silua v porc'. TRE et post: ualuit x lib'. Modo: xv lib'.

Ipse archiep's ten' CERTEHAM. IN FELEBERG HVND'.
Pro iiii solins se defd'. T'ra e' xiiii car'. In d'nio sunt ii^{e}, et lx uill'i cum xv cot' h'nt xv car' et dim'. Ibi ęccl'a et i seruus, et v mold' et dim' de lxx sol', et xxx ac' prati, et silua xxv porc'. TRE et quando recep': ualuit xii lib'. Modo: xxv lib', et tamen reddit xxx lib'.

Ipse archiep's ten' GOMERSHAM. Pro viii solins se defd'. T'ra e' xii car'. In d'nio sunt ii^{e}, et lx uill'i cum viii cot' h'nt xvii car'. Ibi ęccl'a et ii serui, et i mold' de xxv sol', et xii ac' prati. Silua xl porc'. TRE et quando recep': ualuit xii lib'. Modo: xx lib', et tamen reddit xxx lib'.

Ipse archiep's ten' CERTH. Pro iii solins IN CERT HVND'. se defd'. T'ra e' xii car'. In d'nio sunt ii^{e}, et xxxvi uill'i cum xi cot' h'nt xxii car' et dim'. Ibi v serui, et ii mold' de vi solid', et salina de vi den', et xxvii ac' prati. Et silua c porc'. TRE et quando recep': ualuit xii lib'. Modo xx lib', et tamen redd' / xxvii lib'.

Ipse archiep's ten'   IN CALEHELLE HVND'.
LITELCERT. TRE se defd' pro iii solins, et modo pro ii hid' et dim'. T'ra e'   In d'nio sunt ii^{e}, et xix uill'i cum v bord' h'nt vii car'. Ibi ii mold' de v sol' et x den', et xi ac' prati, et silua xv porc'.
De terra huius M̄ ten' Will's de archiep'o dimid' solin, et ibi h't in d'nio i car', cum iiii seruis, et x acras prati, et siluam xx porc'.
Totum M̄ ualeb' TRE et post: c sol'. Modo viii lib' et viii sol' et iiii den'. *Quod Will's ten': appreciatur xl sol'.

DB-Ke-5rb

Ipse archiep's ten' WELLE. TRE se defd' pro vii solins, et modo pro v. T'ra e' xviii car'. In d'nio sunt iiii, et quat' xx^{ti} et unus uill's cum v bord' h'nt xii car' et dim'. Ibi vii serui, et un' mold' de xxx den', et xx ac' prati. Silua quat' xx porc'. TRE: ualeb' xvii lib' et xi sol' et iiii den'. Quando recep': t'ntd'. Modo: xxiiii lib' et iiii den', et tamen redd' xl lib'.
IN LEST DE ESTREIA.   IN ESTREI HVND'.

Ipse archiep's ten' ESTREI. Pro vii solins se defd'. T'ra e'   In d'nio sunt iii car', et lxxii uill'i cum xxii bord' h'nt xxiiii car'. Ibi i molin' et dimid' de xxx *solid', et iii salinę de iiii solid', et xviii ac' prati. Silua: x porc'.
Et in Getinge ten' monachi cantuar' dimid' solin et unum iugum et v acras, et ibi h'nt vi uill'os cum ii car' et dim'.
Int' totum TRE et post ualeb' xxvi lib' et x sol' et iiii den' et i ferding. Modo: xxxvi lib' et x solid' et iiii den' et i ferding.

Ipse archiep's ten' EDESHAM. Pro xvii solins se defd'. T'ra e'   In d'nio ii car' sunt et dim', et c uill'i cum xiiii bord' h'nt xxxvi car'. Ibi xiii ac' prati, et iii serui. Silua ad clausuram.
De terra huius M̄ ten' ii milites de archiep'o iii solins, et ibi h'nt in d'nio iiii car', et xviii uill'i cum v bord' h'nt i car'.
Totum M̄ TRE ualeb' xl lib'. Quando recep': similiter. Modo redd' xlvi lib' et xvi solid' et iiii den', et archiep'o c sol' de *Garsunne.
Quod milites ten' ual' xi lib', et tamen redd' xiii lib'.

Ipse archiep's ten' WERAHORNE.   IN HAME HVND'.
Pro uno solin se defd'. T'ra e' ii car'. *(In d'nio) e' i car', et vi uill'i cum iii bord' h'nt i car'. Ibi xii ac' prati, et silua vi porc'. TRE: et post, ual' xx sol', et modo lx sol'.
IN LIMOWART LEST.   IN BLACHEBORNE HVND'.

Ipse archiep's ten' APELDRES. TRE se defd' pro ii solins, et modo pro uno. T'ra e' viii car'. In d'nio sunt iii car', et xxxvii uill'i cum xli bord' h'nt xi car'. Ibi ęccl'a, et vi piscarię de *(iii s)ol' et iiii den'. Ibi ii ac' prati, et silua vi porc'. TRE et post: ualeb' vi lib'. Modo: xvi lib' et xvii sol' / et vi den'.

Ipse archiep's ten'   IN HVND' DE WI.
unum M̄ quod se defd' pro uno solin TRE, et modo pro dimidio. T'ra ii car'. In d'nio e' una, et iii uill'i cum iiii bord' h'nt ii car' et dimid'. Ibi ęccl'a, et i molin' de ii sol', et ii serui,

et vii ac' prati. Silua x porc'. TRE et post: l sol', modo iiii lib'.

Ipse archiep's ten' ASMESLANT. IN MARESC DE ROMEN'. Pro uno solin se defd'. T'ra e' iii car'. Ibi sunt xxi uill's, h'ntes vii car'. Val' et ualuit semper liii sol'. De hac terra h't Will's folet i iugum, et ual' ei per annum x sol'.

SANDWIC suprascript' est, pertin' ad d'nium monachorum.

:

:

:

DB-Ke-5va

(IIII) (TERRA EP'I ROVECESTRE.)

Ep's Rofensis ten' SVDFLETA. Pro vi solins se defd'. T'ra e' xiii car'. In d'nio e' una car', et xxv uill'i cum ix bord' h'ntes xii car'. Ibi vii serui, et xx ac' prati. Silua x porc'. Modo se defd' pro v solins. Ibi est ęccl'a. TRE et post ualuit xi lib'. Modo xxi lib', et tamen redd' xxiiii lib', et unciam auri. De isto M̄ est in Tonebrige tantum de silua et de terra, quod / appreciatur xx^{ti} sol'.

Isdem ep's ten' ESTANES. TRE (se) defd' pro vi solins, et modo pro iiii solins. T'ra e' xi car'. In d'nio sunt ii^{ę}, et xx uill'i cum xii bord' h'nt xi car'. Ibi ęccl'a et iiii serui, et lxx^{ta}ii^{ę} ac' prati, et un' mold' de vi solid' et viii den', et una piscaria de iii sol' et iiii den'. Silua lx porc'. TRE et post, ualeb' xiii lib', et modo xvi lib', et tamen redd' xx lib', et unam unciam auri, et un' Marsuin. Ricardus de Tonebrige ten' de isto M̄ tant' siluæ quod ual' xv sol'.

Isdem ep's ten' FACHESHAM. Pro ii solins se defd'. T'ra e' In d'nio e' una car', et xv uill'i cum iii bord' h'nt iiii car'. Ibi ęccl'a et iii serui, et ii molini de xv sol', et iiii ac' prati. Silua xxx porc'. TRE et post: ua- lebat vii lib'. Modo viii lib'.

Isdem ep's ten' LANGAFEL, et Anschitillus (pb'r) de eo. Pro uno solin se defd'. T'ra e' In d'nio e' una car', et ix uill'i cum vii bord' h'nt ii car'. Valuit lxx sol', et modo c solid'.

Isdem ep's ten' BRONLEI. Pro vi IN BRONLEI HVND'. solins se defd' TRE, et modo pro iii^{bus}. T'ra e' xiii car'. In d'nio sunt ii^{ę} car', et xxx uill'i cum xxvi bord' h'nt xi car'. Ibi i mold' de iiii solid', et ii ac' prati. Silua c porc'. TRE et post: ualuit xii lib' et x sol'. Modo xviii lib', et tamen reddit xxi lib' ii^{os} solid' minus.

Isdem ep's ten' OLDEHAM. Pro vi solins se defd' TRE, et modo pro tribus. T'ra e' v car'. In d'nio sunt ii^{ę}, et xviii uill'i cum xvi bord' h'nt vi car'. Ibi vi serui, et i piscaria, et *(lx) ac' prati. Silua xx porc'. Ibi ęccl'a. TRE et post: ualuit viii lib'. Modo xii lib'.

Isdem ep's ten' MELLINGETES. Pro iii solins se defd' TRE, et modo pro uno et dimid'. T'ra e' iii car'. In d'nio e' una, et v uill'i cum vi bord' h'nt ii car'. Ibi ęccl'a, et un' mold' de ii solid'. Silua xx porc'. TRE et post: ualuit xl sol', et modo iiii lib'.

Isdem ep's ten' TOTESCLIVE. TRE pro iii solins se defd', et modo pro uno solin. T'ra e' iii car'. In d'nio e' un' solin et una car' ibi, et x uill'i cum ii car'. Ibi ęccl'a, et i seruus, et ii^{ę} ac' prati. Et silua x porc'. TRE et post:

ualuit lx sol', et modo vii lib'.

Isdem ep's ten' ESNOILAND. TRE se defd' pro vi solins, et modo pro iii^{bus}. T'ra e' vi car'. In d'nio sunt ii car', et x uill'i cum vi bord' h'nt vi car'. Ibi ęccl'a et v serui, et *iii^{es} mold' de *(xl) solid', et xxx ac' prati. Silua iiii porc'. TRE et post: ualeb' vi lib', et modo ix lib'.

DB-Ke-5vb

Isdem ep's ten' COCLESTANE. IN ESSAMELE HVND'. Pro ii solins et dimid' se defd' TRE, et modo pro ii^{bus} tant'. T'ra e' vi car'. In d'nio sunt ii^{ę}, et xv uill'i cum ix bord' h'nt v car'. Ibi ęccl'a et ii serui, et i molin' de xxx den', et xx ac' prati. TRE et post: ualeb' iiii lib' et x sol', et modo x lib' et x solid'.

Isdem ep's ten' DANITONE. Pro ii solins se defd' TRE, et modo pro dimid' solin. T'ra e' ii car'. In d'nio e' una, et vi uill'i h'nt ibi i car'. Ibi ęccl'a et iiii serui, et iiii ac' prati. Silua xv porc'. TRE et post: ualeb' c sol', et modo vii lib' et xv solid'.

Isdem ep's ten' HALLINGES. TRE se defd' pro vi solins, et modo pro ii^{bus} et dimid'. T'ra e' vii car'. In d'nio sunt iii car', et xv uill'i cum ix bord' h'nt vi car'. Ibi ęccl'a et ii serui, et xxx^{ta} ac' prati, et silua v porc'. *(TRE et post ualb' vii lib'. Modo xvi lib'. Quod Ricardus ten' in sua leu': / ual' vii sol'.)

Isdem ep's ten' FRANDESBERIE. Pro x solins se defd' TRE, et modo pro vii. T'ra e' xv car'. In d'nio sunt v car', et xl uill'i cum xxviii bord' h'nt xi car'. Ibi ęccl'a et ix serui, et un' molin' de xii sol', et xl ac' prati. Silua *(v) porc'. TRE et post ualeb' viii lib', et modo xxv lib'. *Quod Ricardus ten' in sua leuua: ual' x sol'.

Isdem ep's ten' BORCHETELLE. IN HVND' DE ROVECESTRE. TRE pro ii solins se defd', et modo pro uno solin et dimid'. T'ra e' iiii car'. In d'nio sunt ii^{ę} car', et vi uill'i cum iii car'. Ibi l ac' prati, et ii molini de xx^{ti} solid'. TRE et post: ualeb' vi lib', et modo x lib'.

IN ROVECESTRE habuit ep's et h't *adhuc quat' xx^{ti} mansuras terrę quę pertin' ad Frandesberie et Borcstele *propri(a) eius *maneri(a). TRE et post: ualebant iii lib', modo ualent viii lib', et tamen per annum reddunt xi lib' et xiii sol' et iiii denar'.

Isdem ep's ten' ESTOCHES. TRE se defd' IN HOW HVND'. pro v solins, et modo pro tribus. T'ra e' v car'. In d'nio sunt ii car', et x uill'i cum v bord' h'nt iiii car'. Ibi ęccl'a et *iiii^{or} serui, et iiii ac' prati. TRE et post et modo ual' viii lib' et xx^{ti} den', et tamen reddit qui tenet xiii lib' et xx denar'.

Hoc M̄ fuit et est de episcopatu rofensi, sed Goduinus comes TRE emit illud de duobus ho'ibus qui eum teneb' de ep'o, et eo ignorante facta est hęc uenditio. Postmodum uero regnante W rege, diratiocinauit illud Lanfrancus archiep's contra baiocensem ep'm, et inde est modo saisita rofensis ęccl'a.

:
:
:
:
:
:
:
:
:

:
:
:

DB-Ke-6ra

(V) (TERRA EP'I BAIOCENSIS.)

IN LEST DE SVDTONE. IN ACHESTAN HVND'.

De ep'o Baiocensi ten' Hugo de porth HAGELEI. Pro dimidio solin se defd'. T'ra e' In d'nio sunt ii car', et xiiii uill'i cum iii bord' h'nt iiii car'. Ibi iii serui, et xii ac' prati, et un' mold' de xx sol', et una dena siluę de v porc'. Tot' M̄ ual' modo xv lib' de xx^{ti} in ora. In hoc M̄ ten' unus h'o xx^{ti} acras terrę, ualentes per annum v sol'. Vluret uocatur, nec pertin' ad illud M̄, neque potuit habere d'nm pret' regem.

Helto ten' SVINESCAMP de ep'o. Pro x solins se defd'. T'ra e' xiiii car'. In d'nio sunt iii, et xxxiii uill'i cum iii bord' h'nt xiii car'. Ibi unus miles et x serui, et xl ac' prati. Silua iii *porc', et v piscarię de xxx den', et vi^{ta} que seruit ad hallam, et una Heda de v solid' et iiii den'. De silua huius M̄ tenet Ricardus in sua leuua quod ual' iiii solid'. Totum M̄ ualeb' xx lib', et modo ual' xxxii lib'.

Radulfus filius Turaldi ten' de ep'o ERCLEI. Pro uno solin se defd'. T'ra e' In d'nio sunt ii^{ę} car', et ix uill'i cum vi cot' h'nt iii car'. Ibi iii serui, et silua x porc'. Tot' M̄ ualeb' iii lib', et modo c sol'. Quędam mulier tenuit.

Radulfus ten' de ep'o EDDINTONE. Pro dimid' solin. T'ra e' i car', et ibi e', cum iiii bord', et ii seruis, et ibi i molin de *xx(iii sol'). Totum M̄ appreciatur iiii lib'. TRE parum ualeb'. Lestan tenuit de rege E, et post mortem eius uertit se ad Alnod (cilt), et modo est in calumpnia.

Ansgotus de Rouecestre ten' de ep'o MAPLEDESCAM. Pro dimidio solin. T'ra e' In d'nio e' i car', cum uno uill'o et iiii bord', et iiii seruis. Ibi una acra prati, et silua viii porc', et xvi denar' plus. Valuit iiii lib', et modo cx sol'. Eustan tenuit de rege E.

Adam filius Huberti ten' de ep'o REDLEGE. Pro uno solin se defd'. T'ra e' In d'nio sunt ii car', et vi uill'i cum v bord' h'nt ii car'. Ibi v serui, et dim' acra prati, et una dena siluę quam ten' Ricardus de Tonebrige. Valuit (Man') iii lib', et modo iiii lib' et x sol'. *Siuuard tenuit de rege E.

Hugo de port ten' de ep'o EISSE. Pro tribus solins se defd'. T'ra e' In d'nio e' una car', et xii uill'i cum viii bord' h'nt iii car'. Ibi quidam miles h'ns viii int' seruos et ancillas, et terram ad unam car'. Pręter hoc h't Hugo ii^{os} ho'es tenentes dimid' solin, qui poterant TRE ire quolibet sine licentia. Vna terra uocatur Didele, et alia Soninges. T'ra e' ibi ad unam car', et appreciatur xx sol'. Tot' M̄ appreciabatur vii lib', et modo similit'. Quod Ricardus ten' de Tonebrige: xl sol' appreciatur. Rex h't inde ii^{as} denas, quę appreciantur vii sol'. Godric tenuit de rege E.

Goisfridus de Ros ten' LOLINGESTONE. Pro uno solin se defd'. T'ra e' In d'nio e' una car', et iiii uill'i cum uno cot' h'nt ii car'. Ibi vii serui, et vi ac' pasturę. Silua xx porc'. Quando recep': ualeb' lx sol', et modo c sol'. Rex h't in manu sua quod ual' x solid'. Brixe cilt tenuit de rege E.

DB-Ke-6rb

De ep'o ten' Malgerius LOLINGESTONE. Pro dim' solin se defd'. T'ra e'   In d'nio e' una car', et iii uill'i cum vi bord' h'nt i car'. Ibi v ac' prati. Totum M̄ ualeb' lx sol', modo lxx sol'. De isto M̄ h't Rex quod ual' x solid'. Bruning tenuit de rege E.

Isdem Malgerius ten' in FERLINGEHAM dimid' iugum terrȩ. T'ra e' iii boum. Ibi sunt ii boues, cum uno bord', et ii ac' prati. Valuit et ual' xv sol'. Brunesune tenuit, et potuit cum terra sua uertere se quo uoluit. De hoc M̄ ten' rex quod ual' viii sol'.

Isdem Malgerius ten' in Pinnedene dimid' solin de ep'o. T'ra e' vii boum. Ibi e' una car' cum vi uill'is, et vi ac' prati. Valuit et ual' xvi sol'. Aluret tenuit TRE, et potuit se uertere quo uoluit.

Osbernus pastforeire ten' in Lolingeston dimid' solin de ep'o. T'ra e'   In d'nio e' i car', et iii uill'i cum i bord' *et i seruo h'nt i car'. Ibi v ac' prati. Silua v porc', et un' molin' de xv solid' et cl anguill'. Rex h't siluam pro nouo dono ep'i, et ual' iii sol'. Totum M̄ ualeb' lx sol'. Modo lxxvii sol'. Seuuart sot tenuit TRE, et potuit se uertere cum terra sua quo uoluit.

Wadardus ten' de ep'o dimid' solin in Ferningeham. T'ra e' iii car'. In d'nio sunt ii^{e} car', cum uno uill'o et ii cot', et v seruis. Ibi dimid' mold' de v solins, et iiii ac' prati. Silua v porc'. Excepto *(isto) dim' solin ten' Wadardus dimid' iugum in ead' uilla, quod nunquam se quietauit apud regem. Int' totum ualuit iiii lib', et modo vi lib'. Estan tenuit TRE, et potuit se uertere quo uoluit.

Isd' Wadard ten' de ep'o MALPLESCAMP. Pro dim' solin se defd'. T'ra e' ii car'. Ibi sunt cum i uill'o et iiii bord' et v seruis, et una acra et dim' prati. Silua viii porc' et xvi denar'. Valuit iii lib', et modo vi lib'. Vltanus tenuit sub Heraldo.

Ernulfus de Hesding ten' FERNINGEHAM. Pro iii iugis se defd'. T'ra e' ii car'. Ibi sunt modo vi boues cum ii uill'is et iii bord'. Ibi un' mold' de x sol', et viii ac' prati. Pastura c ouibus. Silua x porc' et xiiii den'. Rex h't de silua huius M̄ quod ual' viii sol'. Totum M̄ ualuit iii lib', et modo xl solid'. Dering tenuit, et potuit se uertere quo uoluit.

Anschitillus de ros ten' TARENT de ep'o. Pro dim' solin se defd'. T'ra e' i car' et dim'. In d'nio e' una, et iiii uill'i cum iiii bord' h'nt i car'. Ibi iii ac' prati, et ii molini de xviii sol'. Silua iii porc'. Rex h't de isto M̄ pro nouo dono ep'i quod ual' x denar'. Totum M̄ ualuit et ual' c sol'. Aluric tenuit de rege E.

In ead' uilla h't isdem *(A) i manerium de ep'o. Pro dim' solin se defd'. T'ra e' i car' et dimid'. Ibi v uill'i et v bord' et un' mold' de xx solid'. Ibi iii ac' prati, et i^{us} seruus. Totum M̄ ualuit lx sol', et modo lxx solid'. Osiert tenuit de rege E.

Isdem Anschitillus ten' de ep'o HORTVNE. Pro uno solin se / defd'.

DB-Ke-6va

T'ra e' iii car', et ibi sunt iiii bord', et un' mold' de v sol', et vi ac' prati. Ibi ęccl'a est, et silua iii porc'. Rex h't pro nouo dono ep'i tant' siluę de isto M̄, quod ual' v sol'. Totum M̄ ualuit iiii lib', et modo vi lib'. Godel de Brixi tenuit, et potuit se uertere cum hac terra quo uoluit.

Isdem Anschitillus ten' de ep'o in eod' M̄ dimid' solin. T'ra e' un' car', et ibi e' in d'nio, et viii uill'i cum vi bord' h'nt i car'. Ibi i molin' de xv sol', et ix ac' prati. Silua v porc'. Totum M̄ ualuit xl sol', et modo lx (sol'). Ording tenuit de rege.

Isdem Anschitillus ten' de ep'o in eod' M̄ unum solin. T'ra e' iii car'. In d'nio est una car', et viii uill'i cum ii car'. Ibi unus seruus, et viii ac' prati, et dim' mold' de v solid'. Silua xv porc'. Totum M̄ ualuit iiii lib', et modo c solid'. Aluuardus tenuit de Heraldo. Hęc iiii^{or} Maneria sunt modo pro uno M̄.   IN LITELAI HVND'.

* Robertus Latin' ten' de ep'o LOISNES. T'ra e' xvii car'. In d'nio e' una, et lx uill'i cum iii bord' h'nt xv car'. Ibi ii serui, et iii cot', et iii piscarię de iiii sol', et xxx ac' prati. Silua xx porc'. TRE: ual' xx lib'. Quando ep's recep': xviii lib', et modo xxii lib', et tamen qui ten' redd' xxx lib'. Hoc M̄ se defd' TRE pro x solins, et modo pro iiii solins. Azor tenuit.

Ansgotus ten' de ep'o HOV, quod se defd' pro uno solin. T'ra e'   In d'nio e' una car', et v uill'i cum i car' et dimid', et un' mold' de x sol'. Ibi ii cot' et unus seruus, et xii ac' prati. Silua iii porc'. TRE ualeb' lx sol'. Quando recep': t'ntd', et modo iiii lib'. Anschil de rege E tenuit.

Abb' S' Augustini ten' de ep'o baiocensi PLVMESTEDE. Pro ii solins et uno iugo se defd'. T'ra v car'. In d'nio e' una car', et xvii uill'i *cum iii bord' h'nt iiii car'. Ibi silua v porc'. TRE: ualeb' x lib'. Quando recep': viii lib', et modo t'ntd', et tamen qui ten' redd' xii lib'. Brixi cilt tenuit de rege E.   IN HELMESTREI HVND'.

Malgerius ten' de ep'o ROCHELEI. Pro uno solin se defd'. T'ra e'   In d'nio e' una car' et dimid', et x uill'i cum x bord' h'nt ii car' et dim'. Ibi i molin' de xii solid'. Silua iii porc'. TRE ualeb' iiii lib'. Quando recep': iii lib', et modo c solid'. Aluuard tenuit de rege E.

Ernulfus de hesding ten' de ep'o CIRESFEL. Pro ii solins se defd'. T'ra e'   In d'nio sunt ii car', et xx uill'i cum iiii bord' h'nt viii car'. Ibi iiii serui, et un' molin' de x sol', et x ac' prati, et silua x porc'. TRE: ualeb' xvi lib', et post: xii lib', et modo xxv lib', et tamen qui ten' redd' xxxv lib'. Tochi tenuit de rege E.

Adam filius Huberti ten' de ep'o SVDCRAI. Pro uno solin se defd'. T'ra e'   In d'nio sunt ii car', et xiiii uill'i cum i bord' h'nt iiii car'. Ibi vi serui, et x ac' prati. Silua x porc'. TRE ualeb' vi lib', et post: iiii lib', et modo x lib'. Toli tenuit de rege E.

Isdem Adam ten' de ep'o WICHEHAM. Pro uno solin se defd'.

DB-Ke-6vb

T'ra e'   In d'nio sunt ii car', et xxiiii uill'i h'nt iiii car'. Ibi xiii serui, et una ęccl'a, et un' molin' de xx den', et una silua de x porc'. TRE ualeb' viii lib', et post: vi lib', et modo xiii lib'. Godric (fil' carle) tenuit de rege E.

Goisfridus de ros ten' de ep'o LASELA. Pro vii solins se defd'. T'ra e' In d'nio sunt iii car', et xxxi uill's cum xiiii bord' h'nt xvi car'. Ibi *x^{cem} serui, et una piscar' de quat' xx^{ti} anguill' et x. Silua lxxv porc'. Totum M̄ ualeb' TRE xxx lib'. Quando recep': xvi lib', et modo xxiiii lib' quod Goisfridus ten'. Ricardus de Tonebrige quod ten' in leuua sua: appreciatur vi lib'. Quod rex tenet de hoc manerio: xxii sol'. Brixi cilt tenuit de rege E.

Anschitil de ros ten' de ep'o CRAIE. Pro dim' solin se defd'. T'ra e' In d'nio e' i car', et vii uill'i cum vi bord' h'nt unam car'. Ibi ęccl'a, et una acra prati, et iii ac' pasturę. TRE et post: ualeb' iiii lib', et modo iii lib'. Leuric tenuit de rege E.

Isdem Anschitillus ten' de ep'o aliam CRAIE. Pro dim' solin se defd'. T'ra e' In d'nio e' una car', et vii uill'i cum v bord' h'nt i car'. Ibi i molin' de xlii den', et v serui. Silua vii porc'. TRE et post: ualuit iiii lib', et modo: iii lib'. / de Alnod cilt. *Hę( ) duę terrę fuer' ii M̄ TRE, et modo sunt in uno M̄. Aluuinus tenuit

IN DIMIDIO LEST DE SVDTONE. IN GRENVIZ HVND'.

Ep's Lisiacensis ten' de ep'o baiocensi GRENVIZ. Pro ii solins se defd'. T'ra e' In d'nio sunt ii car', et *(xxiiii uill'i) h'nt iiii car', et iiii bord' et i cot', et v serui. Ibi iiii mold' de lxx sol', et xxii ac' prati, et xl ac' pasturę. Et silua x porc'. Hi ii^{o} solins TRE fuer' ii M̄. Vnum tenuit Heroldus (com'), et alium Brixi, et modo sunt in uno. TRE et post: (simul) ualebant viii lib', et modo appreciantur xii lib'.

Haimo (uicec') ten' de ep'o ALTEHAM. Pro uno solin et dim' se defd'. T'ra e' xii car'. In d'nio sunt ii car', et xlii uill'i cum xii bord' h'nt xi car'. Ibi ix serui, et xxii ac' prati. Silua l porc'. TRE ualeb' xvi lib'. Quando recep': xii lib', et modo xx lib'. Aluuoldus tenuit de rege.

Filius Turaldi de Rouecest' ten' de ep'o WITENEMERS. Pro uno solin se defd'. T'ra e' iiii car'. In d'nio sunt ii^{e} car', et xi uill'i cum ii cot' h'nt ii car'. Ibi iiii ac' prati. Silua xv porc'. TRE ualeb' c sol'. Quando recep': iiii lib', et modo c sol'. Anschil tenuit de rege E.

Walterius de douuai ten' de ep'o LEE. Pro dim' solin se defd'. T'ra e' iiii car'. In d'nio sunt ii car', et xi uill'i cum ii cot' h'nt ii car'. Ibi ii serui, et v ac' prati. Silua x porc'. TRE et quando ep's recep': ual' iii lib'. Modo: c sol'. Aluuin tenuit / de rege.

Will's filius Ogerii ten' de ep'o CERLETONE. Pro uno solin se defd'. T'ra e' v car'. In d'nio e' i car', et xiii uill'i h'nt iii car'. Ibi ii serui, et viii ac' prati. Silua v porc'. TRE et post, et modo: ual' vii lib'. Hanc terram tenuer' de rege ii^{o} fr's pro ii^{bus} maneriis, Goduin et Aluuard.

Isd' Will's ten' de ep'o CRAI. IN HELMESTREI HVND'. Pro dimid' solin se defd'. T'ra e' In d'nio e' una car', et viii uill'i cum i car' et dimid', et iiii cot', et i molin' de x solid'.

DB-Ke-7ra

Ibi unus seruus, et silua vi porc'. TRE ualeb' iiii lib', et post: iii lib'. Modo: iiii lib'. Goduinus (fot) tenuit de rege E.

Anschitillus ten' de ep'o CROCTVNE. Pro uno solin et uno iugo se defd'. T'ra e' In d'nio nichil est, *sed iii uill'i et iiii bord' ibi sunt. TRE et post ualebat c solid', et modo vi lib'. Aluuinus tenuit hanc terram de rege E, pro duobus M̄.

Gislebertus maminot ten' de ep'o CODEHAM. Pro iiii solins se defd'. T'ra e' x car'. In d'nio sunt iiii, et xv uill'i cum vi bord' h'nt vi car'. Ibi ęccl'a, et xi serui, et ii molini de *xiii(i) solid' et ii denar'. Silua xl porc'. TRE ualeb' xx lib', et post: xvi lib'. Modo: xxiiii lib'.

Isdem Gislebertus ten' de ep'o CHESTAN. Pro dimid' solin se defd'. T'ra e'   In d'nio e' i car', et iiii uill'i cum i car'. Ibi silua v porc'. TRE et post: ualeb' lx sol'. Modo: xl solid'. Sberne biga tenuit de rege E.

Hugo nepos herberti ten' de ep'o SENTLINGE. Pro uno solin et dim' se defd'. T'ra e'   In d'nio sunt ii car', et xx uill'i cum ii car'. Ibi ęccl'a et ix serui, et vi ac' prati, et xx ac' pasturę. Silua viii porc'. TRE ualeb' viii lib', et post: vi lib'. Modo: viii lib'. Bonde tenuit de archiep'o.

Ansgotus de Rouec' ten' de ep'o BACHEHAM.   IN BRVNLEI HD'. Pro ii solins se defd'. T'ra e' viii car'. In d'nio sunt ii, et xxii uill'i cum viii bord' h'nt viii car' et dimid'. Ibi xii ac' prati, et iiii serui, et un' mold', et silua lx porc'. TRE et post: ualeb' ix lib'. Modo: xiii lib'. Anschil tenuit / de rege E.

IN LEST DE ELESFORD.   IN LAVROCHESFEL HD'.

Adam ten' de ep'o LELEBVRNE. Pro ii solins se defd'. T'ra e'   In d'nio sunt iii car', et xvi uill'i cum ii bord' h'nt vii car'. Ibi ęccl'a et x serui, et un' molin' de vii solid', et xii ac' prati. Silua l porc'. TRE: ualeb' viii lib'. Quando recep': vii lib'. Modo: viii lib'. Ricardus de Tonebrige ten' in sua leuua quod ual' xxiiii sol'. Rex ten' pro nouo dono ep'i quod ual' xxiiii solid' et ii den'. Hoc M̄ tenuit Turgis de Goduino comite.

Anschitil ten' de ep'o ELENTVN. Pro uno solin se defd'. T'ra e' iii car'. In d'nio sunt ii, et xv uill'i cum ii bord' h'nt i car' et dimid'. Ibi ęccl'a et ii serui, et dimid' molin' et una dena de xv sol'. Silua viii porc', et una acra prati. TRE ualeb' c sol'. Quando recep': lx sol'. Modo: c solid'. Vluric tenuit de Alnod cilt.

Haimo (uicec') ten' de ep'o DICTVNE. Pro uno solin se defd'. T'ra e' iiii car'. In d'nio sunt ii^{e}, et xx uill'i cum v bord' h'nt iii car'. Ibi ęccl'a et vi serui, et un' molin' de x solid', et viii ac' prati, et xxxv ac' pasturę. Silua vi porc'. TRE: ualeb' viii lib'. Quando recep': c sol'. Modo viii lib'. Sbern tenuit de rege E.

Vitalis ten' de ep'o SIFLETONE. Pro iii iugis se defd'. T'ra e' i car'. In d'nio i car' et dimid', et vi uill'i cum uno bord' h'nt dim' car'. Ibi vi serui, et i molin' de x / solid'.

DB-Ke-7rb

Ibi x ac' prati, et xxx ac' pasturę. TRE ualeb' xl sol'. Quando recep': iiii lib'. Modo: c solid'. Hanc (terram) tenuer' TRE duo ho'es in paragio, Leuuinus et Vluuinus, et potuer' cum terra sua se uertere quo uoluer'.

Radulfus filius Turoldi ten' de ep'o AIGLESSA. Pro iii iugis se defd'. T'ra e'   In d'nio e' i car', et vii uill'i cum xiiii bord' h'nt i car'. Ibi i seruus, et x ac' prati. Silua x porc'. TRE et post: ualeb' iii lib'. Modo iiii lib'. Ricardus quod ten' in sua leuua: xv den'. Rex *v(iii) solid' et v den' pro nouo dono ep'i. Et in Rouecest' habuit ep's iii domos de xxxi denar', quas cepit de isto M̅ in (sua) manu. Hoc M̅ tenuit Alnod cilt.

Hugo de port ten' de ep'o PELLESORDE. Pro dimid' solin se defd'. T'ra e' In d'nio e' i car', et unus uill's cum iiii bord' h'nt iii boues. Ibi ęccl'a et ii serui, et v ac' prati, et una ac' pasturę. TRE ualeb' xx sol'. Quando recep': xxx sol'. Modo: xl sol'. Godric tenuit de rege E.

Isdem Hugo ten' de ep'o RIESCE. Pro ii solins et dim' se defd'. T'ra e' v car'. In d'nio sunt ii^{e}, et x uill'i cum ii bord' h'nt iii car'. Ibi ęccl'a et x serui, et i molin' de x sol', et ix ac' prati. Silua v porc'. TRE ualeb' viii lib'. Quando recep': c sol'. Modo vi lib'. Aluric tenuit de rege E.

Isdem Hugo ten' de ep'o OFEHAM. Pro uno solin se defd'. T'ra e' iii car'. In d'nio nichil. Ibi vi uill'i cum i bord' h'nt ii car'. Ibi i molin' de l den', et iii serui, et iiii ac' prati. Silua x porc'. TRE ualeb' xl sol'. Quando recep': xx sol'. Modo: xxx sol'. Godric tenuit de rege E.

Rannulfus de columbels ten' de ep'o ESSEDENE. Pro uno solin se defd'. T'ra e' In d'nio e' una car', et xix uill'i cum iii bord' h'nt iii car'. Ibi iii serui, et viii ac' prati. TRE: ual' iii lib'. Quando recep': iiii lib'. Modo v lib'. Leuuinus (com') tenuit.

Rotbertus Latin' ten' ad firmam de Rege TOTINTVNE, de nouo dono ep'i baioc'. Pro dim' solin se defd'. T'ra e' unius car' et dim'. In d'nio e' una, et *(i)i(i^{es}) uill'(i) cum ix bord' h'nt dim' car'. Ibi iiii serui, et v ac' prati. Silua ii porc'. TRE ualeb' xxx sol'. Quando recep': xx sol'. Modo xl sol'. Vlnod tenuit de rege E.

Isdem Rotbertus ten' in Totintune ad firmam de rege i iugum, et istud est de nouo dono ep'i baioc', et ibi nil est nisi ii^{e} ac' prati. Val' et ualuit semper x sol'. Goduinus tenuit de rege E.

Radulfus filius Turaldi ten' de ep'o EDDINTVNE. Pro ii solins se defd' *((et dimid')). T'ra e' v car'. In d'nio sunt ii^{e}, et vi uill'i cum ix bord' h'nt i car'. Ibi ęccl'a et x serui, et ii molini de xi solid' et ii den', et xii ac' prati. Silua x porc'. TRE ualeb' viii lib'. Quando recep': c sol'. Modo: vi lib'. Agelred tenuit de rege E.

DB-Ke-7va

Radulfus filius Turoldi ten' de ep'o IN TOLLENTREV HD'. MELETVNE. Pro uno solin et iii iugis se defd'. T'ra e' iiii car'. In d'nio e' una, et xxi uill's cum ii bord' h'nt ii car'. Ibi ęccl'a, et i molin' de xlix den', et Heda de xx solid', et iii serui. TRE ualeb' iiii lib', et post: iii lib'. Modo vi lib'. Ricardus quod ten' in sua leuua: v sol' in una silua. / Leuuinus com' tenuit.

Isdem Radulfus ten' de ep'o LEDESDVNE. Pro ii solins et dimidio et dim' iugo se defd'. T'ra e' vi car'. In d'nio sunt ii^{e}, et xvii uill'i cum iiii bord' h'nt v car'. Ibi ęccl'a et i seruus, et iii ac' prati et dimid'. Silua xx^{ti} porc'. TRE ualeb' vi lib', et post: c solid'. Modo viii lib'. Ricardus quod h't in sua leuua: xx den'. Ep's ten' in sua manu intra ciuitatem *Rouecest' iiii domos ad hoc M̄ pertin', de quibus h't ix sol' et x den'. / Leuuinus (com') ten'

Herbertus filius Iuonis ten' de ep'o GRAVESHAM. Pro ii solins et uno iugo se defd'. T'ra e' iiii car'. In d'nio est una, et iiii uill'i cum viii seruis h'nt ii boues. Ibi ęccl'a et i heda. TRE ualeb' x lib'. Quando recep': t'ntd'. Modo xi lib'. Hoc M̄ fuer' iii[a] M̄ TRE. Leuric et Vluuinus et Goduinus tenuer'. Nunc est in unum.

Wadardus ten' de ep'o NOTESTEDE. Pro ii solins se defd'. T'ra e' ii car'. In d'nio e' una, et ibi iiii bord', et ęccl'a, et iiii serui. Silua iii porc'. TRE ualeb' iiii lib'. Quando recep': iii lib'. Modo v lib'. Vlstan tenuit de rege E.

Anschitilus ten' de ep'o OFEHAM. IN LAVROCHESFEL HD'. Pro uno solin se defd'. T'ra e' In d'nio e' i car', et vi uill'i cum ii bord' h'nt i car'. Ibi iiii serui, et i molin' de x sol', et vii ac' prati. Silua x porc'. Et in ciuitate Rouec' i domus reddens xxx den'. TRE ualeb' M̄ c sol'. Quando recep': iiii lib'. Modo iiii lib' et ix solid'. Ricardus de Tonebrige quod ten': xi sol' ual'. Vluric tenuit de Alnod cilt.

Radulfus de Curbespine ten' de ep'o BERLINGE. Pro vi solins se defd'. T'ra e' In d'nio e' una car', et x uill'i cum xiiii bord' h'nt vi car'. Ibi ęccl'a, et vi serui, et i molin' de x sol' et ccc et xxx anguill', et piscaria de lx anguill'. Ibi xii ac' prati, et pastura l animalibus. Silua xl porc'. TRE ualeb' xii lib'. Quando recep': vi lib'. Modo: xii lib'. Sbern biga tenuit de rege E.

Isdem Radulfus ten' de ep'o BORHAM. Pro vi solins se defd'. T'ra e' viii car'. In d'nio sunt ii, et xv uill'i cum xx bord' h'nt vi car'. Ibi ęccl'a et vii serui, et i molin' de vi sol', et x ac' prati. Silua xx porc'. TRE ualeb' x lib', et quando recep': t'ntd'. Modo: xii lib'. Ep's de Rouecest' h't domos de hoc M̄, et ual' vii solid'. Hoc M̄ tenuit Leuuinus (com') IN LITEFELLE HVND'.

Corbinus ten' de ep'o PECHEHAM. Pro ii solins se defd'. T'ra e' vi car'. In d'nio e' una, et xii uill'i h'nt v car', et viii bord' et v serui, et iii ac' prati. Silua x porc'. TRE et post: ualeb' xii lib'. Modo: viii lib', *(et tamen redd' xii lib'.) Rex h't de hoc M̄

DB-Ke-7vb

tres denas, ubi manent iiii uill'i, et ual' xl sol'. Leuuinus (com') tenuit.

Ricardus de Tonebrige ten' de ep'o HASLOW. Pro vi solins se defd'. T'ra e' xii car'. In d'nio sunt iii, et xlvii uill'i cum xv bord' h'nt xv car'. Ibi ęccl'a et x serui, et ii molini de xi *solid', et xii piscarię de vii solid' et vi den', et xii ac' prati. Silua lx porc'. TRE et post, et modo, ual' xxx lib'. Eddeua tenuit de rege / E.

Radulfus filius Turoldi ten' de ep'o dimid' solin in ESTOCHINGE-BERGE. TRE tenuer' ii liberi ho'es et modo similit', et ual' xx sol'. IN LEST DE ELESFORD. IN WACHELESTAN HVND'.

Ricardus de Tonebrige ten' de ep'o TIVEDELE. Pro uno iugo se defd'. T'ra e' i car', et ibi e' in d'nio, et ęccl'a. Et silua ii porc'. Val' et ualuit semper xv sol'. Eddeua tenuit de rege.

Hugo nepos Herberti ten' de ep'o IN AIHORDE HVND'. HARIARDESHAM. Pro ii solins se defd'. T'ra e' vi car'. In d'nio *( ) xviii uill'i cum x bord' h'nt iiii car'. Ibi ęccl'a et xi serui, et ii molini de xi solid' et vi den', et vii ac' prati.

Silua xv porc'. TRE: ualeb' x lib'. Quando recep': viii lib'. Modo: x lib'. Osuuardus tenuit de rege E.

Isdem Hugo ten' de ep'o FEREBVRNE. Pro uno solin se defd'. T'ra e' ii car'. In d'nio iiii uill'i cum i car' et dimid', et ii molini de xl den'. TRE ualeb' iiii lib'. Post et modo: iii lib'. Aluuinus tenuit de Goduino (com').

Isdem Hugo ten' de ep'o i iugum liberę terrę in SELESBVRNE, et ibi h't dimid' car' cum i bord' et v seruis, et una acra prati et dim'. Val' et ualuit semper xx sol'. Aluuinus tenuit de Goduino comite.

Isdem Hugo et Adeloldus camerarius ten' de ep'o FREDENESTEDE. Pro uno solin se defd'. T'ra e' iii car'. In d'nio iii uill'i h'nt vii boues. Ibi ęccl'a et ii ac' prati et dimid', et silua ii porc'. Val' et ualuit semper xx sol'. Leuuinus tenuit de rege E.

Adelold ten' de ep'o ESLEDES. Pro iii solins se defd'. T'ra e' xii car'. In d'nio sunt ii car', et xxviii uill'i cum viii bord' h'nt vii car'. Ibi ęccl'a et xviii serui. Ibi ii arpendi uineę et viii ac' prati. Silua xx porc', et v molini uillanorum. TRE ualeb' xvi lib'. Similit' quando recep'. Modo xx lib', et tamen reddit xxv lib'. Leuuinus (com') tenuit. De hoc M̄ h't abb' S' Augustini dimid' solin, quod ual' x sol', pro excambio parchi ep'i baioc'. Comes de ow h't iiii denas de isto M̄, quę ual' xx solid'.

Ansgotus de Rouecest' ten' de ep'o AVDINTONE. Pro ii solins se defd'. T'ra e' iii car' et dimid'. In d'nio sunt ii^{e}, et vii uill'i cum v bord' h'nt i car' et dim'. Ibi ęccl'a et iiii serui, et vi ac' prati, et i molin' de iiii sol' et ii den'. Silua x porc'. TRE et post: ualuit iiii lib'. Modo vii lib'. Goduinus et Aluuinus tenuer' de rege E pro ii^{bus} M̄.

Isdem An(s)got ten' de ep'o STOCHINGEBERGE. Pro ii solins se defd'. T'ra e' In d'nio e' i car', et v uill'i cum ix bord' h'nt ii car'. Ibi ęccl'a et ii serui, et i molin' de lxiiii den'. Silua xv porc'. TRE et post, ualuit iiii lib'. Modo vi lib'. Elueua tenuit de rege E.

Hugo de port ten' ALNOITONE. Pro iii solins se defd'. T'ra e' viii car'. In d'nio sunt ii car', et xviii uill'i cum vi bord' h'nt vi car'. Ibi ęccl'a, et viii serui, et ii molini et dim' de xvii / solid'.

DB-Ke-8ra

Ibi v ac' prati. Silua xl porc'. TRE ualeb' ix lib', et t'ntd' quando recep'. Modo x lib', et tamen reddit xii lib'. Huic M̄ adiacent iii mansiones terrę in Rouecestre, et redd't v sol' per annum. Osuuardus tenuit de rege E.

Adam filius Huberti ten' de ep'o SVDTONE. Pro iiii solins se defd'. T'ra e' vii car'. In d'nio sunt ii^{e}, et xviii uill'i cum v bord' h'nt iiii car'. Ibi ęccl'a et iiii ac' prati, et i molin' Silua l porc'. TRE ualeb' xii lib'. Quando recep': x lib'. Modo: xiiii lib', et tamen reddit xviii lib'. Leuuinus (com') tenuit.

Isdem Adam ten' de ep'o CERTH. Pro iii solins se defd'. T'ra e' viii car'. In d'nio e' una, et xx uill'i cum v bord' h'nt vi car'. Ibi ęccl'a et viii serui, et vi ac' prati. Silua l porc'. Ibi iii arpend' uineę, et parcus siluatic' bestiarum. TRE et post, et modo: ual' xii lib'. Alnod (cilt) tenuit.

Isdem Adam ten' de ep'o SVDTONE. Pro uno solin et dimid' se defd'. T'ra e' viii car'. In d'nio sunt ii^{e}, et xv uill'i cum ix bord' h'nt iiii car'. Ibi ęccl'a et x serui, et viii ac' prati. Silua l porc'. TRE et post: ualeb' x lib'. Modo xii lib', et tamen redd' xviii lib'. Leuenot tenuit / de rege E.

Isdem Adam ten' de ep'o BOGELEI. Pro ii solins se defd'. T'ra e' ii car' et dim'. In d'nio e' una car', et ii uill'i cum ii bord' h'nt dimid' car'. Ibi ęccl'a et iiii serui, et i molin' de v solid', et vi ac' prati. Silua xx porc'.
De isto M̄ h't unus h'o Adam un' solin et uocatur Merlea, et ibi h't i car', et iiii uill'os cum i car', et eccl'am, et ii seruos, et siluam iiii porc'.
Totum M̄ TRE ualeb' vi lib', et post: t'ntd'. Modo vii lib'. / Turgis tenuit de rege E.

Isdem Adam ten' de ep'o LANGVELEI. Pro uno solin et dim' se defd'. T'ra e' iiii car'. In d'nio sunt ii^{e}, et vii uill'i cum v bord' h'nt iii car'. Ibi ęccl'a et vii serui, et iii ac' prati. Silua xxv porc'. TRE ualeb' lx sol'. Quando recep': l sol'. Modo: lx solid'. Turgis tenuit de rege E.

Isdem Adam ten' de ep'o OTRINGEDENE. Pro dimid' solin se defd'. T'ra e' ii car'. In d'nio e' una, et ii uill'i cum iiii bord' h'nt dim' car'. Ibi ii serui, et una acra prati. Silua v porc'. TRE et post, ualuit x sol'. Modo xxx sol'.
Huic M̄ pertin' ii mansure terrę in Cantuaria de xii denar'. Aluuardus tenuit de rege E hoc M̄.

Isdem Adam ten' de ep'o ES(T)SELVE. Pro dimid' solin se defd'. T'ra e' i car', et ibi e' in d'nio, cum uno uill'o et uno bord', et v seruis. Ibi iiii ac' prati. Silua iiii porc'.
TRE et post, et modo: ual' xx solid'. Godric tenuit / de rege E.

Will's filius Roberti ten' de ep'o WESTSELVE. Pro uno solin se defd'. T'ra e' iii car' et dimid'. In d'nio sunt ii^{e}, et quidam francig' cum x uill'is et i bord', h'nt i car' et dim'. Ibi v serui, et i acra prati, et un' molin' de xv den'. Silua xv porc'.
TRE et post, et modo: ual' iiii lib'. Eddid tenuit de rege E. Huic M̄ pertineb' in cantuaria TRE una domus, reddens xxv denar'.

DB-Ke-8rb

Hugo nepos Herberti ten' de ep'o BOLTONE. Pro uno solin se defd'. T'ra e' ii car'. In d'nio nichil, sed v uill'i h'nt i car' ibi, et ii ac' prati. Silua xx porc'. Ibi ęccl'a.
TRE et post: ualeb' viii lib'. Modo: vi lib'.
Aluuinus tenuit de Goduino (com').

Isdem Hugo ten' de ep'o GODESELLE. Pro uno solin se defd'. T'ra e' ii car'. In d'nio e' una, et v uill'i h'nt i car' et dim'. Ibi eccl'a, et ii serui, et ii ac' prati, et silua x porc'.
TRE et post, et modo: ual' iiii lib'. Eduuinus tenuit de rege E, et potuit ire cum terra sua quo uoluit.

Isdem Hugo ten' de ep'o WINCHELESMERE.
Pro dimid' solin se defd'. T'ra e' i car', et ibi e' in d'nio cum iii seruis, et ęccl'a, et silua v porc'. Et TRE in cantuaria iii domus pertineb' huic M̄ redd'tes xl den'.
Tot' TRE ualeb' c sol', et post, et modo: xl sol'.
Vluiet tenuit de rege E, et potuit ire quo libuit.

Isdem Hugo ten' de ep'o ESTSELVE. Pro dimid' solin se defd'. T'ra e' i car', et ibi e' in d'nio, cum i uill'o et uno bord', et ii seruis. Ibi iiii ac' prati, et silua iiii porc'.
TRE et post, et modo: ual' xl sol'. Vluiet tenuit de rege E.

Goisfridus de Ros ten' de ep'o OTEHAM. Pro uno solin et uno iugo se defd'. T'ra e' ii car' et dimid'. In d'nio e' una, et ix uill'i cum iii bord' h'nt i car'. Ibi eccl'a, et ii serui, et i molin' de v solid', et iii ac' prati. Silua viii porc'. TRE ualeb' iiii lib'. Quando recep': iii lib'. Modo: iiii lib'. Aluuinus tenuit de rege E.

Rotbertus Latin' ten' ad firmam HERBRETITOV. Adeloldus tenuit de ep'o. Pro uno solin se defd'. T'ra e'   In d'nio e' una car', et ii uill'i cum i bord' h'nt ii a'alia, et ibi iiii ac' prati. TRE et post, (et modo:) ual' lx sol', et tamen est ad firmam pro iiii lib'. Aluricus tenuit de Goduino (com').

Isdem Rotbertus ten' ad firmam BRVNFELLE. Adeloldus tenuit de ep'o. Pro uno solin se defd'. T'ra e'   In d'nio sunt ii^{e} car', et v uill'i cum x bord' h'nt i car' et dim'. Ibi i molin' de vi solid' et viii den', et pastura de xv sol'. Ibi xii serui, et viii ac' prati. Silua xx porc'. TRE et post, ual' iiii lib'. Modo c solid'. Aluuinus tenuit de Goduino (com'). Huic M̄ pertin' quędam libera terra ad iii boues, et ual' v sol'.

Radulfus curbespine ten' de ep'o TVRNEHAM. Pro iii solins se defd'. T'ra e' viii car'. In d'nio e' una, et xvi uill'i cum xviii bord' h'nt iiii car'. Ibi ęccl'a et vi serui, et i molin' de vi solid', et iiii ac' prati. Silua xl porc'. TRE et post, ualeb' x lib'. Modo xii lib', et tamen redd' xiiii. Sbern biga tenuit de rege E.

Isd' Radulfus ten' de ep'o FEREBVRNE. Pro uno solin se defd'. T'ra e'   In d'nio e' una car', et ii uill'i cum i bord', et ii serui, et una *acra prati et dimid'. Silua vi porc'. TRE et post, et modo: ual' xxx solid'. Sbern biga tenuit de rege E.

Odo ten' de ep'o GELINGEHAM. Pro dimid' solin se defd'. T'ra e' i car'. In d'nio sunt ii^{e}, et vi bord' h'nt dim' car'. Ibi i molin' de xvi sol' et vii den', et xiii ac' prati, et viii ac' / pasturę.

DB-Ke-8va

TRE ualeb' xl sol'. Quando recep': xxx sol'. Modo lx sol'.

Rotbertus Latin' ten' ad firmam de ep'o   IN CETEHAM HVND'. CETEHAM. Pro vi solins se defd'. T'ra e' xvi car'. In d'nio sunt iii, et xxxiii uill'i cum iiii bord' h'nt x car'. Ibi ęccl'a et xv serui, et i molin' de xxxii den', et xx ac' prati, et piscarię vi de xii den'. Silua i porc'. TRE et post: ualuit xii lib'. Modo xv lib', et tamen redd' xxxv lib'. Goduinus (com') tenuit.

IN LEST DE EILESFORD.   IN ROVECESTRE HVND'.

Filius Will'i tahum ten' de ep'o DELCE. Pro uno solin et uno iugo se defd'. T'ra e'   In d'nio e' una car', et v uill'i h'nt ii car'. Ibi xii ac' prati. Silua i porc'. TRE et post, ualuit iii lib', et modo lxx sol'. Godricus tenuit de rege E.

Ansgotus de Rouecestre ten' de ep'o DELCE. Pro uno solin se defd'. T'ra e' ii car', et ibi sunt in d'nio, *cum uno uill'o et v bord', et vi seruis. Ibi xii ac' prati, et lx ac' pasturę. TRE et post, et modo: ual' c solid'. Osuuardus tenuit de rege E.

Isdem Ansgotus ten' de ep'o STOCHES.   IN HOV HVND'. Pro ii solins se defd'. T'ra e' ii car', et ibi sunt in d'nio cum vii bord'. Ibi una piscaria de ii solid'. TRE et post: ualuit c solid'. Modo cx solid'. Anschil tenuit de rege E.

Ipse ep's Baiocensis ten' in d'nio HOV. Pro l solins se defd' TRE, et modo pro xxxiii^{bus}. T'ra e' l car'. In d'nio sunt iiii, et c uill'i iii minus cum lxi cot' h'nt xliii car'. Ibi vi ęccl'ę, et xii serui, et xxxii ac' prati. Silua xxx porc'. Totum M̄ TRE ualeb' lx lib'. Quando ep's recep': similit', et modo t'ntd', et tamen qui eum ten' reddit c et xiii lib'. Huic M̄ pertineb' ix domus in Rouecest' ciuitate, et vi solid' reddeb', nunc ablatę sunt. Hoc M̄ tenuit Goduinus comes. De hoc M̄ ten' Ricardus de Tonebrige dimid' solin, et siluam xx porc'. TRE et post, et modo: ual' xl solid'. Adam filius Huberti ten' de eod' M̄ un' solin, et un' iugum de ep'o, et ibi h't unus h'o eius in d'nio dimid' car', et iiii uill'os cum dim' car', et uno cot'. Val' et ualuit xxx solid'. Anschitil de Ros ten' de ipso M̄ iii solins, et ibi h't in d'nio i car', et v uill'i cum xii cot' h'nt i car' et dim'. Ibi v serui, et un' molin' de x solid', et xii ac' prati, et ii piscar' de v sol'. TRE et post, ualeb' vi lib'. Modo vi lib' et v solid'.

Adam ten' de ep'o i iugum in PINPA. IN TVIFERDE HVND'. T'ra e' Ibi h't dim' car' cum ii seruis, et iiii acras prati, et dimid' piscariam sine censu. Silua: vi porc'. TRE ualeb' vi sol', et post, v sol'. Modo: x sol', et tamen redd' / xv sol'. Godricus tenuit de rege E.

Rannulfus de Columbels ten' de ep'o FERLAGA. Pro uno solin se defd'. T'ra e' iiii car'. Rann' non ten' nisi iii^{a} iuga, et ibi h't in d'nio i car', et x uill'os cum iiii cot' h'nt iii car'. Ibi ęccl'a, et vii serui, et i molin' de v sol', et x ac' prati. Silua xv porc'. TRE et post, et modo: ual' vii lib'. Alnod tenuit / de rege. De isto solin ten' Raynerus i iugum de ep'o in M̄ PINPE,

DB-Ke-8vb

et ibi h't i car', cum ix seruis, et iii acras prati. Siluam iiii porc'. TRE (et post) ualeb' xx sol'. Modo: xl solid'. Alnod (cilt) tenuit de rege E.

Haimo ten' de ep'o NEDESTEDE. Pro iii solins se defd'. T'ra e' vi car'. In d'nio e' una, et xiiii uill'i h'nt v car'. Ibi ęccl'a, et xiiii serui, et ii molini de xiiii solid', et piscaria de ii sol', et vii ac' prati. Silua xxxv porc'. TRE ualeb' viii lib', et post: vi lib'. Modo: viii lib' et v sol'. Norman tenuit de rege E. De isto M̄ h't ep's xxx sol' pro ii hagas.

Radulfus filius Turaldi ten' de ep'o OTRINGEBERGE. Pro ii^{bus} solins se defd'. T'ra e' v car'. In d'nio sunt ii^{e}, et vi uill'i cum viii bord' h'nt iii car'. Ibi ęccl'a, et ii molini de iii solid', et ii^{e} ac' prati, et piscaria de xxx anguill'. Silua ii porc'. TRE et post ualuit xl solid'. Modo: vi lib'. Leueua tenuit de rege E. Huic M̄ adiacent iiii hagę in ciuitate, redd' iii sol'.

Hugo de braiboue ten' de ep'o OTRINBERGE. Pro ii solins se defd'. T'ra e' iiii car'. In d'nio e' una, et ix uill'i cum iiii bord' h'nt ii car'. Ibi iii serui, et i molin' de xvi denar', et iii ac' prati. Silua ii porc'. TRE et post: ualuit iiii lib'. Modo: c solid'. Godil tenuit de rege E.

Adeloldus tenuit de ep'o TESTAN, et Robertus modo ten' ad firmam. Pro uno solin se defd'. T'ra e' In d'nio sunt ii^{e} car' et dimid', et vii uill'i cum iii bord' h'nt i car'. Ibi xii serui, et i molin' de iii sol', et viii ac' prati. Silua xx porc'. TRE ualeb' c sol', et post: lx sol'. Modo: c solid'. Eduuardus ten' / de rege E. Hanc terram tenuer' iii fr's TRE pro tribus Maneriis. Nunc est in unum.

Isdem Adeloldus tenuit de ep'o BENEDESTEDE, et Robertus ten' ad firmam. Pro uno iugo se defd'. T'ra e' In d'nio e' i car', cum v seruis, et una acra prati. Silua vi porc'. TRE et post: ualuit xx solid'. Modo: xl sol'. Godricus tenuit de Alnodo (cilt). IN MEDESTAN HD'.

Rannulfus de Columbels ten' de ep'o BERMELIE. Pro uno iugo se defd'. T'ra e' In d'nio e' una car', cum v seruis, et iiii ac' prati. Silua iii porc'. TRE ualeb' xv sol'. Quando recep': xx sol'. Modo: xl sol'. *(Pro vii solins se defdb' TRE. Modo pro v solins.)

Rotbertus Latin' ten' ad firmam BOSELEV. T'ra e' xx car'. In d'nio sunt iii car', et xlvii uill'i cum xi bord' h'nt xvi car'. Ibi iii molini de xxxvi sol' et viii den', et xvi serui, et xx ac' prati. Silua l porc'. TRE et post, ualuit xxv lib'. Modo xxx lib', et tamen Robertus reddit lv lib'. Alnod (cilt) tenuit. De hoc M̄ ten' Helto dim' solin, et ibi h't i car', cum uno bord', et i franc * et ii acras prati, et siluam: vi porc'. Et ual' xl sol'.

Radulfus filius Turaldi ten' de ep'o LITELBROTEHAM. Pro uno solin et dim' se defd'. T'ra e' In d'nio e' i car', et iiii uill'i cum iiii bord' h'nt ii car'. Ibi ii serui, et ii molini de iiii solid', et ii ac' prati. Silua v porc'. TRE et post, ualuit xl sol'. Modo lx sol' et liiii den'. Ricardus de Tonebrige h't in sua Leuua quod ual' xiii sol'. Et siluam l porc'. Et rex h't de eod' M̄ quod ual' xvi den'. Hanc terram TRE tenuer' Goduinus et Eduunus pro ii^{bus} Maner'.

Adam ten' de ep'o CELCA. Pro iii solins se defd'. T'ra e' vii car'. In d'nio sunt ii^{e}, et xiiii uill'i cum vi bord' h'nt v car'. Ibi ęccl'a, et iiii serui, et un' molin' de v solid', et xvi ac' prati. TRE ualeb' vii lib', et post: / c solid'.

DB-Ke-9ra

Modo x lib', et tamen qui (tenet) redd' xiiii lib'. De hoc M̄ est in manu regis quod ual' vii sol', de nouo dono ep'i. In manu sua retinuit ep's in Ciuitate Rouecestre iii hagas, quę ualent l denar'. In Exesse est una hida que iuste ad hoc M̄ pertinet. Goduin filius dudeman tenuit. Modo ten' Rannulfus peurel.

Isdem Adam *( )ten' de ep'o HE(C)HAM. Pro v solins se defd'. T'ra e' xii car'. In d'nio sunt iii car', et xxiiii uill'i cum xii bord', h'nt vi car' et dimid'. Ibi xx serui, et xxx ac' prati. Ibi ęccl'a et i molin' de x sol', et piscaria de iii solid', et in Exesse pastura cc ouibus. TRE ualeb' xii lib', et post vi lib'. Modo: xv lib'. Hanc terram tenuer' TRE Goduin filius carli, et Toli, pro ii Man'.

Isdem Adam ten' de ep'o (in) COLINGE i solin et dimid'. T'ra e' i car' et dim'. In d'nio sunt ii car', et v uill'i h'nt dimid' car'. Ibi iiii serui, et vii ac' prati. Silua x porc'. TRE et post: ualuit xl sol'. Modo: iiii lib'. Ricardus de Tonebrige quod h't in sua leuua: ual' vii *((sol')). Vluuinus tenuit de Leuuino comite.

Isdem Adam ten' de ep'o BICHELEI. Pro dimid' solin se defd'. T'ra e' dim' car'. In d'nio e' dim' car', et unus uill's cum dim' car', et ii bord'. Ibi i molin' de v sol'. *Vluuinus tenuit de / Leuuino com'. TRE et post: ualuit x sol'. Modo xv solid'. IN ESSAMLE HD'.

Radulfus filius Turaldi ten' de ep'o ARCLEI. Pro uno solin se defd'. T'ra e' dim' car', et ibid' sunt adhuc xxx ac' terrę. In d'nio e' una car', et vi uill'i h'nt dimid' car'. Ibi xii ac' prati. TRE et post: ualuit xl sol'. Modo: iiii lib'.

Hunef tenuit de Heraldo (com').

Ansgotus de Rouecest' ten' HANEHEST. Pro dim' solin se defd'. T'ra e' i car'. In d'nio e' una car', et ii uill'i cum iiii seruis. TRE ualeb' xx sol'. Quando recep': xxx sol'. Modo: xl solid'. Goduinus tenuit de Goduino (com').

Ernulfus de Hesding ten' de ep'o CLIVE. Pro dim' solin se defd'. T'ra e'   In d'nio dimid' car', et ii uill'i, et x ac' prati, et pastura c ouium. TRE et post: ual' xxx sol'. Duo fr's tenuer' de rege E, Aluric et Ordric.

Isdem Ernulfus ten' de ep'o HADONE. Pro iii iugis se defd'. T'ra e' i car', et ibi e' in d'nio, et vi uill'i cum i bord' h'nt i car'. Ibi vi ac' prati. TRE et post: ual' l solid'. Modo: lx sol'. Osuuardus tenuit de rege E.

Odo ten' de ep'o in ead' Hadone i iugum. T'ra e' dim' car'. In d'nio nichil est. TRE et post, et modo ual' xx solid'.

Isdem Odo ten' de ep'o COLINGES. Pro dim' solin se defd'. T'ra e' dimid' car'. Ibi e' cum uno bord', et iiii ac' prati. TRE et post, ualuit xx solid'. Modo: xxx solid'. God / tenuit de rege / E.

Helto ten' de ep'o MELESTVN. Pro dimid' solin se defd'. T'ra e' i car', et ibi e' cum v uill'is, et i acra prati. TRE et post: ualuit x solid'. Modo: xxx solid'. Vluuardus (uuit) tenuit de rege E.

IN DIMIDIO LEST DE MIDDELTONE.   IN MILDETONE HVND'.

DB-Ke-9rb

Hugo de port ten' de ep'o TVNESTELLE. Pro iii solins *(solins) et dim' se defd'. T'ra e' iiii car'. In d'nio sunt ii car', et ix uill'i cum i car', et ix serui. Silua x porc', et salina de xii denar'. TRE et post, ualeb' vii lib'. Modo: viii lib'. Osuuard tenuit de rege E.

Isdem Hugo ten' de ep'o CERCE. Pro ii solins se defd'. T'ra e' ii car'. In d'nio e' una, *cum v bord' et uno seruo, et un' molin' de vi solid' et viii den'. Val' *(xxx solid') *((vi lib')). Osuuardus tenuit.

(Id' H ten' de ep'o STEPEDONE. Osuuard teneb' TRE, et tunc se defdb' pro i solin dimidio iugo m[inus.] T'ra e' ii car'. In d'nio e' [una,] cum i seruo et v bord'. Val' xxx solid'.)

* Isdem Hugo ten' de ep'o TANGAS. Pro ii solins se defd'. T'ra e' iii car'. In d'nio sunt ii^{e}, et v uill'i cum i car'. Ibi ęccl'a et iiii serui, et un' molin' de viii solid'. Silua iiii porc'. TRE et post, ualuit vii lib'. Modo: x lib' et x solid'. Osuuardus / tenuit. De istis solins quos Hugo de port h't, tenuit Osuuardus v ad gablum, et iii solins et un' iugum et dimid', quos abstulit uillanis regis.   IN BORWART LEST.   IN BRIGE HVND'.

Ricardus filius Will'i * ten' de ep'o BORNE. Pro vi solins se defd'. T'ra e' viii car'. In d'nio sunt iii car', et xliiii uill'i cum iii bord' h'nt x car'. Ibi ęccl'a, et unus seruus, et iiii molini de xvi solid' et viii den'. Piscaria de vi den'. Pastura unde arauer' extranei ho'es vi acras terrę. Silua iiii porc'. TRE ualeb' xviii lib'. Quando recep': x lib'. Modo xix lib'.

Ipse ep's Baioc' ten' in d'nio HARDES. Pro ii solins se defd'. T'ra e' iiii car'. In d'nio e' una, et ix uill'i cum ii car'. Ibi ęccl'a et v serui. Silua xx porc'. TRE ualeb' vii lib', et post: c sol'. Modo: vii lib', et tamen reddit x lib'. Eduinus tenuit / de rege E.

Isdem ep's ten' in d'nio STELLINGES. Pro uno iugo se defd'. T'ra i car' et dimid'. In d'nio nichil est nisi i bord'. Ibi ęccl'a. Silua ii porc'. TRE ualeb' lx sol', et post et modo: xl solid'. Alret tenuit de rege E.

Isdem ep's ten' (in) d'nio BVRNES. Pro ii solins se defd'. T'ra e' vi car'.

In d'nio sunt ii^{ę}, et xxv uill'i cum iiii bord' h'nt vii car'. Ibi ęccl'a, et vi serui, et un' molin' de xxxviii denar', et una salina de xxx den', et dimid' piscaria iiii den'. De pastura xl den'. Silua vi porc' et dimid'. TRE ualeb' xii lib', et post: vii lib'. Modo: xii lib', et tamen redd' xviii lib'. Quod Hugo de monfort ten': ual' v sol'. / Leuinc tenuit de rege E. Hęc iii^{a} Maneria ep'i Baioc', tenet Rannulfus ad firmam.

Rannulfus de columbels ten' de ep'o HARDES. Pro uno solin se defd'. T'ra e' iiii car'. In d'nio e' dimid' car', et ix uill'i h'nt ii car'. Ibi ęccl'a et viii serui, et xiii ac' prati. Silua iiii porc'. TRE ualeb' vi lib', et post: iiii lib'. Modo: c solid'. Azor tenuit de rege E. IN DONAMESFORD HVND'.

Ipse ep's ten' in d'nio WICHEHAM. Pro iiii solins se defd'. T'ra e' xi car'. In d'nio sunt ii^{ę} car', et xxxvi uill'i cum xxx^{ta}ii cot' h'nt ix car'. Ibi ęccl'a et unus pb'r qui dat xl sol' per ann'. Ibi unus parcus, et ii molini de l solid', et ii^{ę} saline de xxxii denar', et iii piscarię de iiii solid', et xxxii ac' prati. Pastura ad ccc oues, et ad xxxi anim'. Silua quat' xx^{ti} porc'. TRE ualeb' xxv lib'. Quando recep': xx lib'. Modo: xxx lib'. Huic M̄ pertin' in cantuaria iii masurę, redd'tes vi solid' et viii^{to} denar'. Hoc M̄ tenuit Aluredus (biga) *(tenuit) de rege E. Adhuc iacet ad hunc M̄ dimidium solin liberę terrę

DB-Ke-9va

quam Sired tenuit de Alured biga, et modo ten' Goisfridus filius malę terrę de ep'o baioc', et ual' et semper ualuit lx solid'. IN HVNDRET et in ciuitate cantuariensi h't Adam filius Huberti de ep'o iiii domos, et ii^{as} foris ciuitatem, quę reddunt viii solid'. IN EOD' HVND'.

Haimo uicecom' ten' de ep'o LATINTONE. Pro dim' solin se defd'. T'ra e' i car' et dim'. In d'nio e' una, cum ii bord'. Ibi paruum nemus de xii acris pasturę. TRE et post, et modo ual' iii lib'.

Isdem Haimo ten' de ep'o dimidium solin, et est terra iiii car'. In d'nio sunt ii^{ę} car', et xi bord' cum iii car', et xvi ac' siluę minutę. TRE ualeb' c sol', et post vi lib', et modo ix lib'. Has terras TRE tenuer' burgenses cantuarię, et usque ad ep'm baioc' qui ab eis cepit. IN LIMOWART LEST. IN FVLCHESTAN HVND'.

Willelmus de arcis ten' FVLCHESTAN. TRE se defd' pro xl solins, et modo pro xxxix. T'ra e' c et xx^{ti} car'. In d'nio sunt xiiii car', et cc^{ti} et ix^{uem} uill'i et quater xx et iii bord'. Int' omnes h'nt xlv car'. Ibi v ęccl'ę, de quibus h't archiep's lv solid'. Ibi iii serui, et vii molini de ix lib' et xii sol'. Ibi c ac' prati. Silua xl porc'. Hoc M̄ tenuit Goduinus comes.

:

De hoc M̄ ten' Hugo filius Will'i ix solins de terra uillanorum, et ibi h't in d'nio iiii car' et dim', et xxx viii uill'os cum xvii bord' qui h'nt xvi car'. Ibi iii ęccl'ę, et un' molin' et dimid' de xvi solid' et v den', et una salina de xxx den'. Silua vi porc'. Val' xx lib'.

// Walterus de appeuile ten' de hoc M̄ iii iuga et xii acras terrę, et ibi h't i car' in d'nio, et iii uill'os cum i bord'. Val' xxx solid'.

// Aluredus ten' i solin' et xl acras terrę, et ibi h't in d'nio ii car' cum vi bord', et xii acras prati. Val' iiii lib'.

// Walterus filius Engelberti ten' dimid' solin et xl acras, et ibi h't in d'nio i car' cum vii bord', et v ac' prati. Val' xxx solid'.

// Wesman ten' i solin, et ibi h't in d'nio i car', et ii uill'os cum vii bord' h'ntes i car' et dim'. Val' iiii lib'.

// Aluredus dapifer ten' i solin et un' iugum et vi acras terrę, et ibi h't in d'nio i car' cum xi bord'. Val' l solid'.

// Eudo ten' dimid' solin, et ibi h't in d'nio i car' cum iiii bord', et iii ac' prati. Val' xx solid'.

// Bernardus de S' Audoeno iiii solins, et ibi h't in d'nio iii car', et vi uill'i cum xi bord' h'nt ii car'. Ibi iiii serui, et ii molini de xxiiii solid', et xx ac' prati. Silua ii porc'. De una dena et de terra quę data est ab his solins ad firmam exeunt iii lib'. *(Int' totum) Val' ix lib'.

// Baldricus ten' dimid' solin, et ibi h't i car', et ii uill'os cum vi bord' h'nt i car', et un' molin' de xxx den'. Val' xxx sol'.

// Ricardus ten' lviii acras terre, et ibi h't i car' cum v bord'. Val' x sol'. Totum Fulchestan TRE ualeb' c et x lib'. Quando recep': xl lib'. Modo quod h't in d'nio: ual' c lib'. Quod milites ten' *supradicti: / simul ual' xlv lib' / et x sol'.

DB-Ke-9vb

IN HONINBERG HVND'.

Ep's baiocensis ten' in d'nio ALHAM. Pro vi solins se defd'. T'ra e' xxiiii car'. In d'nio sunt v car', et xli uill's cum viii bord' h'nt xviii car'. Ibi ęccl'a et viii serui, et ii molini de vi solid', et xxviii ac' prati. Silua c porc'. TRE et post: ualuit xxx lib', *((modo: xl,)) et tamen reddit l lib'. Hoc M̄ tenuit Edericus de rege E. IN ROVINDEN HVND'.

Adam filius huberti ten' de ep'o i denam de dimid' iugo, quę remansit extra diuisionem hugon' de montfort, et iacuit in Belice. Ibi h't ii uill'os cum dim' car'. Val' et ualuit hoc semper x sol'.

Ansfridus ten' de ep'o in Bochelande IN STOTINGES HVND'. dimid' solin, et ibi h't in d'nio i car' cum uno uill'o. T'ra e' ii car'. TRE ualeb' xx sol'. Quando recep': xxx solid'. Modo: xl sol'. IN ESTREA LEST. IN ESTRE HVND'.

Radulfus de curbespine ten' de ep'o un' iugum in Berfrestone. Ibi una paupercula mulier redd' iii den' et un' obolum. Val' et ualuit semper x sol' hoc iugum.

Rannulfus de Columbels ten' ibi un' iugum, quod in Hardes escotauit, et nunc usque scotum regis non scotauit.

Adeloldus tenuit de ep'o ESWALT. Pro iii solins se defd'. T'ra e' In d'nio e' una car', et vi uill'i cum ii bord' h'nt iii car'. Ibi ii serui, et siluula ad clausuram. TRE ual' ix lib', modo xv. Alnod cit tenuit de rege E.

Osbernus filius Letardi ten' de ep'o i solin in SELINGE. Ibi h't un' uill'm reddentem ii sol'. TRE ualeb' lx sol', et post et modo: xxx solid'. Aluuinus tenuit TRE.

Isdem Osbernus ten' de ep'o POPESELLE. Pro uno solin se defd'. T'ra e' In d'nio sunt ii car', et unus uill's cum iiii bord', h'nt dimid' car'. Hanc terram tenuer' ii° liberi ho'es de rege E. Quidam miles eius ten' dimid' iugum, et ibi h't i car' in d'nio. Totum TRE ualuit lx sol', et post: xx sol'. Modo c solid'.

Radulfus de Curbespine ten' IN BEVSBERGE HVND'. dimid' iugum in Popessale, et ibi h't iii boues.

TRE et post: ualuit iiii sol', modo viii solid'. Vluric tenuit de rege E.

Fulbertus ten' de ep'o BERHAM. Pro vi IN BERHAM HVND'. solins se defd'. T'ra e' xxxii car'. In d'nio sunt iii car', et lii uill'i cum xx cot' h'nt xviii car'. Ibi ęccl'a, et unum molin' de xx solid' et iiii den'. Ibi xxv piscarię de xxxv solid' iiii den' minus. De auera, idest seruitium lx sol'. De herbagio xxvi sol', et xx^{ti} ac' prati. De pasnagio cl porc'.

De isto M̄ dedit ep's unam bereuuicham Herberto filio *luonis, quę uocatur HVHAM, et ibi h't i car' in d'nio, et xii uill'os cum ix car', et xx acras prati.

De eod' quoque M̄ dedit ep's Osberno paisforere i solin, et ii molin' de l sol', et ibi e' in d'nio i car', et iiii uill'i cum i car'.

Totum BERHAM TRE ualeb' xl lib'. Quando ep's recep': similit', et tamen reddebat ei c lib'.

Modo per se Berham ual' xl lib', et Hucham x lib'. Et hoc quod Osbernus h't: vi lib', et terra cuiusdam Rannulfi militis ual' xl sol'.

Hoc M̄ tenuit Stigandus archiep's, sed non erat de archiep'atu, / sed fuit de d'nica firma regis E.

DB-Ke-10ra

Vitalis de ep'o ten' SOANECLIVE. IN WITENESTAPLE HD'. Pro dimid' solin se defd'. T'ra e' i car' et dim'. In d'nio e' i car', cum viii cot', qui redd't iiii sol' et vi den'. Silua xx porc'. TRE ualeb' xxi solid'. Quando Vital' recep': xii sol'. Modo: xxx sol'. Eduuardus (Snoch) tenuit de rege E.

Isdem Vital' ten' de ep'o i iugum in eod' Hund', et ibi h't dimid' car' in d'nio, cum iiii bord', redd' vi solid'. T'ra e' dimid' car. Silua x porc'. TRE et post, ualuit x solid'. Modo: xx solid'. Vlsi tenuit de rege E.

IN LEST DE WIWARLET. IN FAVRESHANT HD'.

Adam ten' de ep'o ORE. Pro ii solins se defd'. T'ra e' iiii car'. In d'nio e' una, et x uill'i cum x bord' h'nt ii car'. Ibi dimid' ęccl'a, et un' molin' de xxii sol', et ii^{e} piscarię sine censu, et i salina *(de) xxviii den'. Silua vi porc'. TRE ualeb' iiii lib', et post: lx sol'. Modo: c solid'. Turgis tenuit de rege E.

Isdem Adam ten' de ep'o STANEFELLE. Pro ii solins se defd'. T'ra e' * [iiii c]ar'. In d'nio e' i car', et x uill'i h'nt ii car'. Ibi ęccl'a, et [vi] serui, et ii ac' prati. Silua lx porc'. TRE ualeb' lx sol', et post: xl sol'. Modo: c solid'. Turgis tenuit de Goduino (com').

Hugo de porth ten' de ep'o NORTONE. Pro iiii solins se dfd'. T'ra e' iiii car'. In d'nio sunt iii car', et xviii uill'i cum vi bord' h'nt v car'. Ibi iii ęccl'ę, et iii molini sine censu, et ii piscar' de xii den'. Silua xl porc'. TRE ualeb' viii lib', et post: vi lib'. Modo: xii lib'. Osuuardus tenuit de rege E. IN FELEBERGE HVND'.

Fulbertus ten' de ep'o CILLEHAM. Pro v solins se defd'. T'ra e' xx car'. In d'nio sunt ii car', et xxxviii uill'i cum xii cot' h'nt xii car'. Ibi ęccl'a et vi molini (et dimid') de vi lib' et viii solid', et ii^{e} piscarię de xvii den', et pastura de xviii sol' et vii den'. In cantuaria ciuitate xiii masurę pertin' huic M̄, redd' xv' solid', et ix ac' prati. Silua quat' xx porc'. TRE ualeb' xl lib', et post: xxx lib'. Modo: xxx lib' similit', et tamen reddeb' ep'o baiocensi quat' xx lib' et xl sol'. Sired tenuit de rege E. IN FAVRESHANT HVND'.

Hugo nepos Herberti ten' de ep'o OSPRINGES. Pro vii solins et dim' se defd'. T'ra e' xx car'. In d'nio *non sunt car'.

Ibi xxix uill'i cum vi bord', h'nt xi car'. Ibi ęccl'a, et i molin' de xi solid' et viii den', et piscaria de x den', et salina de iiii den', et xiii ac' prati. Silua de quat' xx porc'. De terra huius M̄ ten' Herbertus dimid' solin et iii uirg', et ibi h't in d'nio i car', et i uill'm cum x bord' h'ntes i car'. Ricardus de maris ten' dimid' solin de hoc M̄, et ibi h't vi uill'os et i bord' cum i car'. Et quidam Turstinus ten' i iugum, quod redd' v solid'. Totum M̄ TRE ualeb' xx lib'. Quando Herbertus recep': xv lib'. Modo: xx lib'. Huic M̄ pertin' in cantuaria i masura de xxx denar'. *(Hoc M̄ tenuit)

Ansfridus ten' de ep'o CILDRESHAM. Pro uno solin se defd'. T'ra e' iii car'. In d'nio e' una, et iiii uill'i cum ii bord' h'nt i car' et dimid'. Ibi v serui, et ii ac' prati. Silua est sed nil redd'. De hoc M̄ ten' quidam miles terram ad i car'. Int' tot' TRE ualeb' lx sol', et post: xl sol'. Modo: iiii lib'.

DB-Ke-10rb

Isdem Ansfridus ten' de ep'o ERNOLTVN. Pro uno solin se defd'. T'ra e' iii car'. In d'nio e' una, et viii uill'i cum ii car' et dimid'. Ibi ii salinę, et in ciuitate cantuaria i masura de xxi den'. TRE ualeb' iiii lib', et post: xl sol'. Modo: c sol'. Hoc M̄ Burnod de rege E tenuit. De isto M̄ ten' Rannulfus x acras quę iacent iuxta ciuitatem, et reddeb' xlii den' TRE.

Isdem Ansfridus ten' de ep'o MACHEHEVET. Pro uno iugo se defd'. T'ra e' dimid' car'. Ibi sunt ii uill'i redd' l denar'. TRE ualeb' l den', modo ual' lx den'. Seuuold tenuit TRE.

Isdem Anfridus ten' de ep'o BADELESMERE. Pro uno solin se defd'. T'ra e' ii car' et dim'. In d'nio e' una, et x uill'i h'nt i car' et dim'. Ibi ęccl'a, et ii serui, et piscaria de xii den'. Silua iiii porc'. TRE ualeb' lx sol', et post: lx sol'. Modo: iiii lib'. Hoc M̄ reclamat abb' S' Augustini, quia habuit TRE, et hund' attestantur ei. Sed filius ho'is dicit patrem suum se posse uertere ubi uoluerit, et hoc non annu(u)nt monachi.

Isdem Ansfridus ten' de ep'o PERIE. Pro uno iugo se defendeb'. Ibi est unus bord' redd' v den'. TRE et post: et modo: ual' xvi solid'. Wlui tenuit de rege E.

Isdem Ansfridus ten' de ep'o PERIE. Pro dimid' solin se defd'. T'ra e' i car'. Ibi iii bord', et una masura in ciuitate de xvi denar'. TRE et post, et modo ual' xxiiii solid'. Vlueua tenuit / de rege E.

Osbernus ten' de ep'o BOCHELAND. Pro iii iugis se defd'. T'ra e' i car'. In d'nio e' una, et iii uill'i cum ii bord' h'nt dimid' car'. Ibi viii serui. TRE ualeb' iiii lib', et post: iii lib', et modo lxx solid'. / Seuuardus tenuit de rege E.

Isdem Osbernus ten' un' iugum de ep'o in eod' M̄, et pro i iugo se defd'. TRE ualeb' xx sol', et post et modo: ual' x sol'. Leuuard tenuit de rege E.

Hugo de porth ten' de ep'o HERSTE. Pro iii^{bus} iugis se defd'. T'ra e' i car'. In d'nio e' cum ii bord' et ii seruis. TRE et post, ualuit x solid'. Modo: xxx solid'. Osuuardus tenuit de rege E.

Adam ten' de ep'o unum iugum in ORE, et pro i iugo se defd'. T'ra e' i car'. Hanc ten' iii uill'i modo ad firmam, et redd't xx sol', et tantd' semper ualuit. Ibi ęccl'a est. Leuuold tenuit de rege E.

Herfridus ten' TREVELAI. *((Pro iii solins se defnd'.)) T'ra e' viii car'. In d'nio e' una, et xxiiii uill'i cum v bord' h'nt vi car' et dim'. Ibi ęccl'a, et v serui. Silua xx porc'. Et in ciuitate iii hage de xxxii denar'. TRE ualeb' vii lib', et post: vi lib'. Modo: viii lib'. Vlnod tenuit de rege E.

Herbertus tenuit de ep'o NORDESLINGE. T'ra e' i car'. Pro dim' solin se defd'. Ibi ii bord' redd't ii solid'. TRE et post: ualuit xx sol'. Modo: xxv sol'. Turgod tenuit TRE.

Hęc ii^{o} M̄ tenuit Herbertus filius iuonis de ep'o Baioc'.

:

DB-Ke-10va

Turstinus de girunde ten' in Bochelande i iugum de ep'o, et pro i iugo se defd'. Ibi est unus uill's reddens vi solid'. Val' et ualuit semper xii solid'. Turgot tenuit de rege E.

Rogerius filius Anschitil ten' de ep'o ESLINGES. Pro uno solin se defd'. T'ra e' i car'. Ibi e' in d'nio, et unus bord' h't dimid' car'. Ibi ęccl'a et i molin' de x solid', et ii ac' prati. TRE ualeb' lx sol', et post: xx sol'. Modo: xl solid'. Vnlot tenuit de rege E, et potuit ire quo uoluit cum terra.

Fulbertus ten' de ep'o ESLINGES. Pro v solins se defd' TRE, et modo pro ii^{bus}, et sic fecit postquam ep's dedit M̄ Hugoni filio fulberti. T'ra e' vi car'. In d'nio sunt ii car', et *xxx^{ta} uill'i h'nt iii car'. Ibi ęccl'a et xxviii serui, et i molin' de x sol'. Silua xxx porc'. TRE ualeb' x lib', et quando recep': vi lib'. Modo iiii lib', et tamen ep's habuit viii lib'. Sired tenuit de rege E.

Isd' *(Fulbertus) ten' de ep'o DODEHAM. Pro uno solin se defd'. T'ra e'   In d'nio e' una car', et xvii uill'i cum x bord' h'nt ii car'. Ibi ęccl'a et vi serui, et dimid' piscar' de ccc allecibus. Et in cantuaria ciuitate v hagę de vii sol' et x den'. TRE ualeb' x lib'. Ep's misit ad firmam (pro) x lib'. Quando fulbertus recep': vi lib', et modo similit'.   Sired tenuit de rege E.

Ricardus ten' de ep'o RONGOSTONE. Pro uno solin se defd'. T'ra e'   Ibi ii uill'i h'nt i car', et redd't vi sol'. TRE et post, et modo ual' xl solid'. Vluiet tenuit de rege E.

IN FERLEBERGE HD'.

Ansfridus ten' de ep'o HORTONE. Pro dimid' solin se defd'. T'ra e' i car'. Ibi e' in d'nio, et xiii uill'i h'nt dimid' car'. Ibi i seruus, et ii molini de una marka arg', et viii ac' prati, * et c ac' siluę minutę. TRE ualeb' xl [sol', et post:] xxx sol'. Modo: c solid'. Godricus tenu[it de re]ge E.

IN [WI H]VND'.

Adam ten' de ep'o FANNE. Pro dim' solin se defd'. T'ra e' i car' et dim'. In d'nio sunt ii car', et iii uill'i et iii serui, et ę(c)cl'a, et xiii ac' prati. Silua x porc'. TRE: ualeb' iiii lib', et post: xx sol'. Modo: iiii lib'. Hugo de montfort ten' inde quod ual' xx solid'.

Wadardus ten' de ep'o BERCHVELLE. Pro dim' solin se defd'. T'ra e' i car'. Ibi e' in d'nio, et iii uill'i, et iii serui, et un' molin' de xl den', et x ac' prati, et un' alnetum. TRE et post, ualuit xx sol'. Modo xl solid'. Werelm tenuit de rege.

Isdem Wadardus ten' de ep'o CVMBE. Pro uno solin se defd'. T'ra e' ii car'. In d'nio e' una, et ix uill'i cum v bord' h'nt i car' et dimid'. Ibi xiiii ac' prati. Silua v porc'. TRE: ualeb' lx sol', et post: l sol'. Modo: iiii lib', et seruitium unius militis. Leuret de rochinge tenuit de rege E.

Radulfus de curbespine ten' de ep'o BETMONTESTVN. Pro uno solin se defd'. T'ra e' vi car'. In d'nio sunt ii^{e}, et xiii uill'i cum i bord' h'nt iii car'. Ibi xxxiii ac' prati, et silua xl porc'. De isto M̄ ten' Hugo de montfort int' siluam et pasturam quod ualeb' TRE vi lib', et post et modo, t'ntd'. Ailricus tenuit de rege E.

DB-Ke-10vb

Adeloldus tenuit de ep'o DENE. Pro uno solin se defd'. T'ra e' ii car'. In d'nio e' una car', et iiii bord', et ii serui, et una acra prati, et silua vii porc'. De isto solino ten' Radulfus de curbespine i iugum et dimid', quod ual' et ualuit semper x solid'. // Adeloldus habuit dimid' solin et dimid' iugum, et TRE ualeb' xl solid', et post: xx solid'. Modo: xl sol'. Hęc terra est in manu regis. Hanc terram tenuer' Vlnod et Waua et Aluuard et Vlueron de rege E, et erat dispertita in tribus locis. IN CALEHEVE HVND'.

Radulfus de curbespine ten' PIVENTONE de feudo ep'i, et Hugo de eo. Pro uno solin se defd'. T'ra e' v car'. In d'nio e' una et dimid', et vii uill'i cum vii bord' h'nt iii car' et dim'. Ibi ęccl'a, et ix serui, et un' molin' de lv den', et xx ac' prati. Silua lx porc'. TRE ualeb' viii lib', et post: c sol'. Modo: vi lib'. Sbern (biga) tenuit de rege E.

Isd' Radulfus ten' iii denas quę remanser' extra diuisionem Hugon' de montfort, de pistinges M̄, et ibi est un' iugum terrę et una uirga, et ibi sunt ii uill'i. Val' et ualuit semper xv sol'. IN FERLIBERG HD'.

Herfridus ten' de feudo ep'i ESSAMELESFORD. Pro dim' solin se defd'. T'ra e' i car'. In d'nio e' i car', et iii uill'i cum i bord' h'nt i car'. Ibi iii serui, et viii ac' prati. TRE ual' lx sol', et post: xl sol'. Modo: lx solid'. Alret tenuit de rege E.

Osbertus ten' de Will'o filio taum ALDELOSE. IN BILISSOLD HD'. Ibi iacet dimid' solin. T'ra e' ii car'. In d'nio e' una car', et iii uill'i h'nt dimid' car'. TRE ualeb' xxx sol', et post: xx solid'. Modo xl sol'. Hęc terra est de feudo ep'i baioc', et remansit foris diuisionem suam. Godric tenuit de rege E cum BRADEBVRNE M̄. IN LIMOWART LEST. IN OXENAI HVND'.

Osbernus paisfor' ten' de ep'o PALESTREI. Pro iii iugis se defd'. T'ra e' ii car'. In d'nio e' una, et ix bord' h'nt dim' car'. Ibi ęccl'a et ii serui, et x ac' prati, et v piscar' de xii den'. Silua x porc'. TRE et post: ualuit xl sol'. Modo lx solid'. Eduui (pb'r) tenuit de rege E. IN LEST DE ESTREI. IN BEVSBERGE HVND'.

Isdem Osbernus ten' de ep'o xii acras terrę, quę ual' per annum iiii solid'.

Hugo de porth ten' de ep'o PESINGES ET PIHAM. Pro ii solins se defd'. T'ra e' In d'nio ii car' et dimid', et vi uill'i cum xiiii bord' h'nt i car'. TRE ualeb' c sol', et post: nichil. Modo: vi lib'. Lefstan et Leuuin et Eluret et Sired et alii ii tenuer' TRE, et poterant ire quolibet cum terris suis. IN LIMOWART LEST. IN NEVCERCE

Ep's Baiocensis ten' in d'nio BILSVITONE. Pro iiii solins se defd'. T'ra e' xv car'. In d'nio sunt v, et xlvii uill'i cum xxvii bord' h'nt xiiii car'. Ibi ęccl'a et x salinę de c denar', et x ac' prati. Silua l porc', et ii^{e} piscar' de v den'. TRE ualeb' x lib', et post: xxx lib'. Modo: l lib', et tamen reddit de firma lxx lib'. Alnod (cilt) tenuit. In hoc M̄ misit ep's iii^{es} denas, quę remanser' extra diuisionem comitis de ow.

Rotbertus de Romenel ten' de ep'o IN LANTPORT HVND'. AFETTVNE. Pro uno solin se defd'. T'ra e' iii car'. In d'nio e' una, et ix uill'i cum iii bord' h'nt iii car' et dimid'. Ibi ii serui. TRE: ualeb' c sol', et post: l solid', modo iiii lib'.

Isdem Rotbertus ten' de ep'o in Maresc dim' solin, et pro tanto se defd'. T'ra e' ii car'. Ibi xi uill'i cum ii bord' h'nt iii car', et piscariam / de ii solid'.

* (Isd' Robertus h't l burgenses in burgo de ROMENEL, et de eis h't rex omne seruitium, et s't quieti pro seruitio maris ab omni consuetudine pret' tribus, Latrocin', pace infracta, et forstel.)

DB-Ke-11ra

TRE et post ualuit xl sol'. Modo: l sol'. Alsi tenuit / de Goduino (com').

Isdem Robertus ten' de ep'o dimid' solin in Maresc, et pro tanto se defd'. T'ra e' ii car'. In d'nio e' dimid' car', et xv uill'i cum ii bord' h'nt iii car' et dimid'. TRE *et post: ualeb' xxx sol', modo xl sol'. Sex soch'i tenuer' TRE. IN ROVINDENE HVND'.

Isdem Rotbertus ten' de ep'o BENINDENE. Pro dimid' solin se defd'. T'ra e' ii car'. In d'nio e' una *car', et iiii uill'i cum ix bord' h'nt ii car'. Ibi silua v porc', et una ęccl'a. TRE et post, ualuit xl sol'. Modo: l solid'. Osier tenuit de rege E. IN ADILOVTESBRIGE / HVND'.

Isdem Rotbertus ten' de ep'o dimid' iugum, et pro tanto se defd'. Ibi una uidua manet reddens *xiii^{cim} denar' per annum. Val' et ualuit semper x solid'. Duo soch'i tenuer' TRE sine aulis et d'niis.

Isdem Rotbertus ten' de ep'o dimidiam denam de M̄ TITENTONE, quod ten' Hugo de montfort, et ibi h't terram ad dimid' car', et un' uill'm cum iii bord' et dimid' car', et ii^{as} piscar' de v solid'. Val' hoc totum et ualuit xv solid'. Hęc terra est extra diuisionem Hugon'. IN LEST DE ESTREI. IN ESTREI HVND'.

Herbertus ten' ad firmam de rege RINGETONE. De feudo est ep'i. T'ra e' In d'nio sunt ii^{e} car', et iiii uill'i cum vii bord' h'nt ii car' et dimid'. Ibi un' molin' de xl solid'. TRE ualeb' viii lib'. Quando recep': c sol'. Modo viii lib', et tamen reddit xiii lib'. Eduuardus tenuit de rege E.

Adam ten' de feudo ep'i in HAMOLDE dimid' iugum, Riculfus ten' de Adam. Et aliud dimid' iugum de AIMOLDE ten' Herbertus de Hugone nepote Herberti. Hoc utrunque ual' xx sol'.

Hugo ten' EWELLE de ep'o. Pro iii solins IN BEVSBERG HVND'. se defd'. T'ra e' In d'nio e' i car', et xv uill'i cum xii bord' h'nt ii car'. Ibi ii molini de xlvi solid', et iiii ac' prati. Silua iiii porc'. TRE ualeb' xii lib', et post: c sol'. Modo: x lib', et tamen redd' xii lib' et xii solid'. Edricus de Alham tenuit de rege E. De isto M̄ ten' Hugo de Montfort xvii acras terre, et unam denam et dimid', quod appreciatur vii solid'.

Isdem Hugo ten' de ep'o WESCLIVE. Pro ii solins se defd'. T'ra e' In d'nio e' i car', et xvii uill'i h'nt ii car'. TRE ualeb' viii lib'. Quando recep': vi lib'. Modo: viii lib'. De hoc M̄ ten' Hugo de montfort ii molin' de xxviii solid'. Edricus tenuit de rege E.

Isdem (Hugo) ten' SOLTONE de ep'o. Pro uno solin se defd'. T'ra e' In d'nio e' una car', et iii uill'i cum uno bord' redd't iiii solid' et vii *den'. TRE ualeb' xv lib', et post, et modo: xxx solid'. In hoc M̄ mansit Godricus et ten' xx^{ti} acras de alodio suo.

Idem Hugo ten' in DOVERE un' molin', qui reddit xlviii ferlingels de frumento, et non pertin' ulli Manerio.

Ansfridus ten' de feudo ep'i in Leueberge dimid' iugum, et ibi h't i uill'm et i bord'. Val' v solid'. Leuuinus tenuit de rege E.

Ibidem mansit quidam Altet qui tenuit de rege E ii^{as} acras in alodium, et tenuit eas de Ansfrido, et appreciatur vi solid'.

Radulfus de curbespine ten' COLRET de ep'o. T'ra e' In d'nio i car' et dim', et vi uill'i cum vii bord' h'nt ii car'. Ibi ii serui, et iiii ac' prati. Pro ii solins se defd'. TRE ualeb' viii lib', et post: xx solid'. Modo: vi lib'. Molleue tenuit de rege E.

Isdem Radulfus ten' EWELLE. Pro iii solins se defd'. T'ra e' In d'nio e' una car', et v uill'i cum iiii bord' h'nt ii car'. Ibi silua x porc'. De hoc M̄ ten' quidam miles i solin de Radulfo, et ibi h't i car' / cum iii bord'.

DB-Ke-11rb

Totum M̄ TRE ualeb' xii lib', et post: xx sol'. Modo: xl sol', et tamen quod Radulfus h't, reddit iiii lib'. // Hugo de montfort h't cap' manerii, et ibi v molin' et dimid' de vi lib'. / Molleue tenuit de rege E.

Isdem Radulfus ten' de ep'o SVANETONE. Pro ii solins se defd'. T'ra e' In d'nio i car', et ii bord' cum dimid' car'. De hac terra ten' Robertus de barbes i solin, et ibi h't iii uill'os cum dimid' car'. Et quidam Hugo ten' i solin, et h't ibi i car' in d'nio, et un' bord'. TRE ualeb' x lib'. Quando recep': xxx solid'. Modo: xl solid', et tamen redd' iiii lib'. Coloen tenuit de rege E.

Isdem Radulfus ten' de ep'o APLETONE. Pro uno solin se defd'. T'ra e' In d'nio sunt ii^{e} car', cum vi bord'. TRE ualeb' c sol', et post: x sol'. Modo: xl solid'. Ascored tenuit de rege E.

Herfridus ten' de Hugone BROCHESTELE, et est de feudo ep'i. (TRE) Pro uno solin se defd'. T'ra e' In d'nio e' i car', et ii serui. TRE ualeb' lx sol', et post: lx. Modo: xl. Quando Herbertus recep': iii^{a} iuga. Modo: ii^{o} iuga. Vlnod tenuit de rege E.

Turstinus tinel et uxor eius ten' ad firmam de rege W in Leueberge i iugum et v acras, et ibi sunt ii uill'i cum ii bord'. Val' et ualuit semper viii solid'. *Boche tenuit de rege E.

IN LEST DE ESTREI. IN ESTREI HVND'.

Ansfridus ten' de ep'o GOLLESBERGE. Pro ii solins et iii iugis se defd'. T'ra e' In d'nio sunt ii^{e} car', et xxiiii^{or} uill'i TRE ualeb' xii lib', et post: xx sol'. Modo: ix lib'. In Sanduuic h't archiep's xxxii masuras, ad hoc M̄ pertinent' et redd't xlii solid' et viii den'. Et Adeluuoldus h't i iugum quod ual' x solid'.

* Hoc M̄ ten[uer' v] teigni de rege E, et iii^{es} manebant ibi assidu[e. Duo uero] tenebant inde ii^{os} solins, in paragio, sed non m[aneba]nt ibi. Quando Ansfridus recep': fecit un' M̄.

Turstinus ten' de ep'o CHENOLTONE. Pro uno solin se defd'. T'ra e' In d'nio sunt ii car', cum ii bord'. TRE: et post iiii lib'. Modo: vii lib', et tamen reddit viii lib'. Eduuardus / tenuit de rege E.

Osbertus filius Letardi ten' de ep'o BEDESHAM. Pro uno iugo et dim' se defd'. T'ra e' In d'nio e' una car', cum uno uill'o et iiii bord'. TRE: ualeb' lx sol', et post xxx sol'. Modo: l solid'. Godesa tenuit de rege E. In eod' M̄ ten' de ipso osberno x teigni un' solin et dim' iugum, et ibi h'nt ipsi iiii car' et dimid'. TRE ualeb' c solid', et post: xxx solid'. Modo lx solid'.

Ansfridus ten' de ep'o SOLES. Pro uno solin se defd'. T'ra e' In d'nio sunt ii car', et viii uill'i cum dimid' car'. TRE ualeb' c sol', et post: xx sol'. Modo vi lib'. Elmer tenuit de rege E.

Radulfus filius Roberti ten' de ep'o HERTANGE. Pro uno solin se defd'. T'ra e'   In d'nio e' una car', et v uill'i cum ii bord' h'nt ii car'. TRE ualeb' xl solid', et post: x sol'. Modo lx solid'. Eddid tenuit de rege E.

Osbernus ten' de ep'o i iug' et dimid', in eod' hund', et ibi h't vii bord'. TRE ualuit x lib', et post: x solid'. Modo: xxx solid'. Ernold tenuit de rege E.

DB-Ke-11va

IN BEVSBERGE HVND'.

Hugo de montfort ten' de ep'o i solin uacuę terrę extra diuisionem suam, et adiacuit NEVENTONE M̄ quod h't intra suam diuisionem, et ibi h't i bord'. Val' et ualuit semper lx sol'.

Wibertus ten' dimid' iugum   IN ESTREI HVND'. quod iacuit in gildam de DOVERE, et modo defd' se cum terra Osberti filii Letard, et ualet per annum iiii solid'.

Osbernus filius Letard ten' de ep'o HAMA. Pro uno solin se defd'. T'ra e'   In d'nio e' i car', cum uno uill'o et ii bord' et ii seruis. TRE ualeb' l sol', et post: xx sol'. Modo lx sol'. Tres teigni tenuer' de rege E.

Isdem osbernus ten' de ep'o CILLEDENE. Pro uno solin et uno iugo et x acris se defd'. T'ra e'   In d'nio nichil modo, sed ix uill'i h'nt ibi ii car' et dimid'. TRE ualeb' lx sol', et post: xxx sol'. Modo: xl solid'. Goduinus tenuit de rege E et alii v teigni.   Osbernus misit terras eorum in un' M̄.

Aluredus ten' de ep'o MIDELEA. Pro iii iugis et xii acris se defd'. T'ra e' iii car'. In d'nio e' una car' et dim', et v uill'i cum ix bord' h'nt i car'. Ibi ęccl'a, et x ac' prati. Silua x porc'. TRE ualeb' lx sol', et post: xl sol'. Modo: lx sol'. Godricus tenuit de rege E.   IN SVMMERDENE HVND'.

Rotbertus Latin' ten' vi acras terre, et ibi h't dim' car'. Hanc terram tenuit unus soch's. Et de nouo dono ep'i h't in manu regis de Ricardo filio Gisleberti (com') x uill'os cum iii car', et siluam l porc', et inde reddit Rotbertus de firma vi lib'.

Turstinus ten' de ep'o TICHETESTE. Pro uno solin et dim' se defd'. T'ra e'   In d'nio e' i car', cum iiii bord' et et parua siluula. TRE ualeb' iiii lib', et post xl sol'. Modo: c sol'. Edricus de Alham tenuit de rege E.

Isdem Turstinus ten' de ep'o i iugum in WANESBERGE, et ibi sunt ii bord'.   Tochi tenuit de rege E.

Isdem Turstinus ten' de ep'o i iugum in ECE, et ibi sunt iiii bord'. Hęc ii^{o} iuga TRE ualeb' xv sol', et post: x sol'. Modo xx^{ti} sol'.

Osbertus ten' de ep'o i iugum et x acras in MASSEBERGE, et ibi sunt ii uill'i cum dimid' car'. Goduinus tenuit de rege E.

Isdem osbertus ten' de ep'o xv acras in ESMETONE, et ibi manet unus pb'r. Hoc utrunque TRE ualeb' xxx sol', et post: xx sol'. Modo xxx sol'. Sired tenuit de rege E.

IN ESTREI HVND'.

Radulfus de curbespine ten' de ep'o ii solins in WALWALESERE. T'ra e' In d'nio i car' et dim', et xiiii uill'i cum ii car' et dim'. De hac terra h't Robertus dimid' solin, et unam car' ibi. TRE ualeb' vii lib' et x sol', et post l sol'. Modo vii lib'. Wluuard tenuit de rege E.

Osbertus filius Letard ten' de ep'o i iugum in ECE, et ibi sunt iii uill'i. TRE: ualeb' xii sol', et post: vi sol'. Modo: xvi sol'. Bernoltus tenuit de rege E.

Rad' de curbespine ten' de ep'o ESSEWELLE. Pro iii solins se defd'. T'ra e' In d'nio sunt iii car', et unus uill's cum vii bord' h'nt dim' car'. Ibi unus seruus. Val' vi lib'. Molleue tenuit de rege E.

DB-Ke-11vb

Osbernus ten' de ep'o unum M̄ quod tenuer' iii liberi ho'es de rege E. Pro uno solin et dimid' se defd'. T'ra e' In d'nio e' una car', et unus uill's cum uno bord' h't dim' car'. TRE et post, et modo: ual' iiii lib'.

Radulfus de columbers ten' de ep'o SELINGES. Pro uno solin et dimid' se defd'. T'ra e' In d'nio e' una car', et iiii uill'i cum iii bord' h'nt dimid' car', et i car' et dim'. TRE ualeb' iiii lib', et post: xl sol'. Modo: c sol'. Vluuic tenuit de rege E. *( )

Radulfus de curbespine ten' (de ep'o) DANETONE. Pro dimid' solin se defd'. T'ra e' iii car'. In d'nio e' una, et iiii uill'i cum ii bord' h'nt i car'. Ibi ęccl'a, et iiii masurę in cantuaria, reddent' vi sol' un' den' minus. TRE ualeb' lx sol', et post: xx sol'. Modo: lx sol'. Molleue tenuit de rege E.

Isdem Radulfus ten' de ep'o i iugum in Brochestele. Quod Molleue tenuit de rege E, et ibi est unus uill's redd' xxx den'.

*(Radulfus de curbespine ten' xl acras terrę,) IN BEVSBERGE HD'. quas tenuit Molleue de rege E, et ibi est unus uill's reddens vi solid', et tant' ualet.

Rannulfus de ualbadon ten' dimid' iugum in HAMESTEDE, quod tenuer' ii liberi ho'es de rege E in Bochelande, et dicit modo Rannulfus quod ep's baiocensis dedit cuidam suo fr'i. Ibi est unus uill's reddens xxx denar'. *((/ VL' x sol'.)) IN NVNNIBERG HD'.

Anschitil de ros ten' de feudo ep'i ACRES, quod tenuer' duo fr's, et quisque habuit haulam. Modo est pro uno M̄, et pro uno solin se defd'. T'ra e' ii car'. In d'nio e' una car' et dim', et v uill'i cum v bord' h'nt i car'. Silua x porc'. Et ęccl'a. TRE ualeb' xl sol', et post: xxx sol'. Modo: lx sol'.

Rogerius filius anschitil ten' de IN BRICEODE HD'. feudo ep'i HASTINGELAI, quod tenuit Vlnod de rege E, et tunc defd' se pro uno solin, et modo pro iii iugis, quia Hugo de montfort ten' aliam partem intra diuisionem suam. T'ra e' iii car'. In d'nio sunt ii^{e}, et ii uill'i cum vi bord' h'nt i car'. Ibi iiii serui, et silua i porc'. TRE ualeb' lx sol', et post: xxx sol'. Modo lx solid'.

:

:

:

(VI) (TERRA ĘCCL'Ę DE LABATAILGE.)

ABBAS Sc'i MARTINI de loco belli (tenet) M̄ quod uocatur WI, quod TRE et modo se defd' pro vii solins. T'ra e' lii car'.

In d'nio ix car' sunt, et cxiiii uill'i cum xxii bord' h'nt xvii car'. Ibi ęccl'a, et vii serui, et iiii molini de xxiii solid' et viii den', et cxxxiii ac' prati, et silua ccc porc' de pasnagio.
TRE ualeb' quat' xx^{ti} lib' et c solid' et vi sol' et viii den'. Quando recep': cxxv lib' et x sol' de xx^{ti} in ora. Modo: c lib' ad numerum.
Et si abb' habuisset sacas et socas: xx lib' plus appreciaretur.

// Radulfus de curbespina (ten') unam denam et un' iugum de terra soch'orum huius Manerii, redd' de consuetud' vi den'. Et Adelulfus ii^{as} partes unius solin, redd' xii denar'. Et Hugo de montfort h't ii^{o} iuga, redd' ccc anguill' et ii^{os} solid', et sacam et socam in TRE reddebant.

// De xxii hund' pertin' isti M̄ saca et soca, et omnia forisfactura quę iuste pertin' regi.

DB-Ke-12ra

(VII) (TERRA ĘCCL'Ę SC'I AVGVSTINI.)

IN DIMIDIO LEST DE SVDTONE. IN LITELAI HVND'.

ABBAS Sc'i AVGVSTINI h't un' M̄ nomine PLVMSTEDE, quod defd' se pro ii solins et uno iugo. T'ra e' In d'nio e' i car', et xvii uill'i cum vi cot' h'nt vi car'. Ibi silua v porc' de pasnagio. TRE et post: ualuit x lib'. Modo: xii lib', et tamen reddit xiiii lib' et viii solid' et iii den'.

IN LEST DE ELESFORT. IN HAIHORNE HVND'.

Ipse abb' ten' LERTHAM, quod se defd' pro v solins et dimid'. T'ra e' xviii car'. In d'nio sunt ii car', et xl uill'i cum vii bord' h'nt xvi car'. Ibi i seruus, et ii molini de vi solid' et viii den', et viii ac' prati. Et silua *xl porc'. TRE ualeb' xxviii lib', et post: xvi lib'. Modo: xxviii lib'. De hoc M̄ ten' Robertus Latin' un' iugum, quod ualet v solid'.

IN BOROART LEST. IN BRIGE HVND'.

Ipse abb' ten' BORNE, quod se defd' pro uno solin. T'ra e' ii car'. In d'nio e' una, et ix uill'i cum uno bord' h'nt i car'. Ibi ii molini de ix solid' et vi den', et iii ac' prati et dimid'. Silua de v porc'. TRE ualeb' c sol', et post: xl solid'. Modo: c solid'.

Ipse abb' ten' M̄ LANPORT, et ibi est un' solin et un' iug', et semper quietum fuit, et sine consuetudine, et un' iugum iacet in alio hund' quod pertin' isti M̄, et lxx burgenses erant in cantuaria ciuit' huic M̄ pertinent'. In hoc M̄ sunt ii car' et dim' in d'nio, et xxviii uill'i cum lxiii bord' h'nt vi car'. Ibi xvii ac' prati. TRE ualeb' xx lib', et post: xviii lib'. Modo: xxxv lib' et iiii solid'. IN DVNAMESFORT HD'.

Ipse abb' ten' LITEBVRNE, quod se defd' pro vii solins. T'ra e' xii car'. In d'nio sunt iii car', et xxxv uill'i cum xiiii cot' h'nt vi et dim'. Ibi ęccl'a, et xxxviii ac' prati. Silua iiii porc'. TRE ualeb' xx(v) lib', et post: xx lib'. Modo: xxxii lib'.
De isto M̄ h't ep's baioc' in suo parco tant' quod ual' lx sol'.

Ipse abb' ten' WARWINTONE *et ded' ei ep's baiocensis pro excambio *parci sui. Pro dimid' solin et *xlii acris terrę se defd'. T'ra e' i car', et ibi e' in d'nio, cum iii cotar', et xvi ac' prati. TRE: ualeb' iiii lib', et post: xl sol'. Modo: iiii lib'.
Hoc M̄ tenuit Edricus de Sbern biga, et modo ten' Radulfus / de abb'e.

Ipse abb' ten' ESTVRAI IN ESTVRAI HVND'. quod se defd' pro v solins quietis. T'ra e' xii car'. *In d'nio sunt ii car', et *xxxix cum xxxii bord' h'nt xii car'. Ibi ęccl'a, et x molini de viii lib', et vii piscarię de v sol', et xxviii ac' prati. De pasnagio xxx porc'. TRE ualeb' l sol'. Quando abb' recep': xlv lib'. Modo: l lib', et tamen redd' liiii lib'. IN TANET HVND' / S' MILDREDĘ.

Ipse abb' ten' TANET M̄ quod se defd' pro xlviii solins. T'ra e' lxii car'. In d'nio sunt ii, et cl uill'i cum l bord' h'nt lxiii car'. Ibi ęccl'a et unus pb'r

DB-Ke-12rb

qui dat xx solid' per ann'. Ibi una salina, et ii^{e} piscarię de iii den', et un' molin'. TRE ualeb' quat' xx lib'. Quando abb' recep': xl lib'. Modo c lib'. De isto M̄ ten' iii milites tant' de terra uillanorum, quod ual' ix lib' quando pax est in terra, et ibi h'nt iii car'.

Ipse abb' ten' CISTELET, quod pro xii IN CISTELET HVND'. solins se defd'. T'ra e' xxx car'. In d'nio sunt v car', et lxxii uill'i cum lxviii bord' h'nt xxxix car'. Ibi ęccl'a de xii solid', et xiiii serui. Ibi l ac' prati, et xlvii salinę de l summis salis. De pasnag' cxxx porc'. TRE ualeb' liii lib', et post: xl lib'. Modo: lxxviii lib'. Ibi sunt iii arpenni uineę. De isto M̄ ten' iiii francig' milites, quod ual' per ann' xii lib'.

Ipse abb' ten' unum paruum burgum IN FOREWIC HVND'. quod uocatur FOREWIC. Huius burgi ii^{as} partes ded' rex E sc'o Augustino. Terciam uero partem quę fuerat Goduini (com'): ep's baiocensis concessit eid' sc'o annuente rege W. Pro uno se iugo defd'. Ibi fuer' c masurę terrę iiii minus, redd'tes xiii sol'. Modo sunt lxxiii masurę, t'ntd' redd't. TRE et post ualeb' c solid'. Modo: xi lib' et ii solid'.

Ibidem sunt xxiiii ac' terrę, quas semper habuit S' Augustinus, ubi fuer' et sunt vi burgenses redd'tes xxii solid'. In isto burgo ten' archiep's Lanfr' vii masuras terrę, quę TRE seruiebant S' Augustino, modo arch' aufert ei seruitium.

Iuxta ciuitatem cantuar' h't S' Augustinus dimid' solin, quod semper fuit quietum, et ibi e' i car' in d'nio, cum xv bord', et *vi(i) acrę prati. Et ibid' sunt iiii ac' terre quas ten' iiii moniales in elemosina de abb'e, et redd't ii sol' et unam summam farinę. Totum hoc TRE et post, et modo: ual' iiii lib'. IN LEST DE WIWARLET. IN FAVRESHANT HVND'.

Ipse abb' ten' WIRENTONE, quod pro uno solin se defd'. T'ra e' ii car'. In d'nio e' una, et ix uill'i cum i car'. Ibi ii^{e} ac' prati, et v porc' de pasnag' siluę. TRE ualeb' lx sol'. Quando recep': xl sol'. Modo: iiii lib'. IN WI HVND'.

Ipse abb' ten' ESMEREFEL, et Anschitil de eo. Pro uno solin se defd'. T'ra e' i car', et ibi e' in d'nio cum v bord', et vi ac' prati. Silua x porc'. TRE xl sol', et post: xx sol'. Modo: xl sol'.

In DARENDEN ten' Adam de abb'e dimid' solin. T'ra e' dimid' car'. Ibi sunt ii serui, et vii ac' prati. Val' et semper ualuit xx sol'.

Ipse abb' ten' SETLINGES M̄ IN BOLTONE HVND'. sine halla, quod se defd' pro vi solins. T'ra e' xi car'. Nichil in d'nio. Ibi xxx uill'i h'nt x car'. Ibi ęccl'a. TRE ualeb' xv lib'. Quando recep': viii lib'. Modo: xiii lib' / et v solid'.

Ipse abb' ten' dimid' iugum IN CALEHEVE HVND'.

in Rotinge, quod TRE se defd' pro dim' solin. Ibi fuit et est una car' in d'nio. Val' et ualuit semper xv sol'. IN CERT HD'.

Ipse abb' ten' un' iugum RAPENTONE, et Anseredus de eo, et pro uno iugo se defd'. T'ra e' ii car'. *In d'nio e' una, cum iiii bord'. Ibi xi ac' prati, et quarta pars molini de xv den', et silua x porc'. Et adhuc h't ii iuga quę de suo d'nio dedit ei abb', et ibi ii uill'os cum viii bord'. TRE et post: ualuit iii lib'. / Modo: iiii lib'.

DB-Ke-12va

Ansfridus ten' de abb'e CHERINCHEHELLE. IN FERLEBERG HD'. Pro dimid' solin se defd'. T'ra e' i car'. In d'nio sunt ii^{e}, et viii uill'i h'nt i car' et dimid'. TRE et post, ualuit xx^{ti} sol'. Modo xxx^{ta} sol'. IN LEST DE ESTREA. IN CORNELEST HVND'.

Ipse abb' ten' NORBORNE. Pro xxx solins se defd'. T'ra e' liiii car'. In d'nio sunt iii, et lxxix uill'i cum xlii bord' h'nt xxxvii car'. Ibi xl ac' prati, et silua x porc'. *TI
TRE ualeb' quat' xx lib'. Quando recep': xx lib'. Modo: lxxvi lib'.
De terra uillanorum huius M̅ ten' Oidelard i solin, et ibi h't ii car' cum xi bord'. Val' iiii lib'.

// De ead' terra uillanorum ten' Gislebertus ii solins, dimid' iugum minus, et ibi h't i car' et iiii uill'os cum i car'. Val' vi lib'.

// Wadardus ten' de isto M̅ iii solins lx acras minus de terra uillanorum, et ibi h't i car', et viii uill'os cum i car', et ii seruos. Val' ix lib'. Ipse uero nullum seruitium reddit abb'i, nisi xxx sol' quos persoluit in anno.

// Odelinus ten' de ead' terra uillanorum i solin, et ibi h't i car' cum iii bord'. Val' iii lib'.

// Marcherius ten' de ead' terra uillanorum quod ual' viii solid'.

// Osbernus filius Letardi ten' dimid' solin et xi acras prati, de terra uillanorum, quod ual' xxv sol'. Ipse redd' abb'i xv solid'.

// Rannulfus de columbers ten' un' iugum. Val' l den'.

// Rannulfus de ualbadon ten' un' iugum, et redd' inde l den'.

// Item supradictus Oidelardus ten' de hoc M̅ un' solin, et uocatur BEVESFEL, et ibi h't ii car' cum x bord'. Val' vi lib'.

Ipse abb' ten' MVNDINGEHAM. Pro duobus solins et dimid' se defd'. T'ra e' v car'. In hoc M̅ terra quam tenent monachi nunquam geldauit. Et Wadardus ten' ibi terram quę TRE semper geldauit, et illo tempore erat M̅ insimul. Modo h'nt monachi in d'nio iiii car', et xx bord' cum una car', et un' molin' de xvi solid', et siluam iiii^{or} porc'. Ibi ęccl'a. TRE ualeb' xxii lib', et post: x lib'. Pars abb'is: xxvi lib'.
Wadardus h't in d'nio ibi i car', et viii uill'os cum ii^{bus} bord' *h'ntibus iiii car'. Val' et ualuit x lib'.
Nullum seruitium inde reddit nisi xxx solid' per annum abb'i.

Ipse abb' ten' SIBERTESWALT. IN BEVSBERG HVND'. Pro duobus solins se defd'. T'ra e' iiii car'. In d'nio e' una et dim', et xi uill'i cum *vi bord', h'nt ii car' et dim'. Ibi ęccl'a. TRE ualeb' viii lib'. Quando recep': xl sol'. Modo: vi lib', et tamen redd' viii lib'.

Ipse abb' ten' PLATENOVT. Pro uno solin se defd'. T'ra e' In d'nio nichil, sed iiii uill'i cum iii bord' h'nt car' et dimid'. Ibi silua minuta. Radulfus de curbespina h't xxv acras de hac terra. TRE et post, et modo ual' xx solid', tamen appreciatur xl solid', eo quod sit ad firmam.

Ipse abb' ten' PRESTETVNE. Pro v solins IN PRESTETVN / HVND'. se defd'. T'ra e' viii car'. In d'nio sunt ii^{e} car', et xxv uill'i cum xvii bord', h'nt ix car'. Ibi parua siluula.

DB-Ke-12vb

De hoc M̄ ten' Vital' i solin et dim' iugum, et ibi h't in d'nio ii car', et xvii bord' cum dim' car'. Totum M̄ TRE ualeb' x lib'. Quando recep': vi lib'. Modo ual' xiiii lib' quod h't abb'. Quod Vitalis tenet: c solid' ualet.

Ansfridus ten' de abb'e ÆLVETONE. Pro dimid' solin et dim' iugo se defd'. T'ra e' In d'nio e' una car', et iii uill'i cum iii bobus in car'. In isto M̄ ten' Ansfridus dimid' solin de d'nio monachorum, et reddit inde S' Augustino c denar' per annum. Godessa tenuit in alodium, et ded' inde S' Augustino xxv denar' in elemosina, unoquoque anno. TRE ualeb' xl sol', et post: x sol'. Modo: lx solid'.

IN LEST et in hund' de ESTREI, h't S' Augustinus iii uirg' terre, et ibi e' in d'nio i car' cum v bord'. TRE ualeb' x solid', et post: v sol'. Modo: xx solid'. IN LIMOWART LEST. IN STOTINGES HVND'.

Gaufridus ten' BODESHAM de abb'e. Pro uno solin se defd'. T'ra e' ii car', et ibi sunt cum viii bord'. Silua xv porc'. TRE ualeb' iiii lib', et post: xx sol'. Modo: iiii lib'. / Quidam uill's tenuit.

Ipse abb' ten' in LANPORT ii solins et un' iugum. T'ra e' vi car'. Ibi sunt ix uill'i cum iiii bord', h'ntes vi car'. Ibi x ac' prati, et silua ii porc'. TRE ualeb' vi lib', et post: iiii lib'. Modo: viii lib'. IN LEST DE WIWARLET. IN LANGEBRIGE HVND'.

Ipse abb' ten' CHENETONE. TRE se defd' pro iiii solins, et iacuit in BORCHEMERES. T'ra e' x car'. Ibi sunt xxx uill'i h'ntes x car'. Ibi ęccl'a. Vill'i tenuer' TRE. Cum his iiii solins h't S' Augustinus i iugum quietum ab omni scoto regio, et ibi tant' siluę unde exeunt de pasnagio xl porci, aut liiii denar' et un' obol'. Totum hoc TRE ualeb' x lib', et post viii lib'. Modo: xii lib' et x sol'. IN MARESS DE ROMENEL.

Ipse abb' ten' BVRWARMARESC. Pro ii solins et iii iugis se defd'. T'ra e' xii car'. In d'nio sunt iiii, et xliiii uill'i cum v bord' h'nt x car'. TRE ualeb' xx lib', et post: x lib'. Modo: xxx lib'.

Scyra testificatur quod Bedenesmere fuit S' Angustini TRE, et de illo qui eam teneb' habeb' abb' sacam et socam.

:

(VIII) (TERRA SC'I PETRI DE GAND.) IN GRENVIZ HVND'.

ABBAS de Gand ten' de rege LEVESHAM, et de rege E tenuit, et tunc et modo pro ii solins se defd'. T'ra e' xiiii car'. In d'nio sunt ii^{e} car', et l uill'i cum ix bord' h'nt xvii car'. Ibi iii serui, et xi molini cum gablo rusticorum viii lib' et xii solid' redd't. De exitu portus: xl solid'. Ibi xxx ac' prati. De silua: l porci de pasnag'. Totum M̄ TRE ualeb' xvi lib', et post: xii lib'. Modo: xxx^{ta} lib'.

:

:

:

DB-Ke-13ra

:

(IX) (TERRA HVGONIS DE MONTFORT.)

HVGO de montfort ten' un' M̄ ESTWELLE, quod tenuit Frederic de rege E, et pro uno solin se defd'. Tria iuga sunt infra diuisionem Hugonis, et quartum iugum est extra, et est de feudo ep'i Baioc'. T'ra e' iii car' int' totum. In d'nio sunt ii^{e} car', et v uill'i cum v bord' h'nt i car' et dim'. Ibi x serui, et xii ac' prati, et silua TRE ualeb' lxx sol', et post: xxx sol'. Modo: lxx solid'.

Ipse Hugo ten' HAINTONE de rege, quod Vlsi prb'r tenuit de rege E, et pro uno solin se defd'. T'ra e' i car', et ibi e' cum i uill'o et iiii bord', et iii ac' prati. TRE et post: et modo, ual' xx solid'.

IN LEST DE WIWARLET. IN LANGEBRIGE HVND'.

Maigno ten' de Hug' SEIVETONE. Bresibalt tenuit de rege E, et pro dimid' solin se defd'. T'ra e' i car', et ibi e' in d'nio, cum i uill'o et vi bord'. Ibi ęccl'a et pb'r, et un' molin' de x den', et viii ac' prati. TRE ualeb' xxx sol', et post: xx sol'. Modo: xxx solid'.

Isdem Maigno ten' de Hugone ESTEFORT. Turgisus tenuit de Goduino (com'), et pro uno solin se defd'. T'ra e' dimid' car'. In d'nio tamen e' una car', et ii uill'i h'nt i car'. Ibi ii serui, et viii ac' prati. TRE ualeb' xxv solid'. Quando recep': xx sol'. Modo: xxx solid'.

Ipse Hugo ten' ESSELLA. Tres ho'es tenuer' de rege E, et potuer' ire quolibet cum terris suis. Pro iii^{bus} iugis se defd'. T'ra e' i car' et dimid'. Ibi modo iiii uill'i cum ii bord' h'nt i car', et vi acras prati. Totum TRE ualeb' xx solid', et post: xv solid'. Modo: xx solid'.

Aliam ESSETESFORD ten' Maigno de Hugone. Wirelmus tenuit de rege E. Pro uno solin se defd'. T'ra e' iiii car'. In d'nio sunt ii^{e}, et ii uill'i cum xv bord' h'nt iii car'. Ibi ęccl'a et pb'r, et iii serui, et ii molin' de x solid' et ii den'. TRE ualeb' lxx sol', et post: lx sol'. Modo: c sol'.

IN LIMOWART LEST. IN NEWECERCE HVND'.

Isdem Hugo ten' in Maresc de Romenel i iugum. T'ra e' Medietatem huius terrę tenuer' ii^{o} soch'i, et ii^{o} uill'i aliam. Ibi sunt modo iiii uill'i, h'ntes i car'. Hęc terra ualuit et ual' xii solid'.

Isd' Hugo ten' dimid' iugum, quod tenuit unus soch's. Ibi ii bord' sunt modo. Hęc terra appreciatur in Titentone, quia illuc arata est cum d'nicis carrucis.

Hoc testatur hund' et burgenses de Doure, et ho'es abb'is S' Augustini, et Estrea lest: quod terra ETRETONE quam calumniantur canonici S' Martini de Doure super Hugonem de montfort, quod Vluuile Wilde eam tenuit in alodio TRE, et defd' se *pro uno iugo, et ibi h't i car' in d'nio, et v bord' cum i car', et un' molin' de xx solid'. Val' et ualuit x lib'.

Ipse *Hugo ten' ESTBRIGE in d'nio. IN WERDE HVND'. Alsi tenuit de Goduino (com'), et pro uno solin se defd'. T'ra e' vi car'. In d'nio sunt iii car', et ii uill'i cum xxxvi bord' h'nt iiii car'. Ibi viii salinę cum tercia parte nonę salinę de xx solid'. Dimid' piscaria viii den'. Silua de iii porc' de pasnag'. Ibi ii ęccl'ę. TRE et post: ualuit x lib'. Modo: xv lib'.

Bertrannus ten' de Hug' dimid' iug' et dimid' uirgam. Pro tanto se defd'. Adelelmus tenuit de rege E. T'ra e' ad i car'. TRE ualeb' xx^{ti} solid'.

Herueus ten' de Hugone BLACHEMENESTONE. Blacheman

DB-Ke-13rb

tenuit TRE, et pro dimidio solin se defd'. T'ra e' ii car'. In d'nio sunt ibi, et iii uill'i cum x bord' cum i car'. Ibi ęccl'a et unus seruus. TRE ualeb' iiii lib', et post: iii lib'. Modo vi lib'.

Isd' Hugo ten' in Maresc de Romenel un' solin dimid' uirga minus. Pro tanto se defd'. T'ra e' iii car'. Ibi xiiii soch'i h'nt iii car'. TRE ualeb' iiii lib', et post: iii lib'. Modo: c sol'.

Rogerius ten' de Hugone un' iugum in Maresc de Romenel. Pro uno iugo se defd'. Duo soch'i tenuer'. T'ra e' i car', et ibi e' cum iii bord'. TRE ualeb' xxx sol', et post: xv sol'. Modo: / xxx solid'.

Rotbertus ten' de Hugone in eod' Maresch sextam partem unius iugi. Vnus soch's tenuit. Val' et ualuit v solid'. IN HEN HVND'.

Rogerius ten' de Hugone POSTINGES. Sbern (biga) tenuit. Pro duobus solins et dimid' se defd'. T'ra e' xiii car'. In d'nio sunt iii^{es}, et xvi uill'i cum vii bord' h'nt vii car'. Ibi ii ęcclesiolę, et ii molini de vi solid', et xl ac' prati. Silua xl porc'. TRE ualeb' x lib', et post: c solid'. Modo: xiiii lib'. De isto M̄ ten' Radulfus de curbespine iii denas, extra diuisionem sunt, et ual' xv solid'.

Isdem Hugo ten' dimid' solin, quod Aldret (bot) tenuit de rege E sine halla. Pro dimid' solin se defd'. T'ra e' iii car'. Ibi unus uill's cum iiii bord' man', nulla ibi car'. Vn' molin' de xxv denar', et v ac' prati.

Isdem Hugo ten' BELICE. Turgis tenuit de rege E, et pro uno solin se defd'. T'ra e' In d'nio e' una car', et ii^{o} uill'i cum uno bord' h'nt i car'. Ibi iii ac' prati. Hę duę terrę TRE ualeb' lx sol', et post: xx sol'. Modo: lx sol'.

Ipse Hugo ten' unam terram quam IN NEWECERCE HD'. Azor (Rot) tenuit de rege E sine halla. *Pro uno solin se defd'. T'ra e' v car'. Ibi viii uill'i cum iii bord' h'nt ii car'. TRE et post: ualuit viii lib'. Modo: ix lib'.

Ipse Hugo ten' dimid' solin in Maresch de Romenel. Pro tanto se defd'. T'ra e' iiii car'. Duodecim soch'i tenuer' et tenent h'ntes iiii car'. Val' et ualuit lx solid'.

Isdem Hugo ten' in ipso Maresch IN ADELOVESBRIGE HD'. un' iugum. Pro tanto se defd'. T'ra e' ii car'. Ibi sunt xii soch'i cum viii bord' h'ntes ii car'. Hę duę terrę TRE ualeb' cx sol', et post et modo similit'.

IN BLACHEBVRNE HD'.

Ipse Hugo ten' TINTENTONE. Vlnod tenuit de rege E, et tunc defd' se pro uno solin. Modo pro dimidio, quia foris diuisionem est. T'ra e' v car'. In d'nio sunt ii^{ę} car', et xxi uill's cum vi bord' h'nt vii car'. Ibi ęccl'a et ix serui, et iii piscarię de v solid', et xxxviii ac' prati. Silua xl porc'. TRE ualeb' xii lib', et post: vi lib'. Modo: vii lib'.

Isdem Hugo ten' dimid' iugum quod tenuer' v soch'i et modo tenent, h'ntes i car' ibi cum iiii bord'. Val' et ualuit / semper v solid'.

DB-Ke-13va

Herueus ten' de Hugone IN ESTRAITES HD'. SEDLINGES. Osuuard tenuit de rege E. Pro uno solin se defd'. T'ra e' vii car'. In d'nio sunt iii car', et viii uill'i cum xxv bord' h'nt iiii car'. Ibi ii ęccl'ę, et un' molin' de xxx den', et xxxvi ac' prati, et silua de vi porc'. TRE ualeb' viii lib', et post: c solid'. Modo: vii lib'.

Alnod ten' de Hugone HORTONE. IN STOTINGES HD'. Leuuinus tenuit de rege E, et pro dimidio solin se defd'. T'ra e' iii car'. In d'nio sunt ii^{e} car', et v uill'i cum vi bord' h'nt i car' et dimid'. Ibi ęccl'a, et un' molin' de xxv den', et xxiiii ac' prati. Silua x porc'. TRE ualeb' xl sol', et post: xx. Modo: lx sol'. Ibid' ten' Alnod i iugum de Hugone, sed nil ibi est.

Ipse Hugo ten' iii uirg' et dimid' in eod' LEST, quas tenuer' iii soch'i de rege E. Ibi modo unus uill's h't dimid' car' cum iii bord'. Val' et ualuit semper x solid'. IN HAME HVND'.

Will's ten' de Hugone iii^{a} iuga et dimid' uirga in ORLAVESTONE. Hanc terram tenuer' xi soch'i. T'ra e' iii car'. Ibi modo ii car' in d'nio, et xv uill'i cum ix bord' h'nt iii car' et dim'. Ibi ii^{e} ęccl'ę, et xx ac' prati. Silua vi porc'. TRE ualeb' lx sol', et post: xxx sol'. Modo: c solid'.

Radulfus filius Ricardi ten' de Hugone dimid' solin in Rochinges, quod Leuret tenuit de rege E. Pro dimid' solin se defd'. T'ra e' ii car'. Ibi modo xii uill'i h'nt unam car' et dimid'. De silua: i porc'. TRE ualeb' l sol', et post: xxx sol'. Modo: l solid'.

Radulfus ten' de Hug' HORTVN. IN STOTINGES HD'. Duo soch'i tenuer' de rege E, et pro uno iugo et dim' se defd'. T'ra i car' et dim'. In d'nio e' una, cum iiii uill'is, et un' molin' de xxx den', et x ac' prati. De silua vi porc'. TRE ualeb' xl sol', et post: xx sol'. Modo: xxx solid'.

Hugo de manneuile ten' de Hug' IN ESTRAITES HD'. ESTRAITES. Vlnod tenuit de rege E. Pro ii solins se defd'. T'ra e' viii car'. In d'nio sunt ii^{e}, et xi uill'i cum xxv bord' h'nt v car'. Ibi ęccl'a, et vii serui, et xxx ac' prati. TRE ualeb' *(x sol', et post: iiii sol'. Modo: viii *(so)l')((ib'.))

Ansfridus ten' de Hug' i iugum quod tenuit in eod' hund' unus soch's de rege E, et pro uno iugo se defd'. T'ra e' i car'. Ibi e' cum uno uill'o et ii bord', et un' molin' de xxvi den', et viii ac' prati. TRE et modo ual' xl sol'.

Rotbertus cocus ten' de Hugone i iugum quod tenuit unus soch's et pro tanto se defd'. Ibi e' una car' cum uno bord', et iiii ac' prati. TRE et modo ual' xxx solid'.

Gislebertus ten' de Hugone un' iugum IN LANGEBRIGE HD'. quod tenuit quidam soch's de rege E. Val' et ualuit iiii sol'. Nil ibi fuit nec est.

// De Etwelle quam ten' Herbertus filius Iuonis extra diuisionem Hugon', ten' ipse Hugo xiiii acras terrę, infra suam diuisionem, et ual' ii sol'.

DB-Ke-13vb

IN ESTREA LEST. IN BEVSBERGE HVND'.

Ipse Hugo de montfort ten' ETWELLE. Molleue tenuit Pro iii solins se defd', *((et modo: pro i^{o} solin.)) T'ra e' i car', et ibi e' in d'nio, et xix bord' h'nt i car'. Ibi ęccl'a, et iiii molini (et dimid') de iiii lib' et xvi sol' et iiii den', et iiii ac' prati. TRE ualeb' xi lib', et post: iiii lib'. Modo: viii lib'.

Ipse Hugo ten' NEVENTONE. Edericus tenuit de rege E, et pro ii solins se defd' tunc, et modo pro uno quia alius est extra diuisionem. T'ra e' ii car', et ibi sunt in d'nio. Ibi ęccl'a et xxi bord', et iii serui cum iii car'. Ibi iii molini et dimid' de cv solid'. Totum TRE ualeb' xii lib', et post: iii lib'. Modo: xii lib', quod h't Hugo intra diuisionem suam.

Intra diuisionem hanc est unus soch's tenens xvi acras terrę, et ipse idem tenuit de rege E.

In eod' hund' ten' id' Hugo unam partem Iaonei, quę nichil redd' nec reddid', nec ad ullum M̄ iacuit, sed est intra diuisionem suam, et fuit de d'nio regis. *Aluuinus (pb'r) tenut

In eod' hund' h't Fulbertus de Hugone un' molin', et redd' xxiiii sol'.

Herfridus ten' de Hugone POLTONE. Vluuinus tenuit de rege E, et pro uno solin se defd'. T'ra e' ii car'. Ibi sunt iii uill'i et ęcclesiola. TRE ualeb' xl sol', et post: xv sol'. Modo: xxx sol'.

IN WIWART LEST. IN BERISOVT HVND'.

Ipse Hugo ten' BREBVRNE. Godricus de burnes tenuit de rege E, et pro vii solins se defd' tunc, et modo pro v solins et dimid' et dim' iugo, quia alia pars est extra diuisionem Hug', et eam ten' ep's baiocensis. T'ra e' xv car'. In d'nio sunt ii^{e}, et xxxi uill's cum x bord' h'nt x car'. Ibi ęccl'a et viii^{to} serui, et ii molini de vii solid', et xx ac' prati. Silua de xxv porc'. TRE: ualeb' xx lib', et post: viii lib'. Modo: xvi lib'.

In hund' de Certh ten' quędam femina de Hugone i uirgam, quam unus soch's tenuit de rege E. Val' iii solid'.

Ipse Hugo ten' dimid' iugum in TEPINDENE IN BLACHEBVRNE HD'. quod tenuit Norman de rege E, et pro dim' iugo se defd'. Ibi sunt ii^{o} uill'i cum dim' car'. Valuit semper et ual' c denar'.

IN LIMOWART LEST. IN ESTRAITES HD'.

Ipse Hugo ten' SIBORNE. Osiar tenuit de rege E, et pro uno solin se defd' tunc et modo. T'ra e' ii car'. In d'nio e' una, et unus uill's cum iiii bord' h't i car', et ibi unus seruus. TRE ualeb' lx solid', et post: xx sol'. Modo: iiii lib'.

Isdem Hugo h't *(   ) dimid' solin SVANETONE. T'ra e' i car'. Norman tenuit de rege E, et pro tanto se defd'. Ibi iiii uill'i h'nt i car'. Ibi silua de v porc'. TRE ualeb' xxv sol', et post: xv sol'. Modo: xxx sol'.

Nigellus ten' de Hugone un' iugum, et in Aia vii acrę. Vnus soch's tenuit de rege E. T'ra e' i car'. In d'nio e' dimidia car', et vi bord' et ii serui, et v ac' prati. TRE ualeb' xx solid', et post: x sol'. Modo: xxv sol'.

Will's filius Grosse ten' de Hugone BONINTONE. Norman tenuit de rege E, et pro uno solin se defd'. T'ra e' iiii car'. In d'nio e' una, et ix uill'i cum iiii bord' h'nt ii / car'.

DB-Ke-14ra

Ibi ęccl'a et viii serui, et silua viii porc'. TRE ualeb' iiii lib', et post: iii lib'. Modo: c solid'.

Herueus ten' de Hugone OBTREPOLE. Alrebot tenuit de rege E, et pro uno solin se defd'. T'ra e' vi car'. In d'nio est una, et xi uill'i cum ii car', et unus seruus, et x ac' prati, et silua redd' v denar' de pasnagio. *TR TRE ualeb' l solid', et post: xx sol'. Modo: iiii lib'.

IN BLACHEBVRNE HVND' ET IN NEVCERCE HVND'.

Heraldus ten' dimid' solin unam uirgam minus

Sex soch'i tenuer' de rege E, et pro tanto se defd'. T'ra e' v car'. In d'nio sunt ii^{e}, et xxxi bord' h'nt iii car'. Ibi unus seruus. TRE ualeb' lx sol', et post: xxx sol'. Modo: iiii lib' et xv sol'. Et adhuc h't unam denam quę iacuit in FANE manerio Adam. Ibi sunt ii bord', redd'tes xxx denar'. Val' et ualuit semper v sol'.

Ipse Hugo ten' dimid' solin IN BERISCOLT HVND'. in HASTINGELIE. Vlnod tenuit de rege E, et pro tanto se defd'. Modo ten' quidam homo de Hugone, et h't ibi ii bord', reddentes iiii solid'. Valuit semper et ual' x sol'.

Ipse Hugo ten' in d'nio un' iugum et dimid' IN LANGEBRIGE / HD'. in TEVEGATE. God tenuit de rege E. Ibi est modo unus uill's cum i car', et ibi viii ac' prati. TRE: ualeb' xx sol', et post: x sol'. Modo: xx solid'.

In eod' hund' est una uirga terrę in SVESTONE, quam tenuit unus soch's de rege E. Ibi modo est unus bord', xii denar' redd'. TRE ualeb' xxx den', et post: xviii. Modo: iii solid'.

:

:

:

:

(X) (TERRA COMITIS EVSTACHII.)

IN DIMIDIO LEST DE SVDTONE. IN OSTREHAM HVND'.

Comes EVSTACHIVS ten' de rege OISTREHAM. Goduinus (com') tenuit de rege E, et pro iiii solins se defd' tunc et modo. T'ra e' In d'nio sunt ii^{e} car', et xlii uill'i cum vii bord' h'nt xxx car'. Ibi x serui, et un' molin' de v solid', et xvi ac' prati, et de silua: c porc'. TRE ualeb' xxx lib'. Quando recep': xx^{ti}iiii lib'. Modo: xl lib'.

:

IN LEST DE WIWARLET. IN WI HVNDRET.

Ipse comes ten' BOLTVNE. Goduinus com' tenuit, et pro vii solins se defd' tunc et modo. T'ra e' xxxiii car'. In d'nio sunt iii^{es}, et lxvii uill'i cum v bord' h'nt xxx car'. Ibi ęccl'a, et xvii serui, et ii molini de vii solid' et ii denar', et xxvi ac' prati. Silua cc porc'. TRE ualeb' xx lib', et post: xxx lib'. Modo: xl lib'.

:

:

:

:

:

DB-Ke-14rb

:

(XI) (TERRA RICARDI F. GISLEBERTI.) IN TVIFERDE HVND'.

RICARDVS de Tonebrige ten' HALLINGES, et Aldret tenuit de rege E, et tunc et modo defd' se pro ii solins. T'ra e' xvi car'. In d'nio e' una et dimidia, et xvi uill'i cum xii bord' h'nt vi car'. Ibi ii ęccl'ę, et xv serui, et ii molini de xxv solid', et iiii piscarię de mille et septingent' anguill', xx^{ti} minus. Ibi v ac' prati. Et silua cl porc'. TRE et post: ualuit xxx lib'. Modo: xx lib', eo quod terra uastata est a pecunia. IN MEDESTAN HVND'.

Isdem Ricardus ten' BERMELINGE. Alret tenuit de rege E, et tunc et modo pro uno solin se defd'. T'ra e' iiii car'. In d'nio

ii car', et v uill'i cum viii bord' h'nt v car'. Ibi xiii serui, et un' molin' de v solid', et iiii ac' prati. Silua x porc'. TRE ualeb' iiii lib', et post: c solid'. Modo: iiii lib'.
:
:
:

(XII) (TERRA HAMONIS VICECOMITIS.)

IN LEST DE WIWARLET. IN WIT HVND'.

HAIMO uicecom' ten' de rege un' Maner', quod TRE se defd' pro ii solins et dimid', et modo pro uno solin et iii iugis. T'ra e' viii car'. In d'nio v bou' arantes, et xvi uill'i cum xv bord' h'nt x car'. Ibi ęccl'a, et vii serui, et un' molin' de ix solid' et lx anguill'. Ibi xx ac' prati, et silua xxx porc'. TRE ualeb' x lib', et post: vii lib'. Modo: xiiii lib' et vi solid' / et vi den'. De isto M̄ ten' Hugo de montfort iii^{a} iuga et dim'. Val' lx sol'.

IN DIMIDIO LEST DE SVDTONE. IN GRENVIZ HVND'.

Ibi h't Haimo lxiii acras terrę, quę pertin' in HVLVIZ. Will's accipitrarius tenuit de rege E. Ibi sunt xi bord' redd'tes xli denar'. Totum ual' iii lib'.

IN LEST DE ELESFORD. IN LITEFEL HVND'.

Ipse Haimo ten' MAROVRDE. Norman tenuit de rege E, et tunc et modo pro ii solins se defd'. T'ra e' ix car'. In d'nio sunt ii^{ę}, et xxviii uill'i cum xv bord' h'nt x car'. Ibi ęccl'a, et x serui, et ii molini de x solid', et ii^{ę} piscar' de ii solid'. Ibi xx ac' prati, et tant' siluę unde exeunt lx porc', de pasnag'. TRE ualeb' xii lib', et post: x lib'. Modo: xix lib'.

IN LEST DE BOROWART. IN WITESTAPLE HVND'.

Ipse Haimo ten' BLEHEM. Norman tenuit de rege E, et tunc et modo se defd' pro uno solin. T'ra e' iiii car', et xii uill'i h'nt ibi ii car'. In d'nio e' una car'. Ibi ęccl'a, et ii ac' prati, et de pasnag' lx porc'. Ibi una piscaria. TRE ualeb' viii lib', et post et modo: ual' vi lib'.
:
:
:
:
:

DB-Ke-14va

(XIII) (TERRA ALBERTI CAPELLANI.)

* IN DIMIDIO LEST DE MILDETONE. IN MILDETONE HD'.

ALBERTVS capellanus ten' de rege NEWETONE. Sidgar tenuit de regina Eddid, et tunc et modo se defd' pro vii solins et dimid'. T'ra e'
Terra quę fuit in d'nio est ad firmam pro lx solid'. In ipso M̄ *x uill'i cum xlviii bord' h'nt v car'. Ibi xii ac' prati, et iiii denę de silua redd't xxx porc', de pasnag'. Ibi una piscaria seruiens hallę, et ii serui. Siluula parua ad clausuram. Ad hoc M̄ pertin' in cantuaria ciuitate iiii hagę, et ii^{e} in Rouecestre, quę reddeb' lxiiii *denar'. Et de M̄ Mildentone redditur in Neuuetone una consuetudo, idest xxviii pensę caseorum, et de xxviii solins de Mi(l)dentone pertin' in Neuuetone x lib' et x sol', et de alia parte de nouem

solins de Middeltone pertin' in Neutone xxviii pensę caseorum et dimidia, et lviii solid' de gablo ex his nouem solins. Et de his ix solins reddeb' Sigar apud Mildetone Aueram. De hoc M̄ sunt foris iii denę, quę ibi fuer' TRE, sicut hund' testificatur. Tot' M̄ TRE ualeb' xl lib', et post: xxxvi lib'. Modo: xxxiiii^{or} lib'. Archiep's inde h't vi lib', et ep's baioc' iii denas h't. Val' xl sol'. De terra huius M̄ ten' Goisfridus (de ros) unum iugum, et ual' x sol'. Adam filius Huberti tant' silurę unde exeunt xl den' per ann'.

Notes

1va19 Cerlentone] *with* C *written over an* I 1va36 Sired] *with* d *altered from* t 1vb1] *an* r *added between the columns opposite this line* 1vb34 i uill'm] *over an erasure* 1vb44–6] *added at the end of this column and marked for insertion after line 20* 1vb44 et] *written over an* i 2ra40 sequitur ... abierit] *perhaps over an erasure* 2va6 cum] *with* c *written over an* et *sign* 2va20] *an* r *added in the margin opposite this line* 2va43 xvii] *perhaps altered* 2va46 Pro quat'] *with* Pro *perhaps altered and* q *written over an unfinished* et *sign* 2vb9] *small erasure* 2vb23 xxiiii] *over an erasure; also a small erasure between the columns* 2vb34 xxxi sol'] *with* s *perhaps written over a second minim* 2vb25 de iiii] *over an erasure; also a small erasure between the columns* 3ra13 quo facta] *over an erasure* 3ra28 vi] *over an erasure* 3ra29 prati] *with* ti *over an erasure* 3rb6 METLINGES] *with a final* T *erased* 3rb8 v] *perhaps altered* 3rb12 in d'nio] *over an erasure* 3rb33 xi] *with* x *written over a minim* 3rb38 xxv] *small erasure over* xx 3va10 Quod] *with an unwanted stroke through the tail of* Q 3va16 lxiiii] *with* l *over an erasure* 3va28 xxix] *over an erasure; also a small erasure in the margin* 3va31] IN BOROWART LEST *erased but legible* 3va40] *small erasure* 3va50 in noua] *altered from* inoua 3vb24 xl car'] *perhaps inserted into a space* 3vb47 vi] *with a second minim erased* 4rb17] *small erasure* 4rb19 iuga] *with* a *altered from* um 4rb21 xi] *with* i *altered from* v 4rb31 et dimidio] *added above the line, probably by another hand* 4rb31 ix car'] *perhaps inserted into a space* 4rb34 quater xx[ti]] *over an erasure; also a small erasure in the margin* 4rb39 T'ra ... In] *over an erasure; also a small erasure in the margin* 4va2 solin] *should be* solins 4va34 burg's] *should be* burg'sis 4va40–2] *added at the end of this column and marked for insertion after line 11, where there is also a small erasure in the margin* 4vb6 In] *with an unwanted stroke at the top* 4vb15 eod'] *with* o *altered from* a 4vb23 quod] *with an unwanted* i *over* q 4vb23 reddid'] *with* d' *altered from an unfinished* t 4vb40 Quod] *with an unwanted stroke through the tail of* Q 4vb40 Quod] *with an unwanted stroke through the tail of* Q 5ra11 Huic] *with* H *altered from* I 5ra24 anguillis] *perhaps over an erasure* 5ra50 Quod] *with an unwanted stroke through the tail of* Q 5rb11 solid'] *with* s *written over an unwanted stroke, perhaps an unfinished* d 5rb26 Garsunne] *with an unwanted stroke over* u 5rb29 In d'nio] *over an erasure* 5rb36 iii sol'] *with* iii s *over an erasure; also a small erasure between the columns* 5va34 lx] *over an erasure; also a small erasure in the margin* 5va49 iii[es]] *perhaps altered* 5va49 xl] *over an erasure* 5vb13 TRE ... sol'] *inserted in smaller script* 5vb17 v] *over an erasure* 5vb18 Quod] *with the start of an unwanted stroke through the tail of* Q 5vb24 adhuc] *with* h *altered* 5vb25 propria] *with* a *over* os *erased* 5vb25 maneria] *with* a *over* os *erased* 5va30 iiii[or]] *perhaps altered* 6ra13 porc'] *with* p *written over an unfinished ascender* 6ra23 xxiii sol'] *partly over an erasure; a numeral rubbed out in the margin* 6ra35 Siuuard] *with the second* u *altered from* n 6rb17 et] *written over a* c 6rb25 isto] *altered from* hoc *erased* 6rb45 A] *over an erasure* 6va16] *a sentence first added above the line and then erased* 6va30 et] *written over a* c 6vb7 x[cem]] *perhaps altered* 6vb20 Hę] *with a final* c *erased* 6vb23 xxiiii uill'i] *over an erasure* 7ra4 sed] *written over an* et *sign* 7ra10 xiiii] *with the last minim inserted* 7rb10 viii] *with one minim inserted and two added above the line* 7rb38 iii[es] uill'i] *altered from* i uill's 7rb46 et dimid'] *added above the line, probably by another hand* 7va13 Rouecest'] *with* R *written over a* c 7va50 et tamen ... lib'] *added in the lower margin* 7vb4 solid'] *with* d' *written over an* n 7vb15] et *sign erased* 8rb46 acra] *altered from* ac' 8va16 cum] *with* c *written over an* et *sign* 8vb34 Pro ... solins] *added above the line* 8vb40] *small space* 9ra8] *small erasure* 9ra19 sol'] *added at the end of the line, probably by another hand* 9ra23 Vluuinus ... com'] *should be marked as a turn-up* 9rb2 solins] *rubbed out* 9rb7 cum] *with* c *written over an* et *sign* 9rb8 xxx solid' (vi lib')] *with* xxx solid' *cancelled and* vi lib' *added above the line, probably by another hand* 9rb9] *a paragraph added in the outer margin intended for insertion here* 9rb16] *small space* 9rb51 tenuit] *rubbed out* 9va45 Int' totum] *inserted into space* 9va50 supradicti] *with* pra *perhaps altered from* pre 9vb6 modo: xl] *added above the line by another hand* 9vb41 luonis] *should be* Iuonis 10ra13 de] *added in the margin* 10ra16–17] *smeared and partly illegible* 10ra35 non] *with the second* n *written over an ascender* 10ra45 Hoc M̄ tenuit] *rubbed out* 10rb39 Pro iii solins se defnd'] *inserted by another hand* 10va11 xxx[ta]] *perhaps altered* 10va15 Fulbertus] *inserted, perhaps over an erasure* 10va28–30] *blotted and partly illegible* 10vb51–3] *added in the lower margin* 11ra4 et] *written over an unfinished* u 11ra7 car' et] *perhaps altered* 11ra11 xiii[cim] *perhaps altered* 11ra40 den'] *with* d *written over an* s 11rb21 Boche] *with* B *altered from an* I 11rb30–2] *blotted and partly illegible* 11vb9] IN ESTREI HD' *erased* 11vb17 Radulfus ... t'rę] *inserted, perhaps over an erasure* 11vb23 / VL' x sol'] *added above the line by another hand* 12ra13 xl] *altered* 12ra36 et ded'] *with the* et *sign inserted and* d' *altered, perhaps from an unfinished* e 12ra37 parci] *with an unexplained sign above* ci 12ra37 xlii] *perhaps altered* 12ra42 In] *with* I *written over an unfinished* et *sign* 12ra43 xxxix] *with* ix *perhaps altered* 12rb26 vii] *with the second minim inserted* 12rb47 In] *with* I *written over an* et *sign* 12va8 TI] TRE *unfinished* 12va36 h'ntibus] *with* ibus *altered* 12va40 vi] *with* v *perhaps altered* 13ra40 pro] *perhaps altered* 13ra42 Hugo] *with* H *written over a* t 13rb31 Pro] *written over a* T 13va38 x sol' ... viii sol'] *inserted* 13va38 sol'(ib')] *with* so *erased and* ib' *added, probably by another hand* 13vb3 et modo: pro i[o] solin] *inserted by another hand* 13vb17 Aluuinus (pb'r) tenuit] *should be marked as a turn-up* 13vb40] *one word erased, perhaps* hunc 14ra6 TR] TRE *unfinished* 14va1] *the red heading added in the upper margin* 14va7 x] *perhaps altered* 14va12 denar'] *with* d *written over an unfinished* s

Errors in the parliamentary edition

1vb39) *for* Hicham *read* Huham 2ra17) *for* cicuitatem *read* ciuitatem 2ra35) *for* Corcordatum *read* Concordatum 2rb23) *for* Medrediue *read* Medrecliue 3vb47) *for* vii *read* vi 5ra13) *add* et *before* xxiiii 5va15) *for* marsum *read* marsuin 5va22) *for* Anchitillus *read* Anschitillus 6ra14) *for* Silua *read* silua 6va12) *add* et *before* dim' 7ra48) *for* Uttalis *read* Uitalis 7va13) *for* Roucest' *read* Rouecest' 7vb30) *add* de *after* ten' 7vb44) *for* Ansgot *read* An[s]got 7vb48) *delete* de *after* ten' 8va16) *delete* et *before* cum 9rb7) *delete* et *before* cum 9rb51) *add space before* de 9va49) *delete paragraph sign before* Totum 9vb25) *for* xxxx *read* xxx 9vb41) *for* Iuonis *read* luonis 10va23) *add* de *before* rege 10vb7) *for* Wana *read* Waua 11rb51) *for* In *read* in 13ra45) *for* nouæ *read* nonæ 13vb5) *for* xvii *read* xvi 13vb41) *add* et *before* pro

Comments

The following comments relate to some features of the text which vary in kind but have one property in common: they all seem to have originated in this particular manuscript. Most of them (not quite all of them) result from decisions made by the DB scribe, either while the text was being constructed, or while it was being checked. In a manner of speaking, these features are superficial, and the reader may prefer to ignore them, at least at first. But anyone who wants to develop a closer acquaintance with this booklet, or with the DB scribe's way of working, as it is exemplified here, will find these comments helpful, I hope. If they are read at all, they should be read alongside a facsimile.

0r–v) The whole first leaf was left blank (which is why the seventeenth-century numbering begins with the second leaf, not with this one). At the moment when he ruled this leaf, the scribe was assuming that it would be or might be written on; but in the event it was not. There must have been some reason why these two pages stayed blank, but I am doubtful what that reason might have been. If it is right – as I suspect but cannot prove (above, p. 90) – that the scribe wrote the body of the text first, beginning on fo. 2v, before coming back to insert the preliminary section, he may perhaps have miscalculated the number of pages that ought to be reserved for the purpose. At first he assumed that he would need five pages; but then, when the time arrived for the preliminary section to be written, he decided that he could (with only a little difficulty) compress it into three pages; and therefore he chose to start on fo. 1r, not on fo. 0r. But this is not the only possible explanation, and I am far from sure whether it is the best one.

1ra1–3) The first three lines here were also left blank, and again I am doubtful why.

1vb1) In two places, here and at 2va20, the scribe wrote an *r* alongside the text, as a reminder to himself. (It probably stands for *require*, 'find out about this'.) He was telling himself not to forget that something needed to be done – something which he was unable or unwilling to do immediately, but thought that he ought to do at a later stage. I do not see what this could mean except that he was (when he had time) planning to consult the B text. As far as we know, he had no other recourse: if he found some defect in D-Ke, he could only hope that the defect might have originated there (or in C-Ke), and that B-Ke might be immune from it. What defect did he find here? The only problem which I can see is this: the man whose lands are being described (one of the canons of Saint Martin's) is referred to by one name at the start of the paragraph and by a different name halfway through (*Turbatus … isdem Robertus*). If that was the DB scribe's problem, he would (as we happen to know) have found the solution in the B text, where this man was called Robert Trublet (B-Ke / xAug / A4-23v2) – *trublet* (or *turblet*) being French for 'troubled', *turbatus* (or *turbulatus*) in Latin. (There were two canons named Robert; so each of them needed a surname.) Thus, if the DB scribe had got round to consulting the B text, he would presumably have inserted the name *Robertus* before *Turbatus*; and then he would have erased the reminder. From the fact that he did neither of these things, we are entitled to suspect that what he was planning to do was never done. (But I would not think of blaming him much for that.)

1vb44–6) This paragraph (which lacks rubrication) was added at the foot of the column, in slightly smaller script, and marked for insertion after line 20. The wording of the value clause differs from that used in the preceding entries. We would expect it to say *Val' lx sol', TRE: c sol'*; in fact it says *TRE ualb' c sol', modo lx sol'*. Throughout DB-Ke, the shortened form of *ualebat* is *ualeb'*; the scribe switched over from that to *ualb'* while he was writing DB-Sx (Flight 2006, fig. 3).

2ra1) The scribe started writing on the second ruled line, perhaps because he was going to be using large capitals.

2ra40) There is a drastic change of appearance in the middle of this sentence. As far as *fixerit*, the script is unusually large; from *sequitur* onwards, it is small. (Possibly *sequitur … abierit* was written over an erasure; I have not been able to decide.)

2ra43–8) The paragraph beginning with *Quidam* looks as if it was inserted into a space originally intended to stay blank. The ink seems darker; the text seems cramped; and the ruling is disregarded. (The first line floats above the ruling; the next five written lines occupy the space of four ruled lines.) Very probably the paragraph at the bottom of the column (ruled lines 48 9) was already in place before this preceding paragraph was written.

2rb2–48) Here again, after line 8, the ruling is disregarded. (Altogether this paragraph consists of 47 written lines occupying the space of 40 ruled lines.) Possibly the block of text at the foot of this column (ruled lines 43–50) was already in place before the preceding paragraph was supplied; but there is no proof of that. (Not that we could hope for any proof – unless the scribe had misjudged the spacing so badly that he could not prevent a collision from occurring.)

2rb50–7) The last eight ruled lines in this column are occupied by the index, which, as usual, is divided into two sub-columns. When he came to add the red numerals, the scribe allowed himself some ornamental touches of the kind noted by Chaplais (1987, p. 75).

2va2) As soon as he started writing the body of the text, the scribe had to decide how to deal with the fact that Kent was divided into lests as well as hundreds.[26] Characteristically, he dived in and worked out a solution as he went along. In

[26] This was not altogether a new problem for him. In the first two counties that he dealt with, the DB scribe was confronted with similar complications: a two-tier system in Yorkshire, a three-tier system in Lincolnshire. But the headings in DB-YoLi are badly managed; the scribe makes a much more successful job of it here.

chapter 1 he used a whole line for the headings, putting the lest heading on the left and the hundred heading (as usual) on the right. As long as each paragraph needs a double heading, this solution works perfectly; the problem takes on a different complexion in chapter 2, where sometimes only a hundred heading is necessary (below, 3ra42).

2va20) Here again, the scribe wrote an *r* in the margin to remind himself of something. As at 1vb1, I take it that he had some question in mind for which he was hoping to find an answer in the B text, when he had the time to look for it. What that question might have been is hard to say; I can only suggest that he wanted to find out the name of Helto's nephew. Whether B-Ke would have told him that, we have no way of knowing. From the fact that the *r* is still there, we may be inclined in infer that he never actually got round to making the search.

2va31–2) In chapter 1 the scribe left a line or two blank between one paragraph and the next. He did the same in the preliminary section of chapter 2, but stopped doing it after that.

2vb23–5) In several places, an alteration made in the text – a numeral rewritten over an erasure – is accompanied by a small erasure in the margin (or, as here, in the space between the columns). These corrections are significant because they suggest that a systematic check was under way. What was happening was something like this. The scribe knew (as everyone does who has tried the experiment) that Roman numerals are very easily misread; so he worked through his manuscript, checking it against the source text. Every so often, he came across a mistake – and some were such as could not be put right except by means of an erasure. In a case like this, not wanting to lose momentum, he did not stop to make the correction straight away. He marked the number which was wrong, jotted down the right number in the margin as a reminder to himself, and continued with his check. Once that operation was complete, he went back to the beginning and scanned through the manuscript again, looking for his reminders. When he found one, he made the erasure, rewrote the numeral, and finished off by erasing the number in the margin.

3ra42) Here, for the first time, the scribe was starting a new hundred without starting a new lest at the same time; so he had to decide how to deal with the headings. His solution, at first, was to use a whole line, putting the hundred heading on the right as usual, but leaving the space to the left of it blank, as if it was occupied by an invisible lest heading. He did this, I think, because he was wondering whether it might be best to use a double heading every time (which is what I would have recommended, if he had asked my advice). By leaving a blank, he was giving himself the option of inserting the lest headings later, if that was what he made up his mind to do. With two exceptions (3rb11, 3vb46), he continued leaving blanks until he was in sight of the end of chapter 2 (below, 4rb46) – at which point he decided that a hundred heading could be allowed to stand alone. And in consequence the blanks stayed blank.

3rb6) The name was written *METLINGEST* at first, but the final *T* got erased. This did not happen till after the rubrication was in place: the erasure cuts through the red line.

3va10) Here the scribe started writing *Quando*, but stopped himself and altered the word to *Quod*. The same mistake occurs again at 4vb40 (twice in one line), 5ra50 and 5vb18. Apparently the scribe had a phrase in his head – *Quando recep'* – which tended to pop up in places where it was not wanted. But then he got it under control again.

4rb28) This is the point where a question arose which (as far as DB-Ke is concerned) had not arisen previously. If it was necessary to give the name of the TRE tenant, where should this information be put, and how should it be worded? The scribe decided to put it at the end of the paragraph, wording it like this: *Hoc M̄ tenuit A— de B—*; he did that here, and again in the following paragraph (4rb35). But these two entries are exceptional. In the first few chapters, nearly always, it could be taken for granted that the manor was held TRE by the current tenant's predecessor – a previous king (chapter 1), a previous archbishop (chapters 2–3), a previous bishop of Rochester (chapter 4). In chapter 5, on the contrary, every paragraph ought to report the name of the TRE tenant; but the scribe had reached the end of the third paragraph (6ra20) before he woke up to that.

4rb46) The format changes at this point. The space for an invisible lest heading disappears,[27] reappears in the next paragraph (4va1), but then disappears for good, with just a few sporadic exceptions (9vb1, 10va24, 11va39, 13rb41). From 4va6 onwards, the scribe made it a rule that lest headings were not to be inserted except where they were indispensable; but there are, again, a few exceptions to this rule (below, 6vb21).

4va17–18) The first two lines of this paragraph seem to have been inserted. Apparently the scribe left two lines blank here at first (perhaps because he wanted to make sure of the facts), and then filled them in somewhat later, using a thicker pen and blacker ink. The insertion had been made before the rubrication was done.

4va40–2) An added paragraph, marked for insertion after 4va11; it lacks rubrication. The wording of the value clause associates this entry with DB-So and DB-DnCo (above, pp. 91–2).

4vb23) The scribe wrote *qui* but then altered it instantly to *quod*. For him the word *solin* was normally neuter; but his usage is not perfectly consistent. (Despite making this correction, he still wrote *Hunc*, not *Hoc*, in the following sentence.)

5va5) Here the scribe discovered, a moment too late, that he had misstated the assessment clause. Instead of *Pro vi*

[27] In the current stretch of text – the subchapter describing the lands of the archbishop's knights – the lest headings had all gone missing (above, p. 19). Presumably that made it seem all the more pointless to keep leaving spaces for them.

solins se defd' (5va2), he ought to have written something like *TRE se defd' pro vi solins, et modo pro v solins.* His reaction is not what one might expect it to be. Rather than going back and altering what he had written, he interpolated a sentence into the middle of the paragraph (5va5), making no attempt to connect it with the misleading statement three lines above. (We know of at least one reader who was indeed misled (C3 / T1, fo. 170rc).) From indications like this, it can be seen that the scribe was reluctant to do anything which would mar the appearance of the manuscript. Later on, while he was correcting it, he might have no choice but to make erasures and insertions; that could not be helped. While he was writing it, however, he tried to avoid making changes which would look at all unsightly. (There are places, for instance, where the word-order went slightly wrong. Many scribes would have put things right by inserting transposition marks. This scribe disliked doing even that.)

5vb25) The scribe wrote *proprios eius manerios* at first (where *-os* is a masculine inflection), but then erased and corrected the endings, to make *propria eius maneria.* For him the word 'manor' was definitely neuter.

6ra3) Because this is the start of the chapter, the bishop is put in first place and given his title: *De ep'o Baiocensi ten' Hugo de porth ....* If this paragraph were not at the beginning, the wording would be: *Hugo de porth ten' de ep'o ....*

6ra20) The first two paragraphs in chapter 5 fail to give the name of the TRE tenant. Now the scribe decided (or remembered) that this information ought to be included, and from here onwards he made a point of doing so. In almost every paragraph, after stating the value, he concluded with a sentence of this type: *Quaedam mulier tenuit* (6ra20), *Lefstan tenuit de rege E ...* (6ra24), *Eustan tenuit de rege E* (6ra30). Even so, he regarded these statements as a peripheral part of the text: that is why he often allowed them to protrude beyond the ruled space, rather than starting a new line. As the object of the sentence the words *Hoc manerium* are to be understood; the scribe omitted them except where this sentence was separated from the value clause by some other statements (e.g. 7ra34, 7rb13), in which case he needed to make it clear that he had gone back to speaking about the whole manor. Explanatory remarks are sometimes attached to the end, such as *et potuit se uertere quo uoluit* (6rb28). In a case where two or more TRE manors had been merged to make one manor, he usually modified the wording. To avoid repeating the word *manerium*, he preferred to write something like this: *Hanc terram tenuerunt de rege duo fratres pro duobus maneriis* (6vb46). With incidental variations of this kind, the scribe continued in the same way almost as far as the end of chapter 5: *Bernoltus tenuit de rege E* (11va47), *Molleue tenuit de rege E* (11va51). But then he came to a paragraph which set him thinking (below, 11vb1).

6rb1) Because the start of this paragraph coincided with the start of a column, the scribe reversed the wording: *De ep'o ten' Malgerius ....* The coincidence does not recur till 7va1, and the wording is not reversed there – because the scribe forgot, or because he did not think it worth doing the same thing again, that far into the chapter.

6va16) A sentence was added above the line here – and then on second thoughts it was erased. Though I cannot read any part of it, I think it safe to guess that this sentence was the assessment clause, added here in the same way as the one for Boxley (below, 8vb34), presumably by the DB scribe himself. But then it was noticed (by him or by somebody else) that in fact this information had already been included – not in the usual place for it, but near the end of the paragraph – and the addition was erased accordingly. (Some retouching seems to have been needed after that, in the line below.)

6va23) There is a marked change of appearance at this point. By the end of the previous paragraph, the scribe's pen was badly out of trim; here he starts again with a sharpened pen. The interruption causes him to lose concentration: he writes *quod se defd' pro uno solin* instead of *Pro uno solin se defd'.* (He reverts to the normal wording in the next paragraph.) This is the sort of hint which goes to show that the scribe was composing the text at the moment of writing it. (Sometimes, we know, he wrote out a draft version of a paragraph or two, using some spare piece of parchment for the purpose, before committing himself to the final version (Flight 2006, pp. 77–9). But that was not his standard procedure.)

I had hoped that it might be possible, by looking for changes like this, to arrive at some idea of the number of days' work which went into the writing of the DB-Kc text. But I cannot see my way to any useful conclusion.

6vb21) This is the first of four places where we find a lest heading repeated for no obvious reason. The heading at the start of the chapter (6ra2) is still applicable: we do not need to be told that Greenwich hundred is in Sutton half-lest. Redundant lest headings occur twice more in this chapter (7vb9, 8va9) and once in chapter 9 (11rb22). I discuss the significance of these facts elsewhere (above, pp. 16–18).

7vb39) Perhaps the start of a stint.

8rb21) Definitely the start of a stint. The script becomes suddenly smaller.

8va23) The scribe leaves space as if for a hundred heading; but none is needed, because the heading at 8va19 still applies.

8vb9) Perhaps the start of a stint. The next few written lines are too close together; after that the scribe gets the spacing right again.

8vb34) The assessment clause, originally omitted, was added above the line. One detail suggests that it is appreciably later: the abbreviation *se defdb'* for *se defendebat* (preferred to *se defendit*) occurs only once elsewhere in DB-Ke, in the paragraph added in the margin of the opposite page (below, 9rb6–8).

8vb40) 'and one French—' Here the scribe started writing *francig'* (for *francigenam*, 'Frenchman') – but halfway through he changed his mind, decided that some other word would be better, estimated how much space he would need for it, and continued with *et ii acras prati* after that. His intention was to come back later, erase the unfinished word, and substitute the word that he preferred; but he never got round to doing so. The missing word remained missing. We know that it was not *francigenam*; we know how long it was going to be, and what context it had to make sense in; beyond that we are free to guess. (Possibly the word was *militem*, as at 3vb42.)

8vb41) The scribe left space as if for a hundred heading – and should indeed have supplied one.

9rb6–8) When the text was first compiled, the end of this paragraph went missing, together with most of the next one: after writing *Val'*, the scribe lost his place, jumping ahead to the corresponding point in the following paragraph. If the scribe had not gone wrong, the text would look something like this:

Isdem Hugo ten' de ep'o CERCE. Pro ii solins se defd'. T'ra e' ii car'. In d'nio e' una, cum v bord' et uno seruo, et un' molin' de vi solid' et viii den'. Val' [*vi lib'. Osuuardus tenuit.*
Isdem Hugo ten' de ep'o STEPEDONE. Pro i solin dimid' iugo minus se defd'. T'ra e' ii car'. In d'nio e' una, cum v bord' et uno seruo.] *Val' xxx solid'. Osuuardus tenuit.*

By jumping ahead, the scribe lost the last few words of the first paragraph and all but the last few words of the second.

Later – not till after he had rubricated the text – he saw his mistake and added a version of the missing paragraph in the margin:

Id' H. ten' de ep'o STEPEDONE. Osuuard teneb' TRE, et tunc se defdb' pro i solin dimidio iugo minus. T'ra e' ii car'. In d'nio e' una cum i seruo et v bord'. Val' xxx solid'.

Even from its wording, this paragraph is obviously incongruous. The abbreviated verbs, *teneb'* for *tenebat* (preferred to *tenuit*) and *se defdb'* for *se defendebat* (preferred to *se defendit*), associate this addition with aspect 6. It is only towards the end of DB-So that the scribe started using the imperfect for both verbs, *teneb' TRE et geldb'* (Flight 2006, fig. 6). So this paragraph would seem to have been added at around the same time as the one which appears at the end of chapter 2 (4va40).

As well as making this addition, the scribe ought also to have corrected the value that he had mistakenly given for *Cerce*. The adjustment was indeed made – *xxx solid'* was cancelled and *vi lib'* was written above it – but the hand which made it appears to be somebody else's.[28] The sentence *Osuuardus tenuit* was allowed to stand; though attached to this paragraph by mistake, it happened to be correct.

9rb15) The layout is irregular, possibly because the scribe did not realize in time that this line would need to include a lest heading as well as a hundred heading.

9rb16) The space after *Will'i* is a hint (as at 8vb40) that the scribe was intending to erase this word and replace it with a longer one.

10ra16–17) The manuscript has suffered some damage here, towards the inner edge of this leaf (fo. 10 is a singleton), and there are a few words which I cannot in conscience pretend to be able to decipher. I print them, in square brackets, as they were read (unanimously) by Farley, Netherclift and Larking.

10rb39) The assessment clause – *Pro iii solins se defnd'* – was inserted in darker ink, by a hand which I think it quite certain was not the DB scribe's. Apparently the DB scribe had left a space here, and somebody else, sooner or later, supplied the missing information. This corrector used the formula which he could see was normal (except that instead of *defd'* he wrote *defnd'*, an abbreviation which occurs uniquely here); the only new information is the number itself.[29] Where did the information come from? The fact that the DB scribe left a blank here implies that it was not to be found in his source text, i.e. in D-Ke. But it ought to have been present in B-Ke, and we are, I think, permitted to guess that this other scribe went looking for it there – and found it.

10rb50) The last line in this column is gratuitously blank.

10va11) The numeral *xxx* is not distinctly legible. The superscript *ta* seems to prove that it was originally *xxx* (for *triginta*). From that it may have been altered to *xxix*; but the alteration (if made at all) was made so clumsily that the intention is unclear.

10va28–30) This is one of the places where the manuscript got blotted (above, p. 94). I print the illegible words, in square brackets, as they were read by Farley in the 1760s (BL Stowe 851).

10vb7) The *u* in *Waua* is badly shaped; because of some show-through from the recto page it looks more like an *n* at first sight, and that is how Farley read it. But I am sure that *u* is right.

10vb37) The layout is irregular, again perhaps because the scribe did not realize in time that a lest heading would be

[28] Thorn and Thorn (2001, p. 61 and pl. 28) identify this addition as the work of the corrector whom they call scribe B.

[29] The same assessment for this manor is reported by ε (C1-6vb26), and no doubt we can take it to be true as a statement of fact. But I would not wish to argue from this that the addition had been made in DB before ε was compiled. Because a few of the facts appearing in ε do not derive from DB, it is not impossible that the two texts were corrected independently.

needed, as well as a hundred heading. The word *HVND'* could have been turned up or down, but the scribe forgot about it.

10vb51–3) This paragraph was added in the lower margin, at the foot of this column, in smaller, less careful script, after the rubrication had been done. Presumably we are meant to insert it after line 48, but there is no explicit indication of that.

11rb15) Perhaps the start of a stint. The next few written lines are closer together than they should be (and the assessment clause is botched.)

11rb30–2) This is the other place where the manuscript got blotted (above, p. 94). Here again I print the illegible words as they were read by Farley in the 1760s (BL Stowe 851).

11va1) The format goes wrong here. Perhaps the scribe had written *IN* on the left, as if for a lest heading, before realizing that only a hundred heading was required here.

11vb1) This is the entry which prompted the scribe to think of arranging the information rather differently. His source text did not tell him the name of this manor; to make it clear at once which manor was meant he used a *quod* clause: *Osbernus ten' de ep'o unum M̄ quod tenuer' tres liberi homines de rege E.* In the next two paragraphs he reverted to his previous policy, putting the TRE tenant's name right at the end of the paragraph (11vb9, 11vb14). But he was wondering whether it might not be a better idea to put this information just after the name of the manor, and in the next paragraph he decided to make the experiment: *i iugum in Brochestele, Quod Molleue tenuit de rege E* (11vb15, his capital *Q*). He was close to the end of chapter 5 by now, but in the final paragraph we see him still experimenting with this new arrangement: *Hastingelai, quod tenuit Ulnod de rege E, et tunc ...* (11vb30).

By this time, he was sufficently used to following the name of the manor with a *quod* clause that he continued doing the same thing in chapters 6–7, not to introduce the TRE tenant's name (which, as in chapters 1–4, could be taken for granted), but to start the assessment clause: *Wi, quod TRE et modo se defd' pro vii solins* (11vb40), *Plumstede, quod defd' se pro ii solins et uno iugo* (12ra4). But he was generally opposed to using dependent clauses (he was recording facts, not writing a work of literature), and halfway through chapter 7 he reverted to making the assessment clause a sentence by itself (12va1).

Nevertheless, as soon as he reached chapter 9, he resumed the experiment which he had been making at the end of chapter 5: *Estwelle, quod tenuit Frederic de rege E, et pro uno solin se defd'* (13ra3). Having tried it again, he decided that he did prefer this new arrangement; but he dropped the *quod* and started a new sentence instead, putting the TRE tenant's name first: *Seiuetone. Bresibalt tenuit de rege E, et pro dimid' solin se defd'* (13ra13). From this point onwards the arrangement is stable and the wording varies only slightly. The only significant change is the inclusion of an additional phrase in the assessment clause, as it appears in chapters 10–13 (below, 14ra33).

11vb9) A hundred heading has been erased here, but is still partly legible. It looks like *IN ESTREI HD'*. If so, the heading was redundant (the heading at 11va39 still applies), and presumably that is the reason why someone decided to erase it.

11vb17) The scribe rewrote the first line of this paragraph, in darker ink than the surrounding text, probably over an erasure. (That explains why he gave the tenant's name in full, rather than simply saying *Isdem Radulfus*.) The correction had been made before the rubrication was done.

11vb23) The sentence added between the lines, *VL' x sol'*, seems certain to be the work of another hand.

12ra36) The scribe had written *de e*, presumably for *de ep'o baiocensi*, before he changed his mind. (If this manor were held from the bishop, the paragraph would belong in chapter 5, not here.) Improvising, he inserted an *et* sign before *de* and overwrote the unwanted *e* with a large round *d*, so that *de e* became *et ded'*.

12rb24) Space as if for a hundred heading, and probably one is needed.

12va8) The scribe began writing the value clause here, but then decided to start a new line for it instead. It happened twice – here and at 14ra6 – that his pen was already in the middle of the *TRE* formula before he changed his mind. All the way through, the scribe had been somewhat inclined to start a new line when he came to the value clause. (He can be expected to do this, for instance, if the previous line is the end of a sub-paragraph, or if it is already more than about half full.) Though his propensity for doing this is hard to measure, it does seem to be getting stronger towards the end of DB-Ke.

12va37) The start of a stint: the script becomes suddenly smaller.

12vb37–8) Perhaps an addition: the ink seems slightly paler. But these lines were in place before the rubrication was done.

13va19) The start of a stint: the script becomes suddenly smaller.

13vb3) The sentence *et modo: pro i° solin* was inserted by a corrector.[30] As at 10rb39, the DB scribe's behaviour suggests that he was dissatisfied with his source text. He left the previous sentence (*Molleue tenuit*) unfinished; he left most of this line blank. Probably he saw reason to think that some explanatory remark might be needed here – like

[30] The notation for *modo* resembles that used in an addition at 9vb6, written, so it seems safe to say, by the same hand as this.

the one which occurs in the following paragraph (13vb7–8) – but wanted to make sure of the facts before committing himself. This means, I suppose, that he was thinking of taking a look at B-Ke, in the hope that the state of affairs might be described more clearly there than it was in D-Ke. He never got round to doing this himself; but the blank space caught the eye of a corrector and prompted him into making the same search which the DB scribe had meant to make. This curt addition was the outcome of that.

13vb5) The number of shillings is not distinctly legible. Farley read it as *xvii*, without the dot which would normally follow a numeral. It looks like *xvi* (with a dot at the end) to me.

13vb17) The three words at the end of this line seem to have been turned up from the line below; but the sentence was left unfinished and the turn-up sign was not put in.

14ra33) From here onwards, the phrase *tunc et modo* becomes a regular part of the assessment clause. Up until now, we have been expected to assume that the TRE assessment remains valid unless there is some statement to the contrary; now we are told explicitly that it does still apply. The origins of this phrase go back to chapter 9, where the scribe had to explain some changes of assessment resulting from the demarcation of the boundary between the feod of the bishop of Bayeux and the division of Hugo de Montfort. The paragraph for Brabourne (13vb23) shows how he dealt with this. Because he had just mentioned king Edward (*Godricus de burnes tenuit de rege E*), he did not want to use the formula *TRE*; so he used the word *tunc* instead of it: *et pro vii solins se defd' tunc, et modo pro v solins et dimid' et dim' iugo*; and then he went on to say why.[31]

By the time that he started chapter 10, the phrase *tunc et modo* was so much on his mind that he began to use it regularly, even though, as a matter of fact, the assessments were mostly unchanged. For the moment, however, the word-order is unstable. The scribe was still experimenting with different turns of phrase when he reached the end of this booklet:

et pro .. solins se defd' tunc et modo (14ra)
et pro .. solins se defd' tunc et modo
et tunc et modo defd' se pro .. solins (14rb)
et tunc et modo pro .. solins se defd'
et tunc et modo pro .. solins se defd'
et tunc et modo se defd' pro .. solins
et tunc et modo se defd' pro .. solins (14va)

If we want to know the result of this experiment, we need to look at the booklet which was written next, i.e. DB-Sx.

In the end, these changes in the wording of the entries do not amount to much. If the scribe had still been following the same rules that guided him through most of chapter 5, the last paragraph of chapter 12 would look like this:

Ipse Haimo ten' BLEHEM. Pro uno solin se defd'. T'ra e' ...... ual' vi lib'. Norman tenuit de rege E.

In fact it looks like this:

Ipse Haimo ten' BLEHEM. Norman tenuit de rege E, et tunc et modo se defd' pro uno solin. T'ra e' ...... ual' vi lib'.

All that the scribe has done is to rearrange some elements of the text. Except that one fact is made explicit which was only implicit before, the information given remains exactly the same.

Nevertheless, we need to stay alert to changes in the scribe's procedure. They may seem trivial, and yet they may be significant. Microscopic details are what go to show that some of the scribe's additions in DB-Ke are appreciably later than the original text – that they are of roughly the same date as the last booklets to be written – because phrases which the scribe had in his head while he was working on DB-So and DB-DnCo are echoed in some of the additions that he made here (above, 4va40–2, 8vb34, 9rb6–8).

[31] 'Because the other part is outside Hugo's division, and the bishop of Bayeux holds it.'

Chapter 5
Commentary

It is hard to see what limit can be fixed for a commentary on the records of the survey of Kent. If Larking had continued as he started – with a note on the etymology of the name 'Dover' (1869, p. 149) – his commentary would have run to many hundred pages. For my part I regret very much that he did not continue and complete it; but there is a limit on how much can usefully be said by any single person, even by someone as attuned to the subject as Larking. (We might all get on a little faster, perhaps, if editors stopped thinking that their readers expected them to hammer down every nail.) It seems to me a sensible rule – a point of etiquette if nothing more – that a commentary should not exceed the length of the text being commented upon. On one aspect of the evidence, the identification of the place-names, I aim for exhaustive coverage. For the rest, I pick and choose. If I am sure that I have something constructive to say, I allow myself to say it; if not, I hold my peace.

For obvious reasons, this commentary is organized around DB-Ke, the only surviving record of the survey which was intended to cover the entire county. Parallel passages from α and B / xAug are cited in the appropriate places, if they provide some extra information, or some help in understanding DB; for more detailed comparison, the reader should make use of the concordances appended to the relevant chapters. (The same applies to ε, for what little ε is worth.) By analogy with the surviving D booklets, it seems fairly certain that the contents of DB-Ke's preliminary section (1ra–2rb) would have been placed at the end of D-Ke. The DB scribe preferred to put them at the beginning; I have preferred to put them back at the end. This is, in any case, the order of business which I would recommend for anybody new to the subject: start with the main text and save the preliminaries for later.

The adjustments to the lest and hundred headings suggested in Table 1 are taken for granted here. Except where there is some room for doubt, I make no further comment.

I have thought that it might be helpful to mark the identifications which differ significantly from those in the Phillimore edition. For this purpose I have put small asterisks in the * margin – which I hope will be visible enough for those readers who wish to find them, but not too distracting for those who prefer to ignore them.

Index

2rb50–7) 'Here are listed those holding lands in Kent.' Apart from the king himself, this is a list of all the people who hold any land in this county directly from the king. In comparison with other counties of similar size, the number of such tenants is small, because here it was being assumed that every piece of land was, in the absence of definite proof to the contrary, held from the earl of Kent, i.e. from the bishop of Bayeux (below, p. 170).

The ordering of the chapters does not conform exactly to the sequence that we might expect. From the way in which the DB scribe arranged the chapters in other booklets, it is not hard to work out what rules he had in mind (Flight 2006, pp. 137–40); but he did not always apply these rules strictly, and in DB-Ke, perhaps because the number of chapters was small, he allowed himself some laxity. In an ideal ordering, chapter 13 (Albert the chaplain) would follow chapter 8, and chapter 10 (the count of Boulogne) would come before chapter 9.

1. Land of the king

The king had kept only four manors in Kent for himself; but one of them (Dartford) was large, and another (Milton) was gigantic. A fifth manor (Wye) had ceased to be the king's only recently, when it was given to the abbot of Battle (11vb40).

2va3) 'King Willelm holds Tarentefort.' Dartford TQ 5474. Including Woolwich TQ 4379, Chislehurst TQ 4469, Sutton TQ 5570, Wilmington TQ 5372, and Kingsdown TQ 5763.

3) 'for one sulung and a half.' Just once, the scribe tries Latinizing the word for 'sulung' (*pro uno solino et dimidio*); having tried it, he decides against. After this it is always a French word, *solin* in the singular, *solins* in the plural.

12) 'seventy pounds by weight, one hundred and eleven shillings (at the rate) of twenty pence to the ora, and seven pounds and twenty-six pence by count.' The treasury had a number of tricks for insulating the king (as landowner) from his failure (as king) to maintain the value of the currency. 'By weight' presumably meant what it says: the cash was weighed, pound by pound, not counted out, penny by penny. 'Twenty pence to the ora' meant a surcharge of 25 per cent. (An ora was a fifteenth of a pound, so theoretically 16 pence. 'Twenty-five pence to the ounce' or 'fifteen pence to the shilling' would have meant exactly the same thing, but the first formula was the conventional one.) The most stringent rule was 'refined and weighed', which in Kent applied to payments from Milton (2vb10) and Canterbury (2ra15).

15) 'The men of the hundred (of Axstone) testify (this).' A statement obtained by the second team of commissioners from the local jury. Do they know of any assets which ought to belong to this manor lost since the time of king Edward? Yes, they do. In particular, they report some dubious transactions on the part of the TRE sheriff of Kent, Osward. From the language used here – 'lost the sheriffdom' – it would seem that he was removed from office some time before the death of the king; but he did not lose his lands till later. Confiscated from him, they were given *en bloc* to Hugo de Port. By 1086, Hugo had acknowledged that he held his

lands in Kent from the bishop of Bayeux; but I would guess that this was not initially the case. The manor of Hawley mentioned here (line 21) is described in chapter 5 (6ra3).

2va34) 'King W(illelm) holds Elesford.' Aylesford TQ 7258.

40) 'Of this manor Ansgot holds next to Rochester as much land as is worth 1680 pence.' Not identified. Ansgot was the owner of Great Delce (8va15).

42) 'Also the bishop of Rochester, in exchange for the land on which the castle sits, has as much of this land as is worth 208 pence.' Not identified. The Rochester sources say nothing about this exchange – nothing about the land that was lost, nothing about the land that was acquired in compensation.

That silence is a warning. When William Camden came across this passage in DB – it is mentioned for the first time in the fourth edition of the *Britannia* – he took it to prove that the castle at Rochester had been built by the king (Camden 1594, p. 246), not, as he had previously (and rightly) assumed, by the bishop of Bayeux (1590, p. 248). At first sight, it does suggest that; but a single sentence in DB, purposely worded in a neutral manner, is not enough to prove the point. It is perfectly possible that bishop Odo had given this land to the church of Rochester, in the belief that the land was his to give, and that the commissioners themselves had discovered that it was not – that in fact that it was properly part of the manor of Aylesford. (The same reading would apply to the land in Ansgot's possession.) It seems to me that every statement in DB which directly affects the king should be read as if it ended with a question mark: 'This is how things are: is the king willing to let them stay as they are?' In this instance, the silence of the Rochester sources is a strong hint that the king was *not* willing to let things stay as they were.

The itinerant justices who visited the county in the thirteenth century had greater powers than the commissioners who carried out the survey. They were there to try cases, not just to discover and ascertain the facts. Even so, in any case which concerned the king – a plea of *Quo waranto*, for instance – their judgment was only provisional. The report of their proceedings had to end with a clause reserving the right of the king to reopen the case, whenever he felt so inclined: *saluo iure regis, quando inde loqui uoluerit*, or something to that effect (often shortened to *saluo iure regis et cetera*, because, though it had to be said, it almost went without saying).

2va46) 'King W(illelm) holds Middeltune.' Milton (Regis) TQ 9065. By far the largest single manor in Kent. As well as a dozen villages surrounding Milton, it included nearly the whole of the isle of Sheppey; it also included a tract of territory in the Weald (most of Marden TQ 7444 and part of Goudhurst TQ 7237) which came to be called Marden hundred. Almost all the constituent places are known to have had churches of their own at the time of the survey.

2vb3) 'The men of the Weald pay fifty shillings in lieu of guard duties and carrying duties.' (I note in passing that 'cartage' is not a good translation for *avera*: one had to show up with a pack-horse, not a cart.)

6) 'Of this manor Hugo de Port holds 8.25 sulungs which TRE were (associated) with the other sulungs in (the payment of) customs.' The situation is (despite some corruption of the text) more clearly explained in B / xAug: 'Of these 80 sulungs Hugo de Port holds 8.25 sulungs from the bishop of Bayeux', and that leaves 71.75 sulungs to carry the burdens formerly carried by 80 (A4-17v4–9). Hugo's share is separately described by four paragraphs

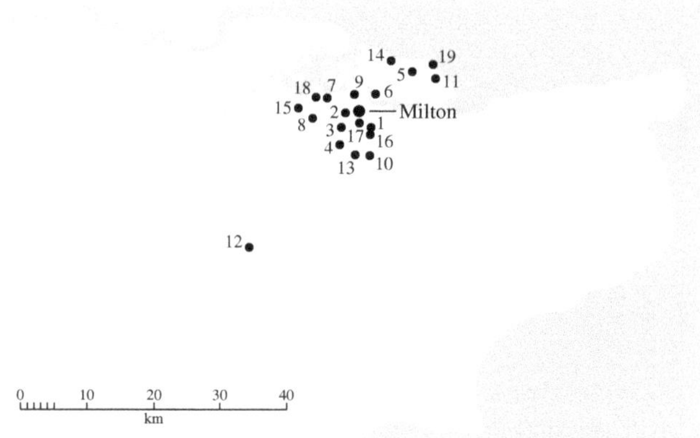

1 Bapchild	8 Hartlip	14 Minster
2 Bobbing	9 Iwade	15 Rainham
3 Borden	10 Kingsdown	16 Rodmersham
4 Bredgar	11 Leysdown	17 Sittingbourne
5 Eastchurch	12 Marden	18 Upchurch
6 Elmley	13 Milstead	19 Warden
7 Lower Halstow		

Figure 4. Places included in the description of Milton.

in chapter 5 (9rb1–15, where the assessments that are given add up to 8.375 sulungs, half a yoke more than the total reported here). All of this land belonged to Osward (the sheriff) TRE; now it held by the bishop of Bayeux, and by Hugo from him. (This is how things are: is the king willing to let them stay as they are?)

10) 'one hundred and forty pounds by fire and weight.' In theory, that is, the treasury would melt down the coins, skim off the dross, and weigh the pure silver that was left: if the king was entitled to a pound, he was entitled to a pound's weight of silver, however many coins that might take. But probably this never happened. (In the twelfth century, the most that the treasury did was test a sample.) On the evidence of an entry in DB-Sx – *l lib' ad arsuram et pensum quae ualent lxv lib'* (fo. 16rb) – this formula was taken to mean a surcharge of 30 per cent.

2vb21) 'King W(illelm) holds Faureshant.' Faversham TR 0161, including Sheldwich TR 0156. Like Milton church (2vb16), Faversham church had been given to Saint Augustine's (Bates 1998, no. 81); DB fails to mention this.

The entire manor passed out of the king's domain in 1148, when it was given by king Stephan to the abbey which he and his wife had founded here. After 1154, not without some delay, his successor decided to let the donation stand (GREx 1156:65).

2. Land of the archbishop of Canterbury

The chapters describing the lands of the archbishopric (including chapter 4) are important not just for their content. This is where we can see most clearly how the survey text evolved from one version to the next. Trying not to repeat what I have said before (above, pp. 18–20), I summarize my thoughts on the subject with the help of a diagram.

In the B text the paragraphs covering the archbishop's manors would have been listed in cadastral order, alternating with paragraphs for other people's manors. Our only good clue to the wording used in B is the selection of extracts made for Saint Augustine's, which includes one of the manors in question here (5ra9). Each paragraph, it seems, started something like this: 'In the hundred of C— the archbishop has a manor N— and it is of the food of the monks of Holy Trinity' (B / xAug / A4-19v15). The lests were indicated too, but I do not have any clear idea how these indications were fitted into the text.

Working from B, the C scribes compiled two booklets: one (C-1) for the manors held by the archbishop and his men, the other (C-2) for the manors assigned to the archbishop's monks. Doing only what they had done many times before, the C scribes would have made sure that these booklets included the cadastral indications (lests as well as hundreds) that were required. It was easy for them to decide which paragraphs belonged in C-2, provided that the B text included the necessary clause ('it is of the food of the monks' or something similar). But if that clause had been omitted, or if it was overlooked, a paragraph which ought to be copied into C-2 would be copied into C-1 instead – and that, I suggest, is how we should explain the fact that one of the monks' manors (Mersham) is, in DB, mistakenly listed among the archbishop's manors (3vb47).

Working from C, the D scribes decided to distribute the contents of C-1 into three separate sections: one (D-1) for the manors held either wholly or partly in domain, a second (D-2) for the manors held by the bishop of Rochester, and a third (D-3) for the manors held by the rest of the archbishop's knights. D-1 was basically a fair copy of C-1 – the scribe had only to omit the paragraphs reserved for the other sections – and the cadastral headings were reproduced successfully (as they were in D-4, an unaltered fair copy of C-2). D-2 and D-3 were concatenations of excerpts, and the scribe or scribes responsible did not make any serious attempt to supply the new cadastral headings made necessary by this re-organization of the text: in these two sections, the lest headings were uniformly absent, and the hundred headings only sporadically present. It was at this stage, I think, while the D text was being written, that some misunderstanding resulted in a serious mistake. The paragraph describing the manor of Teynham ought to have been included (the whole of it) in section D-1. That did not happen. What happened instead was that one of the constituent subparagraphs was included in section D-3, and the rest of the paragraph was lost.

Working from D, the DB scribe was responsible for one more blunder. Not understanding that the bishop of Rochester was one of the archbishop's tenants, he thought that section D-2 was out of place; so he decided that it ought to be moved and made into a separate chapter. D-1 and D-3 became DB-1 and DB-2 (ch. 2); D-4 became DB-3 (ch. 3); and D-2 became DB-4 (ch. 4).

Along these lines, I think, we can understand not just how the text changed its shape, but also how some of its errors came about. It is a great help, of course, that copies survive of a contemporary description of the archbishop's manors, text α, drawn up (as I suppose) by the archbishop's own officials (above, p. 44). We also have a copy (C1, fos. 5va–c) of a schedule of the payments due from the archbishop's domain manors (from all of them, not just the ones in Kent), and this, though not of much relevance here, does give us some useful hints. Thanks to the survival of these documents, we have some means of knowing what DB ought to say, and thus of comparing what it ought to say with what it actually says.

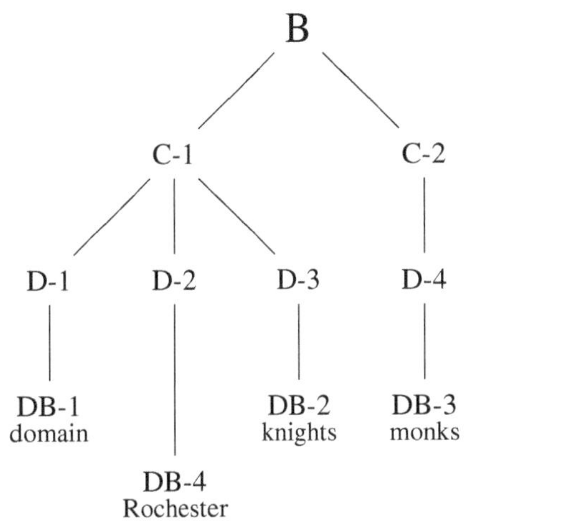

Figure 5. Evolution of the survey text as represented by chapters 2–4 of DB-Ke.

Since 1070 – the previous archbishop having been deposed by the pope's legates and put into prison by the king – the church had been governed by a monk from Italy named Lanfranc, thoroughly competent, and thoroughly trusted by king Willelm. (Before this, Lanfranc had been the first abbot of the monastery founded by duke Willelm, as he then was, in Caen.) With the king's help, the new archbishop was able to recover numerous manors and pieces of land which had passed into private hands (doc. 3). He rebuilt his cathedral church, and the monastery which was attached to it; he founded two hospitals and a church near Canterbury; after 1075 he took control of the bishopric of Rochester, reconstructing that church as well, and founding a new monastery next to it.

In return for the lands which he held from the king, the archbishop was required to supply the king, when the king asked for them, with sixty knights, properly armed and equipped. Like other barons, the archbishop found it convenient to distribute this load among his tenants, requiring some quota of knight's service from them, in return for the lands which they held from him. Surprising as it may seem, obligations of this sort were not among the matters which the survey was designed to investigate, and exact information is not to be looked for in DB.

(A list of the archbishop's knights – which, mostly, can be read as a description of the situation existing in the 1090s – was one of the documents added by later scribes at the end of manuscript C1 (above, p. 39). A later version of this list, extensively revised and annotated, was discovered and printed by Colvin (1964); and this, mostly, can be read as a description of the situation existing in the 1160s. I make use this evidence in identifying some of the places referred to by DB, but do not discuss it any further than that.)

Lanfranc died in 1089, three years after the survey. Over the next 25 years, the archbishopric was in the king's hands for periods which add up to more than half of the time: in 1089–93, until a new archbishop was appointed, in the person of Anselm; in 1097–1100, while Anselm was in exile; in 1103–7, while he was in exile for the second time; and in 1109–14, while the see was vacant again. During these intervals, the king's agents who were managing the property thought only of short-term profits. Since they were aiming to raise as much money as possible for the king, while the opportunity lasted, they might be inclined to strike bargains with the church's tenants which would not be profitable in the longer run; and a passage in Edmer's *Historia novorum* seems to be complaining that this is what they did (ed. Rule 1884, p. 26). On the other hand, for as long as the archbishop remained in his hands, the king had a personal interest in making sure that the church's rights were exerted to the furthest extent, if not even a little further; and in that sense these periods of royal control may actually have helped to consolidate the church's authority over its possessions.

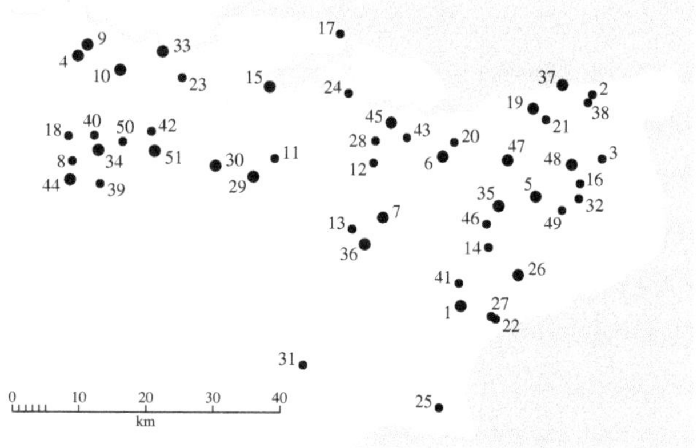

1 Aldington	18 Halstead	35 Petham
2 All Saints	19 Herne	36 Pluckley
3 Ash	20 Hernhill	37 Reculver
4 Bexley	21 Hoath	38 St Nicholas
5 Bishopsbourne	22 West Hythe	39 Sevenoaks
6 Boughton	23 Ifield	40 Shoreham
7 Charing	24 Iwade	41 Smeeth
8 Chevening	25 Lydd	42 Stansted
9 Crayford	26 Lyminge	43 Stone
10 Darenth	27 Lympne	44 Sundridge
11 Detling	28 Lyminge	45 Teynham
12 Doddington	29 Maidstone	46 Waltham
13 Egerton	30 East Malling	47 Westgate
14 Elmsted	31 Newenden	48 Wingham
15 Gillingham	32 Nonington	49 Womenswold
16 Goodnestone	33 Northfleet	50 Woodlands
17 Grain	34 Otford	51 Wrotham

Figure 6. Lands of the archbishop of Canterbury.

This chapter is the only one which starts with a preliminary section – two paragraphs taken out of the cadastral frame (probably by the DB scribe himself). The main text begins at 3ra19.

3ra3) 'In the city of Canterbury the archbishop has twelve townsmen and thirty-two plots of land ... and one mill.' The corresponding passage in α (C1-2va32–7) is part of the description of the manor of Westgate (3va44). Putting the two passages together, we discover that this property was owned collectively by the priests of Saint Gregory's church – a new establishment set up by archbishop Lanfranc on a site outside Northgate. (Its original purpose is explained by Lanfranc's obit (Gibson 1978, p. 228); the church was refounded some forty years later as an Augustinian priory.)

The word which I translate as 'plot of land' is something of a puzzle. In doc. 2 it is *mansio*. In α it is *mansura*, once *mansura terrae* (C1-2va49). In B / xAug, it is usually *mansura* or *mansura terrae* (e.g. A4-22r19); but alternatively it may be *mansio* or (once only and perhaps by error) *mansio terrae* (19r22). In DB the spelling oscillates between *mansura* and *masura*; here again we find the expression *mansura terrae*, as if it seemed necessary for the meaning to be made specific. As the word is used in these texts, however, it always means the same thing, regardless of whether the word *terrae* is attached to it or not: a *mansura* is a plot of land in a city or town (Canterbury, Rochester, Dover). To some degree it can be used interchangeably with *burgensis* (the sort of person expected to own such a plot) or with *domus* (the sort of building expected to stand on such a plot). (The corresponding English word was *haga*, which occurs as a gloss in doc. 2 and several times also in DB.) As far as I can see any sense in this, *mansura* is a hybrid word. In people's minds it was certainly connected with *mansio*; but it was also connected with *mensura*. It meant a measure of land (one plot marked out from the neighbouring plots) which was also a place to live and build a house on.

3ra7) 'Sandwich lies in its own hundred.' Apart from what it tells us about Sandwich, this paragraph is textually important, because versions of it survive in $\alpha 1$ (C4-71vb2–8), $\alpha 2$ (C1-3vb48–c10) and B / xAug (A4-21r16–v2), as well as in DB.

13) 'In the year in which this survey was made, Sandwich paid fifty pounds by way of farm.' The DB scribe thought it necessary to specify the year (he hesitated over the wording that he should use) because he wanted his readers to understand that the information was already out of date. From the second version of text α, we can see what he was getting at: 'Last year it paid fifty pounds ... and this year it it supposed to pay seventy pounds' (C1-3vc4–7). So the statement was true at the time when the survey was conducted, in the middle of one financial year, but – as far as the DB scribe could tell – was no longer true at the time when he was writing, in the middle of the next.

3ra19) 'The archbishop of Canterbury holds in domain Tarent.' Darenth TQ 5671.

22) 'To this manor belong five townsmen in Rochester paying 80 pence.' The connection persisted. In the 1180s, when one such piece of land in the city was given to the monks of Rochester, archbishop Baldwin confirmed the grant 'saving the service due to the manor of Darenth' (Cheney and Jones 1986, no. 303). In the 1220s, after the monks had got possession of the whole manor of Darenth (in exchange for Lambeth), some of the citizens of Rochester were still paying the same rent that had been paid at the time of the survey (*pro quibusdam masagiis in Rofa in medio quadragesime vi sol' et viii d'*, R3, fo. 72v, cf. Thorpe 1788, p. 7, from R4).

24) '... and ten shillings.' This phrase, ostensibly part of the current value ('fifteen pounds and ten shillings'), seems rather to be a fragment of a clause which is found complete in α: 'And ten shillings Ricard has of it inside his castle' (C1-3rc43–4), i.e. the lowy of Tonbridge.

Text α tells us explicitly that the next two manors, Otford and Sundridge, are in a hundred called *Codesede* (C1-3rc14). In the thirteenth century, without doubt, they belonged to Codsheath hundred; but so did Kemsing, which in DB seems to be firmly placed in Helmstree hundred (6vb5). We might think of inserting a hundred heading here, assuming that it was accidentally omitted. Alternatively we might think that DB is right as it stands, and that Otford and Sundridge were (whatever the archbishop might think) regarded by the commissioners as part of Axstone hundred. Or we might think of transposing the heading for Helmstree hundred (3ra42), on the assumption that it got itself misplaced in DB (and Kemsing then would cease to be a problem). It is hard to decide which solution is the best.

3ra26) 'The same archbishop holds Otefort in domain.' Otford TQ 5259. The manor included Shoreham TQ 5261, Halstead TQ 4861, Woodlands TQ 5761, Chevening TQ 4857, Sevenoaks TQ 5354, and a large tract of land in the Weald, where two-thirds of Summerden hundred belonged to the archbishop.

30) 'Of this manor three thegns hold one sulung and a half.' Here and later, the DB scribe saw an opportunity to shorten the text by amalgamating two or more sub-paragraphs; and that, by and large, is what he chose to do. For the details we have to go back to α, where these three thegns are identified by name (C1-3rb48–52).

(All three of them turn out to be foreigners. The DB scribe did not think it absurd to use the Latinized English word *teignus* for a Frenchman. But he did not make a habit of it.)

'What Haimo holds of it.' Probably Chevening – but only if the tenant is Haimo the sheriff (or, not impossibly, his son).

'What Rodbert the interpreter and Gosfrid de Ros hold of it.' Possibly Robert held Halstead (which, with Preston TQ 5262 in Shoreham, belonged later to a family named de Malevile). Goisfrid held Lullingstone (repr. Castle Farm) TQ 5263 in Shoreham (Hasted 3:6): there is no doubt about that. (He also held some land in Wrotham (3rb27).)

3ra36) 'The same archbishop holds Sondresse.' Sundridge TQ 4854. Though they disagree slightly about the amount of it, α, DB and the schedule of farms (C1, fo. 5va) all say that this manor is paying a farm of twenty odd pounds in addition to providing the archbishop with one knight. (None of them explains the reason for this abnormal arrangement.) Around 1170, when we hear of it next (Colvin 1964, p. 15), Sundridge was connected with two manors – Sibton and Eythorne – which had belonged to Robert son of Watso in the 1080s. But it is doubtful how that connection came about.

3ra43) 'The same archbishop holds Bix.' Bexley TQ 4973.

3ra49) 'The same archbishop holds Erhede.' Crayford TQ 5175. The place has changed its name twice. *Erhede* is a good DB spelling of the original name (not to be mistaken, though sometimes it has been, for Erith); after c. 1100 it came to be called Erde (below, p. 242); after c. 1500 it acquired its modern name.

At the time of the survey, Crayford was paying the archbishop twenty-one pounds, seemingly by way of farm (C1-5vb). Though his name is not mentioned in either α or DB, the manor was probably held by Hugo de Port (who, here as elsewhere, would have stepped into the shoes of Osward (C1-3rb28), the TRE sheriff of Kent). He was certainly in possession in the 1090s, but by then the tenure had been changed to knight's service. Crayford descended to Hugo's son Henric (R1, fo. 198v) and beyond (Colvin 1964, p. 30), with the rest of the barony of Port.

* 3rb6) 'The same archbishop holds in domain Metlinges.' East Malling TQ 7057. There is no doubt about it: East Malling belonged to the archbishop; West Malling belonged to the bishop of Rochester and is listed in chapter 4 (5va36).

3rb12) 'The same archbishop holds in domain Norfluet.' Northfleet TQ 6274, including Ifield TQ 6570.

3rb20) 'The same archbishop holds Broteham.' Wrotham TQ 6159, including Stansted TQ 6062. The spelling 'br' for 'wr' occurs in the hundred heading as well as in the main entry, and again at 8vb41; evidently it is not just a momentary slip. I take it to be a French-speaking scribe's attempt to represent the difference that he could hear between [wr] and [r]. A writ of Henric I, as it was copied into Rochester's cartulary (R1, fo. 187r–v), spells the name *broteham* again; the rubric supplied by the scribe (who was fluent in English) has *uuroteham*.

Changing his mind, the DB scribe keeps the Wrotham sub-paragraphs separate; but he still lumps the values together.

25) 'Of this manor Willelm the dispenser holds one sulung.' Probably part of Yaldham TQ 5858 in Wrotham (Hasted 5:15). The tenant seems to be the man who is called Willelm de Wroteham in the list of the archbishop's knights (C1-7rb).

27) 'Of the same manor Goisfrid (de Ros) holds from the archbishop one sulung.' Part of Yaldham TQ 5858 in Wrotham, the manor called East or Great Yaldham (Hasted 5:15). For this and other land (3ra30), Goisfrid owed the service of one knight (C1-7rb). He gave tithes from Yaldham to the monks of Rochester (R1, fo. 189v). Unlike the manors held by Goisfrid from the bishop of Bayeux (6ra46), these lands did not pass to Eudo dapifer. When they are next heard of, they belong to Willelm Malet (d. 1170).

29) 'Of the same manor Farman holds one yoke and a half from the archbishop.' Text α says 'one sulung and a half' (C4-71rb8 = C1-3rc25); since Farman has three ploughs at work here, α is probably right. Possibly this is Ightham TQ 5956 – but only on * the grounds that Ightham ought to be mentioned somewhere and does not seem to be mentioned anywhere else. Farman does not occur in the list of the archbishop's knights: by the time that this list was compiled, Ightham probably belonged to Willelm son of Radulf (Colvin 1964, p. 16).

3rb36) 'The same archbishop holds Meddestane.' Maidstone TQ 7655, including Detling TQ 7958.

41) 'Of this manor three knights hold from the archbishop four sulungs.' Changing his mind again (but this time the decision sticks), the DB scribe amalgamates three sub-paragraphs. The details are in α (C1-3ra49–54):

'Radulf has one sulung.' Preston TQ 7258 in Aylesford. The ten- * ant is Radulf son of Turald (as is clear from doc. 1, and from later evidence connecting Preston with the barony of Talebot).

'Willelm, bishop Gundulf's brother, has two sulungs.' Detling, or part of it. (Gundulf was bishop of Rochester (below, p. 169); the fact that he had a brother named Willelm is recorded only here.)

'Anschitil de Ros has one sulung.' Cossington TQ 7459 in Aylesford.

Detling and Preston ('not far from the river Medway') both appear in the list of manors restored to Christ Church by Willelm I (doc. 3).

48) 'The monks of Canterbury have every year from two men of this manor twenty shillings.' There are two passages in α which seem to correspond with this (C1-3ra54–b3, 4vc43–8), but they differ from one another, and from DB, in some significant respects. The statement most consonant with later evidence is this: 'Wulfric and Cole hold Burgericestune; there is half a sulung there, and from it they pay 100 pence to the altar of Holy Trinity; this half-sulung is included in the ten sulungs of Maidstone' (C1-4vc). Without doubt, the place in question is Burston (repr. Bus- * ton Manor) TQ 7150 in Hunton (Hasted 5:151); the identification was first made by Kilburne (1659, p. 151). The monks of Christ Church continued to receive an annual payment of 100 pence from Burston (below, p. 166).

3va2) 'The same archbishop holds Gelingeham.' Gillingham TQ 7868, including Grain TQ 8876.

7) 'Of this manor a certain Frenchman holds land for one plough.' Part of Gillingham, the manor called West Court TQ 7769 (Hasted 4:231). Text α has this: 'What Anschitil de Ros and Rodbert Brutin own (is worth) forty shillings' (C1-3ra38–40). Anschitil drops out of the picture in DB: this anonymous Frenchman is sure to be Robert Brutin. There is a matching item in the list of the archbishop's knights: 'Robert Brutin, half' (C1-7rb). A man called 'Ricard Brutin of Gillingham' gave tithes from this place to the monks of Rochester (R1, fo. 191r).

3va12) 'The same archbishop holds Roculf.' Reculver TR 2269. As the name is used here, it means something larger than the parish but much smaller than the thirteenth-century manor of Reculver. It is fairly sure to have included Hoath TR 2064; it may also have included the adjoining part of Thanet, All Saints TR 2767 and St Nicholas at Wade TR 2666. The manor is one that had been lost until Lanfranc got it back (doc. 3); there is no hint of that, however, in DB.

* 3va20) 'The same archbishop holds Nortone in domain.' Herne TR 1865 under another name. DB's *Nortone* is a slip of the pen: the name ought to be 'Northwood' (C1-2vc17, cf. C1-5va). This name – or this description, *bi norþan wude*, 'to the north of the wood' – seems to have covered the whole strip of open country, north of the Blean, from Seasalter across to Reculver. It could be applied to Whitstable; it could be applied to Swalecliffe; it could also be applied, as this entry proves, to a place in Reculver hundred. By the thirteenth century, the manor of Northwood had ceased to exist, and there is only one possible explanation for that: it must have been amalgamated with Reculver. So the place called 'Northwood' in 1086 – 'Archbishop's Northwood' (C1-1vc) – must be one of the places which were included in the manor of Reculver later on. By elimination, that has to mean Herne.

As Harold Gough points out to me, it is only by adding the two assessments together – 8 sulungs for Reculver, 13 sulungs for Northwood – that one can come even close to the assessment of 26 sulungs reported in the charter of king Eadred (Sawyer 1968, no. 546) which granted this estate (Reculver in the widest sense) to Christ Church. As far as the mainland is concerned (some of the sulungs were in Thanet), the scope of the grant was fully worked out by Gough (1992): its limits seem to coincide very closely with the outward boundaries of Reculver, Hoath and Herne. Apparently the estate became divided into two equal parts, one of which (Reculver in a narrow sense) was lost for some length of time but eventually recovered. (Its assessment was reduced by 5 sulungs, somewhere along the line.) In the twelfth century, the parts were reunited, and the name Reculver could then revert to its tenth-century meaning.

From the schedule of the archbishop's farms, we discover that the monks of Christ Church were getting a payment of eight pounds from Northwood (*et de hoc gablo habent monachi viii lib'*, C1, fo. 5vb). The payment continued; but by 1179 it was being described as 'eight pounds from Reculver' (*de Raculfre octo libras sterlingorum*, Holtzmann 1936, no. 181). Perhaps it should also be noted, by the way, that a cash payment of 140 pounds from the manors of Reculver and Boughton under Blean is said to have been allocated by archbishop Lanfranc to the two hospitals which he had founded near Canterbury (Cheney and Jones 1986, no. 96, cf. GREx 1167:201); but there is no word of that in either α or DB, presumably because it was not the king's business to know how the archbishop's income was disposed of.

27) 'Of this manor (of Northwood) Vitalis holds from the archbishop three sulungs and one yoke and twelve acres of land.' More details in α: 'Of these sulungs Vitalis of Canterbury has one sulung and one yoke (on the mainland), and in Thanet a sulung and a half; he also has in Macebroc twelve acres, and half a sulung from the archbishop (called) Et ezilamerth' (C1-2vc21–6). (The end of this sentence is hard to construe; I punctuate after 'acres' and take *Et* to mean *Æt*, but the name 'ezilamerth' is still a puzzle.) The history of this holding is well documented (MacMichael 1963, Colvin 1964, Urry 1967). Its centre was at Stourmouth TR 2562 (the church of which was given by Vitalis's son to the monks of Rochester); the land in Thanet was part of Sarre TR 2665. 'Macebroc' is a lost place called Makenbrook (TR 1767 approx.) in Herne (for help in fixing the location of which I am indebted to Harold Gough). *

3va33) 'The same archbishop holds Piteham.' Petham TR 1351, including Waltham TR 1148 and Elmsted TR 1144.

39) 'Of this manor Godefrid and Nigel hold one sulung and a half and a yoke.' The holdings are described separately in α (C1-2vb22–7):

'Of these sulungs Godefrid the steward has half a sulung ... namely Suurtling.' Swarling TR 1352 in Petham.

'... and Nigel has one sulung and one yoke of land.' Whiteacre TR 1147 in Waltham. In the list of the archbishop's knights Nigel (or a descendant of his) appears as Niel de Huatacra (C1-7rb).

By choosing to add these two sub-paragraphs together, the DB scribe commits himself to some arithmetic. He has no trouble with numbers, or with pounds, shillings and pence; but sulungs and yokes are another matter. Here he is adding 'half a sulung' to 'one sulung and one yoke'; and the answer that he gets, though right in its way, is not correctly expressed. It ought to be 'one sulung and three yokes'. Similar solecisms occur below. The scribe knew – what he could see at once, from the text in front of him – that a yoke was smaller than a sulung; but he shows no sign of knowing what fraction of a sulung it was. Even where he ought to do it, he never performs a carry which would prove that he was counting four yokes to a sulung. That is why he ends up with expressions like 'one sulung and six yokes' (3vb3), instead of 'two sulungs and a half', or 'five sulungs and a half and three yokes' (3vb44), instead of 'six sulungs and one yoke'. It is clear from this (but not just from this) that the DB scribe was not acquainted with Kent.

42) 'Of these (nine pounds) the monks get eight shillings a year.' The payment came (and continued to come) from Swarling, 'which belongs to the monks' clothing' (C1-2vb24), i.e. to the chamberer's department.

3va44) 'The same archbishop holds Estursete in domain.' Westgate (repr. Westgate Court) TR 1458, in the western suburb of Canterbury. The hundred which DB calls by the same name was conterminous with the manor; it was later called Westgate hundred, and that name was current before 1109 (Brett and Gribbin 2004, no. 19).

3vb3) 'Of this manor five men of the archbishop's own one sulung and six yokes.' The holdings are noted individually in α (C1-2va9–22, 38–46); the DB scribe keeps Haimo's separate (line 7) but amalgamates the others.

'Of these seven sulungs Godefrid the steward has one sulung from the archbishop, (namely) Tenitune.' Thanington TR 1356. Godefrid occurs twice in the list of the archbishop's knights, apparently because he was, temporarily, in possession of someone else's lands as well as his own (as might happen, for instance, if he had custody of an under-age heir). In one entry he is called Godefrid de Mellinge: this covers Thanington and lands in Sussex (including part of the manor of South Malling) which descended to his heirs. In the other he is called Godefrid de Tanintuna: this covers lands at East Lenham (4va2), Hunton (4vb36) and Swarling (3va39) which followed different trajectories (Colvin 1964, p. 17).

'Also Vitalis has of them one yoke.' Not identified.

'Robert de Hardes holds of them one yoke of land.' Not identified.

'Also Ægelward holds three yokes in Natinduna.' Part of Nackington TR 1554.

'Albold holds of the said sulungs one yoke, (namely) Wic.' Wyke TR 1758 in St Martin's parish (Hasted 11:160, Colvin 1964, p. 37).

7) 'Of the same manor Haimo the sheriff holds half a sulung from the archbishop.' Part of Milton TR 1255.

4ra10–18) 'The same archbishop holds a village which is called Saint Martin. It belongs to (the manor of) Estursete and lies in the same hundred.' This paragraph has got itself misplaced in DB (see below): it ought to be somewhere here. It refers to the tract of land east of the city which was (and continued to be) part of Westgate hundred.

11) 'It defended itself for one sulung and a half.' In fact for one sulung only, as is clear from α (C1-2va23) and from what DB says below (line 17). Half of it was held in domain, the other half by Radulf (called 'the chamberlain' in α). Because the paragraph is out of place, DB has lost sight of the fact that this sulung counts as one of the seven sulungs of Westgate.

Another detached portion of this manor (and of this hundred) was the place which used to be called Harwich TR 1066 (before the name Whitstable shifted itself to this place, leaving the old village to be called Church Street instead). Harwich is the subject of a paper by Baldwin (1993) which, unfortunately, is flawed by a basic error. The author failed to realize (and the experts whom he consulted failed to explain to him) that in Kent (as also in Sussex) the English word 'borough' was used in two different senses – not just different but antithetical senses. The very fact that Harwich was a *borga* (i.e. a subdivision of a hundred) is proof that it was not a *burgus* (i.e. a town). Nevertheless, there is probably some value in Baldwin's suggestion that Harwich superseded Seasalter (5ra15) as a port for Canterbury. Seasalter has the status of a town without the appearance of one; Harwich has the appearance without the status. Possibly Harwich was a new town, established on a site acquired by one of the archbishops, fronting on a sheltered inlet (later a lagoon, then a marsh, and now a golf course), which never reached the point of being formally recognized as a *burgus*. It did, for a time, have a church of its own (below, p. 234); but at some uncertain date the parish was merged with Seasalter – which is why the Seasalter/Whitstable boundary zigzags as it does.

Whitstable itself is not mentioned in DB, but may be silently included in the entry relating to Kingston (9vb35). From that we discover that Kingston had formerly belonged to archbishop Stigand; and possibly the case could be made that Stigand – who is never given credit for much – deserves to be recognized as the founder of Harwich.

3vb10) 'The same archbishop holds in domain Burnes.' Bishopsbourne TR 1852.

3vb16) 'The same archbishop holds in domain Boltune.' Boughton under Blean TR 0458, including Hernhill TR 0660.

3vb23) 'The same archbishop holds in domain Cheringes.' Charing TQ 9549, including Egerton TQ 9047.

23) 'It defended itself for eight shillings.' An uncorrected slip of the pen: the scribe wrote *sol'* for *solins*.

24) 'In domain there is one sulung.' Absent-mindedly, so it seems, the scribe includes an item of information which otherwise he always omits. From this hint, helped out by analogy, we may gather that the D-Ke text said something along these lines: '8 sulungs, land for 40 ploughs, 1 sulung and 4.5 ploughs on the domain, 7 sulungs and 27 ploughs for the men, another 8.5 ploughs can be made'. If the DB scribe had followed his usual policy, that would have been reduced to this: '8 sulungs, land for 40 ploughs, on the domain 4.5 ploughs, the (villains and bordars) have 27 ploughs', and so on. Losing concentration, he wrote *In dominio est unum solin* – and having written it, he let it stand.

3vb29) 'The same archbishop holds Pluchelei.' Pluckley TQ 9245. At the time of the survey, this manor was paying a farm of twenty pounds (C1-3ra29); and the absence of this payment from the schedule of farms (C1, fos. 5va–c) is a hint that the schedule is of slightly later date. By the 1090s, Pluckley had been granted out. It was held by Willelm Folet, as two knight's fees (Colvin 1964, pp. 22–3); and it continued with his descendants (or, at least, with men who used the same surname).

3vb34) Probably here, certainly somewhere, a block of text has gone missing: a heading for Teynham hundred and a paragraph describing Teynham TQ 9663. A sub-paragraph concerning a half-sulung in Sheppey is included in the following section (4va2) – where Teynham hundred comes next after Calehill hundred – but the main entry has been lost.

Teynham was an important manor (this was where the archbishop had his vineyard), and its omission makes a large hole in the map. Only the basic facts are reported by α: 'Teynham is a manor of the archbishop's; in the time of king Edward it defended itself for 5.5 sulungs; similarly now; it is appraised at 50 pounds' (C1-2vc51-4). In the thirteenth century the churches of Lynsted TQ 9460, Doddington TQ 9357, Stone TQ 9861 and Iwade TQ 9067 were all regarded as chapels dependent on Teynham.

3vb35) 'The same archbishop holds Wingheham in domain.' Wingham TR 2457. Another large manor, including Ash TR 2858, Goodnestone TR 2554, Nonington TR 2552, and Womenswold TR 2250.

41) 'Of this manor Willelm de Arcis holds one sulung in Fletes.' Fleet TR 3060 in Ash (Hasted 9:209). Willelm was lord of Folkestone (9va16). Some documents from Christ Church refer to this holding as *Ratebourc* (doc. 1), meaning Richborough; that is just a different name for the same place. The whole area inside the walls of the Roman fort was included in the manor of Fleet (*Feet of fines*, p. 5).

44) 'Of the same manor five men of the archbishop's hold five sulungs and a half and three yokes.' Text α has the details (C1-2vb5–11):

'Vitalis has one sulung.' Walmestone TR 2559 in Wingham.

'Wibert and Arnold have three sulungs.' Probably Goss Hall TR 3058 and Knell TR 2860, both in Ash (Colvin 1964, p. 26).

'Heringod has one sulung less ten acres.' Probably Overland TR 2759 in Ash (Colvin 1964, p. 27). The DB scribe seems to have counted this holding as three yokes; perhaps that is what his source text said.

'Godefrid the crossbowman has one sulung and a half.' Probably Ratling TR 2453 in Nonington (Colvin 1964, p. 25). Not the same man as Godefrid the steward (3vb3).

3vb46) 'In Longbridge hundred.' There is a difficulty with the cadastral headings here. DB seems to say that we are still in Eastry lest, but that is sure to be wrong; a lest heading must have gone missing. Later on, the whole of Longbridge hundred was in Shrewinghope lest, which, by and large, is Wiwarleth lest under another name. In DB some parts of Longbridge hundred – including Kennington (12vb25), Sevington and Ashford (13ra13) – are certainly reckoned to belong to Wiwarleth lest, and possibly that is the heading which we ought to supply here too. It is also possible, however, that the southern part of Longbridge hundred – just like the southern part of Bircholt hundred (4ra3) – fell within Limwar lest at the time of the survey, only later being added to Wiwarleth lest. That is what text α seems to be telling us: speaking of Mersham, it says that 'this manor lies in Limwar leth in the hundred of Longbridge' (C1-4rb36–7). Since DB is certainly defective as it stands, and since α is explicit, I supply the heading accordingly.

3vb47) 'The same archbishop holds in domain Merseham.' Mersham TR 0539. Not one the archbishop's domain manors. It is missing from the list of farms (C1-5va–c); and α (C1-4rb28) seem to prove that it should properly have been listed among the monks' manors in chapter 3. In the thirteenth century, Mersham was supplying the monks with provisions for fourteen days (C4, fo. 69vb).

4ra2) 'In Limwar lest, in Bircholt hundred.' This is the southern part of Bircholt hundred – the part which belonged to the archbishop, the part which was in Limwar lest. The northern part of it was in Wiwarleth lest (13vb22).

4ra3) 'The same archbishop holds Aldintone in domain.' Aldington TR 0736, including Smeeth TR 0739. The manor also included extensive lands in the Weald and in the Marsh. (Lydd TR 0420 was originally part of Aldington; its connection with the Cinque Ports is a later complication.)

4ra10–18) This whole passage is misplaced: it ought to be part of the description of Westgate (3vb9). By some accident it came to be inserted here, in the middle of the Aldington paragraph. It is hard to understand how or when this dislocation occurred. (In DB the stray paragraph is exactly one column too late, but I do not see how that can be significant.) One possible conjecture might run something like this. Aldington's lands in Romney Marsh, which later we find being called Saint Martin's hundred (GREx 1199:68), might perhaps have already been called Saint Martin's at the time of the survey; though this fact is not mentioned in α, it might perhaps have been mentioned in the survey text; and that note might – perhaps – have been misread as an instruction to insert the Westgate sub-paragraph here. (This conjecture arose from my reading of an article by Robertson (1880); but he was starting from the opposite assumption – that α is wrong and that DB is right as it stands. Misled by Somner's description, he thought that α consisted of edited extracts from DB (Robertson 1880, p. 352).) But I doubt whether we can be sure of anything, except that somebody blundered.

4ra19) The interrupted paragraph resumes: 'In Romenel there are four score and five townsmen who belong to the archbishop's manor of Aldington.' Old Romney TR 0325.

This and all other passages that mention Romney appear to relate to Old Romney. There is nothing to indicate what sort of settlement existed (if any did) on the site of (New) Romney TR 0624. The name 'Old Romney', *Vetus Rumenel*, once it starts to occur, proves that both places existed, and that the new one was already the more important of the two: the expectation was that people would take *Rumenel* to mean (New) Romney unless they were told otherwise. By the early thirteenth century, the name *Vetus Rumenel* was appearing frequently; but I have no note of its occurrence before the 1160s (GREx 1165:109). Provisionally it look to me as if (New) Romney was a new town created by one of the early twelfth-century archbishops.

21) 'Of the same manor of Aldinton there lies in Limes half a yoke and half a rod.' Lympne TR 1134, including West Hythe TR 1234.

A rod is one quarter of a yoke, one sixteenth of a sulung. There is no piece of arithmetic to prove the point, but the pattern is clear enough: we hear of half-yokes, but not of any smaller fraction; we hear of one rod and three rods, but not of any larger number. So this is the way to count: one rod, half a yoke, three rods, one yoke, one yoke and one rod, one yoke and a half, one yoke and three rods, half a sulung, and so on. (If one is counting with half-rods, i.e. with thirty-seconds of a sulung, there is another point to watch out for. One does not say 'three rods and a half': the rule is to round up and then subtract. So the right thing to say is 'one yoke less half a rod' (7/32), 'half a sulung less half a rod' (15/32), 'three yokes less half a rod' (23/32), 'one sulung less half a rod' (31/32).)

23) 'There are seven priest there who pay 1740 pence.' A mysterious statement, and we get no help from α in making sense of it. Apparently Lympne church is a minster on the verge of extinction. The 'seven priests' are never heard of again; the church became an ordinary parish church, on a par with the churches formerly subordinate to it (below, p. 228).

26) 'Of the same manor (of Aldington) the count of Eu holds Estotinghes as one manor.' Stowting TR 1241. (DB ignores the fact that Stowting was in Stowting hundred, but has headings which refer to this hundred four times elsewhere.) In α the tenant is named as Willelm de Arcis (C1-2vb34); possibly he held the manor at farm from the count. Nothing much is known about this place before the thirteenth century, when Stephan Harengod (d. 1257) held the hundred of Stowting from the king and the manor of Stowting from the countess of Eu.

4ra32) 'The same archbishop holds in domain Leminges.' Lyminge TR 1640. According to doc. 3, 'the minster of Lyminge with the lands and customs belonging to the same minster' had been lost until they were given back to Christ Church by Willelm I; but we are given no hint of that in either α or DB.

38) 'Of this manor three men of the archbishop's hold two sulungs and a half and half a yoke. Again we find the details in α (C1-2vb50–4):

'Rodbert son of Watso has, of these (seven sulungs), two sulungs in feod.' Sibton TR 1541 in Lyminge. By around 1170 the manor belonged to Thomas son of Thomas son of Bernard (Colvin 1964, p. 15), continuing with his descendants (who adopted fiz Bernard as their surname). They also held Eythorne (5rb22) and Sundridge (3ra36).

'Rodbert de Hardes has half a sulung.' Probably Waddenhall TR 1248 in Waltham, in Stowting hundred (Hasted 9:321); but the known connections of that place point towards Petham (3va33), not towards Lyminge.

'Osbert Pasforera has half a yoke.' Not identified.

One sulung of 'almsland' in Romney Marsh, mentioned here by α (C1-2vb54–c9), is listed by DB at the end of chapter 3 (5rb43).

4ra43 'The same archbishop holds Newedene.' Newenden TQ 8327. In α we are told that Newenden was formerly dependent on Saltwood; it is listed among the monks' lands for that reason (C1-4rc20). It was lost; it was recovered by Lanfranc (doc. 3), but not reunited with Saltwood, nor given back to the monks.

No church is mentioned, either by DB or by the lists printed in chapter 8. Probably Newenden was part of the parish of Sandhurst (d16), only later becoming a small parish by itself. Both churches were in the archbishop's gift in the 1270s (T1, fos. 183v–4v).

Land of his knights

The next stretch of text – which has all the properties of a separate chapter except that it lacks a number – covers those manors which were each held entirely by one of the archbishop's men. The cadastral headings are more than usually defective, but the defects are easily mended.

* 4rb2) 'Ansgot (de Rovecestre) holds from the archbishop Forningeham.' Charton TQ 5566 in Farningham (Hasted 2:518). The name by which this manor came to be called was derived from the Cheritone family, who took their name from Cheriton TR 1836. Willelm de Cheritone was a nephew and one of the heirs of Willelm fiz Helto, Ansgot's grandson (below, p. 262); he is known to have been in possession of this manor by 1184 (Moore 1918, vol. 1, pp. 182–3, Kerling 1973, p. 149, *Curia regis rolls*, vol. 12, p. 503).

4rb9) 'Radulf son of Unspac holds Elesford from the archbishop.' Eynsford TQ 5465. Radulf's descendants used the surname de Einesford; they were men of some importance.

* 4rb17) 'Malger holds from the archbishop three yokes in Orpinton.' Little Orpington (repr. Mayfield Place) in Orpington (Hasted 2:103). The place was in Helmstree hundred (4vb1).

4rb23) 'Haimo the sheriff holds from the archbishop Briestede.' Brasted TQ 4655. Text α puts Brasted in Westerham hundred; later evidence says the same.

4rb30) 'The count of Eu holds from the archbishop Olecumbe.' Ulcombe TQ 8449. Ulcombe was in Eyhorne hundred.

* 4rb37) 'Radulf son of Turald holds Boltone from the archbishop.' Boughton Monchelsea TQ 7749. The identification is certain. As DB says, this half-sulung was counted towards the six sulungs of the monks' manor of Hollingbourne (4vb19).

Possibly here, certainly somewhere, we would expect to find some mention of the manor of Wootton TR 2246 – in Barham (Kinghamford) hundred, in Borwar (Saint Augustine's) lest. This was one of the places given back to Christ Church by Willelm I (doc. 3). The later evidence relating to Wootton was pieced together by Colvin (1964, pp. 25–6); as I read it, the upshot is that in the 1090s Wootton would have belonged to a man named Radulf ('of Eastry', as he is called in the list of the archbishop's knights). But there is no visible trace, in either α or DB, of either Wootton or Radulf.

4rb43) 'Ricard the archbishop's man holds from him Levelant.' Leaveland TR 0054.

4rb46) 'The same Ricard holds from the archbishop Grauenel.' Graveney TR 0562.

4va2) 'Godefrid the steward holds from the archbishop Lerham.' East Lenham TQ 9051 in Lenham (Hasted 5:427), in the part of the parish which belonged to Calehill hundred. (Lenham itself was in Eyhorne hundred; it belonged to Saint Augustine's (12ra10).)

* 4va7) 'The same Godefrid (the steward) holds from the archbishop in Sheppey half a sulung.' Stonepit TQ 9869 in Eastchurch. In the sixteenth century this part of Eastchurch parish was still in Teynham hundred (Lambard 1576, p. 33). The corresponding sentence

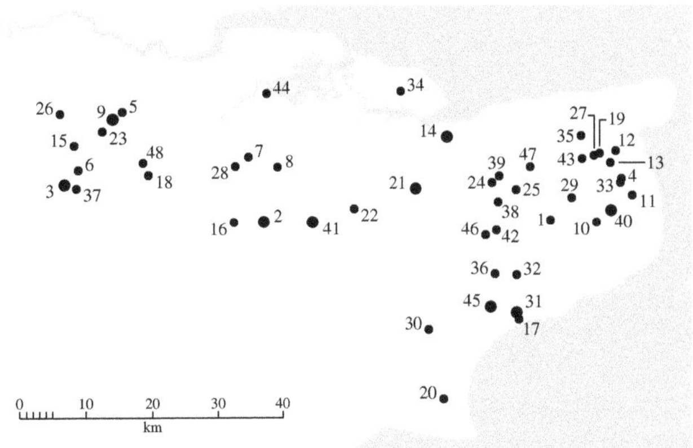

1	Barham	17	Hythe	33	Statenborough
2	Boughton	18	Ightham	34	Stonepit
3	Brasted	19	Knell	35	Stourmouth
4	Buckland	20	Langport	36	Stowting
5	Charton	21	Leaveland	37	Sundridge
6	Chevening	22	East Lenham	38	Swarling
7	Cossington	23	Lullingstone	39	Thanington
8	Detling	24	Milton	40	Tilmanstone
9	Eynsford	25	Nackington	41	Ulcombe
10	Eythorne	26	Little Orpington	42	Waddenhall
11	Finglesham	27	Overland	43	Walmestone
12	Fleet	28	Preston	44	West Court
13	Goss Hall	29	Ratling	45	Westenhanger
14	Graveney	30	Ruckinge	46	Whiteacre
15	Halstead	31	Saltwood	47	Wyke
16	Hunton	32	Sibton	48	Yaldham

Figure 7. Lands of the archbishop's knights.

in α (where the tenant is called Godefrid de Melling) is part of the paragraph for Teynham, the rest of which is missing from DB. As far as the land in Sheppey is concerned, α adds only one fact: 'Osward held this (half) sulung from the archbishop in the time of king Edward' (C1-3ra4).

Land at Stonepit, valued at 960 pence, was recovered by archbishop Ricard in 1177 (GREx 1177:203). It had lapsed to the king in 1165, with other lands of Radulf Picot's (GREx 1165:108). I do not know how it had come to belong to him.

4va10) 'Osbern son of Letard holds one yoke from the archbishop in Bocoland.' Probably Buckland TR 3156 in Woodnesborough (Hasted 10:130). In α this yoke is mentioned just briefly, in a sort of footnote attached to the Eastry paragraph (C1-3vb45); there may have been some doubt about its status. Tithes from a place called Buckland, presumably this place, had previously been given by Osbern to Saint Augustine's (Bates 1998, pp. 352–3).

4va40) 'Willelm (Folet) holds from the archbishop Tilemanestone.' Tilmanstone TR 3051. This and Willelm's other lands near Eastry are involved in some obscurity. The corresponding stretch of text in α differs significantly between one version and the other (C4-71va31–40, C1-3vb24–44); it was, apparently, only in the second version that Willelm's name was mentioned. None of these lands continued with his descendants. By the 1170s, Tilmanstone was linked with the barony of Crevequer (Colvin 1964, p. 11).

4va12) 'Willelm Folet holds from the archbishop Flenguessam.' Probably Finglesham TR 3353 in Northbourne (Hasted 9:595); but the identification depends only on the resemblance of the name. Finglesham, later, like the rest of Northbourne, belonged to Saint Augustine's.

4va14) The same Willelm (Folet) holds Estenberge from the archbishop.' Statenborough TR 3155 in Eastry (Hasted 10:111).

4va16) 'These lands.' Referring to 4va12 and 4va14. The value clause covers them both.

4va17) 'Hugo de Montfort holds from the archbishop Salteode.' Saltwood TR 1535, including the town of Hythe TR 1634. From Hugo this manor descended to his son, Robert de Montfort, who gave Saltwood church to the monks of Le Bec, for the subordinate priory of Saint-Philbert-sur-Risle (Brett and Gribbin 2004, no. 34, cf. Saltman 1956, no. 297). After Robert's death, archbishop Anselm got possession of Saltwood and restored it to the monks (Brett and Gribbin 2004, no. 17). But that is not even nearly the end of the story.

The town of Hythe is mentioned only twice in DB. All we are told is that there were 225 townsmen belonging to Saltwood (line 22) and six belonging to Lyminge (4ra36).

* 4va25) 'Willelm de Eddesham holds from the archbishop Berewic as one manor.' Westenhanger TR 1136 under another name (a name which survives as Berwick TR 1235 in Lympne). The history of Westenhanger was thoroughly muddled by Philipott (1659, pp. 302–3); Hasted (8:68–72) added to the confusion; and versions of his account are still in circulation (e.g. Martin and Martin 2001). There was only one manor here, with a name which was variably spelt and misspelt: a good thirteenth-century form would be *Ostringehangre*. Between the 1160s and the 1240s it was held from the archbishop by the family of Auberville (whose principal holding was the second-tier barony of Swingfield); through Joanna de Auberville (who had also inherited a share of the second-tier barony of Eynsford) the right descended to her son (by her second husband), Nicol de Crioil (d. 1303).

4va30) 'Robert de Romenel holds from the archbishop Langport.' Old Langport (lost) in Lydd TR 0420 (Hasted 8:425). The exact site of the manor is not known to me. Hasted puts it 'at the eastern part of this parish, near New Romney,' and gives the name of the current owner. Perhaps someone can find an estate map.

4va40) The paragraph added here is marked for insertion before 4va12 (see above).

3. Land of the archbishop's monks

Because of a decision made by the C scribes (above, p. 18), the paragraphs describing the manors assigned to the Canterbury monks came to form the contents of a separate chapter in DB. (Because of an error committed by the C scribes, one manor which ought to have been listed here – Mersham (3vb47) – came to be included in chapter 2 instead.) As we find them described in α, the monks' manors are classified further: some of them are earmarked 'for the monk's food' (i.e. they belong to the cellarer's department), some 'for their clothing' (i.e. the chamberer's department). That information seems to have been carried forward into the B text – but these were internal arrangements, of no concern to the king, and DB says nothing about them.

The existence of this separate chapter reflects an understanding that the monks were, to some significant extent, independent from the archbishop. Perhaps not at first, but at any rate after he had appointed his own man as prior, archbishop Lanfranc seems to have allowed the monks to manage their own affairs. A letter of his, surviving accidentally, makes it clear that he regarded the monks' manors as belonging in a separate category from his own (Clover and Gibson 1979, p. 170); but the division was not recorded in any formal document. After 1103, the monks of Rochester had a charter sealed by the king, archbishop and bishop which explicitly put them in possession of some of the church's manor. (By the 1140s, the bishop of Rochester was being sued by the monks of Rochester for flouting the terms of this charter.) The monks of Canterbury had no similar charter. (They did acquire a copy of the relevant sections of DB (above, p. 92), but it is doubtful what weight that evidence would have carried before the late twelfth century. Until then, DB did not have any special status. If it was read at all, it was read as a description of how things happened to have stood at the time of the survey, not as a prescription for how things ought to stand.) In any case, the devil is in the details. Were there some items of business about which the archbishop had to be consulted? Did he have some right of veto? If the monks were mismanaging their property, was the archbishop entitled to intervene? In the end, it means little to say that the monks were independent. The question is: in what respects? to what degree?

From the monks' point of view, these questions became especially acute when the archbishopric was in the king's hands – as it was bound to be from time to time, whenever an archbishop died; as it might also be on other occasions, if the king and the archbishop fell out. When the king's agents moved in to manage the archbishop's manors, should they, or should they not, take possession of the monks' manors too? As might be expected, the king's agents took one view, and the monks took the other. But there was nothing that the monks could do, beyond feeling sorry for themselves. It was archbishop Willelm (1123–36) – whose election the monks had bitterly resented because he was not a monk himself – who first attempted to provide them with some protection. In 1126, when he obtained a papal privilege for the monks, he saw to it that the text included a clause prohibiting 'that wicked and detestable custom' by which their property was exposed 'to devastation and plunder' after the death of an archbishop (Holtzmann 1936, no. 9). Could Lanfranc not have done something similar, fifty years before?

There is one minor point which seems worth noting. A subsequent privilege, dated 1179, confirming the possessions of the chamberer's department, includes a list of cash payments which came from ten manors in Kent (plus one in Essex) outside the monks' domain (Holtzmann 1936, no. 181, repeated in no. 250). All the same items occur in a schedule of incoming payments headed 'Gablum maneriorum' (C4, fos. 69vb–70ra, cf. T1, fos. 172r–v). Since some of them match up exactly with payments noted in DB, perhaps the reader may like to see the whole list: Reculver (1920 pence), Farningham (1440), Burston (100), Berwick (240), Graveney (240), Swarling (96), Warehorne (240), Kennington (243), Hunton (1440), Pett (25). (I cannot say why the Christ Church monks were in receipt of a payment from Kennington (12vb25).)

4vb2) 'The archbishop of Canterbury holds Orpintun.' Orpington TQ 4666. A large manor, including St Mary Cray TQ 4768, Hayes TQ 4066, Downe TQ 4361, and Knockholt TQ 4658. Part of Orpington is listed separately in chapter 2 (4rb17), because it was held by one of the archbishop's knights.

In α the Orpington paragraph ends with a sort of footnote: 'And of these same sulungs Dirman has half a sulung at Keston' (C1-4vb41). Part of Keston TQ 4162 continued to belong to the monks – they got nothing from it, as far as I can see, except a payment of 120 pence (C4, fo. 69vb) – but I cannot fix the site of it.

4vb9) 'The same archbishop holds Pecheham.' East Peckham TQ 6652.

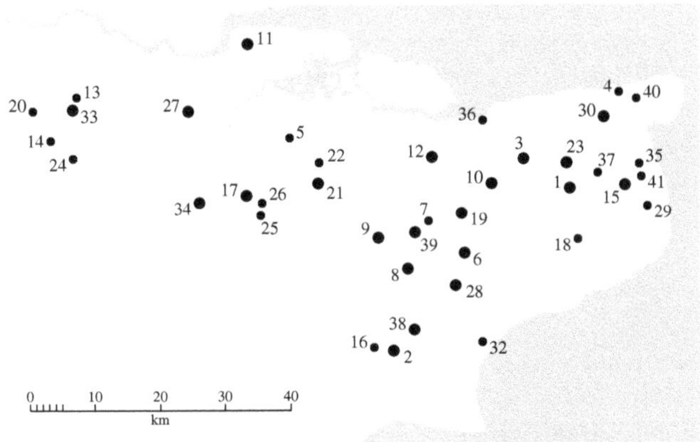

1 Adisham
2 Appledore
3 Barton
4 Birchington
5 Bredhurst
6 Brook
7 Challock
8 Great Chart
9 Little Chart
10 Chartham
11 Cliffe
12 Copton
13 St Mary Cray
14 Downe
15 Eastry
16 Ebony
17 East Farleigh
18 Geddinge
19 Godmersham
20 Hayes
21 Hollingbourne
22 Hucking
23 Ickham
24 Knockholt
25 Linton
26 Loose
27 Meopham
28 Mersham
29 Great Mongeham
30 Monkton
31 Orgarswick
32 Orpington
33 East Peckham
34 Sandwich
35 Seasalter
36 Staple
37 Warehorne
38 Westwell
39 Woodchurch
40 Worth

Figure 8. Lands of the archbishop's monks.

13) 'Of the land of this manor a man of the archbishop's holds half a sulung.' Part of Stockenbury TQ 6749 in East Peckham (Lawrence 1983). The circumstances are more clearly explained in α: Edric, who held this half-sulung from king Edward, used to pay his geld (*scottum*) at East Peckham; but he did so of his own volition, not because the land belonged to Holy Trinity or the monks (C1-4vb1–6).

15) 'Of the same manor Ricard de Tonebrige holds two sulungs and one yoke.' Probably in or near Yalding TQ 6950. Three places are mentioned in doc. 1 as being in dispute between the archbishop and Ricard (called simply that, but certainly to be identified as Ricard son of Gislebert). In the past they had been owned by Adalred – evidently Æthelred of Yalding (14rb3) – and now they were owned by Ricard; but it is stated that Adalred had held them from the archbishop (meaning Stigand) and implied that Ricard ought to do the same – either that or else relinquish possession. This entry in DB tells us what the outcome was: Ricard retained possession (seemingly in gavelkind), as the archbishop's tenant. But it is clear that there was still some friction. In DB this holding of Ricard's is valued separately from the archbishop's; and α complains that 'Ricard has never paid tax for these two sulungs and this yoke during the time that he has owned them' (C1-4va9).

4vb19) 'The same archbishop holds Hoilingeborde.' Hollingbourne TQ 8455, including Bredhurst TQ 7962 and Hucking TQ 8458. A thirteenth-century list still counts six sulungs for Hollingbourne (Brooks 1994, p. 368): that includes two sulungs at Goddington TQ 8654 in Harrietsham and half a sulung at 'Archbishop's Boughton', i.e. Boughton Monchelsea TQ 7749. This half-sulung is listed separately in chapter 2 (4rb37).

23) 'To this manor belongs half a sulung which has never paid tax. The bishop of Bayeux holds this from the archbishop by (payment of) gavel.' Not identified.

4vb25) 'The same archbishop holds Mepeham.' Meopham TQ 6466.

4vb31) 'The same archbishop holds Ferlaga.' East Farleigh TQ 7353, including Linton TQ 7550 as well as Hunton TQ 7249 and Loose TQ 7552 (see below). East Farleigh itself was in Rochester diocese; so was Hunton. Later evidence puts Linton and Loose in Canterbury diocese: Linton was a parish by itself, Loose church was a chapel of Maidstone. There may have been some adjustment of the diocesan boundary here. (A small detached portion of East Farleigh (TQ 7651) is shown on the six-inch map: this is the only isolated portion of either diocese.)

36) 'Of the land of this manor Godefrid holds half a sulung in feod.' The tenant is Godefrid the steward (C1-4va37), and the land he held was Hunton (C1-4vc35).

40) 'What Abel the monk holds.' The facts are spelt out in α: 'And what Abel the monk holds of it by order of the archbishop is appraised at six pounds' (C1-4va32). And again: 'Loose is the monks' manor, and (it is earmarked) for their clothing. It defended itself for one sulung, which Abel the monk holds, and he pays a farm to the monks. This sulung belongs in the six sulungs of (East) Farleigh' (C1-4vc21).

It is not clear whether the DB scribe understood that Abel was a monk. When he uses the abbreviation m^o, he normally expects us to read it as *modo*, 'now'. But it was also accepted shorthand for *monachus*, 'monk', and is occasionally used by the DB scribe in that sense: *Hertaldus* m^o *S' Trinitatis* (DB-Mx-128vb), *tenent* m^o *S' Nicolai* (DB-Bd-214vb).

4vb42) 'The same archbishop holds Cliue.' Cliffe TQ 7376.

4vb47) 'The same archbishop holds Monocstune.' Monkton TR 2765, including Birchington TR 3069 and Woodchurch TR 3268.

5ra3) 'The same archbishop holds Gecham.' Ickham TR 2258.

8) 'Of the land of this manor Willelm his man holds as much as is worth seven pounds.' Ruckinge TR 0233 (in Newchurch hundred). More details in α: 'And what Willelm de Hedesham has of it, namely one sulung at Rocinges, is worth seven pounds' (C1-3vc46). This is one of the places recovered by archbishop Lanfranc (doc. 3). The tenant is the same man who held Westenhanger (4va25), but that manor follows a different trajectory. Ruckinge, when next we hear of it, was held from the archbishop, as one knight's fee, by Willelm son of Radulf (i.e. the son of the man who held Eynsford (4rb9) in 1086).

5ra9) 'The same archbishop holds Nordeude.' Northwood (repr. Barton) TR 1558, in the north-eastern suburb of Canterbury. The manor is called 'Northwood' both here and in α (C1-3vb3); the thirteenth-century scribes who worked on a copy of the latter text show no sign of feeling uncomfortable with this name (C4-71va22). It seems likely, therefore, that *Norgate* (xAug / A4-19v15) was a miscorrection made at Saint Augustine's. But in any case the identification is certain.

5ra15) 'In the same Borwar lest there lies a small town by the name of Seseltre which properly belongs to the archbishop's kitchen, (but, as things stand now,) someone named Blize holds (it) from the monks.' Seasalter TR 0964. From this and the parallel entry in α (C1-3vc52), it is clear that Seasalter was a special case. It is a borough, though only a small one; it is not in any hundred; by implication it is not assessed for geld (though there is land there for two ploughs). Apparently Seasalter was a town that had died, retaining the name and something of the status that went with it, despite ceasing to function as a town. I have already noted the suggestion (Baldwin 1993) that trade was diverted to a new port called Harwich which was part of the archbishop's manor of Westgate (3va44).

The tenant's name is (or would be, but for a slip of the pen) Blittære in α/C1 (3vc54). This was also the name of the man in charge of building operations at Saint Augustine's in September 1091: *praestantissimus artificum magister templique spectabilis dictator Blitherus* (Gocelin, *De translatione sancti Augustini*, lib. 1, cap. 9). Presumably the man is the same; but I do not know quite what one can make of that.

* 5ra21) 'The same archbishop holds Prestetone.' Copton TR 0159 in Preston (Hasted 6:532).

5ra26) 'The same archbishop holds Certeham.' Chartham TR 1055.

5ra32) 'The same archbishop holds Gomersham.' Godmersham TR 0650, including Challock TR 0149.

5ra37) 'The same archbishop holds Certh.' Great Chart TQ 9741.

5ra42) 'The same archbishop holds Litelcert.' Little Chart TQ 9346.

* 47) 'Of the land of this manor Willelm holds from the archbishop half a sulung.' More details in α, where the tenant is called Willelm son of Hermenfrid and the land that he holds is called *Pette* (C1-4ra34). This Willelm occurs only once elsewhere, in a list of the archbishop's knights (C1-7rb); there is no entry to match this one in later lists. Despite the name, the place in question is not to be identified with Pett TQ 9649, which was part of the manor of Charing (3vb23). There is only one clue that I can find, and I do not know how far it can be trusted. Philipott (1659, p. 106) speaks of a manor called Pett, somewhere in Little Chart, which belonged at the time to the Darells of Calehill and paid a token rent to the Dean and Chapter of Canterbury. But Hasted does not mention it.

5rb1) 'The same archbishop holds Welle.' Westwell TQ 9947.

5rb8) 'The same archbishop holds Estrei.' Eastry TR 3154, including Worth TR 3356. Four places described in chapter 2 were or had been connected with the manor of Eastry (4va10–16, 4va40–2).

13) 'And in Getinge the monks of Canterbury hold half a sulung and one yoke and five acres.' Geddinge TR 2346 in Wootton (Hasted 9:369). In Hasted's time this part of Wootton was still considered to belong to Eastry hundred.

5rb18) DB seems to be saying that Adisham is in Eastry hundred – which is not impossible, but on the face of it not very likely. The places just north of Adisham – Ickham (5ra3) and Littlebourne (12ra30) – are both explicitly put in Downhamford hundred, which was part of Borwar (Saint Augustine's) lest; in the thirteenth century the same was true for Adisham. But α says no less explicitly that Adisham is in Eastry lest, as well as being a 'hundred in itself' (C1-3vc34–6). Apparently there must have been some change in the cadastral pattern here, but it is hard to be sure what was happening.

5rb18) 'The same archbishop holds Edesham.' Adisham TR 2254, including Staple TR 2656 (in a detached portion of Downhamford hundred) and Great Mongeham TR 3451 (in Cornilo hundred).

22) 'Of the land of this manor two knights hold from the archbishop three sulungs.' This is the only paragraph in chapter 3 where the DB scribe had occasion to do what he had already done fairly consistently in chapter 2 – add sub-paragraphs together. The two knights are named and their holdings described in α (C1-3vc28–34):

'Of these (seventeen) sulungs (of Adisham) Rodbert son of Watso has two, namely Egedorn.' Eythorne TR 2749 (in Eastry hundred), later held, like Sibton in Lyminge (4ra38), by the fiz Bernard family (Colvin 1964, pp. 15–16). This holding became attached to the archbishop's manor of Wingham (3vb35).

'... and Roger holds one (sulung) at Beraham.' Barham TR 2050 (in Barham hundred, as DB calls it, afterwards Kinghamford hundred). The tenant is the man called 'Roger the butler' in the list of the archbishop's knights (C1-7rb); his successors used the surname 'de Bereham'. This holding became attached to the archbishop's manor of Bishopsbourne (3vb10).

5rb28) 'The same archbishop holds Werahorne.' Warehorne TQ 9832. Though α does not say so, it is not unlikely that this manor had been leased out. Later, the monks got nothing from it except a payment of 240 pence (C4, fo. 70ra).

5rb32) 'In Limwar lest, in Blackbourne hundred.' The 'seven hundreds of the Weald' are a conspicuous feature of the thirteenth-century landscape (below, p. 265), but their earlier history is obscure. Of the seven only three are mentioned in DB: Blackbourne, Rolvenden (9vb7, 11ra5) and Selbrittenden (4ra42). Whether the others existed or not cannot be said with certainty; but I would be strongly inclined to assume that they did. Only Blackbourne hundred is explicitly assigned to a lest – we are told three times that it belongs to Limwar lest (1va15, 2rb5, 5rb32) – but no doubt the same was true for as many of the others as existed.

5rb33) 'The same archbishop holds Apeldres.' Appledore TQ 9529, including Ebony TQ 9229. Said by α to be held at farm by Robert de Romenel (C1-4ra41).

5rb38) '(In Wye hundred) the same archbishop holds a manor.' Brook TR 0644. More details, including the name of the place, in α (C1-4rb51). Like Appledore, this manor was held at farm by Robert de Romenel.

5rb43) '(In Romney Marsh) the same archbishop holds Asmeslant.' Four yokes of land in Romney Marsh, collectively called 'almsland', detached from the manor of Lyminge and assigned to the monks of Christ Church. Text α has two passages referring to this land, the longer of which spells out the facts like this: 'Of this sulung Willelm Folet has one yoke, namely Sturtune, and of the same sulung the said Robert (son of Watso) has (the other) three yokes, namely Ordgaresuuice, Cassetuisle, and Eadruneland' (C1-2vb54–c9). The only straightforward identification here is Orgarswick TR 0830 (in Worth hundred).

5rb47) 'Sandwich is described above; it belongs to the monks' domain.' Referring back to 3ra7.

4. Land of the bishop of Rochester

From the 1070s onwards, the bishop of Rochester was appointed by the archbishop, not by the king. With respect to the lands that he owned, he was one of the archbishop's tenants. For reasons indicated elsewhere (above, p 20), the DB scribe failed to realize this fact: he took it for granted that the bishop of Rochester, like every other bishop, held his lands directly from the king. Throughout this chapter, therefore, the reader needs to remember that DB is inadvertently misrepresenting the situation. Instead of 'The bishop

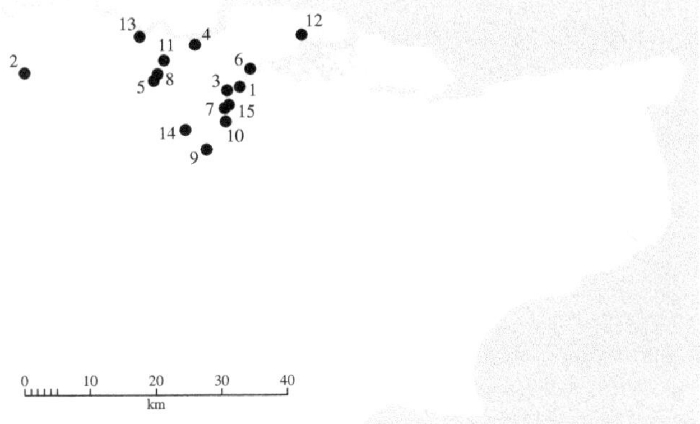

1	Borstal	6	Frindsbury	11	Southfleet
2	Bromley	7	Halling	12	Stoke
3	Cuxton	8	Longfield	13	Stone
4	Denton	9	West Malling	14	Trottiscliffe
5	Fawkham	10	Snodland	15	Wouldham

Figure 9. Lands of the bishop of Rochester.

of Rochester holds Southfleet', the first paragraph ought to say 'From the archbishop of Canterbury the bishop of Rochester holds Southfleet'; and every other paragraph ought to start: 'The same bishop holds from the same archbishop . . .'. It should also be borne in mind that the cadastral headings for this chapter are abnormally defective (above, p. 19); but those which are missing are easy to restore.

Outside Kent, the bishop owned only manor: Freckenham in Suffolk (D-Sk-381r), recovered for the church of Rochester by archbishop Lanfranc. One other valuable property, the manor of Haddenham in Buckinghamshire (DB-Bu-143vb), was bought by Lanfranc from the king, with the intention of donating it to Rochester; but the purchase had to be renegotiated with Willelm II, and the donation was not finalized till then (R1, fos. 212r–13r).

The bishop at the time of the survey was a monk from Le Bec named Gundulf, appointed by Lanfranc in 1077. Working together (though not as equal partners), the archbishop and bishop rebuilt the cathedral church and established a monastery next to it, like the one which already existed in Canterbury. The first monks are said (reliably, I think) to have arrived in 1083 (R3, fos. 27v, 30v–1r, Flight 1997a, p. 78), and a share of the church's lands was earmarked for their subsistence. Originally that share consisted of Frindsbury (5vb14), Stoke (5vb28), Southfleet (5va2), Denton (5vb6) and Fawkham (5va17) in Kent, and Freckenham in Suffolk. When Freckenham was found to be too remote, Lanfranc was asked to give permission for a change in this arrangement: the bishop took that manor back, and the monks got Wouldham in exchange for it (R1, fo. 172r–v). By 1103, when the allocation was formally recorded for the first time, in a charter sealed by the king, archbishop and bishop (Johnson and Cronne 1956, no. 363), the monks had lost Fawkham as well – but they had made some gains which outweighed that loss, including the manor of Haddenham. From the point of view of the commissioners conducting the survey, these arrangements were of no interest (above, p. 45), and there is not one word about them in DB.

As the archbishop's tenant, the bishop was required to provide him with ten knights – these ten being counted towards the sixty knights which the archbishop had to find for the king (C1-7rb). On this topic too, for the same reason, DB is uninformative. If somebody had sat down, twenty years after the survey, and composed a description of the Rochester manors modelled on α's description of the Canterbury manors (above, p. 43), he would have found himself writing quite a number of sentences like this: 'Of these ten sulungs of Frindsbury, Goisfrid Talebot has half a sulung called Wickham which he holds from the bishop in feod of the land of the monks.' (The place in question here is Wickham TQ 7267 in Strood, known to have been given to Goisfrid by bishop Gundulf (R1, fo. 186r), presumably not till after 1088.) Unluckily nobody thought of writing such a text, nor anything resembling it. It is arguable, perhaps, that the creation of holdings for the bishop's knights did not get started before the 1090s; but DB's silence proves nothing.

5va2) 'The bishop of Rochester holds Sudfleta.' Southfleet TQ 6171.

7) '. . . and an ounce of gold.' The twelfth-century exchequer took an ounce of gold to be equivalent to 180 pence (e.g. GREx 1186:192), i.e. nine times as much as an ounce of silver.

5va9) 'The same bishop holds Estanes.' Stone TQ 5774.

15) '. . . and one porpoise.' The DB scribe wrote this as a French word, *marsuin* here, *marsuins* (plural) in DB-Sx (17va). At Gillingham, at around this time, a porpoise was reckoned to be worth 48 pence (*et iiii sol' pro i marsuino* (C1-5vb).

5va17) 'The same bishop holds Fachesham.' Fawkham TQ 5968. A manor redeemed by Lanfranc from the king (R1, fos. 172v–3r). The original plan (Lanfranc's, by the way, not Gundulf's) was that Fawkham should supply a fortnight's food for the monks; but that arrangement did not last. When heard of next, this manor was held as two knight's fees by Godefrid de Falcheham. (That information comes from a list of the bishop's knights copied into the cartulary by a mid twelfth-century scribe (R1, fo. 217r) – the same man, it seems, who rewrote part of the list of parish churches (220v). The two leaves in question are a sheet which was substituted for one of the original sheets (Flight 1997a, p. 20); so the scribe may have been recopying this list from the sheet which was being discarded.)

5va22) 'The same bishop holds Langafel.' Longfield TQ 6069.

22) '. . . and Anschitil the priest (holds) from him.' This is the only place in chapter 4 where DB takes a second step down the ladder of tenure. The bishop's tenant is presumably to be identified as Anschitil archdeacon of Canterbury, whose existence is securely attested (e.g. R1, fo. 184v), and who seems to have been responsible for both dioceses. (Anschitil 'archdeacon of Rochester' occurs only in spurious documents; though Brett (1996, p. 19) is inclined to believe in him, for my part I feel fairly sure that he is a ghost.) In the thirteenth century and later, the manor of Longfield was regarded as a perquisite of the archdeaconry of Rochester.

5va25) 'The same bishop holds Bronlei.' Bromley TQ 4069.

5va31) 'The same bishop holds Oldeham.' Wouldham TQ 7164.

5va36) 'The same bishop holds Mellingetes.' West Malling TQ *
6757.

5va41) 'The same bishop holds Totescliue.' Trottiscliffe TQ 6460.

41) 'TRE it defended itself for three sulungs, and now for one sulung.' But there was some difference of opinion on this point, as we discover from $\alpha 2$ and $\alpha 3$ (above, p. 70).

Bishop Gundulf appears to have set his sights on the adjoining land to the west – 1.5 sulungs called Little Wrotham – in Wrotham hundred. At the time of the survey, it was held by Radulf son of Turald (8vb41). After 1088 it came to belong to Goisfrid Talebot, and he gave it, or half of it, to the church of Rochester. A writ of Henric I, confirming this donation (Johnson and Cronne 1956, no. 647), specifies that only 'a half of Little Wrotham' is concerned; but the indications are that both halves were acquired, possibly on separate occasions. (There is no evidence, later on, connecting this place with the barony of Talebot; Rochester's list of benefactors says flatly that Goisfrid 'gave Little Wrotham' (R3, fo. 82r, Thorpe 1769, p. 116); and in 1236 the holding is said to consist of 1.5 carucates (*Feet of fines*, p. 126).) More often than not, it was called Trottiscliffe – which is some excuse, perhaps, for the ignorance displayed by Flight (1997a, p. 285). Until the 1270s, it was held as half a knight's fee from the bishop of Rochester; then, in complicated circumstances (Thorpe 1769, pp. 660–1, Larking 1868, pp 334–8), the tenant was ousted and the bishop got possession. On the map it is represented by Wrotham Water TQ 6259 in Wrotham (Hasted 4:553).

5va46) 'The same bishop holds Esnoiland.' Snodland TQ 7061.

5vb1) 'The same bishop holds Coclestane.' Cuxton TQ 7066.

5vb6) 'The same bishop holds Danitone.' Denton TQ 6673. One of two manors reclaimed for the church by archbishop Lanfranc (doc. 3).

5vb10) 'The same bishop holds Hallinges.' Halling TQ 7063.

5vb14) 'The same bishop holds Frandesberie.' Frindsbury TQ 7469.

5vb19) 'The same bishop holds Borchetelle.' Borstal TQ 7267 in St Margaret's parish (Hasted 4:164).

5vb24) 'In Rochester the bishop (of Rochester) owned (TRE) and still owns (now) eighty plots of land which belong to Frindsbury and Borstal, his own manors.' Apparently a single rent-collector was responsible for all these plots; perhaps a share of the proceeds went to the monks, Frindsbury being one of the manors which came to belong to them.

5vb28) 'The same bishop holds Estoches.' Stoke TQ 8275.

33) 'This manor was and is the bishopric of Rochester's, but earl Godwin in the time of king Edward bought it from the two men who held it from the (then) bishop. This sale was made without his (the bishop's) knowledge. Afterwards, however, in the reign of king Willelm, archbishop Lanfranc proved his right to it against the bishop of Bayeux, and the church of Rochester is now in possession of it.' Stoke and Denton (5vb6) are the two manors said to have been recovered for the church of Rochester by archbishop Lanfranc (doc. 3). The inclusion of this statement about Stoke (taken together with the absence of any similar statement about Denton) suggests that its ownership was still in contention at the time of the survey. I take it that the bishop of Bayeux had not altogether renounced his claim on this manor, and that archbishop Lanfranc and bishop Gundulf seized the opportunity (when the second team of commissioners came round) to have their version of the facts put on record. In 1088, once Odo had forfeited his lands, the case was decided by default in Rochester's favour.

5. Land of the bishop of Bayeux

Apart from B / xAug, this chapter is our best proxy for B-Ke. Allowing for the fact that half of the paragraphs have been omitted (because they belong in some other chapter), allowing for the fact that the paragraphs which remain have been shortened and reworded by the DB scribe, what we are looking at here is a third-hand copy of the B text for Kent. It is, in principle, still organized cadastrally, lest by lest and hundred by hundred. (If anyone had thought to start reorganizing it along feodal lines, the first step would have been to find the paragraphs relating to the domain manors and collect them together at the front of the chapter; and that has not been done.) On the other hand, the cadastral arrangement is not perfectly preserved here, as it is in B / xAug. In the second half of this chapter, we find ourselves jumping haphazardly between one lest and another. Because the same thing happens in other chapters (in every chapter where there was scope for it to happen), it is clear that this disorder originated in the C text. For one reason or another, the scribes responsible for that version of the text were following an order which was cadastral up to a point, but subject to some disruption. I suggest no specific explanation for this (one would have to begin by deciding whether the phenomenon is peculiar to C-Ke or whether it tended to affect the C text generally); but the result that we see is similar to what we might expect to see if some quires of the B text had got themselves shuffled, before the C text was compiled.

The size of this chapter – it is as long as all the others put together – is one sign of the special status enjoyed in this county by the bishop of Bayeux, by reason of his appointment as earl of Kent. There is another sign of it too. In many counties, the text tails off into a succession of short chapters (or sections of an omnibus chapter) covering the lands of people who owned very little, perhaps just a single small manor, but held what they did own directly from the king. That does not happen here. In Kent the presumption was that every manor (not counting the king's) was held from the bishop of Bayeux, unless there was indisputable evidence to the contrary. Only a few people could prove that the presumption did not apply to them – the archbishop, three abbots, one priest, four barons – and that is why DB-Ke has relatively few chapters, and why it does not tail off towards the end. (The shape that the text would take, if the bishop were factored out, can be visualized with the help of text ε (chapter 6) – or, more concretely, with the help of an early twelfth-century list of the king's tenants in chief (Flight 2005).)

In the years following the conquest, once the initial grab for land was over, many adjustments were needed before the new order was solidly bedded down. Bishop Odo could not help but be at the centre of things. In eastern Kent his interests collided with those of Hugo de Montfort, in western Kent with those of Ricard de Tonebrige; but it seems clear from DB that compromises had been worked out, well before the time of the survey, and had proved to be stable enough.

After 1070, Odo had many more differences to settle, both with the new archbishop and with the new abbot of Saint Augustine's. If we focus on the contemporary evidence (ignoring the fictionalized accounts which were current a generation later), we will be struck by the amicable way in which matters of this kind were dealt with. If either party thought it necessary for the facts to be investigated more thoroughly, the case was taken to the county court, or to the hundred court (doc. 1); as far as we know, the bishop was invariably content to abide by the verdict of the court, and to make sure that his men did too, even if the land in question had been stolen from the church long before 1066. He was, after all, a bishop. And he understood how hard it could be for a church to hold onto its possessions when the rule of law broke down.

There was no occasion for DB to mention the fact – which in any case everyone knew – that bishop Odo had been arrested in 1082 and kept in prison ever since. He had not forfeited his lands: the assumption was that he might, one day, be released and reinstated. But all the manors which he held in domain had been taken into the king's hands, and we can see from DB (which did need to mention this) that they are being managed, for the time being, by men who answer to the king.

For the most part, the bishop's men were left in possession of the lands which he had distributed among them. There were some exceptions, however. One of his men, Adelold the chamberlain, had certainly been dispossessed, in or after 1082, presumably because he was implicated in the bishop's crimes. Except for one slip of the pen (7vb30), he is invariably referred to in the past tense: 'Adelold used to hold' (but does not hold any longer). Since we happen to know that he was still alive after 1087 – he was one of the people who, once the king was dead, caused trouble for the nuns of Caen (Haskins 1918, p. 63) – we can safely infer that he had lost his English possessions and been banished from the country. It would be up to the bishop to decide what should be done with these lands; since the bishop was, for the moment, incapable of making decisions, they were (as they should be) in the king's hands meanwhile. Two other men of the bishop's, Turald de Rovecestre and Herbert son of Ivo, seem to be caught in limbo: sometimes they are spoken of in the present tense (which seems enough to prove that they were both alive at the time), sometimes in the past tense. Though the evidence is hard to grasp, it looks as if they had also offended the king, but not as unforgivably as Adelold: they were allowed to keep their lands but told to stay out of England. By the time of the survey, the result was (so it seems) that Turald had transferred his lands to his son, and Herbert his to his nephew.

To allude very briefly to the sequel, the bishop was kept in prison till September 1087, when the king on his deathbed gave orders for his release. (The chroniclers put some gloomy prognostications into the old king's mouth, as of course they would: unlike the king, they knew what was going to happen next.) By the end of the year Odo was back in England, in attendance on his nephew, the new king. To what extent he was able to reestablish control over his lands and his men is far from clear; but at least he did regain possession of his castle at Rochester. The ineffectual rebellions which broke out in the early months of 1088 were, by all accounts, chiefly inspired by him. With the capture of Rochester castle by the king, Odo's career in England was finally brought to an end. He was allowed to return to Normandy, but his title and lands were all confiscated. He was never forgiven, never seen in England again.

After 1088, though some of the bishop's men survived the storm, a large amount of land became available for reallocation: the bishop's domain manors (other than those which belonged to the earldom of Kent), the lands of Adelold the chamberlain, the lands which were confiscated now (so it seems) from several other men (including Turald de Rovecestre's son and Herbert son of Ivo's nephew). Sooner or later (probably very soon), the forfeited lands were given to supporters of the king – some of them unknown in Kent at the time of the survey – whose loyalty had earned them a reward. The scale of this redistribution would not be matched again, except during the reign of king Stephan; and most of the changes which happened at that time were reversed in the reign of his successor.

When the bishop of Bayeux died, in 1097, it was at least faintly possible that the earldom of Kent – the title and the lands annexed to it – might be given to his nephew Willelm, count of Mortain (who was certainly his heir, if there was any inheritance). Apparently count Willelm did make a bid for the earldom, only to be rebuffed by Henric I. Soon afterwards, the battle of Tinchebray (September 1106), where he fought on the losing side and was taken prisoner, extinguished all his hopes. Throughout the twelfth century, the earldom of Kent was left vacant; and the assets which went with it remained in the king's hands, dribbling away over time (Flight 1998).

6ra3) 'From the bishop of Bayeux Hugo de Port holds Hagelei.' Hawley TQ 5472 in Sutton (Hasted 2:353). Previously part of the manor of Dartford (2va21); the value clause includes a surcharge which only the king could demand.

6ra10) 'Helto holds Suinescamp from the bishop.' Swanscombe TQ 6073. Later the head of the barony of Talebot (below, p. 262).

6ra17) 'Radulf son of Turald holds from the bishop Erclei.' Hartley TQ 6166.

6ra21) '(The same) Radulf (son of Turald) holds from the bishop * Eddintone.' Part of Dartford, the manor which came to be called Bicknors TQ 5473 (Hasted 2:308), treated as part of Addington (7rb45).

6ra26) 'Ansgot de Rovecestre holds from the bishop Mapledescam.' Part of Maplescombe TQ 5663.

6ra31) 'Adam son of Hubert holds from the bishop Redlege.' Ridley TQ 6163.

6ra36) 'Hugo de Port holds from the bishop Eisse.' Ash TQ 6064.

6ra46) 'Goisfrid de Ros holds (from the bishop) Lolingestone.' Part of Lullingstone TQ 5264, the manor called Lullingstone Ros (Hasted 2:541).

6rb1) 'From the bishop Malger holds Lolingestone.' Lullingstane * TQ 5265. The name Lullingstane is 'Lulling's stone': it was not the same place as Lullingstone, 'Lulling's estate', but did tend to get confused with it.

6rb6) 'The same Malger holds in Ferlingeham (from the bishop) half a yoke of land.' Part of Farningham TQ 5466.

6rb11) 'The same Malger holds in Pinnedene half a sulung from the bishop.' Pinden TQ 5969 in Horton (Hasted 2:504).

6rb15) 'Osbern Pastforeire holds in Lolingeston half a sulung from the bishop.' Part of Lullingstone TQ 5264, the manor called Lullingstone Peyforer (Hasted 2:541).

6rb22) 'Wadard holds from the bishop half a sulung in Ferningeham.' Part of Farningham TQ 5466.

6rb29) 'The same Wadard holds from the bishop Malplescamp.' Maplescombe TQ 5663.

6rb33) 'Ernulf de Hesding holds (from the bishop) Ferningeham.' Part of Farningham TQ 5466.

6rb39) 'Anschitil de Ros holds Tarent from the bishop.' Darenth TQ 5671.

6rb45) 'In the same vill the same A(nschitil de Ros) has a manor from the bishop.' Part of Darenth TQ 5671.

6rb50) 'The same Anschitil (de Ros) holds from the bishop Hortune.' Horton (Kirby) TQ 5668. Anschitil occurs only once outside Kent, holding Tatsfield TQ 4156 in Surrey from the bishop of

xAug	DB		sulungs
	6va16	Erith	10
	3ra49	Crayford	4
	6va23	Howbury	1
17r9	6va28	East Wickham	2.25
17r11	12ra3	Plumstead	2.25
		?	.5

Table 16. Manors in Littleleigh hundred.

Bayeux (DB-Su-31va). Horton was the manor which came to be regarded as the head of the barony of Ros (below, p. 261).

6va6) 'The same Anschitil (de Ros) holds from the bishop in the same manor half a sulung.' Part of Horton TQ 5668.

6va10) 'The same Anschitil (de Ros) holds from the bishop in the same manor one sulung.' Part of Horton TQ 5668.

6va14) 'These four manors are now (counted) as one manor.' It is not clear what this means. 'Three' would make sense; 'five' would make sense; but which are the 'four' manors that we are supposed to be counting? The abnormal wording of 6rb45 should perhaps be taken as a hint that this paragraph was interpolated into the text (conjecturally by the second team of commissioners), and that 'four' ought to have been altered to 'five' accordingly.

6va15) 'In Littleleigh hundred.' If anyone were sanguine enough to think of reconstructing the B text, or of discovering some numerical pattern in the geld assessments, this hundred would be a good place to start. There are only five paragraphs to deal with, three of them in chapter 5, one each in chapters 2 and 7. Without running any serious risk, we can reassemble them into the order shown in Table 16; and from this it will seem quite likely that Littleleigh hundred carried (or had once carried) an assessment of 20 sulungs, divided among three places: 10 sulungs for Erith, 5 sulungs for Crayford (in a wide sense), 5 sulungs for Plumstead (in a wide sense). The only snag is that half a sulung has gone missing, and various explanations might be suggested for that, if it seemed worth making the effort to think them up.

* 6va16) 'Robert Latiner holds from the bishop Loisnes.' Erith TQ 5078. Apparently Erith was one of the bishop's domain manors, currently being administered for the king by Robert. As as Boxley (8vb34), that seems to have caused some difficulty, reflected by the misplacement of the assessment clause. What happened, I would guess, is that in some version of the text this clause was cancelled (by someone who supposed that a manor in the king's hands should not have to pay geld) but then written back in again (by someone who was sure that it should), where there happened to be space for it.

6va23) 'Ansgot (de Rovecestre) holds from the bishop Hou.' Howbury TQ 5276 in Crayford (Hasted 2:277).

* 6va28) 'The abbot of St Augustine's holds from the bishop of Bayeux Plumestede.' East Wickham TQ 4676, treated as part of Plumstead (12ra3). A charter of bishop Odo's, not closely datable, refers to the land described here. Because it ends with a one-line subscription by the king, the text was printed by Bates (1998, pp. 352–3); so I have not printed it again. The donations made and confirmed by the bishop are (i) half of the village of Plumstead, (ii) the land called 'Smethetone' (below, p. 183), and (iii) the tithes given to the abbey by some of his men, Adelold *cubicularius*, Osbern son of Letard and Osbern Paisforere. With regard to East Wickham, the charter does not tell the whole story. It seems clear from the sequel that the bishop's man, Anschitil de Ros, kept possession of the land by becoming the abbot's tenant.

6va34) 'Malger holds from the bishop Rochelei.' Ruxley TQ 4870.

6va39) 'Ernulf de Hesding holds from the bishop Ciresfel.' Chelsfield TQ 4763. Later the head of a small second-tier barony (below, p. 258).

6va45) 'Adam son of Hubert holds from the bishop Sudcrai.' St * Paul's Cray TQ 4769. The identification is certain. North Cray and Foots Cray appear below (6vb12, 6vb48); St Mary Cray TQ 4768 does not appear because it was part of Orpington (4vb2); St Paul's Cray is the place which is later found belonging to the honour of Eudo the steward. In the list of parish churches (chapter 8) this place is called *Rodulfescræi*; presumably this refers to Radulf the butler (6va50).

6va50) 'The same Adam (son of Hubert) holds from the bishop Wicheham.' West Wickham TQ 3864. Though DB does not say so, the manor had probably already been granted out to one of Adam's men, Radulf the butler; St Paul's Cray (6va45) and Cooling (9ra15) belonged to him as well.

Part of West Wickham was in Surrey at the time, and is described separately there: this is the land in Wallington hundred held for one hide by Adam son of Hubert from the bishop of Bayeux (DB-Sy-31vb). As was first seen by Davis (1934), the county boundary was realigned in 1176, at the instance of Radulf's grandson (above, p. 4).

6vb5) 'Goisfrid de Ros holds from the bishop Lasela.' Kems- * ing TQ 5558, including Seal TQ 5556. All three of the manors which belonged to Goisfrid de Ros in 1086 – Kemsing, Lullingstone (6ra46), Otham (8rb21) – were subsequently acquired by Eudo the steward (d. 1119). The two smaller manors continued to be held by a family named de Ros, presumably descended from a relative of Goisfrid's; Kemsing was held by Eudo in domain.

6vb12) 'Anschitil de Ros holds from the bishop Craie.' North Cray TQ 4871.

6vb16) 'The same Anschitil (de Ros) holds from the bishop a sec- * ond Craie.' Part of North Cray TQ 4871.

6vb20) 'These two lands (6vb12, 6vb16) were two manors in the time of king Edward. Now they have been made into one manor.' Both entries refer to North Cray; it is the first one which mentions the church.

6vb22) 'The bishop of Lisieux holds from the bishop of Bayeux * Grenuiz.' West Greenwich, meaning Deptford TQ 3777. (East Greenwich, meaning Greenwich TQ 3877, belonged to the monks of Gent, and is silently included with Lewisham (12vb41).)

Gislebert Maminot, bishop of Lisieux (1077–1101), held land from the king in several counties, from the bishop of Bayeux in Kent, Surrey (DB-Sy-31va–b) and Buckinghamshire (DB-Bu-144rb, 145ra bis), and from the bishop of London in Middlesex (DB-Mx-127va). These holdings were Gislebert's personal property (the church of Lisieux had no claim on them). Most of them are later found belonging to the barony of Maminot, of which West Greenwich was the head (below, p. 257).

6vb29) 'Haimo the sheriff holds from the bishop Alteham.' Eltham TQ 4274.

* 6vb34) 'The son of Turald de Rovecestre holds from the bishop Witenemers.' Kidbrooke TQ 4076 under another name. DB's *Witenemers* seems to be a bad spelling of the name which turns up later as Writtlemarsh, and then (from the sixteenth century onwards) as Wricklemarsh TQ 4075 in Charlton (Hasted 1:426, Egan 1993); it survives now only as a street-name. (Though frequently misspelt, by Hasted and others, it does not have an 's' in the middle.)

In DB-Ke this is the only place where Radulf son of Turald is referred to as 'Turald of Rochester's son', rather than by his own name. In D-Ex, however, he is 'Turold's son' more often than 'Radulf' (D-Ex-22v–5v); and that seems to me to suggest quite strongly that he held his lands, not in his own right, but as his father's assignee.

6vb39) 'Walter de Dowai holds from the bishop Lee.' Lee TQ 3975. Walter de Dowai (often called 'Walscin', a diminutive form of the name) was not one of bishop Odo's clients. He was an important man, holding manors in several counties directly from the king; and it is strange to find him here, holding just one small manor in Kent as a tenant of the bishop of Bayeux. But in fact, if I read the signs correctly, this was not his only property in Kent. It looks to me as if Walter was holding the manor of Lewisham at farm from the abbot of Gent (12vb41); and this paragraph relating to Lee should, I think, be interpreted in that light, as the expression of some unresolved dispute between the abbot and the bishop of Bayeux. The abbot was claiming (so I suppose) that this half-sulung at Lee was properly part of Lewisham. Until the case could be settled, Walter was in possession of it; but he was recorded provisionally as the bishop's, not the abbot's, tenant.

Nothing is heard later of any claim on the part of the abbot. It is said (and seems likely to be true) that Walter's granddaughter Juliana was still in possession of Lee in the time of king Henric II. By the 1180s, however, the manor had come to belong to the Essex-based baron Gilebert de Montfichet (*Curia regis rolls*, vol. 4, p. 174) – it is, I would guess, a relevant fact that he was married to one of the daughters of Ricard de Luci – and it continued with his descendants, despite a suit brought against them by Juliana's grandson (vol. 11, p. 516).

6vb43) 'Willelm son of Oger holds from the bishop Cerletone.' Charlton TQ 4177. The same man owned a prebend in Saint Martin's of Dover (1va23); he also occurs as one of the bishop's tenants in Buckinghamshire (DB-Bu-144va).

After 1088, Charlton was acquired by Robert Bloet (the king's chancellor until his promotion to the bishopric of Lincoln in 1093) and subsequently given by him to the monks of Bermondsey (Smith 1980, no. 6, Davis 1913, no. 340).

6vb48) 'The same Willelm (son of Oger) holds from the bishop Crai.' Foots Cray TQ 4771. The TRE tenant is named as Goduin Fot (7ra2); the place-name is *Fotescræi* in the list of parish churches (chapter 8).

7ra3) 'Anschitill holds from the bishop Croctune.' Crofton TQ 4566 in Orpington (Hasted 2:101).

7ra8) 'Gislebert Maminot holds from the bishop Codeham.' Cudham TQ 4459. A namesake of the bishop of Lisieux (6vb22), and doubtless a close relative of his. He also held a large manor in Buckinghamshire, that too from the bishop of Bayeux (DB-Bu-144vb). Like bishop Gislebert's, this man's lands became part of the barony of Maminot.

7ra13) 'The same Gislebert (Maminot) holds from the bishop Chestan.' Keston TQ 4162.

7ra17) 'Hugo nephew of Herbert holds from the bishop Sentlinge.' Sandling (or Sentling) in St Mary Cray TQ 4768 (Hasted 2:114). Text α has a paragraph describing this manor (C1-4vb44), presumably because the archbishop had not altogether despaired of getting it back. But the claim was never made good. With Hugo's other lands, Sandling resurfaces later as part of the honour of Peverel of Dover.

21) 'Bonde held it from the archbishop.' In α the TRE tenant is differently named: Ælfgeat in C1, Wulfgeat in C4. (One or other of the coloured initials is wrong. Since a man named *Uluiet* appears in DB as Hugo's predecessor at two other manors (8rb11, 8rb17), C4 is probably right.)

7ra22) 'Ansgot de Rovecestre holds from the bishop Bacheham.' Beckenham TQ 3769.

7ra28) 'Adam (son of Hubert) holds from the bishop Leleburne.' Leybourne TQ 6858.

7ra36) 'Anschitil (de Ros) holds from the bishop Elentun.' Allington TQ 7457.

7ra42) 'Haimo the sheriff holds from the bishop Dictune.' Ditton TQ 7058.

7ra48) 'Vitalis holds from the bishop Sifletone.' Siffleton (lost) in Ditton TQ 7058 (Hasted 4:457).

7rb6) 'Radulf son of Turold holds from the bishop Aiglessa.' Eccles (lost) in Aylesford (Hasted 4:432).

7rb14) 'Hugo de Port holds from the bishop Pellesorde.' Paddlesworth TQ 6862.

7rb20) 'The same Hugo (de Port) holds from the bishop Riesce.' Ryarsh TQ 6759.

7rb26) 'The same Hugo (de Port) holds from the bishop Ofeham.' Part of Offham TQ 6658.

7rb31) 'Rannulf de Columbels holds from the bishop Essedene.' Nashenden TQ 7365 in St Margaret's (Hasted 4:166). The spelling is bad: a good DB spelling would be *Nessendene*. Local scribes were still writing the name with initial *hn* or *nh* in the second half of the twelfth century.

The manor is correctly placed in Larkfield hundred; only much later did it come to be included in the liberty of the city of Rochester, as that was demarcated in the fifteenth century.

7rb36) 'Rotbert Latiner holds at farm from the king Totintune.' Tottington TQ 7360 in Aylesford (Hasted 4:431).

37) 'of the new gift of the bishop of Bayeux'. There are seventeen entries in chapter 5 which note that the king has possession of some land which might have been expected to belong to the bishop; in nine instances the land is said explicitly to be 'of the bishop's new gift'. (The word 'gift', no doubt, is a euphemism: the king has requisitioned the land, and the bishop has made no objection.) This entry for Tottington is the only one in which a whole manor is concerned. Elsewhere the king has acquired just some part of the manor, sometimes only a very small part. By and large, the statements referring to these acquisitions of the king's resemble those which refer to the creation of the lowy of Tonbridge; in fact, in four instances the same manor which has lost

some land to the king has also lost some land to Ricard son of Gislebert.

I do not know that anyone has ever suggested an explanation for these entries. It occurs to me that they may (mostly) relate to the creation of a hunting reserve for the king – specifically the park called Bockingfold (Hasted 5:163). (The name survives as Bockingfold TQ 7044 in Yalding.) The core of this park, I would guess, was a tract of woodland that belonged to the manor of Tottington; but it would also have included outlying portions of numerous other manors, just as the lowy of Tonbridge did. Not much later, both the park and the manor of Tottington would have been given to Haimo the sheriff; and from him they would have descended eventually to Hamo de Crevequer (d. 1263), who is known to have owned them both. (Hamo held Bockingfold in domain; one of his men held Tottington.) This seems a promising idea to me, but it needs to be worked out.

7rb42) 'The same Rotbert (Latiner) holds in Totintune at farm from the king one yoke.' Part of Tottington TQ 7360 in Aylesford.

7rb45) 'Radulf son of Turald holds from the bishop Eddintune.' Addington TQ 6558.

7va1) '(The same) Radulf son of Turold holds from the bishop Meletune.' Milton TQ 6573.

7va7) 'The same Radulf (son of Turold) holds from the bishop Ledesdune.' Luddesdown TQ 6666.

7va15) 'Herbert son of Ivo holds from the bishop Grauesham.' Gravesend TQ 6373.

7va21) 'Wadard holds from the bishop Notestede.' Nurstead TQ 6468.

7va25) 'Anschitil (de Ros) holds from the bishop Ofeham.' Offham TQ 6658.

7va33) 'Radulf de Curbespine holds from the bishop Berlinge.' Birling TQ 6860.

7va40) 'The same Radulf (de Curbespine) holds from the bishop Borham.' Burham TQ 7161.

45) 'The bishop of Rochester has the houses of this manor; they are worth seven shillings.' To be read alongside a document dating from c. 1120 (R1, fos. 198v–9v) in which Radulf the clerk, on certain conditions, surrenders the rents from various properties, in and around Rochester, which are paid to him because he has possession of Wouldham church. One of the items is this: 'From five acres belonging to the church of Wouldham in exchange for the cemetery of Burham, seven shillings and four pence.' (The tenants are named: they pay 16, 48, and 24 pence respectively.) I take this to mean that bishop Gundulf had allowed Burham church to have its own cemetery, subject to some compensation for Wouldham church, and that these plots of land in the city (with the arable land attached to them) were given to the bishop for that purpose.

7va47) 'Corbin holds from the bishop Pecheham.' West Peckham TQ 6452.

7vb2) 'Ricard de Tonebrige holds from the bishop Haslow.' Hadlow TQ 6349. This entry and the entry for Tudeley (7vb10) are the visible results of a compromise worked out between Ricard son of Gislebert and the bishop of Bayeux. Ricard has conceded that these two manors are outside the lowy of Tonbridge: they are held by him from the bishop, and they are covered by the regular system of local government, belonging respectively to Littlefield and Watchlingstone hundreds.

7vb7) 'Radulf son of Turold holds from the bishop half a sulung in Estochingeberge.' Stockenbury TQ 6749 in East Peckham (Hasted 5:102).

7vb10) 'Ricard de Tonebrige holds from the bishop Tiuedele.' Tudeley TQ 6245. This is the only explicit mention of a place in Watchlingstone hundred.

7vb13) 'Hugo nephew of Herbert holds from the bishop Hariardesham.' Harrietsham TQ 8753. (In 1262, when the owner of this manor leased it to someone else for a term of seven years, he reserved to himself the advowsons of two churches, Harrietsham and Staplehurst (*Calendar of patent rolls 1258–66*, p. 265). I mention this because the history of Staplehurst TQ 7842 is very obscure, and this seems to be one of the earliest known facts.)

7vb19) 'The same Hugo (nephew of Herbert) holds from the bishop Fereburne.' East Fairbourne (repr. Fairbourne Manor Farm) TQ 8651 in Harrietsham (Hasted 5:450).

7vb23) 'The same Hugo (nephew of Herbert) holds from the bishop one yoke of free land in Selesburne.' Not identified, but probably not far from Goddington TQ 8654 in Harrietsham. A payment due to the prior of Christ Church is said to arise from Goddington and 'Seldresbourne' (*Calendar of inquisitions post mortem*, vol. 6, p. 109). *

7vb26) 'The same Hugo (nephew of Herbert) and Adelold the chamberlain hold from the bishop Fredenestede.' Frinsted TQ 8957. Hugo's holding is Wrinsted TQ 8955 in Frinsted (Hasted 5:556), with a distant dependency at Ashurst TQ 5139 in Watchlingstone hundred. Adelold's holding had presumably been confiscated, with the rest of his lands, before 1086. Some time later, it seems to have been divided between Haimo (son of Haimo) the sheriff and Willelm de Albigni. Haimo's share, Yoke (repr. Yoke's Court) TQ 8956 in Frinsted, came to belong to the barony of Crevequer; it was held jointly with a manor in Lullingstone (6rb15) by the Peyforer family. Willelm's share, Frinsted itself, came to belong to the honour of the earl of Arundel; in or shortly before the 1230s, it was owned by a man named Hamo de Wode. The holding disintegrated from the 1230s onwards, as Hamo's daughters sold it off piece by piece. The owner of Yoke acquired most of the land (*Feet of fines*, p. 138 etc.), but not Frinsted church, which was bought by the owner of Wrinsted (p. 252).

7vb30) 'Adelold (used to hold) from the bishop Esledes.' Leeds TQ 8253. Though DB has *ten'*, as if for *tenet*, 'holds', B/xAug has *tenebat* (17r15); and the past tense is certainly right. It is clear that Adelold had been dispossessed, and that his manors were all, as xAug says of Leeds, 'in the king's hands'.

36) 'Of this manor the abbot of Saint Augustine's has half a sulung ... in exchange for the bishop of Bayeux's park.' The bishop's park was at Trenley TR 1959 in Wickhambreaux (9rb43). The land given to the abbot in exchange was at Garrington TR 2056 in Littlebourne (12ra36); but I cannot explain how that could be regarded as being 'of the manor' of Leeds.

37) 'The count of Eu has four dens of this manor.' In Sussex, says B/xAug (17r19).

7vb39) 'Ansgot de Rovecestre holds from the bishop Audintone.' Aldington TQ 8157.

7vb44) 'The same Ansgot (de Rovecestre) holds from the bishop Stochingeberge.' Stockbury TQ 8461. As well as his lands in Kent, Ansgot held the large manor of Preston (Bissett) SP 6529 in Buckinghamshire (DB-Bu-144vb, where he is called Ansgot de Ros). After 1088, Stockbury became the head of a small first-tier barony, which had a rather complicated history (below, p. 262).

* 7vb48) 'Hugo de Port holds (from the bishop) Alnoitone.' Elnothington TQ 8356 in Hollingbourne (Hasted 5:465, Grove 1985). Later the head of the barony of Port in Kent (below, p. 261).

8ra5) 'Adam son of Hubert holds from the bishop Sudtone.' Sutton (Valence) TQ 8049.

8ra10) 'The same Adam (son of Hubert) holds from the bishop Certh.' Chart Sutton TQ 8049.

8ra15) 'The same Adam (son of Hubert) holds from the bishop Sudtone.' East Sutton TQ 8249.

8ra20) 'The same Adam (son of Hubert) holds from the bishop Bogelei.' Bowley TQ 8949 in Boughton Malherbe (Hasted 5:411).

24) 'Of this manor (Bowley) a man of Adam's has one sulung. It is called Merlea.' Marley TQ 8853 in Harrietsham. ('A man of Adam's', like *unus homo eius* (8va35), not 'a man (called) Adam': the name *Adam* is often not declined.) Tithes from Bowley and Marley were given by Adam to Anschitil archdeacon of Canterbury, and by Anschitil to the monks of Rochester; the donation was later confirmed by Adam's brother, Eudo the steward (R1, fos. 184r–v, 196r).

8ra28) 'The same Adam (son of Hubert) holds from the bishop Languelei.' Langley TQ 8051.

8ra33) 'The same Adam (son of Hubert) holds from the bishop Otringedene.' Otterden TQ 9454.

8ra39) 'The same Adam (son of Hubert) holds from the bishop Estselue.' Old (Middle) Shelve TQ 9251 in Lenham (Hasted 5:434).

8ra43) 'Willelm son of Robert holds from the bishop Westselue.' New (West) Shelve TQ 9151 in Lenham (Hasted 5:432).

8rb1) 'Hugo nephew of Herbert holds from the bishop Boltone.' Boughton Malherbe TQ 8849.

8rb6) 'The same Hugo (nephew of Herbert) holds from the bishop Godeselle.' Wormshill TQ 8857. Medieval spellings of the place-name are strangely variable: sometimes the place is *Wormeselle*, sometimes *Wodneselle*. The DB form seems to be a bad French spelling of the latter name.

8rb11) 'The same Hugo (nephew of Herbert) holds from the bishop Winchelesmere.' Wichling TQ 9155 under another name. The identification is certain. Except for the 'n', DB's spelling is good: the place was called 'W(h)icklesmere' or something similar. The modern name starts appearing in the thirteenth century.

* 8rb17) 'The same Hugo (nephew of Herbert) holds from the bishop Estselue.' East Shelve (repr. Cobham Farm) TQ 9351 in Lenham (Hasted 5:435).

8rb21) 'Goisfrid de Ros holds from the bishop Oteham.' Otham TQ 7854.

8rb26) 'Rotbertus Latiner holds at farm Herbretitou. Adelold used to hold it from the bishop.' Harbilton (lost) in Harrietsham TQ 8753 (Hasted 5:454).

8rb31) 'The same Rotbert (Latiner) holds at farm Brunfelle. Adelold used to hold it from the bishop.' Broomfield TQ 8352.

8rb38) 'Radulf (de) Curbespine holds from the bishop Turneham.' Thurnham TQ 8057.

8rb44) 'The same Radulf (de Curbespine) holds from the bishop Fereburne.' West Fairbourne TQ 8552 approx. in Harrietsham (Hasted 5:452).

8rb48) 'Odo holds from the bishop Gelingeham.' Grange TQ 7968 * in Gillingham (Hasted 4:236). Like Bekesbourne (9rb30), Grange came to be connected with Hastings, and was eventually absorbed into the liberty of the Cinque Ports.

8va2) 'Rotbert Latiner holds at farm from the bishop Ceteham.' Chatham TQ 7568. Though DB does not make this clear, Chatham was one of bishop Odo's domain manors, temporarily in the king's hands and being managed by Robert Latiner. More precisely, I think we can be sure that this was one of the manors (like Hoo and Boxley) annexed to the earldom of Kent. While Odo was in possession of Chatham, he gave a small piece of land to the church of Rochester, as a site for the monks' garden; and the trouble caused later by that donation (docs. 13–14) proves that the manor was only conditionally his. After 1088 (unlike Hoo and Boxley), Chatham became detached from the earldom. At some date it must have been given to Haimo the sheriff; with Leeds (7vb30) and other lands, it passed from him to Robert de Crevequer.

8va10) 'The son of Willelm Tahum holds from the bishop Delce.' Little (Upper) Delce TQ 7466 in St Margaret's (Hasted 4:171). Possibly the wording implies that Willelm's son is under age (10vb21).

8va15) 'Ansgot de Rovecestre holds from the bishop Delce.' Great (Lower) Delce TQ 7467 in St Margaret's (Hasted 4:168).

8va19) 'The same Ansgot (de Rouecestre) holds from the bishop * Stoches.' Malmaynes TQ 8175 in Stoke (Hasted 4:39).

8va23) 'The same bishop of Bayeux holds in domain Hou.' Hoo TQ 7871, including Allhallows TQ 8377, Saint Mary Hoo TQ 8076, (High) Halstow TQ 7775, Shorne TQ 6971, and Cobham TQ 6668. A large manor, held by Odo – as is proved by the twelfth-century exchequer rolls (Flight 1998) – by right of the earldom of Kent. It is not clear who had charge of this manor at the time of the survey. Robert Latiner is connected with Hoo by a slightly later document from Rochester (doc. 14), but may not have moved in till after 1088, when Odo was dispossessed.

24) 'It defended itself TRE for fifty sulungs, and now for thirty-three.' A charter of Robert Bardulf for the monks of Reading, dating from 1205 or just before (Kemp 1986, no. 400), includes some arithmetic which (as Kemp pointed out) goes to prove that on the manor of Hoo, at that time, people were counting six yokes to one sulung. As far as I know, this evidence stands alone; but it is perfectly explicit. In the light of that, this apparent reduction in the assessment for Hoo could be interpreted as follows. It was agreed that there were 200 yokes here; the question was how one should convert that number into a number of sulungs. Did one apply the rule and divide by four (on the assumption there were four pairs of oxen in a plough-team)? Or did one make an exception for Hoo (where the soil was so heavy that there had to be six pairs of oxen) and divide by six accordingly? From two entries in the exchequer roll for 1130 (Flight 2005, p. 373), it is clear what the answer was: when it came to the payment of geld, there were four yokes in a sulung, and Hoo was no exception.

* 32) 'Of this manor Ricard de Tonebrige holds half a sulung and woodland for twenty pigs.' Presumably the block of land around Oxen Hoath TQ 6352 in West Peckham (Hasted 5:63) which continued to be regarded as part of the hundred of Hoo.

34) 'Adam son of Hubert holds of the same manor one sulung and one yoke from the bishop.' Not identified.

37) 'Anschitil de Ros holds of the same manor three sulungs.' Not identified.

* 8va41) 'Adam holds from the bishop one yoke in Pinpa.' Part of Pimpe (lost) in Yalding TQ 6950 or Nettlestead TQ 6852 (see below). This Adam is identified by ε with Adam son of Hubert, but I would not rely on that.

8va46) 'Rannulf de Columbels holds from the bishop Ferlaga.' West Farleigh TQ 7153.

51) 'Of this sulung Rainer holds one yoke from the bishop in the manor (called) Pinpe.'

The last subparagraph seems to imply that there ought to be a separate entry for Pimpe. Later evidence would lead us to look for it in chapter 11, but it is not to be found there, nor anywhere else. Pimpe is a lost place, apparently close to the boundary between Yalding TQ 6950 and Nettlestead TQ 6852 (Hasted 5:121). (It is definitely not the same place as Pimp's Court TQ 7552 in East Farleigh (Hasted 4:378): that is a house named after the family who took their name from Pimpe.)

8vb3) 'Haimo (the sheriff) holds from the bishop Nedestede.' Nettlestead TQ 6852.

8vb9) 'Radulf son of Turald holds from the bishop Otringeberge.' Wateringbury TQ 6853.

8vb15) 'Hugo de Braiboue holds from the bishop Otrinberge.' Part of Wateringbury, including Canon Court TQ 6854 (Hasted 5:113).

8vb20) 'Adelold used to hold from the bishop Testan, and Robert now holds (it) at farm.' Teston TQ 7053. Here and in the next paragraph, DB has the past tense, rightly: Adelold has lost possession. Probably the man in charge now is Robert Latiner; but it could be some other Robert.

25) 'Three brothers held this land TRE as three manors; now it (has been made) into one.' A puzzling remark: we have just been told that Teston was held by Edward TRE; so what does 'this land' mean? Possibly a paragraph has gone missing.

8vb26) 'The same Adelold used to hold from the bishop Benedestede, and Robert (now) holds (it) at farm.' Bensted (lost) in Hunton TQ 7249 (Hasted 5:148).

8vb30) 'Rannulf de Columbels holds from the bishop Bermelie.' West Barming TQ 7153.

8vb34) 'Rotbert Latiner holds at farm Boseleu.' Boxley TQ 7758. Another manor held by bishop Odo by right of the earldom of Kent (Flight 1998).

39) 'Of this manor Helto holds half a sulung.' Probably Weavering TQ 7855 in Boxley (Hasted 4:340).

* 8vb41) 'Radulf son of Turald holds from the bishop Litelbroteham.' Wrotham Water TQ 6259 in Wrotham (Hasted 4:553). The subsequent history of this manor is summarized above, in connection with the paragraph for Trottiscliffe (5va41).

8vb49) 'Adam (son of Hubert) holds from the bishop Celca.' Part of Chalk TQ 6872. This is the manor called East Chalk (repr. East Court Manor), the history of which is well documented – and quite distinct from that of West Chalk (see below). East Chalk became separated from the honour of Eudo the steward. It was acquired by Hamo de Sancto Claro (as is proved by GREx 1130:67); with Hamo's granddaughter Gunnora it passed to Willelm de Lanvalein (d. 1180); with Willelm's great-granddaughter Hawisia it passed to Johan de Burgo (d. 1275); and by him it was given to the monks of Bermondsey.

6) 'In Essex there is one hide which rightfully belongs to this manor. Godwin son of Dudeman used to hold it; now Rannulf Pevrel holds it.' Not identified.

The other part of Chalk, the manor called West Chalk, is missing from DB. We know enough about its history to be fairly certain that it was already a separate manor at the time of the survey; by some accident, somewhere along the line, the paragraph describing it got dropped. Also missing from DB is any mention of the part of Strood which became Temple Manor TQ 7368. It seems likely (I think) that this part of Strood was once part of the manor of West Chalk and would therefore have been included in the same missing paragraph. (If not, we are going to have to suspect that more than one paragraph is missing from Shamell hundred.)

Both places were in the king's hands before 1108. Tithes from Strood and Chalk were given to the monks of Rochester by Henric I (Johnson and Cronne 1956, no. 517); it is clear from the sequel that the places in question were what later became Temple Manor and West Chalk. A list of the tithes paid to the monks c. 1220 includes both items: 'of the tithe of the domain of Hugo de Neville in Chalk' we get one half, the parish church the other (R3, fo. 124v); 'from the Templars' grange in Strood' we get the whole tithe of the domain (fo. 125v).

This part of Strood seems to have remained in the king's possession until 1159, which is when it was given to the Templars (GREx 1159:58). By becoming the owners of this manor, the Templars also became the owners of Shamell hundred.

West Chalk became the property of Gervais de Cornhelle, who appears in the exchequer roll for 1165 charged with a share of the cost of the the 'army of Wales' *pro terra de Chalcra* (GREx 1165:106). From Gervais (d. 1183–4) it descended to his son Henric (d. 1192–3), and then to Henric's daughter's husband, Hugo de Neville (d. 1234). From Hugo's son it was bought by Johan de Cobeham (last occ. 1251); after that it continued with Johan's descendants till 1364, when it became part of the endowment of Cobham college.

9ra8) 'The same Adam (son of Hubert) holds from the bishop Hecham.' Lillechurch (repr. Church Street) TQ 7174 under another name. Like East Chalk (8vb49), this manor parted company with the honour of Eudo the steward. It was acquired by Eustachius count of Boulogne (d. 1125), whose daughter Mathildis (d. 1152), the wife of king Stephan, used it to found a priory for their daughter. In the twelfth century the place was always called Lillechurch; the name Higham resurfaced in the thirteenth century, alternating with Lillechurch at first, but eventually becoming the normal name.

The identification seems secure, but there is some reason to hesitate, because Rochester's list of parish churches has separate entries for *Lilecirce* and *Heahham* (i34–5). I do not understand that.

9ra15) 'The same Adam (son of Hubert) holds from the bishop in Colinge one sulung and a half.' Cooling TQ 7575.

9ra21) 'The same Adam (son of Hubert) holds from the bishop Bichelei.' Beckley TQ 7074 in Chalk (Hasted 3:462).

9ra25) 'Radulf son of Turald holds from the bishop Arclei.' Oakleigh TQ 7274 in Higham (Hasted 3:487). Willelm de Cloville, with his lord Goisfrid Talebot's assent, gave tithes from this place to the monks of Rochester (R1, fo. 186r).

9ra30) 'Ansgot de Rovecestre holds (from the bishop) Hanehest.' Presumably Henhurst TQ 6669 in Cobham (Hasted 3:425). Tithes from that place were given to the monks of Rochester by Gocelin de Henherste (R1, fo. 186r, R3, fo. 82v), but I do not know whose tenant he was. The next recorded owner is Willelm de Lanvalei (GREx 1169:161, R2, fo. 157v): by that time the exchequer seems to have been regarding Henhurst as part of the manor of Hoo (8va23).

9ra34) 'Ernulf de Hesding holds from the bishop Cliue.' Part of Cliffe TQ 7376.

* 9ra38) 'The same Ernulf (de Hesding) holds from the bishop Hadone.' Part of Strood TQ 7369, including the manor which came to be called Boncakes (Hasted 3:551). The name used for this place by DB did not survive.

9ra42) 'Odo holds from the bishop in the same Hadone one yoke.' Presumably part of Strood TQ 7369.

9ra44) 'The same Odo holds from the bishop Colinges.' Part of Cooling TQ 7575.

9ra47) Helto holds from the bishop Melestun.' Merston TQ 7072.

9rb1) 'Hugo de Port holds from the bishop Tunestelle.' Tunstall TQ 8961.

* 9rb6) 'The same Hugo (de Port) holds from the bishop Cerce.' Not identified. There is one (and only one) manor in Milton hundred belonging to the barony of Port which appears to be missing from DB, namely Murston TQ 9264. Is it possible that *Cerce* might be Murston under another name?

* 9rb8–9) 'The same Hugo (de Port) holds from the bishop Stepedone.' A lost place in Eastchurch TQ 9871 called something like *Stapindune*. Around 1200, the monks of Christ Church were receiving a payment of 48 pence a year in lieu of the tithes of this place; the money was paid to them by the monks of Les Dunes (a Cistercian house in West Flanders), who, by that time, were the owners of Eastchurch church. (*De Stapindune, iiii sol'. Hos reddunt monachi de Dunes, et sunt in Scapeia decime iste prope Estcherche* (C4, fo. 52Ar).)

9rb9) 'The same Hugo (de Port) holds from the bishop Tangas.' Tonge TQ 9364. This became the head of a second-tier barony (below, p. 261).

9rb13) 'Of these sulungs which Hugo de Port has, Osward held five for gavel and three sulungs and one yoke and a half which he took away from the king's villains.' In Milton hundred (2va46) as at Dartford (2va3), Hugo de Port got possession of the lands which had been held TRE by Osward the sheriff. DB appears to be saying that some of this land (3.375 sulungs) should by rights be given back to the king.

It follows from the arithmetic that half a sulung less half a yoke equals one yoke and a half, and hence that four yokes make one sulung.

9rb16) 'Ricard son of Willelm holds from the bishop Borne.' Patrixbourne TR 1855. Later the head of the barony of Patric (below, p. 259).

9rb22) 'The same bishop of Bayeux holds in domain Hardes.' Upper Hardres TR 1550.

9rb26) 'The same bishop holds in domain Stellinges.' Stelling TR 1448. Later evidence puts Stelling in Stowting hundred; probably it is only listed under Bridge hundred here because it was dependent on Upper Hardres. The abbot of Saint Augustine's believed that Stelling ought to belong to him (doc. 4); but he seems to have let the claim drop (there is no word of it in DB, nor even in xAug), perhaps in return for the donations made by the bishop (Bates 1998, pp. 351, 352–3).

9rb30) 'The same bishop holds in domain Burnes.' Bekesbourne TR 1955.

9rb37) '(As to) these three manors of the bishop of Bayeux, Rannulf holds (them) at farm.' Presumably this is Rannulf de Columbels, the tenant of Lower Hardres (9rb38), who has engaged to look after the bishop's domain manors close by (Upper Hardres, Stelling, Bekesbourne) and pay a share of the proceeds to the king.

9rb38) 'Rannulf de Columbels holds from the bishop Hardes.' Lower Hardres TR 1553.

9rb43) 'The same bishop holds in domain Wicheham.' Wickhambreaux TR 2258.

46) 'There is a park there.' Trenley Park TR 1959 in a detached portion of Wickhambreaux (Hasted 9:162). Some of the land which went into the park was acquired by the bishop from the abbot of Saint Augustine's (12ra36). Another 25 acres were acquired from the archbishop, who got four dens in exchange (Bates 1998, pp. 332–3).

52) 'In addition there belongs to this manor half a sulung of free land.' Not identified.

9va3) 'In the hundred (of Canterbury), in(side) the city of Canterbury, Adam son of Hubert has from the bishop four houses, and two (more) outside the city, which pay 96 pence.'

9va6) 'Haimo the sheriff holds from the bishop Latintone.' Nackington TR 1554. Despite the bad spelling – a good DB spelling of the name would be *Natindone* (the modern form is a corruption) – there is no doubt about the identification.

9va10) 'The same Haimo (the sheriff) holds from the bishop half a sulung.' Probably part of Milton TR 1255.

9va13) 'The townsmen of Canterbury held these lands TRE, and (continued to hold them) till (after the arrival of) the bishop of Bayeux, who took (the lands) from them.' Referring to the two half-sulungs held by Haimo (9va6, 9va10). This is a complaint registered with the second team of commissioners by the men of the city.

9va16) 'Willelm de Arcis holds Fulchestan.' Folkestone TR 2235, together with all its dependencies (below, p. 249).

This stretch of text (9va16–50) is anomalous: it is the only subchapter contained in chapter 5. It begins with a fancy initial (a 'U' overlapped by a 'V') of the size which elsewhere is only used for the first entry in a chapter: the scribe is warning us straight away that Folkestone is a special case. Everywhere else in chapter 5, the manors are listed in approximately cadastral order; to find the manors held by one particular man, we have to scan through the text, just as the compiler of ε had to do (below, pp. 203–4). But here we find the entire barony of Folkestone brought together and entered under a single heading.

Folkestone had once been a minster, a similar establishment to Saint Martin's of Dover. It was wealthier than Dover – 40 sulungs worth 110 pounds versus 24 sulungs worth 61 pounds – and it possessed one important asset with which Dover could not compete, the shrine of a resident saint. (This was Saint Eanswitha, about whom practically nothing was known, though it was generally agreed that she was the daughter of king Eadbald (d. 640).) By the first half of the eleventh century, the minster had ceased to function, surviving only as a source of income for a well-connected priest. The story as we hear it from the monks of Christ Church (who took the view that the minster's endowment ought to have defaulted to them) is that Folkestone was given by king Cnut (d. 1035) to a priest named Eadsige, and some time later (after Eadsige's promotion to the archbishopric in 1038) sold by him to earl Godwine. Here as elsewhere (at Hoo, for instance), it is unclear from DB what happened to this manor after Godwine's death in 1053; perhaps we may assume that it passed to one of his sons. In any event, it became available for redistribution after 1066.

The minster was not reestablished. Folkestone came to belong to Willelm de Arcis; it was recorded as his in 1086; and it passed to his descendants. In 1095, Willelm's widow and his daughter and daughter's husband were all involved in negotiations with the abbot of Lonlay which led to the foundation of a small priory here; its endowment consisted of a very small share of the endowment of the vanished minster.

Willelm de Arcis was not one of the adventurers who owed their advancement entirely to the bishop of Bayeux. He was an important man in Normandy, taking his name from Arques-la-Bataille in Seine-Maritime; he owned land in Suffolk too which was held directly from the king (D-Sk-431v). It sounds to me as if Willelm was claiming to hold Folkestone from the king, rather than from the bishop. As things stood in 1086, the case had been deferred indefinitely because the bishop was in prison, but Willelm was not prepared to let the matter go unrecorded; and his protest was made forcefully enough to affect the compilation of the survey text. What we would have found in D, I suspect, is a subchapter drafted in such a way that it could be relabelled as a separate chapter, if the case was eventually decided in Willelm's favour; and what we find in DB is a version of that, perhaps quite drastically abridged. (The scribe seems to be determined not to let it overflow into the next column.) Two years later, the bishop forfeited all his English possessions; and that had the incidental effect of settling the Folkestone case.

Two small details may take on some significance in this light. First, the DB scribe does not actually say that Willelm holds Folkestone from the bishop of Bayeux: that is implied by the fact that this stretch of text forms part of chapter 5, but generally the scribe makes the point explicit by including the words *de ep'o*, and he does not do that here. Second, the man who compiled an epitome of DB, after the rebellion of 1088, seems to think that Folkestone needs special treatment. When he starts reorganizing the contents of chapter 5, the very first thing he does – even before listing the bishop's domain manors – is to register the fact that Willelm de Arcis holds Folkestone (ε/C1-6rb11).

20) 'There are five churches there, from which the archbishop gets 660 pence.' This is the only surviving trace of Folkestone's former status as a minster (see below): like Saint Martin's of Dover, it had paid the archbishop a lump sum for the churches which were under its control. Which five churches these were, I cannot say.

24) 'Of this manor ... ' This begins a sequence of ten paragraphs listing the lands which Willelm has distributed among his men. Not a single place-name is mentioned. Without guidance of that kind, it is (as far as I can see) impossible to make any definite connections between the men who are named here and the men who occur in 1166 as tenants of Willelm's great-grandson.

24) 'Hugo son of Willelm holds nine sulungs of villains' land.' Because this holding is the largest, it ought to be the easiest to identify. Of the holdings recorded in 1166, no single one is comparable in size with this; but there are two relatively large and approximately equal holdings which add up to something of about the size that we are looking for. My guess would be that the second-tier baronies of Swingfield TR 2343 and Cheriton TR 1836 (held in 1166 by Willelm de Alberville and Willelm de Cherintone respectively) were created by halving the land of Hugo son of Willelm (as might happen if a man left no son but two daughters). I see nothing to prove it, however.

29) 'Walter de Appevile holds of this manor three yokes and twelve acres of land.'

31) 'Alvred holds one sulung and forty acres of land.

33) 'Walter son of Engelbert holds half a sulung and forty acres of land.'

35) 'Wesman holds one sulung.'

37) 'Alvred the steward holds one sulung and one yoke and six acres of land.' Interesting as a piece of arithmetic: if one wanted to say '256 acres', this was the way to say it.

39) 'Eudo holds half a sulung.'

41) 'Bernard de Sancto Audoeno holds four sulungs.' Bernard occurs in Suffolk too, holding Clopton TM 2252 from Willelm de Arcis (D-Sk-431v).

46) 'Baldric holds half a sulung.'

48) 'Ricard holds fifty-eight acres.'

49) 'The whole of Folkestone in the time of king Edward was worth one hundred and ten pounds. When (Willelm) got possession, (it was worth) fifty pounds. Now what (Willelm) has in domain is worth one hundred pounds, (and) what the knights hold (who are) listed above is together worth forty-five pounds and ten shillings.' A striking example of the unexplained fluctuations in value which are sometimes taken as a measure of the impact of the conquest. Folkestone's value had dropped from 26400 pence to 12000 pence, but has now rebounded to 34920 pence, well above its TRE level.

The manor of Newington TR 1837 (below, p. 249) has gone missing from DB, perhaps because there was some doubt as to how it should be listed. In the 1090s it was held by Beatrix, the widow of Willelm de Arcis, not in dower (in which case it would have reverted to her husband's heirs as soon as she died), but apparently as property which she was free to dispose of. It came to belong to her daughter's second husband, Manasser count of Guînes (Flight 2005, p. 366); and it continued to belong to the counts of Guînes, despite the fact that the counts who succeeded Manasser were not lineally descended from him.

9vb2) 'The bishop of Bayeux holds in domain Alham.' Elham TR 1743. We are not told who is currently in charge of this manor.

9vb8) '(In Rolvenden hundred) Adam son of Hubert holds from the bishop one den of half a yoke, which stayed outside Hugo de Montfort's division; it used to belong to Belice.' In other words, it used to be attached to a manor in Heane hundred (13rb26) but is now agreed to belong to the feod of the bishop of Bayeux.

9vb11) 'Ansfrid holds from the bishop in Bochelande half a sulung.' Not identified. No one has been able to find a Buckland in Stowting hundred. Probably the tenant is Ansfrid Masleclerc, as the compiler of ε either knew or guessed to be the case (C1-6rc7).

9vb15) 'Radulf de Curbespine holds from the bishop one yoke in Berfrestone.' Part of Barfrestone TR 2650.

9vb18) 'Rannulf de Columbels holds there (in Barfrestone) one yoke which used to pay its geld in (Lower) Hardres (9rb38); till now it has not paid geld.' An attempt to explain some discrepancy in the geld account for Eastry hundred; but I cannot pretend that it makes much sense to me.

9vb20) 'Adelold used to hold from the bishop Eswalt.' Part of Easole TR 2652 in Nonington (Hasted 9:254).

9vb24) 'Osbern son of Letard holds from the bishop one sulung in Selinge.' Part of Shelving TR 3056 in Woodnesborough (Hasted 10:125).

* 9vb27) 'The same Osbern (son of Letard) holds from the bishop Popeselle.' Part of Popeshall TR 2847 in Coldred (Hasted 9:389). This is the part which is later found belonging to the barony of Port. It was called Popeshall in the thirteenth century, South Popeshall in the fourteenth. Like the rest of Popeshall, it was in Bewsborough hundred.

* 9vb32) 'Radulf de Curbespine holds half a yoke in Popessale.' Part of Popeshall TR 2847 in Coldred. This is the part which is later found belonging to the barony of Maminot. It was called North Popeshall in the thirteenth century, Popeshall in the fourteenth. (But by then there was a third manor here, later called North or Little Popeshall, which seems to have split off from this one.)

By the twelfth century Popeshall had a church (its site is known) which was regarded as a chapel of Coldred (11ra49). Both churches were given to the monks of Dover by Walkelin Maminot, probably in 1154×61 (Holtzmann 1936, no. 220).

* 9vb35) 'Fulbert holds from the bishop Berham.' Kingston TR 1951. As Ward pointed out (1933, pp. 82–3), the name Barham could be used in a broad sense, and here it refers to Kingston. (Barham itself belonged to the archbishop (3vb10).) But Kingston was a large manor, with a number of outlying members. Hougham is mentioned by name below (because it was causing trouble); Ringwould TR 3548 and Whitstable TR 1166 are probably also covered by this entry (or else they have been omitted). They were certainly both part of the barony of Chilham, and certainly both held in domain; but I have no record of them earlier than 1185, when Johan de Dovre had to pay to regain possession after the death of his uncle Hugo's widow (GREx 1185:232).

38) 'There are 25 fish-weirs.' Possibly at Whitstable.

41) 'Of this manor the bishop (of Bayeux) gave an outlier to Herbert son of Ivo; it is called Huham.' Hougham TR 2739. Fulbert is complaining that part of his inheritance was given away by the bishop, during the time that he had custody of it. Apparently Fulbert got Hougham back; it certainly did belong to his descendants.

44) 'Also of the same manor the bishop gave Osbern Paisforere one sulung.' Not identified.

46) 'The whole of Kingston TRE was worth 40 pounds; when the bishop (of Bayeux) got possession (it was worth) the same, and yet it used to pay him 100 pounds.' As at Chilham (10ra31) and Eastling (10va9), the bishop is accused of overexploiting the manor while it was in his hands.

49) 'The land of a knight named Rannulf is worth 40 shillings.' This holding has not been mentioned before; probably that means that Rannulf was given the land by Fulbert, not by the bishop of Bayeux. By elimination, this may perhaps be Tappington TR 2046 in Denton (Hasted 9:361).

50) 'Archbishop Stigand held this manor. It did not belong to the archbishopric, however, but to the domain farm of king Edward.' This seems to be an echo of some earlier dispute between bishop Odo and archbishop Lanfranc, decided in Odo's favour: the manor was found to have been Stigand's personal property, given to him by king Edward.

10ra1) 'Vitalis from the bishop holds Soaneclive.' Part of Swalecliffe TR 1367. Most of Swalecliffe belonged to Saint Augustine's, and is silently included under Sturry (12ra41); here we find that one piece of it had passed into private hands. The monks still had their eyes on this piece, however, as is clear from the fact that the corresponding entry from B-Ke is included in xAug (A4-20v23).

10ra6) 'The same Vitalis holds from the bishop one yoke in the same (Whitstable) hundred.' Not identified.

10ra10) 'Adam holds from the bishop Ore.' Oare TR 0063. Another yoke in Oare, also held by Adam, is listed separately below (10rb35). Oare's history runs with that of Stalisfield (10ra15); despite the distance between them, Oare church was regarded as a chapel of Stalisfield church.

10ra15) 'The same Adam holds from the bishop Stanefelle.' Stalisfield TQ 9652. The DB spelling is bad, but the link with Oare (10ra10) makes the identification certain.

The compiler of ε took this Adam to be the same person as Adam son of Hubert (C1-6rb36). Probably that was a guess, and I doubt whether it was a good guess: there is nothing in the later history of these places to confirm it. After Adam, the next recorded owner of Stalisfield is a man named Hunfrid Canuth, who, before 1108 (R1, fo. 196r), gave a portion of tithes from this place to the monks of Rochester (R1, fo. 190r). That gift was renewed by D(rogo) de Monci (Thorpe 1769, p. 620, from R2, fo. 143v) – who (to my knowledge) is not otherwise connected with Kent.

An entry in the exchequer roll for 1162 proves that Oare by then was owned by the Flemish financier Willelm Cade (d. 1164×6); both Stalisfield and Oare are known to have belonged later to one of Willelm's sons, Arnold Cade. (French-speaking English scribes were inclined to write his name as 'Ernulf' – which presumably means that the final consonant was not being pronounced.) It was Arnold who gave (perhaps sold) both churches to the canons of Saint Gregory's (Woodcock 1956, no. 32), saving the payment due to the Rochester monks. And it was Arnold who gave both manors to the Hospitallers – which probably means that he used them to secure a loan and lost them by failing to repay it. The Hospitallers were in possession by 1191, as can be inferred from an entry in the exchequer roll for that year (GREx 1191:146).

10ra19) 'Hugo de Porth holds from the bishop Nortone.' Norton TQ 9661. This entry also covers Newnham TQ 9557, Boardfield

TQ 9352, Davington TR 0161, and Harty TR 0266. The 'three churches' would be Norton, Newnham, and one of the others, possibly Davington.

The TRE tenant, Osward, is the man referred to elsewhere as 'Osward de Nordtone' (1va6) and 'Osward the sheriff' (2va19); here, as is frequently (but perhaps not always) the case, he has been succeeded by Hugo de Port. It is not to be inferred from this (Green 1990, p. 50) that Hugo succeeded Osward as sheriff of Kent. Hugo got Osward's lands; but the lands did not go with the job. Besides, we know that Osward had lost the job before 1066 (2va23–4).

This holding became a small second-tier barony, the head of which was no longer at Norton but at Newnham. The first recorded owner, Hugo son of Fulco (also called Hugo de Niwenham), was probably in possession by 1110, when he witnessed a charter of Henric de Port (R1, fo. 198v). Hugo gave Norton church to the monks of Rochester (fo. 190v) – or led them to believe that he had done so. His son, Fulco son of Hugo (also called Fulco de Niwenham), gave Newnham church to the monks of Faversham – or led them to believe that he had done so (Cheney and John 1986, no. 467A). Once the dust had settled, Norton church came to belong to the bishop (not the monks) of Rochester; and the other four churches all came to belong to the prioress and convent of Davington.

10ra25) 'Fulbert holds from the bishop Cilleham.' Chilham TR 0653, including Molash TR 0252. After 1088, Chilham became the head of a first-tier barony. Fulbert, who survived for another forty years, was sometimes called 'de Chileham', sometimes 'de Dovre'. The latter surname – apparently derived, not from Dover, but from a village of that name in Normandy, Douvres-la-Délivrande – was the one which his descendants used. In DB, however, Fulbert is always just Fulbert.

31) 'Now (it is worth) thirty pounds … and yet it used to pay the bishop of Bayeux four score pounds and forty shillings.' As in the entries for Kingston (9vb35), Eastling (10va9) and Luddenham (10va15), it seems to be implied that Fulbert's manors had been in the bishop's hands for some time (presumably because Fulbert was under age), and had been made to pay extortionate farms (nearly three times too much, in the case of Chilham).

10ra34) 'Hugo nephew of Herbert holds from the bishop Ospringes.' Ospringe TR 0060. After 1088, this became the head of the barony of Willelm Pevrel of Dover.

10ra46) 'Ansfrid (Masleclerc) holds from the bishop Cildresham.' A lost place, subsequently part of the manor of Westwood TR 0159 in Preston (Hasted 6:536).

By about 1150, Helto son of Ricard (occ. 1130–66) had come into possession of a one-third share of the lands which had formerly belonged to Ansfrid Masleclerc. By trying to turn Sheldwich TR 0156 into a separate parish, he got into a dispute with the monks of Saint Augustine's, the owners of Faversham church (below, p. 227). Having failed in that attempt, he appeased the monks by giving them (with his wife's assent) sixteen acres of land of his domain of *Serichesam* and all the tithes of his domain of *Ernodintuna* (Turner and Salter 1915–24, pp. 507–8). In a slightly later document the names are spelt *Sceldrichesham* and *Ernoldintone* (Morey and Brooke 1967, pp. 405–6). It seems that there may be some connection between *Sceldrichesham* and Sheldwich, but I cannot get a grip on it.

* 10rb1) 'The same Ansfrid (Masleclerc) holds from the bishop Ernoltun.' The same comment as for *Cildresham*.

10rb8) 'The same Ansfrid (Masleclerc) holds from the bishop Macheheuet.' Macknade TQ 0260 in Preston (Hasted 6:537).

10rb11) 'The same Ansfrid (Masleclerc) holds from the bishop Badelesmere.' Badlesmere TR 0155.

10rb15) '(As to) this manor, the abbot of Saint Augustine's claims it because (his predecessor) owned it TRE, and (the men of) the hundred testify in his favour. But the man's son (i.e. the son of the TRE tenant) says that his father could turn himself where he wished (i.e. could choose his own lord). This the monks do not agree with.' More details in B / xAug (A4-18r1), and in a sentence appended to DB's chapter 7 (12vb37). The sequel is unknown, except that the monks did not get possession of Badlesmere.

This makes a poignant picture: a disinherited Englishman watching from the sidelines while the newcomers squabble over land which ought to be his. Perhaps so – but we cannot be sure that this sentence in DB gives us all the relevant facts. A bastard son, even if everyone knew who his father was, would not have stood to inherit the land, regardless of the outcome of the battle of Hastings.

10rb18) 'The same Ansfrid (Masleclerc) holds from the bishop Perie.' Part of Perry TR 0160 in Preston (Hasted 6:539). *

10rb21) 'The same Ansfrid (Masleclerc) holds from the bishop (another) Perie.' Same comment.

10rb24) 'Osbern (Paisforere) holds from the bishop Bocheland.' Buckland TQ 9762. Osbern gave tithes from this place to Saint Augustine's (Bates 1998, pp. 352–3).

10rb28) 'The same Osbern (Paisforere) holds one yoke from the bishop (which is now) in the same manor'.

10rb31) 'Hugo de Porth holds from the bishop Herste.' A lost place called Hurst (Hasted 6:145), represented on the six-inch map by a detached portion of Murston parish (TQ 9962). The identification is certain. *

10rb35) 'Adam (son of Hubert) holds from the bishop one yoke in Ore.' Part of Oare TR 0063. The larger part, also held by Adam, has already been described (10ra10).

10rb39) 'Herfrid holds from the bishop Treuelai.' Throwley TQ 9955.

10rb45) 'Herbert (son of Ivo) used to hold from the bishop Nordeslinge.' Part of Eastling TQ 9656. We are not told who is currently in possession.

10rb49) '(As to) these two manors, Herbert son of Ivo used to hold them from the bishop of Bayeux'. Referring back to 10rb39 and 10rb45; but the statement is redundant, as far as the latter paragraph is concerned.

10va1) 'Turstin de Girunde holds in Bochelande one yoke from the bishop.' Presumably part of Buckland TQ 9762, but I cannot trace its history. The same Turstin occurs as one of the bishop's tenants in Buckinghamshire, holding Dunton SP 8224 and Foscote SP 7135 from the bishop of Bayeux (DB-Bu-144vb). His descendants are found holding three knight's fees of the honour of Peverel of Dover – two for the manors in Buckinghamshire, the third for Wrinsted in Kent (7vb26). It is not known when or how they got possession of Wrinsted; but Hamo de Girunda occurs in Kent in 1165, making a payment which represents three knight's fees (GREx 1165:106).

10va4) 'Roger son of Anschitil holds from the bishop Eslinges.' Probably Goodnestone TR 0461 with the name misreported (perhaps through confusion with the following entry). Roger's name links this manor with Hastingleigh (11vb29), and later evidence establishes a link between Hastingleigh and Goodnestone in Faversham hundred (below, p. 257).

10va9) 'Fulbert holds from the bishop Eslinges.' Eastling TQ 9656.

9) 'It defended itself for 5 sulungs TRE; now (it defends itself) for 2 (sulungs), and has done so since the bishop (of Bayeux) gave the manor to Hugo son of Fulbert.' This seems to mean that Eastling was originally given to Hugo son of Fulbert, and that from him it has descended to Fulbert. Though this is the only mention of Hugo in DB, he is also mentioned in the records of Saint Augustine's, in connection with Sibertswold (doc. 5). I take it that he was Fulbert's father (or possibly his uncle or elder brother).

14) 'Now (it is worth) four pounds, and yet the bishop used to get eight pounds.' Taken together with the Chilham entry (10ra25), this seems to mean that the manor was in the bishop's hands for some length of time, after the death of the original tenant, before Fulbert was given possession.

10va15) 'The same Fulbert holds from the bishop Dodeham.' Luddenham TQ 9963. (In ε there are duplicate entries for this manor (C1-6vb6–7), one with initial 'D' (as in DB), the other with 'L' (correctly).)

19) 'The bishop put it out to farm for ten pounds.' Another excessive payment demanded by the bishop, while he had Fulbert's inheritance in his custody.

* 10va21) 'Ricard holds from the bishop Rongostone.' Probably the same as a lost place in Faversham hundred called *Ruggeston'* in 1242, *Rugeston'* in 1346. (The identification with Ringlestone TQ 8755 in Hollingbourne, suggested as an afterthought by Hasted (6:568), has nothing to recommend it.)

10va25) 'Ansfrid (Masleclerc) holds from the bishop Hortone.' Horton TR 1155 in Chartham (Hasted 7:312).

10va30) 'Adam (son of Hubert) holds from the bishop Fanne.' Fanscombe TR 0746 approx. in Wye. (This is the manor held by Muriela de Sumery in 1242, by Johan Sumery in 1346.)

34) 'Hugo de Montfort holds of (this manor) what is worth twenty shillings.' Including a den now attached to the manor of Kenardington (14ra9).

There is a group of small manors in this neighbourhood – Aldglose (10vb21), Coombe (10va40), Grove, Fanscombe – of which Hasted (8:29) reports the names but gives no adequate account, perhaps because he could not get access to the archive of Saint Thomas's hospital in Southwark, to which by that time these manors had come to belong.

The hospital's records – a useful collection, so far as one can judge from the catalogue – are now in the London Metropolitan Archives; possibly someone might like to take a look at them.

10va35) 'Wadard holds from the bishop Berchuelle.' Buckwell TR 0448 in Boughton Aluph (Hasted 7:390).

10va40) 'The same Wadard holds from the bishop Cumbe.' Coombe TR 0846 approx. in Hastingleigh. (This is the manor held by Philip de Cumbe in 1242, by Thomas de Cumbe in 1346.)

* 10va45) 'Radulf de Curbespine holds from the bishop Betmontestun.' A lost place called Beamonston TQ 9948 approx. in Westwell (Hasted 7:417).

10vb1) 'Adelold used to hold from the bishop Dene.' Dean Court TQ 9848 in Westwell (Hasted 7:420).

3) 'Of this sulung Radulf de Curbespine holds one yoke and a half, . . . and Adelold had (in addition to that) half a sulung and half a yoke.' Further proof that there are four yokes in a sulung.

6) 'This land is in the king's hands.' Meaning the part not given to Radulf de Curbespine.

10vb9) 'Radulf de Curbespine holds Piuentone of the bishop's feod, and Hugo (holds it) from him.' Pivington TQ 9146. The unusual wording (echoed in the next three paragraphs) implies that there is something peculiar about this manor; I think we are expected to understand that Hugo means Hugo de Montfort. But Pivington is later found running with the rest of Radulf's lands.

10vb14) 'The same Radulf (de Curbespine) holds three dens which got left out of Hugo de Montfort's division.' They used to be part of Hugo's manor of Postling (13rb14); now they are not.

10vb17) 'Herfrid holds of the bishop's feod Essamelesford.' Shalmsford TR 0954 in Chartham (Hasted 7:308). Another place which was on the borderline between the bishop's feod and Hugo de Montfort's division. Later on, though the categories changed, Shalmsford remained on the edge: uniquely here, the honour of Peverel of Dover intersected with the honour of the Constabulary.

10vb21) 'Osbert holds from Willelm son of Taum Aldelose. Aldglose (lost) in Hastingleigh TR 1044 (Hasted 8:29). Another complicated story, and the report we are given is so condensed that it is hard to make much sense of it. Willelm occurs elsewhere as 'the son of Willelm Tahum' (8va10); apparently father and son were both called Willelm, and the father had the surname *taon* (meaning 'gadfly'). Possibly 'Osbert' (who may or may not be the same person as Osbern Paisforere) has the manor in custody while the son is under age.

24) 'This land is of the feod of the bishop of Bayeux and got left out of his (i.e. Hugo de Montfort's) division.' Another place affected by the demarcation between the bishop's feod and Hugo's division: TRE it was part of Brabourne (13vb23); now it is separate, and therefore separately assessed.

10vb27) 'Osbern Paisforere holds from the bishop Palestrei.' Palstre TQ 8828 in Wittersham (Hasted 8:488).

10vb32) 'The same Osbern (Paisforere) has twelve acres of land.' This entry reads like an interpolation, an addition made to the B text by the second team of commissioners. It should perhaps have been attached to the preceding paragraph, as the compiler of ε appears to have thought (C1-6rc14).

10vb33) 'Hugo de Porth holds from the bishop Pesinges and Piham.' Pising (lost) and Pineham TR 3145 in Whitfield (Hasted 9:552).

10vb38) 'The bishop of Bayeux holds in domain Bilsuitone.' Bilsington TR 0434. As with Elham (9vb2), we are not told who has custody. After 1088, both manors were given to Willelm de Albigni (below, p. 248).

43) 'Into this manor the bishop put three dens which were left out of the count of Eu's division.' As with Hugo de Montfort's division, some demarcation had been worked out between the bishop's

feod and count Robert's division; but this is the only place where we find any mention of it. Since the count held nothing in Kent directly from the king, the presumption is that these dens had been attached to one of his Sussex manors. When they became part of the bishop's feod, the bishop decided to attach them to the manor of Bilsington.

* 10vb45) 'Rotbert de Romenel holds from the bishop Afettune.' A lost place in Old Romney TR 0325. The name occurs as *Effetone* in the thirteenth century (*Book of fees*, p. 1345); the DB form, odd though it looks, is not seriously wrong.

10vb51) 'The same Robert (de Romenel) has fifty townsmen in the town of Romenel.' Old Romney TR 0325. This paragraph was added at the foot of the column, apparently intended for insertion here.

10vb49) 'The same Rotbert (de Romenel) holds from the bishop in the Marsh half a sulung.' (This paragraph is interrupted by the passage added at the foot of the column: it continues at 11ra1.)

11ra2) 'The same Robert (de Romenel) holds from the bishop half a sulung in the marsh.'

11ra6) 'The same Rotbert (de Romenel) holds from the bishop Benindene.' Benenden TQ 8032. The manor is stated to be in Rolvenden hundred; it is stated to have a church; so the identification can be regarded as certain. But Benenden did not belong to Robert's descendants.

11ra10) '(In Aloesbridge hundred) the same Rotbert (de Romenel) holds from the bishop half a yoke.'

11ra13) '(Also in Aloesbridge hundred) the same Rotbert (de Romenel) holds from the bishop half a den (which used to be part) of the manor of Titentone which Hugo de Montfort holds. ... This land is outside Hugo's division.' Though called 'half a den', this land is under the plough. It used to be attached to Tinton (13rb42); now it is separate, and part of the bishop's feod. (It ought to have an assessment, but no figure is given.)

11ra18) 'Herbert holds at farm from the king Ringetone; it is of the bishop's feod.' Ringleton TR 2957 in Woodnesborough (Hasted 10:135). Though DB does not say so, this is one of the manors confiscated from Adelold the chamberlain. Tithes from Ringleton, Knowlton (11rb33) and Tickenhurst (11va26) were given to Saint Augustine's by Adelold (doc. 10); at the time, it seems, he was holding all these manors in domain.

11ra23) 'Adam holds of the bishop's feod in Hamolde half a yoke, (and) Riculf holds (it) from Adam. (As for) the other half yoke of Aimolde, Herbert holds (it) from Hugo nephew of Herbert.' Hamwold TR 2855 in Woodnesborough (Hasted 10:132). This reads like an interpolation made by the second team of commissioners, reporting the basic facts for a yoke which had been overlooked. The identification has to be right, but the history of the place is very obscure.

11ra26) 'Hugo holds Ewelle from the bishop.' Ewell TR 2844. This is Hugo, the nephew of Herbert son of Ivo, as is clear from the cross-reference in chapter 9 (13va49), and from the subsequent history of this and the next few places. (The compiler of ε mistook this 'Hugo' for Hugo de Port (C1-6va19).) The manor in question here is the one which was subsequently given to the Templars (below, p. 260).

11ra33) 'The same Hugo (nephew of Herbert) holds from the bishop Wescliue.' West Cliffe TR 3444.

11ra38) 'The same Hugo (nephew of Herbert) holds Soltone from the bishop.' Solton TR 3345 in West Cliffe (Hasted 9:422).

11ra43) 'The same Hugo holds in Dover one mill which pays 48 quarters of wheat; it does not belong to any manor.' The same mill complained of by the men of Dover (1ra44).

The word 'ferlingel' occurs only this once in DB-Ke (except that 'ferding' (5rb16) is almost the same). Apparently it meant a larger quantity than a seam; one schedule which I have seen (Canterbury Cathedral Archives, Reg. H, fo. 25v) takes it to be equivalent to 1.75 seams. At that rate, if a seam was 16 bushels, a ferlingel was 28 bushels.

11ra45) 'Ansfrid holds of the bishop's feod in Leueberge half a yoke.' Not identified. No one has found a place of this name anywhere in Bewsborough hundred (or anywhere else, for that matter). Probably the tenant is Ansfrid Masleclerc, as ε supposes it to be (6rc6), but that cannot be confirmed.

11ra49) 'Radulf de Curbespine holds Colret from the bishop.' Coldred TR 2747.

11ra54) 'The same Radulf (de Curbespine) holds (from the bishop) Ewelle.' La Cressoniere (repr. Kearsney) TR 2843 in River (Hasted 9:442). *

57) 'Of this manor a certain knight holds one sulung from Radulf.' Here and in the next paragraph, DB descends one rung further than usual down the feodal ladder. Probably this means that the commissioners had been especially careful here, so as to make sure that the bishop's feod and Hugo's division were accurately distinguished.

2) 'Hugo de Montfort has the head of the manor.' Hugo's manor is La Riviere (repr. River), as listed in chapter 9 (13vb2); both paragraphs report the same name for the TRE tenant. Apparently what used to be a single manor has been split between Radulf and Hugo.

11rb4) 'The same Radulf (de Curbespine) holds from the bishop Suanetone.' Swanton TR 2444 in Lydden (Hasted 8:129).

7) 'Of this land Robert de Barbes holds one sulung, ... and someone called Hugo holds one sulung.' In other words, this manor has been split between two of Radulf's men. Probably Hugo is *quidam Hugo* to make sure that he cannot be mistaken for Hugo de Montfort.

11rb11) 'The same Radulf (de Curbespine) holds from the bishop Apletone.' Appleton TR 3447 in a detached part of Waldershare (Hasted 10:57).

11rb15) 'Herfrid holds from Hugo (nephew of Herbert) Brochestele; it is (part) of the bishop's feod.' A lost place called Borstall (or Brostall) in Ewell TR 2844. It was given to the Templars in 1246 (*Feet of fines*, p. 190). The manor survived as a separate entity – it is called Borestall Banks by Philipott (1659, p. 149), Temple alias Boswell Banks by Hasted (9:434) – but I have not been able to fix the site of it. If anyone has seen an estate map, I hope they will be kind enough to let me know.

11rb19) 'Turstin Tinel and his wife hold at farm from king W(illelm) in Leueberge one yoke and five acres.' The same lost place in Bewsborough hundred of which another half-yoke is listed above (11ra45). The wording of this entry is anomalous; I suspect that it may have been rewritten by the second team of commissioners.

11rb23) 'Ansfrid (Masleclerc) holds from the bishop Gollesberge.' Woodnesborough TR 3056. Despite DB's bad spelling, the identification is certain.

27) 'In Sandwich the archbishop has thirty-two plots of land belonging to this manor . . . and Adelwold has one yoke.'

30) 'Five thegns held this manor from king Edward. Three of them lived there permanently. Two of them held two sulungs of it, jointly with the others, but did not live there. When Ansfrid got possession, he made it into one manor.' This paragraph, partly illegible now, was still fully legible in the 1760s (above, p. 94).

11rb33) 'Turstin holds from the bishop Chenoltone.' Knowlton TR 2853. Tithes from Knowlton were among those given to Saint Augustine's by Adelold the chamberlain (11ra18). As at Tickenhurst (11va26), Turstin is said to hold from the bishop; but it seems more likely that he had been given custody by the king, in the same way that Adelold's other manors had been put out to farm. (The phrase *decimam totius terre Turstini* occurs in the surviving copies of bishop Odo's charter (Bates 1998, pp. 352–3), but it should, I think, be construed as a gloss, not part of the original text.)

11rb36) 'Osbert (i.e. Osbern) son of Letard holds from the bishop Bedesham.' Betteshanger TR 3152, including Barfrestone TR 2650. 'Osbert' here, 'the same Osbern' four lines below. The DB scribe oscillates between these spellings of the name, presumably because in French he was pronouncing it [oz'ber], only adding the extra consonant at the moment when he turned it into Latin and wrote it down. (Similarly, because the first 't' in 'Ro(t)bert' comes and goes, I would guess that he was pronouncing this name [ro'ber].)

The spelling of the place-name is bad, but the identification is good. Osbern gave tithes from this place to Saint Augustine's (Bates 1998, pp. 352–3, where the place-name is spelt *Bedesan*).

40) 'In the same manor ten thegns hold from the same Osbern one sulung and half a yoke.' Probably this is Barfrestone, divided into several pieces.

11rb43) 'Ansfrid (Masleclerc) holds from the bishop Soles.' Soles TR 2550 in Nonington (Hasted 9:256).

11rb47) 'Radulf son of Robert holds from the bishop Hertange.' Hartanger (lost) in Barfrestone TR 2650 (Hasted 10:74).

11rb51) 'Osbern holds from the bishop one yoke and a half in the same (Eastry) hundred.' Not identified. Possibly Osbern son of Letard, though the compiler of ε did not think so (6vb34).

11va2) '(In Bewsborough hundred) Hugo de Montfort holds from the bishop one sulung of empty land. (It is) outside his division, (even though) it used to belong to the manor of Neventone (13vb7) which he has inside his division.' Not identified. The entry is out of place, and the wording is anomalous: I think we can be sure that this is an addition made by the second team of commissioners. We are being warned that there is a sulung here which might be mistaken for part of Hugo's division. That is not the case: uniquely for this sulung, Hugo is the bishop's tenant.

11va5) 'Wibert holds half a yoke (in Eastry hundred) which used to belong to the gild of Dover.' Not identified. This entry again seems sure to have been added by the second team of commissioners.

11va8) 'Osbern son of Letard holds from the bishop Hama.' Ham TR 3254.

11va12) 'The same Osbern (son of Letard) holds from the bishop Cilledene.' Chillenden TR 2653.

11va17) 'Alvred holds from the bishop Midelea.' Not identified. * (The suggestion that this might be Midley TR 0323 in Romney Marsh has nothing to be said in its favour. Midley was part of the manor of Aghne (repr. Court Lodge) TR 0224 in Old Romney (Hasted 8:441) belonging to the monks of Christ Church; it was connected with Mersham (3vb47), not Eastry.)

11va21) 'In Summerden hundred.' The only mention of this hundred in DB, prefixed to a mysterious paragraph which seems to relate to some adjustment affecting the westward limits of the lowy of Tonbridge. It ought to have been included much sooner, under Sutton half-lest. I take it that this entry was inserted into the B text by the second team of commissioners. Perhaps it was jotted down in some convenient space (which happened to be in the middle of Eastry hundred), with the intention, never fulfilled, of rewriting it later in its proper place.

22) 'Rotbert Latiner holds six acres of land.' Presumably somewhere in the eastern part of Summerden hundred, which belonged to the manor of Dartford. (The archbishop owned most of the hundred; the king owned this part.)

23) 'Also, of the bishop's new gift, he has, in the king's hand, from Ricard son of count Gislebert, (some arable land and some woodland), and from it he pays by way of farm six pounds.' I am far from sure that I understand the nature of this transaction. Apparently the bishop had held this land from Ricard son of Gislebert, but had relinquished possession to the king. In any case the outcome is that Robert Latiner is managing this property on the king's behalf.

11va26) 'Turstin holds from the bishop Ticheteste.' Tickenhurst TR 2954 in Northbourne (Hasted 9:593). This place follows the same trajectory as Knowlton (11rb33).

11va30) 'The same Turstin holds from the bishop one yoke in Wanesberge.' Part of Woodnesborough TR 3056.

11va32) 'The same Turstin holds from the bishop one yoke in Ece.' Part of Each TR 3058 in Woodnesborough.

11va33) 'These two yokes.' Referring to 11va30 and 11va32.

11va34) 'Osbert holds from the bishop one yoke and ten acres in Masseberge.' (Part of) Marshborough TR 3057 in Woodnesborough. If ε can be trusted (I think it can be), this is Osbern Paisforere (C1-6rc15).

11va36) 'The same Osbert holds from the bishop fifteen acres in * Esmetone.' Part of a lost place called *Smethetune*, possibly near Shingleton TR 2852 in Eastry. The spelling *Esmetone* has been variously interpreted. I take it to be a syncopated form of *Esmedetone*, which in turn is to be construed as a French form of *Smethetune*. If the name survives at all, it ought to be something like 'Smeaton'.

The rest of *Smethetune* belonged to Saint Augustine's, and is silently included in DB's description of Northbourne (12va23). It is mentioned frequently in the abbey's records. As was noted by Ward (1933, p. 65), a passage in the twelfth-century *Noticia terrarum* (above, p. 73), associates it with a place called Shrinkling: *Inter smethetune et scrinclinge est unum solin'* (A4, fo. 13r). It is said – and seems to be true – that Shrinkling is the same place as Shingleton (Hasted 10:105).

11va40) 'Radulf de Curbespine holds from the bishop two sulungs in Walwalesere.' Waldershare TR 2948.

11va45) 'Osber(n) son of Letard holds from the bishop one yoke in Ece.' Part of Each TR 3058 in Woodnesborough.

11va48) 'Radulf de Curbespine holds from the bishop Essewelle.' Easole TR 2652 in Nonington (Hasted 9:254).

The parish of Nonington was bisected by a hundred boundary, and that, in this part of Kent, is a rather unusual phenomenon (above, p. 10). Nonington church was in Wingham hundred, but the eastern half of its parish (except for a block of land around Kittington TR 2751) belonged to Eastry hundred. Possibly this might be taken to mean that Easole was a separate parish at the time when the hundreds were formed.

11vb1) 'Osbern holds from the bishop a manor (in Eastry hundred).' Not identified. (In ε this manor is mentioned twice – not just among the lands of Osbern son of Letard (C1-6va30), but also among those of Osbern Paisforere (6rc16). This is one of the indications which tend to prove that some guesswork went into the compilation of that text.)

11vb5) 'Ra(nn)ulf de Columbers holds from the bishop Selinges.' Part of Shelving TR 3056 in Woodnesborough (Hasted 10:125). Probably DB's 'Radulf' is just a slip of the pen (perhaps an anticipation of the next paragraph) – but it not impossible that Rannulf had a relative named Radulf.

11vb10) 'Radulf de Curbespine holds from the bishop Danetone.' Denton TR 2146.

11vb15) 'The same Radulf (de Curbespine) holds from the bishop one yoke in Brochestele.' A lost place in Ewell TR 2844, already mentioned once (11rb15).

11vb17) 'Radulf de Curbespine holds forty acres of land (in Bewsborough hundred).'

* 11vb20) 'Rannulf de Valbadon holds half a yoke in Hamestede ... and Rannulf now says that the bishop of Bayeux gave it to a brother of his.' Not identified, but apparently in Bewsborough hundred. A puzzling little entry, which looks as if it was added by the second team of commissioners. Rannulf's brother, the previous owner, was named Reinald de Valbadon: he is accused of stealing four acres of *Hemstede* which ought to be Saint Augustine's (doc. 4). Rannulf himself occurs once more in DB-Ke, as the tenant of a yoke belonging to the manor of Northbourne (12va24).

Rannulf de Valbadon – the same man or another man with the same name – was still holding half a yoke, directly from the king, in about 1120 (Flight 2005, p. 372).

The two paragraphs which follow look as if they got dropped to the end of this chapter, perhaps by accident, perhaps because it had been doubted for a moment whether they were 'of the bishop's feod' or not. The hundred headings were supplied; the lest headings were not. Acrise, no doubt, was in Limwar lest. Hastingleigh, lying to the north of Brabourne (13vb23), was presumably in Wiwarleth lest.

11vb24) 'Anschitil de Ros holds of the bishop's feod Acres.' Acrise TR 1942.

11vb29) 'Roger son of Anschitil holds of the bishop's feod Hastingelai.' Hastingleigh TR 1044. (Excluding half a sulung which belonged to Hugo de Montfort (14ra15).) Together with Goodnestone (10va4), Hastingleigh became part of the second-tier barony

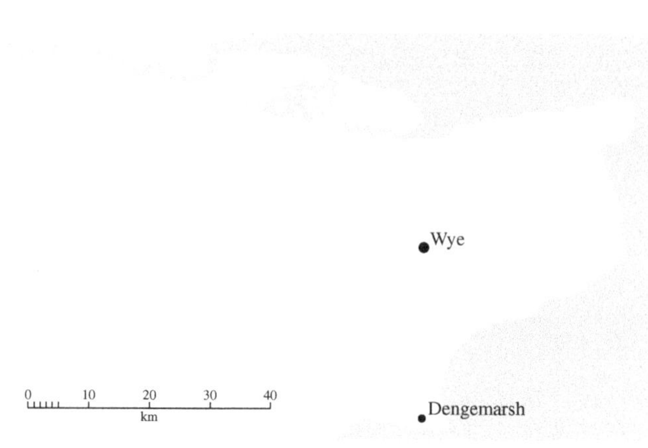

Figure 10. Lands of the abbey of Battle.

of Weston Turville (Buckinghamshire), which itself was part of the honour of the earl of Leicester (below, p. 257).

6. Land of the church of Battle

The abbey of Saint Martin of the Battle was founded by king Willelm on the site of the victory to which he owed his crown. One valuable manor in Kent became part of its endowment.

11vb40) 'The abbot of St Martin's of the place of battle holds a manor which is called Wi.' Wye TR 0546. A large manor, extending beyond both the parish and the hundred with which it shared its name. Dengemarsh TR 0518 in Lydd was originally part of Wye, though later it came to be regarded as a separate manor.

Some useful thirteenth-century documentation concerning the manor of Wye was put into print by Scargill-Bird (1887) and Muhlfeld (1933). DB's description should be read in light of that.

7. Land of Saint Augustine's church

The monastery founded by Saint Augustine on a site just outside the walls of the city of Canterbury had maintained a continuous existence ever since. In 1070, the previous abbot having deserted his post and fled to Denmark, a Norman monk named Scotland, from the monastery of Le Mont-Saint-Michel, was appointed in his place. Like Lanfranc, he had to steer his church through difficult waters; and there are several surviving documents which illustrate the course he took (docs. 4–8). He also started rebuilding the church itself, on a grand scale. We do not know when the work began; but we do know exactly how far it had advanced by the time of Scotland's death in 1087.

Except perhaps for some property in London, the abbey owned nothing outside Kent; except for one, all of its manors were in the eastern half of Kent (within the diocese of Canterbury). In return for these lands, the abbot was required to provide the king with fifteen knights, whenever the king might ask for them.

One word of warning. The reader should realize that, in some respects, the history of Saint Augustine's is highly problematic. The abbey's own historians – Thomas Sprott, who was writing at the end of the thirteenth century, Willelm Thorne, who revised and continued Sprott's chronicle a hundred years later – are notoriously unreliable. With regard to what happened in the years just after the survey, following the death of abbot Scotland, much damage has been done by a mischievous piece of pseudo-history concocted by one of the monks of Christ Church in about 1120. To cut

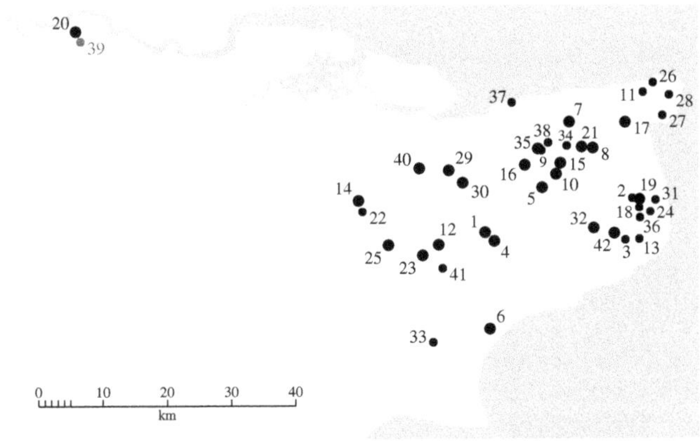

1	Ashenfield	15	Littlebourne	29	Selling
2	Little Betteshanger	16	Longport	30	Shillingheld
3	Bewsfield	17	Minster	31	Sholden
4	Bodsham	18	Little Mongeham	32	Sibertswold
5	Bridge	19	Northbourne	33	Snave
6	Burmarsh	20	Plumstead	34	Stodmarsh
7	Chislet	21	Preston	35	Sturry
8	Elmstone	22	Rayton	36	Sutton
9	Fordwich	23	Repton	37	Swalecliffe
10	Garrington	24	Ripple	38	Westbere
11	Hengrove	25	Rooting	39	East Wickham
12	Kennington	26	St John	40	Wilderton
13	East Langdon	27	St Laurence	41	Willesborough
14	Lenham	28	St Peter	42	Wlatenholt

Figure 11. Lands of the abbey of Saint Augustine.

a long story short, the gist of it is that the abbey's monks – having mutinied once too often – were all evicted, and that monks were brought in from Christ Church to replace them. Camouflaged in excerpts from a genuine text (which, unhappily, does not survive in any better form than this), the narrative was planted in a copy of the 'Anglo-Saxon Chronicle' (Cambridge, Corpus Christi College 173, fo. 32v); and there it sat for many years, doing no harm to anyone. (The monks of Saint Augustine's became aware of its existence but did not think it worth refuting.) After the dissolution, however, it came to the attention of a post-medieval generation of historians, who, lacking a medieval sense of humour, took it at face value. From Parker (1572, pp. 99–100) onwards, numerous versions of the story have found their way into the literature, all of them derived, directly or indirectly, from this single manuscript. (Usually the story is given some slight twist, to make it seem a little less incredible: in Parker's version, for instance, only some of the monks are expelled, and the monks who replace them are 'new monks', not monks from Christ Church.) For anyone who knows when their leg is being pulled, the story is obviously fiction. The abbey did not become metamorphosed into a cell of Christ Church. If proof of that is needed, the reader has only to look at the writings of Gocelin – especially at his report on the excavations carried out at Saint Augustine's in 1091, in the time of abbot Wido (1087–93).

12ra3) 'The abbot of Saint Augustine's has a manor by the name of Plumstede.' Plumstead TQ 4578. The abbot also owned East Wickham TQ 4676, but there he held from the bishop of Bayeux (6va28), not directly from the king.

12ra10) 'The same abbot holds Lertham.' Lenham TQ 8952. The spelling is odd, but there is no doubt about the identification.

15) 'Of this manor Robert Latiner holds one yoke.' Possibly Rayton (repr. Chapel Farm) TQ 9050 in Lenham, which showed some tendency to slip out of the abbey's possession (Johnson and Cronne 1956, no. 1283). (This yoke should apparently be counted separately from the 5.5 sulungs of Lenham; so I infer from doc. 11.)

12ra17) 'The same abbot holds Borne.' Bridge TR 1854. The *
identification was made by Ward (1933, p. 64), on the evidence of doc. 11.

12ra22) '(In Canterbury hundred) the same abbot holds a manor (called) Lanport.' Longport (repr. Barton Court) TR 1557 outside Canterbury. Portions of this manor in Stowting hundred are listed separately below (12vb20).

12ra30) 'The same abbot holds Liteburne.' Littlebourne TR 2157, including Stodmarsh TR 2260.

35) 'Of this manor the bishop of Bayeux has in his park as much as is worth 60 shillings.'

12ra36) 'The same abbot holds Warwintone.' Garrington TR 2056 in Littlebourne (Hasted 9:152).

36) 'The bishop of Bayeux gave it (Garrington) to him (the abbot) in exchange for his (the bishop's) park.' The park which the bishop had made for himself was at Trenley TR 1959 in Wickhambreaux (9rb43).

12ra41) 'The same abbot holds Esturai.' Sturry TR 1760, including Swalecliffe TR 1367.

12ra48) 'The same abbot holds (Saint Mildred's) manor of Tanet.' Minster TR 3164. This entry covers the whole of the eastern half of Thanet, except for six sulungs which were connected with Chislet (12rb6), not with Minster.

This entry ought to cover Stonar TR 3358 as well; if it does, it suggests that there was no commercial activity there in the 1080s, at least none from which the abbot made a profit. A text originating at Christ Church, the report of a trial held at Sandwich in 1127, describes how a parasitic settlement at Stonar had 'recently' come into existence: huts were built along the shore, and the abbot's men began collecting tolls which ought to have been paid to Christ Church's officers in Sandwich; they also began running an unlicensed ferry, to carry men and goods from Thanet across the river (Stenton 1964, p. 116). A charter of Henric I, confirming the abbot and monks of Saint Augustine's in their possession of Stonar, 'the land and the whole shore as far as the middle of the river', refers back to an earlier trial, in the time of Willelm II, 'between the men of London and the men of abbot Wido' (Johnson and Cronne 1956, no. 1644, citing Davis 1913, no. 372). So the settlement at Stonar seems to have been founded – on land which the abbot claimed as his – by traders from London who wanted to do business in Sandwich without paying the usual tolls.

In B/xAug, not in DB, there is a record of some property belonging to the abbot in Sandwich itself: thirty plots of land and a church (A4-21r23). The church in question is Saint Peter's.

12rb6) 'The same abbot holds Cistelet.' Chislet TR 2264, including Westbere TR 1961. Also a large tract of woodland, from East Blean Wood TR 1864 across to West Blean Wood TR 1664, represented by a detached portion of Chislet parish on the six-inch map.
Half of the manor described here was in Thanet, at Hengrove TR *
3368 in St John's.

6) 'which defended itself for 12 sulungs.' A passage in xAug (perhaps derived from B-Ke, perhaps an interpolation) says that six of these sulungs are at Margate (A4-20v8); a twelfth-century

list of sulungs has separate but successive entries for Margate and Chislet, 6 and 6.25 sulungs respectively (doc. 11).

The mainland portion of the manor is mapped by Tatton-Brown (1997, p. 138). For identifying the portion in Thanet, the crucial evidence – kindly pointed out to me by Harold Gough – comes from a passage in the thirteenth-century 'Black Book' (ed. Turner and Salter 1915–24, pp. 25–6): 'Furthermore there are at Margate in the parish of Saint John's five sulungs and fifty acres which belong to Hengrove' (*Sunt preterea apud Meregate in parochia sancti Iohannis v sullingi et l acre qui pertinent ad Hengraue*). By this time the connection with Chislet seems to have been broken (any payments or deliveries that had to be made were being made either to Minster or to the abbey itself), and the assessment had been adjusted downwards, from 6 to 5.25 sulungs, just as the assessment for Minster had been reduced from 48 to 45.75 sulungs; but it is clear that the Hengrove sulungs were being counted separately from the Minster sulungs. (The due called 'horsaver' is payable at the rate of 16 pence per sulung, and the total is reported to be 816 pence: that is the equivalent of 45.75 + 5.25 = 51 sulungs.) As late as 1441, in a document printed by Lewis (1723, app. pp. 29–34), Hengrove was still being treated as a separate manor from Minster (and the assessments had been reduced even further by then, to 42.44 and 4.75 sulungs).

9) 'forty-seven salterns paying fifty seams of salt.' The word 'seam' occurs only twice in DB-Ke, here as a measure of salt, below as a measure of flour (12rb27). In French it was *some*, from the Latin (originally Greek) word *sagma*, 'pack-saddle'. Some people were aware of that; but nearly always, in writing as well as in speech, this word became merged with *some* from *summa*, 'sum'.

A seam was properly a measure of weight – it was the load which a pack-horse could carry – but there were rules for converting it into a measure of volume. At Aldington in the 1280s, a seam of salt was equal to 8 bushels (Witney 2000, p. 242). (It could also be converted into money: at Folkestone in the 1260s, a seam of salt was priced at 20 pence (Larking 1860, p. 256).)

12rb13) 'The same abbot holds a small town which is called Forewic.' Fordwich TR 1859.

14) 'King Edward gave two thirds of this town to Saint Augustine. As for the third which had been earl Godwin's, the bishop of Bayeux granted it to the same saint, with the king's assent.' A writ of the bishop's, addressed to archbishop Lanfranc, sheriff Haimo and others, is the record of this donation (Bates 1998, p. 351).

22) 'In this town (of Fordwich) archbishop Lanfranc holds seven measures of land which TRE paid service to Saint Augustine. Now the archbishop is depriving him (the saint) of the service.' A complaint from the abbot: the archbishop's tenants are refusing to pay their share.

12rb24) 'Next to the city of Canterbury Saint Augustine has half a sulung which has always been quit (i.e. exempt from paying geld).'

26) 'In the same place there are four acres of land which four nuns hold in alms from the abbot.' Urry (1967, pp. 662–3) sees this as the earliest reference to the priory of Saint Sepulchre.

27) 'one seam of flour.' Possibly 16 bushels. (At Folkestone in the 1260s there were 16 bushels in a seam of oats (Larking 1860, p. 262).) It is not clear how the nuns were expected to come by this quantity of flour.

12rb30) 'The same abbot holds Wirentone.' Wilderton (repr. Pidgeon Cottage) TQ 9957 in Throwley (Hasted 6:453).

12rb34) 'The same abbot holds Esmerefel, and Anschitil (holds it) from him.' Ashenfield TR 0947 in Waltham (Hasted 9:324). DB's spelling of the place-name is better than the modern spelling: the first element is the man's name Æscmer. In B / xAug the tenant is called Anschitil 'the marshal' (A4-18r8). (The compiler of ε identified him with Anschitil de Ros (C1-6rb50). Possibly that is right; but the manor did not pass to Anschitil's descendants.)

12rb37) 'In Darenden Adam holds from the abbot half a sulung.' *
A lost place in Wye hundred, mentioned fairly often in the records of Saint Augustine's, where the usual spelling of the name is *Dernedene*. I have not been able to establish its location.

12rb39) 'The same abbot holds Setlinges.' Selling TR 0356.

12rb43) 'The same abbot holds half a yoke in Rotinge.' Rooting TQ 9445 in Pluckley (Hasted 7:472).

12rb46) 'The same abbot holds one yoke (called) Rapentone, and Ansered (holds it) from him.' Repton TQ 9943 in Ashford (Hasted 7:531). The assessment seems to be misreported by DB. Twelfth-century lists count one sulung here: *Ad Repetune i suling'* (doc. 11), *habet Rapetone unum solinum* (A4-13r). Later on, this holding is linked with Little Betteshanger (12vb13).

12va1) 'Ansfrid (Masleclerc) holds from the abbot Cherinchehelle.' Shillingheld (repr. Shillinghold Wood) TR 0654 in Chilham (Hasted 7:283). DB's spelling of the place-name is wild, but the identification is certain; the site is (or was until the 1960s) marked by visible earthworks. B / xAug gives the tenant's surname (A4-18r11).

12va5) 'The same abbot holds Norborne.' Northbourne TR 3352. In the largest sense the manor included (Little) Mongeham (12va27), Bewsfield (12va25), Ripple TR 3550, (East) Langdon TR 3346, Sholden TR 3552, Elmstone (12vb5), the lost *Smethetone* (12va23), and 'other members' too (of which Sutton TR 3349 was certainly one); so defined, it was assessed at 36 sulungs (doc. 11). But DB has separate entries for several of those places.

10) 'Of the villains' land of this manor, Oidelard holds one sulung.' Oidelard was the abbot's steward (doc. 8); he also held part of Bewsfield (12va25).

12) 'Of the same villains' land, Gislebert holds two sulungs less half a yoke.' This land was at Sholden and Bewsfield (A4-12r).

14) 'Wadard holds of this manor three sulungs less sixty acres of the villains' land.' Wadard is the same man who held Maplescombe (6rb29) and other places from the bishop of Bayeux. By agreement with abbot Scotland, he had been given (or, more probably, allowed to keep) five sulungs of land 'around Northbourne', but only for his own lifetime (doc. 6). Some of that land is recorded here, some of it in the next paragraph. (The rent of thirty shillings, though mentioned twice in DB, covered all five sulungs.) Later, despite the terms of the lease, Wadard's successor, Manasser Arsic, got possession of the land, but abbot Hugo succeeded in dislodging him (Johnson and Cronne 1956, no. 944). Wadard's land was at Ripple and East Langdon.

18) 'Odelin holds of the same villains' land one sulung.' Odo called Odelin was one of the abbot's knights. The land he held was at Sutton (Turner and Salter 1915–24, p. 433).

20) 'Marcher holds of the same villains' land what is worth eight shillings.'

21) 'Osbern son of Letard holds half a sulung ... of the villains' land.' Another man of bishop Odo's with whom the abbot had had to come to terms.

A subparagraph seems to have gone missing here, relating to a man named Acard who owned land worth twenty shillings (B / xAug / A4-21v11).

23) 'Rannulf de Columbers holds one yoke.' This is the land at *Smethetone* which, for a time, was wrongfully occupied by Rannulf (doc. 4). Bishop Odo 'gave it back' (Bates 1998, pp. 352–3): in other words, he renounced any claim on the land, as far as he himself was concerned. His man remained in possession, becoming the abbot's tenant.

24) 'Rannulf de Valbadon holds one yoke.' An interpolation in xAug says that 'this is the land which Simon de Holte holds' (A4-21v7). Simon de Holt (occ. 1236–58) was the second husband of Emma, daughter and heir of Stephan de Denintone, who took his surname from Denton (11vb10).

25) 'Also the Oidelard mentioned above (12va10) holds of this manor one sulung; it is called Beuesfel.' Bewsfield (repr. Church Whitfield) TR 3145. In medieval records the church and parish were always called Bewsfield; Whitfield was the name of a manor in this parish, not recognizably recorded in DB.

* 12va27) 'The same abbot holds Mundingeham.' Little Mongeham TR 3350. (Great Mongeham was part of the manor of Adisham (5rb18) belonging to the monks of Christ Church.)

Probably here, certainly somewhere, there ought to be an entry for Ripple TR 3550. In xAug we find a shortened version of the entry as it appeared in B, and the facts reported there are these: 'Ripple TRE was held by Wlmer from the abbot and answered for one sulung and a half; now it is held from the abbot by Ansfrid Masleclerc; it pays 100 pence a year to Saint Augustine's and 100 pence a year to Saint Martin's (of Dover); the whole manor is worth eight pounds' (A4-21v22).

In DB, Ripple is mentioned only incidentally (as *Ripe* or *Ripa*) in the description of the lands of Saint Martin's (2rb17); the main entry has gone missing. The difficulty does not end there, because it seems that there must have been another manor in Ripple, held by Ansfrid Masleclerc from the bishop of Bayeux, which is also missing from DB. It is first heard of in about 1230, when – with other lands which had once belonged to Ansfrid – it was reported to owe a castleguard rent to Dover (120 pence every 24 weeks).

12va38) 'The same abbot holds Siberteswalt.' Sibertswold TR 2647. Abbot Scotland had given this manor on a lifetime lease to Hugo son of Fulbert – whom I take to have been the father of Fulbert de Dovre (10va9) – for a rent of twenty shillings (doc. 5). By 1086 Hugo was dead, and apparently the lease had not been renewed in Fulbert's favour: to judge from this entry (and from the corresponding entry in xAug (A4-22r4)), the manor was in the abbot's domain at the time. But that was not the end of the story. Sooner or later, Fulbert or his descendants recovered possession of Sibertswold, paying the abbot a rent of 20 shillings (until 1232, when the rent was increased to 24 shillings (*Feet of fines*, pp. 114–15)); they sold the place in 1257 (pp. 286–7).

12va43) 'The same abbot holds Platenout.' A lost place called *Wlatenholt*, probably represented by Waddling Wood TR 2946 in Coldred. (The name is 'Wadholt Wood' on the first-edition six-inch map; that has been replaced by 'Waddling Wood' on the current map.) The identification, first made by Wallenberg (1934), looks sure to be right; but it needs to be worked out a little further.

12va48) 'In Preston hundred.' This hundred is a problem. It consisted only of these two manors of the abbot's, Preston and Elmstone. DB appears to be placing it in Eastry lest (the heading at 12va4 should still apply), but later evidence puts it squarely in Borwar (Saint Augustine's) lest. There are two possibilities. Either we take the evidence as we find it, inferring that Preston hundred was, at some later date, taken out of Eastry lest and put into Borwar lest. Or else we insert a lest heading here, on the assumption that it was accidentally omitted from DB. It is far from clear to me which option should be preferred. Since some decision is required, I have assumed, provisionally, that DB is right as it stands.

12va48) 'The same abbot holds Prestetune.' Preston TR 2460.

1) 'Of this manor Vitalis holds one sulung and half a yoke.' The tenant is the same man who held from the archbishop (3va27) and the bishop of Bayeux (7ra48). This land at Preston passed to his son, Haimo son of Vitalis (doc. 11), but I cannot trace it further.

12vb5) 'Ansfrid holds from the abbot Æluetone.' Approximately the same as Elmstone TR 2660. In the abbey's records this name is very variably spelt: at its simplest it resembles the DB form, but forms like *Eluiedetone* and *Ælfgidetone* go to prove that it means 'Ælfgyth's estate'. The modern name is different: it derives (the spelling is thoroughly deceptive) from 'Ægelmer's estate'.

The tenant is Ansfrid Masleclerc. Together with Ripple, this manor was given to Ansfrid by abbot Scotland (doc. 7), on similar terms to those negotiated with Wadard (doc. 6). In return, Ansfrid donated tithes from five manors held by him from the bishop of Bayeux.

7) 'with three oxen in a plough.' The wording is odd, and probably the text is corrupt. I would guess that *in car'* is a misreading of *iii car'*, and that *iii bobus* was meant as a correction of that.

8) 'In this manor Ansfrid holds half a sulung of the monks' domain.' Possibly this is Elmstone in a stricter sense, i.e. the place to which the name originally belonged.

12vb13) 'In the lest (of Eastry) and in the hundred of Eastry Saint Augustine has three rods of land.' This reads like one of the entries added by the second team of commissioners. Apparently this land had been overlooked at first, perhaps because there was doubt which hundred it belonged to. The holding in question can be identified as Little Betteshanger TR 3252 in Northbourne (Hasted 9:591). The early twelfth-century list of sulungs makes a connection between these three rods and Repton (12rb46): 'Willelm de Rapintune holds three rods in the hundred of Eastry' (doc. 11). (This proves that DB's 'three rods' is right and that xAug's 'three yokes' is wrong.) In 1242, when Repton belonged to Walter de Dene (*Book of fees*, p. 660), half a fee in Betteshanger was held from him by Petrus de Betlesangre (p. 656). By 1253 we find this holding being counted as part of Cornilo hundred, like the rest of Northbourne. *

12vb17) 'Gaufrid holds Bodesham from the abbot.' Bodsham TR 1045 in Elmsted (Hasted 8:40).

12vb20) 'The same abbot holds in Lanport two sulungs and one yoke.' Several pieces of land in Stowting hundred, regarded as limbs of the manor of Longport (12ra22). The twelfth-century *Noticia terrarum* identifies them by name; the list includes (part of) Elmsted TR 1144 and (part of) Horton TR 1240 (A4-13r). *

12vb25) 'The same abbot holds Chenetone.' Kennington TR 0245, including Willesborough TR 0241.

25) 'TRE ... it belonged to Borchemeres.' I do not understand what this means. *Borchemeres* is usually supposed to be Burmarsh, the place described in the following paragraph (12vb33); but the names are very differently spelt, and the places are very far apart. Besides, if one place did belong to the other, one would have expected Burmarsh to belong to Kennington (as Dengemarsh belonged to Wye), not vice versa. It seems unlikely to me that *Borchemeres* and *Burwarmaresc* are the same place; at most I might be willing to believe that the names became confused, during the compilation of the survey text.

12vb33) '(In Romney Marsh) the same abbot holds Burwarmaresc.' Burmarsh TR 1032, including Snave TR 0129. The DB spelling is good; the usual twelfth-century spelling was something like *Burwarmareis*. The parallel passage in xAug seems to be saying that Burmarsh is in Blackbourne hundred (A4-24r15), but I do not see how that could possibly be right; I would rather suppose that the text is defective at this point.

12vb37) 'The shire testifies that Bedenesmere used to be Saint Augustine's TRE.' A note relating to the manor of Badlesmere TR 0155 in Faversham hundred, held by Ansfrid Masleclerc from the bishop of Bayeux (10rb11). This is a complaint from the abbot put on record by the second team of commissioners.

8. Land of Saint Peter of Gent

The ancient monastery of Saint Peter of Gent (Saint-Pierre-du-Mont-Blandin) owned only one manor in England, and that manor was in Kent. As we discover from DB, the monks had been in possession TRE, and were still in possession at the time of the survey; they remained so (at least in theory) until the fifteenth century. (In ε the abbey is called 'Saint Wandrille's' (C1-6rb5). It was indeed one of the places which claimed to possess the body of that seventh-century saint, but it was never known by that name, as far as I am aware.)

At the time of the survey, if I read the signs correctly, the manor was held at farm by Walter de Dowai. DB says nothing about that, apparently because arrangements of this kind were regarded as private matters, not needing to be reported to the king; but Walter does occur close by at Lee (6vb39), as a tenant of the bishop of Bayeux. Given that, and given that a link between Lee and Lewisham persists, I think we catch a hint of some unresolved disagreement between the bishop and the abbot of Gent concerning the ownership of that half-sulung. Walter's son Robert, who used the surname de Bantone, did certainly get hold of Lewisham: the abbot had to take him to court to recover possession of the manor (Johnson and Cronne 1956, no. 934). But it was claimed (and seems likely to be true) that Robert had Lewisham given back to him, to hold at fee-farm from the abbot. Robert's daughter Juliana is said to have held Lee, and may have held Lewisham too.

(The evidence from which I piece this story together comes mostly from the record of two lawsuits instigated by Juliana's grandson, Willelm Painel (d. 1228). In 1219 he sued the abbot of Gent, asserting a right to hold Lewisham at fee-farm (*Curia regis rolls*, vol. 8, p. 44); in 1223–5 he sued the owners of Lee (vol. 11, p. 516), who paid him 80 marks to drop the case (*Feet of fines*, p. 84).)

12vb41) 'The abbot of Gent holds from the king Leuesham.' Lewisham TQ 3774, including Greenwich TQ 3877.

Somehow or other, the manor came to be held by Gervais de Cornhelle, who formally renounced any right to it, for himself and his heirs, in 1160×6 (in a batch of three documents summarized by

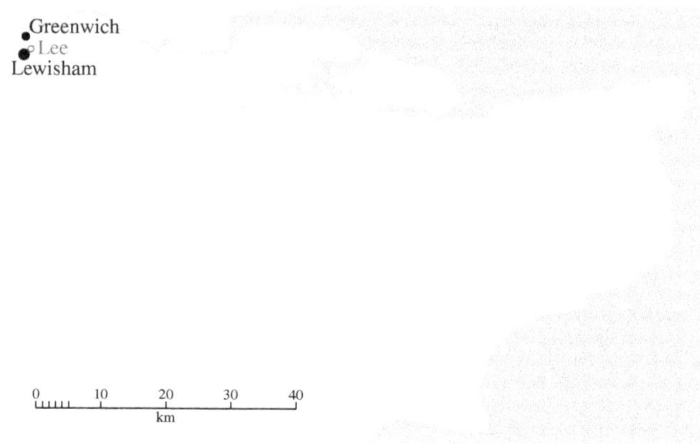

Figure 12. Lands of the abbey of Saint Peter of Gent.

Round 1899, pp. 504–5). Presumably this means that the monks of Gent had decided to buy Gervais out and take the manor into their own hands. They established a small priory there: I infer that it was founded in the 1160s, but have no proof of its existence before the 1190s.

9. Land of Hugo de Montfort

The king's constable, Hugo de Montfort, had acquired a vast estate in England, all of it in the eastern part of the country (below, p. 252). In Kent he had built himself a castle at Saltwood, overlooking the port of Hythe. To provide this castle with a garrison, Hugo had (so it seems) been authorized to get possession of some quantity of land, or number of manors, to be distributed among his knights. Unlike the lowy of Tonbridge, the lands which thus became attached to Saltwood castle did not form a solid block: they were interspersed with lands belonging to other lords. Either at the time or later, after things had settled down, much negotiation had to take place between Hugo and the bishop of Bayeux, before the limits of Hugo's 'division' were adequately defined; there are numerous passages in DB which reflect that process of adjustment. More awkward still, Saltwood turned out to be one of the manors on which archbishop Lanfranc had an undeniable claim. In order to keep possession of it, Hugo had had to acknowledge that he held it from the archbishop; and therefore we find it listed in chapter 2 (4va17).

From the mid twelfth century onwards, there is a respectable amount of surviving documentation relating to the honour of the Constabulary (as Hugo's lands had come to be called). Despite that, the identification of the places named in the following chapter is more than usually problematic. As in other chapters, many identifications are perfectly straightforward; but the ratio of difficult names is higher here than elsewhere. Conversely, some of the places named frequently in later documents are not easy to match up with any of the holdings that we find described in DB. To be brief, it looks as if the honour underwent some fairly extensive reorganization, after the 1080s.

That means, I think, that in dealing with this chapter we need to be especially careful not to jump to conclusions. We should, for example, take warning from some imprudent comments of Ward's (1933, pp. 71–2), where one very dubious identification (of 14vb7 *Neventone*) was used to justify another (of 13rb26 *Belice*).

13ra3) 'Hugo de Montfort holds a manor (called) Estwelle.' Eastwell TR 0047.

4) 'Three yokes (out of four) are inside Hugo's division. The fourth yoke is outside; it is (part) of the feod of the bishop of Bayeux.'

13ra9) 'The same Hugo holds Haintone from the king.' Hampton TR 0743 in the part of Brabourne which belonged to Wye hundred (Hasted 8:22). The record of a lawsuit in 1227 says much about the history of this holding (Maitland 1887, vol. 3, pp. 596–7).

13ra13) 'Maigno holds from Hugo Seiuetone.' Sevington TR 0340. The DB spelling is good: it should be read as five syllables, 'se-i-ve-to-ne', meaning 'Sægifu's estate'.

13ra17) 'The same Maigno holds from Hugo Estefort.' Part of Ashford TR 0142, possibly East Stour TR 0242.

13ra21) 'The same Hugo holds Essella.' Not identified, but possibly part of Ashford. The final *a* is the DB scribe's way of warning us that he has copied the name as he found it, not understanding what English name might be represented by this spelling.

13ra25) 'Another Essetesford Maigno holds from Hugo.' Ashford TR 0142. This is the manor which possesses a church.

13ra31) '(In Newchurch hundred) the same Hugo holds in Romney Marsh one yoke.'

13ra35) 'The same Hugo holds half a yoke ... This land is appraised in Tinton.' Explaining why no value is reported for this yoke: its value is included in the total reported for Tinton (13rb42). (Why Tinton in particular? Because the domain ploughs from that manor are brought over to plough this land.)

13ra37) A misplaced entry (it belongs in Bewsborough hundred), curiously botched as well. It starts off with a summary of the facts of the case, as they were recorded by the second team of commissioners, and then runs on into a paragraph of the normal sort.

37) 'This (is what) the hundred (of Bewsborough) testifies, and the townsmen of Dover, and the abbot of Saint Augustine's men, and Eastry lest, with regard to the land (called) Etretone.' Atterton (repr. Archers Court) TR 3045 in River (Hasted 9:439). (My translation assumes that *quod* should be emended to *quoad*.)

39) 'that Wulwi (called) le Wilde held it in alod TRE.' Wulwi had been one of the canons of Saint Martin's, the owner of the prebend which now belonged to Godric (1vb41). By saying that he held this piece of land 'in alod', the jurors are saying that the canons have no claim on it: it was Wulwi's personal property, not Saint Martin's.

13ra42) The same Hugo holds Estbrige in domain.' Eastbridge TR 0732.

13ra48) '(In Worth hundred) Bertran holds from Hugo half a yoke and half a rod.'

13ra50) 'Herveus holds from Hugo Blachemenestone.' Blackmanstone TR 0729. This manor took its name from the TRE tenant.

13rb5) 'The same Hugo holds in Romney Marsh one sulung less half a rod.' The phrase 'in Romney Marsh' ought perhaps to have been written as a cadastral heading (as at 5rb43, 12vb32). On that assumption, this manor would not have to be looked for in Worth hundred.

13rb8) 'Roger holds from Hugo one yoke in Romney Marsh.'

13rb11) 'Rotbert holds from Hugo in the same Marsh a sixth part of a yoke.'

13rb14) 'Roger holds from Hugo Postinges.' Postling TR 1439.

20) 'Of this manor Radulf de Curbespine has three dens; they are outside Hugo's division'. And therefore we find them listed in chapter 5, as part of the bishop's feod (10vb14).

13rb22) '(In Heane hundred) the same Hugo holds half a sulung.' This piece of land is valued jointly with the next one.

13rb26) 'The same Hugo holds Belice.' Not identified. Though the place cannot be the same, the name may perhaps be connected with Beachborough TR 1638 in Newington (Hasted 8:202), the first element of which was written 'belch' till more decorous spellings, either 'beech' or 'beach', prevailed.

13rb30) '(In Newchurch hundred) the same Hugo holds a (piece of) land.'

13rb34) 'The same Hugo holds half a sulung in Romney Marsh.'

13rb37) '(In Aloesbridge hundred) the same Hugo holds in the same Marsh one yoke.'

13rb40) 'These two lands.' These words do not make sense. Perhaps they were repeated by error (from 13rb29).

13rb42) 'The same Hugo holds Tintentone.' Tinton TQ 9832 in Warehorne (Hasted 8:368).

13rb49) '(In Blackbourne hundred) the same Hugo holds half a yoke.'

13va1) 'Herveus holds from Hugo Sedlinges.' Sellindge TR 0938. An outlying portion of the manor (repr. Sellinge Farm TR 0829) is mapped and discussed by Ward (1936, pp. 24–7).

13va8) 'Alnod holds from Hugo Hortone.' Horton TR 1240. After becoming reannexed to the domain, Horton provided the site for a Cluniac priory founded by Hugo's daughter, Adelina, and her third husband, Robert de Ver (d. 1151). Charters recording the donations made by them and their tenants are a valuable source of information about the history of the honour.

13va14) 'In the same place (Horton) Alnod holds one yoke from Hugo, but there is nothing there.'

13va15) 'The same Hugo holds three rods and a half in the same (Limwar) lest.' Text ε says, perhaps rightly, that this land is in Street hundred (C1-6vc54).

13va19) 'Willelm holds from Hugo Orlauestone.' Orlestone TR 0034. Probably including Shadoxhurst TQ 9737, the church of which, in 1240, was given by Willelm de Ordlawestune to the Trinitarian friars (*Feet of fines*, pp. 153–4).

13va24) 'Radulf son of Ricard holds from Hugo half a sulung in Rochinges.' Part of Ruckinge TR 0233.

13va29) 'Radulf holds from Hugo Hortun.' Part of Horton TR 1240.

13va34) 'Hugo de Manneuile holds from Hugo Estraites.' Street (repr. Court-at-Street) TR 0935 in Lympne (Hasted 8:292)

13va39) '(In Street hundred) Ansfrid holds from Hugo one yoke.'

13va43) 'Rotbert the cook holds from Hugo one yoke.'

13va46) '(In Longbridge hundred) Gislebert holds from Hugo one yoke.' Apparently in part of Longbridge hundred which belonged to Limwar lest (3vb34).

13va49) 'Of Etwelle which Herbert son of Ivo holds outside Hugo's division, the same Hugo holds fourteen acres inside his division.' Herbert's manor of Ewell was part of the bishop's feod (11ra26).

* 13vb2) 'The same Hugo de Montfort holds Etwelle.' La Riviere (repr. River) TR 2943. (Not Ewell except in a large sense, as Ward (1933, p. 70) pointed out.)

* 13vb7) 'The same Hugo holds Neuentone.' A lost place in Bewsborough hundred. Presumably the sulung which has been deducted from the assessment is the one already listed in chapter 5 (11va2). The existence of the church mentioned here is confirmed by an entry in one of C1's lists (a7). Beyond that we get no help.

13vb13) 'Inside this division there is a sokeman holding sixteen acres of land.'

13vb15) 'In the same (Bewsborough) hundred the same Hugo holds one share of Iaonei ... which did not belong to any manor but is (now) inside his division; it used to be (part) of the king's domain.' A very carefully worded paragraph, the meaning of which, even so, is hard to grasp.

13vb18) 'In the same hundred Fulbert has from Hugo one mill.' The unfinished sentence in the line above should be taken to refer to this mill.

13vb19) 'Herfrid holds from Hugo Poltone.' Poulton TR 2741. The tenant may be the same man who occurs at Throwley and elsewhere (10rb39, 10vb17, 11rb15) as a tenant of the bishop of Bayeux; but Poulton did not follow the same trajectory as his other lands.

13vb22) 'In Wiwar(leth) lest, in Bircholt hundred.' Here we have it stated explicitly that Bircholt hundred in in Wiwarleth lest. This is the northern half-hundred (Bircholt Barony, as opposed to Bircholt Franchise), recorded later as part of Shrewinghope lest. Knowing that Brabourne was in Wiwarleth lest, we can be confident that the same was true (as later) for places lying to the north of it – Hastingleigh (11vb29, 14ra15) and Aldglose (10vb21).

13vb23) 'The same Hugo holds Breburne.' Brabourne TR 1041.

24) 'It defended itself for 7 sulungs then, (but) now for 5.625 sulungs, because the other part is outside Hugo's division and the bishop of Bayeux holds it.' As we learn from chapter 5, the 'other part' included Aldglose (10vb21); but that does not fully account for this reduction.

13vb30) 'In the hundred of Chart some woman holds from Hugo one rod.'

13vb32) 'The same Hugo holds half a yoke in Tepindene.' Tiffenden TQ 9036 in High Halden (Hasted 7:222).

13vb36) '(In Street hundred) the same Hugo holds Siborne.' Not identified. Ward (1935, p. 148) has a tentative suggestion.

* 13vb40) 'The same Hugo has half a sulung (called) Suanetone.' Not identified. Here again, Ward (1935, p. 148) ventures a suggestion. The abbot of Saint Augustine's thought that a yoke here ought to belong to him (doc. 4).

13vb44) 'Nigel holds from Hugo one yoke.' The following phrase, 'and in Aia (there are) seven acres', should be read as a parenthesis.

13vb48) 'Willelm son of Grossa holds from Hugo Bonintone.' Bonnington TR 0534.

14ra3) 'Herveus holds from Hugo Obtrepole.' Otterpool TR 1046 in Lympne (Hasted 8:290).

14ra9) '(In Blackbourne hundred and in Newchurch hundred) * Herald holds half a sulung less one rod.' To be identified with confidence as the manor of Kenardington TQ 9732 in Blackbourne hundred, with the land called Cockride (Hasted 8:348) attached to it in Newchurch hundred. From the late twelfth century onwards, the descent of the manor is well documented.

13) 'In addition he has one den which used to belong to Fane, Adam's manor.' Meaning the manor of Fanscombe in Wye hundred belonging to Adam son of Hubert (10va30).

14ra15) 'The same Hugo holds half a sulung in Hastingelie.' Part of Hastingleigh TR 1044. The larger part belonged to the bishop of Bayeux (11vb29).

14ra19) 'The same Hugo holds in domain one yoke and a half in Teuegate.' (Part of) Evegate TR 0639 in Smeeth (Hasted 8:3). Explicitly in Longbridge hundred here, though later on the whole of Smeeth was in Bircholt Franchise hundred.

14ra23) 'In the same (Longbridge) hundred there is a rod of land in Suestone.' Not identified. In ε we find the place-name transformed into *Westtune* (C1-6vc20); but that was probably just a guess, and in any case gets us nowhere.

10. Land of count Eustachius

After 1066, the count of Boulogne acquired a vast estate in England (below, p. 250). In Kent, however, the part of the country closest to Boulogne, he did not gain much of a foothold; there was, one would guess, a policy behind that fact.

14ra32) 'Count Eustachius holds from the king Oistreham.' Westerham TQ 4454, including Edenbridge TQ 4446.

14ra40) 'The same count holds Boltune.' Boughton Aluph TR 0348.

11. Land of Ricard son of Gislebert

Ricard de Tonebrige, son of Gislebert count of Brionne, was an important man both in Normandy and in England. The map of his possessions in Kent – the lands which became the honour of the earls of Clare (below, p. 252) – looks like the fossilized result of an (otherwise unrecorded) episode in duke Willelm's westward advance through Kent in late 1066. Ricard, it seems, was sent on a foray up the river Medway, with orders to find a good site for a castle and get himself dug in. He reached Yalding, and probably thought of stopping at that point; but then he carried on as far as Tonbridge, and chose to build his castle there. After the conquest had been completed, it came to be understood that every piece of land within a specified distance from the castle (roughly 3–4 miles) had now become Ricard's property. The territory thus defined was called the lowy of Tonbridge (above, p. 12). Its population stayed in place; but all rents and services due from the local peasants, regardless of to whom they had been paid in the past, were now payable to Ricard.

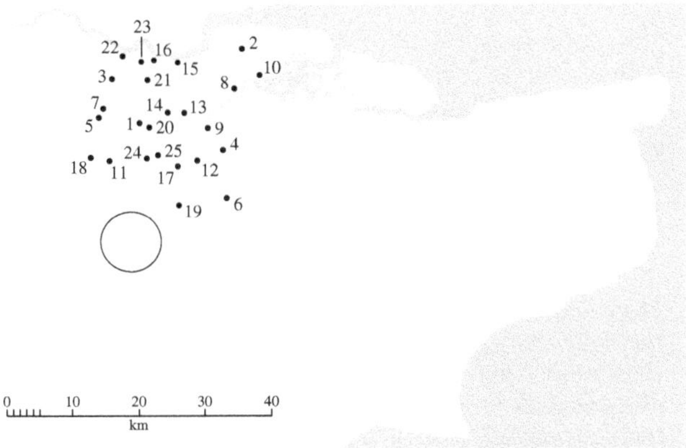

1 Ash	10 Hoo	18 Otford
2 Cooling	11 Kemsing	19 East Peckham
3 Darenth	12 Leybourne	20 Ridley
4 Eccles	13 Luddesdown	21 Southfleet
5 Eynsford	14 Meopham	22 Stone
6 East Farleigh	15 Milton	23 Swanscombe
7 Farningham	16 Northfleet	24 Wrotham
8 Frindsbury	17 Offham	25 Little Wrotham
9 Halling		

Figure 13. Places known to have been affected by the creation of the lowy of Tonbridge.

For the simple reason (so I suppose) that it was not considered to be part of Kent, the lowy of Tonbridge is not described in DB-Ke. But it is mentioned incidentally in many paragraphs, where assets are reported to have been lost to Ricard. Indirectly, the creation of the lowy preserved an interesting snapshot of the pattern of tenure in Kent. If one chose a point in the Weald and drew a circle around it with a radius of 5 km or thereabouts, that circle would include pieces of land belonging to numerous manors in northern Kent. Since the record as we find it in DB is certainly not complete – by and large, it was only the archbishop and the bishop of Rochester who were still nursing a grievance, and even one of the archbishop's complaints got lost (3ra24) – we are missing some of the complexity of the pattern; but what we can see is remarkable enough. (A similar snapshot was produced, I think, by the creation of a park for the king at Bockingfold (7rb37), but the evidence there is harder to decipher.)

Those lands of Ricard's which we find described in DB are those which lay outside the lowy. He held two manors directly from the king, and those are listed in this chapter. In addition he owned two manors for which he had acknowledged himself to be the tenant of the bishop of Bayeux (7vb2, 7vb10); and he held some other land too, either from the bishop (8va32) or from the archbishop of Canterbury (4vb15).

14rb3) 'Ricard de Tonebrige holds Hallinges.' Yalding TQ 6950, including Brenchley TQ 6741.

14rb11) 'The same Ricard (de Tonebrige) holds Bermelinge.' East Barming TQ 7154.

12. Land of Haimo the sheriff

Haimo, called 'the sheriff', or sometimes 'the steward' (because he was, at least nominally, one of the king's household officers), was not a powerful baron like Hugo de Montfort or Ricard de Tonebrige – but in Kent he was a man of importance. There is no good evidence to fix the date of his appointment as sheriff; from the fact that no other post-conquest sheriff is ever mentioned, either in the records of the survey or elsewhere, it is probably fair to infer that Haimo was put in charge straight away, as soon as the machinery of government began to function again. He kept the job until he died, a year or two after the survey. (That he was dead by the early part of 1088 can be deduced, I think, from a Rochester document (Davis 1913, no. 451), mistakenly listed by me (Flight 1997a, no. 504) as a writ of Willelm I.)

As sheriff, Haimo was in receipt of payments from Canterbury (2ra15) and from three of the king's manors (2va14, 2va39, 2vb12); but the sheriffdom (unlike the earldom) did not have any lands annexed to it. The manors listed in this chapter were Haimo's personal property; he also held at least two manors from the archbishop of Canterbury (3vb7, 4rb23) and five from the bishop of Bayeux (6vb29, 7ra42, 8vb3, 9va6, 9va10).

14rb21) 'Haimo the sheriff holds from the king a manor.' Crundale TR 0848. The DB scribe does not know the name of this manor but leaves a space for it; ε supplies the name *Dramword* (C1-6vb51). That name survives as Trimworth Manor TR 0649 in Crundale (Hasted 7:373). In the twelfth century it seems to have been used as an alternative name for Crundale. The church is called Crundale in the 1150s (Saltman 1956, no. 36) and 1180s (Cheney and Jones 1986, no. 147), Trimworth in the 1190s (Cheney and John 1986, no. 519, reciting a charter of Hamo de Valoignes), Crundale in an endorsement on this last document. In the fourteenth century it could still be said that Crundale was 'in Trimworth', rather than vice versa. *

28) 'Of this manor Hugo de Montfort holds three yokes and a half.' Apparently a complaint from Haimo; but as usual DB's language is neutral.

14rb30) 'There (in Greenwich hundred) Haimo has sixty-three acres of land which belong in Huluiz.' Part of Woolwich TQ 4379.

14rb34) 'The same Haimo holds Marourde.' Mereworth TQ 6653.

14rb41) 'The same Haimo holds Blehem.' Blean TR 1260. A shortened version of this paragraph, as it appeared in the B text, is included in the excerpts made for Saint Augustine's (A4-20v21); apparently the abbot thought he had some claim on this manor, but the claim was never made good.

The arable land (enough for four ploughs) consisted of a clearing carved out of Blean wood, on either side of the road between Canterbury and Whitstable. About Blean wood itself DB has nothing to tell us. I wish that I could say something to fill up the gap, but I hardly know more than was known already to Hasted (9:2). The Blean appears in the record largely as a place from which people in Canterbury could get firewood – an unexciting but indispensable commodity. By the 1520s, when the schoolmaster John Twine settled in Canterbury and started exploring the countryside, foxes and badgers were the only animals left in the Blean which might interest a hunter; but he was told that there had been wild boars there too, not that long before (Twine 1590, lib. 2, p. 101).

13. Land of Albert the chaplain

What this chapter describes is the endowment of a dead minster. There are hints of that in DB; but the clearest evidence comes from a somewhat earlier document, the report of an inquiry into the assets of Newington church (doc. 2). Looking at that document – and taking advantage of the hint given at the end of it, that the arrangements existing here bore some resemblance to those existing in the church of Saint Martin's of Dover – it is not difficult to see that Newington church, at some uncertain point in the past, had been manned by seven priests, who were endowed accordingly with seven sulungs of land. (In other words, this minster was one-third the size of Saint Martin's.) Each priest was entitled to four 'shares' – perhaps quarterly payments, perhaps payments charged on the individual yokes (either way the shares would come in multiples of four). Two of the priests were nominated by the archbishop, and one by the abbot of Saint Augustine's; the other four, by implication, were nominated by the king (or, possibly, by whoever owned the manor of Milton).

Those arrangements, though still dimly remembered, had long since been allowed to lapse. By the simple expedient of leaving the posts unfilled, the archbishop and the abbot had appropriated twelve of the shares, leasing out the land which went with them. The other sixteen shares, as doc. 2 puts it, were 'theirs who serve in the church'; but it would seem that they all belonged to a man named Swithgar, put in possession by queen Eadgyth (below, 14va3). Probably it was this man's death which prompted the inquiry of which doc. 2 is the outcome.

The result did not satisfy the abbot of Saint Augustine's. At his instigation the matter was brought before a meeting of the county court, and a different conclusion was reached: eight shares, not four, ought to belong to the abbot. A writ from the king ratifies and gives effect to that decision (Bates 1998, no. 88). Though we are not explicitly told this, it seems clear that the abbot's gain was the archbishop's loss: by the time of the survey the archbishop was the owner of four shares (C1-3va10, cf. doc. 3), not of eight as in doc. 2.

As we find it described in DB, Newington is just another manor, involved in some peculiar relationships with the king's manor of Milton, but otherwise normal enough. Not much later, it passed into lay hands: the next owners whose names we know are Radulf Goiz (C1, fo. 7rb, Johnson and Cronne 1956, no. 1157), Avelina (Brett and Gribbin 2004, p. 80), and Ricard de Luci (d. 1179), her son. Sooner or later, the archbishops waived their claim to a share of the proceeds from Newington (not without getting something in return). The monks of Saint Augustine's did not. One of their registers, the 'Black Book' (ed. Turner and Salter 1915–24), has page after page of information about Newington, including much about cheese.

14va2) 'Albert the chaplain holds from the king Newetone.' Newington TQ 8665.

3) 'Sidgar held (it) from queen Eddid.' The man's name is written *Suidgar* in B / xAug (A4-17v15) and should be read, I suppose, as Swithgar. The queen is Eadgyth, king Edward's widow, who died in 1075. I take this as a hint that she had (at least for a while) been in possession of Milton.

5) 'The land which was in domain is (now) at farm.' In other words, Albert has leased it out, because he has no thought of coming to live here.

10) 'To this manor belong four haws in the city of Canterbury and two in Rochester which (together) paid 64 pence.' B / xAug has only this: 'There are two haws in Rochester which the bishop of Bayeux used to hold; (now) they pay to this manor 24 pence' (A4-17v20). The earlier account in doc. 2 is more detailed and slightly different: 'Two haws in Rochester which pay 24 pence. Also three haws in the city of Canterbury on the west side of Eastbridge; (they) and the church which is there pay 30 pence.' Since then, it seems, a fourth haw in Canterbury, paying another 10 pence, had been annexed to Newington. Urry (1967, p. 76) suggested that the church in question was Saint Peter's; I would think that it might rather be All Saints, on the other side of Eastbridge.

12) 'From the manor of Milton there is paid to Newington a custom (in the shape of) 28 weighs of cheese.' Originally intended, no doubt, for the priests' subsistence: four weighs for each of them each year. The cheese was issued at Milton on 1 August (Turner and Salter 1915–24, p. 289).

13) 'From 28 sulungs of Milton there belongs to Newington (a payment of) ten pounds and ten shillings.' Divided by seven, that is 360 pence, about a penny a day.

14) 'From another part, (comprising) nine sulungs, of Milton there belong to Newington 28.5 weighs of cheese.' Doc. 2 confirms that there were indeed two distinct consignments of cheese, but does not mention the extra half-weigh. This second consignment came 'from Sheppey and from *Binnen ea*' (which I can only suggest may perhaps have been another name for Elmley). By the thirteenth century, though these cheeses were still being paid to the court of Newington, the total had decreased: 11 weighs and a fraction were payable on 24 June, another 5 weighs and a fraction on 29 September (Turner and Salter 1915–24, pp. 288–9). From the arithmetic there, it can be proved that a weigh of cheese was equal to 24 pounds. Its nominal value was 72 pence, 3 pence a pound.

21) 'The archbishop gets six pounds from it.' From the lessee of the land which was attached to his four shares. It is clear from B / xAug that the archbishop's holding was being valued separately from Albert's (A4-17va17).

The abbot's eight shares are not mentioned (except by an interpolated sentence in xAug), perhaps because Albert was still contesting that claim, despite the writ cited above. There was certainly some further litigation in the time of Willelm II, but the only record of it is a passing reference – *sicut iudicatum fuit tempore fratris mei in tribus comitatibus apud Suthuuercam*, 'as was judged in my brother's time, in a meeting of three counties at Southwark' – in a writ of Henric I (Johnson and Cronne 1956, no. 1157).

Dover

1ra4–49) The stretch of text that stands first in DB is a survey of the town of Dover, to be read in parallel with B / xAug / A4-22r6–v15. In B the town is called a *burgum*; but the DB scribe consistently calls it a *villa*, which seems for him to denote a status higher than an ordinary *burgum* but lower than a *civitas*. Like the inhabitants of Canterbury and Rochester, the inhabitants of Dover are called *burgenses* (of course they could not be called *villani*), and the plots of land on which their houses stand are called *mansurae* or *masurae*.

4–21) 'Dover in the time of king Edward.' The opening section is all in the past tense: this is how things used to be.

4–8) '(It) used to pay eighteen pounds; of this money the king got two shares and earl Godwin got one share. Separately from this, the canons of Saint Martin's got another half.' Very badly expressed, but in the light of later evidence the meaning is clear enough. The money in question here is not the farm of the town (that is dealt with below): it is the revenue arising from the toll that was paid by people using the harbour. Of this, we are told, one third belonged to the king, one sixth to the earl, and one half to the canons of Saint Martin's. (The sum quoted, 18 pounds, is explicitly the amount shared between the king and the earl; by implication the canons got the same amount again as their share.) After 1088 the earl's share lapsed to the king; after 1139 the canon's share passed to the monks of Saint Martin's priory; from then onwards, therefore, the king and the monks got half each.

The king could, and sometimes did, grant exemption from the toll of Dover; but the exemption applied only to his half, not to the monks' half. A writ of Henric II which spells this out was printed by Larking (1869, p. 5*, cf. Haines 1930, p. 215). In 1249 the abbot of Le Bec, who was already exempt from paying the king's half of the toll, paid the prior of Saint Martin's 15 marks to get himself, his monks and his men exempted from paying the monks' half as well (*Feet of fines*, p. 229).

9–11) 'The men of the town provided the king with twenty ships once a year for fifteen days; in each ship there were twenty-one men. They did this because he had forgiven them sac and soc.' A crucial episode in the prehistory of the Cinque Ports: through some collective negotiation, the men of Dover had come to an agreement with king Edward. The king would let them keep the money which would otherwise have been paid to him by way of sac and soc. In return, the men of Dover would provide a fleet of twenty ships at their own expense – but only once a year and only for fifteen days. (After that, if the king still needed the ships, he would have to bear the cost himself.)

12–16) 'When the king's messengers came to Dover, they gave three pence in winter and two pence in summer for carrying a horse across. The men of the town supplied a skipper and one other man to help. If anything else was needed, it was hired with his (the messenger's) money.'

16–19) 'From the feast of Saint Michael (29 September) until the feast of Saint Andrew (30 November) the king's truce existed in the town. If anyone broke it, the king's reeve received a communal fine.' This was the herring season – as is proved, for instance, by a charter of archbishop Theobald (Saltman 1956, no. 91). The theory was that at this time of year many of the men of the town would be away from home, fishing in the North Sea (Great Yarmouth came into existence as a seasonal outpost used by ships from Dover and elsewhere); so the king's peace ought to be maintained with extra vigour in their absence.

19–21) 'Anyone who dwelt permanently in the town and paid a custom to the king was exempt from toll throughout the whole of England.'

21–2) 'All these customs existed there when king Willelm came to England.' Referring back to lines 4–21.

23–5) 'At the time of his first arrival in England the town got burnt, and therefore it has not been possible for its value to be computed, (so as to say) how much it was worth when the bishop of Bayeux got possession of it.' The king's biographer, Willelm of Poitiers, makes mention of this fire at Dover (ed. Davis and Chibnall 1998, pp. 142–5), and confirms what we may gather from DB, that bishop Odo was put in charge of the town (pp. 164–5).

25–8) 'Now it is appraised at 40 pounds. The reeve, however, pays 54 pounds from it, to the king 24 pounds of pence which are 20 to the ora, and to the earl 30 pounds by count.' The payment that the reeve is making to the king is subject to a surcharge of 25 per cent (above, p. 157); the payment that he is making to the earl (or would be making to the earl, if the earl were not in prison) is taken at face value.

29–49) The following section is a list of the grievances brought to the commissioners' attention by the men of Dover.

29–44) 'In Dover there are twenty-nine plots of land from which the king has lost the custom (i.e. some payment which ought to be made to him).' In this section the word *mansura* is used interchangeably with *domus*, 'house' or 'building'. These plots or houses are only mentioned because they are causing a problem: we have no way of knowing what proportion they represent of the total number of houses in Dover at the time. Except in three cases, described in more detail at the end (lines 38–44), the facts are not disputed. It is agreed who owns these houses; it is agreed that the custom has not been paid; the question is whether it ought to have been paid or not. Though this is not said, I think we may assume that these were all new buildings, erected on sites left empty by the fire; so the question would be whether there were any obligations, rooted in the ground, which revived as soon as the sites were redeveloped.

For the moment, nothing can be done towards settling this question, because the men concerned – eleven of them, some owning more than one house – all invoke the protection of the bishop of Bayeux. It was one of the disadvantages of keeping the bishop in prison (where he was, legally speaking, a non-person) that his men could avoid answering for their alleged misdeeds by shifting the blame onto him.

30–7) First the straightforward cases (adding up to 26 houses). Of the men named here, one is a first-tier baron, Hugo de Montfort, holding a house in Dover as the bishop's tenant; four are important second-tier barons; and four are canons of Saint Martin's church. The remaining two, Durand and Modbert's son (called Gosfrid son of Modbert in B / xAug), are not mentioned anywhere else.

31–3) 'Willelm son of Tedald, ... Willelm son of Oger, ... Robert Niger, ... Willelm son of Goisfrid.' These men are all canons of Saint Martin's church, each holding one of the prebends listed below (1va–b). All of them, no doubt, were appointed by bishop Odo.

33–4) 'Willelm son of Goisfrid (has) three (plots of land) on which used to be the gihalla of the men of the town.' B / xAug is more informative: 'Willelm son of Gaufrid has a gidhalla which the men of the town have lost possession of. This (gidhalla) was the king's alms. There are three houses there' (A4-22v2). Presumably this means that there is a merchants' guild in Dover which used to have its own hall (on a site donated, free of charge, by an unnamed king). But the hall has ceased to exist (perhaps because it was burnt down in 1066) and three newly-built houses occupy the site of it.

38–44) Now for the three difficult cases.

38–40) 'Concerning that plot of land which Rannulf de Columbels holds which used to be a certain outlaw's: they (the men of Dover) are agreed that half the land is the king's.' B / xAug puts it like this: 'Rannulf de Columbels has fifteen acres of land (which used to be) a certain outlaw's, from which the king (should have) half the gavel and half the land, as they all say' (A4-22v6).

40–2) 'Hunfrid (called) Loripes (i.e. bandy-legged) holds one plot of land of which half the forfeit was the king's.' A similar case to the previous one, so it seems.

42–4) 'Roger de Ostreham has built a house alongside the king's waterway and till now has withheld the king's custom. There was no house there TRE.' B / xAug has this version: 'Roger de Oistresham has built a house on the waterway and the king's land without permission from anyone; he gets the gavel from it and the king gets nothing.' This Roger is mentioned only here. Ostreham may be Westerham (14ra32); alternatively it may be Ouistreham in Normandy.

44–9) And finally this complaint from the men of Dover, presented in the exaggerated language which was normal in such a case. 'At the entrance of Dover harbour there is a mill which is breaking to pieces almost all the ships (that pass), by reason of the great disturbance of the sea (that it causes). It is doing very great harm to the king and the men (of Dover). It was not there TRE. Concerning this (mill), Herbert's nephew says that the bishop of Bayeux gave his uncle, Herbert son of Ivo, permission for it to be built.' B / xAug tells the story like this: 'Herbert son of Ivo built a mill at the entrance of the harbour, where ships are all being broken to pieces by reason of the disturbance of the sea currents. Hugo, Herbert's nephew, says that the bishop of Bayeux gave his uncle permission for this. The men of the town, for their part, say that it is causing harm to the king and to his men' (A4-22v8).

48) 'Herbert's nephew.' Proved by B / xAug to be the same person as Hugo nephew of Herbert.

The king's laws

1rb1–43) 'The king's laws (that are) listed below.' To be read in parallel with B / xAug (A4-24r17–5r5). This stretch of text is hard to get a grip on. As is obvious from the names in lines 19–21, the facts reported are the facts which obtained in the time of king Edward. But here we find them reported in the future tense: if somebody commits a certain offence, he *will* pay a fine to the king. (This is clearer still in the Latin, where the future perfect is used in an 'if' clause like this: 'if somebody *will* have committed such and such an offence'.) Though the jurors are drawing on their knowledge of the past, they are projecting this knowledge into the future. The question which has been put to them has been framed hypothetically. If the king were to decide that the laws of king Edward should be put back into effect (the implication being that they are not in effect at the moment), what would the consequences be? Not to mince words, what profit would the king stand to make?

The jurors' answer, as it was written down, is all the more difficult to understand because it is back to front. It begins with the abnormal cases; the normal cases are left to the end and covered by a single sentence. If we read it in reverse, it makes more sense. There is some range of offences – we are not told what they are – which incur a penalty of 100 shillings (1200 pence). In some circumstances the king will get this money; in others he will not. If the king's officers have apprehended the culprit on the spot – if they have challenged him ('I arrest you in the name of the king') and bailed him to appear in the king's court – the fine will go to the king; otherwise it will go to the lord whose man the culprit is. (It is casually assumed that everyone will have a lord.) Breach of the peace is one exception to the rule, but only because the fine for this offence is heavier, 8 pounds (1920 pence). A more important exception is the one explained to us first: encroachments on the king's highway incur the standard fine, but this money will go the king in every case. Even if the culprit has left the scene without being bailed, the king's officer will pursue him, all the way to his home if necessary, and demand the money from him.

If we imagine all the verbs put into the past tense, this can be read (with only the usual degree of caution) as an account of how things stood in the time of king Edward. It is manifestly *not* to be read as an account of how things stood at the time of the survey.

1–3) '(These laws) are agreed on by the men of four lests, that is, Borwar lest, Eastry lest, Limwar lest and Wiwar lest.' The meeting at which this question came up – a meeting convened by the second team of commissioners – was attended only by these four lests, and that fact had to be recorded. The eastern lests were answerable for the truth of the statements set down; the other three lests were not. But twice we are told explicitly that the statement being made applies to the whole county (lines 15, 30).

In this county, so it appears, the commissioners departed from the policy followed elsewhere by holding more than one meeting – one for the eastern lests, another (or perhaps two others) for the lests not represented here. There is a remark below which perhaps becomes significant in this context: the men of the eastern lests are not obliged to travel further west than Penenden for a meeting of the county court (line 40). What happened, I suspect, was this. Not wishing to travel further than necessary, the commissioners wrote to the sheriff ordering him to convene a meeting at some place which they had chosen in western Kent; the sheriff replied that he was doubtful whether he could enforce the attendance of people from the more distant parts of the county; and a change of plan ensued.

3–10) 'If anyone makes a fence or ditch by which the king's public road is made narrower, or (if anyone) fells into the road a tree standing outside the road and removes a branch or any foliage from it, for each of these offences he will pay the king one hundred shillings. Even if he has gone home without being arrested or put on bail, the king's officer will pursue him just the same, and the fine of one hundred shillings will be paid.' B / xAug has more details: 'If any man makes a fence or ditch by which the king's road is narrowed, or if he makes a hole in the roadway or sets a post, or if he fells a tree standing within the roadway, or if he fells a tree standing outside the roadway so as to let it fall inside and afterwards removes without permission a branch or any foliage or the tree itself, ... ' (A4-24r18).

10–13) 'Concerning breach of the peace: if anyone commits it and is charged with the offence or put on bail (while he is still) on the road, a fine of eight pounds will be payable to the king. If not (i.e. if he is not arrested on the spot), he will be quit towards the king, (but) not towards the lord whose man he is.'

13–14) 'Concerning other offences: the same as for breach of the peace, but a fine of one hundred shillings will be paid.' Here and in line 10, the word *emendare* seems to be used in a quasi-passive construction: not 'he (the culprit) will pay the fine', but 'one will pay the fine', meaning 'the fine will be paid'.

14–39) The verbs now shift into the present tense, but we are still being told what was true in the past.

14–16) 'The king has (the right to) these fines over all alodiers of the whole county of Kent, and over their men.' The word *alodiarius* occurs only twice in DB-Ke, here and two lines below; *alodia* or *alodium* turns up occasionally in the main text, always with reference to the time of king Edward. Comparing lines 16–17 with lines 23–4, we may infer that the French word *alodier* was thought apt for those thegns of king Edward's 'who had their sac and soc'. But these words would never gain much currency in England.

16–17) 'And (note that) when an alodier dies, the king gets the relief of the land.' This is to be read as a parenthetical remark, duplicating lines 23–4, not as the start of a new paragraph. As in B / xAug, the sense runs on from 'and over their men' (line 16) to 'except for the land of Holy Trinity' (line 18).

18–19) 'Except for the land of Holy Trinity, Saint Augustine's and Saint Martin's.' These churches have the right to any fines incurred by their men.

19–22) 'Also except for these people ... (a list of eight names). Over these the king has the right to the fine only from their own heads.' That is, only for offences which they have committed personally. These are alodiers of the highest status, distinguished as such by the fact that they get the fines for offences committed by their men. Godric's surname comes from Brabourne (13vb23), Siret's from Chilham (10ra25).

23–4) '(The king) gets the relief of the lands of those who have their sac and soc.' This is a separate sentence, beginning with a large ampersand. The French word *relief* meant the payment due from an heir before he could get possession.

24–30) 'And from these lands ... (a list of sixteen names) the king has the right to the fine for these offences: assault inside a man's home, breach of the (king's) peace, robbery on the (king's) highway.' A sudden descent into detail. The jurors have been asked a question which they cannot answer in general terms, only by running through a list of the places concerned. I take it that this passage, like lines 39–50, is an attempt to ascertain exactly which rights the king might be thought to have given away, when he gave Wye to the monks of Battle, and which he might be thought to have kept for himself.

The places which can be identified are all in Wiwarleth lest; except for the last one they are all in Faversham hundred. Buckland (10rb24, 10rb28, 10va1), Hurst (10rb31), Oare (10rb35), Harty TR 0266, not mentioned elsewhere in DB, Macknade (10rb8), Perry (10rb18, 10rb21), Throwley (10rb39), Ospringe (10ra34), and Horton (10va25) in Felborough hundred.

30–3) 'Concerning adultery: throughout the whole of Kent the king gets (the fine from) the man and the archbishop gets (the fine from) the woman, except for the land of Holy Trinity, Saint Augustine's and Saint Martin's, from which the king gets nothing.'

33–4) 'Concerning a thief who is condemned to death: the king gets half of his chattels.'

34–5) 'Anyone who takes an outlaw into his home without the king's permission: the king gets the fine for this offence.' DB uses the Latin word *exul*; B / xAug uses a latinized form of the English word, *uthlagus*. 'Concerning an outlaw: someone who is outlawed, anyone who takes him into his home without permission, ... ' (A4-24v19).

36–9) 'From the lands mentioned above, of Alnod Cild and those like him, the king gets guard duty for six days at Canterbury or at Sandwich, and they (the men performing this duty) get food and drink there from the king. If they do not get it, they go away without (incurring any) penalty.' A misplaced remark referring back to lines 19–22.

39–42) The future tense reasserts itself here.

39–41) 'If they (the men of these four lests) are summoned to a meeting of the shire, they will go as far as Penenden, not further. If they do not attend, (they will be fined one hundred shillings each).'

41–2) 'For this offence (failing to attend the shire court) and for all the others, the king will get one hundred shillings.' Referring back to lines 13–14.

42) 'Except for breach of the peace, for which the fine to be paid is eight pounds.' Referring back to lines 10–12.

43) '(Except also) concerning the roads, as is written above.' Referring back to lines 3–10.

1rb44–50) This is marked as a new paragraph, and seems clearly to represent a change of subject. The issue here is what customs the king may still be entitled to claim from lands belonging to the manor or hundred of Wye, even though the manor itself has been given to the abbey of Battle. It seems to be thought that he is still entitled to 'inward' (that word occurs only once elsewhere in DB-Ke, in connection with Milton) – either to the service itself, if he comes into Kent, or else to some payment in lieu of it (in cash or in kind, as the case may be). But the details are very obscure. None of the places named here can be identified.

48–50) 'These lands belong to Wye. The men of these lands used to guard the king at Canterbury or Sandwich for three days, if the king happened to come there.' The second sentence is emphatically in the past tense: this is the way things were, not the way they are. In B / xAug the passage continues: 'And if anyone had failed to stand guard, he would have had to pay a fine to the king of one hundred shillings' (A4-25r11). This is the reply to a hypothetical question put by the commissioners. In effect, the jurors are admitting that the king would be within his rights to demand a fine from each of these places, with respect to every occasion on which he had visited Canterbury or Sandwich during the last twenty years.

Alodiers in West Kent

1va1–7) 'In the lest of Sutton and the lest of Aylesford these people had sac and soc ... (followed by a list of fifteen TRE names).' Some of the proper names are spelt better in B / xAug (A4-25r12–17). Adelold took his surname from Eltham (6vb29), Anschil from Beckenham (7ra22), Azor from Lessness (6va16), Ordinc from Horton Kirby (6va6), Levenot from East Sutton (8ra15), Edward from Teston (8vb20), Osward (the sheriff) from Norton (10ra19), Alret from Yalding (14rb3). *Cillesfelle* must presumably be Chelsfield (6va39), though Esbern is not mentioned there; *Otrinberge* must presumably be Wateringbury (8vb9, 8vb15), though neither Ulestan nor Levric is mentioned there. 'Hazelholt' is a riddle which I am still not able to solve (below, p. 242). The existence of this list is proof that the commissioners had asked for it; but it is not so clear why the information was thought to be worth having. Apparently it was still an open question how far the new owners of these lands were entitled to the same sort of privileges enjoyed by their previous owners.

Canterbury

Having decided to use the rest of fo. 1v for a survey of the lands of Saint Martin's of Dover (see below), the DB scribe starts the next page with an account of the city of Canterbury (2ra2–48). B / xAug has a longer version of it (A4-18r22–19v6), including some passages entirely absent from DB. For guidance in making sense of this whole section, Urry's (1967) book cannot be too highly recommended.

2ra2–8) 'In the city of Canterbury king Edward had 51 townsmen paying gavel.... Now the townsmen paying gavel are 19 (in number). Of the other 32 that there used to be, 11 were destroyed in (the digging of) the city ditch, and the archbishop has 7 of them and the abbot of Saint Augustine's the other 14, by way of exchange for the castle.' The language is misleading: though DB seems to be counting heads, it is really counting tenements. In an urban context, gavel is a ground-rent; the obligation to pay it goes with the ownership of a particular piece of land. The king has lost 32 payments, 11 of them because the plots of land no longer exist (they vanished when the ditch was dug) and the others because the gavel is now being paid to someone else. Seven townsmen have been told to pay their gavel to the archbishop, fourteen to pay it to the abbot, in compensation for property lost when a site was requisitioned for the castle. From Saint Augustine's a memorandum survives of the payments of gavel acquired by the abbey for this reason (Urry 1967, p. 445). By the reckoning used there, the total was made up of eleven payments, mostly of 10 or 12 pence. In addition – DB does not tell us this – the king gave abbot Scotland two churches in the city, Saint Mary's 'in front of the castle' and Saint Andrew's.

According to B / xAug, the 51 townsmen used to pay a total of 929 pence of gavel (A4-18r23), of which the 32 who have now been lost used to pay 482 pence (19r11). (So the 19 who are left ought to be paying 447 pence between them.)

6) '... the city ditch.' B / xAug has 'the castle ditch' (A4-19r13), which seems to make better sense.

14–15) '(Altogether the city) is now reckoned to be worth 50 pounds, but at present the man in charge is paying 30 pounds refined and weighed and 24 pounds by count.' Though DB does not say this, we can be sure that the payments reported here were respectively the king's and the earl's. By 1156 both payments had been reduced, but they were still being accounted for separately. A sum of 29 pounds of 'white' pennies (which conventionally meant a surcharge of 5 per cent) was included in the farm of the county; a sum of 20 pounds (of pennies taken at face value) was included in 'the farm of the land of the bishop of Bayeux' – which, as this evidence helps to prove (Flight 1998, pp. 73–4), was the farm of the assets annexed to the earldom of Kent.

38) '... outside the city, as far as one league and three perches and three feet.' It appears from B / xAug (A4-19r3) that DB has run together two different dimensions: the first (one league) is a length, measured from the gate of the city; the second (three perches and three feet) is a breadth, measured from one or other side of the road. A league was 12 furlongs; a furlong (which the DB scribe calls a *quarentena*) was 40 perches. As I understand it, therefore, we are being told that the king's prerogative extends over a strip of land on either side of each of the main roads leading out of the city, to a distance of 480 perches from the city gate, and to a distance of 3 perches (plus a fraction) from the road.

How many feet made a perch is hard to say. In Romney Marsh, in the thirteenth century, the standard perch was 20 feet long (Dugdale 1662, p. 19); but the very fact that it seemed necessary to specify the length tends to prove that not all perches were the same. The width quoted in DB may perhaps have been converted from a measurement of three perches taken with a perch which was one foot longer than normal.

38–41) 'If anyone digs a hole or sets a post within the limits of these public roads, inside or outside the city, the king's reeve (is to) follow him wherever he goes and take the fine on the king's behalf.' Very similar to the statement already reported for the county at large (1rb3–10). Here too, though *sequitur* is present (for consistency it ought to be *sequetur*), the other verbs are all in the future tense. (For DB's *palum fixerit*, B has *sudem miserit*, 'puts a stake'.)

45) '... before archbishop Lanfranc and the bishop of Bayeux.' B / xAug / A4 omits the first name (probably by accident) and adds three more names at the end: Hugo de Montfort, the count of Eu, and Ricard son of Gislebert (18v9).

Rochester

The city of Rochester is disposed of in two lines. Except for the most basic information (how much is it worth?), we are told nothing about it. The reason for that is simple: the city belonged entirely to the earl of Kent. With the earl in prison, the revenue due to him had defaulted to the king; but otherwise the king had no interest in the place.

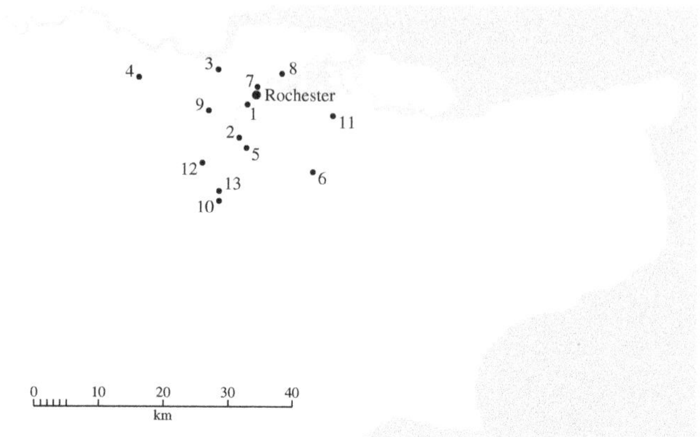

1 Borstal	6 Elnothington	10 Nettlestead
2 Burham	7 Frindsbury	11 Newington
3 Chalk	8 Hoo	12 Offham
4 Darenth	9 Luddesdown	13 Wateringbury
5 Eccles		

Figure 14. Manors owning plots of land in the city of Rochester.

In the main text of DB-Ke, a dozen paragraphs mention the fact that some plots of land in Rochester were counted as assets of the manor in question (or had been so counted, until the bishop of Bayeux cut the connection). A joint total of 80 such plots is reported for the two closest manors, Frindsbury and Borstal (5vb24); otherwise the numbers are small. I do not know that there is much to be learned from this map, or from the similar map which might be drawn for Canterbury. (One place would appear on both maps, namely Newington (14va10).) But perhaps it gives a vague idea of the distance over which a small urban centre like Rochester could exert some attraction.

2ra49) 'When he (the bishop) got possession.' Meaning the bishop of Bayeux. That is how the passage was interpreted by Hasted and Larking – more recently also by Eales (1992, p. 31) – and that is how it ought to be interpreted. There are many things that I would cheerfully admit to feeling doubtful about, but I have no doubt about this. From the twelfth-century exchequer rolls, it can be proved that 'the farm of the city of Rochester' was one of the components included in 'the farm of the land of the bishop of Bayeux' (Flight 1998, pp. 78–81). The bishop got possession of Rochester for the same reason that he got possession of Hoo (8va28) and Boxley (8vb34) – because he was earl of Kent.

Saint Martin's of Dover

The church of Saint Martin in Dover was an ancient minster – how ancient we do not know. Beda does not mention its existence. The story that we hear, very much later, is that the church was founded by king Wictred (who died in 725), on a site that had been chosen by Saint Martin himself; there may be some truth in that. Almost nothing is known about the history of the church – except for the appearance which it makes in the records of the survey – up until the moment when the church itself and all its possessions were given by Henric I to archbishop Willelm (Johnson and Cronne 1956, no. 1736). (The gift was made to commemorate the dededication of Christ Church in May 1130, but the charter was not issued till April 1132.) The archbishop began building a new

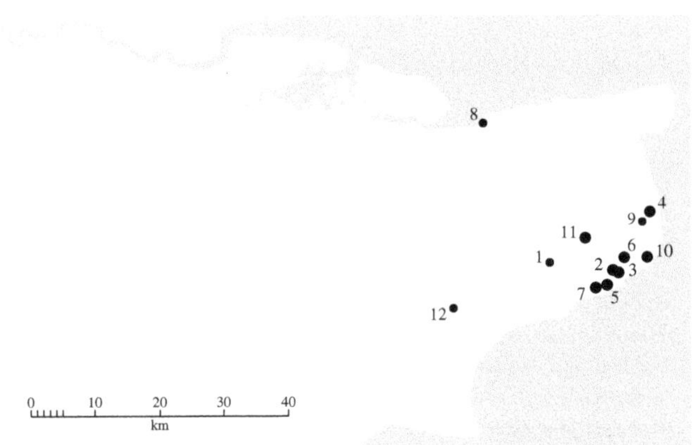

Figure 15. Lands of the church of Saint Martin of Dover.

church, outside the town to the north-west, planning to establish in it a community of regular canons; but he died in 1136 without completing the project.

Three years later, in defiance of his known intentions, a detachment of monks from Christ Church was put in possession of this new church: they formed what came to be called the priory of Saint Martin. The priests who owned shares of the old church were not ousted immediately (as is proved by a document in BL Cotton Claud. D. x, fo. 273v); but they were, by one means or another, made to disappear during the 1140s. (A charter of archbishop Theobald, not later than 1148, speaks of them in the past tense (Saltman 1956, no. 86).) The whole endowment of the old minster, with the church itself, thus passed into the hands of the monks.

As things stood in 1086, the establishment was old, but the building which housed it was not. Though most of the fabric of the church was torn down in the sixteenth century, enough remained of the eastern limb for its design to be worked out and recorded in the 1840s (Plumptre 1861); and the nave was excavated, almost completely, in the 1970s (Philp 2003). The church turns out to have been a large romanesque building, striking similar in plan to the new church built at Saint Augustine's by abbot Scotland, though with a shorter nave. In light of the written evidence, there seems to be no doubt what this means: the church was entirely rebuilt by bishop Odo, after he became its proprietor (less bluntly, its 'patron' or 'advocate'). Presumably that happened quite soon after 1066; and the possibility thus exists that it was Odo – not archbishop Lanfranc, not abbot Scotland – who set the pattern of total demolition and total reconstruction to which other post-conquest bishops and abbots felt obliged to conform.

From later evidence, we discover that there were in fact three churches here, joined together to make a single structure, but otherwise independent from one another. Each of them had its own parish. As well as the church of Saint Martin, which occupied the centre of the building, there were the churches of Saint Nicholas and Saint John the Baptist, which each occupied one of the transepts (*in duabus alis eiusdem ecclesie*, Reg. Winchelsey, ed. Graham 1917–56, p. 888). The priest who served Saint Martin's church had the high-sounding title 'archpriest', but in fact he was just a curate, appointed and paid a stipend by the monks. The other two priests were of higher standing than him; they had to be formally presented by the prior and convent (who owned the patronage of both churches) and formally instituted by the archbishop, in the same way as the rectors of other parish churches. There is explicit evidence for all this from the fourteenth century onwards (Robertson 1893); allusions to the same arrangement can be found in some earlier documents, dating from the early thirteenth (Major 1950, no. 106) and from the late twelfth century (*ueterem ... ecclesiam beati Martini, cum parochiis ... ad ipsam ... pertinenti[bu]s*, Cheney and Jones 1986, no. 125).

Despite its antiquity, despite its location in the centre of a major port, Saint Martin's of Dover seems never to have achieved any special prominence. There was no resident saint, no tomb which might have been thought worth noting in any guidebook for pilgrims. A church of this significance must certainly have had an archive – but not a single document survives. Evidently the monks who arrived on the scene in 1139 did not get possession of the old church's archive. Its loss is the chief reason why the history of Dover – not just the church but also the town – is so thoroughly obscure. But at least it is clear, from the records of the survey, that the minster was in a flourishing condition in the time of king Edward; and that, in itself, is a rather remarkable fact.

Though some encroachments are complained of (2rb40–8), the church's possessions remained largely intact. In the time of king Edward, there were reckoned to be 24 sulungs on which the canons owed geld. (They also possessed some land on which no geld was payable.) Most of their geldable land (21 sulungs) was located in Eastry lest, in Cornilo and Bewsborough hundreds, much of it quite close to Dover; the rest (3 sulungs) was in Limwarleth lest, further away to the west. Apart from their land, the canons had been granted two valuable privileges. They were entitled to a half share of the toll paid by people passing through the port (1ra7–8); and they were also entitled to a one-third share of the toll of the weekly market (2rb21). After 1139, all of these assets came into the hands of the monks of Dover.

Out of this endowment, until the 1130s, the church supported a corporation of secular canons, 22 of them or some such number, each of whom owned a share of the church's profits, which in B and DB is called a prebend. Before 1066, the property was owned and administered communally (1va16), and a prebend consisted (so it seems) of a dividend paid in cash. Since then, however, the bishop of Bayeux had changed things: each prebend now consisted of a portion of the church's land, the proceeds from which were paid directly to the canon who owned it. One prebend was in the archbishop's gift; one was at the disposal of the abbot of Saint Augustine's. But these were just courtesy arrangements: it was the bishop of Bayeux who (until he was imprisoned) controlled the church's affairs.

Twenty years on from 1066, the church's personnel had changed considerably, as one would expect; but there was, even so, a fair measure of continuity (Table 17). In three cases the man owning a prebend has owned it since before 1066; in four cases the man who owns it in 1086 is the son – in a fifth case the brother – of the man who owned it before 1066. Evidently it had been a normal thing, in the time of king Edward, for priests to be married men; for as long as that remained true, there was naturally some tendency for prebends to become hereditary. On the other hand, a majority of the canons are newcomers, to judge from their names; and among them is the man who appears at the top of the list, presumably the head of the community. There has been no purge; but prebends falling vacant have, more often than not, been given to foreign priests. Four of the canons, all with emphatically Norman names (three Willelms, one Robert), can be said for certain to be clients of the bishop of Bayeux, because their names appear in a list of his men owning houses in the town (1ra31–3). During the last few years, however, because the bishop was in prison, the king would have been within his rights to make an appointment, if any vacancy occurred; and perhaps that may have happened.

After 1088, when the bishop of Bayeux lost all his English possessions, the minster lapsed to the king, Willelm II; sooner or later, the king gave it to Rannulf Flambard. (That is, he gave as much as was his to give, the patronage of the church – the right to appoint a new canon, when one of the prebends fell vacant; the right to enjoy the income from this prebend, for as long as the vacancy might happen to last.) Rannulf retained the patronage after his own promotion to the bishopric of Durham (in May 1099); and copies of two writs of Henric I relating to Saint Martin's survive accidentally at Durham for that reason (Craster 1930, pp. 47, 50–1, Johnson and Cronne 1956, nos. 562, 570). (The reader should be warned that this evidence has sometimes been wilfully misinterpreted.) It was Rannulf's death, in September 1128, which made it possible for archbishop Willelm to put in his bid for the patronage of Saint Martin's.

In 1086, when the survey was conducted, it took two attempts to make sense of Saint Martin's possessions. Because the monks of Saint Augustine's had an interest in these matters, we are lucky enough to possess a version of the text as it appeared in B-Ke, where the description of all of these lands was included under Bewsborough hundred (perhaps with cross-references elsewhere). The report produced at this first attempt was rejected, probably because the numbers did not add up. It seems that one of the prebends had been overlooked (1vb44); with or without it, the number of sulungs listed here was well short of the total of 24 which had to be accounted for. So a further attempt was made, and this produced two things: a corrected version of the report which had appeared in B, and a new report which began by explaining why four sulungs were missing from the original report. These two reports would have been copied into D-Ke, probably at the back of it; the DB scribe preferred to put them at the front, with the other introductory matter, arranging them on the page in such a way as to distinguish them from the main blocks of text. In a word, they look like two overgrown footnotes.

1va11–15) 'In the lest of Eastry the canons of Saint Martin's in the time of king Edward owned 21 sulungs, in Cornilo hundred and in Bewsborough hundred. In the lest of Limwarleth they owned three sulungs, one in Street hundred, the second in Bircholt hundred and the third in Blackbourne hundred.' The sulungs in Eastry lest are mostly accounted for by the following list (1va19–b43). Of the places mentioned by name, Charlton TR 3142, Buckland TR 3042, Guston TR 3244, St Margaret at Cliffe TR 3544, Sibertswold TR 2647, Farthingloe TR 2940 in Hougham, and Hougham TR 2739 were all in Bewsborough hundred; only Deal TR 3651 was in Cornilo hundred. The three sulungs in Limwarleth lest are not dealt with till later (2rb5–13).

16–17) 'In the time of king Edward the prebends were common property; they paid 61 pounds altogether. Now they are shared out individually, through (the agency of) the bishop of Bayeux.' In B / xAug this reads: 'and when the bishop of Bayeux arrived, he divided the prebends among the canons of the church, as it seemed good to him' (A4-22v21–2).

1va18–b43) A list of the separate prebends created by bishop Odo. Comparing this with the parallel stretch of text in B-Ke, as that is represented by xAug, we can see that the DB scribe was doing what he usually did – reorganizing the data and using his own form of words. For example, in B / xAug the TRE value comes first, *et ualebat tunc x sol' et modo xx sol'*, but in DB the order is reversed (except in the added paragraph at the end), *Val' xx sol', TRE: x sol'*. In the first paragraph the scribe was experimenting. He tried starting the entry like this: 'R— holds a manor as a prebend, it is called C—, and it defends itself for one sulung.' But then he decided to cut things short, and in subsequent paragraphs the wording becomes: 'In C— holds R— one sulung.'

In each paragraph the scribe has put the TRE owner at the end, in a sentence which takes this shape: 'L— held (it) as a prebend.' But that is to misrepresent the situation. L— did not own this sulung: he owned the prebend to which R— has now succeeded, the prebend to which this particular sulung has now been allocated.

It is true, more often than not, that a prebend comprises one sulung of land; but there are many exceptions to the rule. If we take the numbers as we find them in DB, counting 200 acres to the sulung (2rb31) and excluding the added paragraph (1vb44), the total comes to 3697.5 acres, 18.4875 sulungs. There are two adjustments which we may wish to think of making. If we deduct 10 acres from one entry (1vb5) and count three yokes instead of three rods in another (1vb21), we can make the total come to 3800 acres, 19 sulungs exactly; and probably that is the number which we ought to be aiming for. Adding one sulung which seems to have been overlooked at first (1vb44) and one sulung still held in common (2rb2), we get a total of 21 sulungs in Eastry lest, the number initially reported (1va12).

22) 'Lewin held (it) as a prebend.' The name is *Lifwynus* in B / xAug (A4-23r1). To be identified, no doubt, with the man who appears at the head of the Dover community witnessing a charter of archbishop Eadsige, *Leofwine preost and eall se hired on Doferan* (Robertson 1956, no. 108).

1vb5) '... and 25 acres in addition.' We may wish to think of emending 25 to 15, which would reduce the total to exactly one sulung. But the error, if it was one, existed already in the B text (xAug / A4-23v5).

17) 'Willelm the Poitevin.' Not to be identified with the author Willelm of Poitiers (ed. Davis and Chibnall 1998), who would be referred to by his title, archdeacon of Lisieux. (Besides, he tells us himself that he was not particularly well acquainted with bishop Odo; and a passage in which he has occasion to speak about Dover he confuses the town and the castle.)

21) '... three rods.' B / xAug has 'three yokes' (A4-23v16). In abbreviated form, *uirg'* and *iug'*, the words are easily confused. The same discrepancy occurs once elsewhere (12vb13), and in that instance it can be be proved that DB's reading is the right one. But a prebend consisting of only three rods seems disproportionately small; and the reported value (720 pence) is the same as that of some whole sulungs. So DB seems sure to be wrong here.

23–4) 'In Bewsborough hundred and in Cornilo hundred ... the abbot of Saint Augustine's holds one sulung.' The land in Bewsborough hundred was part of Guston, as we can discover from B / xAug (A4-23v19); in DB this name has dropped out.

44) 'In Sibertesuuald Ulstan son of Ulwin holds one sulung.' This is an added entry, marked for insertion at line 21. By and large it follows the same template that the scribe had used for the preceding entries, but it diverges in two respects: it omits the phrase *in d'nio*, and it treats the value clause differently (instead of *Val' lx sol', TRE: c sol'*, we get *TRE ualb' c sol', modo lx sol'*.) Since this paragraph is missing from B / xAug, it seems likely that the entry originated later than the rest, i.e. not until the further inquiry was made from which the second block of text resulted.

	who owns it now?	who owned it TRE?	acres	
1va19	Radulf de Sancto Sansone	Levwin	200	
23	Willelm son of Oger	Sired	200	
28	Alwi	himself	200	
31	Ulric	Elric	50 + 25 = 75	
35	Sired	his father	200	
39	Radulf	Alric	200	
42	Alred	his father	200	
45	Robert Niger	Esmelt king Edward's chaplain	200	
48	Walter (de Cambremer)	S(with)gar	200	
1vb1	Robert Turbatus	(Swithgar and) Goldstan	100 + 100 = 200	
5	Edwin	himself	100 + 25 + 85 = 210	? 200
11	archdeacon Anschitil	archbishop Stigand	200 + 50 + 50 = 300	
17	Willelm the Poitevin	—	112 + 88 = 200	
21	Adelold	himself	37.5	? 150
24	abbot of St Augustine's	his predecessor	200	
27	Willelm son of Tedald	Derinc son of Sired	125	
30	Sigar	his father	75	
33	Nigel the doctor	Spirites	75	
36	Willelm son of Gaufrid	Sired	200	
39	Baldwin	Edwin (his brother)	200	
41	Godric (latimarius)	(Oswin silvagius)	200	
44	Ulstan son of Ulwin	his father	200	

Table 17. The prebends of Saint Martin's of Dover, as described in DB-Ke. (Brackets distinguish a few details missing from DB which can be retrieved from B / xAug.)

More about Saint Martin's

The stretch of text which I have kept till last (2rb1–48) is the stretch which I take to be the latest component of all. (There is nothing corresponding with it in B / xAug.) As I understand the evidence, the second team of commissioners refused to approve the description of Saint Martin's property, as it appeared in the B text. They notified the king accordingly. We might be willing to guess that much; but in fact we happen to know that this is what the commissioners were expected to do in such circumstances, because a contemporary witness, Robert bishop of Hereford, tells us precisely that (Stevenson 1907). Bishop Robert does not inform us what the sequel would be: we are invited to assume that something would happen, but have to guess what it might be. I take it that the king sent somebody to Dover – perhaps one of his officials, from his court or from his treasury – with orders to investigate the matter in detail and make sure that all the relevant facts were properly recorded. Whoever he was, there is nothing to suggest that this person consulted a jury: it seems that he confined himself to interrogating the canons.

His report begins well enough, by identifying the four sulungs which had previously been omitted; but then it degenerates into an incoherent collection of miscellaneous remarks. (In the form in which it survives – as a copy of a copy – some passages float free from any context in which they would make sense.) The original schedule would, I suppose, have been submitted to the treasury. To become part of the official record of the survey, it would have to be copied into D-Ke; and from there it was copied into DB-Ke. The copy in D was presumably (errors aside) an exact reproduction of the original, so far as the scribe could decipher it. The copy in DB may perhaps have differed from D to some extent, but I doubt whether the differences amounted to much. There is little scope here for the DB scribe to edit the text, substituting the formulas that he prefers for the formulas found in D. There are, on the other hand, numerous disjointed remarks which might easily have been omitted, if the scribe had been intending to shorten the text, but which in fact were not omitted.

One oddity distinguishing this stretch of text is the fact that the word for sulung appears in a Latin form. In the rest of DB-Ke, not excluding the description of the Dover prebends, the DB scribe treats it as a French word. But here the word is Latinized, inconsistently as neuter *solinum* or masculine *solinus*, and declined according to the context. This anomaly, I think, is the DB scribe's way of warning his readers that he is copying this stretch of text as he finds it, without trying to improve it. He is telling us, in other words, that he is conscious of its defects and is not accountable for them.

2rb2–5) 'Of the communal property of Saint Martin's three canons together have one sulung and sixteen acres.' Not identified, but presumably close to Dover. The third canon named here, Sewen, has not been mentioned before.

5–16) 'Concerning Limwarleth lest.' The next paragraphs supply details about the three sulungs in Limwarleth lest referred to in the previous report (1va13–15) but not covered by the description of the prebends – the reason being (as we now discover) that they, like the sulung just mentioned, are still held in common.

5–7) 'One sulung in Blackbourne hundred.' Not identified.

7–11) 'In Street hundred belongs one sulung of Stanetdeste. ... In Bircholt hundred (belongs) one sulung of Stanestede.' That is, the holding comprises two sulungs, one on either side of the hundred boundary. The property in question is what later became the manor of Poulton Stansted in Aldington: the identification was made by Larking (1869, p. 186, cf. Haines 1930, p. 455). The name Stansted seems to be lost, but Poulton TR 0536 appears on the first-edition six-inch map (to the north of Poulton Wood).

13) 'In Brensete a little piece of land.' Possibly part of Brenzett TR 0027, but that does not seem likely to me.

15–16) 'The canons of Saint Martin's have the four sulungs mentioned above as their communal property, both the woodland and the arable land.' Referring back to lines 2–13.

17–30) The next section consists of a collection of memoranda, in no particular order. The man who drew up this report was aiming to make a note of everything of any conceivable interest to the king; and this is the result.

* 17) 'The land (called) Nordeuuode.' Comprising 50 acres, as we are told below (2rb35). This is what became the manor of Norwood in Whitstable TR 1166: the identification was made by Larking (1869, p. 187, cf. Haines 1930, p. 455). The name Norwood continued appearing in leases of the priory lands as late as the eighteenth century (Haines 1930, p. 138), but seems to have dropped off the map.

* 17) '. . . and the land (called) Ripe.' Comprising 100 acres (2rb34). Part of Ripple TR 3550, from which 100 pence a year was payable to Saint Martin's (B / xAug / A4-24r2). This evidence seems convincing enough; but there is (as far as I am aware) no subsequent trace of any such payment from Ripple.

* 17) '. . . and the land (called) Brandet.' Comprising 100 acres (2rb35). Brandred (repr. Blandred Farm) TR 2043 in Acrise (Hasted 8:114-15). Identified by Larking (1869, p. 187).

21) 'The toll of Dover TRE was worth eight pounds; now it is worth twenty-two pounds.' By exclusion, this seems to refer to the toll of the Saturday market, one third of which belonged to the monks after 1139, and had presumably belonged to the canons before that.

22) 'Three churches at Dover pay thirty-six shillings and eight pence.' In the thirteenth century and later, there were three parish churches in Dover which paid a pension to the monks: Saint Mary's (20 shillings), Saint Peter's (11 shillings), and Saint James's (6 shillings). Since those payments add up to 37 shillings, almost the same as the sum reported in DB, it would be hard to resist the conclusion that those were the churches in question. (A possible reference to the pension from Saint Peter's occurs in the original report (1va25).) The existence of Saint Peter's and Saint Mary's is proved by their appearance in the list of parish churches belonging to Saint Martin's of Dover (below, p. 228); the existence of Saint James's (which was on the far side of the river) cannot be confirmed until about 1180, but from then onwards it is regularly mentioned together with the other two.

29) 'From this community the archbishop gets fifty-five shillings every year.' This payment appears in a list of 'the archbishop's Easter customs from priests and churches' (below, p. 229); until Lanfranc changed things, it had been paid partly in kind.

31-2) 'In the communal land of Saint Martin there are four hundred acres and a half which make two sulungs and a half.' This sentence has been much discussed and variously interpreted. I am inclined to cut the knot by assuming that the clause *quae f(ac)iunt duos solinos* was added in the margin of the original, and that the scribe who wrote it used a caret mark, both in the margin and in the body of the text, which looked something like '/^{d}'. (I am thinking of one analogy in particular – the notation used by scribe mu when he was making additions to a version of the Wiltshire geld account (Darlington 1955, opp. p. 181).) Hypothetically this caret mark was misread as '7 d' and miscopied as *et dimid'*, 'and a half'. On this view, we were (until someone made nonsense of it) simply being told that there are 200 acres in a sulung. If the ideal acre measured 4 by 40 perches, the ideal sulung would be a rectangle measuring 200 perches (5 furlongs) in one direction and 160 perches (4 furlongs) in the other.

32–3) 'This land (the four hundred acres just mentioned) has never paid anything by way of custom or tax, because the twenty-four sulungs answer for all these things.' In other words, the canons own two exempt sulungs, in addition to their 24 geldable sulungs.

37–9) 'All these things, if the canons owned them as it would be right (for them to own them), would be worth to them sixty pounds a year (14400 pence). At present they are only getting forty-seven pounds and six shillings and four pence (11356 pence).' An attempt to sum up the state of the canons' finances; but it is hard to see what these numbers mean. The items listed above (lines 2-28) add up to 11495 pence. Possibly some items were altered or inserted, after the total had been calculated.

40–4) Next a list of the encroachments from which the canons claim to have suffered since 1066.

46–8) And finally a note of a twenty-year-old grievance which the canons are hoping to bring to the king's attention.

Chapter 6
An epitome of DB-Ke

Of the documents copied into manuscript C1 by the original scribe (above, pp. 36–7), the one which he chose to put last is a long and tedious list (5vc–7ra) which aims to answer three questions. Who are the barons holding land from the king in Kent? Which manors does each of them own? And for how many sulungs is each of these manors assessed? Two other copies of the same text are known, later and less reliable than the one in C1, but (as I shall argue shortly) not derived from it. Like C1, they both originated in Canterbury.

This text has no title. I propose to call it ε (which, if the reader wishes, can be taken to be short for 'epitome'). At least in the version known to us, ε is manifestly a Canterbury text. That is clear, not just from the provenance of the surviving copies, but also from one negative fact: it excludes the lands of the archbishopric (the lands of the archbishop and his knights, the lands of the archbishop's monks, the lands of the bishop of Rochester). In some sense, therefore, it must be true that ε was complementary to a pre-existing Canterbury text which already contained the same sort of information for the archbishop's own lands. It was not desired to duplicate that information: what ε contains is what that other text did not contain.

Almost without exception, every item of information reported in ε can be matched with an entry in DB-Ke. Long stretches of text consist of nothing but statistical data – personal names, place-names, numbers of sulungs and yokes – of which it can only be said that they are mostly in factual agreement with DB; but here and there the text includes properly constructed clauses and sentences which provide an adequate basis for textual comparison. The very first paragraph (5vc38–45) will tell us where we stand:

Rex tenet derteford. Hoc manerium se defendit pro i sull' et dim'. De ipso manerio ablata est hageli, quę se defendit pro dim' sull'. Hanc terram tenet hugo de port, et liiii agris terrę.

When this is collated with the corresponding paragraphs in DB-Ke (2va3-30), it becomes clear at once that there is some textual relationship existing between ε and DB. The wording of one text is influenced by that of the other. Given that, there are only two possible explanations: either ε (or some form of ε) existed first, and DB was expanded from it; or else DB existed first, and ε was contracted from it. Though several historians have managed to persuade themselves otherwise, this second explanation is obviously the right one.[1] The evidence will be discussed in more detail below, but it will do no harm to state the conclusion now. There are some extraneous elements, which help to give this text such slight interest as it possesses. In bulk, however, ε is derived from DB-Ke.

The copy of ε in C1 is typical of this scribe's work (above, p. 36). It looks as if it was written very slowly and very carefully. There are a few of his pig-headed readings (such as 6vb1 *Fremgaham* with *m* for *ni*, 6vc8 *Bernuelinges* with *nu* for *m*), and several heavy-handed corrections which look as if they may have been reproduced from the exemplar. (Not counting slips of the pen, only one correction is definitely not inherited: at 6va33 the scribe miscopied *ii* as *iii*; but then he (or somebody) noticed the mistake and put it right by erasing the third minim.) One unsatisfactory feature of this copy, also quite possibly derived from the exemplar, is its inconsistent format. The scribe begins by starting a new paragraph for each section of the text, a new line for each item of information; but he soon abandons that plan. Most of the text is written out in a more or less continuous stream, and readers are left to navigate through it by themselves. Here and there, the scribe leaves a blank line or inserts a coloured initial, as if to mark the beginning of a new section; but these divisions seem to be quite arbitrary, more distracting than helpful.

As for the other two copies, these are they:

C5 = Canterbury, Dean and Chapter, Reg. P, fos. 29v–33r (early thirteenth century), badly damaged around the edges

T1 = London, Lambeth Palace Library 1212, fos. 170r–172r (late thirteenth century).

[1] As far as I know, the first hint that ε might not derive from DB occurs in a paper by Douglas (1936, p. 254). (At that time the text was still unpublished, except in Neilson's (1932b) translation, but Douglas was already acquainted with the manuscript.) He changed his mind later on (Douglas 1944, p. 27), but the hint was pursued by others (Sawyer 1955, Hoyt 1962, Kreisler 1967, Harvey 1971, 1975), with dire results. The crux of the argument is supposed to be this. In DB we are told that Upper Delce belongs to Willelm Tahum's son (8va10); in ε we are told that it belongs to Willelm Tahum (6vb37); therefore ε is earlier than DB. It is hard to know what to say about an argument as fatuous as this. Perhaps one might start by asking for an answer to this question: What was the name of Willelm Tahum's son? Unless we can be sure that his name was not Willelm, we cannot be sure that 'the son of Willelm Tahum' and 'Willelm Tahum' were not the same person. (In 1242 'the heir of Willelm de Swantone' held half a knight's fee in Swanton; in 1253 'Willelm de Swantone' held the same half fee; are we supposed to infer from this that time had been running backwards?)

(C1)	A1	C5	T1			
	201v	28v	166v	88	Johnson and Cronne 1956, no. 756	(1)
	201v	28v–9r	170r	89	Brett and Gribbin 2004, no. 16	
		29r–v	170r	90	*De Derenta, ii sull'* ...	(2)
		29v–33r	170r–2r	91	ε (first copy)	
			172r–v	92	schedule of monks' farms	
(1ra–vb)			172v–3r	93–6	lists of churches	(3)
(1vc)			173r	97	list of Romescot payments	
(2rb–c)			173r–v	98	epitome of α	
(2va–5rc)			173v–6v	99	α	(4)
(5va)			176v	100	excerpts from DB-Ke	
(5va–c)			176v–7r	101	schedule of archbishop's farms	
(5vc–7ra)				102	ε (second copy)	(5)
(7rb–c)			177r	103	list of archbishop's knights	

Table 18. Additions made at the end of the lost cartulary, C3, as represented in the three surviving copies, A1, C5 and T1. Notes: (1) Items 88–9 are the last two paragraphs in Fleming's (1997) edition of C3 / C5. The numbering of the items is hers for these two, mine from item 90 onwards. (2) This is the list printed from T1 by Hoyt (1962); I have commented on it already (above, pp. 92–4). (3) Printed from C1 below (chapter 8). (4) Printed from C1 above (chapter 2). (5) Attested only by the corrections added to T1's copy of item 91.

In both manuscripts, ε forms one component of a very much larger text – a twelfth-century cartulary compiled from an assortment of documents preserved in the Christ Church archive (Appendix I). More precisely, it is one of a succession of documents which look as if they were added at the end of the cartulary, on various occasions (Table 18). As far as we can judge, ε was not included in the original compilation, and hence does not occur in the earliest surviving copy of C3, a twelfth-century manuscript from Saint Augustine's (A1): it was added to the cartulary later, perhaps not until the early thirteenth century, and hence occurs only in the two more recent copies (C5 and T1).

As soon as one starts collating C5 and T1 with C1 and DB, it becomes obvious that C3's copy of ε was a rather inaccurate copy. Since its errors are of no interest, all I have done is to tabulate some sample variants which tend to prove the point (Table 19).[2] These variants are not all equally convincing; some of them, taken one by one, would not be convincing at all. But taken together they amount to proof that there were numerous errors occurring in C3 (and therefore in C5 and T1) which do not occur in C1. In C3's defence, however, it ought to be said that all the errors are small ones; there are no large mistakes.

These questions are of slight importance. They would hardly be worth discussing if there did not also exist a small class of variants tending to prove that C3 was not copied from C1. In two places at least, C3 has a better reading. (1) At 6ra45, where C1 has *pro i sull'*, C3 has *pro i iugo* – and it is C3 which agrees with DB (12rb47). Furthermore, the subtotal given at 6ra50 will not work out correctly unless we read *iugo* here. The indications are, therefore, that *sull'* was an error originating in C1. (2) In this same subtotal, where C1 has *et iiii uirg'*, C3 has *et iii uirg'* – and again it is C3 which is right. The only rods that enter into this total are the *iii uirgę terrę* in Eastry hundred listed at 6ra41, and that numeral is given as *iii* by C1, as well as by C3 and DB. Again the signs are that *iiii* was an error originating in C1. These are the only straightforward instances; there are some smaller details (in the spelling of place-names, for example) which might be thought to point in the same direction, but I would not think of relying far on them.

We are trying to identify errors in what is generally a very good copy with the help of what was generally a rather bad copy; so it is not surprising that the results we get are meagre. Even so, I think that they suffice to prove the point – that C3 was not copied from C1. Given that, given that the converse is also (quite certainly) true, we are entitled to infer the existence of a lost copy, say ε′, from which C1 and C3 both derive (Fig. 16). From ε′ the text was copied into C1, with very few errors (only two that we can detect); and later it was copied into C3, with many small errors but no large ones. From C3 it was eventually copied twice again, into C5 and later into T1.

Reconstructing the text of ε′ means choosing between C1 and C3 / C5T1, wherever they disagree. In principle C1 and C3 are of equal value; in practice they are not. C1 is an early copy, surviving just as it was written; C3 is a relatively late copy, demonstrably not a very good one, surviving only in proxy form as two even later copies (one of which is damaged and partially illegible). On points of substance we can usually decide between C1 and C3 by referring to

[2] In making this selection I insist on C5 being legible, and on C5 and T1 agreeing more or less exactly, so that C3's reading is definitely known. I also require there to be a parallel passage in DB, so that we have some basis for deciding, from the textual evidence alone, whether C1 or C3 is right.

	C1	C3 / C5T1	DB-Ke
6ra14	i sull' et i iug'	i sull'	unum solin et unum iug'
18	Waruuintune	Garwintune	Waruuintone
30	ii sull' et dim'	ii sull'	duobus solins et dimid'
6rc1	Macheuet	Machefeld	Macheheuet
2	i iug'	i sull'	uno iugo
32	Fredenestede	Frede	Fredenestede
45	Piuentune	Pinnenentune	Piuentone
6va16	dim' iug' minus	i iug' minus	dimidio iugo minus
38	ii sull' et dim' et dim' iug'	ii sull' et dim' iug'	ii solins et dimidio et dim' iugo
46	iii iug'	iiii iug'	iii iugis
51	Hastingeleg	Astingeleg	Hastingelai
6vb5	vi sull'	v sull'	vi solins
34	Hertange	Bertange	Hertange
39	Hou	Honwe	Hou
52	lx et iii	xlxiii	lxiii
6vc24	tenuit	tenet	tenuit
25	Azorrot	Azor	Azor Rot
34	Bertrannus	Bretrammus	Bertrannus
43	Radulfus filius Ricardi	Radulfus	Radulfus filius Ricardi
7ra2	hundred de cert	hundrede cert	hund' de Certh

Table 19. Selected variants resulting from errors in C3 / C5T1.

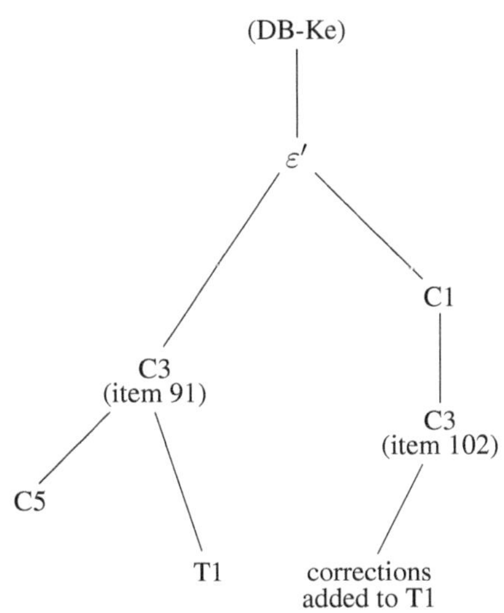

Figure 16. Stemma for the epitome of DB-Ke.

the parallel passage in DB (or by some other criterion); and almost always, as we have seen, the verdict is in favour of C1. But there are many points of detail which cannot be decided.[3]

There is one final complication, but we need not spend much time on it. Some time after C3 was copied into C5, somebody copied the whole of C1 into C3 (except perhaps for the batch of late twelfth-century documents at the end). By the late thirteenth century, C3 had thus come to contain two copies of ε. As I list the contents in Table 18, these copies are item 91 (copied into C3 directly from ε') and item 102 (copied into C3 together with the rest of C1). When the main scribe of T1 (the man who did most of the work) made his copy of C3, he transcribed the first item automatically; but then, when he came to item 102, he recognized it as a repeat of item 91 and declined to transcribe it again. If that had been the end of the story, we should not have been sure that the second copy existed. (In other words, we should not have been able to say which scribe omitted ε: the scribe who copied C1 into C3, or the scribe who copied C3 into T1.) But there is a coda which proves the point for us: a second scribe (the man who supplied the finishing touches to T1) went to the trouble of collating the two copies, and some readings taken from item 102 were added by him to his colleague's copy of item 91.[4] Because they were derived, at second hand, from a manuscript which happens to survive, these added readings have no textual value; from our point of view, they tend only to confuse the issue.

Apart from abbreviation, the creation of ε involved extensive reorganization. For that reason, I think, the man who created it deserved to be called its author. To construct a paragraph like this one:

Hugo de port t'n' Hageleg pro dim' sull', Eisce iii sull', Dideleg et Somniges pro dim' sull', Pellesword pro dim' sull', Resce pro ii sull' et dimid', Offeham pro i sull', Aln-

[3] For instance, it happens more than twenty times that C3 has the preposition *pro* – as in *Haslo pro vi sull'* – and C1 does not have it. Each time we are left in doubt whether *pro* was added by C3 or omitted by C1.

[4] Kreisler (1967) was first to see that some of the corrections in T1 were taken from an C1-like copy of the same text. At 6ra45, this second scribe replaced the reading *iugo* derived from C3 (which is right) with the reading *sull'* derived from C1 (which is wrong). So the copy being used to check the text was C1-like in the specific sense that it shared this error of C1's.

odentune pro iii sull', Tunestele pro iii sull' et dim', Cert pro ii sull', Tanges pro ii sull', Stependune pro i sull' dim' iug' minus, Nordtune pro iiii sull', Herst pro ii iug', Pesinges et Piham pro ii sull', Eawelle pro iii sull', Westcliue pro ii sull', Soltune pro i sull' (6va8–20),

what the author had to do was to scan through the relevant chapter of DB-Ke (i.e. chapter 5) looking for an entry which starts with an 'H'.[5] (The DB scribe had made the initials conspicuous, precisely for the purpose of aiding in a search of this kind.) If this 'H' was a Hugo, and if this Hugo was the right Hugo, he extracted the data he needed from this entry – the place-name and the number of sulungs. Then he checked to see whether the next entry began with an 'I', for *Isdem Hugo*. If it did, he dealt with that entry in the same way; if it did not, he resumed his scan in search of the next 'H'. In this paragraph, the order of the items agrees with the order of the corresponding entries in DB; but that is not always the case.[6] The author, it seems, was unconcerned whether he preserved the DB sequence or not. If he found it convenient to keep the order, he kept it; if he did not, he had no qualms about changing it.

As anyone who tries repeating the experiment will find, this is a wearisome task, easy enough to describe, but hard to execute without making mistakes. Nevertheless, very few of DB's entries fail to reappear in ε. Some of the omissions are surprising. The important manor of Ospringe, for example, is prominently present in DB (10ra34), but absent from ε. (We would expect to find it at 6vb12–18.) It is not to be assumed that all of ε's omissions are simple blunders; as with some of the manors which are surprisingly absent from DB (such as Teynham and Newington), there may have been some temporary doubt regarding the status of Ospringe which caused the author to hesitate. But mistakes may have been made, by the author or by subsequent copyists. With a highly repetitive text like this, it is very easy to lose one's place, skipping from one entry to the next.

As well as some risk of an entry being omitted, there was also some risk of an entry being duplicated – listed somewhere, and then, by error, listed again somewhere else. Three definite instances of duplication occur. (1) An entry in DB reports that the abbot of St Augustine's holds a manor called *Esmerefel* in Wye hundred, and that a man named Ansketil holds this manor from the abbot (12rb34). In ε we find a matching entry in the place where we expect to find it, among the lands of the abbey (6ra43); but we also find this place listed among the lands of Anschitil de Ros (6rb50). A comment is attached to the latter entry pointing out that this item has been listed twice.[7] (2) DB has an entry for a nameless manor in Eastry hundred held from the bishop of Bayeux by a man named Osbern (11vb1). This manor is listed twice in ε, both among the lands of Osbern Paisforere (6rc16) and among the lands of Osbern son of Letard (6va30). Because DB supplied no place-name, ε's author thought it necessary to include some descriptive phrase, and in both places the phrase that is used is in verbal agreement with DB: 'holds a manor from the bishop'. (3) Among the lands of Folbert (de Dovre), one of the items listed in ε is *Dudeham pro i sull'* (6vb7). That comes from DB, where the name is spelt *Dodeham* (10va15). Without doubt, the place in question is Luddenham, and the 'D' is a scribal error. But ε has another entry for Luddenham, and here the name is spelt correctly, *Ludenham pro i sull'* (6vb6). It seems that somebody checked through this paragraph, expecting to find an entry for Luddenham, failed to recognize the *Dodeham* entry as the one which he was looking for, and decided to supply the item that he thought was missing.

These instances of duplication are all instructive – the third especially so, because it proves that somebody working on this text had access to another source of information, and used that source, once at least, for correcting an error that he thought he had found in ε. For us, that introduces some doubt. Where ε and DB disagree on some point of fact, by and large we are going to assume that ε has fallen into error; but there is a chance that ε may have been deliberately corrected, by someone who knew (or thought he knew) that the facts were misreported by DB. It appears, furthermore, that some guesswork went into the making of ε; and the author has the advantage of us here. We cannot tell that he is guessing – rather than reporting what he knows to be true – so long as his guesses are right; and even if he guesses wrongly, we will not be able to catch him at it unless he contradicts himself, or unless he is contradicted by other evidence.

Despite these ambiguities, it is clear that there are some particles of information occurring in ε which do not derive from DB. Apart from the *Ludenham* entry, there are two entries in ε which would be expected to correspond, but do not correspond, with whole paragraphs in DB: among the lands of Adam son of Hubert, *Eluentune pro i sull'* (6rb33); among the lands of Osbern Paisforere, *In hertege i iug' et dim'* (6rc18).[8] Other details supplied by ε include an assessment missing from DB (6vb26) and a name for a manor which is nameless in DB (6vb51). Finally, a

[5] The entries in DB which went to make up this paragraph in ε can be found at 6ra3, 6ra36, 7rb41, 7vb48, 9rb1, 10ra19, 10rb31, 10vb33, 11ra26. The last batch of entries (beginning with *Eawelle*) is included here by error: the Hugo who owned these places was Hugo nephew of Herbert, not Hugo de Port.

[6] For example, in the paragraph listing the lands of Radulf de Curbespine (6rc38-52) the items correspond with entries in DB at 11vb10, 7va40, 11vb15, 9vb32, 9vb15, 7va33, 8rb38, 10va45, 10vb9, 11ra49, 8rb44, 11rb11, 11va40, 11va48, 9vb18. There is some doubt about the last item, which again I take to have been included by error: the yoke mentioned in DB belonged to a different 'R' – Rannulf de Columbels, not Radulf de Curbespine.

[7] But that did not prevent it from being counted twice, by whoever added up the numbers (see below).

[8] The second item was regarded by Hoyt (1962, p. 194) as a garbled version (duplicating 6vb34) of an entry in DB (11rb51), but that seems very unlikely; I do not see how the first item could be explained away (assuming that one wished to do so).

few items which do derive from DB are listed under headings where nothing in DB would justify them being listed. Sometimes we can be sure that ε is wrong; sometimes we cannot decide; but in one instance at least we can be sure that ε is right. The manor of Boxley, in DB, is reported to be temporarily in the possession of Robert Latiner (8vb34). In ε, however, as Hoyt (1962, p. 196) pointed out, it is listed among the domain manors of the bishop of Bayeux (6rb51). That has to be correct, because Boxley was one of the manors held by the bishop in right of the earldom of Kent (Flight 1998); but neither we nor the author of ε could discover this by reading DB. The author must have had some other means of knowing where Boxley ought to be listed; and he must have been willing to act on that knowledge, regardless of what DB said or failed to say.

One feature of ε that is not derived from DB is derived from ε itself – more precisely, from an earlier version of ε, distinguished from the existing version precisely by the absence of this feature. Somebody started working through the text, adding up the itemized assessments and recording subtotals at intervals. But apparently he did not complete the task: subtotals cease appearing halfway through. (In ε as we have it, these subtotals have been integrated into the main text; perhaps they were originally added in the margins.) For us, they are helpful in more than one way, most obviously because they provide some check on the accuracy of the transmitted text, so far as the numbers are concerned.

It is certain, then, that some additional information was incorporated into ε, somewhere along the line between DB and ε'. Where this information came from is another question. Some of it might have come from a written source, unaffected by the errors of DB; some of it might have come from local knowledge; but how can we hope to decide? The question needs to be asked, even so, because it links up with other questions relating to the history of this text. When and where did ε originate? How far did it change its shape in the period of time before we first catch sight of it? In particular, did there ever exist a version of this text which included – what the surviving version does not include – the lands of the archbishopric? We are not going to know what value we can place on ε unless we can find some answer to these questions.

I propose to cut the knot by arguing, straight away, that ε originated in the king's treasury. There are three points which seem to me to favour this conclusion; I see none which count against it.

First, there is this sentence (6rb8–9) covering the lands of the church of Saint Martin's of Dover:

Tota terra sc'i martini de douere se defendit in cent pro xx et iiii sull'.

Though the wording is not derived from DB, the information could have been, and presumably was: one merely has to add the 21 sulungs in Eastry lest to the 3 sulungs in Limwar lest (DB-1va12–14). (Alternatively, if one looks more closely, one can find the total, 24 sulungs, reported later on (2rb33).) The striking fact is the inclusion of the words 'in Kent'.[9] This phrase is triply superfluous. The canons of Saint Martin's did not own any land outside Kent; if they had done so, that land would not have been assessed in sulungs; and in any case it would not have been necessary to allude to the fact in a text which deals exclusively with this one county (and which reminds us of that in every line, as often as it speaks of sulungs and yokes). Nobody from Kent would have thought of saying 'in Kent'; whoever composed this sentence had larger thoughts on his mind.

Second, in dealing with two of DB's chapters, the author of ε reorganized the entries. He worked through the chapter twice. On the first pass he extracted the information he wanted for the manors held in domain; on the second pass he did the same for the manors held by subtenants. There is nothing in ε to explain this, but the result makes it clear what has happened: the extracts both from chapter 7 (Saint Augustine's) and from chapter 9 (Hugo de Montfort) have been deliberately reorganized in this way. In DB-Ke itself, in chapter 2, the same thing has happened: the lands held by the archbishop's knights have been separated from the lands held by the archbishop in domain and moved to the end of the chapter. A government scribe, thinking that this was a useful distinction to make, applied it to this chapter. The author of ε had the same idea and put it into practice on chapters 7 and 9.[10] From government's point of view, that distinction made a difference: when a baron died, or if he lost his lands, the domain manors would fall into the king's hands, but the other manors would not.

Third, in his handling of sulungs and yokes, the author of ε commits the type of error that we also meet in DB. In places where several entries have been condensed into one, the DB scribe is found using odd expressions – 'one sulung and six yokes' (instead of 'two sulungs and a half'), 'five sulungs and a half and three yokes' (instead of 'six sulungs and one yoke') – which betray his ignorance of Kentish matters. Similar solecisms occur in ε, both in the text derived from DB and in the subtotals which came to be interpolated into it. Here and there, two quantities which are stated separately in DB have been added together, and that has resulted in expressions like 'half a sulung and one yoke' (instead of 'three yokes') or 'four yokes' (instead of 'one sulung'). As for the subtotals, whoever worked them out did certainly understand that four yokes made one sulung; the answers that he got were arithmetically correct, but they were not expressed as they should have been.[11] Someone

[9] It is an odd fact that the words *in cent* are omitted from Douglas's transcription, which is otherwise close to perfect.

[10] Whether this distinction should be made or not is a question which the DB scribe did not resolve. In DB-Ke, the lands of the bishop of Bayeux (chapter 5) are all listed in a loosely cadastral order, the domain manors not being separated from the rest. In DB-Ox, by contrast, the bishop's domain manors have been brought to the head of the chapter.

[11] It appears that he had his abacus set up with a column for counting half-

who could speak of 'half a sulung and one yoke' or of 'two yokes and a half' was not someone from Kent.

This seems to me to add up to a fairly convincing case in favour of the view that ε was produced in the treasury. There is only one other option, after all: to suppose that ε was compiled by somebody from Canterbury – one of the archbishop's clerks or one of the monks – given unlimited access to DB.[12] It is easy to believe that a visiting scribe might have been given permission to consult DB-Ke, and to copy some passages from it which affected the archbishop directly. Apparently that did happen (above, p. 36). It is not hard to believe that he might also have been allowed to make a copy of ε, if ε already existed. But it seems very difficult to believe that a visiting scribe would have had the opportunity to make an epitome of his own, or indeed that he would have had any wish to do so. Up to a point, it was desirable to know one's neighbours' business: the surviving version of ε would not survive if that had not been true. But was it so desirable that one of the archbishop's clerks (or one of the monks) would have wanted to invest his own time in extracting all this information from DB-Ke? I find it hard to think so.

What happened, I take it, was this. Some treasury scribe was set the task of epitomizing DB-Ke. His remit was to extract every reference to sulungs and yokes (and smaller quantities too, where they occurred), and to organize the information under the names of the tenants who were, or had recently been, in possession of the land in question. In its original form, so we may suppose, ε did include extracts from chapters 2–4. Based in Winchester, the author of ε would not have been able to draw on local knowledge: any extraneous information incorporated into ε, by the author himself or by correctors, would presumably have come from written records available in the treasury.[13] One source which would certainly have been available is D-Ke, the full-scale version of the survey of Kent, the source text for DB-Ke. If occasionally ε was checked against D, it might reabsorb a few facts which the DB scribe had omitted.

By this time, the bishop of Bayeux had lost his English estates, and those of his men who had kept their lands were

sulungs alongside the column for counting yokes. With that set-up, the quantity 'three yokes' will not occur. Wherever that expression is found in ε, it is being quoted from DB.

Honour of Eudo the steward. Adam son of Hubert (6rb24–40), Goisfrid de Ros (6rb40–2)

Barony of Crevequer. Ansfrid Masleclerc (6rb53–c7), Malger (6rc8–11), Osbern Paisforere (6rc11–18), Rannulf de Columbels (6rc20–4)

Barony of Maminot. Radulf de Curbespine (6rc38–52), bishop of Lisieux (6rc53–4), Gislebert Maminot (6rc54–va2)

Barony of Port. Hugo de Port (6va8–20), Osbern son of Letard (6va23–31)

Barony of Talebot. Radulf son of Turold (6va32–42), Helto (6va42–4)

Barony of Peverel of Dover. Herbert son of Ivo (6vb10–11), Hugo nephew of Herbert (6vb12–18), Herfrid (6vb24–8)

Honour of the earl of Gloucester. Haimo the sheriff (6vb51–c3), Vitalis (6vc3–6)

Table 20. Twelfth-century baronies and the corresponding sections of ε.

now holding them directly from the king. The transformation of the feudal landscape of Kent which followed from the failed rebellion of 1088 is a subject on which we are very poorly informed; but some of the consequences are reflected in this text.

There were, at the time of the survey, two barons in Kent – Ricard de Tonebrige and Haimo the sheriff – who held some of their lands from the king (chapters 11 and 12 respectively) and some from the bishop of Bayeux. In DB-Ke, despite the fact that the bishop was in prison at the time, the lands which he owned are all still listed as his, and Ricard and Haimo appear as his subtenants (scattered entries in chapter 5). In ε, by contrast, the lands which they used to hold from the bishop are listed together with the lands which they have always held from the king. (Here again the author says nothing to explain what he is doing, but the result is its own explanation.)

That is not all. In Table 20 I give a partial list of the baronies existing in Kent in the latter half of the reign of Henric I, around 40 years after the survey, with in each case a list of the tenants who held these lands from the bishop of Bayeux in 1086. (The baronies listed are those – only those but all of those – for which more than one predecessor can be identified in DB.) Comparing this table with ε, the reader will find a large measure of congruence. From the ordering of the paragraphs (an ordering which is not dictated by DB), it can be seen that the author of ε already had some idea how things had been reorganized, or how they were likely to be reorganized, in the aftermath of 1088.[14]

[12] There is perhaps a third alternative which ought to be considered – that the author of ε was working for the sheriff of Kent. I see nothing to be said in favour of this suggestion; the evidence that indicates an ignorance of Kentish matters seems to tell strongly against it.

[13] It has often been said that the spellings of place-names appearing in ε have a more conventional look than the simplified spellings of DB; and that is true, to some extent. The impression I get (and impressions are all that one can hope to get, from evidence of this kind) is that the author of ε disapproved of the orthography invented by the DB scribe, but understood it well enough to guess at the English names hidden behind the spellings that he found in DB. Often he guessed correctly, and in that case the spelling which he used will resemble that used by local scribes familiar with the name. But often his guess was wrong – and these unsuccessful guesses go to prove that he was guessing all the time.

[14] Not all the bishop's men became the king's barons: some became the men of other barons. The author of ε seems to be aware that Goisfrid de Ros in now the man of Adam son of Hubert, that Osbern son of Letard is now the man of Hugo de Port, that Vitalis is now the man of Haimo the sheriff. These are all changes that we might expect to see happening, in the light of later evidence.

Apart from the names of the barons and the names of their manors, the only information which interested the author of ε was the number of sulungs for which each manor was assessed – the number of sulungs for which it had to pay geld. All questions concerning the payment of geld were supposed to have been settled by the survey of 1086; after 1088, they were at risk of being opened up again. Furthermore, new questions arose – not only but especially in Kent – which would not have been relevant before 1088. Of the manors held by Hugo de Port, for example, which were held in domain, and which were held by his men? Now that Hugo was holding his lands in Kent directly from the king,[15] that distinction became significant, because Hugo would expect to be allowed a share of the geld; but it had not been significant in 1086, and the information that the treasury needed could not be found in the records of the survey.

Without a new survey, the treasury could not know exactly how things were working out on the ground. We cannot expect the author of ε to achieve or even to think of achieving the impossible. Being where he was, having the resources that he had, he did what could be done. He produced a sketch showing what DB-Ke would have looked like if the circumstances had been different. If the bishop of Bayeux had lost his lands a few years before the survey, rather than a few years afterwards, this – hypothetically, in rough outline – is the landscape which the commissioners would have discovered.

That is an interesting experiment, and it does not surprise me that archbishop Lanfranc was (so it appears) interested in seeing the result. An emissary of the archbishop's was sent to Winchester, gained access to the original, and made a copy of it. He omitted one long stretch of text (which told him nothing that he did not already know); by deciding to do that he created a new version of ε.[16] For the rest he transcribed the text quite accurately, as far as we can judge. Within a few years, this transcript was in Canterbury. There it was copied into C1. And there it survived for some considerable length of time – long enough to be copied once again, into the monks' cartulary – before finally ceasing to exist.

I print the text line for line, as it appears in C1, following the same conventions as for α (above, p. 46). The sort of tabular format which is used for the first part of the text in C1 is used throughout in C3; but I would guess that this was an improvement made by the C3 scribe, and that C1 was reproducing ε' more exactly, in this as in other respects. In two places (6ra45, 6ra51), C3 has a reading which is demonstrably better than C1's, and I have put these readings into the text, marking them off with square brackets. For the rest, I have not judged it necessary to burden the text with notes reporting all the variant readings to be found in C3 (where C3 can be reconstructed) or in C5 or T1 or both (where it cannot).[17] In theory it is true that some of these readings may be better than C1's; but the better readings are lost in the background noise, and we have no means of filtering them out.

Because so much of the text is just a meagre epitome of DB, I have thought that the reader would be likely to approve if I make some visual distinction between what is second-hand and what is new. As much of the text as was taken from DB is printed here in grey; those elements which were were not (or not straightforwardly) derived from DB are printed in black. The reader will thus be able to see them at a glance – and see at a glance that they do not amount to much.

As for the concordances (below, pp. 212–13), I print them with reluctance. It is hard to imagine that much use will ever be made of them; I hope that it will not be. Nevertheless, I suppose that they had better be published, because otherwise somebody may feel obliged to do the work again; and that is a distressing thought to me. This text, though it has some points of interest, does not deserve more than a small share of anyone else's attention.

[15] The words 'in Kent' are not redundant. In Hampshire and elsewhere, Hugo de Port owned land which he had held from the king since before 1086; in the geld accounts for 1085–6 we find him claiming a deduction with respect to a manor of his in Dorset (Exeter Cathedral Library 3500, fos. 20r, 24r). So Hugo knew the rules; and he would certainly have thought himself entitled, after 1088, to similar deductions with respect to his manors in Kent, so far as they were held in domain.

[16] It is not impossible, however, that the decision to omit this stretch of text was made by the C1 scribe. There is a gap, perhaps a significant gap, at the point where the omission occurs (6ra6–9).

[17] I have transcripts of both manuscripts on file, and anybody who would like to have copies should feel free to ask for them.

ε / C1-5vc

(R) ex tenet derteford. Hoc manerium se defendit pro i sull’ et dim’. De ipso manerio ablata est hageli, quę se defendit pro dim’ sull’. Hanc terram tenet hugo de port, et liiii agris terrę plus.
(H) eilesford se defendit pro i sull’.
(M) ildeltune se defendit pro quater xx sull’. Estra hos sunt in dominio iiii sull’. De ipso manerio tenet prędictus hugo viii sull’ et i *iug(um), quę tempore E regis erant in consuetu-

ε / C1-6ra

dine cum aliis sull’.
(F) euersham se defendit pro vii sull’.
(H) arum summa terrarum sunt c sull’ et i et dimid’ et i iugum.
:
:
:
(Ę) ccl’a sc’i augustini tenet plumstede, et defendit se pro ii sull’ et i iug’.
(L) enham pro v sull’ et dim’.
(*) urnes pro i sull’.
(I) n langeport est i sull’ et i iug’ quod semper fuit quietum et sine consuetudine.
(*) itelburne pro vii sull’.
(W) arwintune pro dim’ sull’ et xlii agris terrę.
(S) turege pro v sull’.
(*) anet pro xl et viii sull’.
(C) istele pro xii sull’.
(F) orwic pro i iug’. Iuxta ciuitatem est dim’ sull’ quod semper fuit quietum.
(W) iretune pro i sull’.
(S) edling pro vi sull’.
(I) n rocinge pro dim’ sull’.
(N) *or(d)burne pro xxx sull’.
(M) *undi(n)geham pro ii sull’ et dim’.
(I) n isto manerio terra monachorum nunquam geldauit sed alia *gelda(b)it.
(S) ubrihtesweald pro ii sull’.
(P) latenout pro i sull’.
(P) restetune pro v sull’.
(C) henetune pro iiii sull’.
(B) urwaremersce pro ii sull’ et iii iug’.
(I) n langeport ii sull’ et i iug’.
(I) n estreie hundret iii uirgę terrę.
(E) smerefeld pro i sull’.
(I) n derendene dim’ sull’.
(*R) apintune pro i *[iug’].
(C) heringelle pro dim’ sull’.
(E) luentune pro dim’ sull’ et dim’ iug’. (B)odesham pro i sull’.
:
(T) ota summa istarum terrarum est c et xl iiii sull’ et i iug’ et *[iii] uirg’ et xvi agros.
:
:

ε / C1-6rb

(Ę) ccl’a sc’i martini de bello tenet manerium quod uocatur Wi, quod se defendit semper pro vii sull’.
:
(Ę) ccl’a **sc’i wandregisili** *de gent tenet liofesham, quod se defendit pro ii sull’.
(T) ota terra sc’i martini de douere se defendit in cent pro xx et iiii sull’.
:
(W) yllelmus de archis tenet **de ep’o** folcestane quod se defendit pro xl sull’. **Idem** ep’s baiocensis tenet how quod se defendit pro l sull’. **Boxelei pro vii sull’.** Hardes pro ii sull’. Stellinges pro i iug’. Burnes pro ii sull’. Wicham pro iiii sull’. Ad istud manerium iacet dim’ sull’ liberę terrę. Heleham pro vi sull’. Bildsuidetune pro iiii sull’.
(T) ota summa est c sull’ et xv et dim’ et i iug’.
Adam filius huberti tenet Redlege pro i sull’. Sudcreie pro i sull’. Wycham pro i sull’. Lilleburne pro ii sull’. **In pimpa i iug’.** Sudtune pro iiii sull’. Item sudtune pro i sull’ et dim’. Cert pro iii sull’. Boclege pro ii sull’. Langelege pro i sull’ et dim’. Ottringedene

pro dim' sull'. Eastselue pro dim' sull'. **Eluentune pro i sull'.** Celca pro iii sull'. Helcaham pro v sull'. In colinga i sull' et dim'. Bicceleg pro dim' sull'. **Stanefeld pro ii sull'. Ores pro ii sull'. Item Ores pro i iug'.** Fanne pro dim' sull'. **In hammolde dim' iug',** et in Bellinge i dene de dim' iug'. Gosfridus de ros t'n' Lolinge tune pro i sull'. Lausele pro vii sull'. Otteham pro dim' sull' et i iug'. Anscetillus de ros t'n' Tarent pro dim' sull', et Item aliud dim' sull'. Hortune pro i sull', et Item i sull' et dim'. Craie pro dim' sull'. Item Craie pro dim' sull'. Croctune pro i sull' et i iug'. Elentune pro i sull'. Offaham pro i sull'. *Hacris pro i sull'. **Eastmeretel pro i sull'. Istud manerium t'n' Anscetillus de ros de abbate. Tota summa est l et ii sull' et dim' et i iug'.** Ansfridus masleclerc t'n' Cyldresham pro i sull'. Ernoldin-

ε / C1-6rc

tune pro i sull'. Macheuet pro i iug'. Badelesmere pro i sull'. Pirie pro i iug'. Item pirie pro dim' sull'. Hortune pro dim' sull'. Wodnesberga pro ii sull' et iii iug'. Endleueberga pro dim' iug'. Soles pro i sull'. In boclande dim' sull'. Malgir t'n' Lolingestune pro dim' sull'. Frenigeham pro dim' iug'. Pinnedene pro dim' sull'. Rocesleg pro i sull'. Osbertus paisforire t'n' Lolingestune pro dim' sull'. Bocland pro iiii iug'. Ealdehlosa pro dim' sull'. Palestrege pro iii iug' et xii agris. In maseberga i iug' et x agros. In emmetune xv agros. **Et i manerium t'n' de ep'o pro i sull' et dim'. In hertege i iug' et dim'.**

:

(R) annulfus de columbes t'n' Sedlinges pro i sull' et dim'. Eiscedene pro i sull'. Fernlege pro i sull'. Bermeling pro i iug'. Hardes pro i sull'.

Rodbertus latimir tenet Hlosnes pro x sull'. Totintune pro dim' sull' et i iug'. Herebrichtestune pro i sull'. Brumfeld pro i sull', et ibi est terra iii boum libera. Cetteham pro vi sull', et in quodam alio loco t'n' vi agros. Adeloldus camerarius t'n' Hledes pro iii sull'. Fredenesstede pro i sull'. Testane pro i sull'. Bedenestede pro i iug'. Eastweald pro iii sull'. **Tota summa xl et vii sull' et dim' et i iug' et terra iii boum et x et viii agros.**

Radulfus de curbespine tenet Danintune pro dim' sull'. Boraham pro vi sull'. In braceshela i iug', et ibi prope in quodam manerio xl agros. In poplesheale dim' iug'. In berefredestune i iug'. Berlinges vi sull'. Torneham iii sull'. Bemundestune pro i sull'. Piuentune pro i sull'. In pistinges i iug' et i uirg'. Colred ii sull'. Eawelle iii sull'. Sumetune ii sull'. Fereburne i sull'. Appletune i sull'. Walmerescore pro ii sull'. Eastwelle pro iii sull'. **Item i iug' quod olim scottau' in hardes.**

Ep's de lisois t'n' grenuwic pro ii sull'. Gyllebertus maminot tenet

ε / C1-6va

Codeham pro iiii sull'. Cestane pro dim' sull'. **Summa xxx et ix sull' et dim' iug' et xl agros et i uirg'.** Willelmus filius rodberti tenet Westselue pro i sull'. Willelmus filius ogeri t'n' Cerletune pro i sull'. Craie pro dim' sull'. Hugo de port t'n' Hageleg pro dim' sull'. Eisce iii sull'. Dideleg et Somniges pro dim' sull'. Pellesword pro dim' sull'. Resce pro ii sull' et dimid'. Offeham pro i sull'. Alnodentune pro iii sull'. Tunestele pro iii sull' et dim'. Cert pro ii sull'. Tanges pro ii sull'. Stependune pro i sull' dim' iug' minus. Nordtune pro iiii sull'. Herst pro iii iug'. Pesinges et Piham pro ii sull'. **Eawelle pro iii sull'. Westcliue pro ii sull'. Soltune pro i sull'. Summa xxx et iiii sull' et ii iug' et dim', et l et iiii agros, quę olim fuerunt in derteford.** Osbernus filius litardi t'n' Hammes pro i sull'. *Cylle(n)dene pro i sull' et i iug' et x agris. In Ecche i iug'. In selling' i iug'. Poplesheale i sull'. Bedesham pro i iug' et dim', et Ibi idem habet i sull' et dim' iug'. Vnum manerium t'n' de ep'o quod se defendit pro i sull' et dim'. Radulfus filius turoldi t'n' Ercleie pro i sull'. Edintune pro *ii sull' et dim'. Wyttunemersc pro i sull'. Eiglesse pro iii iug' et alter Edintune pro dim' sull'. Melintune pro i sull' et iii iug'. Lellesdune pro ii sull' et dim' et dim' iug'. Estotingeberga pro ii sull'. Ottringeberga pro ii sull'. Litelwroteham pro i sull' et dim'. Hercleie pro i sull'. Healt tenet Suanes camp x sull'. Melestane pro dim' sull'. **Summa xxx ii sull' et i iug' et dim' et x agros.**

Eluredus t'n' Middelei pro iii iug'. Thurstanus t'n' Ticstede pro i sull' et dim'. In Wanneberga i iug', et in Heche i iug'. In Endleuaberga i iug' et v agros.

Rogerius filius Anscetilli t'n' Hastingeleg pro i sull'. Eastlinges pro i sull'. Rannulf' de ualbadun t'n' Hamstede pro dim' iug'.

ε / C1-6vb

Wadardus t'n' Fremgaham pro dim' sull'. Meaplesham pro dim' sull'. Notstede pro ii sull'. Bercefeld pro dim' sull'. Cumbe pro i sull'. Folbertus t'n' Bereham pro vi sull'. Cyleham pro v sull'. **Ludenham pro i sull'.** Eastlinges pro v sull'. Dudeham pro i sull'. Walterius de doai t'n' Leahei pro dim' sull'. Corbin t'n' Pecham pro ii sull'. Herbertus filius Iuonis t'n' Grauesand pro ii sull' et i iug'. Hugo nepos herberti t'n' Boctune pro ii sull'. Godeshelle pro i sull'. Wincelesmere pro dim' sull'. Eastselue pro dim' sull'. Feresburne pro i sull'. Herietesham pro ii sull'. Selesburne pro i iug' libere terrę. Sedlinges pro i sull' et dim'. Odo tenet Colinges pro dim' sull' et **in quodam loco** i iug' ***et iii.** Gelingaham pro dim' sull'. Hugo de braiban t'n' Ottringeberga pro ii sull'. Ricardus filius Willelm' t'n' Burnes pro vi sull'. Herefrid' t'n' Brocesele pro i sull'. Scamelesford pro dim' sull'. Trulege pro iii sull'. Ryngestune **pro iii sull'**. Nordheslinges pro dim' sull'. Rodbertus de rumenel t'n' Offetune pro i sull'. Bennedene pro dim' sull' et dim' iug'. In maresc dim' sull'. Et item in eodem maresc dim' sull', et in Titentune dim' dene. Radulf' filius Rodberti tenet Hertange pro i sull', et Osbernus i iug' et dim'. Et item Ibi Hugo de munford i sull', et Wybert' dim' iug'. Wyll' de Taum t'n' Dele pro i sull' et i iug'. *An(s)god tenet Mapeldrescamp pro dim' sull'. Hou pro i sull'. Becheham pro ii sull'. Aldintune pro ii sull'. Stocingabere pro ii sull'. Delce pro i sull'. Stoces pro ii sull'. Henneherste pro dim' sull'. Arnulf' de hesding ten' Cliue pro dim' sull'. Hadune pro iii iug'. Frenigaham pro iii iug'. *Celest(f)eld pro ii sull'.

:

Comes eustachius ten' Ostreham pro iiii sull'. Boctune pro vii sull'. Haymo uicecomes t'n' ***Dramwo(r)d** pro ii sull' et dim'. In hulewic lx et iii agros. Marcword ii sull'. Blen i sull'. Healteham i sull' et dim'.

ε / C1-6vc

Dictune i sull'. Neadesstede iii sull'. Latindune dim' sull' et ibi prope dim' sull'. Vital' t'n' Suealescliue pro dim' sull'. *Siu(l)e(d)etune pro dim' sull' et item i iug'.

Rycardus de tonebrig' tenet Hallinges pro ii sull'. Bernuelinges i sull'. Haslo vi sull'. Tiuedele i iug'.

Hugo de *mun(d)ford tenet Estwelle pro i sull'. Hantune i sull'. Eiselle iii iug'. East brige i sull'. Titentune i sull'. Eawelle iii sull'. Diuentune ii sull'. Bradeburne vii sull'. Siburne i sull'. Suanetune dim' sull'. Hestingelege dim' sull'. In tiuegate i iug' et dim'. In Westtune i uirg' terrę. In Tipendene dim' iug'. In Titentune dim' iug'. In Maresc de rumenel dim' sull' et i iug'.

Bilec i sull' et i terram quam tenuit Azorrot T R E pro i sull' et alia terra quam Ægelred big t'n' T R E pro dim' sull', et In maresc de Rumenel i sull' dim' uirg' min'. Item ibidem t'n' i iug' et dim' iug'. Main ten' Siuledtune pro dim' sull'. Escedes ford pro i sull'. Herueus tenet Blacemannestune pro dim' sull'. Bertrannus t'n' in quodam loco dim' iug' et dim' uirg' terrę. Rogerius in maresc de rumenel i iug', et Rodbertus sextam partem i iugi. Rogerius t'n' Postling pro ii sull' et dim'. Herueus Sedling pro i sull'. Alnodus t'n' Hortune pro dim' sull'. Wyll' In Ordlauestune iii iug' et dim' uirg' terrę. Radulfus filius Ricard' t'n' Rocinges pro dim' sull'. Radulf' Hortune pro i iug' et dim'. Hugo de mendeuile t'n' Estrates pro ii sull'. Herefridus t'n' Poltune pro i sull'. Nigellus t'n' In Aie i iug' et vii agros terrę. Wyll' filius grossę t'n' Bonintune pro i sull'. Herueus t'n' Otrepol pro i sull'. Healaldus t'n' dim' sull' i uirg' minus, et i dene. Hugo tenet **In Stretes hundred** iii uirg'

ε / C1-7ra

terrę et dim', et Item Alnodus i iug', et In hundred de cert i uirg' terrę quam quędam femina t'n' de hugone, et Alibi xvi agros terrę quos quidam sokemann' t'n' de eodem hugone. Ansfridus tenet In Stretes hundred i iug', et alibi Rodbertus *(cocus) i iug', et Gyslebertus adhuc i iug', et Idem hugo xiiii agros terrę.

Notes

5vc53 iugum] *with* um *above* o 6ra13] *a black* b *in the margin* 6ra17] *a black* l *in the margin* 6ra21] *a black* T *in the margin* 6ra29 ( )ordburne] *with* d *inserted* 6ra30 ( )undingeham] *with the second* n *inserted* 6ra33 geldabit] *with* b *altered from* u 6ra45] *a green* r *in the margin; the initial itself is blue* 6ra45 iugo] *C3/C5T1 rightly* : sull' *C1* 6ra51 iii] *C3/C5T1 rightly* : iiii *C1* 6rb5 de] *with* d *written over a* g 6rb49] Hac ris *joined with a dash* 6va25 Cyllendene] *with the first* n *inserted* 6va33 ii] *with a third minim erased* 6vb20 et iii] *perhaps should be* et in 6vb38 Ansgod] *with* s *inserted* 6vb47 Celestfeld] *with* f *inserted* 6vb51 Dramword] *with the second* r *inserted* 6vc5 Siuledetune] *with* l *inserted and* d *altered from* ll 6vc11 mundford] *with the first* d *inserted* 7ra8 cocus] *written above* Rodbertus

Concordance 1
ε / C1 collated with DB-Ke

5vc38	2va3
46	34
48	46
6ra2	2vb21
9	12ra3
12	10
13	17
14	22
17	30
18	36
20	41
21	48
22	12rb6
23	13
23	24
26	30
27	39
28	43
29	12va5
30	27
34	38
35	43
36	48
37	12vb25
38	33
40	20
41	13
43	12rb34
44	37
45	46
46	12va1
47	12vb5
48	17
6rb1	11vb40
5	12vb41
8	1va12–14
11	9va16
13	8va23
15	8vb34
15	9rb22
16	26
16	30
17	43
19	9vb2
20	10vb38
24	6ra31
25	6va45
26	50
26	7ra28
27	8va41
28	8ra5
28	15
29	10
30	20
30	28
31	33
32	39
33	—
33	8vb49
34	9ra8
34	15
35	21
36	10ra15
36	10
37	10rb35
37	10va30
38	11ra23
39	9vb8
40	6ra46
41	6vb5
42	8rb21
43	6rb39
44	45
45	50
45	6va6 + 10
46	6vb12
46	16
47	7ra3
48	36
49	7va25
49	11vb24
50	12rb34
53	10ra46
54	10rb1
6rc1	8
2	11
3	18
3	21
4	10va25
5	11rb23
6	11ra45
6	11rb43
7	9vb11
8	6rb1
9	6
10	11
10	6va34
11	6rb15
12	10rb24 + 28
13	10vb21
14	27 + 32
15	11va34
16	36
16	11vb1
18	—
20	11vb5
21	7rb31
22	8va46
23	8vb30
23	9rb38
25	6va16
26	7rb36 + 42
27	8rb26
28	31
29	8va2
30	11va22
31	7vb30
32	26
33	8vb20
34	26
34	9vb20
38	11vb10
39	7va40
40	11vb15
41	17
42	9vb32
43	15
43	7va33
44	8rb38
45	10va45
45	10vb9
46	14
47	11ra49
47	54
48	11rb4
48	8rb44
49	11rb11
50	11va40
51	48
51	9vb18
53	6vb22
54	7ra8
6va1	13
4	8ra43
6	6vb43
7	48
8	6ra3
9	36
10	7rb14
11	20
12	26
12	7vb48
13	9rb1
14	6
15	9
15	margin
16	10ra19
17	10rb31
18	10vb33
19	11ra26
19	33
20	38
23	11va8
25	12
26	45
27	9vb24
27	27
28	11rb36
29	40
30	11vb1
32	66ra17
33	7rb45
34	6vb34
35	7rb6
35	6ra21
36	7va1
37	7
38	7vb7
39	8vb9
40	41
41	9ra25
42	6ra10
43	9ra47
46	11va17
47	11va26
48	30
49	32
49	11rb19
51	11vb29
52	10va4
53	11vb20
6vb1	6rb22
2	29
3	7va21
3	10va35
4	40
4	9vb35
5	10ra25
6	10va15
6	9
7	15
8	6vb39
9	7va47
10	7va15
12	8rb1
13	6
14	11
14	17
15	7vb19
16	13
17	23
18	7ra17
18	9ra44
19	42
20	8rb48
21	8vb15
22	9rb16
24	11rb15
25	10vb17
26	10rb39
26	11ra18
27	10rb45
28	10vb45
29	11ra6 + 10
30	10vb49
31	11ra2
32	13
33	11rb47
34	51
35	11va2
36	5
37	8va10
38	6ra26
39	6va23
40	7ra22
40	7vb39
41	44
42	8va15
42	19
43	9ra30
44	9ra34
45	38
46	6rb33
47	6va39
49	14ra32
50	40
51	14rb21
52	30
53	34
54	41
54	6vb29
6vc1	7ra42
1	8vb3
2	9va6
3	10
3	10ra1
5	7ra48
5	10ra6
7	14rb3
8	11
9	7vb2
10	10
11	13ra3
12	9
13	21
13	42
14	13rb42
15	13vb2
15	7
16	23
17	36
17	40
18	14ra15
19	19
20	23
20	13vb32
21	13rb49
22	34 + 37
24	26
24	30
26	22
27	5
29	13ra31 + 35
30	13
31	25
32	50
34	48
35	13rb8
37	11
38	14
39	13va1
40	8
41	19
43	24
44	29
45	34
47	13vb19
48	44
49	48
51	14ra3
52	9
53	13va15
7ra1	14
2	13vb30
4	13
7	13va39
8	43
9	46
10	49

Concordance 2
DB-Ke collated with ε / C1

2va3	5vc38
34	46
46	48
2vb21	6ra2
3ra–5vb	—
6ra3	6va8
10	42
17	32
21	35
26	6vb38
31	6rb24
36	6va9
46	6rb40
6rb1	6rc8
6	9
11	10
15	11
22	6vb1
29	2
33	46
39	6rb43
45	44
50	45
6va6 + 10	45
16	6rc25
23	6vb39
28	—
34	6rc10
39	6vb47
45	6rb25
50	26
6vb5	41
12	46
16	46
22	6rc53
29	6vb54
34	6va34
39	6vb8
43	6va6
48	7
7ra3	6rb47
8	6rc54
13	6va1
17	6vb18
22	40
28	6rb26
36	48
42	6vc1
48	5
7rb6	6va35
14	10
20	11
26	12
31	6rc21
36 + 42	26
45	6va33
7va1	36
7	37
15	6vb10
21	3
25	6rb49
33	6rc43
40	39
47	6vb9
7vb2	6vc9
7	6va38
10	6vc10
13	6vb16
19	15
23	17
26	6rc32
30	31
39	6vb40
44	41
48	6va12
8ra5	6rb28
10	29
15	28
20	30
28	30
33	31
39	32
43	6va4
8rb1	6vb12
6	13
11	14
17	14
21	6rb42
26	6rc27
31	28
38	44
44	48
48	6vb20
8va2	6rc29
10	6vb37
15	42
19	42
23	6rb13
41	27
46	6rc22
8vb3	6vc1
9	6va39
15	6vb21
20	6rc33
26	34
30	23
34	6rb15
41	6va40
49	6rb33
9ra8	34
15	34
21	35
25	6va41
30	6vb43
34	44
38	45
42	19
44	18
47	6va43
9rb1	13
6	14
margin	15
9	15
16	6vb22
22	6rb15
26	16
30	16
38	6rc23
43	6rb17
9va6	6vc2
10	3
16	6rb11
9vb2	19
8	39
11	6rc7
15	43
18	51
20	34
24	6va27
27	27
32	6rc42
35	6vb4
10ra1	6vc3
6	5
10	6rb36
15	36
19	6va16
25	6vb5
34	—
46	6rb53
10rb1	54
8	6rc1
11	2
18	3
21	3
24 + 28	12
31	6va17
35	6rb37
39	6vb26
45	27
10va1	—
4	6va52
9	6vb6
15	7
21	—
25	6rc4
30	6rb37
35	6vb3
40	4
45	6rc45
10vb1	—
9	6rc45
14	46
17	6vb25
21	6rc13
27 + 32	14
33	6va18
38	6rb20
45	6vb28
49	30
11ra2	31
6 + 10	29
13	32
18	26
23	6rb38
26	6va19
33	19
38	20
45	6rc6
49	47
54	47
11rb4	48
11	49
15	6vb24
19	6va49
23	6rc5
33	—
36	6va28
40	29
43	6rc6
47	6vb33
51	34
11va2	35
5	36
8	6va23
12	25
17	46
22	6rc30
26	6va47
30	48
32	49
34	6rc15
36	16
40	50
45	6va26
48	6rc51
11vb1	6va30
5	6rc20
10	38
15	40
17	41
20	6va53
24	6rb49
29	6va51
40	6rb1
12ra3	6ra9
10	12
17	13
22	14
30	17
36	18
41	20
48	21
12rb6	22
13	23
24	23
30	26
34	43
37	44
39	27
43	28
46	45
12va1	46
5	29
27	30
38	34
43	35
48	36
12vb5	47
13	41
17	48
20	40
25	37
33	38
41	6rb5
13ra3	6vc11
9	12
13	30
17	–
21	13
25	31
31 + 35	29
42	13
48	34
50	32
13rb5	27
8	35
11	37
14	38
22	26
26	24
30	24
34 + 37	22
42	14
49	21
13va1	39
8	40
14	7ra1
15	6vc53
19	41
24	43
29	44
34	45
13va39	7ra7
43	8
46	9
49	10
13vb2	6vc15
7	15
13	7ra4
19	6vc47
23	16
30	7ra2
32	6vc20
36	17
40	17
44	48
48	49
14ra3	51
9	52
15	18
19	19
23	20
32	6vb49
40	50
14rb3	6vc7
11	8
21	6vb51
30	52
34	53
41	54
14va3	—

Chapter 7
Supporting documents

The decisions involved in compiling this chapter were made over a period of several years, and I can hardly remember what my reasoning was in every single case. Over time, a stable solution seemed to emerge: there were no documents inside the line which I thought should be ejected, no documents outside the line which I thought should be admitted. One rule which I did decide to follow was not to print any of the documents which can be found in Bates's (1998) edition of the 'acta' (loosely defined) of Willelm I. I would cheerfully have broken this rule if any of the documents in question were directly connected with the survey of Kent; but in fact none of them are. The documents printed below are all significant, for one reason or another. It seems to me that they should all be studied closely by anyone interested in the survey of Kent, or more generally in the history of the county over the period 1066–1100. So I hope that the reader will find it helpful to have them assembled here.

Documents from Christ Church

Apart from the documents which were copied into manuscript C1 (above, pp. 36–7), the Christ Church archive has rather little to offer. The three disparate documents printed below tell us nothing about the survey itself; but they are all of considerable interest, each of them in its own way. Two of the manuscripts cited here, C5 and T1, can be found described elsewhere (Appendix I). In referring to T1, I distinguish between the two scribes who contributed to this manuscript. Scribe 1 did the bulk of the work; scribe 2 supplied the finishing touches.

1

A formal record of the business transacted at a meeting of the shire court.

Fulchestan, de beneficio regis est. Ratebourc de archiepiscopatu est, et edzinus dedit goduino. Stepeberga de archiepiscopatu est, et ecclesia christi erat inde saisita quando rex mare transiuit, modo episcopus baiocensis habet. In tilemanestun quando rex mare transiuit erat ecclesia christi saisita de ducentis iugeribus terrae, et in fenglesham de centum iugeribus, et in elme de uiginti quinque iugeribus, et modo ea osbernus ab episcopo tenet. Totesham alnod child de monachis tenebat quando rex mare transiuit, et firmam inde reddebat, et modo episcopus habet. Torentun uiginti quinque iugera habet et ecclesia habebat quando rex mare transiuit, et modo episcopus habebat sed dimisit. Witriscesham ecclesia christi habebat quando rex mare transiuit, et modo osbernus paisforere ab episcopo habet. Auuentingesherst, et edruneland, et aduuoluuinden, ecclesia tenebat quando rex mare transiuit, et firmam inde habebat, et modo Robertus de romenel ab episcopo habet. Prestitun alnod child ab archiepiscopo tenebat quando rex mare transiuit, et firmam reddebat, et modo turoldus ab episcopo habet. Godricus decanus dedit fratri suo quartam partem solingi quod pertinebat ad cliuam, et modo robertus uuillelmus ab episcopo habet. Sunderhirsc de archiepiscopatu est, et archiepiscopus dedit goduino, et episcopus modo habet. Langport et neuuenden de archiepiscopatu est, et archiepiscopus dedit goduino, et episcopus statim in placito cognouit esse de ecclesia. Saltoda de archiepiscopatu est, et archiepiscopus dedit goduino, et modo hugo de dono regis habet. Fecit archiepiscopus [a]Lanfranchus alios clamores super episcopum et super hugonem, sed in hundretis debent diffiniri. Pimpe et chintun, et uuestaldingis adalredus de archiepiscopo tenebat, et modo Richardus habet. Penesherst de archiepiscopatu est, et archiepiscopus tenebat quando rex mare transiuit, et censum et firmam inde habebat. Tertium denarium de comitatu archiepiscopus qui ante edzinum fuit habuit. Tempore edzini rex eduuardus dedit goduino. Terras omnes quę pertinent ad archiepiscopatum et ad abbatiam sancti Augustini, et terras comitis Goduini, testati sunt esse liberas ab omni consuetudine regia, [b]pre[ter illas antiqu]as uias quę uadunt de ciuitate ad ciuitatem, et de mercato ad mercatum, et de portu maris ad alium portum. De illa calumnia quam episcopus Odo fecit de pratis archiepiscopi et sancti Augustini, iudicauerunt omnes quod [c]iniusticiam haberet, et prata utriusque ecclesię sicut ceterę terrę libera esse deberent. Terra Goduini damę ad ecclesiam sancti augustini pertinet, et quando rex mare transiuit ecclesia de terra illa seruicium habebat, et modo hugo de dono regis habet.

BL, Cotton Aug. ii. 36 (facsimile Douglas 1933), with endorsements (1) *Scriptum de terris quas antiquitus habuit cantuariensis ecclesia. Latine*, (2) *Quod archiepiscopus antiquitus habebat tercium denarium de comitatu cantie, et hoc iure ipsius esse debet*; T1, fo. 168r–v, with serial number *C* (scribe 1) and heading *Transcriptum cuiusdam scedule (ueteris) memorialis de maneriis quibusdam archiepiscopatus tempore Lanfranci* (scribe 2); Birch 1887, pp. 293–6; Douglas 1933, pp. 51–2

[a] *partly in capitals,* LanFRaNchVS [b] *the original damaged by water and partly illegible; the missing words supplied from T1* [c] in iusticia *birch, douglas*

Date: soon after 1070. The only certain bounds are 1070 and 1082, the arrival of archbishop Lanfranc and the imprisonment of bishop Odo; but presumably Lanfranc would have acted as soon as he

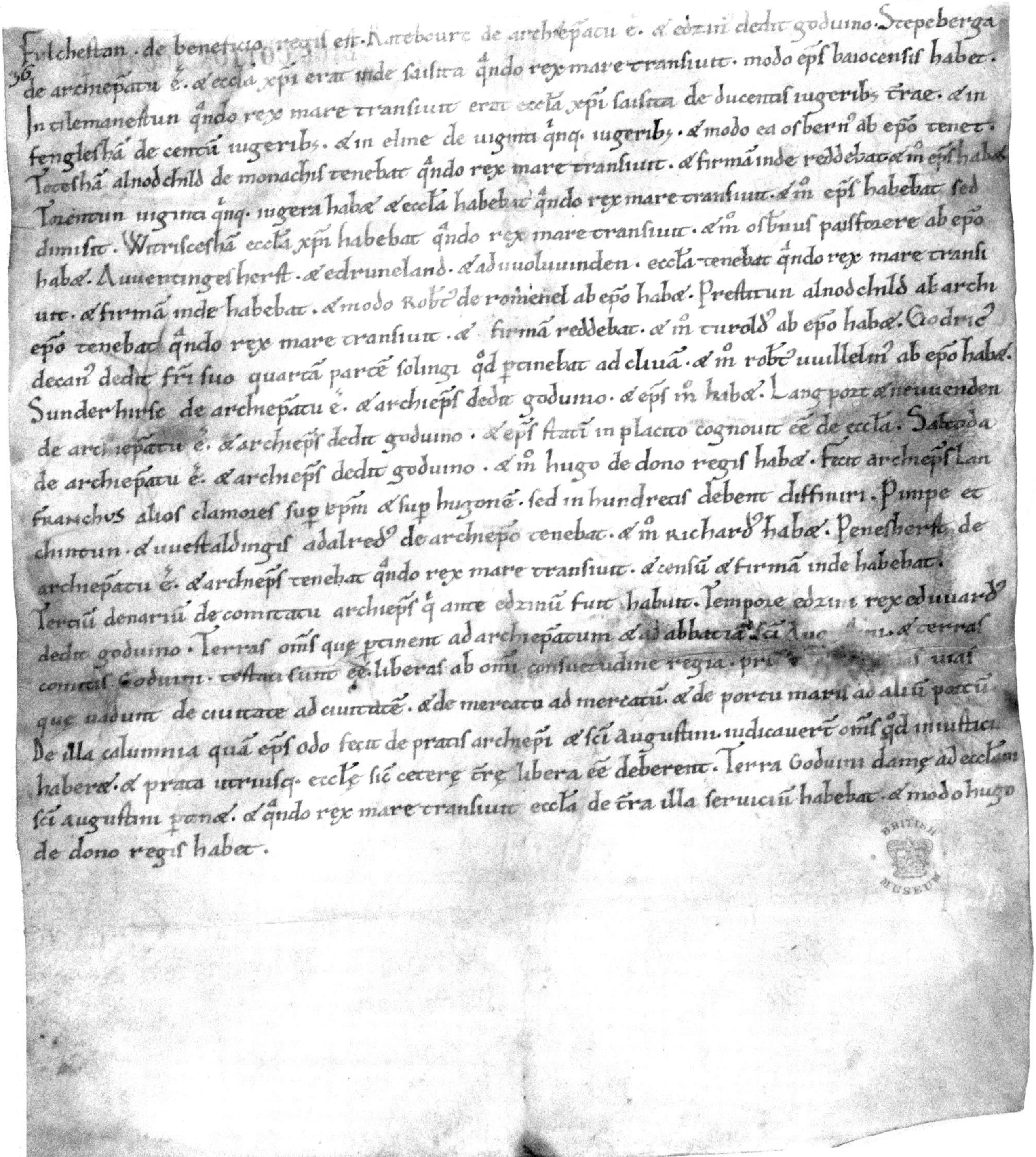

Folchestan . de beneficio regis est. Ratebourc de archiepatu e. et edzui dedit goduino. Stepeberga
de archiepatu e. et eccla xpi erat inde saisita qndo rex mare transiuit. modo eps baiocensis habet.
In tilemanestun qndo rex mare transiuit erat eccla xpi saisita de ducentis iugeribus trae. et in
fenglesha de centu iugeribus. et in elme de uiginti qnq. iugeribus. et modo ea osbern ab epo tenet.
Tecesha alnodchild de monachis tenebat qndo rex mare transiuit. et firma inde reddebat. et m eps habet.
Inetun uiginti qnq. iugera habet et eccla habebat qndo rex mare transiuit. et m eps habebat sed
dimisit. Wrtisceshā eccla xpi habebat qndo rex mare transiuit. et m osbnus paisforere ab epo
habet. Auuentingesherst . et edruneland . et aduuoluuinden . eccla tenebat qndo rex mare transi
uit. et firma inde habebat. et modo Robt de romenel ab epo habet. Prestetun alnodchild ab archi
epo tenebat qndo rex mare transiuit. et firma reddebat. et m turold ab epo habet. Godric
decan dedit fri suo quarta parte solingi qd ptinebat ad eliua. et m robt uuillelm ab epo habet.
Sunderhurse de archiepatu e. et archieps dedit goduino. et eps m habet. Langport et neuuenden
de archiepatu e. et archieps dedit goduino . et eps stati in placito cognouit ee de eccla. Saltcoda
de archiepatu e. et archieps dedit goduino . et m hugo de dono regis habet. Fecit archieps Lan
franchus alios clamores sup epm et sup hugone. sed in hundretis debent diffiniri. Pimpe et
chintun . et uuestaldingis adalred de archiepo tenebat. et m richard habet. Penesherst de
archiepatu e. et archieps tenebat qndo rex mare transiuit. et censu et firma inde habebat.
Terciu denariu de comitatu archieps q ante edzuinu fuit habuit. Tempore edzui rex eduuard
dedit goduino. Terras oms que ptinent ad archiepatum et ad abbatia sci Aug [illegible] et terras
comitis Goduini. testati sunt ee liberas ab omi consuetudine regia. pri [illegible] uias
que uadunt de ciuitate ad ciuitate. et de mercato ad mercatu. et de portu maris ad aliu portu.
De illa calumnia qua eps odo fecit de pratis archiepi et sci augustini iudicauert omis qd iniustici
haberet. et prata utriusq. eccle sic cetere tre libera ee deberent. Terra Goduini dampne ad ecclam
sci augustini ptinet. et qndo rex mare transiuit eccla de tra illa seruiciu habebat. et modo hugo
de dono regis habet.

Figure 17. British Library, Cotton Aug. ii. 36. (The original measures 210 by 185 mm.)

could. There are some signs which seem to favour an early date. At the time when this text was written, 'the archbishop' still meant Stigand; if one meant 'archbishop Lanfranc', one had to say so. The legally significant date was 'when the king crossed the sea', not 'the day when king Edward was alive and dead'.

This is the only document printed here which survives as an original. It consists of an oblong sheet of parchment (210 × 185 mm) with 25 lines of text written on one side of it. Below the last written line there seem to be two more ruled lines; the rest of the sheet is blank. The writing extends very nearly from edge to edge, with only the narrowest of margins. There are no corrections: this is obviously a fair copy, taken from an exemplar which was probably not so tidy. (Several sentences end with the clause 'and now the bishop has it' (or something similar to that). One sentence ends 'and now the bishop had it but has handed it over'. In the exemplar, I imagine, *habet* had been altered to *habebat sed dimisit.*)

The scribe is a known individual (Webber 1995, p. 148). He wrote two other surviving documents, one of them a writ of bishop Odo for Christ Church (Bates 1998, p. 328); he also wrote a short inscription – which includes the words 'I, Lanfranc' – in a book donated to Christ Church by the archbishop.[1] The hand is not Lanfranc's own;[2] but the man who wrote this inscription was, at least for part of his career, Lanfranc's alter ego.[3]

Originally this document was longer than it is now – by how much it is impossible to say. Because the script is rather small, in proportion to the spacing of the lines, and (more particularly) because the descenders are quite short, it would be possible to make a horizontal cut, between any given line and the next, without touching the text, or almost so; and clearly that is what someone decided to do. In consequence the first surviving line is very close to the upper edge; and the tallest characters – the *F* in *Fulchestan*, the *R* and the *b* in *Ratebourc*, the abbreviation mark in *e'* for *est* – have all been sliced off at the top. Once the document had been cut in two, the upper part was discarded, and only the lower part was kept. It was folded up for safety (there are four horizontal creases and one vertical) and labelled for ease of reference.[4] In other words, it was now being treated as a formal document, fit to be preserved in the archive.

I print the text from the original, checking it against the two previous editions (Birch 1887, Douglas 1933), and against the copy in manuscript T1, the existence of which was first noted by Du Boulay (1966). As well as making some adjustments to the text, Du Boulay provided an English translation of it (1966, pp. 38–9); but I think that he misidentified some of the place-names. (Preston is certainly the place in Aylesford (DB-Ke-3rb41); Cliffe is presumably the manor of that name (4vb42).)

[1] *Hunc librum dato precio emptum ego LANFRANCVS archiepiscopus de beccensi cenobio in anglicam terram deferri feci et ecclesię Christi dedi. Siquis eum de iure prętatę ecclesię abstulerit, anathema sit* (Ker 1960, pl. 5).

[2] Lanfranc's handwriting is represented by the subscription which he added to one version of the primacy agreement of 1072 (Bates 1998, pp. 309–10) – *Ego Lanfrancus dorobernensis archiepiscopus subscripsi* – and that is not the same as this. Here again, I am grateful to Tessa Webber for her advice.

[3] A monk of Le Bec named Gundulf is known to have been brought over to England and employed in Lanfranc's household (until he was appointed to the bishopric of Rochester in 1077). Is it worth considering the possibility that this might be Gundulf's hand?

[4] The first endorsement is the work of a twelfth-century scribe who seems to have been responsible for a thorough reorganization of the Christ Church archive. It would be useful to know the date of the latest documents which passed through his hands.

2

The report of an inquiry into the lands and other assets belonging to Newington church.

[a]Hee sunt consuetudines et terre que pertinent ad ecclesiam de [b]Niuuentune. Septem sulinges terre. Septem dennas in silua que uocatur uueald. Vna (1) piscacio in loco qui dicitur Bædinge. Viginti et octo pensas casei de Middeltune, et uiginti et octo (2) pensas casei de Scapeia [c]et de Binnen ea. Viginti quatuor libras denariorum, hoc est [d]gablum de terra septem sulinge. Ecclesia sancte Sexburge in Scapeia debet predicte ecclesie unoquoque anno decem solidos. [e]Ecclesia quoque de Merandenne ad illam pertinet. Due [f]mansiones in Hrofecestr' que reddunt ii solidos. Tres quoque (3) mansiones in ciuitate Cantuuarie in occidentali parte Eastbrigge et ecclesia que [g]est ibi reddunt triginta denarios. Sex (4) carra de uuald. Homines quoque de uuald debent unam (5) domum estiualem [h][facere] aut uiginti solidos dare. In eadem ecclesia sunt uiginti et octo partes. Octo partes sunt archiepiscopi et ecclesie Christi. Quatuor sancti Augustini. [i]Sedecim [j]partes sunt eorum qui seruiunt in eadem ecclesia. Brihtmundus tenuit partem archiepiscopi et dedit ei unoquoque anno octo libras. Leofsinus auunculus eiusdem Brihtmundi tenuit partem abbatis et dedit [k]ei iiii libras. In ecclesia quoque sancti Martini Doffris ecclesia Christi et archiepiscopus habet iiii partes. Et abbas duas.

(1) piscacio [l]quod dicitur anglice 'uuere' (2) pensas [m]quod anglice dicitur 'uuægian' (3) mansiones [n]idest 'hagan' (4) carra de uuald quod anglice dicitur 'gaueluuænas' (5) domum estiualem quod anglice dicitur 'sumer hus'

T1, fos. 167v–8r, with serial number *XCIX* (scribe 1) and heading *Consuetudines de Newenton'* (scribe 2); C5, fo. 28v, no heading (damaged by fire); Fleming 1997, pp. 151–2 (very inaccurate), from C5

[a] (h)ee *T1 (with cue for rubricator)* : ( )e *C5* [b] Nuuentune *T1* : Niwentune *C5* [c] *a hairline added in T1 by scribe 2 suggests starting a new sentence here* [d] gablum *T1 altered to* gabulum *by scribe 2* : gabla *C5* [e] *a small erasure before* ecclesia *T1* [f] mansiones in Hrofecestr' *T1* : etiam in Rofecestra mansiones *C5 (perhaps misreading a transposition mark)* [g] est ibi *T1* : *transp. C5* [h] facere *my conjecture* : *om. T1, C5* [i] Sedecim *T1 altered to* Sexdecim *by scribe 2* : xvi *C5* [j] partes sunt *T1* : *om. C5* [k] ei *T1* : *om. C5* [l] quod dicitur *T1* : que dicitur que dicitur *C5* [m] *gloss om. C5* [n] *gloss om. C5*

Date: 1070×86. Presumably after the arrival of archbishop Lanfranc, and probably not long after. Certainly earlier than 1086.

This is one of the documents which were copied into the lost cartulary, C3, and subsequently copied from there into these two surviving manuscripts, C5 and T1 (below, Appendix I). Without hesitation I print the text from T1, which though later than C5 is generally much more reliable; it is also in excellent condition, unlike

C5, which in places is illegible. (C5's variant readings are numerous but not of any interest; I cite only a few of them.) As it appears in T1, the text is the work of scribe 1, but several corrections were made to it by scribe 2. It was he who inserted the heading here; he also wrote the matching entry in the table of contents: *XCIX. Consuetudines et terre ecclesie de Newentun'* (fo. 148v).

Two features of the text are vaguely problematic. First, the punctuation is unsatisfactory – inadequate at the beginning, excessive towards the end. Seeing the problem, scribe 2 went through the underpunctuated section, adding vertical hairlines where he thought he saw a break in the sense. Though at one point I disagree with him (note *c*), on the whole it seems clear that he had caught the intended meaning, and I have followed his lead. Second, there are five explanatory remarks – glosses which give the English equivalent for some Latin word employed in a technical sense. Because some of these glosses are awkwardly placed (and because two of them are missing from C5), it seems doubtful whether they are properly part of the text; so I have thought it best to cut them out and place them at the end.

The contents of this document are paraphrased by Du Boulay (1966, pp. 176–7); I discuss them further in the commentary, in relation to DB's chapter 13 (14va3).

3

An obituary notice of Willelm I, who restored to the church of Canterbury almost all the lands which had been taken away from it, in Kent, Surrey, London, Middlesex, Buckinghamshire, Oxfordshire, Suffolk and Essex.

Obiit WILLELMUS rex anglorum. Hic reddidit ęcclesię Christi omnes fere terras antiquis et modernis temporibus a iure ipsius ęcclesię ablatas. Quarum terrarum nomina hęc sunt. In cantia, Raculf, Sandwic, Rateburch, Wudetun, Monasterium de limminge cum terris et consuetudinibus ad ipsum monasterium pertinentibus, Saltwude cum burgo hethe ad saltwude pertinente, Langport, Niwendene, Rokinge, Detlinge, Prestentune non longe a fluuio medeweie sitam, Sunderherste, Earhethe, Orpentun, Ainesford, Denintun, Stocke, Quattuor prebendas de niwentune, et preter hęc omnia multas alias modicas terras tam in insulis quam extra insulas in cantia sitas. (Stocke uero et denentun LANFRANCUS archiepiscopus reddidit ęcclesię Sancti ANDREĘ, quia de iure ipsius ęcclesię antiquitus fuerunt.) In suthrege, Murtelac. Lundonię monasterium Sanctę MARIĘ cum terris et domibus quas Liuinguus presbiter et uxor illius lundonię habuerunt. In mildelsexum, Hergam, Heisam. In buckingeham scire, Risbergam, Healtun. In oxenaford scire, Niwentun. In suthfolke, Frakenham. (Hanc uillam LANFRANCUS archiepiscopus reddidit ęcclesię Sancti ANDREĘ, quia antiquitus ad ipsam ęcclesiam pertinebat.) In eastsexum, Stistede, Stanbrigge. Hęc omnia reddidit pro deo et pro salute animę suę gratis et sine ullo pretio.

Dart 1726, app. p. ii, from BL, Cotton Claudius C. vi, fo. 165v; Bandinel 1813, p. 109, from the same; Le Patourel 1948, pp. 24–6, from the same

Date: 1087. Presumably composed immediately after the king's death in September that year.

This document would not have existed in separate form (unless perhaps the author wrote out a draft of it on some spare piece of parchment); it would have been entered in the church's martyrology – the book where the monks recorded their benefactors' names – so that it could be read aloud each year, on the anniversary of the king's death. I reproduce the text as it was printed by Le Patourel, replacing *&* with *et* and adjusting the punctuation (but not the capitalization). Also I have bracketed two sentences which read like afterthoughts.

As far as Kent is concerned, the places listed (not all of them identified correctly by Le Patourel) are Reculver, Sandwich, Fleet (called Richborough) in Ash, Wootton, Lyminge, Saltwood and Hythe, Langport in Lydd, Newenden, Ruckinge, Detling, Preston in Aylesford, Sundridge, Crayford, part of Orpington, Eynsford, Denton and Stoke (these two restored by Lanfranc to the church of Rochester), and four prebends in Newington church.

Documents from Saint Augustine's

The dissolution of Saint Augustine's abbey, in July 1538, appears to have resulted in the total destruction of its archive. In consequence, the only documents known to us are those which had been copied into the abbey's cartularies and registers, which (or some of which) had a happier fate. The textual relationships existing between these manuscripts are a tangle which no one has unravelled very far; in the comments which follow, I focus as narrowly as possible on the particular stretches of text which have some interest for us, and what I say should be regarded as tentative.

It is clear that the monks retained in their possession a remarkable collection of documents dating from the late eleventh century – from the time of abbots Scolland (1070–87) and Wido (1087–93), and from the scandalously long period, after Wido's death, when the abbey was left without an abbot (1093–1107). Of course they were careful to keep important documents, such as charters and writs of Willelm I,[5] Willelm II, or Odo bishop of Bayeux.[6] But documents of much less significance were also preserved – two small memoranda, for instance, relating to the compensation received by abbot Scolland for assets which vanished when a tract of land in Canterbury was seized as a site for the castle.[7] But it must not be forgotten that they exist only in the form of thirteenth-century and fourteenth-century copies, some of which may be several steps removed from the originals. Much more so than documents from Christ Church or Rochester, documents from Saint Augustine's have a fuzzy quality to them; and this is something which has to be allowed for in deciding how far to trust them.[8]

These are the manuscripts and stretches of text which come into question here.

[5] These were all edited by Bates (1998, nos. 80–4, 87–8).

[6] A writ and a charter of bishop Odo's were also edited by Bates (1998, pp. 351–3). (The charter has a line at the end of it added by the king.)

[7] They were printed by Urry (1967, p. 445), from manuscripts A2 and A4 (see below); I have not thought it necessary to print them again.

[8] This applies, not just to the documents printed here, but also to the abbey's pre-conquest (or ostensibly pre-conquest) charters, all of which – with the exception of the forged papal letters – were edited by Kelly (1995).

A2 = BL, Royal 1 B. xi, fos. 145v–7v, a collection of lists and memoranda relating to the abbey's property, entered on five blank pages at the end of a mid twelfth-century copy of the Gospels (Warner and Gilson 1921, vol. 1, p. 12; Dodwell 1954, p. 34). A single stretch of text, written by an early thirteenth-century hand. The same documents, in very nearly the same sequence, turn up again in A4 (see below). Among them are the lists of parish churches which are printed in chapter 8 (where the reader will find some more detailed description of these two manuscripts); two of the other items are printed below (docs. 10–11).

A3 = BL, Cotton Julius D. ii, fos. 84–103, 114–33, 104–13 (five quires of 10 leaves each, the third bound after the fifth). Two stretches of text, the second beginning at 130v15. Both stretches were written by the same hand, that of a very competent scribe active in about 1230, but the second stretch (130v–3v + 104r–9v) is distinguished by the absence of rubrication, and by the fact that as far as 108r it runs parallel with a substretch of text in A5 (see below). Five items from A3 are printed below (docs. 4–8); all of them come from (what ought to be) the final quire.

A4 = National Archives, E 164/27, fos. 2r–48r. The rest of the book (see below) dates from about 1320, but this section may perhaps be somewhat earlier. Two stretches of text, distinguished by a change of hand at 27r10. The first stretch contains all the items of interest for us, most importantly the series of excerpts from the B-Ke text (chapter 3). Of the documents printed below, three appear in this manuscript. One which occurs in shortened form in A3 occurs at full length here (doc. 4). It is included in a substretch of text (2r–8r) which represents a partial calendar of the abbey's archive, compiled (so it seems) from a boxful of documents tied up in bundles but otherwise not kept in order (above, p. 73). The two documents printed from A2 occur in A4 as well (docs. 10–11), included in a substretch of text (11v–17r) which from 14r onwards runs parallel with A2.[9]

A5 = National Archives, E 164/27, fos. 48r–191v, written by three collaborating scribes in about 1320. Four of the documents printed below occur in this manuscript, one of them only here (doc. 9). Two items (docs. 6–7) come from a substretch of text (76v–87r) which from 79v onwards runs parallel with A3. Within the specified bounds, both manuscripts seem to consist of excerpts from a mid twelfth-century cartulary.[10] The other two items (docs. 8–9) appear to have been copied from the originals; at least I can see no reason not to think so.

[9] A note added by a fifteenth-century hand against the beginning of this substretch tells us that it was 'extracted from the textus of Saint Adrian' (fo. 11v). That is the name which we find being used, from the late thirteenth century onwards, for what was regarded as the abbey's most important register. There seems to be only one surviving manuscript which might perhaps be identified as a fragment of that register: I mean BL Cotton Vitellius A. ii, fos. 3–19.

[10] Because there are only two copies – not three, as in the case of the Christ Church cartulary (Appendix I) – the evidence is ambiguous by definition, and the exemplar cannot be adequately reconstructed. Of the items occurring in both copies, the latest are two charters of Henric I (Johnson and Cronne 1956, nos. 1283, 873); of those occurring only in A5, the latest is a charter of Stephan (Cronne and Davis 1968, no. 163); of those occurring only in A3, the latest are a batch of documents dating from the period 1175–8, when the abbot-elect was working hard to repair the damage done by his predecessor – and, at the same time, trying to avoid being humiliated by the archbishop. This last batch looks as if it may have been inserted subsequently (in the same way that a batch of documents was copied onto the blank pages at the end of manuscript C1); my guess would be that the cartulary was originally compiled in the time of abbot Hugo II (1126–51). It may have been, or may have become, another component of the textus of Saint Adrian (see previous note).

Most of the following documents are referred to by the abbey's earliest chronicler, Thomas Sprott, who was at work towards the end of the thirteenth century, perhaps even a little later. Except for the first few paragraphs (Dugdale 1655, p. 23 = Bandinel 1813, p. 126), Sprott's chronicle has not been published in its original form; but large portions of the text – including all the passages of interest for us – were translated into English by Stevens (1722, pp. 303–22).

4

A list of the pieces of land stolen from Saint Augustine since 1066.

Iste sunt terrule quas ab antiquo tempore et in diebus Eadwordi regis sanctus Augustinus habuit, set sibi potestas diuitum eas contradicentibus fratribus abstulit. Unum iugum quod uocatur Suanetum sibi Hugo de mundford iniuste usurpauit, et xxx agros quos Godwine punter linde east bricce tenebat, et unum iugum de Hortune, et Ængestsele quod Wlfric pullehare de sancto Augustino tenebat, et terram Ælfsi tumbe sune, de qua sanctus Augustinus solebat habere seruitia. [a][Willelmus de arces habet dimidium aratrum atte Broke quod Siric habuit. Ricardus de tonnebrigge habet illud de Bearmlince. Robertus de somerie habet Sourtherst et Herreferynge, duoden' l agros Aelfgidetone. Randulfus de columbeal et terram que uocatur Smethetune. De Acrisc dimidium aratrum habet Ranulfus frater Godefridi de eo. xxv agros tenet Petrus de Aelgidetune. xxv agros tenet Ranulfus de corbespyn de Yatenholte. Et Reginaldus de albedone tenet quatuor agros de Hemstede. Et Osbernus tenet Betlesangre. Et comes Cancie possidet Scellynge.]

A3, fo. 108r, incomplete, with space for heading but none supplied; A4, fo. 2v, no heading; Kelly 1995, pp. cx–xi, from A4 (as far as *quod Siric habuit*)

[a] et c' *A3, omitting the rest*

Date: 1070×82. Presumably later than abbot Scolland's arrival in 1070; earlier than bishop Odo's fall from power.

The text is not in good shape. There are places where both scribes seem to be copying sequences of characters without understanding what they mean (and the A3 scribe gives up the struggle halfway through). I am in the same quandary: I can more or less read what the manuscripts say, but there are places where the sense of it escapes me. Despite that, most of the text is comprehensible, and I am sure that it deserves to be published in full. I print it from A3, as far as A3 goes; the rest is from A4 (which, as the reader should bear in mind, is rather carelessly written).[11]

[11] This is the closest that I would be willing to come to a translation: 'These are pieces of land which Saint Augustine used to own in ancient times, and in the time of king Eadward; but the power of rich men has taken them away from him, despite the brothers' protests. Hugo de Montfort has unjustly usurped for himself a yoke which is called Swanton, and 30 acres of Eastbridge which Godwine ... used to hold, and a yoke of Horton, and Hinxhill which Wulfric ... used to hold from Saint Augustine, and the land of Ælfsi ... from which Saint Augustine used to get services. Willelm de Arcis owns a half ploughland at Brook which Siric used to own. Ricard de Tonebrige owns ... Barming. Robert de Someri owns ... two dens (?), 50 acres (of) 'Ælvetune' ... Rannulf de Columbels ... the land which is called 'Smedetune'. Godefrid's brother Rannulf has

This seems to be an aide-mémoire drawn up for abbot Scolland's benefit, at a time when he was trying to recover Saint Augustine's lost property. Since it is clear from doc. 1 that some of the abbot's grievances were discussed at Penenden in 1072, we may be tempted to suppose that the present document was drawn up at about that time; but the evidence does not seem adequate to justify this conclusion. (It should be noted, by the way, that the manor of Badlesmere, to which the abbot advanced a claim in 1086 (DB-Ke-10rb15, 12vb37), is not mentioned here.)

5

An agreement between abbot Scotland and Hugo son of Fulbert. Hugo gets possession of two sulungs at Sibertswold, on condition that he pays the abbot 20 shillings each year on the feast of Saint Andrew and gives tithes of all his proceeds from the domain. He is to keep the land properly stocked and manage it well. After his death, it is to revert to Saint Augustine, in whose cemetery he has chosen to be buried.

Conuentio inter Scollandum abbatem et monachos sancti Augustini cum Hugone filio Fulberti. Accepit ipse Hugo terram duorum solingiorum Suibertesweald, ea conditione, quod dabit ipse per singulos annos xx solidos in festo sancti Andree abbati et fratribus, et dabit decimam omnium rerum suarum que in eadem terra fuerint, scilicet messium, ouium, lane, porcorum, animalium, caseorum et ceterorum que ipse in dominio habuerit. Francigene quicumque de terra illa quicquam ab eo tenuerint eandem prescriptam conuentionem quam et ipse custodient. Angli uero ibidem degentes consuetam annonam reddent, usque dum legittime ab omnibus Angligenis decima reddatur, et ipsi eam tunc daturi. Terram uero istam debet ipse Hugo bene uestire et domibus et animalibus et bene agricolari. Et si contigerit sibi obitus, habeat totam terram cum uestitura in dominium sanctus Augustinus, in cuius cimiterio delegit sibi sepulturam, et omnium propriarum rerum donationem. Ipse autem seruiet abbati et fratribus fideliter sicut miles eorum. Consuetudines tamen quas hactenus reddidit terra illa regi in operibus castellorum uel quod dicunt scot uel aliarum rerum reddet. Nomina testium, Hildegarus decanus, [a]......

A3, fo. 104v, with space for heading but none supplied; summarized A4, fo. 3v

[a] et c' *A3, omitting the rest*

Date: 1070×9. Probably not much later than 1070. Presumably of the same date as doc. 6, which is earlier than doc. 7, which is fairly sure to be earlier than doc. 8, which is dated 1079.

Unlike archbishop Lanfranc (who arrived in England just a few months later than him), abbot Scolland liked to get his business dealings recorded in writing, and docs. 5–7 are a consequence of that. He has had to negotiate agreements with three of bishop Odo's men: Hugo son of Fulbert, Wadard, Ansfrid Masleclerc. All three (so we may assume) had put themselves into possession of land which properly belonged to Saint Augustine, and the abbot had to make the best terms with them that he could. The resulting agreements were probably all drawn up in duplicate, though there is nothing in the wording to indicate that. This agreement with Hugo was apparently the only one which included a list of witnesses; unfortunately the A3 scribe cut the list short (as he usually did) and the first name alone is preserved. I have no idea who Hildegar the dean may have been.

Two matters referred to incidentally here are, I think, of some larger significance. First, we find it being taken for granted that pieces of these manors are likely to be given to foreign immigrants, *Francigene*. (Perhaps this has already happened; the abbot would not admit that gifts made previously were valid.) Such immigrants, it seems, were numerous enough to be found just about everywhere; and those who are known to us by name were probably not more than a small proportion of the total number. Second, while these immigrants are expected to pay tithes, the English do not do the same. They pay something; there is some custom which they recognize; but they do not pay tithes in any sense of the word which abbot Scolland understands. Though he disapproves of it, he does not have the authority himself to overturn this custom. Nevertheless, he is expecting that some change will be made – and that means, I suppose, that archbishop Lanfranc was known to be considering the matter.

The first two agreements (docs. 5–6) are framed in identical terms – from which we may infer that Hugo and Wadard had formed a united front against the abbot. In return for an acknowledgment that it was Saint Augustine's, each of them was allowed to keep the land that was in his possession, for his lifetime, at a modest rent. After his death, it would become part of Saint Augustine's domain. No doubt there was some expectation that the lease would be renewed in favour of the man's heir; but the abbot did not commit himself to that.

Sibertswold, the manor in question here, was back in the abbot's hands by 1086 (DB-Ke-12va38). Fulbert de Dovre – Hugo's heir, presumably his son – was not in possession of it. But there are signs that Fulbert had only quite recently come into his inheritance, and perhaps he had not yet had time to come to terms with the abbot. That is doubtful; but Sibertswold did certainly belong to Fulbert's descendants.

6

An agreement between abbot Scotland and Wadard the knight. Wadard gets possession of five sulungs around Northbourne, on condition that he pays the abbot 30 shillings each year at Whitsun and gives tithes of all his proceeds from the domain. He is to keep the land properly stocked and manage it well. After his death, it is to revert to Saint Augustine, in whose cemetery he has chosen to be buried.

Conuentio inter Scollandum abbatem et monachos sancti Augustini cum Wadardo milite. Accepit ipse Wadardus terram quinque solingiorum circa Norburnam uillam, ea conditione, quod dabit ipse per singulos annos xxx solidos in pentecosten [a]abbati, et dabit decimam omnium rerum suarum que in eadem terra [b]fuerint, scilicet messium, ouium, lane, porcorum, animalium, caseorum et ceterorum que ipse in [c]dominio habuerit. Francigene [d]quicumque de

from him a half ploughland of Acrise. Petrus holds 25 acres of 'Ælvetune'. Ra(d)ulf de Curbespine holds 25 acres of 'Wlatenholt'. Reginald de (V)albadon holds 4 acres of 'Hemstede'. Osbern holds Betteshanger. The earl of Kent is in possession of Stelling.'

terra illa [e]quicquam ab eo tenuerint, [f]...... Angli uero ibidem degentes consuetam annonam [g]reddent, usque dum legittime ab omnibus Angligenis decima reddatur, et ipsi eam tunc daturi. Terram uero istam debet ipse Wadardus bene uestire et domibus et animalibus et bene agricolari. Et si contigerit sibi obitus, habeat totam terram cum [h]uestitura in dominium sanctus Augustinus, in cuius cimiterio delegit [i]sibi sepulturam, et omnium propriarum rerum donationem. Ipse autem seruiet abbati et fratribus fideliter sicut miles eorum. Consuetudines tamen quas [j]hactenus reddidit terra illa regi in operibus castellorum uel quod dicunt scot uel aliarum rerum reddet.

A3, fo. 107v, with space for heading but none supplied; A5, fo. 85r, with heading *De terra Wadardi militis circa Northbourne*; summarized A4, fo. 2r

[a] abbati et fratribus *doc. 5* [b] fiunt *A5* [c] domo *A3* [d] quecunque *A5* [e] quicunque *A5* [f] eandem prescriptam conuentionem quam et ipse custodient *doc. 5* : *om. A3, A5* [g] reddent *doc. 5* : redent *A3* : reddant *A5* [h] uestura *A5* [i] *om. A5* [j] actenus *A3*

Date: 1070×9. Earlier than doc. 7, which is fairly sure to be earlier than doc. 8.

It is a textual point worth noting that both copies omit the second half of the sentence which begins with *Francigene*. (The A5 scribe tried to knock some sense into what was left by changing two of the words; he did not succeed.) Otherwise the wording is identical, mutatis mutandis, with that of the abbot's agreement with Hugo son of Fulbert (doc. 5). In DB we find Wadard listed as the abbot's tenant for part of Northbourne (12va14) and part of Little Mongeham (12va35); the fact that he pays the abbot 30 shillings is mentioned twice.

7

An agreement between abbot Scotland and Ansfrid Masleclerc. Ansfrid gets possession of two named lands, on condition that he does service to Saint Augustine's and pays the customs which the land ought to pay; he is also to pay tithes, on the same terms as Wadard. In addition, he agrees to give tithes from five places which he holds from the bishop (of Bayeux); the bishop's assent to this is noted.

Hec [a]conuentio est inter abbatem Scollandum et Ansfridum qui dicitur Masleclerc. Accepit ipse terram que dicitur Riple et terram de Aluatuna a supradicto abbate, ea conditione, ut seruiat inde sancto Augustino et abbati et fratribus et reddat consuetudines quas terra reddere debet. Reddat autem decimam frugum suarum rerum, sicut reddit Wadardus. De quinque etiam suis uillis, id est Hortun, Lega, Ernoltuna, Sceldrisham, Oslacestune, quas possidet [b]ab episcopo, ipso annuente, similiter [c]dat decimam tam frugum quam omnium animalium suorum et ceterarum rerum sancto Augustino, preter [d]gabulum et forisfacturas. Si qui Franci fuerint in istis terris, decimam dabunt. Angli uero secundum suum morem faciant, donec melius fit.

A3, fos. 107v–8r, with space for heading but none supplied; A5, fo. 85r–v, with heading *De terra de Ripple et Aluetuna*; summarized A4, fo. 2r

[a] est conuencio *A5* [b] de *A5* [c] dat *A3, A5 (read* det *or* dabit*)* [d] ga *A5 (at end of line)*

Date: 1070×9. It refers back to the abbot's agreement with Wadard (doc. 6); from the fact that Wadard and Ansfrid are named as witnesses in the next document, it appears that they had both come to terms with the abbot before 1079.

The place-names here are uncommonly problematic. Ripple was described in B-Ke (xAug has a shortened version of that paragraph) but dropped out of the text, somewhere alone the line between B and DB. *Aluatuna* is *Æluetone* in DB (12vb5), but can only be loosely identified on the ground. As for the five manors held by Ansfrid from the bishop of Bayeux (called simply 'the bishop'), only the first is straightforward: this is Horton in Chartham (10va25). *Ernoltuna* and *Sceldrisham* are recorded as Ansfrid's property in DB (10rb1, 10ra46) but have not been adequately identified. *Lega* and *Oslacestune* are puzzles which I cannot solve.

8

The record of a donation made by Herbert son of Ivo, with the assent of his lord, bishop Odo, earl of Kent, in return for his being made a brother of abbot Scotland and the brothers of Saint Augustine's. His donation consists of the tithes from five of his manors, the names of which are given; tithes of all tithable goods are to be paid to Saint Augustine, or one hundred shillings in cash each year, if that is what the abbot decides.

Anno dominice incarnationis millesimo septuagesimo nono, regnante glorioso rege Anglorum Willelmo et Odone Baiocarum pontifice Cantie comitatum tenente, domino quoque [a]abbate Scollando sancti Augustini monasterium regente, Herbertus Iuonis filius petiit a [b]supradicto abbate et fratribus loci quatinus illorum efficeretur frater, eumque suis precibus die ac nocte domino commendarent. Quod iam dictus abbas una cum fratribus benignissime annuit. Pro qua re isdem Herbertus, concedente Odone pontifice Cantie comite domino suo, dedit sancto Augustino et domino abbati Scollando et fratribus decimas quinque mansionum, quarum nomina subter [c]annectimus, ut [d]posterorum nostrorum memoriis commendentur. Est ergo una harum ad Cliue, altera ad Æuuella, tercia uero ad Ospringes, quarta ad Hergedesham, quinta ad [e][Wildene]. De his quinque mansionibus totam plenam decimam omnium rerum de quibus recte datur decima sancto dedit Augustino, uel per singulos annos centum nummorum solidos. Istud in arbitrio et uoluntate iam dicti abbatis constituit. Huius igitur donationis nomina testium qui affuerunt hic annotamus, scilicet Reginaldus, Wadardus, [f][Ansfridus masleclerc, Odilardus dapifer abbatis, Gauufridus filii Gauslini, et preter hos affuit omnis sepedicti abbatis familia.]

A3, fo. 108r, with space for a heading but none supplied; A5, fos. 148v–9r, with heading *Donacio decimarum Herberti sancto Augustino*; summarized A4, fo. 2r

[a] *om. A5* [b] iam dicto *A5* [c] anectimus *A3* : anneximus *A5* [d] posteriorum *A3* [e] Wildene *A5* : Langedune *A3 (*Langedone *A4*, Langetune *doc. 10)* [f] et c' *A3, omitting the rest*

Date: explicitly 1079, when Willelm was king of the English, Odo bishop of Bayeux was earl of Kent, and Scolland was abbot of Saint Augustine's.

This seems to be a genuine donation, inspired by nothing beyond the declared motive – a wish to be remembered in the monks' prayers. The manors in question are Solton in West Cliffe (DB-Ke-11ra38), (Temple) Ewell (11ra26), Ospringe (10ra34), Harrietsham (7vb13), and apparently Wilden in Bedfordshire (DB-Bd-209vb). (At some later stage, the monks seem to have decided that the fifth manor was (part of) (East or West) Langdon; but I do not see how that could be right.) By 1086, all of these places had passed into the possession of Herbert's nephew Hugo; DB-Bd makes it clear that Hugo holds from his uncle, who holds from the bishop of Bayeux, and no doubt the same was true for the manors in Kent, though DB-Ke does not say so. The tithes (and the optional 1200 pence) were all lost, soon after 1088, when the lands from which they were supposed to come were given to Willelm Pevrel (doc. 10).

9

A writ of Willelm II (Davis 1913, no. 351) addressed to Haimo the steward, ordering him to see to it that the abbot of Saint Augustine's continues to receive the tithes which were being paid on the day when the king's father was alive and dead, regardless of to whom the king has given the land from which the tithes arise; also to see to it that the abbot is put back into possession of the land of which Anschitil has dispossessed him.

Willelmus rex [a]Angl(orum) H(aimoni) dap(ifero) salutem. Fac ut abbas sancti Augustini habeat omnes decimas quas sanctus Augustinus habebat ea die qua pater meus fuit uiuus et mortuus, cuicunque ego postea dederim terras de quibus decime exeunt, et quicquid sibi ablatum est fac sibi reddi cum iusticia. Et de terra de qua Anschitillus dissaisiuit eum postquam ipse recepit abbaciam fac eum resaisiri, et michi et sibi fac inde iusticiam, si iniuria facta est. T(este) R(oberto) can(cellario).

A5, fo. 148r–v, with heading *Willelmus i de decimis beati Augustini*; Davis 1913, p. 133

[a] Anglie *A5*

Date: 1088×93. Later than the redistribution which followed from the rebellion of 1088. The unnamed abbot has to be Wido, who died in 1093.

The next document gives some indication of the tithes which were in contention. As to the dispute with Anschitil (de Ros), it seems that the land causing trouble was East Wickham – i.e. the half of Plumstead held by the previous abbot from the bishop of Bayeux (DB-Ke-6va28). A mid twelfth-century list of Saint Augustine's's lands complains that 'the other part of Plumstead ... has now unjustly been taken away from him' (A4, fo. 11v); but some compromise was eventually worked out, with the result that Anschitil's descendants are found holding East Wickham at fee-farm from the abbot and convent.

10

A list of the tithes donated to Saint Augustine by Herbert son of Ivo and others which are no longer being paid.

Herebertus filius iuonis dedit decimas de v maneriis suis, Osprenge scilicet et Cliue et Welle et Hergetesham et Langetune, et assederat erga abbatem per c sol'. Sed postquam Willelmus peuerel habuit honorem abstulit totum [a]santo. Willelmus de albeneio aufert S' Augustino decimas iii maneriorum, scilicet [b](Con(l)tune) Cnoltune et Ringeltune et Tikenherste, quas dedit Aþeloldus S' Augustino cum concessu regis Willelmi et episcopi baiocensis. Et Rogerius de maineres aufert decimam de Eswelle quam dedit similiter Aðeloldus eodem concessu. Decima paisforie de Boclande et de Doura, iste et alie quamplures decime iniuste detinentur.

A2, fo. 147v, no heading; A4, fos. 15v–16r, no heading

[a] *sic A2* [b] Contune *corrected and then cancelled instantly A2*

Date: probably c. 1090, but possibly somewhat later.

Herbert's donation is recorded by doc. 8, Adelold's by a charter of bishop Odo (Bates 1998, p. 353). Willelm Pevrel and Willelm de Albigni were among the men rewarded with grants of land in Kent after 1088. Presumably the same was true for Roger de Maineres, but this memorandum is (to my knowledge) the only trace of his existence.

11

An early twelfth-century list of the abbey's lands.

Breuis recapitulatio.
De S' Mildreda xlviii solini.
Ad Meregate vi solini.
Ad Cistelet vi solini et i iugum.
Ad Sturaie v solini cum Swalecliue.
Ad Langeport i solin' et [a](ii) iuga silicet Iuentune et Lichesore.
Ad Norburne et Muningeham et Bewesfeld, Riple, Langedune, Scoueldune, Ælfiuetune, Smethetun' cum aliis omnibus menbris xxxvi suling.
Ad Prestune v soling et xv acres cum terra Haimonis filii uitalis.
Ad Litleburne vii solin.
Ad Leanham v soling' et dimid' et i iugum.
Ad Sellinges vi suling'.
Ad Kenetune et Wiuelesberege iiii soling' et iii^{a} iuga.
Ad Suiberteswald ii soling.
Ad Wilrintune i soling.
Ad Brege i suling.
Ad Dene dimid' soling.
De terra demesune iii^{a} iuga, inter marasc et superiorem terram.
Ad Repetune i suling'.
Lizeline de Snaue dimid' suling.
Ad Sceldinglelde dim' soling'.

Ad Gildinge i solin.
Ad Bodesham i soling.
Ad Æsmeresfeld i soling.
Ad Plumstede ii soling et i iugum.
Ad Dernedane dim' soling.
Ad Marasc ii soling et iii[a] iuga et unus miles scilicet Robertus de S' leodogario tenet dim' iug'.
Ad Forwiz i iugum.
De terra Wolnod tretun i iug' et dim'.
Ad Sturtune et Rotinge i iugum et dim'.
De terra [b](Colring) Colgrin i iugum.
Willelmus de Rapintune tenet iii uirgas in hundred de Æstrie.

A2, fo. 147ra–b, with heading *Solini de abbatia*; A4, fos. 16v–17r, with title replaced by heading *Breuis recapitulacio solinorum*

[a] ii *on erasure A2* [b] Colring *cancelled instantly A2*

Date: not earlier than c. 1090, not later than c. 1130.

The dating depends on the comment attached to the entry for Preston, 'including the land of Haimo son of Vitalis' (which one could easily regard as an afterthought, if one were inclined to complicate the issue). The Vitalis who held part of Preston in 1086 (DB-Ke-12vb1) was the same man who occurs elsewhere as a tenant both of the archbishop and of the bishop of Bayeux. He was dead by 1108; his son Haimo was dead by 1137.

Loosely speaking, this list is a generation later than 1086; I print it because it appears to have some independent value. As far as I can see, there is nothing in the arrangement or wording of the entries which connects this list with the records of the survey. The title 'A short recapitulation' suggests that it was originally compiled from, and placed at the end of, a survey of the abbey's manors – possibly a new survey commissioned by abbot Hugo (1107–26).[12]

Documents from Rochester

We have the monks of Rochester to thank for preserving two important documents: a version of the Rochester section of text α (chapter 2), and a list of the parish churches existing in the diocese of Rochester (chapter 8). For the rest, there are only four documents which I take to be worth printing here, and they are only rather distantly relevant. Two of them (docs. 12 and 15) tell us something about the disruption caused by the creation of the lowy of Tonbridge; the others (docs. 13–14) relate to a donation made by the bishop of Bayeux, while he had possession of Chatham, which after 1088 was declared to be illicit.

Four manuscripts are cited here, the last two of them only incidentally. These are they:

R1 = Strood, Medway Archives, DRc / R1, fos. 119–235 (c. 1120);

R2 = BL, Cotton Domitian x, fos. 92–211 (early thirteenth century);

R3 = BL, Cotton Vespasian A. xxii (early thirteenth century);

[12] The record of this private survey, if there was such a thing, might also be the source for some of the components in the *Noticia terrarum* (above, p. 73) which are not derived from either B-Ke or DB-Ke.

R4 = Strood, DRc / R2, fos. 9–52, 'Custumale Roffense' (mid thirteenth century).

All four are described in Flight (1997a); as far as R1 is concerned, the pertinent facts have already been repeated once (above, pp. 39–40), and I refrain from repeating them again.

12

An agreement between bishop Gundulf and Gislebert son of Ricard, made in the presence of archbishop Lanfranc, concerning the lands in the lowy of Tonbridge which belong to the church of Rochester.

Hęc est conuentio quę facta est Cantuarię in presentia domni archiepiscopi Lanfranci atque eo precipiente scripta, inter Gundulfum episcopum et Gislebertum de tunebrigge. Iudicio ipsius domni archiepiscopi debet Gislebertus unoquoque anno dare l solidos domno episcopo Gundulfo pro terra sancti Andreę quam ipse Gislebertus habet, quoadusque dabit ei tantum de alia terra sua unde habeat per singulos annos l solidos uel ualens. Testante eodem archiepiscopo Lanfranco, et episcopo Willelmo de Dunhelma, et abbate Gisleberto Westmonasterii, et abbate Paulo sancti Albani, et Haimone uicecomite de Cantorberia, et Bertranno de uirduno, et maxima parte de familia ipsius domni archiepiscopi.

R1, fo. 175r, with heading *De conuentione inter Gundulfum et Gislebertum*; printed most recently by Brett and Gribbin 2004, p. 11

Date: 1086$\times$8. At the time of the survey, Gislebert's father was still in possession, and the issue referred to here was unresolved. The bishop of Durham was exiled in 1088, not returning to England till after Lanfranc was dead.

This is a temporary settlement of a dispute echoed in several paragraphs of DB-Ke; it arose from the fact that the lowy of Tonbridge had swallowed up outlying portions of some of the bishop's manors. A final settlement, involving some chicanery on Gislebert's part, was arrived at some years later (doc. 15).

13

A writ of Willelm II (Davis 1913, no. 355) addressed to Haimo the sheriff and his officers of Hoo, concerning the land belonging to the reeveship of Chatham which was given to the monks of Rochester by the bishop of Bayeux (1088$\times$94)

Willelmus rex Anglorum, Haimoni uicecomiti et omnibus ministris suis de Hou, salutem. Sciatis me concessisse monachis sancti Andreę rofensis ęcclesię terram illam quę pertinet ad pręposituram de Ceteham, et quam ipsi monachi infra ortum suum habent inclusam, ea conuentione quod ipsi monachi pro anima patris mei ducentas missas cantare debent, et episcopus Gundulfus pro illa terra debet dare de alia terra sua quę ualeat quantum ipsa ualebat tempore quo episcopus baiocensis concessit eam eisdem monachis.

Testibus, Walchelino episcopo, et Rodberto cancellario, et Rannulfo capellano, apud Bricestoc.

R1, fo. 211v, with space for a heading but none supplied; R2, fo. 183r, with heading *De terra ubi uinea est*;[13] Thorpe 1769, p. 209, from R2

Date: 1088×94. Later than 'the battle of Rochester' (doc. 14). The chancellor is Robert Bloet, who was made bishop of Lincoln in 1094. Probably 1089×93, while the archbishopric was vacant.

This writ, combined with the consequential writ of bishop Gundulf (doc. 14), gives us a glimpse of some of the adjustments which followed from the fall of Odo bishop of Bayeux. The manor of Hoo, which had belonged to the bishop by right of the earldom of Kent, was back in the king's hands now; and the sheriff had sent in some of his officers to manage it. (From doc. 14 we discover their names, and the fact that they were answerable to the sheriff; here the word *suis* is ambiguous.) Hoo was their base, but their sphere of operations included the city of Rochester (which had also belonged to bishop Odo by right of the earldom) and the manor of Chatham.

On the evidence of this writ, I think it has to be inferred that Chatham too, at the time, was regarded as one of the manors appropriated to the earldom of Kent. It had not been given to the bishop of Bayeux outright: it had been given to him in trust – and now it turned out that he broken that trust by giving away some of its assets. The particular case that we hear about (there may have been others) concerns a piece of land which Odo had given to the church of Rochester, 'for the monks to make their garden there' (doc. 14).[14] But this land, as the king was now informed, was one of the perquisites which went with the reeveship of Chatham, and ought not to have been given away. The king was magnanimous enough not to insist on the land being given back; instead he demanded a piece of land of equal value, by way of compensation. He also expected the monks to sing two hundred masses for his father's soul. (Some time later, Chatham was given – given outright – to Haimo the sheriff, and its value was deducted from the value of the earldom. That had happened before any record of 'the farm of the land of the bishop of Bayeux' found its way into the surviving exchequer rolls (Flight 1998).)

14

A writ of Gundulf bishop of Rochester addressed to sheriff Haimo and the barons of Kent, concerning three acres of the land of Borstal which he has given to the king in exchange for the three acres given to the church and monks by Odo bishop of Bayeux.

Gundulfus rofensium gratia dei episopus, Haimoni uicecomiti et omnibus baronibus regis de Cænt francigenis et anglis, salutem et benedictionem dei et suam quantum potest. Volo uos omnes scire me iam quietum esse aduersus regem de illa cambitione terrę quam ei promisi post uuærram Rofę, pro illis tribus acris quos Odo baiocensis episcopus dedit ęcclesię sancti Andreę et monachis nostris ad faciendum ibi ortum suum iuxta murum deforis uersus australem partem ciuitatis forinsecus, qui iam inclusi sunt muro circumquaque. Et illos tres acros terrę quos pro illis tribus dedi regi in cambitionem liberaui iam ministris uicecomitis, Rodberto scilicet de sc'o amando, et Rodberto latimier, et Ælfuuino [a]fratre eius preposito de Cetham, et Grentoni de Rouecestra, de nostra dominica terra de Burchestealla, presentibus testibus istis, Ansgoto de rouecestra, Gosfrido talebot, Goisfrido de ros, [b]Radulfo pincerna Adę, Rodulfo clerico, et aliis multis de nostra familia et de ciuibus eiusdem uillę.

R1, fos. 211v–12r, with space for a heading but none supplied; R2, fo. 183r–v, with heading *De eadem* (i.e. *De terra ubi uinea est*); Thorpe 1769, p. 526, from R2

[a] *sic R1, R2* [b] Radulfo *with* l *corrected R1*

Date: 1088×94 or a little later. Presumably not more than slightly later than doc. 13; at any rate earlier than 1100.

There are some interesting names here. Robert Latimier (his surname distinctly so spelt) is still active, though here he appears as one of sheriff Haimo's officers.[15] He has a brother, Ælfwin, who is reeve of Chatham; Grento is reeve of Rochester (R1, fo. 189v). Among the witnesses, Goisfrid Talebot is one of the new men rewarded for their support in 1088, and Radulf the butler is a tenant of Adam son of Hubert's.

15

A writ of Gislebert son of Ricard addressed to sheriff Rannulf and the barons of Surrey, concerning the land given by his man Othin to the church of Saint Andrew of Rochester.

Gilebertus filius Ricardi, Rannulfo uicecomiti et omnibus baronibus francigenis et anglis de comitatu de Suthereia, salutem. Sciatis quod ego dedi ecclesie sancti Andree de Rouecestra terram Othini hominis mei de Bullocchesfelda, pro cambitione illius terre quam habeo de eodem sancto infra leugam meam de Tunebrige, liberam et quietam ab omni consuetudine que ad me pertinet. Et hanc donationem meam facio cum filio eiusdem Othini ad faciendum [a][eum] monachum ibi, pro anima patris mei et matris mee, et pro salute anime mee. Et isti sunt testes, Anselmus archiepiscopus [b]......

[13] There is also a copy in the charter roll for 1275 (*Calendar of Charter Rolls*, vol. 2, p. 194)

[14] The location of the piece of land given by bishop Odo remains uncertain. From doc. 14 we learn that it consisted of three acres, 'next to the wall (of the city) on the outside'. By 1088 it had been surrounded with a wall of its own. The rubric in R2 identifies this land as 'the land where the vineyard is': that made sense in about 1220, but does not convey any definite meaning to us. Just a few years later, in 1225, a new ditch was dug around the city; and in consequence of that, very probably, a new site would have had to be found for the vineyard . (To the south of the southernmost wall around the cathedral precinct, there is a public garden called 'The Vines'. Until someone convinces me otherwise – the earliest occurrence of the name known to me dates from 1759 (*Archaeologia Cantiana*, 15 (1883), 123) – I shall go on assuming that it was invented by some local antiquary in the eighteenth century.)

[15] Robert died during Anselm's lifetime, i.e. before 1109 (R1, fo. 183r). His widow had some complicated dealings with the monks of Rochester (R1, fos. 200v–1r).

R2, fo. 140r, with heading *De terra de Bullocchesfeld'*.

[a] eum *om. R2* [b] et c' *R2, omitting the rest*

Date: probably 1093×7. Anselm was in England at the time, and Gislebert would have wanted to get this matter settled as soon as he could. Other possible dates are 1100×3 and 1107×9.

There also exists an inflated version of this document (supposed original, Strood, DRc / T373; R2, fo. 139r–v; Thorpe 1769, p. 590, from R2). It seems sure to be a forgery (though I cannot say that I have looked at it very closely), but the witness list – which includes the name of Godefrid prior of Winchester (1082–1107) – may possibly be genuine.

In hard fact, this is a donation by Othin, payment for his son's admission as a monk. To make this donation he needs his lord's assent – but Gislebert, instead of just assenting, represents it as his own donation, and as a fulfilment of the promise that he had made (doc. 12).[16] (He glosses over the fact that the donation is worth less than 50 shillings.) Nothing further is known of Othin's son. A rent of 480 pence from *Bullocesfelde* is said to have been earmarked for the monks' clothing by bishop Gundulf (R1, fo. 196r); it is listed *c.* 1220 among the chamberer's rents (R3, fos. 101v, 102r; R4, fos. 51r, 52r, from R3; Thorpe 1788, p. 27 from R4).[17]

[16] A man called Odin, presumably the same, occurs in Surrey as a tenant of Gislebert's father at the time of the survey: he held 2.5 hides belonging to the manor of Bletchingley TQ 3250 (DB-Sy-34va). (His name is *Odmus* in the printed text, but the Phillimore edition assumes that it ought to be *Odinus* – and rightly so, as this document would seem to prove.)

[17] I have not identified 'Bullocksfield', but apparently it was somewhere in the parish of Bletchingley (R3, fo. 102v).

Chapter 8
Early lists of parish churches in Kent

Across most of England and Wales, the distribution of parish churches is not adequately documented before the late thirteenth century. Kent is the sole exception. For both of the Kentish dioceses, long lists of parish churches survive which date from before 1200, some of them even from before 1100.

Since the 1930s, the existence of these lists has been widely known, and their value has been widely recognized. In particular, a pair of articles by Gordon Ward (1932, 1933) made most of the evidence easily accessible. The majority of the churches named were successfully identified by him. There are some outright errors, and some of the guesswork seems extravagant to me. On the whole, however, Ward did an admirable job, and only a few loose ends require any further comment.

Eleven texts are printed below. Five of them (a–e) come from Christ Church, three (f–h) from Saint Augustine's; those lists relate to the diocese of Canterbury. For the diocese of Rochester one composite text exists, the three components of which (i–k) need to be treated separately.

Most of these texts are explicitly concerned with money. In the view of their respective compilers, they were not so much lists of parish churches as lists of payments due from parish priests. Especially for the archbishop, payments of this kind added up to a considerable sum.[1] List (c) is a record of the arrangements which Lanfranc found in place, when he first arrived (i.e. in 1070). The churches appearing in this list – there are fourteen of them, but possibly one has been omitted (see below) – had all been required to pay an annual tribute to Christ Church. List (d) is a record of the new arrangements introduced by Lanfranc. Essentially he made two changes: he replaced payments in kind with payments in cash, and he imposed a similar charge on a large number of other churches which had not previously been liable. The individual charges vary greatly, between one church and another, and it seems by and large impossible to say how the payment due from each church was determined. But a chrism fee of 7 pence was certainly one of the items which entered into the reckoning.

Chrism was a mixture of olive-oil and balsam, consecrated in a very solemn way, reserved for a small number of special uses.[2] The commonest use – the only everyday use, so to speak – was in the rite of baptism: without chrism a baby could not be properly baptized. For that reason every parish priest needed a supply of chrism; but he could not make it himself. Only a bishop – only a bishop assisted by a suitable number of priests and deacons – could perform the ceremony which turned the raw ingredients into chrism. It seems to have been the normal practice, perhaps the universal practice, for chrism to be made on the Thursday before Easter.[3] The arrangements for its distribution are not so clear; they may perhaps have varied from diocese to diocese, and from time to time.[4]

The exchange of money for chrism was frowned upon; in the end it was forbidden.[5] But clearly Lanfranc had no qualms about it.[6] If it was traditional for parish priests to make some payment, at the same time that they received their chrism, he took it for granted that such payments would continue.[7] There was, after all, some benefit in the transaction. By coming to Canterbury and paying his fee, a parish priest was recognizing the archbishop as *his* bishop; by allowing a quantity of chrism to be given to him, the archbishop was recognizing this priest as one of *his* priests. Repeated every year, the inward flow of silver, no less than the outward flow of chrism, helped to unify the diocese.

Over time, as sensibilities changed, the name 'chrism pennies' dropped out of use: it seemed safer to call them 'synod pennies' instead. As far as the diocese of Rochester is concerned, we know that the payments in question were granted to the monks of Rochester by bishop Ernulf (1115–24). It is not clear what Ernulf called them;[8] but in the

[1] The total for list (d) is 3615 pence.

[2] Chrism was not the same thing as holy oil: it was much holier than that.

[3] We happen to know, for instance, that in 1187 the chrism for the diocese of Canterbury was consecrated on 26 March, which was indeed the Thursday before Easter. On this occasion the ceremony took place in London (Gervasius, *Chronicle*, ed. Stubbs 1879–80, vol. 1, p. 360); since the bishop of London had died a few weeks earlier, the archbishop was presumably making chrism for that diocese as well as for his own.

[4] What happened in 1187 was that the chrism, once it had been consecrated, was carried to Canterbury and then, 'in the usual way', distributed by the sacrist.

[5] The last word on the subject was spoken by the Second Lateran Council in 1139. After that, it could not be doubted but that the giving or receiving of money for chrism was prohibited.

[6] His attitude emerges most clearly from a letter which he wrote to bishop Stigand of Chichester (Clover and Gibson 1979, no. 30).

[7] *Crisma tantum a uobis accipiant, et ea que antiquitus instituta sunt in crismatis acceptione persoluant.*

[8] In Ernulf's charter, as it survives, the payments are called 'the pennies which parish priests are accustomed to pay either when they receive chrism

1140s, when the monks applied to the pope for a confirmation of this grant, 'synod pennies' was the expression that they used.[9] Similarly – though it does not seem to be known exactly when or how – the chrism pennies from the diocese of Canterbury came to belong to the monks of Christ Church; and there too we find them being called 'synod pennies'.[10]

In Lanfranc's time, there were numerous churches in the diocese of Canterbury which did not get their chrism directly from Christ Church. They got it instead from a 'mother church' to which they were subordinate.[11] Arrangements of this kind were presumably justified by history (or pseudo-history): the 'mother church', once upon a time, was the only church within its sphere; as new parishes were formed, new churches built, the 'mother church' continued to exert some superiority over them. There are various ways in which that superiority could find expression, but one of them might be – for a time clearly was – a special role for the mother church in mediating the distribution of chrism. In that respect, large parts of the diocese were not directly under the archbishop's supervision. Indeed, to judge from list (a), Lanfranc had no very accurate idea what churches actually existed in his bishopric, other than those which paid a tribute to Christ Church; he seems to have had no list at all of the churches that belonged to Saint Augustine's.

Arrangements of this kind, even if Lanfranc allowed them to persist, seem largely to have been dismantled not much later. Some vestiges did survive: in the language which became normal later, one church might be said to be a 'chapel' of another church. In the 1080s, ten churches 'belonged' to Lyminge, and two of them, two hundred years later, were still regarded as 'chapels' of Lyminge (Paddlesworth and Stanford). Within the diocese of Rochester, similar relationships show up – most notably with respect to extensive manors like Dartford, Orpington, Shoreham, Hoo – which are, we may suppose, the attenuated traces of arrangements similar to those which had existed in eastern Kent. But a list of the chrism fees due to Rochester, no later than the 1120s, takes no notice of these complications. As far as the distribution of chrism was concerned, it was already the rule that every parish priest should present himself in Rochester and pay his money there.

In the diocese of Canterbury, there were – apart from Christ Church itself – only two churches which remained conspicuously higher in status than the rest: Saint Augustine's and Saint Martin's of Dover. Saint Martin's dwindled away in the 1130s: its endowment was transferred to the newly founded priory, outside the town, and the old church became just one more parish church (or, more precisely, three parish churches under one roof). Saint Augustine's did not dwindle away. In the course of time, however, as other 'mother churches' lost status, the special privileges claimed by the abbey became increasingly obtrusive. The archbishops and the monks of Christ Church began to feel insulted by the abbey's pretensions; the abbots and the monks, for their part, had to find new ways to maintain their independence, and to justify rights which in the past had been taken for granted. Neither side was willing to yield, and disputes kept flaring up.

This levelling process cleared the ground for the erection of new administrative structures. Both bishoprics came to be divided into deaneries, eleven for Canterbury, four for Rochester. Though the details do not become clear until much later, there are casual references which prove the existence of deaneries as far back as the 1140s – except that then they were called not deaneries but chapters.[12] In the diocese of Canterbury only one of these new groupings (the deanery of Sutton) coincides at all closely with a group of churches appearing in list (a); but even in this case the resemblance is not exact, and I do not see that anything follows from it.

At around the same time, the map of parishes seems to have crystallized out into something very close to the late medieval (and post-medieval) configuration. Of the lists that are printed here, those which date from the mid or late twelfth century contain very few surprises: almost without exception, the parish churches which existed at that time are the same churches which existed a hundred years later. Rare instances can be found of churches which ceased to exist after the twelfth century, or of chapels which were later made into independent churches with parishes of their own; but minor adjustments of this kind continued to occur after the late thirteenth century, and it is only to be expected that some would have occurred in the course of the preceding hundred years.

or when they attend the synod', *denarios quos presbiteri parochiani solent reddere uel quando crisma accipiunt, uel ad synodum conueniunt* (R1, fo. 197r). But this is a replacement leaf, and it is not impossible (I would say not unlikely) that the wording has been altered.

[9] Eugenius III for prior Brien and the monks of Rochester, dd. 25 Feb. 1146: *Concessionem autem uobis rationabiliter factam ab Ernulfo bone memorie episcopo uestro de sinodalibus denariis et scripti eius pagina confirmatam, ratam esse censemus* (R1, fo. 206r).

[10] Saltman 1956, no. 49, Cheney and Jones 1986, no. 76, both from Reg. H, fo. 26r.

[11] It is hard to be sure what language is best to use here. The documents themselves are not helpful. The churches dependent on Saint Martin's, for example, are merely said to 'belong' to it, which might mean almost anything. List (f) from Saint Augustine's uses the word 'mother' – but promptly mixes its metaphors by calling the dependent churches 'limbs'. The word 'minster' would certainly be suitable in some cases, but I think we ought to be careful not to use this term too loosely.

[12] It seems likely that the chapters were created, or given definite shape, in the time of archbishop Theobald (1139–61). A charter of archbishop Theobald concerning Graveney church is addressed to 'archdeacon Walter and the whole chapter of Teynham' (Saltman 1956, no. 252, dated 1143×8); I read this as a reference to what was later called the deanery of Ospringe. In other charters of Theobald's there are references to 'the whole chapter of the city of Canterbury' (no. 36), 'all clerics of the chapter of Dover' (no. 97), and 'the whole chapter of Reculver' (no. 146), i.e. the deaneries of Canterbury, Dover and Westbere respectively. By the 1170s, it was understood that each chapter would have its own dean, elected (in some sense) from among its members, answerable (in the first instance) to the archdeacon (Cheney and Jones 1986, nos. 75–6).

In the earliest lists, those which date from the early twelfth century or before, the proportion of problematic names is distinctly larger. The map, it seems, was still in a fairly fluid state at the time. New churches were being built; but there was also some tendency for old churches to disappear. Gains and losses are likely to go together: when a new church is built, some existing church will lose part of its parish, part of its congregation, part of its income. Unless there is someone in control, someone who can prevent the construction of new churches where the consequences are likely to be more negative than positive, it is more or less bound to happen that some old churches will cease to be viable.

Nobody was in control. A conscientious bishop would doubtless do his best to encourage the building of new churches, where new churches were needed, but he had no power to make this happen, except on the manors which belonged to him and his church. The initiative had to come from the lord of the manor; and generally this means that it came from an individual layman, who had no reason to weigh the wider consequences. It was taken for granted (so I suppose) that any lord was entitled to build himself a church, if that was what he wanted to do. Some people might grumble, but they had no right to complain. Of course the plan could not be carried through without the local bishop's assent: it was the bishop who would have to consecrate the church, once it had been built; it was the bishop who would have to install the first priest. But how could the bishop refuse, once he was presented with a fait accompli? Was it not a commendable act to build a church?

There are only two documented cases known to me of an attempt to carve a new parish out of an old one. Both cases are relatively late, and the very fact that we know about them tends to prove that they are not typical; but they are instructive nevertheless. The first relates to Sheldwich. The lord of the manor, Helto son of Ricard,[13] built a church here, expecting that it would become the centre of a separate parish. But he met with determined opposition. The monks of Saint Augustine's, as owners of Faversham church, had interests which they were prepared to defend, whatever the cost might be. In the end, Helto backed down. He agreed that his church was only a chapel, subordinate to Faversham church, of which, he admitted, he was himself a parishioner; he apologized for the trouble that he had caused; he paid compensation.[14] In a similar case, twenty years later, the lord of Leaveland came up against the monks of Saint Bertin's, who were the owners of Throwley church.[15] Like Helto, Nathanael de Levelande was beaten into submission. In the longer run, however, Leaveland did become a separate parish, independent from Throwley.

As I hope to have said enough to show, the documents which follow are of interest in their own right, not just because they help to elucidate the records of the survey. For present purposes, however, their importance lies in the fact that they give us an entirely independent picture of the distribution of settlement in Kent, in the late eleventh century or not long after that.

Parish churches in the diocese of Canterbury: lists (a–e)

The first two pages of manuscript C1 (above, p. 36) are occupied by lists of churches which add up to give us an overview of the diocese of Canterbury as it existed in the time of archbishop Lanfranc. Though these lists have been printed more than once, I imagine that it may be found helpful if I print them again.

The list which I place first – in the manuscript it is placed third – is the one which poses most problems. As Ward (1933, p. 68) said, it is 'full of difficulties of identification'. He made that remark about the first paragraph, but it also applies to the three paragraphs which follow; and even in the rest of the list an occasional entry occurs which is perplexing. There are so many enigmas, it seems to me, that this list cannot be taken to describe the situation existing in the 1080s. It looks back to a time (perhaps in the early eleventh century) when the diocese comprised eleven (or more) large parishes, each with its own mother church. The mother churches are all easy to identify: it is the subordinate churches (plus the churches named in the final paragraph) which in many cases would seem to have disappeared (or changed their names) by the time that any other evidence becomes available. For some reason, the changes seem to have been most drastic in the eastern and southern parts of the diocese; but some change had happened everywhere.

List (c), as we are explicitly told, is a record of certain arrangements which existed at the time of Lanfranc's arrival in Canterbury – arrangements, that is, which were current in the 1060s. At that time, it seems, there were, apart from Saint Augustine's, fourteen churches – including nine that are mentioned in list (a) – which paid a tribute to Christ Church at Easter. The tribute due from Saint Augustine's is itemized separately in list (b); we hear a great deal about it, from the 1120s onwards, as the monks there exerted every effort to get it abolished. List (d), of which again we are explicitly told that it describes the new arrangements introduced by Lanfranc, is relatively straightforward. There are a few problematic entries – but the same is true for twelfth-century lists as well.

The fifth list, (e), has not been printed before. It comes from manuscript C4, i.e. from the same booklet, written in about

[13] Helto was the grandson of the Malger who held Ruxley in 1086 (DB-Ke-6va34). As well as his grandfather's lands, he had also acquired (perhaps through his wife) a one-third share of the lands which in 1086 belonged to Ansfrid Masleclerc; that is how he came to own Sheldwich.

[14] The story comes mostly from two documents: a charter of Helto son of Ricard (Turner and Salter 1915–24, pp. 507–8) and a letter of pope Adrianus IV (Hardwick 1858, pp. 406–7).

[15] Cheney and Jones 1986, no. 203, and other documents printed by Larking (1861) from the cartulary of Saint Bertin's.

1215, which also contains a copy of a somewhat discrepant version of text α (above, p. 33). The leaves have been damaged by water towards the top: the black ink was unaffected, but the red ink used for the headings dissolved, to the extent that in places it has vanished altogether. This list is basically a modified version of list (d), with the churches rearranged into groups – groups which were called chapters in the twelfth century, but which came to be called deaneries later. Because the entries are organized geographically, identification becomes much easier than it would be if only list (d) was available.

As for the lists which come from C1, I have treated them more loosely than text α, not reproducing the format of the original or distinguishing the coloured initials; otherwise the transcription is as accurate as I can make it. (A 'w' with a dot beneath it represents the *p*-like character called 'wyn'.) Misreadings of the kind to which this scribe is prone (above, p. 36) occur quite frequently in lists (a) and (d), but I have not thought it necessary to note them.

List (a)

(a1) Iste ȩccl'ȩ pertinent ad sc'm martinum de doforis.	Dover, St Martin
(a2) Sc'i petri.	Dover, St Peter
(a3) Sc'ȩ mariȩ.	Dover, St Mary
(a4) Infra ciuitatem, v monasteria.	?
(a5) Ceorletun.	Charlton
(a6) Denetun.	Denton
(a7) Niẉantun.	?
(a8) *Æ ẉellan, ii ȩccl'as.	? Ewell and River
(a9) *Itum, *æ ẉellan.	?
(a10) Ẉaltun.	?
(a11) Cliue.	? St Margaret at Cliffe
(a12) Burnan.	?
(a13) Cliue.	? West Cliffe
(a14) Gutiestun.	Guston
(a15) Ad folcestan pertinent.	Folkestone
(a16) Aẉoluescyrce.	?
(a17) Bilicean.	?
(a18) Ciricetun.	Cheriton
(a19) Sumafeld.	Swingfield
(a20) Ealhham.	Alkham
(a21) Fleota.	Fleet in Ash
(a22) Huhcham.	Hougham
(a23) Achalt.	?
(a24) Hleodæna.	Lydden
(a25) Wulferestun.	? Wolverton in Alkham
(a26) Ad limenam.	Lympne
(a27) Laurentiuscirce.	?
(a28) Martini ȩccl'a.	?
(a29) Iue circe.	Ivychurch
(a30) Bennede circ'.	?
(a31) Hlide.	Lydd
(a32) Siẉoldescirc'.	?
(a33) Niẉan circ'.	Newchurch
(a34) In hyðe, ii eccl'ȩ.	Hythe
(a35) Ælsiescirc'.	? Eastbridge
(a36) Blacemannes c'.	Blackmanstone
(a37) Mertumnes c'.	?
(a38) Deman, c.	Dymchurch
(a39) Ordgares. *(c.)	Orgarswick
(a40) Bilsẉiðetun.	Bilsington
(a41) Bunnigtun.	Bonnington
(a42) Ealditun.	Aldington
(a43) Stræta.	Street in Lympne
(a44) Sellinge.	Sellindge
(a45) Kyngestun.	?
(a46) Vndetun.	?
(a47) Sẉirgildan, c'.	?
(a48) Ad limminges.	Lyminge
(a49) Wihtricesham.	Wittersham
(a50) Petri ȩccl'a.	?
(a51) Martinescirce.	?
(a52) Stanford.	Stanford
(a53) Hortune.	Horton
(a54) Stutinge.	Stowting
(a55) Birichalt.	Bircholt
(a56) Steallinge.	Stelling
(a57) Aqus.	Acrise
(a58) Ẉeadlesẉurðe.	Paddlesworth
(a59) Ad middeltune.	Milton
(a60) Norðcip'.	?
(a61) Legesdun.	Leysdown
(a62) Rodmæresham.	Rodmersham
(a63) Milstede.	Milstead
(a64) Tunsteal.	Tunstall
(a65) Bacelde.	Bapchild
(a66) Bradegare.	Bredgar
(a67) Bobinge.	Bobbing
(a68) Tanga.	Tonge
(a69) Eastcyrce.	Eastchurch
(a70) Ad niẉantunum.	Newington
(a71) Heordlyp.	Hartlip
(a72) Rænham.	Rainham
(a73) Vpcyrcean.	Upchurch
(a74) Stacabere.	Stockbury
(a75) Halgastaẉ.	Halstow
(a76) Sexburgamynster.	Minster (in Sheppey)
(a77) Niẉecyrce.	?
(a78) Ad tænham.	Teynham
(a79) Duddingtun.	Doddington
(a80) Stane.	Stone
(a81) Cillinge.	?
(a82) Ætþamgeræde.	Iwade
(a83) Ad ẉingeham.	Wingham
(a84) Æsce.	Ash
(a85) Nunningitun.	Nonington
(a86) Rytlinge.	Ratling in Nonington

(a87) Ẉimlingẉeald. Womenswold
(a88) Ẉielmestun. Walmestone in Wingham
(a89) Eadredestun. ?

(a90) Ad mægdestane. Maidstone
(a91) Boxlea. Boxley
(a92) Dytlinge. Detling
(a93) Thornham. Thurnham
(a94) Ealdingtun. Aldington
(a95) Holingaburna. Hollingbourne
(a96) Ẉelcumeẉeg. ?
(a97) Leanham. Lenham
(a98) Boctun. Boughton Malherbe
(a99) Wulacumba. Ulcombe
(a100) Hlyda. Leeds
(a101) Langalea. Langley
(a102) Suðtun. Sutton
(a103) Cert. Chart Sutton
(a104) Hedekaruna. Headcorn
(a105) Fridenastede. Frinsted
(a106) Gmðhyrste. Goudhurst
(a107) Mæredæn. Marden

(a108) Ad Wy. Wye
(a109) Æscedefford. Ashford
(a110) Crundala. Crundale
(a111) Broca. Brook
(a112) Dreamwurðe. Trimworth in Crundale
(a113) Haenostesyle. Hinxhill
(a114) Brixiestun. ?
(a115) Ẉyllan. Eastwell
(a116) Haudkashyrste. Hawkhurst

(a117) Ad cyrringe. Charing
(a118) Eardingtun. Egerton

(a119) *Ebben ea. Ebony
(a120) Ẉylmingtun. ?
(a121) Cealueloca. Challock
(a122) Brygge. Bridge
(a123) Berham. Barham
(a124) Alter berham. ? Kingston
(a125) Monasterium æthyrnan. ?
(a126) Garẉynnetun. Garrington in Littlebourne
(a127) Natindune. Nackington
(a128) Haranhylle. Hernhill

C1, fo. 1rc–va

(a8) Æ wellan *so written, perhaps imitating an erasure in the exemplar* (a9) *presumably* Iterum *misread* æ wellan *again so written* (a39) c *inserted, perhaps by another hand* (a119) *three lines left blank before this*

List (b)

(b) Hęc sunt quę debentur de sc'o augustino singulis annis ęccl'ę xp'i.
(b1) Secretarius *(sc'i aug') vii d' super altare xp'i ponet, aut secretario *(ęccl'e xp'i) in manu dabit.
(b2) Abbas, uel qui in loco abbatis fuerit per idoneos ministros debet mittere ad ęccl'am xp'i xxx panes tales, ut iiii ualeant semper unum denarium, et ii optimos multones, et iii amphoras plenas, ii de meda, et tertiam de ceruisa, et sescentos denarios. Ista omnia debent persolui in cęna d'ni.

C1, fo. 1rc

(b2) sc'i aug' *written above* Secretarius ęccl'e xp'i *written above* secretario

List (c)

(c) Hęc est institutio antiqua ante aduentum domni Lanfranci archiep'i (c1) de middeltune, ii sestres mellis, et ii multones, et viii agnos, et lx panes, et xii d', et in pentecostes dc denarios.
(c2) De megdestane, i sestarium mellis, et viii agnos, et lx panes, et xii d' ad uinum, et xiiii d' ad oleum.
(c3) Simili modo dabatur de Cyrringe. De ẉy, Tænham, Ẉingeham, Estrege.
(c4) De liminges, i sestarium mellis, et ii uerueces, et xxx panes, et vii d'.
(c5) De apeldre, i sestarium mell', et xxx panes, et iiii agnos, et vii d' ad oleum, et vi ad uinum.
(c6) De doforis, i sestarium mell', et xxx panes, et ii multones, et vii d', et dc denarios.
(c7) De *folkestane, i sestarium mell', et xxx panes, et ii uerueces, et vii denarios, et sescentos denar'.
(c8) De duobus boctunis, de unoquoque, iiii agnos, et xxx panes, et xiii den'.
(c9) Similiter de rokinge.
(c10) Sed beatę memorię lanfrancus *ut in antea scriptum est ordinauit et instituit.

C1, fo. 1vb

(c7) fol(k)estane *corrected* (c10) ut in antea scriptum est *referring to list (d)*

List (d)

(d) Hę sunt consuetudines archiep'i in pascha de presbiteris et ęcclesiis.
(d1) De middeltune, x sol' iiii denarios minus. Milton
(d2) De mægdestane, x sol' iiii d' minus. Maidstone
(d3) De Cyrringe, x sol' iiii d' minus. Charing
(d4) De Wy similiter. Wye
(d5) De tænham, ii sol'. Teynham
(d6) De wingeham, ii sol'. Wingham
(d7) De eastrege, x sol' iiii d' minus. Eastry
(d8) De limminges, xxxii d'. Lyminge
(d9) De apeldre, vii sol'. Appledore
(d10) De doforis, lv sol'. Dover, St Martin
(d11) De folcestane, l sol'. Folkestone
(d12) De boctune, xxviii d'. Boughton under Blean
(d13) De alio boctune, xxviii d'. Boughton Aluph
(d14) De rumenea, xxxii d'. ?
(d15) De rokynges, xxviii d'. Ruckinge

(d16) De sandhyrste xxviii d'. Sandhurst
(d17) De ruluindænne, xxviii d'. Rolvenden
(d18) De wndecyrce, xxviii d'. Woodchurch
(d19) De binnigdænne, xxviii d'. Benenden
(d20) De sealtwude, xxviii d'. Saltwood
(d21) De wodnesbeorge, xxviii d'. Woodnesborough
(d22) De leocham, xxviii d'. Ickham
(d23) De biscopestune, xxviii d'. Bishopsbourne
(d24) De welle, xxviii d'. Westwell
(d25) De grauenea, xxviii d'. Graveney
(d26) De berewic, xxviii d'. Harwich in Seasalter
(d27) De prestentune, xxviii d'. Preston
(d28) De ospringe, xxviii d'. Ospringe
(d29) De fæuresham, xxviii d'. Faversham
(d30) De wicham, xxviii d'. Wickhambreaux
(d31) De certeham, xxviii d'. Chartham
(d32) De Godmæresham, xxviii d'. Godmersham
(d33) De cilleham, xxviii d'. Chilham
(d34) De mundingham, xxviii d'. Great Mongeham
(d35) De merseham, xxviii d'. Mersham
(d36) De Cnoltune, xxviii d'. Knowlton
(d37) De sandwic, xxviii d'. Sandwich
(d38) De burna, xxviii d'. Patrixbourne
(d39) De burna, xxviii d'. Bekesbourne
(d40) De bradeburna, xxviii d'. Brabourne
(d41) De cranebroca, xxviii d'. Cranbrook
(d42) De wealemere, xxviii d'. Walmer
(d43) De Colredan, xxviii d'. Coldred
(d44) De middelea, xxviii d'. ?
(d45) De fordwic, xxviii d'. Fordwich
(d46) De werhorna, xxviii d'. Warehorne
(d47) De wealdwarescare, xxviii d'. Waldershare
(d48) De *Cyllindænne, xxviii d'. Chillenden
(d49) De trulege, xxviii d'. Throwley
(d50) De æslinge, xxviii d'. Eastling
(d51) De ælham, xxviii d'. Elham
(d52) De hardan, xxviii d'. Upper Hardres
(d53) De *desham, xxviii d'. Adisham
(d54) De tilemannestune, xxviii d'. Tilmanstone
(d55) De smiðatune, xxviii d'. ?
(d56) De hyruuerðestun, xxviii d'. Barfrestone
(d57) De cert, xxviii d'. Great Chart
(d58) De bædericesdænne, xxviii d'. Bethersden
(d59) De hadmwoldungdenne, xxviii d'. Halden
(d60) De wealtham et pytham, xxviii d'. Waltham and Petham
(d61) De rumenea, xxxi d'. Old Romney
(d62) De haðfelde, x d'. Hothfield
(d63) De plucelea, x d'. Pluckley
(d64) De Niwantune, vii d'. Newington (near Milton)
(d65) De kynigtune, vii d'. Kennington
(d66) De syrran, vii d'. Sarre
(d67) De heortege, vii d'. Harty
(d68) De bidindænne, vii d'. Biddenden
(d69) De Sturmude, vii d'. Stourmouth
(d70) De *rætte, vii d'. Fleet in Ash
(d71) De Sæsealtre, vii d'. Seasalter
(d72) De bæðdesmere, vii d'. Badlesmere
(d73) De hamme, vii d'. Ham
(d74) De bereham, vii d'. Barham
(d75) De Ottrindænne, vii d'. Otterden
(d76) De pytte, iii d'. Pett
(d77) De denentune, vii d'. Davington
(d78) De luddenham, vii d'. Luddenham
(d79) De Oran, vii d'. Oare
(d80) De piuingtune, vii d'. Pivington
(d81) De blean, xii d'. Blean
(d82) De Norðtune, vii d'. Norton
(d83) De kynardingtune, xii d'. Kenardington
(d84) De Elmestede, xii d'. Elmsted
(d85) De Eardlanestune, vii d'. Orlestone
(d86) De hæstingelege, xii d'. Hastingleigh
(d87) De Sineredænne, vii d'. Smarden

C1, fo. 1ra–b

(d48) Cy(ll)indænne *corrected* (d53) E *omitted* (d70) r(æ)tte *corrected*

List (e)

(De sinodalibus soluend' ad *[octau'] Pentecost'.)
(De cap'lo de douor')
(e1) E[ccle]sia de douoria, [l]v sol' Dover, St Martin
(e2) Folkestane, lv sol' Folkestone
Summa c et x sol'
(De cap'lo de sandwico)
(e3) Eccl'ia S' mar' de sandwic, xiiii den' Sandwich, St Mary
(e4) Eccl'ia S' clem' in sandwic, xiiii d' Sandwich, St Clement
(e5) Bethleshangre, iii dener' ob' Betteshanger
(e6) Wodnesberge, xxviii den' Woodnesborough
(e7) Estreia, ix sol' viii den' Eastry
(e8) Wrthe, vii d' Worth
(e9) Cnoltune, xxviii d' Knowlton
(e10) Haurne, iii den' ob' Ham
(e11) Berefreistune, vii d' Barfrestone
(e12) Muningeham, xii d' Great Mongeham
(e13) Riple, vii d' Ripple
(e14) Colrede, xxi d' Coldred
(e15) Walemere, xxviii d' Walmer
(e16) Waldwaressare, xxviii d' Waldershare
(e17) Redlindwad, vii d' Ringwould
(e18) Tilemanestune, xxviii d' Tilmanstone
Summa xxix sol' iiii d'
(De cap'lo de cerringe)
(e19) Cerringe, ix sol' viii d' Charing
(e20) *Stalefeld, vii den' Stalisfield
(e21) Welle, xxviii den' Westwell
(e22) Chert, xxviii d' Great Chart
(e23) *Bederichesdenne, xxviii d' Bethersden
(e24) Sandherste, xxviii d' Sandhurst
(e25) Ruluindenne, xxviii d' Rolvenden
(e26) Benindenne, xxviii d' Benenden
(e27) Cranebroke, xxviii d' Cranbrook
(e28) Smeredenne, vii den' Smarden
(e29) Bidindenne, vii den' Biddenden

(e30) Plukele, x den'	Pluckley
(e31) *Hatfelde, x den'	Hothfield
(e32) Lithlechert, vii d'	Little Chart
(e33) Kenintune, vii d'	Kennington
(e34) Hathewoldindenne, xxviii d'	Halden
(e35) Piuintune, vii den'	Pivington
(e36) Petthe, iii dener'	Pett
Summa xxxiii sol' ix d'	
(De cap'lo de *......)	
(e37) Tyrelesbu[rne], xxviii dener'	Patrixbourne
(e38) Liuingesburne, vii dener'	Bekesbourne
(e39) Wiccham, xxviii dener'	Wickhambreaux
(e40) Sturmuthe, vii dener'	Stourmouth
(e41) Wingeham, ii sol'	Wingham
(e42) Iecham, xxviii dener'	Ickham
(e43) Lithlewelle, vii den'	? Well in Ickham
(e44) Chilindenne, xiiii d'	Chillenden
(e45) Edesham, xxviii den'	Adisham
(e46) Rettheburch, vii d'	Fleet in Ash
Summa xiiii sol' x d'	
(De cap'lo de limminge)	
(e47) Limminge, xxxii d'	Lyminge
(e48) Bradeburne, xxviii den'	Brabourne
(e49) Elmestede, xii dener'	Elmsted
(e50) *Hastingelege, xii den'	Hastingleigh
(e51) Elham, xxviii den'	Elham
Summa ix sol' iiii d'	
(De cap'lo de tenham)	
(e52) Thenham, ii sol'	Teynham
(e53) Feueresham, xxviii d'	Faversham
(e54) Trulege, xxviii d'	Throwley
(e55) Eslinge, xxviii d'	Eastling
(e56) Osprenge, xxviii d'	Ospringe
(e57) Niwentune, vii d'	Newington
(e58) Middeltune, ix sol' viii d'	Milton
(e59) Bissopesboctune, xxviii d'	Boughton under Blean
(e60) Grauene, xxviii d'	Graveney
(e61) *Herteie, vii d'	Harty
(e62) Prestune, xxviii d'	Preston
(e63) Northune, vii d'	Norton
(e64) Ludenham, vii d'	Luddenham
(e65) Niweham, vii d'	Newnham
(e66) Bedelesmere, vii d'	Badlesmere
(e67) Ore, vii d'	Oare
(e68) Deuintune, vii d'	Davington
(e69) Otringedenne, vii d'	Otterden
Summa xxxiii sol' iii d'	
(De cap'lo de burnes)	
(e70) Certham, xxviii d'	Chartham
(e71) Chileham, xxviii d'	Chilham
(e72) Godmeresham, xxviii d'	Godmersham
(e73) Wy, ix sol' viii d'	Wye
(e74) Waltham, xiiii d'	Waltham
(e75) Pettham, *xiiii d'	Petham
(e76) Hardre, xxviii d'	Upper Hardres
(e77) Bissopesburne, xxviii d'	Bishopsbourne
(e78) Bereham, vii d'	Barham
(e79) Yrlesboctune, xxviii d'	Boughton Aluph
Summa xxvi sol' vii d'	
(De cap'lo de limene)	
(e80) Saltwde, xxviii d'	Saltwood
(e81) Merseham, xxviii d'	Mersham
(e82) Wdecherche, xxviii d'	Woodchurch
(e83) Apeldre, ii sol'	Appledore
(e84) Kenardintune, xii d'	Kenardington
(e85) Werehorne, xxviii d'	Warehorne
(e86) *Ordhlauestune, vii d'	Orlestone
(e87) Rokinge, xxviii d'	Ruckinge
(e88) Rumene, xxxi d'	Old Romney
(e89) Baldriesherste, iii d'	Hurst
Summa xviii sol' i d'	
(De cap'lo de raculue)	
(e90) Herewik, xxviii d'	Harwich in Seasalter
(e91) Sesautre, vii d'	Seasalter
(e92) Muneketune, xxviii d'	Monkton
(e93) Serre, vii d'	Sarre
(e94) Thettecherche, vii d'	? Woodchurch
Summa vi sol' v d'	
(De cap'lo de meidestane)	
(e95) Meidestane, ix sol' viii d'	Maidstone
(e96) Chert de suttune, vii d'	Chart Sutton
Summa x sol' iii d'	
(De cap'lo de cantuaria)	
(e97) Blen, xii d'	Blean
(e98) Fordwic, xxviii d'	Fordwich
Summa iii sol' iiii den'	
Summa tocius xiiii li' xiiii sol' ii den'	

C4, fo. 61va–c

(e) octau' *almost dissolved away, but this appears to be the only possible reading* (e20) Stalefe(l)d *with* l *inserted* (e23) Beder(i)chesdenne *with one letter corrected* (e31) Ha::tfelde *with one letter erased* (e37–46) *the end of the heading dissolved away, except for one ascender, perhaps the* h *of* Wingeham (e50) Hastingele::ge *with one letter erased* (e61) Herteige *with* g *marked for deletion* (e75) xxiii *corrected to* xiiii (e86) Ordhaluestune *with* al *marked for transposition*

Comments

(a2–4) The crux is entry (a4), 'Inside the city, five churches.' Ward took 'the city' to mean Dover – and therefore he had to reject the obvious identifications for entries (a2) and (a3). But Dover was not a city. In a list drawn up for the archbishop, 'the city' should surely mean Canterbury. There were numerous churches in Canterbury, but none of them had any recorded connection with Dover, as far as I am aware. I do not see the way out of this difficulty.

(a7) The difficulties involved in identifying this entry as Newington (near Hythe) were understood well enough by Ward (1933, pp. 69–70). He decided to ignore them; I think that he was wrong to do so.

(a9) Ward read *Itu'* as a place-name: he took it to be a very bad spelling for Eythorne. But no doubt it is an error for *It'u'*, meaning *iterum*, 'again'.

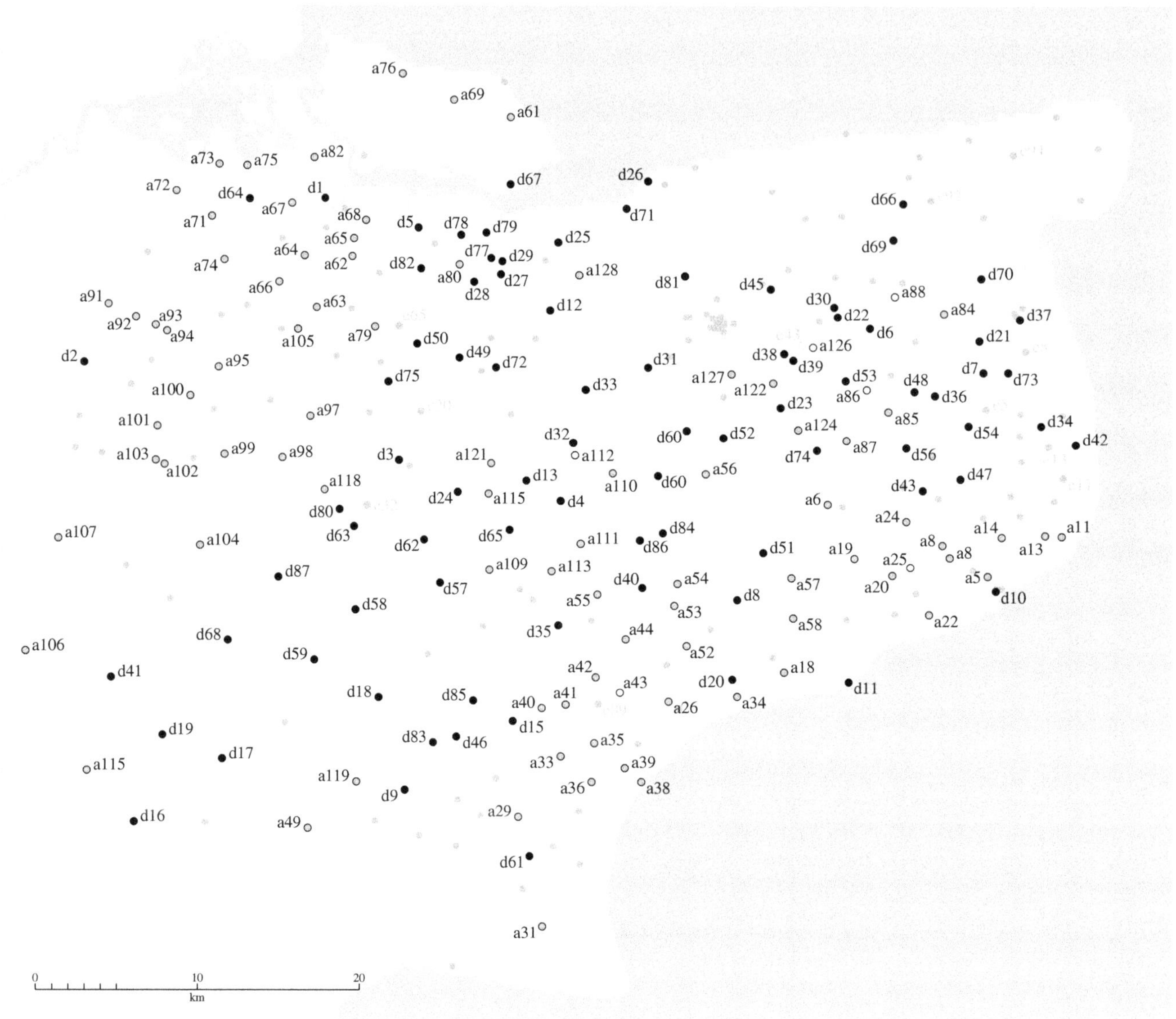

Figure 18. Parish churches in the diocese of Canterbury.

(a12) Ward's suggestion, Northbourne, is out of the question. Northbourne was a mother church in its own right, belonging to Saint Augustine's (f10).

(a15) By the 1080s, the endowment of the minster at Folkestone had been transformed into the barony of Folkestone (above, p. 178). DB says that there are five churches there belonging to Willelm de Arcis (9va20), and three more belonging to one of Willelm's men (9va27). List (a) has eleven churches.

(a26) Lympne occurs only here: it is not included in list (c), nor in list (d) – unless I am right to suspect that it appears there in a garbled form (d14).

(a27–8) I doubt whether Ward's identifications are tenable. If New Romney existed, it would only have had one church, Saint Nicholas's; but in fact the town's existence (as far as I can see) is not securely attested before the mid twelfth century.

(a34) 'In Hythe, two churches.' The statement is clear; its meaning is not. Ward suggested Hythe and West Hythe, but I doubt whether anyone would have thought of saying that West Hythe was 'in Hythe'. (A 'hythe' is a port, as DB explains (2va8) – a place where it is permitted for ships to be loaded and unloaded. Hythe was the port of Saltwood; West Hythe was the port of Lympne.) Hythe itself – Saltwood's hythe – was already a town in the 1080s (DB-Ke-4va22); it must have had a church; it may perhaps have had two.

(a35) Ward pointed out that a man named Alsi (Ælfsige) was the TRE tenant of Eastbridge (DB-Ke-13ra43). But in fact there are said to be two churches there (13ra46), and that adds another complication.

(a45) Ward suggested that this might be Kingsnorth, with the name misspelt. For the reasons indicated below (d74), I doubt whether that can be right.

(a46) Ward took this to be Wootton, with the name misspelt. That is not impossible, but it seems very doubtful to me.

(a47) Not Swarling: the names are only vaguely similar. But I have no alternative suggestion.

(a57) As Ward observed, the name must be *Acris* with insular *r* misread (the long stroke combined with *c* to make *q*, the short stroke with *i* to make *u*).

(a59–69) A later list of the churches subordinate to Milton survives from Saint Augustine's; it is printed below as list (fm). Once we have deleted the items which are obviously the same in both lists, the residue is this:

(a60) Norðcip'	(fm1) Due ecclesie in Scapaie
(a61) Legesdun	(fm3) Morinistune
(a69) Eastcyrce	(fm9) Sithingeburne

It seems clear that Leysdown and Eastchurch are the 'two churches in Sheppey' (though there is perhaps some room for doubt about Eastchurch); so *Norðcip'* may be Murston or Sittingbourne under another name. Or it may be a different church again – one which had ceased to exist by the twelfth century. On any reading of the evidence, it looks as if at least one new church was built, somewhere in the ambit of Milton, after list (a) was compiled.

(a70–7) A parallel list is available for Newington too; it is printed below as list (fn). The residual entries are these:

(a76) Sexburgamynster	(fn1) Due ecclesie in Scapeia
(a77) Niẉecyrce	(fn7) Bordenne

So *Niẉecyrce* might be the second of the 'two churches in Sheppey' (presumably Warden, since Leysdown and Eastchurch have already been accounted for); or it might be Borden under another name; or it might be a church which subsequently ceased to exist. I see no way of advancing beyond this point.

(a81) Not Selling, which belonged to Saint Augustine's (f34). We know which churches were subordinate to Teynham in the thirteenth century: Doddington, Lynsted, Stone, Iwade. Is it possible that 'Chilling' might be Lynsted under another name?

(a82) A misreading of *Æt þam gewæde*, 'at the ford'.

(a89) Possibly Goodnestone under another name ('Eadred's estate' instead of 'Godwine's estate'). Certainly Goodnestone was one of the churches subordinate to Wingham later.

(a96) If we trace out this sequence of entries on the map, it looks as if *Welcumeweg* might be Harrietsham under another name. Is there any evidence which might corroborate that? (Ward got it into his head that *Welcume* was a bad spelling for Ulcombe, but that is very unlikely.)

(a110, a112) Later on, Trimworth was just an alternative name for Crundale church (e.g. Cheney and John 1986, no. 519); but here it is listed separately.

(a119–28) After three blank lines (perhaps the scribe's way of signalling some discontinuity in the exemplar), the list ends with a puzzling assortment of entries, the sense of which is hard to see. Perhaps it should be read in the same sort of light as the sub-list of 'chapels' appended to list (i).

(a120) Ward (1933, p. 82, 1936, p. 19) proposed identifying this Wilmington as the place of that name in Sellindge. That may be right; but Ward's treatment of the evidence is cavalier, and the case needs to be looked at again more carefully.

(a121) Challock, later, was dependent on Boughton Aluph.

(a121) Barham, later, was dependent on Bishopsbourne.

(a125) Possibly Herne; but why make a point of calling it 'the church at Herne'? (Herne, later, was dependent on Reculver.)

(a126) Garrington, later, was a chapel dependent on Littlebourne; but presumably that would not have been the case before it was given to Saint Augustine's by the bishop of Bayeux (DB-Ke-12ra36).

(a128) Hernhill, later, was dependent on Boughton under Blean.

(b2) The phrase *in loco abbatis* does not have as much significance as Ward (1933, p. 68) wanted to read into it. Even in the normal course of events, the abbot would often be away from his abbey, for one reason or another. In particular, he would be expected to attend the king's Easter court, whenever the king was in England.

(b2) Here and in list (c), the word *multo* means 'ram'; it is a colloquial synonym for *aries*.

(c9) Comparison with list (d) suggests that one name (d14) may have been omitted here.

(c10) The comment here, 'as is written before', refers to list (d), which the man who put these documents in order (so that they could be copied into this manuscript) chose to place before list (c). The expression 'of blessed memory' is also important: it is proof that Lanfranc was already dead when the documents were put in order.

(d1) This payment of 116 pence from Milton church is itemized by list (fm). It comprises (i) a payment of 7 pence for chrism from each of twelve subordinate churches and (ii) a payment of 32 pence from the mother church itself. (List (fm) does not just give the same total: it uses the same odd formula, 'ten shillings less four pence'.) The second payment is, no doubt, a commutation of the tribute that was previously paid in kind (c1); the tribute due from Saint Augustine's was similarly commuted for a payment of 36 pence (b2). As for the chrism pennies, it does not seem to be literally true that there were twelve churches dependent on Milton. List (a) has only ten churches; list (fm) can only contrive to reach a total of twelve by including one church which is not subordinate to Milton and by ignoring one church which pays half the normal amount. Twelve appears to be a symbolic number, expressive of the church's status; and that will explain why four other churches – Maidstone, Charing, Wye, Eastry – are charged with exactly the same payment.

(d11) No doubt the payment was 55 shillings, the same as for Dover. That is the amount mentioned in DB (9va20), and list (e) concurs.

(d12–13) The corresponding entries in list (e) are 'Bishop's Boughton' (e59) and 'Earl's Boughton' (e79), the 'earl' in question being the count of Boulogne.

(d14) This entry is puzzling, not just because it is identical (give or take one minim) with a later entry (d61), but also because it comes near the end of a sequence of entries (d1–15) which is otherwise identical with the sequence in list (c). We get no help from list (e), which has no matching entry – but that fact itself is significant.

I strongly suspect that this is a garbled reference to the minster at Lympne (a26), missing from lists (c) and (e) because it no longer counted as a minster (DB-Ke-4ra23).

(d23) List (e) spells the name correctly (e77).

(d26) Identified by Ward initially as Berwick in Lympne (1933, p. 63), then as Westenhanger (1935, p. 147), which did certainly have a church of its own in the thirteenth century. But the corresponding entry in list (e) spells the name *Herewik* and puts the church in Reculver chapter (e90). The place in question must presumably be Harwich (a detached portion of the archbishop's manor of Westgate), located on the boundary between Seasalter and Whitstable.

(d37) In list (e) this payment is split between two churches, Saint Mary's and Saint Clement's (e3–4). There was a third church in Sandwich, Saint Peter's, but that belonged to Saint Augustine's (f30, g2). (Later it belonged only half to the abbey and half to the men of Sandwich.)

(d38, d39) These identifications are transposable; but I cannot see that it is going to make any difference which *burna* is which.

(d44) Presumably the lost place in Bewsborough hundred of which DB records the existence, plus the fact that it possessed a church (DB-Ke-11va17). There is no matching entry in list (e).

(d55) A lost place in Eastry hundred belonging to Saint Augustine's (below, p. 237). There is no matching entry in list (e).

(d56) List (e) spells the name more correctly (e11).

(d74) This is an instructive case. Ward identified *Bereham* as Barham, and list (e) confirms that he was right. Having done that, he had to think of alternative identifications for *Berham* and *alter Berham* (a123–4). (Here he was assuming that a church which appears in list (a) cannot (unless it is a mother church) appear again in list (d). That is true on the whole, but I would hesitate to push the assumption to the limit.) Pointing out, quite rightly, that the name 'Barham' could be used in a very large sense, he identified *Berham* as Bishopsbourne and 'the other *Berham*' as Kingston (which is indeed called Barham in DB). Having done that, however, he had to find an alternative identification for *Kyngestun* (a45). Might it perhaps be Kingsnorth misspelt? (The answer to that is, almost certainly, no. In the light of its later history, we can feel fairly sure that Kingsnorth, if it appeared here at all, would appear in the list of churches subordinate to Wye.) Uncertainties ramify, therefore, and may magnify themselves as they do so. Ward was not unaware of this danger, but it seems to me that he underestimated it.

(d76) List (e) puts this church in Charing chapter (e36). From the late thirteenth century onwards, the existence of a church called Pett is well attested – in 1281 the patronage belonged to one Stephan Girard of Romney – but its location is uncertain. As far as I can see, there is no reason to associate it with the manor called Pett or Pett's (repr. Pett Place) TQ 9649 in Charing. The ruined chapel there, mentioned by Ward (1933, p. 66), is thought by some to be an eighteenth-century sham.

(d77) List (e) spells the name more correctly and puts the church in Teynham chapter (e68).

(e) Most of the entries in this list can be matched with entries in list (d), but three items have gone missing (d14, d44, d55) and twelve new items have been added (e5, e8, e13, e17, e20, e32, e43, e65, e89, e92, e94, e96). The arithmetic is all correct, except that the grand total is one shilling short.

(e37) As far as I know, this is the only evidence that Patrixbourne was once called 'Tirel's Bourne'.

(e94) The name, I suppose, means 'thatch church'; perhaps it was another name for Woodchurch. The romescot list in manuscript C1 includes an item for *tenet tete circe* (1vc13-14).

Index

d1, e58 Minster (in Sheppey) a76 Great Mongeham d34, e12 Monkton (in Thanet) e92 Nackington a127 Newchurch a33 Newington (near Milton) a70, d64, e57 Newnham e65 *Niwantun* a7 *Niwecyrce* a77 Nonington a85 *Northcip'* a60 Norton d82, e63 Oare d79, e67 Orgarswick a39 Orlestone d85, e86 Ospringe d28, e56 Otterden d75, e69 Paddlesworth a58 Patrixbourne d38, e37 Petham d60, e75 *Petri aecclesia* a50 Pett d76, e36 Pivington d80, e35 Pluckley d63, e30 Preston (near Faversham) d27, e62 Rainham a72 Ratling in Nonington a86 Richborough, see Fleet Ringwould e17 Ripple e13 River a8 Rodmersham a62 Rolvenden d17, e25 Old Romney d61, e88 Ruckinge c9, d15, e87 *Rumenea* d14 Saint Margaret at Cliffe a11 Saltwood d20, e80 Sandhurst d16, e24 Sandwich d37, e3–4 Sarre d66, e93 Seasalter d71, e91 Sellindge a44 *Siwoldes circe* a32 Smarden d87, e28 *Smithatune* d55 Stalisfield e20 Stanford a52 Stelling a56 Stockbury a74 Stone (near Faversham) a80 Stourmouth d69, e40 Stowting a54 Street in Lympne a43 Sutton (Valence) a102 Swingfield a19 *Swirgildan circe* a47 Teynham a78, c3, d5, e52 Throwley d49, e54 Thurnham a93 Tilmanstone d54, e18 Tonge a68 Trimworth in Crundale a112 Tunstall a64 Ulcombe a99 *Undetun* a46 Upchurch a73 Waldershare d47, e16 Walmer d42, e15 Walmestone in Wingham a88 Waltham d60, e74 *Waltun* a10 Warehorne d46, e85 *Welcumeweg* a96 Well in Ickham e43 Westwell d24, e21 Wickhambreaux d30, e39 Wingham a83, c3, d6, e41 Wittersham a49 Wolverton in Alkham a25 Womenswold a87 Woodchurch d18, e82 Woodchurch (in Thanet) e94 Woodnesborough d21, e6 Worth e8 Wye a108, c3, d4, e73

Parish churches in the diocese of Canterbury belonging to Saint Augustine's: lists (f–h)

As Ward saw, the lists contained in the Christ Church manuscript C1 are systematically defective in one respect: they omit nearly all of the churches which belonged to the abbey of Saint Augustine's. In the hope of making good the deficiency, Ward looked at one of the abbey's own registers – the so-called 'White Book' – and in it he discovered a copy of a twelfth-century list of the abbey's churches. Thanks to him, this list was put into print for the first time.

There are, in fact, two surviving copies of this list, and the copy which Ward did not get to see is generally more satisfactory than the copy which he did. These are the copies, identified by the same codes that have already been used (above, p. 218) for the two manuscripts in question.

A2 = British Library, Royal 1 B. xi, fos. 145v–6v (early thirteenth century)

A4 = National Archives, E 164/27, fos. 14v–15r (early fourteenth century), printed by Ward (1933, pp. 84–8)

We can take it as given that these copies are independent, i.e. that neither was copied from the other. (That A2 was not copied from A4 is obvious; that A4 was not copied from A2 will appear below.)

As far as we can tell (above, p. 218), the exemplar from which these two copies derive was a cartulary compiled in the time of abbot Hugo II (1126–51). One entry (f25) mentions king Stephan but does not mention Henric II; perhaps we might venture to infer from this that the list describes the situation existing in about the middle of the twelfth century. That was Ward's suggestion, and I am inclined to agree. But texts of this kind are liable to be altered and annotated repeatedly, whenever somebody thinks that they need to be brought up to date, and we have no means of deciding which elements are original and which are not.

In principle these copies are of equal value, but the earlier copy, A2, has the advantage of being better organized. As it appears here, the main text consists of three paragraphs, the headings of which are as follows: (f) *De Eclesiis*, (g) *De Eclesiis denarios cirsmales reddentes*, (h) *De Eclesiis Censualibus*. (This is how the headings are written in A2; the scribe had his own ideas about spelling and a weak grasp on Latin grammar.) There are also two subsidiary paragraphs, each of which, in this copy, was deliberately placed at the bottom of a page, in the same manner as a footnote: (fm) *Capelle de Middeltune*, (fn) *Capelle de Niwintune*. That is all perfectly clear. In A4, only list (h) remains roughly the same; the other four paragraphs are welded together into one. The two subsidiary paragraphs have been interpolated into the main text, and most of list (g) has been omitted, the information being written instead between the lines of list (f). One can see that the scribe was trying to produce a simplified version of the text; one can understand why he thought that this would be a good idea. But in the end he only succeeded in confusing things.

In one respect, nevertheless, this copy is more reliable than A2. The order of the entries in list (f) differs greatly between one copy and the other, apparently because there was some ambiguity in the layout of the exemplar which these scribes interpreted differently. Though I have not been able to work this out in full, it seems clear that the exemplar had part of list (f) arranged something like this:

	Eccl'a S' Laurencii.
Eccl'a de Litleburne.	Eccl'a S' Nicholai ad Stanores.
Eccl'a de Stodmerse.	Eccl'a S' Petri ad Sanwiz.
Eccl'a de Forwiz.	Eccl'a de Feuresham.
Eccl'a de Sturaie.	Eccl'a de Sithingeburne.
Eccl'a de Cistelet.	Eccl'a de Mildeltune cum omnibus capellis suis dono regum Willelmi Henrici, Stephani.
Capella de Bere.	
Eccl'a S' Marie in Taneto.	
Eccl'a S' Petri.	Eccl'a de Sellinges.
Eccl'a S' Ioh' baptiste.	Eccl'a de Swaleweclive.

The A2 scribe read these entries line by line; the A4 scribe read them column by column – and that is certainly the way in which they were meant to be read.

Though the title does not say so, the compiler of list (f) was confining his attention to the diocese of Canterbury: the monks owned a church in west Kent too – Plumstead (with the chapel of East Wickham) – but that is not included here. With one exception (f16), the churches named can all be identified without the slightest trouble, and there is little to add to what was said by Ward. The names that appear in lists (g) and (h) are mostly repeated from list (f). This third list, (h), was not published by Ward but does have some points of interest; I print the section relating to churches, but not the subsequent section concerning tithes.

By and large, the following text is taken from A2; but there are some changes which I have felt it permissible to make. In list (f), for the reasons explained above, I have altered the order of the entries, to align it with the order in A4; and I have omitted a few phrases, missing from A4, which look like interpolations, some of them being derived from list (h). Also, all the way through, I have disregarded A2's eccentric spelling. Variant readings from A4 are cited only selectively, where they seem to be useful.

List (f)

(f) He sunt ecclesie de *tenatura sancti Augustini. *
*(f1) *In ciuitate Cantuaria ecclesia sancti Pauli apostoli ante portam ipsius sancti Augustini ecclesie,
(f2) Ecclesia sancte Marie ante portam castelli,
(f3) Ecclesia sancti sepulcri, *
(f4) Ecclesia sancti Laurencii, *
(f5) Ecclesia sancte Mildrede,
(f6) Ecclesia sancti Iohannis baptiste,
(f7) Ecclesia sancte Margarete,
(f8) Ecclesia sancti Andree,
(f9) Ecclesia omnium sanctorum infra Eastbrege.

(f10) Ad Norburne ecclesia sancti Augustini, mater ecclesiarum eiusdem uille.	Northbourne
Huic subiacet	
(f11) Ecclesia de Munigham,	Little Mongeham
(f12) Ecclesia de Sutune,	Sutton
(f13) Ecclesia de Soueldune,	Sholden
(f14) Ecclesia de Siberteswalde,	Sibertswold
(f15) Ecclesia de Bewesfed,	Bewsfield
(f16) Ecclesia de Smethetune,	?
(f17) Ecclesia de Langedune, *	East Langdon
(f18) Capella de Riple,	Ripple
*et sunt membrum de Norburne.	
(f19) Ecclesia de Litleburne.	Littlebourne
(f20) Ecclesia de Stodmerse.	Stodmarsh
(f21) Ecclesia de Forwiz.	Fordwich
(f22) Ecclesia de Sturaie.	Sturry
(f23) Ecclesia de Cistelet.	Chislet
(f24) Capella de Bere.	Westbere
(f25) Ecclesia sancte Marie in Taneto. *	Minster
(f26) Ecclesia sancti Petri.	
(f27) Ecclesia sancti Iohannis baptiste.	
(f28) Ecclesia sancti Laurencii.	
(f29) Ecclesia sancti Nicholai ad Stanores.	Stonar
(f30) Ecclesia sancti Petri ad Sanwiz.	Sandwich
(f31) Ecclesia de Feuresham. *	Faversham
*(f32) Ecclesia de Sithingeburne.	?
(f33) Ecclesia de Mildeltune cum omnibus capellis suis dono regum Willelmi, Henrici, Stephani. *	Milton
(f34) Ecclesia de Sellinges.	Selling
(f35) Ecclesia de Swaleweclíue.	Swalecliffe
(f36) Ecclesia de Prestune. *	Preston
(f37) Ecclesia de Laenham.	Lenham
(f38) Capella de Reietune.	Rayton in Lenham
(f39) Ecclesia de *Keitune.	Kennington
(f40) Ecclesia de Wiuelesberge.	Willesborough
(f41) Ecclesia de Burwaremareis. *	Burmarsh
(f42) Ecclesia de Snaues.	Snave
(f43) Ecclesia de Brogcerece.	Brookland
(f44) Ecclesia de Demecirege. *	Dymchurch
(f45) Ecclesia de *Oxenaie.	Stone
(f46) Ecclesia de Tandordenne.	Tenterden
(f47) Ecclesia de Firtindenne.	Frittenden

A2, fos. 145v–6r; A4, fos. 14v–15r

(title) tenura *A4* de Canterburia et extra *add. A4* (f1–47) *ordered in A2 as follows*: 1, 5–6, 2–4, 7–13, 28, 19, 29, 20, 30, 21, 31, 22, 32, 23, 33, 24–6, 34, 27, 35, 18, 16–17, 36–40, 14–15, 41, 44, 42–3, 45–7 (f1) In ciuitate Cantuaria *om. A4* (f3) (xii d') *add. A2, from h12* (f4) hospitale *add. A4* (f17) candelam duarum librarum *add. A2, from h14* (after f18) et sunt menbra ecl'e de Norburne *A2, after f15* : et sunt menbrum de Norburne *A2, after f17* : et sunt membrum de Northbourn' *A4, after f18* (f25) et S' Mildrede *add. A2* (f31) iiii lib' *add. A2, from h2* : capella de Cheldewich *add. A4* (f32) *the whole entry cancelled A4* (after f33) *lists fm and fn interpolated here A4* (f36) talentum i *add. A2, from h11* (f39) Kenington' *A4* (f41) ii sol' *add. A2, from h13* (f44) i ecl'a *add. A2, nonsensically* (f45) Stones in Oxoniaie *A4*

(fm) Iste sunt capelle matris ecclesie de Middeltune de dominio regis, et ibi accipiunt crisma et ibi reddunt denarios.

(fm1) Due ecclesie in Scapaie que reddunt xiiii d'.	Leysdown and Eastchurch
(fm2) Elmeleia est insula permodica et reddit iii d' et ob'.	Elmley
(fm3) Morinistune, vii d'.	Murston
(fm4) Tanges, vii d'.	Tonge
(fm5) Bachechilde, vii d'.	Bapchild
(fm6) Rodmeresham, vii d'.	Rodmersham
(fm7) Milestede, vii d'.	Milstead
(fm8) Bradegare, vii d'.	Bredgar
(fm9) Sithingeburne, vii d'.	Sittingbourne
(fm10) Bobbinge, vii d'.	Bobbing
(fm11) Tunstalle, vii d'.	Tunstall
(fm12) Bichenore, vii d'.	Bicknor

Set non pertinet ad Middeltune, licet ibi accipiat oleum et reddat denarios.
(fm13) Ipsa mater ecclesia, xxxii d'.
*Summa, x sol' iiii d' minus.

A2, fo. 145v (as footnote); A4, fo. 14v (as part of list (f))

(after fm13) Summa ... minus *om. A4*

(fn) Iste sunt capelle ecclesie de Niwintune oleum *ibi accipientes et denarios reddentes.

(fn1) Due ecclesie in Scapeia.	Minster and Warden
(fn2) Renham.	Rainham
(fn3) Upcherege.	Upchurch
(fn4) Halegesto.	Halstow
(fn5) Stogingeberi.	Stockbury
(fn6) Herdlepe.	Hartlip
(fn7) Bordenne.	Borden

A2, fo. 146r (as footnote); A4, fos. 14v–15r (as part of list (f))

(title) ibi vid' Midd' *A4*

List (g)

(g) Iste sunt ecclesie que solent reddere septenos denarios singulis annis.
*(g1) Tres ecclesie de Taneto, xxi d'.
(g2) Ecclesia sancti Petri de Sanwiz, vii d'.
(g3) Ecclesia de Siberteswald, vii d'.
(g4) Due ecclesie de Norburne, xiiii d'.
(g5) De Litleburne de ii ecclesiis, xiiii d'.
(g6) De Prestune ecclesia, vii d'.
(g7) De Cistelet pro ii ecclesiis, xiiii d'.
(g8) De Sturaie, vii d'.
(g9) Ecclesia de Swalewecliue, vii d'.
(g10) Ecclesia de Sellinges, vii d'.
(g11) Ecclesia de Bauesfeld, vii d'.
(g12) Ecclesia de Wiuelesberge, vii d'.
(g13) Ecclesia del Mareis, vii d'.
(g14) Brocecerege, vii d'.
(g15) Ecclesia de Oxeneie, vii d'.
(g16) Ecclesia de Snaues, vii d'.
(g17) Ecclesia de Tantuardanne, vii d'.
(g18) Ecclesia de Fridindenne, vii d'.
(g19) Ecclesia de Muniggeham, vii d'.
*(g20) Ecclesia de Kenigtune, vii d'. Uno anno reddit hic et alio ecclesie sancte trinitatis, ubi oleum recipit: ibi reddit.
(g21) Similiter ecclesia de Smedetune solebat reddere vii d', set permissione detinentur.
(g22) Sunt autem quedam de istis ecclesiis que reddunt denarios crismales ecclesie sancti saluatoris singulis annis, quo uero modo hoc fiat nisi negligentia nostra nescitur. He sunt ecclesia de Laianham, ecclesia de Forwiz, ecclesia de Feuresham, ecclesia de Mildeltune, ecclesia de Newentune, et si que sunt alie.

A2, fo. 146r; A4, fos. 14v–15r

(g1–19) *these data mostly inserted by A4 between the lines of list (f), with the remark* Memorandum quod denarii crismales signantur supra (g20–2) *attached by A4 to the end of list (f), beginning* Item memorandum quod ecclesia de Keningtone reddit huic ecclesie uno anno et alio anno . . .

List (h)

(h) Iste sunt ecclesie censuales sancto Augustino *. . .
(h1) Prebenda de Douoria, xx sol'.
(h2) Ecclesia de Feuresham sancte Marie, iiii lib', et abbatia, iiii lib'.
(h3) Sancta Margareta, iii sol'.
(h4) Sancta Mildreda, medietatem de his que apportantur. Sed modo nisi x sol'.
(h5) Ecclesia de Fordwiz, x solidos.
(h6) Ecclesia de Leanham, iii sol'.
(h7) Ecclesia de Newentune, ad parcamenum.
(h8) Ecclesia de Middeltune, xl sol' super altare, et de decimis x lib' de dominio regis.
(h9) De tribus capellis de Taneto, vi sol'.
(h10) De ecclesia de Sellinges, iii sol'.
(h11) Ecclesia de Prestune, i talentum.
(h12) Ecclesia de sancto sepulcro, xii d'.
(h13) Ecclesia de Burwarmareis, ii sol'.
(h14) Ecclesia de Langedune, candelam ii librarum.
(h15) Ecclesia sancti Andree in ciuitate, candelam ii librarum.
(h16) Ecclesia *de Swalecliue, in festiuitate sancti Augustini, candelam ii librarum.
(h17) Ecclesia omnium sanctorum de Eastbrege, candelam unius libre.
(h18) Ecclesia de Stanore, candelam ii librarum.
(h19) Ecclesia de Fismanne, candelam unius libre.
(h20) Ecclesia de Snaues, candelam unius libre.

A2, fo. 146r–v; A4, fo. 15r

(title) et decime a fidelibus dei oblate *add. A2, A4, but I omit that stretch of text* (h16) de *om. A2*

Comments

(f1–9) The list begins with nine churches in Canterbury. Two of them (f2, f8) were, we know (because A2 and A4 tell us so), given to the abbey by Willelm I, in compensation for the income lost from land requisitioned for the castle (Urry 1967, p. 445). Apart from that, the significant features of this list would seem to be that Saint Sepulchre and Saint Laurence are included, and that Saint Edmund and Saint Mary Magdalene are not (though the last church does appear, under the name 'Fishmanchurch', in list (h)).

(f16) Everything that is known about the church of *Smethetune* can be summed up in a few lines. Archbishop Lanfranc made it pay a tribute of 28 pence (d55). Here it is listed, without comment, among the churches subordinate to Northbourne. List (g) says that it used to pay a chrism fee of 7 pence, alternately to Saint Augustine's and to Christ Church, but that the payment is no longer being made (g21). After that, as far as I am aware, *Smethetune* disappears – not just the church but also the place-name itself.

(f31) Only A4 mentions the chapel of Sheldwich.

(f32) A puzzling entry, not because there is any doubt about the identification, but because there is no other evidence suggesting that Saint Augustine's was ever in possession of Sittingbourne

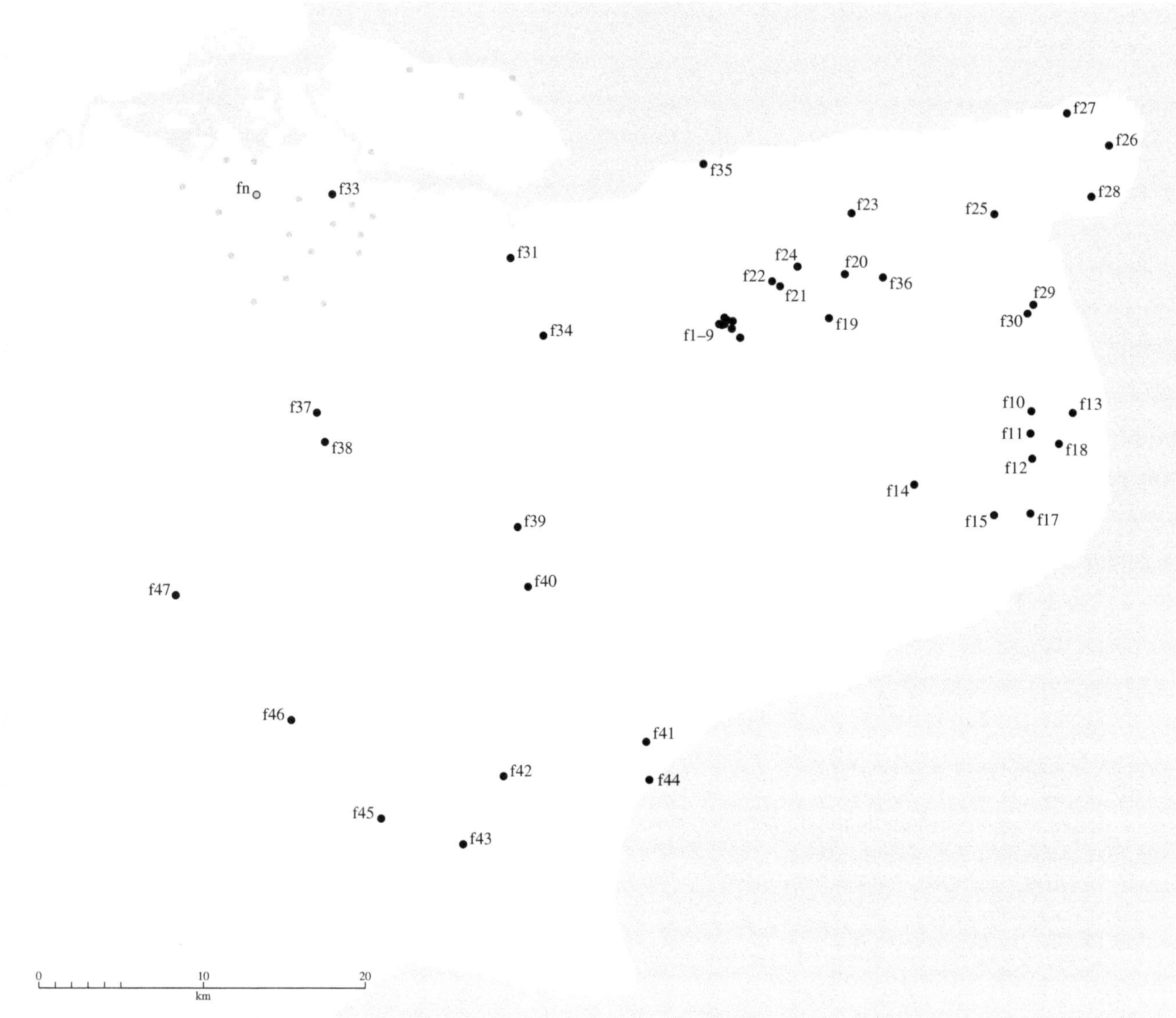

Figure 19. Parish churches in the diocese of Canterbury belonging to Saint Augustine's.

church. Probably this item (which is cancelled in A4) was included here by error; perhaps it resulted from some ambiguity in the exemplar, an item which was properly part of list (fm) looking as if it might be part of list (f).

(fm) This sub-list is included because the monks of Saint Augustine's, by becoming the owners of Milton church (it was given to them by Willelm I), had acquired some rights over its dependent churches. This meant, at the very least, that the chrism pence were payable to them: the priests of the churches on this list all had to go to Milton to get their chrism. Beyond that, it is not very clear – perhaps it was not very clear to the monks themselves – what rights they ought to enjoy; but certainly some tithes in other parishes were claimed to belong to Milton, by reason of its status as the mother church.

(fm1) These 'two churches in Sheppey' are, I suppose, the churches called *Legesdun* and *Eastcyrce* in list (a).

(fm2) 'Elmley is a very small island' (and therefore gets a discount of 50 per cent). This item is not included in the total.

(fm12) 'Bicknor is not subordinate to Milton, even though it gets its chrism and pays its pence there.' The meaning of this sentence, made doubtful by errors of transcription in A4, is perfectly clear in A2. It applies to this entry alone. As a matter of convenience, Bicknor gets its chrism from Milton; unlike the other churches on the list, it is not obliged to do so.

(fn) From the inclusion of this sub-list, and from entries below (g22, h7), it seems certain that list (f) did once contain an entry for Newington church, probably just after Milton. The entry was cancelled – and list (fn) ought to have been cancelled too but was not. So the footnote survives, without the entry to which it ought to be attached. (Plainly the title means that these churches have to obtain their chrism from Newington; A4's interpolation is disingenuous.)

(fn1) These 'two churches in Sheppey' have to be the two not covered by list (fm). Minster is certainly one of them, *Sexburgamynster* in list (a); Warden is probably the other.

(g1–21) Most of these payments are inserted by A4 between the lines of list (f). Six are omitted, probably just by mistake: (g2, g6, g9–10, g13, g20). Those payments which consist of some multiple of 7 pence are divided and allotted as follows: (g1) to (f26–8), (g4) to (f12–13), (g5) to (f19–20), (g7) to (f23–4).

(g20–2) The list ends with some interesting comments. In the compiler's view, it ought to be an iron rule that the abbey's churches get their chrism from the abbey, but in fact there are some exceptions. Kennington (f39) gets its chrism from Christ Church in alternate years; the same used to be true for *Smedetune* (f16), but now it does not pay any chrism fee at all. More distressing still, some of the abbey's churches – five that he is aware of – get their chrism from Christ Church every year: Lenham (f37), Fordwich (f21), Faversham (f31), Milton (f33), Newington (fn). (As Ward saw, that is the reason why all of these churches occur once or more in lists (a–e).) He does not know how this was allowed to happen; the thought occurs to him that some churches, after ceasing to pay their chrism fees to the abbey, may have been lost altogether. That is the meaning of the final phrase, 'and, not impossibly, others'.

(h) In A4 this list has been edited extensively, possibly by the A4 scribe himself. The items have been reordered; some have been shortened, and some have been dropped altogether. But the list was a dead letter by the time that this copy was made. In 1237, under pressure from the archbishop, the abbot and convent agreed to relinquish almost all such payments, in return for a twenty-mark share of the income of either Preston or Selling church, whichever fell vacant first (Turner and Salter 1915–24, pp. 534–7). The agreement took effect in 1242 – it was Preston which had fallen vacant – and the document assigning the monks their share includes a list of the payments which they were giving up (pp. 539–41). Mostly they match with entries in one or other version of list (h), but in detail there are numerous discrepancies.

(h1) In the 1140s, when the abbot and monks were coming to terms with archbishop Theobald, they gave him two mills in Dover and twenty shillings from their prebend in Saint Martin's church (Hardwick 1858, pp. 390–1). The twenty shillings that appear in this list are, I suppose, the balance which remained with them.

Index

Parish churches in the diocese of Rochester: lists (i–k)

A list of the parish churches belonging to the diocese of Rochester was copied into the twelfth-century Rochester cartulary, the same manuscript cited previously as R1 (above, p. 39). The entries were printed and discussed individually by Ward (1932), and there is little to say beyond what was said by him, with regard to the identifications.

As it survives (R1, fos. 220v–2r), this list is a composite text, put together over a period of several decades.

The earliest and largest component, list (i), is a list which was included in the original cartulary, written in the 1120s. But it was not allowed to survive in its pristine form.[16] The beginning of the list, possibly one whole page, disappeared when a leaf was cut out; and the portion which survives has been altered and added to by later hands. Several of the original entries have been erased, for reasons we can only guess at.

The second component, list (j), is a partial list written by a later scribe on the last page (220v) of a newly inserted sheet (fos. 217 + 220).[17] The hand is clumsy and undistinguished; it seems to me to date from the late twelfth century.[18] Presumably this scribe was making a copy of the portion of list (i) which was about to be discarded; but the fact that he took the trouble to write this page out again seems to imply that he intended to make some changes in the text, and we have no means of knowing what those changes were. Presumably also he was under the impression that this new list, combined with the remainder of the old list, would add up to a complete description of the diocese; but he was not quite right about that.

[16] This manuscript suffered much mutilation at the hands of later scribes (Flight 1997a, pp. 31–3).

[17] Some portions of the text relating to Rochester bridge were rewritten in a similar fashion (Flight 1997b, pp. 2–3) – by a better but rather similar hand, so far as the Latin version is concerned (fo. 164v).

[18] Late rather than mid twelfth century, I would think – mainly because of the *de* ligature, which occurs three times (always at the end of a line) in the word *den'*. (The same scribe wrote a list of the bishop's knights (fo. 217r), but did not use this ligature there.)

Both lists were annotated by a third scribe, who wrote the names of several churches and chapels in the margin, using a variety of symbols to connect them with entries in the main text. These notes vary in appearance, some being written with a finer pen than others, but they are, I think, all the work of a single hand; I take them to date from the end of the twelfth or beginning of the thirteenth century. Taken together, they constitute the third component, list (k).

The original list does not seem to have been organized in any meaningful way. There is, for instance, no correlation between the ordering of the entries here and the organization into deaneries recorded later, not even with respect to the deanery of Shoreham: the archbishop's churches are included in this list, haphazardly interspersed among the others. There is some vague tendency for neighbouring churches to be juxtaposed (e.g. Ridley, Ash, Hartley), but that is hardly a surprise: no doubt it would sometimes happen that priests who were neighbours made the journey together and paid their fees, upon arrival, one after the other. So perhaps the order is just the accidental order in which the chrism fees came to be paid (with a few accidental exceptions) on one particular occasion.[19]

In its final composite form, this list agrees very closely with the list that can be compiled, from the bishops' registers and other sources, for the fourteenth century and later (Flight 2000). Most of the churches named here can be identified without the slightest difficulty. But there are a few surprises. Several churches which are fairly certain to have existed at the time are absent;[20] on the other hand, some names which are present here do not turn up again in later records. In list (j) there is only one such entry; in list (i) there are several (and would perhaps have been more, if some had not been erased); and the impression we get, here as in east Kent, is that the map of parishes was still in a slightly fluid state at the beginning of the twelfth century, solidifying by the end of it.

This fluidity is most evident in the section of list (i) which carries the subheading *De capellis*, 'Concerning chapels'. What meaning this distinction was intended to convey is not clear. For the scribe who added the marginal notes, calling a church a chapel meant that it was dependent on some other church; but a church which was a chapel in that sense would not be expected to need a separate supply of chrism. The churches called chapels here appear to have an independent existence. Some are paying at a reduced rate; some, apparently, are not paying anything (or at least not paying this year), but still, for some reason, need to be included in the list. Some of these chapels evolved into parish churches; the majority did not.

[19] I read no sigificance into the fact that the list begins with Tonbridge, not with a church near Rochester. Even so, it is striking that the next six churches to be listed were all, like Tonbridge, connected with the honour of Clare; the same was true for the first entry in the list of chapels.

[20] The churches which I think we might expect to find are these: West Farleigh, Hayes, Keston, Kingsdown, Longfield; also the altar of St Nicholas in the cathedral church. Hayes and Keston may perhaps be missing because they were still subordinate to Orpington. The other omissions appear to be accidental.

List (i)

(i1) *[ ]	?
(i2) *[ ]	?
(i3) Erde *(uel earhethe), ix d'.	Crayford
(i4) Wilmentuna, ix.	Wilmington
(i5) Lullingestuna, ix den'.	Lullingstone
(i6) Le, ix den'.	Lee
(i7) Mæruurtha, ix den'.	Mereworth
(i8) Westerham, ix den'.	Westerham
(i9) Watlande, ix den'.	Woodlands
(i10) Ciuilinga, ix den'.	Chevening
(i11) Æinesford, ix den'.	Eynsford
(i12) Cimisinga, ix den'.	Kemsing
(i13) Wicham, ix den'.	West Wickham
(i14) Bradesteda, ix den'.	Brasted
(i15) Færningeham, ix den'.	Farningham
(i16) Hæselholte, ix den'.	?
(i17) Readlega, ix den'.	Ridley
(i18) Æisce, ix den'.	Ash
(i19) Herclei, ix den'.	Hartley
(i20) Sundererserce, ix den'.	Sundridge
(i21) Mapeldreskampe, ix den'.	Maplescombe
(i22) Heure, ix den'.	Hever
(i23) Scorham, ix den'.	Shoreham
(i24) Hludesdune, ix den'.	Luddesdown
(i25) Otteford, ix den'.	Otford
(i26) Rokesle, ix den'.	Ruxley
(i27) Leleburna, ix den'.	Leybourne
(i28) Culinga, ix den'.	Cooling
(i29) Iuelda, ix den'.	Ifield
(i30) Cidingestane, ix den'.	Chiddingstone
(i31) Terstana, ix den'.	Teston
(i32) Æilentune, ix d'.	Allington
(i33) Freondesbyri, ix den'.	Frindsbury
(i34) Lilecirce, ix den'.	Higham
(i35) Heahham, ix den'.	?
(i36) Cobbeham, ix den'.	Cobham
(i37) Scorene, ix den'.	Shorne
(i38) Halgesto, ix den'.	Halstow
(i39) Hnutstede, ix den'.	Nurstead
(i40) Sc'a wereburh de hou, ix den'.	Hoo
(i41) Dereuuoldes treow, ix den'.	?
(i42) Ordmæres circe de hou, ix den'.	?
(i43) *Do[ ]des circe, ix d'.	Dode
(i44) Deremannes circe de hou, ix den'.	?
(i45) Cliue, ix den'.	Cliffe
(i46) Falkenham, ix den'.	Fawkham
(i47) Denituna, ix den'.	Denton
(i48) Meletuna, ix den'.	Milton
(i49) Grauesænde, ix den'.	Gravesend
(i50) *Eadelmesbre(g)ge, ix den'.	Edenbridge
(i51) Stokes, ix den'.	Stoke
(i52) Grean, ix den'.	Grain
(i53) Cilesfeld, ix den'.	Chelsfield

(i54) Celca, ix den'.	Chalk
(i55) Northcræi, ix den'.	North Cray
(i56) Rodulfescræi, ix d'.	St Paul's Cray
(i57) Fotescræi, ix den'.	Foots Cray
(i58) Norðfleotes, ix den'.	Northfleet
(i59) Suðfleotes, ix den'.	Southfleet
(i60) Bixle, ix d'.	Bexley
(i61) Suaneskampe, ix den'.	Swanscombe
(i62) Haltesteda, ix d'.	Halstead
(i63) Derente, ix den'.	Darenth
(i64) *[ ]	?
(i65) Derteford, ix den'.	Dartford
(i66) Suð derente, *ix den'.	? South Darenth in Horton
(i67) Suðtuna, ix den'.	Sutton
(i68) Stanes, ix den'.	Stone
(i69) Orpintuna, ix den'.	Orpington
(i70) Hortune, ix den'.	Horton
(i71) Plumstede, ix den'.	Plumstead
(i72) Bromlega, ix den'.	Bromley
(i73) Æltheham, ix den'.	Eltham
(i74) Wicham, ix den'.	East Wickham
(i75) Cerlentune, ix den'.	Charlton
(i76) Greneuuic, ix den'.	Greenwich
(i77) West greneuuic, ix den'.	Deptford
(i78) Wleuuic, ix den'.	Woolwich
(i79) Gillingeham, ix den'.	Gillingham
(i80) Bearmlinges, ix den'.	East Barming
(i81) *[ ] ix den'.	?
(i82) Seouenaca, ix d'.	Sevenoaks
(i83) Meallingetes, ix d'.	West Malling

De capellis.

(i84) Bitteberga reddit *sex denarios.	Bidborough
(i85) Chitebroc, vi den'.	Kidbrooke
(i86) Comba, vi d'.	? Westcombe in Greenwich
(i87) Strodes, vi den'.	Strood
(i88) Capella de hou, vi den'.	Howbury in Crayford
(i89) *[ ]	?
(i90) *[ ]	?
(i91) Halgelei, vi den'.	Hawley in Sutton
(i92) Æslingeham, vi den'.	Islingham in Frindsbury
(i93) West cliue, vi den'.	? West Court in Cliffe
(i94) *Gre[ ]nic, vi den'.	Grange in Gillingham
(i95) Stanstede, vi d'.	Stansted
(i96) *Thorninduna, vi d'.	?
(i97) *Liṇdisinge, vi d'.	Lidsing in Gillingham
(i98) Mersctuna, vi d'.	Merston
(i99) Lullingestana, vi den'.	Lullingstane
(i100) Hescendena.	Nashenden in St Margaret's
(i101) Bearmlingetes, vi den'.	West Barming
(i102) Cusintune.	Cossington in Aylesford
(i103) *Bean(t)esteda. *	Bensted in Hunton
(i104) Cretenersce.	? Greatness in Sevenoaks
(i105) Sciburna.	Shipbourne
(i106) Helle. *(vi d')	St Margarets in Darenth
(i107) Fearnberga. *(vi den')	Farnborough
(i108) Sc's Leonardus.	St Leonard's in West Malling
(i109) Lilintuna.	Linton
(i110) Sc'a Maria de castello.	?

R1, fos. 221r–2r

(i1–2) *probably two entries erased* (i3) uel earhethe *written above* Erde (i50) Eadelmesbre(g)ge *corrected* (i64) *one entry erased* (i66) vi *added above* ix *by a different hand* (i81) *one entry partly erased* (i84) sex *dotted out and* Sed modo ix *added above it by a different hand* (i89–90) *probably two entries erased* (i96) *this item cancelled, doubtless by a different hand* (i97) Li(n)disinge *with* n *dotted out* (i103) Bean(t)esteda *with* t *inserted* *in the space after this,* Craie *inserted by a different hand* (i106) vi d' *added at the end of a line* (i107) vi den' *inserted into a space*

List (j)

(j) De numero ecclesiarum rofensis episcopatus, et de *reddittibus quos singule reddunt quando accipiunt sanctum crisma a matre ecclesia episcopatus.

(j1) Tonebrigga reddit nouem denarios.	Tonbridge
(j2) Barindena, ix den'.	Barden in Tonbridge
(j3) Ealdinga, ix den'.	Yalding
(j4) Lega, ix den'.	Leigh
(j5) Bræncesle, ix den'.	Brenchley
(j6) Horsbundenne, ix den'.	Horsmonden
(j7) Theudelei, ix den'.	Tudeley
(j8) Lamburherste, ix den'.	Lamberhurst
(j9) Peppingeberia, ix den'.	Pembury
(j10) Speldherste, ix den'.	Speldhurst
(j11) Wotringaberia, ix den'.	Wateringbury
(j12) East pecham, ix den'.	East Peckham
(j13) West pecham, ix den'.	West Peckham
(j14) East fearnlega, ix den'.	East Farleigh
(j15) Becceham, ix den'.	Beckenham
(j16) Trottescliui, ix den'.	Trottiscliffe
(j17) Ciselherste, ix den'.	Chislehurst
(j18) *Cuclena, ix den'.	Cowden
(j19) Æischerste, ix den'.	Ashurst
(j20) Æilesford, ix den'.	Aylesford
(j21) Berlingis, ix den'.	Birling
(j22) Meallingis, ix den'.	East Malling
(j23) Codeham, ix den'.	Cudham
(j24) Reierse, ix den'.	Ryarsh
(j25) Offeham, ix den'.	Offham
(j26) Dictuna, ix den'.	Ditton
(j27) Huntintune, ix den'.	Hunton
(j28) Netlesteda, ix den'.	Nettlestead
(j29) Burcham, ix den'.	Burham
(j30) Wldeham, ix den'.	Wouldham
(j31) Sc'a margarita, ix den'.	Rochester, St Margaret
(j32) Cætham ix den'.	Chatham
(j33) Sc's Clemens, ix den'.	Rochester, St Clement
(j34) Cuclestena, ix den'.	Cuxton
(j35) Hallingis, ix den'.	Halling
(j36) Snodilande, ix den'.	Snodland
(j37) Wroteham, ix den'.	Wrotham
(j38) Meapeham, ix den'.	Meopham
(j39) Pennesherste, ix den'.	Penshurst

(j40) Ehteham, ix den'. Ightham
(j41) Eadintuna, ix den'. Addington
(j42) Lisna, ix den'. Erith
(j43) *Leueseham, ix den'. Lewisham

R1, fo. 220v

(title) reddittibus *so spelt* (j18) Cuclena *so spelt in error for* Cudena (j43) *this entry overflows into the bottom margin*

List (k)

(k1) Beantesteda ⟶ (j3)
(k2) Bitteberga ⟶ (j4)
(k3) Lilintuna ⟶ (j14)
(k4) Cap' anfridi ⟶ (j16) ?
(k5) Cusintuna ⟶ (j20)
(k6) pædlesuurtha ⟶ (j21) Paddlesworth
(k7) Hescindena ⟶ (j31)
(k8) *Stanteda ⟶ (j37)
(k9) cap' Ho ⟶ (i3)
(k10) Lullingestana ⟶ (i5)
(k11) Sela ⟶ (i12) Seal
(k12) Strodes, Æslingeham, Thorndun ⟶ (i33)
(k13) *Mercstune ⟶ (i37)
(k14) Westcliue ⟶ (i45)
(k15) cap' Fearnberga ⟶ (i53)
(k16) Gretenersce ⟶ (i62)
(k17) Helle ⟶ (i63)
(k18) Craie * St Mary Cray
(k19) chitebroc ⟶ (i75)
(k20) comba ⟶ (i76)
(k21) Grenic, Lidisinga ⟶ (i79)
(k22) Bearmlingetes ⟶ (i80)
(k23) Sc's Leonardus ⟶ (i83)

R1, fos. 220v–1v, marginal annotation

(k8) *so spelt in error for* Stansteda (k13) *so spelt in error for* Mersctune (k18) *should be* ⟶ (i69)

Comments

(i3) Crayford has changed its name twice. The name 'Earhethe', used by DB, seems to have been obsolescent by c. 1100. 'Erde' was taking its place; and that remained the usual name till c. 1500.

(i13, i74) There are two churches here called 'Wickham', and the only hesitation comes in deciding which is which. The second Wickham occurs among a group of churches which otherwise all lie in the north-west corner of Kent; so probably that is East Wickham.

(i16) The name 'Hazelholt' is a puzzle, and I am no closer to solving it than I was ten years ago (Flight 1997b, p. 20). Ward proposed to identify it with Hadlow. Though his reasons were mostly wrong, the conclusion may be partly right. It seems possible that 'Hazelholt' and Hadlow were alternative names for the same place. There are two lines of argument. First, a woman named Eadgyth of Hazelholt is mentioned in DB as one of the people in West Kent who had sac and soc in the time of king Edward (DB-Ke-1va7). That being so, her name would be expected to occur in the main text too – and the only possible identification is with the woman who owned Hadlow and Tudeley (7vb6, 7vb12). (This woman's name is written *Eddeua*, and that is the DB scribe's spelling for Eadgifu, not Eadgyth; but the names are similar enough that they might become confused.) Second, since Hadlow is stated to have a church (DB-Ke-7vb4), it ought to appear in this list – and the only possible identification is with the church called 'Hazelholt' here. Given all this, one can understand why Ward felt impelled to identify 'Hazelholt' with Hadlow. I feel the same impulse myself, but am still not ready to give way to it. Someone should take a fresh look at the problem, paying particular attention (so I suggest) to the records of the manor of West Peckham.

(i34, i35) Higham church was always called 'Lillechurch' until c. 1200; the new name begins appearing in the thirteenth century. The church called 'Higham' here seems to have disappeared: presumably its parish was merged with that of Lillechurch, its name surviving and eventually becoming more popular than that one.

(i41) An interesting name, but I cannot identify the place.

(i42, i44) Probably Allhallows and St Mary Hoo, but there is no evidence to settle it, let alone to say which is which.

(i43) Despite its being sandwiched between entries connected with Hoo, the identification of this entry seems secure. As late as the fourteenth century, Dode was still sometimes called 'Dodechurch'.

(i56) The name 'Rodulf's Cray' occurs only this once, but the identification is certain. Rodulf (or Radulf) was butler to Adam son of Hubert (R1, fo. 212r), who held St Paul's Cray in 1086 (DB-Ke-6va45), and later to Adam's brother, Eudo the steward (R1, fo. 184v).

(i74) Probably East Wickham (see above).

(i84) The annotation 'But now nine (pence)' reflects the fact that Bidborough was detached from Leigh and made into a separate parish in 1219 (Thorpe 1769, pp. 166–7).

(i87) Strood was in Frindsbury until the 1190s, when it was made a separate parish.

(i96) 'Thorndown' was in Frindsbury, towards the boundary with Cooling. An early thirteenth-century Rochester manuscript has the name *Torindun'* glossed *videlicet Chetindon'* by a later hand R3, fo. 66v, printed, incorrectly, by Thorpe 1788, p. 2). This suggests that the name was falling out of use, and that the place was approximately or partly the same as Chattenden TQ 7572 in Frindsbury.

(i103) The place has disappeared, and I cannot locate it accurately enough to map it. A marginal note (k1) associates Bensted with Yalding; but Bensted was in Hunton later.

(i104) A marginal note (k16) associates Greatness with Halstead; but Greatness was in Sevenoaks later.

(i109) Linton is listed as a chapel here, and a marginal note (k3) connects it with East Farleigh; but Linton, later, was in Canterbury diocese.

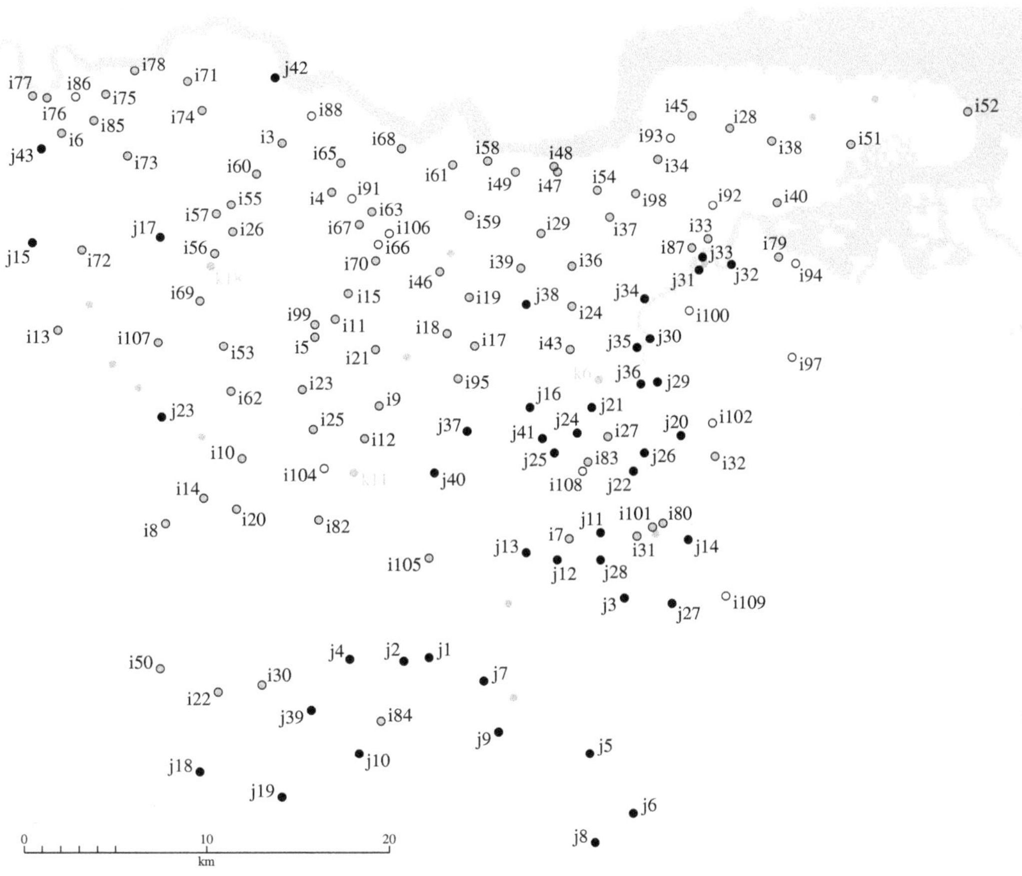

Figure 20. Parish churches in the diocese of Rochester.

(j2) This entry is the only oddity in list (j). Ward thought that the place in question had to be Barden, and I think that he was right; but there is no other evidence of a church existing there.

(k1–23) The arrow means that this marginal entry is keyed to an entry in the preexisting text.

(k4) If this chapel is correctly linked with Trottiscliffe, it is to be identified with the manor, variously called Trottiscliffe or Little Wrotham, which is represented on the map by Wrotham Water. In that case 'Anfrid' would be Ansfrid the steward (occ. 1108–37); the manor continued with his descendants (Conway 1911) for the next hundred years (*Feet of fines*, p. 126). But the chapel is not heard of again.

(k6) Paddlesworth, linked with Birling here, was, later, an independent church.

Index

Chapter 9
Thirteenth-century baronies in Kent

After 1086, we have to wait a long time before we find another document giving us a view of the feudal landscape of Kent which is both detailed and approximately complete. To be precise, we have to wait until 1242, when the king demanded a subsidy – called (in the jargon of the time) 'the aid for the king's crossing into Gascony' – to be paid by everyone who held land by knight's service.

Like any lesser lord, the king had the right to demand an 'aid' from his men on certain special occasions – when his eldest son was knighted, for instance, or when his eldest daughter got married. Kings had exercised this right in the past, and would exercise it again in the future; what makes this particular aid important is the manner in which was collected.

On previous occasions, the demand had always been addressed to the king's tenants in chief. The exchequer held them responsible for paying the money. (Those who had tenants of their own would collect a share of the money from them, as they would do from theirs, and so on down the line. But that was their business, not the exchequer's.) Most recently, this was how 'the aid for marrying the king's sister', charged at the rate of 320 pence for each knight's fee, had been collected in 1235–6. In the account which appeared in the exchequer roll (*Book of fees*, pp. 569–70), each barony is covered by a single entry which gives only the minimum amount of information. The whole barony of Chilham, for example, is condensed into this:

Ricard fiz le rei (owes) 4800 pence for fourteen fees of ancient feoffment, plus one fee of recent feoffment, of the honour of Fulbert de Dovre.[1]

That corresponds with an entry in the account of 'the aid for marrying the king's daughter', levied at the rate of 160 pence per fee, as far back as 1168 (GREx 1168, pp. 212–13):

Hugo de Dovre (owes) 2240 pence for (fourteen) knights of ancient feoffment. The same (Hugo) owes 160 pence (for one knight) of recent feoffment.

And that is based on Hugo's reply to a writ sent out to each of the king's tenants in chief in 1166, demanding a list of the names of each of this tenant's knights (E 164/12, ed. Hearne 1728, pp. 55–6).[2] By the 1230s, the exchequer thus had good reasons for suspecting that its information was seriously out of date, even if the facts had been truthfully reported in the first place, and that the king might be losing money to which he was entitled.[3]

In 1242, the collectors were given new instructions. They were to inquire, hundred by hundred, which manors were held by knight's service, and who was the tenant of each; and they were to demand payment, at the rate of 480 pence per fee, directly from this man. In a word, they were told to get to the bottom of things. Apparently they were under orders to stay away from the hundred of Milton, and from the lands of the archbishopric (which was in the king's hands at the time); otherwise they seem to have carried out their investigations throughout the whole of Kent.

The account which the collectors drew up would have consisted of some hundreds of individual entries,[4] each of which (by analogy with later accounts) would have been worded something like this:

Shrewinghope lest. ... Felborough hundred. ... From Eudo de Sellingehelde, for half a fee in Chilham which he holds from Ricard fiz le rei, and which Ricard holds from the lord king, 240 pence.[5]

The original account, regrettably, does not survive. But there are two derivative versions of the text, produced inside the exchequer, which aim to put the information into a

[1] Ricard fiz le rei (d. 1246) was a bastard son of king Johan's; he had acquired the barony by marrying Fulbert's daughter (below, p. 251). The formulas *de veteri feffamento, de novo feffamento* date back to the early years of Henric II (see below): they distinguish fees created before 1135 (i.e. before the day when the first king Henric was alive and dead) from fees created in the time of the usurper, Stephan.

[2] The text is garbled towards the end. It ought to read: *Summa xi mil' et dim', et super dominium meum ii milites et dim'. De nouo feodamento. Willelmus* .... (The lords of Chilham had created fewer knight's fees than the number of knights which they had to find for the king; so they had to make up the deficit out of their own resources. That is what is meant by the formula *super dominium meum*.) Hugo submitted a separate reply (pp. 253–4) relating to the share of a barony in Cambridgeshire which had come to him through his wife.

[3] Between 1172 and 1230, demands for *escuage* were dealt with in just the same way – charged to the king's tenants in chief, and based on the numbers of knight's fees reported in 1166. The distinction between an *aide* and an *escuage* was not sharply drawn: an *aide*, one might say, became an *escuage* if it was levied at the rate of so much for each *escu* (meaning 'shield'), i.e. for each knight's fee.

[4] By my reckoning, there are 348 entries in the surviving versions of this account. From a comparison with the account for 1253–4 (see below), I infer that the number of missing entries is probably close to 60 – perhaps 5 for Milton hundred, rather more than 50 for the archbishopric.

[5] The manor in question is Shillingheld TR 0654 in Chilham (Hasted 7:283). The occupant in 1166 was Elias de Silinghalde, who held half a knight's fee from Hugo de Dovre. In this instance, therefore, the inquiry turned up nothing new.

form which will be useful for future reference. Some slight changes have been made in the wording of the entries:

Eudo de Sellingehelde holds half a fee in Chilham from Ricard fiz le rei, and Ricard holds it from the lord king.[6]

More significantly, the entries have been reorganized. In the same sort of way that the B text of the survey of 1086 was transformed into the D text, the entries derived from the collectors' account have been extracted from their cadastral frame, so as to be inserted into a feodal frame. In the earlier of the two surviving versions (*Book of fees*, pp. 654–70), the hundreds have disappeared but the division into lests is retained; in the final version (pp. 670–83) the lests have disappeared as well, and the fees belonging to each barony have been grouped together, in a loosely cadastral order. The barony of Chilham, for instance, has been reconstituted under the heading 'Fees of Ricard fiz le rei and Roesia his wife'. In order for this to be done, more than twenty entries had to be pulled together, from five different hundreds, in three different lests.

In putting itself to so much trouble, the exchequer was evidently working on the assumption that future aids would be collected in the traditional way, from the king's tenants in chief: the only difference would be be that in future the assessments would be based on the facts ascertained in 1242. But that was not what happened. Subsequent aids, so far as we have any record of them, were collected in the same way as the aid of 1242 – lest by lest, hundred by hundred, directly from the tenant who was in possession.[7] From the exchequer's point of view, this reorganization of the text turned out to be a waste of time; from our point of view it was decidely a change for the worse, because the loss of the cadastral frame makes it harder to identify the manors which are named. Nevertheless, with the help of other evidence, almost every entry can be put back into the right lest and hundred. As for the entries which were deliberately omitted – principally those for the archbishop's knights – we know enough to guess what these entries would have said, if they had been included.

[6] In fact both versions omit this last clause, letting it be taken for granted. That happens frequently but not always. Here is an entry which makes it explicit that the chain of tenure ends with the king: 'Michael de Hestingele holds three quarters of a fee there (in Hastingleigh) from the heir of Willelm de Turville, and he (holds it) from the earl of Leicester, and he (holds it) from the lord king.'

[7] Though I have made it a rule not to cite any evidence later than 1242 (except where it cannot be helped), I attach a list of these later aids, with notes of the documentation relating to Kent, in case the reader wishes to pursue this line of inquiry. (1) *Aide pour fille marier*, 240 pence per fee, collected in 1245–6. No surviving record. (2) *Aide pour faire fils chevalier*, 480 pence per fee, collected in 1253–4. A poor copy of a version of the account was printed by Greenstreet (1878). (3) *Aide pour fille marier*, 480 pence per fee, authorized by parliament in 1290 but not collected till 1302–3 (*Calendar of patent rolls 1301–7*, 76–7). Some version of this account appears to be represented by a seventeenth-century copy in BL Lansdowne 309, fos. 3v–13v. The heading was quoted by Greenstreet (1876, pp. 108–9), who also printed a few extracts (1877, pp. 376–9); the full text has yet to be published. (4) *Aide pour faire fils chevalier*, 480 pence per fee, collected in 1346–7. The collectors' account survives in the original (together with various copies and derivative versions); the full text was edited by Greenstreet (1876), and again by the PRO (*Feudal aids*, pp. 20–52). Except where the collectors had made some new discovery, each entry in this account was based on one of the entries in the account of the aid of 1302–3, which itself was based (or intended to be based) on the aid of 1245–6. So each entry may be said to encapsulate a hundred years of history.

Bridging the gap between 1086 and 1242 is not an easy task. Until the end of the twelfth century, when the records of central government begin to proliferate, the evidence is thin at best, and very unevenly distributed. To trace the history of individual manors is practically impossible: a few isolated hints are the most that can be hoped for. Even to trace the history of the first-tier baronies can sometimes be very difficult. Quite often, one item of evidence may be all that stands between us and utter ignorance;[8] on occasion we can find no evidence at all, and guesswork is all that we are left with.

In the following paragraphs, I give outline sketches of the history of all the first-tier baronies which were represented in Kent. By and large I have not thought it necessary to cite the evidence in detail. Such as it is, it is mostly well enough known and well enough understood, and Sanders's (1963) book will point the reader in the right direction. Where footnotes occur in any number, that should be taken to imply that the standard accounts seem seriously defective to me, because they have overlooked or misunderstood some significant pieces of evidence. The small-scale maps are intended to give some idea of the extent of each barony, so far as Kent is concerned. They are, of necessity, simplified to some degree. Here and there, where the dots are tightly clustered, a small manor which could have been marked on the map has had to be omitted for lack of space; but I have not omitted any manor which can be recognized in DB-Ke.

My chief purpose is a simple one: to let the reader know what evidence exists which can clinch the identification of places named in DB-Ke, or in the other records of the survey of Kent. As soon as one starts discussing this evidence, however, one cannot help but notice how it bears on other questions. It is not my intention, now or ever, to write a comprehensive account of the feodal history of Kent; but there are two topics in particular which I have made a point of mentioning, wherever there is something to be said.

First, I have tried to explain how the system of castle-guard worked, with respect to the castles at Dover and Rochester. (There is, as far as I am aware, no indication that a similar system existed for the castle at Canterbury.) The arrangements in place at Dover were designed to provide the castle, all year round, with a garrison of no less than 22 knights. (I simplify slightly: full particulars are given below.) For each four-week spell of duty, four knights were supplied by the honour of the Constabulary, three each by the baronies of Averenches, Chilham, Arsic, Peverel and

[8] One neglected source, a sixteenth-century copy of an early twelfth-century list of the holders of land in Kent (Flight 2005), will, I venture to hope, not be neglected any longer.

Maminot, two by the barony of Port, and one by the barony of Crevequer. The arrangements concerning Rochester are not so well documented, but it seems that three baronies – Talebot, Patric, Stockbury – were expected to provide the castle with a small garrison, perhaps of four knights. By the time that any detailed information becomes available, both systems had become fossilized. Nobody performed the service that was theoretically due from them, in person or by deputy; all that was required was the payment of a sum of money. At Dover, 'one knight' (i.e. the service of one knight for four weeks) meant a payment of 120 pence (roughly 4 pence a day); at Rochester it meant a payment of 144 pence (roughly 5 pence a day).

Second, I have done what I can to elucidate the history of each barony during the reign of king Stephan (1135–54).[9] Drastic changes occurred during this period; but most of these changes were deliberately reversed, after 1154, following the death of Stephan and the accession of Henric II. In these circumstances, because the changes did not take permanent effect, we are all the more likely to be left in ignorance of them.

By 1138, the country was slipping into civil war. Gladly or not, people had to choose sides. Several Kentish barons renounced their allegiance to the king: they left the country, or at least they left Kent, and their baronies were confiscated. The king and his wife, queen Mathildis (countess of Boulogne in her own right), were, it seems, prepared to pay almost any price to maintain their lines of communication with the continent, and the man who benefited most was Willelm de Ipre (the bastard son of the younger son of Robert I, count of Flanders).[10] Nearly everything in Kent that the king had to give passed into Willelm's possession: the city of Canterbury, the royal manors, the manors which went with the earldom of Kent, and at least two of the confiscated baronies as well (Ospringe, Chilham). If the barony built up by Willelm had descended to a son of his, that son would have been by far the most important man in Kent (and doubtless he would have aspired to the title of earl). But that was not to be.

Throughout the rest of Stephan's reign, even in the critical year of 1141 (when the king himself was held prisoner, and the empress and her supporters were briefly in possession of London), Kent was little touched by the war. The machinery of government continued to function – but it functioned under a system of military rule, exerted by the king's castellans: Willelm de Ipre at Canterbury, Radulf fiz le comte at Rochester,[11] Pharamus de Boulogne at Dover.

During the 1140s, Willelm de Ipre expressed the gratitude he felt for his newly acquired possessions by founding a Cistercian abbey; the site that he chose for it was the manor of Boxley (one of the manors belonging to the earldom of Kent).[12] At about the same time, the king and queen were planning the foundation of an abbey of Cluniac monks (on the model, no doubt, of the abbey of Reading, founded by Henric I), and the site that they chose was in Kent – the royal manor of Faversham.[13] (That manor had been given to Willelm de Ipre, but now he agreed to give it back to the king, in exchange for other land of equal value.) The first monks (who came from Bermondsey) arrived in 1148, though the buildings were far from finished at the time.[14] Dying within the space of two years (1152–4), the queen, her elder son, and her husband the king were all buried in the abbey church.

Once Stephan was dead, Henric II succeeded to the throne without opposition. Those barons who had supported the usurper were, by and large, allowed to keep their lands, so far as they could prove that they had been in possession (or that their predecessors had been) on the day when the first king Henric was alive and dead. Those barons who had been dispossessed by Stephan (or whose predecessors had been) were reinstated, on the same terms, with little or no delay. The monks of Faversham were allowed to keep that manor; though the king, before becoming king, had promised to respect their rights, there were, no doubt, some anxious moments before it became clear that this was one of the promises which the king meant to keep (GREx 1156:65). The monks of Boxley were kept in suspense a little longer, but then it was decided that they too should be allowed to stay (GREx 1157:102). As for Willelm de Ipre, the barony which he had built up was dismantled, not all at once but piece by piece, during the first few years of the new king's reign. Chilham was given back to its rightful owner; the other lands were repossessed by the king.[15] Within four years or so, except at Faversham and Boxley, every trace of Stephan's usurpation had been erased.

Many charters, very probably, were thrown away, at around this time, because they had become worthless. But some charters did survive – sometimes in places where one might hardly think of looking for them. There was, for example, an important file of documents relating to two parish churches in Kent preserved in the archive of the abbey of

[9] An article by Eales (1985) is helpful in supplying the background, but seems to me to keep circling the subject without getting down to business.

[10] The article 'William of Ypres' in the *Oxford Dictionary of National Biography* (2004) is Eales's work again.

[11] Radulf's identity has caused some bafflement (even his existence has been doubted), but I take him to be the same Radulf who is recorded elsewhere – the document in question is discussed by Round (1901, pp. 164–5) – as a son of count Eustachius III (which means that he must have been an illegitimate half-brother of the queen's).

[12] The Rochester annals date the foundation to 1143 (R3, fo. 29v). This was and remained the only house of Cistercian monks in Kent. The plan was recovered by excavation in 1971–2 (Tester 1974).

[13] Though the abbey was Cluniac in inspiration, archbishop Theobald required all links with the Cluniac order to be broken before he would bless the first abbot.

[14] In fact they were never finished – not, at least, on anything like the scale originally intended. The site was partly excavated in 1965 (Philp 1968).

[15] Some of them – Dartford, Hoo, Ospringe – were given to another Willelm, the king's younger brother. He might also have aspired to be earl of Kent (there was even a time when it looked as if he might become king of Ireland); but he died, unmarried, in 1164, and his lands reverted to the king.

Saint Bertin, in the town of Saint-Omer. And it is – by the way – a curious fact that Edward Hasted was one of the last people to see the original charters (almost all of which were shortly to be destroyed). Fleeing from his creditors in 1790, Hasted settled in Saint-Omer; and, while he was there, he took the opportunity (as of course he would) to consult the abbey's archive.

Adam fiz Willelm

This is a puzzling case. From the 1230s onwards, it becomes clear that a few manors in Kent belong to a second-tier barony based in Hertfordshire, and that this barony owes a small amount of castleguard rent to Dover. I have no idea how this had come about. The first name to occur in connection with Dover is Adam fiz Willelm (d. 1236); but in Hertfordshire (not in Kent) the history of the barony can be traced back to a man of the same name who was a tenant of the bishop of Bayeux in 1086.

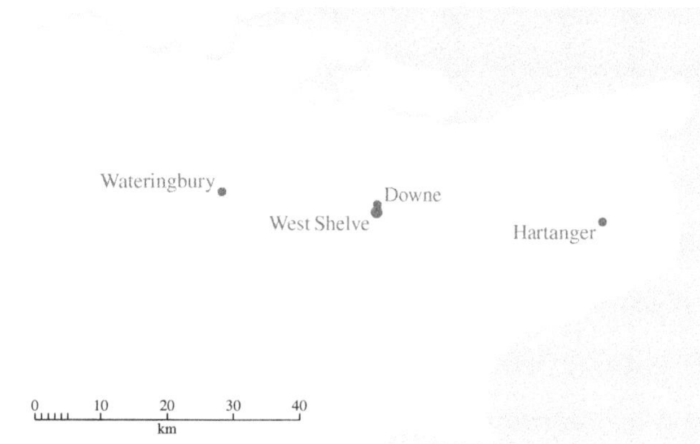

In 1242 the barony belonged to Simon fiz Adam (occ. 1241–53); his overlord was Walter fiz Robert (d. 1258). Of the manors in Kent, West Shelve was held in domain; the others were granted out. Downe and Hartanger owed castleguard at Dover; so did the manor of Graveley in Hertfordshire.[16]

Albigni, *see* Arundel

Arsic

The lands which in 1086 were held from the bishop of Bayeux by Wadard (including five manors in Kent) became the property of a family named Arsic. The head of the barony was at Cogges in Oxfordshire. After Wadard, the first recorded owner is Manasser Arsic (occ. 1101–10); it does not seem to be known who he was, or how he had got possession. His last male descendant was Robert Arsic (d. 1230). After Robert's death, the inheritance was divided between his two daughters, Johanna and Alexandra, both of whom were to be married more than once. Their mother, Sibilla, was still alive, and so was their aunt Margareta (their father's elder brother's widow), and each was in possession of a share of the Arsic lands by way of dower. The manor of Cogges had just recently been sold (to Walter de Grey, archbishop of York), and nothing much was left, beyond the service from the knight's fees.

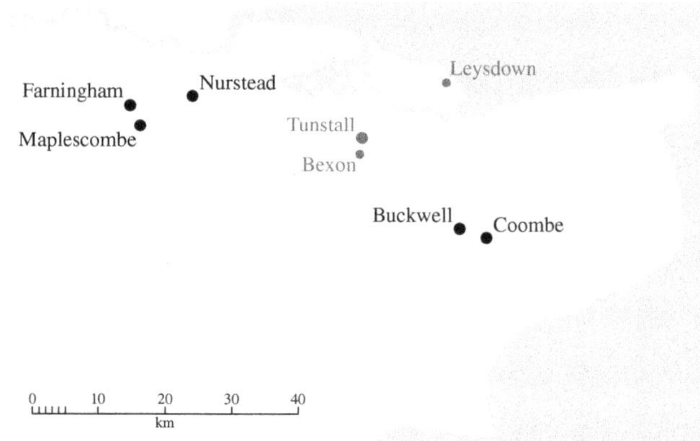

This was one of the baronies which owed castleguard at Dover: for every 4-week spell, it was (in theory) required to supply three knights. The service was distributed among 18 knight's fees (including the five in Kent): they were organized into six teams of three knights each, working on a 24-week rota.

The five manors in Kent which had belonged to Wadard were all granted out, before 1135, for one knight's fee apiece. In unknown circumstances, before 1166, the Arsics got possession of a sixth manor, Tunstall, which they held from the barony of Port. There were assets in Sheppey which went with this manor, apparently including Leysdown church, which was given (perhaps sold) by Robert Arsic to the canons of Saint Radegund's. Tunstall with all its remaining assets was sold in 1227 (to Hubert de Burgh, earl of Kent, and his wife Margareta).

As things stood in 1242, Johanna's husband was Stephan Simeon, and Alexandra's was Thomas de la Haye (d. 1246).

Arundel

Three of the domain manors surrendered by the bishop of Bayeux in 1088 – Elham, Bilsington, Knowlton – were granted to Willelm de Albigni (d. 1139). It is likely that they were given to him almost at once; but the earliest evidence which proves that he had possession is a writ of Henric I dating from 1102×8.

By that time, half of Bilsington – the half which came to be called Over Bilsington – had set out on a separate trajectory. It appears that Willelm gave it to his daughter Olivia as her marriage portion.[17] By means unknown to me, it came to belong to Willelm de Courci (d. 1186); Robert de Courci (occ. 1189–1226) got possession in 1189 – but lost

[16] There was no rota. Each fee paid 10 shillings twice a year, at fixed dates. In the case of Hartanger, for instance, the rents fell due a fortnight before Christmas and a fortnight before Midsummer.

[17] The parish church, which went with this half of Bilsington, was given by her husband, Radulf de la Haye, to the monks of Lessay.

it in 1204, when Over Bilsington was confiscated. After that, though not without difficulty, the earl of Arundel – Willelm de Albigni's descendant – recovered possession of the manor.

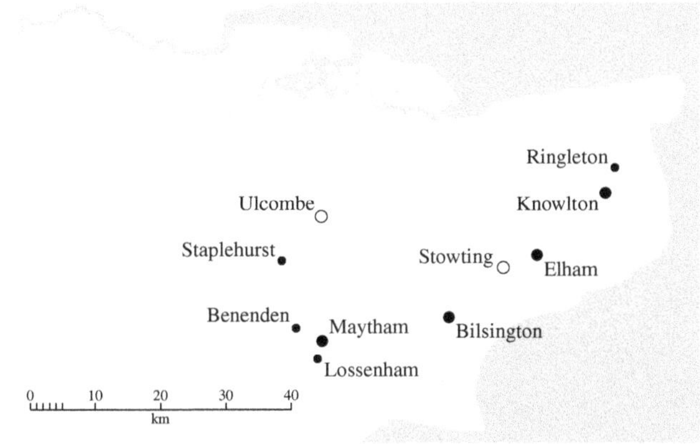

All of the other lands in Kent passed from Willelm to his son, Willelm de Albigni (d. 1176), first earl of Arundel. They were given by him to his daughter, Adelicia, when she became the wife of Johan count of Eu (d. 1170). The count was already the owner of two manors in Kent – Stowting and Ulcombe – which were held from the archbishop; now he became the owner of two more manors, and also of the service from eleven knight's fees (all of which were old fees, i.e. fees which had existed since before 1135).

By the 1220s, the Albigni lands in Kent (except for Over Bilsington) were all in the possession of Johan and Adelicia's granddaughter, Adelicia countess of Eu (d. 1246). (She had been married once; but her husband died in 1219 and she stayed single after that.) When Adelicia's daughter Mathildis got married, some of these assets – Nether Bilsington and most of the knight's fees – were given to her and her husband, Hunfrid de Bohun earl of Hereford (d. 1275).[18] The rest – Elham and a few of the knight's fees – continued to belong to the countess of Eu herself.[19]

Two subordinate holdings are large enough to be regarded as second-tier baronies. One was based on Knowlton; in 1166 it belonged to Alan Pirot, but its history before that is (at least to me) obscure. The other was based on Great Maytham in Rolvenden: this seems to be the holding which belonged before 1108 to Radulf de Chieresburh (identified as Willelm de Albigni's steward), in 1166 to Petrus de Cesaris burgo.

In 1242, most of the knight's fees in Kent were held from the earl of Hereford. Directly or indirectly, all of them were held from the countess of Eu, and by her from the earl of Arundel. Knowlton belonged to Radulf Perot; Maytham had been divided between two sisters, Orabilis and Helewisa, the daughters and coheirs of Radulf de Meyhamme. At Stowting, one knight's fee was held from the countess of Eu, and by the countess from the archbishop. At Ulcombe the countess's interest had just recently been bought out, and the tenant was now holding directly from the archbishop.

Aumale, *see* Marescal

Averenches

The barony centred on Folkestone has a relatively well-recorded history, worked out in detail by Stapleton (1844). In 1086 it belonged to Willelm de Arques (*de Arcis*). With Willelm's daughter Emma it passed to Nigel de Muneville (occ. 1095);[20] with Nigel's daughter Mathildis it passed to Rualon de Averenches (occ. 1125–30), and then to Rualon's son, Willelm de Averenches (occ. 1142–76). Willelm stayed loyal to king Stephan,[21] but seems to have had no difficulty coming to terms with the new regime after 1154. From him the barony passed to his descendants. The male line ended with Willelm (d. 1236) – the son of Willelm de Averenches (d. 1230) – who died before coming of age; and the inheritance then went to his sister Mathildis, who was the wife of Hamo de Crevequer (d. 1263).

Though linked with Folkestone, the manor of Newington follows a different trajectory. It is missing from DB. In 1095 it belonged to Beatrix, the widow of Willelm de Arques; the next recorded owner is Manasser count of Guînes, the second husband of Beatrix's daughter Emma.[22] Like Willelm de Averenches, Ernald count of Guînes stayed loyal to king Stephan,[23] but came to terms with Henric II.[24] (He was staying at Newington when he died, in 1169.) His successors kept possession of the manor – of the whole of it till 1202, of half of it till 1223×7, when count Baldwin III was bought out by Hubert de Burgh.

Folkestone was one of the baronies which owed castleguard at Dover. For each four-week spell, it was required to supply three knights. The load was shared among 21 knights, organized in seven teams of three, working to a 28-week

[18] They sold their part of Bilsington in 1237×40, but retained the service from the knight's fees for themselves and their heirs.

[19] Until she was dispossessed in 1244.

[20] Nigel had some land of his own in Northamptonshire, where he was a tenant of the count of Mortain's. (That helps to explain why the knight's fees in Kent were claimed to be smaller than normal (below, note 25), as was agreed to be true for the fees created by the count.) He and Emma gave Folkestone church to the abbey of Lonlay.

[21] The empress promised to dispossess him in favour of somebody else; but she was never in a position to keep that promise.

[22] Manasser and Emma gave Newington church to the abbey of nuns founded by them in Guînes. Two churches dependent on Newington, Brenzett and Promhill, were covered by this grant.

[23] He witnesses a charter of Willelm de Ipre for the monks of Christ Church (Urry 1967, no. XIV). (The second witness is Radulf fiz le comte – not the son of *this* count (the wording does not say that), but rather, as I suppose, a son of the late count of Boulogne.)

[24] A Premonstratensian house at Blackwose seems to have owed its foundation to count Ernald. Though its history is an almost total blank, there is proof that the house was in existence before 1154 (GREx 1169:110–11). At first it was a dependency of the abbey of Lavendon in Buckinghamshire; but eventually it was taken over by Saint Radegund's.

rota. It is at least roughly true to say that 15 of these fees were in Kent, six of them 'beyond the Thames'.[25]

There were two second-tier baronies, based on Swingfield and Cheriton respectively, but their early histories are obscure. At Swingfield the first recorded owner is Willelm de Auberville (occ. 1166–95);[26] he also held Westenhanger from the archbishop. Towards the end of his life, by means which I do not understand, he acquired a small share of the small barony of Stockbury,[27] in consequence of which he became a first-tier baron. At Cheriton the first recorded owner is Odo de Cheritone (occ. 1135–58). Coincidentally another share of the barony of Stockbury went to Odo's descendant Willelm de Cheritone (d. 1233); so he too became a first-tier baron.

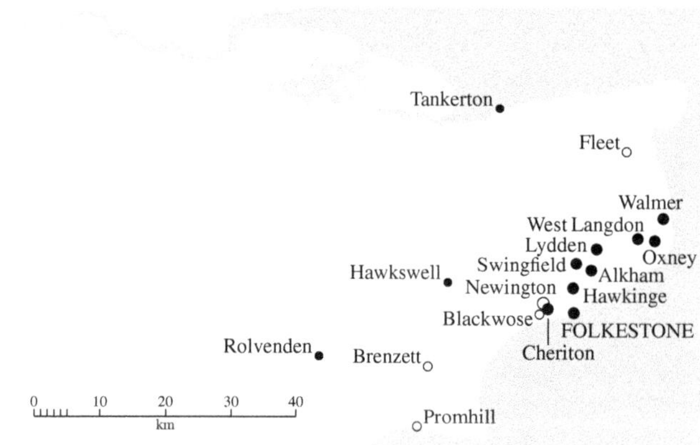

In 1242 the barony of Folkestone belonged to Hamo de Crevequer.[28] Swingfield belonged to Willelm de Auberville (d. 1248), Cheriton to master Odo de Cheritone (d. 1247). Half of Newington was owned jointly by the earl and countess of Kent, Hubert de Burgh (d. 1243) and Margareta (d. 1259). (Count Baldwin was trying to get it back, but he did not succeed.)

Boulogne

Eustachius II, count of Boulogne, having fought on the winning side in 1066, was rewarded with extensive estates in England. The count became the owner of scattered manors in several counties (among them Westerham and Boughton Aluph in Kent), but Essex is where the bulk of the lands and the head of the honour lay. Eustachius's wife, countess Ida, had a small number of manors in her own possession; in the records of the survey she seems to be assumed to be holding them directly from the king, independently from her husband.

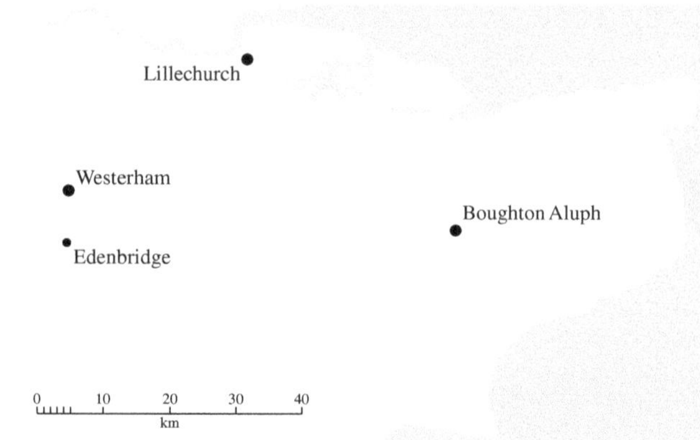

When Eustachius died, he was succeeded as count by his eldest son, Eustachius III.[29] For several years, for as long as Willelm II was king, the new count was not able to get possession of his father's lands in England (perhaps because the king had not forgiven him for participating in the rebellion of 1088); but the next king was more amenable. In 1101–2, king Henric allowed the count to inherit his father's lands; he also arranged for the count to marry his own wife's sister Maria. When Eustachius's mother, countess Ida, died in 1113, he inherited her lands as well; and he enlarged the honour still further, after 1119, by buying some of the manors (Lillechurch in Kent was one) which had lapsed to the king after the death of Eudo the steward.

Eustachius III had no son: his heir was his daughter Mathildis. Shortly before he died in 1125, Eustachius arranged for her to marry king Henric's nephew, Stephan count of Mortain. Ten years later, Stephan became king of England. From the charters that she issued during the time that she was queen, it is clear that Mathildis had control of her own inheritance. Like any baron, she might ask the king to ratify some donation that she had made; but the donation was hers to make, if it came out of the assets of the honour of Boulogne.

Mathildis died in 1152, and the county of Boulogne and its English lands passed to her two sons successively: first to Eustachius IV, who died in the following year (and who, if he had lived longer, might have hoped to be the next king of England), and then to Willelm, who died in 1159. Like his brother, Willelm died childless, and the next heir was his sister, Maria, who happened to be a nun – abbess, in fact, of Romsey in Hampshire. She was brought out of the cloister and married to a younger brother of the count of Flanders; having borne two children, she retired from the world again. (Her thoughts about all this are not recorded, unless they find some echo in the poetry that she wrote.)

[25] The fees in Kent were claimed to be smaller than a normal knight's fee, and entitled to some discount accordingly. Some credence was given to this claim. In the scutage of 1218, for example, the barony was charged at a reduced rate for 15 fees, at the full rate for six 'beyond the Thames'. (Willelm de Averenches seems to have been expecting a discount of 40 per cent; the Exchequer allowed him a discount of 37.5 per cent.)

[26] Willelm de Auberville founded the abbey of Langdon, giving it the churches of West Langdon, Walmer, Oxney and Lydden.

[27] The share for which Anfrid de Canci finished paying in 1186.

[28] Hamo remained in possession until he died, under the rule which the lawyers called the courtesy of England (because it did not apply in France). Then the barony was divided between his and Mathildis's four daughters.

[29] The date of Eustachius II's death is uncertain. From references in version E of the English chronicle, I think it is clear that he died between 1088 and 1096, and that Eustachius III (away on crusade for three years after that) did not get possession of the English lands – still referred to then as 'his father's' – till after 1101.

Both of her children were girls: if either had been a boy, the future might have been different. In the event, once the honour of Boulogne had lapsed to the crown with the death of count Willelm, it never left the king's hands again. Its tenants were said (for as long as this language had any meaning) to be 'holding in chief of the king as of the honour of Boulogne'.

In the time of count Eustachius III, the manors in Kent were apparently held in domain. At Boughton Aluph, two serjeanties were created, the holders of which were required to serve the count as cook and falconer respectively; nothing is heard of these serjeanties before the thirteenth century, but their creation must go back to a time when the count was expecting to spend some of his time at Boughton, needing to be fed and amused while he was there. The parish churches of Boughton and Westerham were both given to the Cluniac priory of Le Wast, not far from Boulogne; an annual payment of 20 pounds out of the revenue from Boughton was given to the hospital of Saint Mary Magdalene in Boulogne itself.

Not much later, both manors were granted out. It is known that Westerham was disposed of by queen Mathildis; probably the same applies to Boughton Aluph.

Lillechurch became the endowment of a small community of nuns.[30] Like some other small religious houses, the priory here was juxtaposed to an existing parish church. Inconveniently, the church had been given to the monks of Colchester (presumably by their founder, Eudo the steward), but queen Mathildis was able to get it back by arranging an exchange. The first prioress was Mathildis's daughter Maria, who had come over to England accompanied by a party of nuns from the abbey of Saint-Sulpice-la-Forêt in Brittany, which, presumably, is where she had been completing her education (and learning the Breton folk-tales which she turned into French verse).[31] Though Maria moved on within a few years, becoming abbess of Romsey (see above), the priory of Lillechurch continued to exist – as a dependency of Saint-Sulpice until the 1230s, independently after that.

In 1242 the honour was in the king's hands. Robert de Canville (d. 1291–2) held Westerham for two knight's fees; he also owned Fobbing in Essex. Elias de Boutone (d. 1247) held Boughton Aluph for one knight's fee. (He was the son of Alulf de Boutone (d. 1214×17), from whom this Boughton took its distinguishing name.)

[30] A few years earlier, Mathildis had promised to give Lillechurch to Willelm de Ipre, in exchange for Faversham; but that exchange did not take place – or, if it did, was renegotiated soon afterwards.

[31] Here I am assuming, *en passant*, that Stephan and Mathildis's daughter was the poet known to historians of French literature as 'Marie de France'. The identification was suggested (but not as strongly as it might have been) by Knapton (1978).

Chilham

Chilham in 1086 was held from the bishop of Bayeux by Fulbert (occ. 1086–1120) – sometimes called 'de Chileham', sometimes 'de Dovre' (a name which seems to be derived, not from Dover, but from a place in Normandy, now Douvres-la-Délivrande). After 1088, Fulbert remained in possession, holding directly from the king. He was succeeded by his son, Hugo de Dovre (occ. 1127–70), sometimes called 'de Chileham' or 'son of Fulbert'. Hugo was dispossessed by king Stephan, and all or some of his lands (probably all of them) were given to Willelm de Ipre.[32] After 1154, Willelm was dispossessed in his turn, and Hugo recovered his inheritance.[33] When Hugo died, in 1170–1, the barony passed to his nephew, Johan de Dovre (d. 1189–90);[34] from him it passed to his son, Fulbert de Dovre, who came of age in 1198 and died in 1202–3, leaving one daughter as his heir.

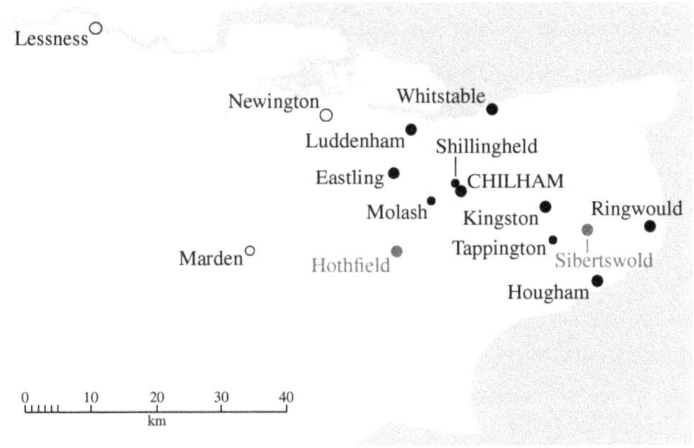

Apart from the barony of Chilham itself, the lords of Chilham held Hothfield from the archbishop, Sibertswold from the abbot of Saint Augustine's. Johan de Dovre's wife Roesia (d. 1211–12) was a daughter of the eldest son of Ricard de Luci (d. 1179).[35] Eventually that meant that her granddaughter, also named Roesia, inherited a share of Ricard de Luci's lands, which included two manors in Kent, Lessness and Newington; but the story is a complicated one, and – since it has no particular relevance – I refrain from telling it here.

This was another barony which owed castleguard at Dover. The load was shared among 15 knights, organized in five teams of three, working to a 20-week rota.

[32] We only know this because Willelm de Ipre gave Chilham church to the monks of Saint Bertin; and we only know that because Hugo de Dovre, after being reinstated, allowed the donation to stand – though of course he represented it as his own donation, ignoring Willelm's existence.

[33] He also got possession of his wife Mathildis's inheritance, a share of some of the lands which had belonged to her brother, Willelm Pevrel (below, Peverel of Dover).

[34] The youngest son of Hugo's younger brother, Willelm de Dovre (occ. 1141–5).

[35] Ricard de Luci founded the abbey of Lessness, giving it the western half of this manor and two parish churches which were his to give, Newington and Marden. (Not Lessness church itself, which already belonged to the canons of Holy Trinity, London.)

In 1242 the barony belonged to Fulbert's daughter Roesia (d. 1261) and her husband – a bastard son of king Johan's, Ricard fiz le rei (d. 1246). (He was sometimes called 'de Chileham', occasionally 'de Warenne', that being his mother's name.) It seems that they were living separately by this time. Roesia held half of Lessness in domain (the half which did not belong to the canons of Lessness). The manor of Newington had also been split in half: one portion was owned by Roesia's nephew Gaufrid de Luci (d. 1252), the other by the heirs of Roesia's grandmother's sister.

Clare

All of the lands which in 1086 belonged to Ricard son of count Gislebert continued with his descendants. Only a small proportion of these lands lay in Kent: Tonbridge with its castle and lowy, and a handful of other manors, none very far from Tonbridge, two of which had been held by Ricard from the bishop of Bayeux.[36] Ricard's great-grandson, Gilebert (d. 1152), was made an earl by king Stephan: he used the title earl of Hertford, sometimes earl of Clare. (He fell out with the king in 1147, but the estrangement did not last long.) When he died, the honour passed to his younger brother, Roger earl of Hertford (d. 1173).[37]

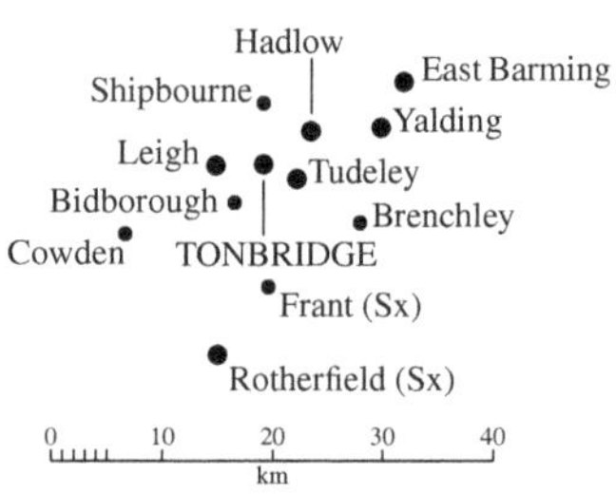

Two generations later, the descent of the earldom of Hertford intersected with that of the earldom of Gloucester. Gilebert de Clare (d. 1230) inherited both earldoms, Hertford from his father, Gloucester from his mother. His title was earl of Gloucester and Hertford; less formally he was often called the earl of Gloucester, sometimes the earl of Clare. (It was known well enough, by the people who needed to know, that these titles all referred to a single person.)

When the earl died in 1230, his son and heir was only eight years old. Assuming that the son remained alive (as in fact he did), this meant that both honours would be in the king's hands for the next thirteen years (except for the share assigned to the late earl's widow by way of dower). The vultures soon started arriving. In 1235 the archbishop of Canterbury got a charter from the king which granted him custody of Tonbridge and Brasted during the heir's minority – not just on this occasion, but on any similar occasion in the future. Brasted was part of the honour of Gloucester and had always been held from the archbishop, since before 1086; archbishop Edmund was within his rights to ask for the custody of it.[38] But the archbishop had no right whatever to ask for the custody of Tonbridge. It was outrageous of him to apply for it, outrageous of the king to grant it. In effect, this charter meant that the earl was now the archbishop's tenant, not the king's, so far as the lowy of Tonbridge was concerned. Assuming that the archbishop remained alive, the earl would be obliged to come to terms with him before he could get possession of this portion of his inheritance. Fortunately for the earl, the archbishop did not remain alive. He died in 1240. Tonbridge fell back into the king's hands; and it stayed there long enough for the earl to get full possession in 1243, while there was still no archbishop to interfere. (The earl realized, no doubt, that eventually he would have to come to terms with the new archbishop; but now he would be negotiating from a position of strength.)[39]

In 1242, the honour of Clare was still theoretically in the king's hands; but it appears that the earl of Gloucester had already been put in possession, even though the formal transfer could not take place before August 1243.

Constabulary

The honour of the Constabulary, as it was defined in the thirteenth century, coincided very nearly with the vast assemblage of lands in England – in Kent, Essex, Suffolk and Norfolk – acquired by Hugo de Montfort in the aftermath of 1066. Hugo had served the duke of Normandy as one of his hereditary constables; he was to serve the king of England in the same capacity. From him, the office and the lands which went with it descended to his son, Robert de Montfort.[40] Falling into disgrace, Robert was dispossessed in 1107, and the inheritance passed to his sister, Adelina, with whom it was granted out twice: firstly to Simon de Molins (occ. c. 1120), secondly to Robert de Ver (occ. 1127–51).[41]

[36] The manor of Rotherfield in Sussex, forfeited by the bishop of Bayeux in 1088, was shortly aferwards acquired by Ricard's son Gislebert (R1, fo. 182v = Davis 1913, no. 450).

[37] Roger's son, Ricard earl of Hertford (d. 1217) was the founder of Tonbridge priory. By an arrangement negotiated with the pope in 1191, the priory was exempted, not just from the bishop of Rochester's jurisdiction, but also from the archbishop's. In the earl's view, so I suppose, it seemed right for the priory to have a special status, consonant with the special status enjoyed by the lowy of Tonbridge.

[38] Even in this respect, however, I am doubtful whether he could cite any favourable precedent. In 1183, after the death of a previous earl of Gloucester, it is clear that the king got custody of Brasted – and kept it.

[39] An agreement was finally worked out in 1258. The earl was not exactly the innocent victim of other people's machinations. By questionable means, his great-grandfather had acquired the hereditary bailiffdom of the hundreds of Littlefield and Watchlingstone, and the earl was stealthily annexing both hundreds to the lowy of Tonbridge. There are several reports about this in the hundred rolls; the men of Wrotham hundred seem to have been best informed.

[40] It was Robert who gave Saltwood church to the monks of Le Bec.

[41] Robert de Ver and Adelina were the founders of the Cluniac priory at Horton.

When war broke out, Robert stayed loyal to king Stephan: he was frequently in attendance on the king, up until 1151, which presumably is when he died. His wife was apparently already dead, never having had any children; so the question arose as to who now had the strongest claim on the inheritance.

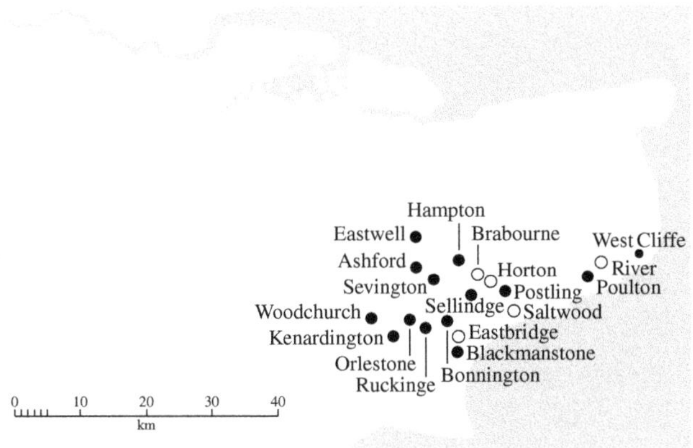

Two claimants came forward. One was Gislebert de Gant (d. 1156), who could prove (if I understand the case correctly) that he was the grandson of a sister of Hugo de Montfort's. The other was Henric de Essexe, who could prove (I think) that his mother was a sister of Adelina's, previously overlooked. On that reading of the evidence, Henric was the nearer heir.[42] In the short run, nevertheless, it was Gislebert de Gant who got possession; and he remained in possession for long enough to give away large parts of the domain.[43] But Henric de Essexe succeeded in ousting him, and was in possession of both the office and the honour before the change of regime in 1154. Nine years later, Henric was dispossessed – in circumstances so ignominious that the honour seems to have reverted to the king absolutely. No other descendant of Hugo de Montfort's was ever allowed to have it.[44]

The lands in Kent formed a compact group, deliberately clustered (so it seems) around Hugo's own castle at Saltwood. This choice of a site for the castle proved to have been unfortunate, because Saltwood was one of the places which archbishop Lanfranc began trying to recover for the church of Canterbury. The sensible solution would have been for Hugo to give the archbishop some land in exchange; instead it was agreed that he should hold the land as the archbishop's tenant, owing him four knights' service, and that was a recipe for trouble.[45]

By the mid thirteenth century, the domain manors had all become separated from the honour. Saltwood was back with the archbishop; Brabourne had been given to the count of Aumale (below, Marescal); River (mostly) belonged to the abbey of Saint Radegund's, Eastbridge to the Maison-Dieu of Dover. What remained were the knight's fees, of which there were roughly 21 in Kent, out of a total of 58 or so.[46] Presumably there had once been a time when the fees in Kent were expected to provide a garrison for Saltwood castle; but nothing is heard about that. They were certainly expected to help in defending the king's castle at Dover. Castleguard rents were payable there by the entire honour, which, for this purpose, was reckoned to consist of 56 knight's fees:[47] the fees were organized into 13 teams, nine of four knights each and four of five. It looks as if a 56-week rota (14 teams of four) had been modified to make it coincide with an ordinary financial year.[48]

In 1242 the honour of the Constabulary (or of Hagenet, or of Le Perche) was, as much as was left of it, in the king's hands.

Crevequer

On the death of Haimo the sheriff, after 1114, the large estate which he had built up was divided into two portions. One portion went to the earl of Gloucester, whose wife is known to have been Haimo's niece. The other portion, possibly retained by the king for a while, was sooner or later granted to Robert de Crevequer (last occ. 1140), whose wife Roesia was (so I suppose) another niece of Haimo's. He was certainly in possession by 1129.[49] Haimo had also held a number of manors from the archbishop, in return for six knights' service; these manors were similarly shared out between the earl and Robert.

[42] In fact, under the rules which applied in the thirteenth century, he would already have been in possession of the whole honour: Adelina would have got only half of it, and her husband would have lost this half as soon as Adelina died. But the rules were more flexible in the twelfth century; or at least kings tended to act as if they were. In this particular case, the king might have taken the view that the honour could not be divided because it was linked with the constableship: he would not want two halves of a constable; nor would he want one constable with only half the estate.

[43] A fact which emerges – as Round observed – from a schedule attached to the exchequer roll for 1169. Quite possibly the schedule understates the case. There may have been other grants made by Gislebert which fail to appear on this list because they had been revoked, by Henric de Essexe before 1163, or by the king since then.

[44] It was subsequently granted out from time to time, but not with permanent effect. For one period (between 1189 and 1217) it belonged to the counts of Le Perche; that is why, in the thirteenth century, the honour is often referred to as the honour of Le Perche. It was also called the honour of Hagenet – a perverse French spelling for Haughley in Suffolk, regarded as the head of the honour.

[45] Far more complicated, but less well recorded (the only evidence consists of casual remarks in DB), was the business of deciding exactly which pieces of land fell inside Hugo's division, exactly which fell outside, in the feod of the bishop of Bayeux.

[46] *Book of fees*, pp. 1464–6, a list put together in 1232–3.

[47] There was also an odd shilling, probably a rent of some other kind absorbed into the list of castleguard rents via the fiction that it represented one-tenth of a knight.

[48] For as long as the system was performing its original function, a 52-week rota would be the very thing to avoid, because it would mean, for instance, that the knights who have to spend Christmas at Dover this year will have to do the same next year, and forever. With any other multiple of 4, the spells of duty travel around the year, and in the long run any hardships are evenly shared.

[49] Robert de Crevequer founded an Augustinian priory on part of the manor of Leeds. The priory was in existence before 1136; its records are an important source of information concerning the Crevequer family and their tenants.

Robert de Crevequer stayed loyal to king Stephan. He and his brother Elias (d. 1162) found a new sphere of activity in Suffolk, where they were given the manor of Mildenhall, to look after, or perhaps to keep. After 1154, Robert's son Daniel de Crevequer (d. 1177) lost his lands for a while; but he was back in possession by 1156, though only of the lands in Kent. (The Crevequer connection with Mildenhall lasted until 1163, but was broken off after that.)[50]

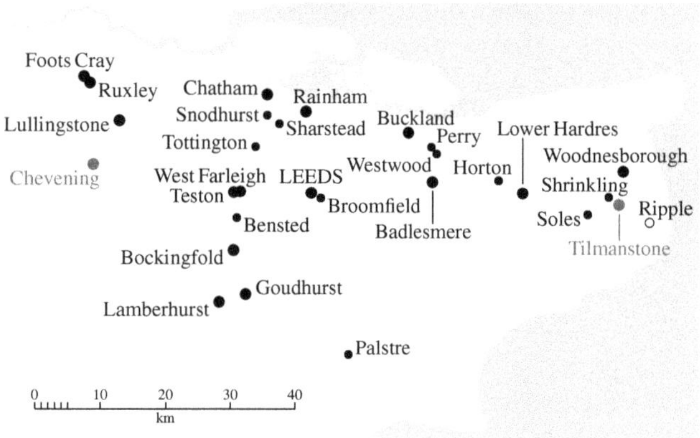

The barony consisted of 14 knight's fees (not counting the service of three knights owed to the archbishop). Two further fees, said to have once been owned by Robert de Crevequer, were claimed by his descendants; but the claim was not made good.[51] Ruxley and Badlesmere might perhaps be regarded as second-tier baronies; but I doubt whether either would meet the definition (unless it were framed so loosely as to be meaningless) before the late thirteenth century.

To a limited extent, the barony of Crevequer owed castleguard at Dover.[52] It seems clear that the lands on which this liability lay were the lands which in 1086 had belonged to Ansfrid Masleclerc.[53] After 1088, Ansfrid became a tenant of Haimo the sheriff's, owing him (so it seems) the service of five or six knights; after Haimo's death, these five or six knight's fees were all included in the share of his estate which became the barony of Crevequer. At some later date (before 1166), Ansfrid's lands were split into three portions (presumably because they were divided among three daughters), and each portion had to pay a corresponding share of the castleguard rent due to Dover.

In 1242 the barony belonged to Hamo de Crevequer (d. 1263). Through his wife Mathildis (his second wife, not the mother of his heirs), he also had possession of the barony of Folkestone (above, Averenches).

Eu, *see* Arundel

Eudo the steward, *see* fiz Gerold

fiz Bernard

Tonge was a second-tier barony included in the barony of Port (see below). Its first recorded owner, Radulf Picot (d. 1165), was a man of some note. He served as sheriff of Kent under both Stephan and Henric II, till being superseded after December 1160. (He incurred a heavy fine then, another in 1165.) In 1156–7 he was given the manor of Kingsdown,[54] in return for the service of half a knight, and that was enough (if the king chose to insist on his prerogative) to make him a first-tier baron.

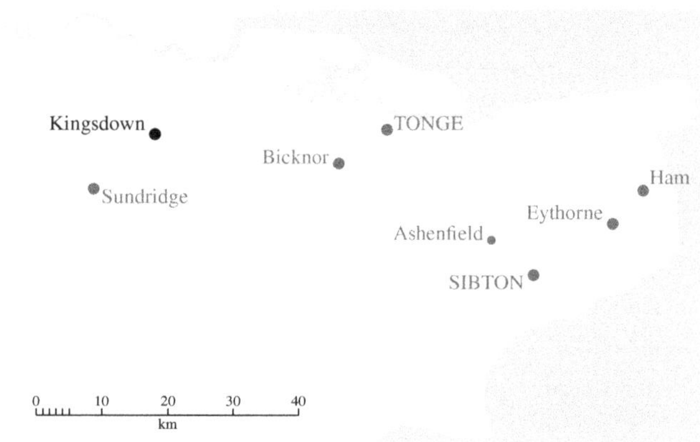

Radulf's heir was his daughter, Eugenia (last occ. 1201).[55] Her first husband was Willelm Malet (d. 1170), with whom she had no children.[56] Her second was Thomas fiz Bernard (d. 1184), with whom she had three sons and one daughter (facts which were put on record in 1185, because by then her status as a marriageable widow made her a person of interest to the king). This marriage united Tonge with the group of manors – principally Sibton in Lyminge – which were held by Thomas from the archbishop of Canterbury.[57]

In 1242, this barony was waiting to be inherited by the heir of Radulf fiz Bernard (d. 1238). Custody of the lands had

[50] While it lasted, it caused friction with the monks of Battle, who were the owners of Mildenhall church.

[51] One fee each for Nashenden and West Barming. In 1242 they were both held directly from the king.

[52] The arithmetic is odd: from one four-week spell to the next, the rent alternated between 120 pence (for one knight) and 80 pence (for two-thirds of a knight). Though the total number of fees is equal to five, the payments were stretched out over a 24-week rota. Probably this means that the number of fees had been reduced from six to five before Ansfrid's lands were partitioned (see below).

[53] One item on the list, *Rokesle*, seems to be an exception; but I think that it refers to the Ruxley family (which acquired a share of Ansfrid's lands), not to Ruxley itself. (In other words, I take it be a shorthand expression for 'the heir of Robert de Rokesle'.) Another item, Ripple, is also something of a puzzle; I refer to it in the commentary (above, p. 187).

[54] The place in Axstone hundred. The consequent deduction appears in the exchequer roll for 1157 (GREx 1157:101).

[55] It turned out that she was not his only daughter. An elder daughter, Adelicia, appeared out of nowhere in 1190, demanding a share of the inheritance. But she seems to have been dead by 1203, and her share was reunited with Eugenia's.

[56] In an absent-minded moment, Round assumed that Eugenia was the mother of Willelm's son Gilbert Malet (d. 1195), but that cannot be true: Gilbert must have been the son of a previous wife of Willelm's. It appears that he and his stepmother were of nearly the same age.

[57] By marrying judiciously, the fiz Bernards were able to acquire some further property in the course of the next two generations; I have not marked these acquisitions on the map.

been granted to Imbert le Pugeis, who was or became the second husband of Radulf's widow Johanna.

fiz Gerold

After the death of Eudo the steward, in November 1119, his vast estate fell into the hands of the king. In Kent it included all the manors which in 1086 had been held from the bishop of Bayeux by Adam fiz Hubert, Eudo's brother, or by Goisfrid de Ros. Small portions of the honour were subsequently granted out: one batch of manors went to the count of Boulogne (see above), another to Hamo de Seint Cleir (below, Lanvalei).[58] But the bulk of it remained intact, and in the king's hands, till after 1154.[59]

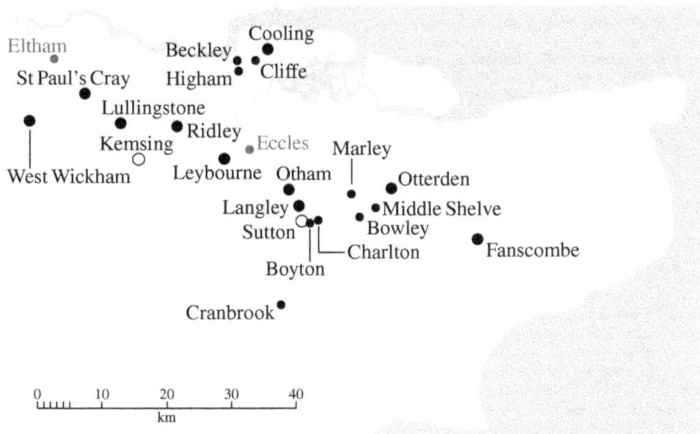

In 1155, the new king gave most of the honour to Warin fiz Gerold (d. 1158), one of the household officials whom he had brought over from Normandy; he also made Warin a chamberlain of the exchequer.[60] A few years later Warin died – and what happened next is involved in much obscurity. We know that Warin left a widow (see below). We also know that Warin left an heir: his name is uncertain, but his existence is proved by a charter of Warin's brother, Henric fiz Gerold.[61] We know that the heir was male; we know that his relationship with Warin was closer than a brother's; therefore he must have been Warin's son.[62] We do not know when he was born, or how old he was when his father died; no later than 1166 he was old enough to get married. He had two children, both boys, born in 1167 and 1173 respectively. And he was dead by 1183, when his widow Mathildis incurred a debt at the exchequer 'for having her land and the custody of her son's land'.[63]

Meanwhile, ever since Warin's death in 1158, somebody had had to fill his place in the exchequer. His brother, Henric fiz Gerold, took over at first; when Henric died, in 1173–4,[64] he was succeeded by his son, Warin fiz Henric. Though no hint of this can be found in the exchequer rolls, I think it has to be concluded that Henric was deputizing for his nephew, Warin for his cousin. In 1166 it was Henric who submitted a list of the knight's fees belonging to this barony; in 1168, when this list and the others like it were used for levying an aid of one mark per fee, it was Henric who incurred the debt.[65] While Henric was alive, the entry was carried forward from year to year without anything being paid; but the debt was later transferred to his son, and he was required to start paying.[66] Off the record, I suppose, it was understood that he was making the payments on behalf of his cousin; when his cousin died, the payments ceased.

The cousin's widow, Mathildis de Caisnet, was an heiress in her own right. That is why she appears in a list of marriageable ladies drawn up in 1185; and that is where we learn about her sons, 18 and 12 years old. The elder son would come of age in 1188: he would expect to inherit his father's land then, his mother's land when she died. The younger son was not of much interest to anyone at the time.

A man named Henric fiz Gerold makes his first appearance in the exchequer rolls in the roll for 1190.[67] He was charged scutage for a block of 53 knight's fees (minus a fraction), which, though not named, is sure to be the honour of Eudo the steward. He is given the title chamberlain; and the exchequer assumed at first that this debt would be written off because Henric was entitled to 'the liberty of the exchequer. Then it had second thoughts and charged him with the debt; but no money was actually paid.[68] This Henric's

[58] Similarly, when the king was minded to make a donation to the canons of Leeds, he gave them Chart Sutton church (Johnson and Cronne 1956, no. 1942).

[59] A charter issued by the soon-to-be king, Henric duke of Normandy, granted the entire honour, in Normandy and England, 'to Robert son of the earl of Gloucester, my kinsman' (Crouch 1988). This Robert, I take it, was earl Robert's younger son (brother of the present earl), whose existence (and whose legitimacy) is vouched for by a charter of his mother's (Patterson 1973, no. 171). But in any case this charter was only a promise, so far as the lands in England were concerned, and the promise was not kept. The most puzzling fact, it seems to me, is the fact that this charter survived.

[60] The king's charter is printed by Richardson and Sayles (1963, p. 437).

[61] In or soon after 1158, fulfilling a bequest of Warin's, Henric donated some land in Sutton to the monks of Rochester (R2, fos. 143v–4r). The charter is carefully worded: the king has authorized Henric to act, but the monks are to understand that some other land of equal value may eventually be substituted for this, at the discretion of 'the king or my brother Warin's heir'.

[62] Or possibly his grandson. He may perhaps have been under age at first, but that is not the whole story. There is some secret here which nobody saw fit to share with us. My guess would be that Warin's heir was (legally speaking) an idiot – not capable of performing his duties at the exchequer, nor of managing his own affairs.

[63] GREx 1183:103, under Oxfordshire. The remainder of this debt was charged to Warin fiz Gerold in 1199 (below, note 70).

[64] This is when Henric's name is replaced by his son's in the sequence of entries relating to Sparsholt in Berkshire (GREx 1174:112). Sparsholt is one of the properties which had been granted to Warin fiz Gerold in 1155 (above, note 60); apparently it must have been taken away from Warin's heir and given to Henric instead.

[65] GREx 1168:38, under Essex and Hertfordshire.

[66] Warin fiz Henric cleared most of this debt between 1178 and 1182. The remainder was charged to Warin fiz Gerold in 1199.

[67] Here and later, I think that fiz Gerold should be read as a surname, not as an indication that his father's name was Gerold.

[68] GREx 1190:109, under Essex and Hertfordshire. In 1192 the debt was transferred to Warin fiz Henric (GREx 1192:170), but still no money was paid; and then finally it was transferred to Warin fiz Gerold.

first appearance turned out to be his only appearance. I take it that he was Mathildis's elder son, of age by 1190 (as we would expect him to be), but dead by 1192.

A man named Warin fiz Gerold (not called chamberlain) makes his first appearance – the first of many – in the roll for 1194. He was charged scutage for a block of 54 knight's fees (minus a fraction), explicitly called 'the feod of Eudo the steward'.[69] From here onwards, we are back on solid ground. Warin fiz Gerold (d. 1216) was Mathildis's younger son, just recently come of age.[70]

Two manors in Kent, Kemsing and Sutton (i.e. Sutton Valence), are known to have been held in domain by Warin fiz Gerold (d. 1158). Kemsing was part of the dower assigned by Warin to his wife, in case she should survive him, as she did. (She was still alive in 1166.) In the normal course of events, the manor would revert to her husband's heirs on her death; but that is not what happened. By 1169, Kemsing was in the king's hands, and was expected to remain there (GREx 1170:160). The history of Sutton is less clear;[71] but it certainly began by belonging to Warin,[72] ended by belonging to the king. By 1200, both manors had been granted out again (below, Marescal), and their trajectory never reconverged with that of the fiz Gerold inheritance. The loss of these two domain manors is (so I imagine) part of the mystery surrounding Warin's heir.[73]

The number of knight's fees in Kent was probably about 16, slightly below one-third of the total number. Most of these fees are accounted for by two second-tier baronies. One was based at Cooling: it belonged to a family which used the surname le Botiller (*pincerna* in Latin), already established here in about 1090 (doc. 14). The other was based at Leybourne: its early history is obscure, but its owners became important men in the thirteenth century.

In 1242 the honour belonged to Margeria de Reviers (d. 1252), the daughter of Warin fiz Gerold (d. 1216). (The surname she used was that of her first husband, Baldwin de Reviers (d. 1216), the father of her son. As for her second husband, she seems to have preferred to forget him.) Apart from the manors which were held directly from the king, some part of Eltham (I do not know which part) was held from the earl of Gloucester, and Eccles was held from Warin de Montchenesi (below, Talebot). Cooling was waiting to be inherited by the heir of Willelm le Botiller; Leybourne belonged to Roger de Leiburne (d. 1250).

Fobert de Dovre, *see* Chilham

Folkestone, *see* Averenches

Gloucester

The property in Kent and Surrey which came to be included in the honour of the earl of Gloucester had all belonged previously to Haimo the sheriff – the younger Haimo, that is. On his death, somewhere between 1114 and 1129, the lands that he held from the king were divided half and half. One portion went to Robert earl of Gloucester (d. 1147), the husband of Haimo's brother's daughter Mabilia (d. 1157); the other portion went to Robert de Crevequer (see above). (The lands which Haimo had held from the archbishop were divided in the same way.) After 1138, the earl was in rebellion against king Stephan. It seems safe to assume that the king dispossessed him, so far as he was capable of doing so (as he would have been in Kent and Surrey); but the earl's son and successor, Willelm earl of Gloucester (d. 1183), was back in possession by 1157.

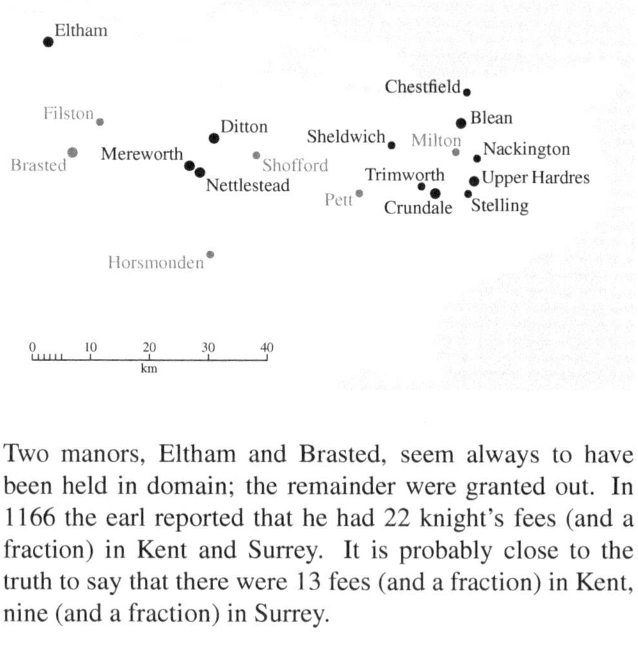

Two manors, Eltham and Brasted, seem always to have been held in domain; the remainder were granted out. In 1166 the earl reported that he had 22 knight's fees (and a fraction) in Kent and Surrey. It is probably close to the truth to say that there were 13 fees (and a fraction) in Kent, nine (and a fraction) in Surrey.

In 1242 the honour of Gloucester was waiting to be inherited by Ricard earl of Gloucester and Hertford (d. 1262), who would not come of age till August 1243. The knight's fees in Kent, however, had all been included in the package of assets granted to Ricard's mother Isabella by way of dower. Though Isabella was dead by now (she died in 1240), her second husband, Ricard count of Poitou and earl of Cornwall (d. 1272), was entitled to keep possession of her dower for his own lifetime, by the rule called the courtesy of England. He did certainly still have possession in 1242 (but appears to have relinquished it soon afterwards).

[69] GREx 1194:37, under Essex and Hertfordshire. Payments were made in this and the following year.

[70] Mathildis herself disappears from the record after 1192. She was certainly dead by 1199, when Warin was charged with two debts which she had failed to pay off – explicitly 'his mother's' debts (GREx 1199:229, under Oxfordshire).

[71] Unlike Kemsing, it is not mentioned by name in the charter of 1155 (above, note 60).

[72] As is proved by Henric fiz Gerold's charter for Rochester (above, note 61).

[73] In other words, I suspect that these manors were the price which had to be paid in order to preserve the rest of the inheritance for the next generation.

Guînes, *see* Averenches

Hagenet, Haughley, *see* Constabulary

Lanvalei

A small batch of the manors which had lapsed to the king on the death of Eudo dapifer (above, fiz Gerold) was used to form a barony for Hamo de Seint Cleir (occ. 1130). The package included one manor in Kent, East Chalk. This is the barony which later came to belong to Willelm de Lanvalein (d. 1180), who acquired it by marrying Hamo's granddaughter. Willelm was in possession by 1156.

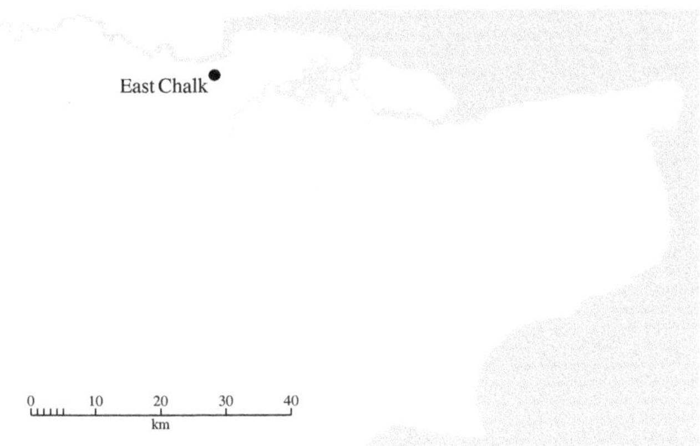

In 1242 East Chalk belonged to Johan de Burgh (d. 1275), whose wife Hawisia was the daughter of Willelm de Lanvalei (d. 1215).

Leicester

In circumstances of which I know nothing, two manors in Kent came to belong to a second-tier barony based at Weston Turville in Buckinghamshire, which itself was part of the honour of the earl of Leicester. The Leicester connection can be traced back to about 1120, but I have no detailed information earlier than an entry in the exchequer roll for 1219.

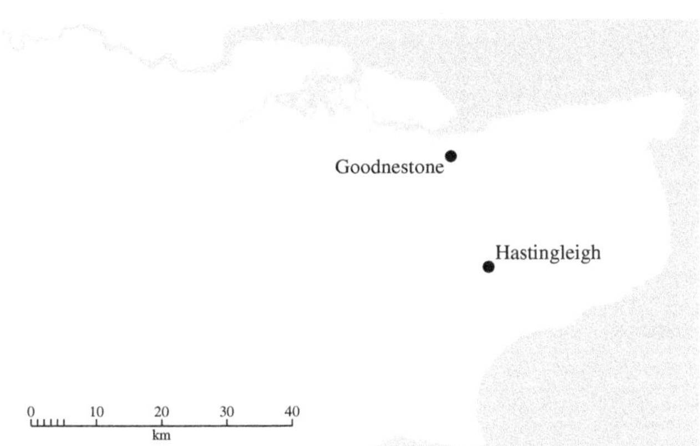

In 1242 the manors in Kent were held by their tenants from Simon de Turville (or 'from the heir of Willelm de Turville'), and by him from the earl of Leicester, Simon de Montfort (d. 1265).

Luci, *see* Chilham

Maminot

By 1100, the lands which in 1086 were held from the bishop of Bayeux by two or three related men – Radulf de Curbespine, Gislebert Maminot bishop of Lisieux, and possibly another Gislebert Maminot (whom the DB scribe seems to regard, rightly or wrongly, as a different person from the bishop of Lisieux) – had coalesced to form a single barony, held directly from the king. The first recorded owner is Hugo Maminot (occ. 1100–1). It is not known when he died; probably the barony was in the king's hands for some time before Hugo's son, Walkelin Maminot (first occ. 1131), was old enough to inherit.[74] In or soon after 1138, Walkelin was dispossessed by king Stephan; whether his lands were kept by the king or given to somebody else, is, again, not known. Soon after the accession of Henric II, Walkelin was reinstated: he was certainly back in England, presumably back in possession, by 1155.

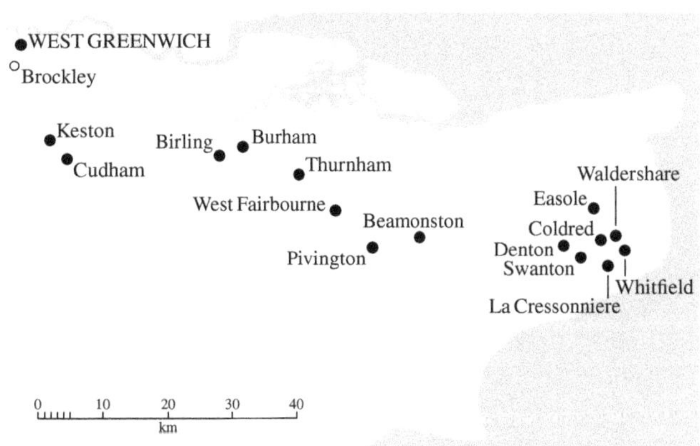

We can be sure that Walkelin died in 1170.[75] What happened next (I think) is that his widow kept possession of the estate – the whole of the domain, not just the portion to which she would be entitled by way of dower. The widow, Juliana, was a woman with powerful connections. She was a sister of Alberic de Ver earl of Oxford (d. 1194). Before becoming Walkelin's wife, she had been married to Hugo Bigod earl of Norfolk (d. 1177); though that marriage had been (so we have to infer) dissolved, Juliana was still allowed to call herself countess, and it was her son, not the son of Hugo's second wife, who eventually inherited the earldom. When she married Walkelin, she was (I think)

[74] That Walkelin was Hugo's son is proved by evidence from Rochester (R3, fo. 82v). It is often said that there were two men named Walkelin Maminot, father and son. The only basis for this statement is a one-line entry in the Bermondsey annals – a late and far from perfectly reliable source – mentioning a donation made, supposedly in 1157, by 'Walkelin Mammynot son of Walkelin Mammynot' (ed. Luard 1866, p. 440). Possibly this can be accepted as proof that Walkelin had a son; but it certainly does not suffice to prove that the son ever had possession of the whole barony. (For a start, it fails to prove that he was legitimate.)

[75] More precisely, between June and September 1170. This can be deduced from the sequence of entries in the exchequer rolls relating to the lestage of Hastings (the collection of which had been subcontracted to Walkelin since 1158). There is other evidence which goes to prove that Walkelin was dead before 1176 (see below).

given joint ownership of the estate, on terms which meant that Walkelin's heirs would not inherit till after she was dead.[76] This sort of arrangement, though not uncommon in the thirteenth century and afterwards, seems to have caused some bafflement at the time, at least inside the exchequer. As late as 1177, somebody was paying off the debts which Walkelin had left unsettled, and the fact that he had been dead for some years made no difference to the wording of the entries that appear in the exchequer rolls. Juliana was certainly still alive in 1185, probably dead by 1190.[77]

By that time, the exchequer had finally recognized the existence of 'the heirs of Walkelin Maminot'; by 1194 it was treating Galfrid de Sai (d. 1214) as their representative.[78] Galfrid's claim on the barony came through his wife, Adelidis. How she was related to Walkelin is not spelt out; but it seems to have been recognized, by those who knew the facts, that she was undeniably his heir (or one of them). Her first husband was Hugo de Periers (d. 1176);[79] by 1180 she was married to Galfrid de Sai. By 1194 Adelidis and Galfrid had got possession of the barony of Maminot, and from that point onwards its history is clear.[80]

The barony owed castleguard at Dover, supplying three knights for each four-week spell of duty. The load was shared among 24 knights, organized in eight teams of three, working on a 32-week rota. As nearly as I can count them, there were 15 knight's fees in Kent; the rest were widely scattered, from Sussex to Northamptonshire.[81] Among the subordinate holdings, none comprising more than three knight's fees, Thurnham is the only one which might be regarded as a second-tier barony;[82] but it was cut up into five pieces after the death of Stephan de Turneham (d. 1214).

[76] Countess Juliana and her steward, Michael de Turneham, founded a Premonstratensian house at Brockley in about 1180; her charter is printed by Caley and Ellis (1817–30, vol. 6, p. 913).

[77] Her death, I take it, is what triggered the litigation between Michael Belet and Galfrid de Sai reflected by an entry in the exchequer roll for 1190.

[78] As late as 1199, however, the exchequer was still doubtful whether Galfrid de Sai was accountable for the entire barony.

[79] A donation to the canons of Combwell by one of the Maminot tenants was made 'with the assent of my lord Hugo de Periers and his wife Adelidis' (Faussett 1866, p. 197). (This charter proves that Walkelin Maminot was already dead.)

[80] As for the canons of Brockley (see above), they seem to have been made an offer they could not refuse. Galfrid would let them keep their land; he would even be willing to give them West Greenwich church; but he would not let them stay where they were. By 1208 they had removed themselves from Brockley and settled at Bayham instead, on a site provided by Robert de Turneham (d. 1211).

[81] Outside Kent, the places which shared the load were Leckhampstead in Buckinghamshire (1 knight), Kimpton in Hertfordshire (2), Gayhurst in Buckinghamshire (1), Hartwell in Northamptonshire (2), Brandeston in Suffolk and Hatcham (in Deptford) in Surrey (2), and Brettinghurst (in Camberwell) in Surrey (1).

[82] Robert de Turneham (d. 1195) was the founder of the abbey of Combwell, in existence by 1168. (It was downgraded to a priory later.) Many of Combwell's early charters survive as originals, often with the seals still attached. They were printed by Faussett (1862–72).

In 1242 the barony belonged to Willelm de Say (d. 1272), the grandson of Galfrid de Sai and Adelidis. He also owned the barony of Patric, which had been acquired by his father (see below).

Marescal

Three large manors in Kent which happened to have lapsed to the king were acquired by Baldwin de Bethune (d. 1212), called count of Aumale because he was married to the countess. Two of these manors, Kemsing and Sutton, are known to have belonged to Warin fiz Gerold (d. 1158); it is a puzzle to know how they had come to belong to the king, rather than to Warin's heirs (above, fiz Gerold). Brabourne is in a different case: this was part of the honour of the Constabulary, forfeited in 1163, and the king could do as he pleased with it. Probably the grant was made in 1197; certainly Baldwin was in possession by 1199.

Baldwin's heir was his daughter Alicia,[83] the wife of Willelm Marescal (d. 1231). Apparently the manors in Kent must have been regranted to Willelm, on terms which meant that they would pass to his heirs, whether or not they were his wife's heirs too. Willelm succeeded his father as earl of Pembroke in 1219. Alicia had died by then, without having any children; and in 1224 he got married again, to the king's sister Alienora. The marriage settlement guaranteed her possession for life of a share of the Marescal estate, including the manors in Kent.

Willelm's father, Willelm Marescal (d. 1219), by acquiring the earldom of Pembroke in 1199, seems also to have acquired a claim to the overlordship of the second-tier barony of Chelsfield. This is another puzzle. Around 1120, Chelsfield belonged (as it would be expected to belong) to Patric de Caources (the successor of Ernulf de Hesding, who owned it in 1086). Some twenty years later, however, when a donation was made to the monks of Reading by a Chelsfield tenant, the grant was confirmed in the first place by Ernulf de Chelesfeld, in the second place by Gilebert earl of Pembroke (d. 1148–9).[84] If Ernulf became the earl's man in the time of king Stephan, as appears to be the case, it is

[83] His wife the countess's heir was her son by a previous marriage.

[84] These charters are printed by Kemp (1986, nos. 249–50).

hard to see how the earl's claim to the overlordship could be maintained. In the short run it was not: by 1166 we find Ernulf's son, Simon de Chelesfeld, listed among the men of Patric de Caources's grandson, Pagan de Montdublel. But eventually, somehow, the Pembroke claim was made good.

In 1242, the Marescal property in Kent was all held by Alienora's second husband, Simon de Montfort earl of Leicester (d. 1265); it would not revert to the Marescal heirs till Alienora was dead (she died in 1275). Chelsfield, by this time, had been divided into three portions; the respective tenants all answered to the earl of Leicester.

Montchenesi, *see* Talebot

Moubrai

Two manors in Kent which were owned by Hugo de Port in 1086 ceased to belong to the barony of Port. It is known that they were held by Willelm Patric (d. 1174), and, for a time, by Willelm's son and heir, Ingelram Patric (d. 1190–1); but it was Willelm's youngest son, Eudo Patric (d. 1212–13) who eventually got possession of Ash, and he or his heirs got possession of Ryarsh too. Those are the known facts. What they appear to mean is that Willelm Patric was married twice, and that Ash and Ryarsh were the marriage portion which came with his second wife – hypothetically a sister or daughter of Johan de Port (d. 1168). His eldest surviving son would inherit the barony of Patric; but Eudo, as the son of this second wife, would stand to inherit his mother's marriage portion.[85]

It is something of a surprise to find that Ryarsh and Ash paid castleguard rents to Rochester. Presumably they incurred this charge while they were in the possession of Willelm Patric, even though, strictly speaking, they were not part of his barony.

In 1242 both manors belonged to Roger de Moubrai (d. 1266), who was the grandson of Eudo Patric's sister Mabilia. Ryarsh was still held in domain; Ash had been granted out.

[85] Possibly Paddlesworth was part of the same package, but it did not pass to Eudo or Eudo's heirs.

Patric

Patrixbourne became the head of a small barony, the early history of which is even more than usually obscure. Before it had any connection with the name Patric, it seems to have passed through the hands of at least two previous owners.

One item of evidence associates Walter Tirel with Upper Delce (R1, fo. 194v); another item associates Tirel de Maineres with a holding in Kent (assessed at 15.875 sulungs altogether) which has to be what later became the barony of Patric (Flight 2005, p. 371). In a twelfth-century list of parish churches, Patrixbourne itself is called 'Tirel's Bourne' (above, p. 231). These are just pieces of a puzzle; how they fit together can only be conjectured. It is possible that Tirel was a nephew (or grandson) of Walter Tirel, named after his uncle (or grandfather), but that is just a guess. What we do know for certain is that Tirel de Maineres was dispossessed of whatever land he owned in England, in or soon after 1124.

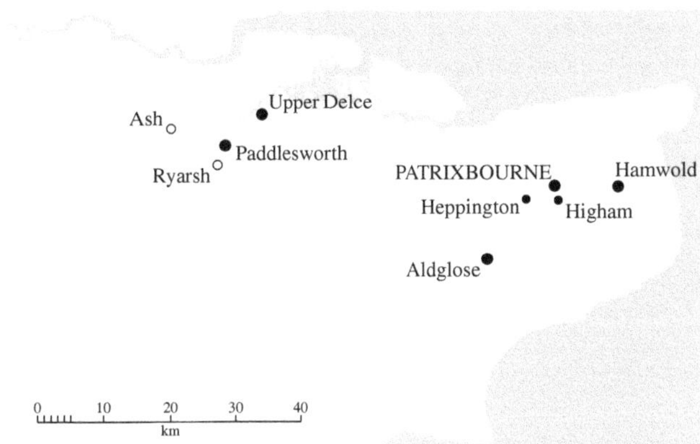

Within the next few years, Willelm Patric (d. 1174) was, for a price, given the lands which had been confiscated from Tirel. He was certainly in possession by 1129; with a possible interruption in the time of king Stephan, he remained in possession until the 1170s. He also acquired, perhaps by marriage, two manors in Kent which did not become part of the barony of Patric (above, Moubrai), and possibly Paddlesworth, which did.

At the time of his death, Willelm had been dispossessed, because of his involvement in the rebellion of 1173–4; but eventually the barony was recovered by his second son, Ingelram Patric (d. 1190–1). When Ingelram died, the inheritance was divided between his two daughters. Their respective husbands, Radulf Teissun and Johan de Praels, were dispossessed in 1204–5,[86] and within the next few years the whole barony came to belong to Galfrid de Sai (d. 1230). (Galfrid's father, Galfrid de Sai (d. 1214), was holding the barony of Maminot in right of his wife (see above); upon his death, the younger Galfrid got possession of that barony too.)

[86] Johan de Praels had given his half of the manor of Patrixbourne, including the church, to the canons of Beaulieu in Normandy. For a price, they were allowed to keep it.

The barony owed castleguard at Rochester, for which purpose it was reckoned to consist of 15 knight's fees (representing a rent of 9 pounds).

In 1242, the barony was owned by Galfrid's son, Willelm de Say (d. 1272), who also owned the barony of Maminot. The record does not distinguish between Patric and Maminot fees; with the help of other evidence, however, most fees can be assigned to one barony or the other.[87]

Pembroke, *see* Marescal

le Perche, *see* Constabulary

Peverel of Dover

Willelm Pevrel (occ. 1100–30), called 'of Dover' to distinguish him from two other men of the same name, was the eldest of three brothers who all became settled in England. Willelm got possession of the lands, mostly in Kent, which in 1086 belonged to Herbert fiz Ivo, to Herbert's nephew Hugo, or to a man named Herfrid, who seems also to have been connected somehow (possibly by marriage) with Herbert. After 1088, Herfrid retained his lands (chiefly Throwley in Kent and Gatton in Surrey) but became Willelm Pevrel's man.

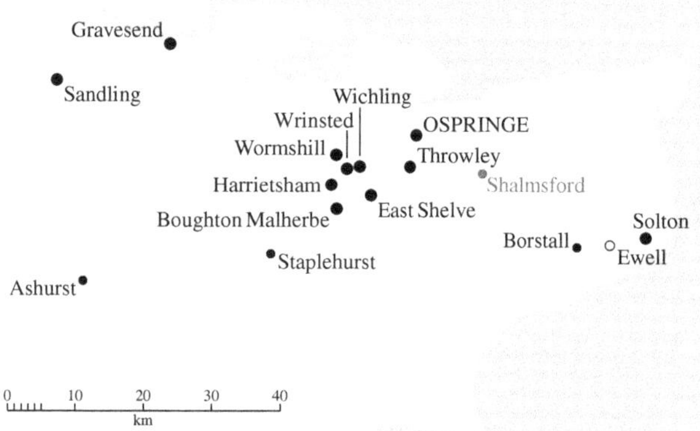

For a short time, the barony was held by Willelm Pevrel's nephew and namesake; but he was dispossessed, in or soon after 1138.[88] (It happens to be known that Herfrid's son Hamo was also dispossessed.)[89] The whole barony seems then to have been given to Willelm de Ipre.[90] After 1154, Willelm de Ipre was dispossessed in his turn, and the barony was given to yet another Willelm, the younger brother of king Henric II. He died in 1164. The barony fell back into the king's hands, and on this occasion it stayed there. It came to be called the honour of Peverel of Dover.

One of the manors in Kent, Ewell, ceased to be part of the barony when it was given to the Templars. (In fact, it was given twice: by the elder Willelm Pevrel and by Willelm the king's brother. Presumably this means that the Templars lost it for a time, but then managed to persuade the king's brother to let them have it back.) Ospringe was held in domain; the other manors were all granted out.

When people spoke of the honour of Peverel of Dover, they did not always mean exactly the same thing; but usually they meant the knight's fees which owed attendance at the court of Ospringe, or (a little more narrowly) the knight's fees which owed castleguard at Dover. As to that, the barony was expected to supply three knights every month; the workload was distributed over 15 knight's fees, organized in five teams of three,[91] working to a 20-week rota. Most of these fees were in Kent; the rest were in Surrey, Essex and Buckinghamshire.

In 1242 the honour was still in the king's hands. Throwley belonged to Robert de Gattone (that having become, by now, the usual surname).

Peverel of London

Two manors in Kent which in 1086 belonged to Ansgot de Rovecestre did not pass to his descendants. Instead they became merged with the package of lands, mostly in Essex, which in 1086 belonged to Rannulf Pevrel. It is not known how this happened. One guess might be that Ansgot married his daughter to Rannulf's son, giving her these two manors as her marriage portion; but there are other imaginable explanations. At all events, the entire holding lapsed to the king on the death of Rannulf's son Willelm. It came to be known as the honour of Peverel of London.

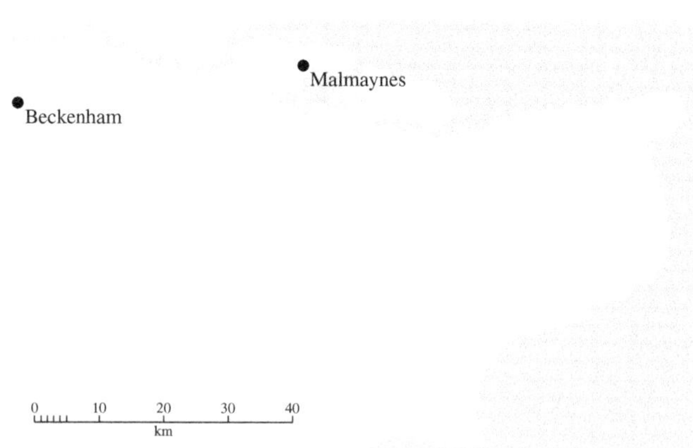

The manors in question are Beckenham and Stoke (i.e. the portion of Stoke which did not belong to the church of

[87] But I am not sure about Paddlesworth or Hamwold.

[88] His heirs were eventually able to recover the lands which the younger Willelm had inherited from his father, Pagan Pevrel, and from his uncle Hamo, but not of the lands which had belonged to his uncle Willelm. I take this to mean that Willelm was given possession of the former lands by king Henric, of the latter by king Stephan.

[89] That he joined the rebellion is proved by his appearance as a witness in a charter of Willelm Pevrel's (Rees 1975, no. 25). Hamo fiz Herfrid was sometimes called Hamo de Trulege, sometimes Hamo de Gattone.

[90] Willelm de Ipre gave Throwley church to the abbey of Saint Bertin. As in the case of Chilham church, it should be remembered that we only know about this because Hamo fiz Herfrid, after being reinstated, allowed the donation to stand.

[91] Something had gone wrong, however, and one team consisted of only 2.25 knights.

Rochester). Half of Beckenham (the northern half) seems to have been held in domain until being granted out by Henric II: the first recorded owner is Willelm fiz Erneis (occ. 1168). The other half of Beckenham (the half which came to be called Langley Park), together with Stoke, became the property of a family whose name, in its earliest appearance, is *Malesmæins* (R1, fo. 186r); I take that to mean *mal es meains*, 'pain in the wounds'. (But thirteenth-century scribes spell the name in various ways, not seeming to know or care about its etymology.) That surname attached itself to the manor in Stoke.

In 1242 the northern half of Beckenham was held from the king for one knight's fee by Ricard de la Rokele (d. 1277). (In modern spelling the name would be 'de la Roquelle'; in Latin it is 'de Rupella'.) One fee in Stoke and half a fee in Beckenham were held by Henric Malemeins (occ. 1227–62) from his cousin Johanna's husband, Willelm Aguillon (d. 1244), Johanna representing the senior branch of the family. It was Henric who revived his twelfth-century predecessors' surname; neither his father nor his grandfather had used it.[92]

Port

The manors which in 1086 were held by Hugo de Port, mostly from the king or from the bishop of Bayeux, continued to belong to his descendants (perhaps with some interruption during the time of king Stephan). Adam de Port (d. 1213) was the last to use that surname. His son Willelm (d. 1239) called himself de Seint Jehan,[93] and his descendants did the same.

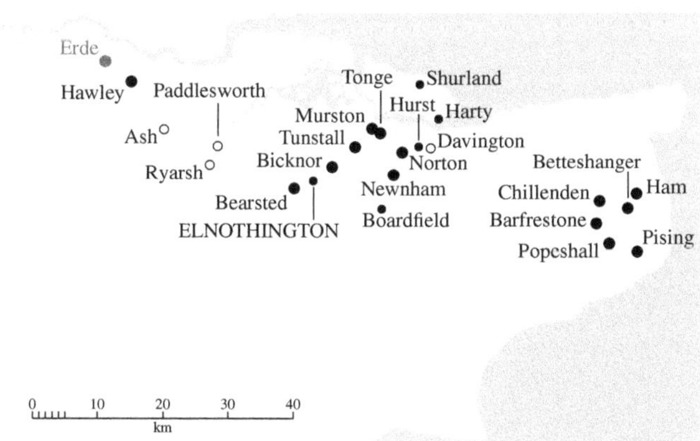

Except for Erde (i.e. Crayford), which was held from the archbishop, Hugo's manors in Kent were all held from the bishop of Bayeux till 1088, from the king after that. To some extent they seem to have been treated as a block by themselves, distinct from the rest of the barony: there was a separate court for the tenants in Kent, which met at Elnothington – a lost place located by Grove (1985). Two or three manors became detached from the barony of Port during the twelfth century (above, Moubrai), but otherwise nothing much changed.

Two of the subordinate holdings are large enough that they can be regarded as second-tier baronies. One was based at Norton and Newnham, its first recorded owner being Hugo fiz Fulco (occ. 1110–15).[94] The other was based at Tonge: its first recorded owner, Radulf Picot (d. 1165), acquired one additional manor which was held directly from the king, and that promoted him to first-tier status (above, fiz Bernard).

Most of the manors in Kent – but not the second-tier barony of Norton – owed castleguard at Dover; so did the manor of Clothall in Hertfordshire, which seems to have been regarded as an outlying member of the barony of Port in Kent. The service was shared among twelve knight's fees, organized into six teams of two knights each, working to a 24-week rota.

In 1242 the barony of Port belonged to Robert de Seint Jehan (d. 1267). Norton was held by Robert de Champaigne; Tonge was waiting to be inherited by the heir of Radulf fiz Bernard (d. 1239).

Ros

The lands which in 1086 belonged to Anschitil de Ros (occ. 1086–96) continued with his descendants. They formed the small barony of Horton, rated at seven knight's fees. It ceased to be a first-tier barony when it was granted to archbishop Willelm in 1136; but its status was the cause of much dispute, from the 1160s onwards, until finally the archbishop's claim was recognized by king Johan in 1202.

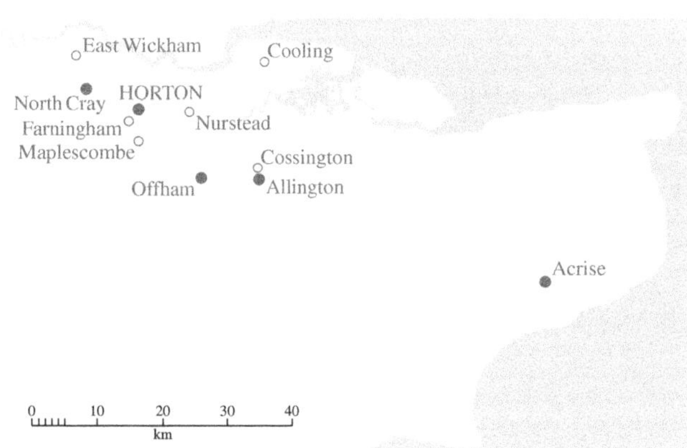

The lords of Horton owned East Wickham, which was held at fee-farm from the abbot of Saint Augustine's; they also held some other lands from the archbishop, separately from

[92] Henric's father was Alan fiz Henric, the second son of Henric fiz Ailwin (d. 1212), mayor of London. His mother was Orabilis de Meyhamme; by 1253 he had inherited her half of the second-tier barony of Maytham (above, Arundel).

[93] Because he had inherited the barony of Halnaker in Sussex from his mother's uncle, Willelm de Seint Jehan (d. 1202).

[94] His son, Fulco fiz Hugo, was the founder of Davington priory, a small house of Benedictine nuns, to whom he gave the churches of Davington, Harty, Newnham and Boardfield. (It is frequently said that the priory was founded in the eighteenth year of king Stephan (1153). That assertion appears to originate with Southouse (1671); but I have not seen this book, and cannot say how far it should be trusted.)

the barony.[95] In addition they had inserted themselves (I do not know when or how) into the chain of tenure on some of the Arsic fees.

In 1242 the barony belonged to the last of the male line, Ricard de Ros (d. 1244×6), who ended his life in a state of financial embarrassment. After his death the inheritance was divided between his sisters.

Say, *see* Maminot, Patric

Stockbury

The lands which in 1086 belonged to Ansgot de Rovecestre have a complicated history. Stockbury and a few other manors were held from the bishop of Bayeux till 1088, from the king after that; part of Farningham (the manor which came to be called Charton) was held from the archbishop. Though the evidence is very thin, the barony seems to have descended smoothly to Ansgot's son, Helto fiz Ansgot (occ. c. 1120), and to Helto's son, Willelm fiz Helto (first occ. 1145×50).

But then something happened. By 1159, the barony (or part of it) belonged to Manasser Biset (d. 1177), one of the new king's stewards. Some years later (while Manasser was still alive), the name Ernulf Biset (occ. 1165–87) starts to appear; and Willelm fiz Helto reappears in the record at about the same time. What these facts appear to mean is that Willelm was dispossessed by Henric II, and that his lands were given to Manasser Biset. After some lapse of time, Willelm was reconciled with the king and allowed to recover his lands, if he could come to terms with the new owner. In fact he recovered only half of the barony; the other half – comprising Delce and half of Aldington, together with the manor of Preston Bissett in Buckinghamshire – continued to belong to a branch of the Biset family.[96]

After the death of Willelm fiz Helto (d. 1179), his half of the barony was divided between his three sisters or their respective heirs. One of these heirs, Willelm de Cheritone (d. 1233), succeeded in regaining possession of Delce; he tried to oust the Bisets from their other manors as well, but in that he did not succeed.

The barony owed castleguard at Rochester, to the amount of seven knight's fees; the service was commuted, as normal, for a payment of 12 shillings per year per fee.[97]

[95] Including Toppesfield TM 0241 in Suffolk – not to be confused (though sometimes it has been) with Toppesfield TL 7337 in Essex, which was part of the honour of Boulogne.

[96] Evidently a younger branch. Most of Manasser's lands descended to his son and heir, Henric Biset (d. 1208).

[97] As far as I can work it out, the arrangement was for each third of Stockbury to pay 14 shillings, for Great Delce to pay 18 shillings, and for Preston Bissett to pay 24 shillings. That makes the total what it ought to be, 84 shillings a year.

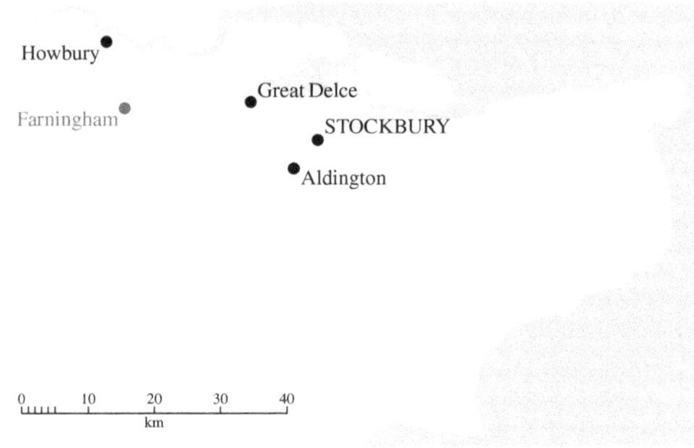

In 1242, the lands inherited from Willelm fiz Helto are found belonging to Willelm de Auberville (d. 1248), master Odo de Cheritone (d. 1247), and Robert de Setvans (d. 1253). Half of Aldington belonged to Arnold Biset.

Talebot

The barony of Talebot was formed from the lands which in 1086 belonged to two men (possibly uncle and nephew) who were tenants of the bishop of Bayeux: Helto, who owned land in Kent and Buckinghamshire, and Radulf fiz Turald, who owned land in Kent and Essex. It appears that they were both dispossessed in 1088. The new owner, Goisfrid Talebot, makes his first appearance no more than a few years later (above, doc. 14).

When Goisfrid died, in or shortly before 1130, he was succeeded by his son, also called Goisfrid Talebot. The younger Goisfrid was dispossessed in 1138; he was one of the rebel barons who joined forces in Gloucester soon after that. Still fighting against the king, he died in 1140.

His next heir was Cecilia Talebot. Though we are not told explicitly how she was related to him, it seems to have been understood, by everyone aware of the facts, that she was indeed the heir to the barony of Talebot. Cecilia was married three times. Her first husband, Roger earl of Hereford (d. 1155), was another member of the rebel alliance; it seems unlikely that he ever got possession of his wife's inheritance.[98] Her second husband, Willelm de Peitiers (occ. 1156–62), a bastard half-brother of queen Eleanor, did certainly get possession; so did her third, Walter de Maiene (occ. 1166–88).

By 1187, it was obvious that Cecilia was never going to have children, and the question came up as to who would inherit the barony after her. At this point it became expedient to remember that she had a younger sister, Agnes by name, who had been ignored till now. With Cecilia and Walter's consent, half of the barony was given to Agnes; when she died, in 1190–1, it passed to her son, Willelm de Montchenesi (d. 1204). Cecilia survived meanwhile – Cecilia countess of Hereford, as she was still allowed to call

[98] But he did find some reason for changing sides in 1152.

herself. She died in 1207–8, and the half of the barony which she had kept could then be reunited with the other half. As soon as Willelm's son Warin came of age, in 1214, he got possession of the entire inheritance.

The barony was centred at Swanscombe. As well as the lands which were held directly from the king, it included a few manors which were held from the archbishop or the bishop of Rochester. In the case of Preston, the connection can be traced back to the 1070s, i.e. to the time of Radulf fiz Turald's father, Turald de Rovecestre.

Talebot was the largest of three baronies which paid castle-guard rents at Rochester. A payment of 18 pounds was due each year: that represents the service of 30 knight's fees, commuted at the rate of 12 shillings per fee. In addition the barony of Patric owed service for 15 fees, the barony of Stockbury for seven (see above). It is, I take it, not coincidental that these numbers add up to a multiple of 13. The theory was, so it seems, that 52 knights – 13 teams of four knights each – owed a four-week spell of duty in Rochester once in every year.

In 1242 the barony of Talebot was still in the possession of Warin de Montchenesi (d. 1255).

Willelm fiz Helto, *see* Stockbury

Chapter 10
Thirteenth-century lests and hundreds

By the thirteenth century, when extensive documentation first becomes available, Kent was organized into six lests and more than 60 hundreds. Despite some ambiguities (such as whether Canterbury and Rochester should be counted as hundreds or not), the multiplicity of sources makes it fairly easy to filter out the flaws of each, and so to construct a synopsis of the county's administrative structure (Table 21) which would probably have been accepted by all parties – the local population, the sheriff and his agents, the king's justices making one of their excursions into Kent – as an accurate description of the state of affairs existing at the time.

It is not to be thought that this structure covered every square inch of Kent. In the thirteenth century, the lowy of Tonbridge was not part of the county at all: it was, in a manner of speaking, a county by itself (see below). Canterbury and Rochester were always special – Canterbury always more so. At least for some purposes, Rochester could still be counted as a hundred,[1] and I include it in the table for that reason; but the city of Canterbury already stood apart. Those places which could claim to share in the privileges of the Cinque Ports (see below) were, ipso facto, not part of any hundred.[2] For all practical purposes, they had ceased to be part of Kent. To complicate things further, there were half a dozen places which – seemingly because they had attracted such aggregations of people that they needed police officers of their own – had been detached from the hundreds to which they had once belonged and recognized as separate entities called, in Latin, 'villatas'.[3] This means, in a manner of speaking, that a place like Dartford had become a hundred by itself; but in general that manner of speaking was avoided, and Dartford remained a 'villata'.[4] It had its own constables; the constables of Axstone hundred had no authority here. These exceptions were important (vitally important, perhaps, for someone who knew that one of the sheriff's officers was trying to find him), but they had not multiplied to such a degree that the rule itself was made meaningless. It was true in theory, it was still largely true in fact, that the county was divided into lests, which themselves were subdivided into hundreds.

Though I do not wish to complicate matters unnecessarily, it ought also to be understood that the hundreds in their turn were subdivided. They each comprised some number of smaller units, for which in Kent the usual Latin name was *borga*. Probably the English name ought to be 'borrow'; but modern writers started calling them 'boroughs' (Kilburne 1659, pp. 126–7, for example), and that is the name which stuck. After the king's justices had visited Kent in 1219, a large crop of entries referring to boroughs turned up in the exchequer roll for the following year (GREx 1220, pp. 162–9). Here each borough is identified by the name of the man who heads it.[5] At this date, perhaps, a borough was still something like a club, free to choose its own members, free to reject any would-be member whom it did not trust. By the 1270s, a borough was not a club. It was a tract of land, marked off by recognized boundaries from the adjoining boroughs, and known by the name of some place in it. Any man living within this tract of land – whether he liked it or not, whether his neighbours liked it or not – was required to be a member. In principle, it was the business of the sheriff's turn (see below) to make sure that every adult male was sworn into a borough. At this level, however, exceptions to the rule were widespread. In numerous instances, a borough was the property of some lord who had the right to summon his men to his own court, and to stop them from attending the sheriff's turn or the hundred court or both.

Kent was the only county which had divisions called lests. In Latin records (the only records that exist) the word we find used is *lestus* – sometimes *lestum*, but (in contexts where one can tell the difference) more often masculine than neuter. By the late thirteenth century,the spelling was shifting to *lastus*, presumably in line with some shift in the

[1] Because it included much more than just the built-up area in and around the city; specifically because it included two manors – Great Delce and Little Delce – which were held by knight's service.

[2] Two places called hundreds in DB, Sandwich and Fordwich, were swallowed up into the liberty of the Cinque Ports.

[3] Latin *villata* representing French *vilee* (three syllables, 'vee-lay-uh'). In the hundred rolls of 1274–5 (ed. Illingworth 1812) five such places are recognized: Newenden, Malling, Brasted, Lessness (= Erith), and Dartford. Except for Lessness (which was sooner or later reabsorbed into Littleleigh hundred), these 'villatas' all survived into the nineteenth century, just long enough to be mapped by the Ordnance Survey. The 'villata' of Seasalter is a very special case (see below).

[4] By Kilburne's time, Dartford had come to be recognized as a hundred by itself, called the hundred of Dartford and Wilmington. In Lambard's time, however, it seems still to have been a 'villata', to be mapped as if it were still part of Axstone hundred.

[5] For example, *Ricardus filius Berengeri cum borga sua ... i m' quia non habuit quem plegiauerat*, 'Ricard son of Berenger with his borga (owes) 160 pence because he did not have whom he had pledged', i.e. did not have with him in court a person that he had gone surety for (GREx 1220, pp. 167–8).

Saint Augustine's	Heddling	Shepway	Shrewinghope	Aylesford	Sutton
Kinghamford	Cornilo	Oxney	Felborough	Toltingtrough	Westerham
Bridge	Bewsborough	Aloesbridge	Wye	Little Barnfield	Summerden
Ringslow	Eastry	Langport	Faversham	Larkfield	Axstone
Whitstable	Wingham	Worth	Calehill	Shamell	Codsheath
Downhamford		Newchurch	Boughton	Hoo	Blackheath
Westgate		Ham	Chart	Chatham	Littleleigh
Blengate		Street	Longbridge	Twyford	Bromley
Preston		Heane	Bircholt Barony	Rochester	Ruxley
Petham		Loningborough	Teynham	Wrotham	
		Stowting		Brenchley	
		Bircholt Franchise	The seven hundreds	Littlefield	
		Saint Martin's	Rolvenden	Watchlingstone	
		Folkestone	Barkley	Maidstone	
			Cranbrook	Eyhorne	
			Selbrittenden		
			Tenterden		
			Blackbourne		
			Great Barnfield		
			The hundred of Milton		
			Milton		
			Marden		

Table 21. The thirteenth-century lests and hundreds of Kent. Based on a record dating from 1253 (Greenstreet 1878), but verified from other sources.

pronunciation;[6] by the fourteenth century this was the normal spelling. The Latin word, we can safely assume, represents a French word, *lest* becoming *last*, which in turn represents an English word. Possibly the English word was *hlæst*, meaning 'load' (above, p. 5): in any case – whether it is the same word or just a similar word – its evolution runs along parallel lines. English *hlæst* (neuter) became *lest* or *last* (masculine) in French; French *lest* or *last* became *lestus* or *lastus* (of uncertain gender) in Latin (or, more correctly, in French disguised as Latin).[7] The English word 'last' meaning 'load' survived unchanged, at least in some specialized senses. In the nineteenth century, there were people who still knew what was meant by a last of herrings.[8] The English word 'last' meaning 'part of Kent' did not survive. Its disappearance is a conundrum which I wish I understood better.

As to the names, there is no approved spelling for 'Heddling', and the reader should not feel obliged to write it (or pronounce it) in the same way that I do. In the records it is usually *Hedeling'*. There is (or was) a Haddling Wood (TR 3047), partly in Waldershare but mostly in a detached part of Northbourne, which perhaps preserves the name (Hull 1955). Between 'Shepway' and 'Shipway' the choice is hard to make. Those writers on whom I would generally rely the most (Somner, Kilburne, Hasted, Furley) all preferred the 'i' spelling;[9] but medieval usage is inconsistent, and modern usage seems to have settled on 'Shepway'. In preference to 'Sherwinhope' (Lambard 1576), I use the name 'Shrewinghope', which accords more closely with the medieval spellings.[10] The lest of Saint Augustine's apparently got its name from the fact that its meetings took place outside the abbey gate: certainly they did take place here in the sixteenth century (Hull 1955). In no sense (let this be said plainly) were the abbot and monks the owners of the lest.[11]

Each lest was managed by an agent of the sheriff's, a bailiff, *ballivus lesti*.[12] Since it seems to have been the usual arrangement for Heddling lest to have the same bailiff as Saint Augustine's lest (which eased the way, no doubt, for Heddling to disappear, as it eventually did), there were five appointments to be made, and the sheriff was the man who made them. (There was also a bailiff for Milton hundred and a bailiff for the Seven Hundreds, but these appoint-

[6] In the hundred rolls, dating from 1274–5, spellings with 'e' and 'a' are of roughly equal frequency.

[7] The fluctuation in gender is a good hint that the Latin word came from French (which had only two genders), not directly from English (which, like Latin, had three). This is a common phenomenon: it affects the word *hundredus* too, to look no further than that. (By addition of the helpful affix *-age*, French *lest* produced *lestage*, *lestagium* in mock-Latin.)

[8] The short answer was 10,000 herrings – but by law one had to add 20 per cent, and then another 10 per cent on top of that. So the purchaser expected to find 13,200 herrings in each last.

[9] To some degree, the preference for 'i' reflects a bias in favour of the etymology which it makes appear more plausible. A place of such importance in the history of the Cinque Ports (see below) should surely have a name evocative of a fleet of ships, not of a flock of sheep.

[10] Such as *Shrewinghop'* (Hershey 2004, pp. 209, 224), *Schrewynghop'* (Book of fees, p. 1380).

[11] A statement of Lambard's which I have quoted elsewhere – that the abbey had 'iurisdiction ouer a whole Last of thirteene Hundreds' (1576, pp. 248–9) – is simply not true.

[12] There was also a coroner for each lest, as well as one for Milton hundred and one each for Canterbury and Rochester (Putnam 1933, pp. 106–8).

ments were, it seems, not normally the sheriff's to make. These officers were chosen by the king – or, in the case of Milton, by whoever was lord or lady of the manor at the time.) A would-be bailiff had to promise to pay the sheriff a fixed sum of money every year by way of farm. The exact figure was (one would guess) a confidential matter; but it was generally supposed, by the people who suffered the consequences, that the bailiffs' farms were being driven upwards, during the thirteenth century, by competition for these posts. Once appointed, the bailiff had to make a profit out of his bailiwick – some margin for himself on top of what was needed to satisfy the sheriff. In 1274–5, when local juries were invited to speak out, they were uniformly indignant in denouncing the bailiffs' misdeeds.

Twice a year, each lest was summoned to a meeting with the sheriff. In the thirteenth century, it was expected of every sheriff that he should make a tour of this kind, once within four weeks after Michaelmas, and again within four weeks after Easter. In most counties, this meant that the sheriff would preside over a special session of each hundred court, where a local jury would be selected, sworn in, and required to answer a long list of questions (Cam 1930, pp. 118–28). In Kent, however, with more than sixty hundreds, it was simply not practicable for the sheriff to visit them all within the time allowed. What he did instead was to visit every lest. (It does not follow that the lests were created for this purpose. Perhaps they were; perhaps they were created for some other purpose and then found to be useful for this one. Either way, the existence of the lests made possible what would otherwise have been impossible.)

Little is known about the conduct of the sheriff's turn. With the exception of one sixteenth-century document (see below), there are no surviving records; but the turn is referred to quite often, incidentally, in records of other kinds. Broadly speaking, the turn seems to have worked in the same sort of way as a visit by the king's justices, but on a smaller scale. The justices visited each county in the circuit that had been assigned to them; the sheriff of Kent visited each lest. The justices expected to be met by a delegation from every hundred; the sheriff expected to be met by a delegation from every borough. (Apparently it would be more accurate to think of a lest as a group of boroughs, not as a group of hundreds.) In some respects, of course, the proceedings were very different. A visit by the king's justices was a painfully protracted business, repeated only at intervals of several years. The sheriff's turn was completed quickly, and happened twice a year. The king's justices admitted no exceptions – not even for the lowy of Tonbridge and the Cinque Ports, which were, however, allowed to be special cases. But there were numerous boroughs which the sheriff could not compel to appear at his turn, because the lord to whom they belonged had the right to hold a court for his own tenants, to deal with the business which the sheriff was dealing with elsewhere.[13]

By the fourteenth century – to speak briefly of some subsequent changes affecting the lasts – the name 'Shrewinghope' was being replaced by 'Scray'.[14] Eventually that became the normal name; but the old one was not forgotten, and it was well enough understood that the two names were synonymous. For some purposes, the last of Heddling was often lumped in together with Saint Augustine's. In the accounts of the aid of 1346, for instance, the heading *lastus sancti Augustini* covers both lasts, and the Heddling hundreds are interspersed among those which did properly belong to the other last. Looking at fourteenth-century records like this, we might easily get the idea that the last of Heddling had already ceased to exist; but in fact it was still there. As late as the beginning of the sixteenth century, it was still customary for the sheriff of Kent to make his twice-yearly tour, though by then there was little business left for these meetings to transact (Hull 1955);[15] and even that late (April and October 1509) the turn comprised six meetings – that is, it included a separate meeting for the last of Heddling.

By the late sixteenth century the lath of Heddling had finally been swallowed up by Saint Augustine's, and the number of laths – I switch to the English word here – had been reduced from six to five.[16] The bailiwicks, however, were tending to increase in number. In the thirteenth century, by and large, a bailiwick had been conterminous with a lath; the sixteenth-century bailiwicks were generally smaller than that, and the boundaries between them did not always respect the boundaries between the laths.[17] There were reckoned to be twelve bailiwicks in the late sixteenth century (Lambard 1596), fourteen in the mid seventeenth (Kilburne 1659).[18] As the laths became fragmented, their functions all devolved on these smaller units. Twice a

[13] One document worth noting is an agreement made in 1316 by the abbot and convent of Saint Augustine's with their tenants in Chislet (copied into Thorne's Chronicle, ed. Twysden 1652, cols. 2033–4). The men of Chislet wanted no demands to be made on them in excess of those which would have been made by the sheriff, had they been attending the sheriff's turn. In particular, they wanted it understood that they did not have to appear en masse at these special sessions of the abbot's court: a delegation of five – the elected head and four of the other inhabitants – was to suffice. By and large, the abbot conceded their demands.

[14] It has sometimes been thought that *Scra* was originally a written abbreviation for *Scrawinhope* or some such spelling. This seems unlikely to me, but I cannot be sure that it is wrong.

[15] Some of the business had been transferred to the shire court, some taken over by the justices of the peace. But the turn was a source of income for the sheriff and continued for that reason at least. I do not know when it stopped happening.

[16] There is no mention of Heddling in the first edition of Lambard's book (1576); in the second edition 'Lath of Hedelinth' is said to have been an alternative name for 'Lathe of Saint Augustines' (Lambard 1596, p. 36). That error can be found repeated by later writers.

[17] Thus, by Kilburne's time, the bailiwick of Twyford (which was mostly in the lath of Aylesford) had captured Marden hundred from the lath of Scray, and the bailiwick of Stowting (mostly in the lath of Scray) had captured Bewsborough hundred from the lath of Saint Augustine's (Kilburne 1659, p. 318).

[18] By Kilburne's time the bailiwick of Sutton had been split in half, and the hundred of Ruxley had been split between the two new bailiwicks (Kilburne 1659, pp. 328–9). Otherwise it remained true that a bailiwick was a group of (whole) hundreds.

year, for instance, as the time came round for the West Kent quarter-sessions (Kilburne 1659, pp. 375–7), the sheriff issued orders requiring the attendance of the bailiff of Sutton Dartford and the bailiff of Sutton Bromley: there was no such person, no such thing, as the bailiff or bailiffdom of the lath of Sutton. The bailiwicks were where the work got done; the laths had become mere names.

A similar process, working along different lines, produced the divisions by which the justices of the peace distributed responsibility among themselves. By Lambard's time, Sutton lath had been split into two divisions, Aylesford lath into three (Lambard 1596, pp. 31–5). By Kilburne's time, Scray lath had been broken up as well: five hundreds had been added to the division of justices of the lath of Shepway,[19] and the hundreds that were left were formed into two new entities, the upper and lower divisions of the lath of Scray (Kilburne 1659, pp. 304–18). And yet, despite their names, these divisions are rather to be regarded as groups of parishes. If we look more closely, we find that the boundaries between them do not respect the boundaries of either hundreds or laths: they follow the parish boundaries. In some parts of Kent, it was common for a parish to be split between two or more hundreds, which might quite possibly belong to different laths. Lenham, for example, was partly in the hundred of Eyhorne but partly in the hundred of Calehill. The latter part of Lenham was in the lath of Scray (and might have been in the division of justices of the lath of Shepway). But in fact the whole parish was in just one division, the east division of justices of the lath of Aylesford (Kilburne 1659, p. 166).[20] If people wanted to report a crime, they did not need to ask themselves which lath (or which hundred or which borough) the crime had been committed in; the fact that it had been committed in their parish was the only fact which mattered. In this respect too, the laths by now were nothing more than names.

Unlike the laths, the hundreds were not withering away. In the late thirteenth century it seems to have been taken for granted (not just in Kent) that the hundred court would need to convene every three weeks.[21] Cases which could not be settled here were referred upwards, not to the lest (which was not a court of law), but to the shire, the county court for Kent. Then and later, the county court normally met on every fourth Monday (Palmer 1982, pp. 10–11).[22] The first session after Michaelmas was, it seems, always held on Penenden Heath; for other sessions the venue varied – sometimes Penenden, sometimes Canterbury or Rochester, sometimes some suitable place near Milton, but not Milton itself. (As far as the evidence goes, the court never met anywhere in western Kent: the rule which we find stated in DB – 'no further west than Penenden' – was apparently obeyed, but interpreted to mean 'no further west than the Medway'.)

Exactly how many hundreds there were, even at a given point in time, is often difficult to say, because the answer will depend on how one chooses to deal with certain ambiguities. For example, some of these units are more or less consistently called 'half-hundreds', and should perhaps be counted as such, not as whole hundreds. But probably we shall prefer to ignore that distinction, which was significant in only one context. When the king's justices descended on the county, a hundred became a 'half-hundred' if it was allowed to be represented by a jury of six, rather than the normal twelve. For the rest of the time, in all respects, it was a hundred like any other. (Great Barnfield on these occasions was sometimes, perhaps always, represented by a six-man jury; but that did not prevent it from being counted as one of the Seven Hundreds.) In the thirteenth century, Marden hundred (or half-hundred) had an awkwardly ambiguous status, to some degree still subordinate to Milton hundred, yet also to some degree independent from it. But this was the only borderline case of the kind. The list of thirteenth-century hundreds given in Table 21 consists of 66 entries. As well as Marden, Rochester hundred might perhaps be cancelled (see above); otherwise the list is solid.

Subsequent changes are few, and of only local effect. Philip Simonson's map of Kent, published in 1596 (below, p. 269), has a box of text that includes a numbered list of of the hundreds existing at the time. The list includes Marden; it does not include Rochester, which, by this time, had definitely ceased to exist (see below). Two pairs of adjoining hundreds have coalesced. Chart hundred and Longbridge hundred have become the single hundred of Chart and Longbridge; Bridge hundred and Petham hundred have also merged. (A few hundreds with some obvious internal cleavage have sprouted double names – thus Bromley hundred has come to be called the hundred of Bromley and Beckenham – but that makes no difference to the total.) So Simonson's list consists of 63 hundreds.[23] By Kilburne's time, two new hundreds have been added – the hundred of Dartford and Wilmington (formerly just a town), the hundred of the Isle of Sheppey (formerly a subdivision of Mil-

[19] For Kilburne, this did not mean that these hundreds had ceased to belong to the lath of Scray. For Hasted it did mean that; so the lath of Scray, as he describes it, can hardly any longer be recognized as DB's lest of Wiwarleth.

[20] Why this division rather than the other? Because the parish church stood in Eyhorne hundred: 'where a parish is in two hundreds, the justices . . . do usually take that parish into their division by the hundred where the church of that parish standeth' (Kilburne 1659, p. 318). This is not an answer, but is the beginning of one.

[21] From the hundred rolls, for instance, we discover that the towns of Hartley and Swanscombe are no longer attending the twice-yearly meetings of the lest of Sutton or the three-weekly meetings of the hundred of Axstone, as they used to do (*solebant facere sectam bis per annum ad lastum de Sutton' et ad hundredum de Acstan' de iii septimanis in iii septimanas*).

[22] The earliest exact date on record is for a meeting which took place at Canterbury on 20 December 1176, chaired by the deputy sheriff, Johan de Cardif. That day was a Monday: it fits into the same four-week cycle as the dates of the meetings noted by Palmer for 1253–4. The court was still meeting on a Monday in the sixteenth century, but by Hasted's time the day had been changed to Wednesday.

[23] His numbering runs up to 64 because it includes the lowy of Tonbridge.

ton hundred) – and thus there are 65 hundreds in his list.[24] Except that the Isle of Sheppey has ceased to be a separate hundred, Hasted's list is exactly the same as Kilburne's. It should be noted that none of these totals include the lowy of Tonbridge, which was hardly any different from a hundred by now (see below) but was not called by that name. Since the facts should all be readily accessible (Lambard 1576, 1596, Simonson 1596, Kilburne 1659, Hasted 1797–1801), I say no more about them here.

As police districts, each having one or two constables elected from among the inhabitants, the medieval hundreds maintained a functional existence until the nineteenth century. By good luck, this means that they survived just long enough to come under the scrutiny of the Ordnance Survey. The first-edition six-inch maps, published (as far as Kent is concerned) between 1869 and 1882, were meticulous in tracing out all the hundred boundaries.[25] But then, in the aftermath of the local government act of 1888, these medieval arrangements were all swept away, and the hundreds disappeared from the map.

The Five Ports – Hastings in Sussex, Sandwich, Dover, Hythe and Romney in Kent – stood outside this administrative structure. Their inhabitants answered to no sheriff, still less to any inferior official like the bailiff of a hundred. In return for providing the king once a year with a fleet of 57 ships (21 each from Hastings and Dover, five each from the other three ports), they enjoyed an extraordinary assortment of privileges; and the inhabitants of other ports and landing-places, eager to participate in these privileges, were willing to take on some share of the responsibility.[26] Already in the thirteenth century, the men of Faversham were responsible for finding one of Dover's quota of ships, the men of Folkestone another, and the men of Lydd for finding one of Romney's quota. Hastings especially had shed so much of its load that by this time two other Sussex ports – Winchelsea and Rye – were supplying larger numbers of ships than Hastings itself: in effect the Five Ports had become the Seven Ports, but the old name was never dropped. On one occasion (only one that I know of), the men of the Cinque Ports were had up before the justices who visited Kent. That happened in summer 1219.[27] By the late thirteenth century, the men of the Ports had been explicitly released from answering to the itinerant justices;[28] there were no pleas which they could not deal with in their own courts – if necessary in their highest court, the court which met at Shepway under the presidency of the king's permanent representative, the Lord Warden. After that, to the extent that successive kings were willing to let it happen, the liberty of the Cinque Ports was continually encroaching on the county of Kent. The largest single expansion occurred in the fifteenth century, when, with the approval of Henry VI, the men of Tenterden entered into a partnership with the men of Rye which had the effect of extending the liberty of the Ports, not just over the town, but over the whole hundred of Tenterden.

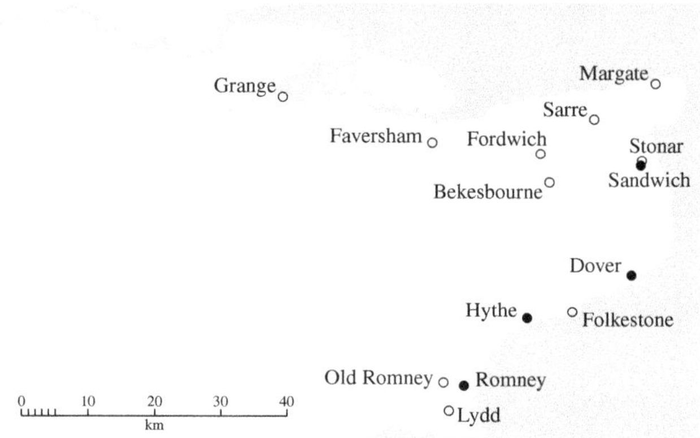

The city of Canterbury ceased to be part of the county. In 1461 it was formally separated from Kent and made into a county by itself. (The castle, however, never having been regarded as part of the city, continued to be part of Kent.) Rochester could not aim as high as that, but the citizens did achieve a large measure of control over their own affairs; and the liberty of the city of Rochester, as it was demarcated in 1446 and 1461, superseded the hundred of Rochester. (In addition, the liberty covered all the lower reaches of the river Medway, from Sheerness upstream as far as a place in Burham called Hawkwood.) A number of other towns in Kent – Gravesend, Maidstone, Sittingbourne, Ashford – set out along a similar path, but each of them has its own story,[29] and there is nothing that can usefully be said about them in the space of a few words. Anyone who wants to know, for instance, how the town of Maidstone ceased to be part of the hundred of Maidstone, and how it came to be regarded as the capital of Kent, will need to consult a history of the place (Newton 1741, Clark and Murfin 1995).

The lowy of Tonbridge came down in the world – a very long way down. In the thirteenth century, the earl of Gloucester and his officials were steadfast in asserting the lowy's special status. The sheriff of Kent had no authority

[24] Kilburne 1659, pp. 330–48; his numbering goes wrong when it reaches Marden (p. 341)

[25] Unless the misunderstanding is mine, there seems to have been some indecision whether 'Longport hundred' should be mapped separately (as in sheet 84) or merged into a larger entity called 'St Martins Longport hundred' (as in sheet 81). In Kilburne's understanding of the facts, Langport hundred covered part of Hope, the whole of Lydd, and part of Old Romney, with the churches of Hope and Lydd (Kilburne 1659, p. 339). But Lydd's status is problematic. Despite its being covered by the Cinque Ports umbrella (see below), Kilburne and Hasted regarded it as part of Langport hundred; the Ordnance Survey did not.

[26] A different explanation applies to two manors in Kent – Bekesbourne and Grange – which became attached to Hastings. I mention those cases in the commentary (DB-Ke-8rb48, 9rb30).

[27] As is proved by a batch of entries appearing in the next year's exchequer roll (GREx 1220, pp. 167–8). Probably this means that the justices held a separate session at Shepway, but I have seen no proof of that.

[28] A liberty first conceded by Henric III, in a charter dated 20 May 1260 (Giraud 1905), and confirmed by Edward I in 1278.

[29] The most unique of them all is the town of Queenborough, founded by Edward III as an adjunct to the newly-built castle.

there. The king's justices were welcome (how could they not be?) to visit the lowy of Tonbridge at any time. If the king chose to send the same justices to visit the lowy that he was sending to visit Kent, that, of course, was his decision to make. But the commission which these justices carried with them had to make explicit mention of the lowy of Tonbridge; and they had to hold a separate session at Tonbridge itself. Once the earl had conceded (as he did in 1258) that he held the lowy of Tonbridge from the archbishop, not from the king, it became difficult for him to justify the claim for its special status – a status which could certainly not have been granted by the archbishop (who did not claim it for himself, with respect to his domain lands, and in any case could not have conferred it upon one of his tenants). For some length of time, inertia prevailed over logic. The itinerant justices who visited Kent in 1262–3 held a separate session at Tonbridge (*Feet of fines*, p. 343); so did the justices who visited Kent in 1271 (pp. 390–1); but sooner or later that practice was discontinued.[30] By the seventeeth century, the lowy of Tonbridge had been fully integrated into the administrative structure of the county. It was part of Kent; it was part of the lath of Aylesford; it was part of the south division of that lath. For all practical purposes, the lowy was just another hundred, distinguished only by its name (and by the fact that it had four constables to police it, no regular hundred having more than two). Jointly with Watchlingstone hundred, it formed the bailiwick of the lowy of Tonbridge – which might just as well have been called the bailiwick of Tonbridge, except (so it seems) that people enjoyed using the more euphonious name.

Lastly, a word about Seasalter, a monument, if ever there was one, to inertia. In the eleventh century, Seasalter was already a peculiar place (DB-Ke-5ra15), a town without any townlike characteristics, in Borwar lest yet not in any hundred. This has to mean that Seasalter was, in a manner of speaking, a hundred by itself – but nobody ever thought of calling it one (perhaps because, even in Kent, even a half-hundred could not be quite as small as this). In Lambard's time, in Kilburne's time, Seasalter still had just the same status, described in different language: it was part of Saint Augustine's lath, but was counted as a separate town. ('It is in no Hundred, but hath a Constable of it self' (Kilburne 1659, p. 242).) And in the nineteenth century, when the six-inch map was surveyed, Seasalter was still the same peculiar place that it had been for eight hundred years.

The coda consists of five short pieces which some readers may perhaps find instructive or entertaining.

(1) Early maps of Kent

Both as works of art and as historical documents, early printed maps have attracted a good deal of attention, reflected in numerous books and articles of which I have to confess to being very largely ignorant (my excuse being that I am interested only in maps of Kent, and only incidentally in them). Most of the people named below are the subject of articles in ODNB,[31] and the references cited there will point any reader who wants to know more in the right direction.

Saxton 1575. The earliest printed map which represents Kent with tolerable accuracy and with a respectable amount of detail is a map of the four south-eastern counties (Kent, Sussex, Surrey, Middlesex) drawn by Christopher Saxton (occ. 1573–98). It was one of a series of maps covering the whole of England and Wales, completed and formally published in 1579. This particular plate was engraved (by Remigius Hogenbergius) in 1575; some finishing touches were added in 1577–8. The portion covering Kent was reproduced by Livett (1938), for purposes of comparison with the maps which follow.

Anonymous. The earliest separate map of Kent is also the first to show the ancient 'lathes': it makes a point of mentioning their existence in its title, 'The Shyre of Kent, Diuided into the five Lathes therof' (Box 1926, Livett 1938). It was copied from Saxton's map,[32] probably without permission; the engraver made a space for his name beneath the scale, but never wrote anything into it. There are some original elements (Livett 1938, pp. 268–70), most conspicuously the dotted lines showing the 'lathe' boundaries. (In one place a more densely dotted line is the start of an attempt to show the hundred boundaries as well.) It seems likely that this map was published in 1576–7 (before Saxton was awarded a monopoly), on the expectation that people who bought Lambard's book (1576) might also wish to buy a map of the county; and the circumstantial evidence suggests to me that Lambard himself was involved in its publication.[33] The plates survived for more than fifty years. With a few additions, this map was reissued to accompany a pamphlet called *The inrichment of the Weald of Kent*, first published in 1625 but reprinted at intervals from 1631 till 1664.[34] The third and latest version of the map is one which shows the main roads (Box 1927).

Simonson 1596. Far more accurate than either of the previous maps is the half-inch map surveyed and drawn by Philip Simonson (d. 1598) of Rochester. It was engraved (in London) by Charles Whitwell (occ. 1582–1611), as two

[30] 'Long since discontinued', says Kilburne (1659, p. 277). Of the very large number of final concords authorized by the king's justices in 1313–14 (Greenstreet 1877–80), none is dated at Tonbridge.

[31] Alternatively they can be searched for on the web. The reader who googles "charles whitwell" or "peter stent" will know as much as I do about these men.

[32] This was proved by Livett (1938). The engraver, he thought, was the same man who made two of the plates for Saxton's atlas, Northamptonshire ... Huntingdonshire (1576) and Worcestershire (1577).

[33] A sketch-map drawn by Lambard, 'Carde of the Beacons in Kent' (BL Add. 62935), dated 1585, took its outlines from this anonymous map. An engraved version of this map of Lambard's was included in the second edition (1596) of his book.

[34] The three places added in this version of the map (Box 1926, p. 90) are all places mentioned in the pamphlet (Jackson 1625). Chafford was the home of the dedicatee, Sir George Rivers (d. 1630).

sheets to be joined down the middle, and first published in 1596 – that is, at around the same time as the second edition of Lambard's book. The title refers back to that of the anonymous map: Simonson's map is called 'A NEW DESCRIPTION OF KENT Divided into the fyue Lathes therof' (Hannen 1914, Livett 1938). Lambard recommends it to his readers in glowing terms (1596, pp. 220–1); though he does not exactly say so, I think we may be sure that he had helped to get this map published. (Lambard and Simonson were both connected with Rochester Bridge – Lambard had been a member of the governing body since 1585, Simonson was appointed paymaster in 1593 (Hannen 1915) – and presumably that was how they became acquainted.) Copies of this map in its original form are very rare; almost all the surviving specimens – including the one reproduced by Hannen (1914) – carry the added imprint of the London printseller Peter Stent (occ. 1642–65), who had evidently somehow got possession of the plates.[35] Mostly these copies survive through having been bound into copies of Thomas Philipott's *Villare Cantianum* (1659, reprinted 1664).

Norden 1605. The next map, dated 1605, was drawn by John Norden (d. 1625) and engraved by William Kip (occ. 1597–1618). It is a very pretty piece of work. Mostly it was copied from Simonson's map, but some of the detail is different. It was specifically designed as an illustration for William Camden's *Britannia* – it was included in the folio edition of the Latin text (1607) and in the English translation (1610, reprinted 1637) – and many of the new labels (such as DVROLENVM and PORTVS LEMANVS) were obviously added in compliance with instructions from Camden. This map of Norden's does not appear to have ever been published separately in any form.[36] Perhaps for that reason, it had no progeny.

Speed 1611. The map which set the pattern was the one published by John Speed (1551/2–1629) in his atlas called *The theatre of the empire of Great Britaine* (1611). Like the other plates, this one was engraved for Speed in Amsterdam, in the workship of Joost de Hondt, alias Jodocus Hondius (1563–1612). Not counting the insets around the edges (coats of arms of the earls of Kent, bird's-eye views of Canterbury and Rochester), this map, in its original form, was hardly anything more than a somewhat inaccurate, somewhat simplified copy of Simonson's map. Within a few years, it had picked up some additions from Norden's map (REGULBIUM is one which can be seen at a glance), but after that it seems to have stayed the same.[37] With the rest of Speed's atlas, this map of Kent was frequently reprinted; and it was very frequently copied by later generations of cartographers – who, whether they knew it or not, were copying a rather poor copy of Simonson's map, enhanced with some antiquarian details copied from Norden's map.

(2) Laths or lathes?

The word is LATH, or ought to be. It should rhyme with BATH, not BATHE. 'Lathe' is a sixteenth-century spelling, mistakenly resuscitated in the nineteenth century. Since then, everyone who has had occasion to use the word has got into the habit, not just of misspelling it, but also of mispronouncing it.

For anyone who has ever tried reading a sixteenth-century book (or who has ever used the expression 'olde worlde'), it will come as no surprise to be told that the word LATH was often spelt 'lathe' at the time. That is true, in the first place, of official records. In a series of documents dating from 1584–95 (ed. Thomson 1926, pp. 66–98), the spelling oscillates between 'lath' and 'lathe' – except in the plural, where it is always 'lathes'.[38] When the word LATH crossed over from the language of officialdom into the language of scholarship, and from manuscript into print, the variability in spelling travelled with it.

William Lambard's *Perambulation of Kent* is the book which introduced the word LATH to the learned world. In the first edition, especially in the stretch of text which Lambard called 'The particular of Kent' (1576, pp. 24–47),[39] the word is almost always spelt 'lathe'.[40] On the other hand, in a block of text which was added in the second edition – a list of the justices of the peace for Kent who were resident in the county (1596, pp. 31–5) – the spelling is always 'lath'. Those two editions were seen through the press by Lambard; a third edition was published in 1656, long after his death. Though substantially the same as the second edition, it is visually very different (it was set in Roman, not black-letter type), and a fairly serious effort was made to regularize the spelling. Here, almost always, LATH was spelt 'lath', regardless of how it had been spelt in the second edition. The compositor who set this edition had probably never met the word before, but he knew what rule to apply.[41] When he came across an unfamiliar word in an old book, he had to ask himself whether the spelling was consistent or not. If the final 'e' was always there, he should

[35] At Stent's instigation, the map was embellished with inset views of Dover and Rye. A later state adds Stent's address, 'at the white Horse in giltspure street', and the date '1659'.

[36] A description of Kent written by Norden, of the kind which accompanied his published maps, was, by Nicolson (1696, pp. 39–40), reported to exist in manuscript. I have not tried to track it down.

[37] The only variation that I can see affects the imprint, added for the 1627 edition (at the bottom centre, to the right of the stylized representation of the battle of Hastings), altered for subsequent editions in 1650 and 1676.

[38] This batch of documents was assembled by Sir Roger Twysden from among his family papers: they survived from the time when his grandfather was one of Lord Cobham's deputy lieutenants.

[39] This is a summarized English version of the accounts submitted to the exchequer by the collectors of the 'fifteenth and tenth' of 1570–1 (above, p. 6). Lambard's book had been under construction for several years; this block of text was one of the last components to be added.

[40] In this stretch of text there is only one exception, 'Summe of this whole Lath' (1576, p. 31). The second edition has 'Sum of this whole Lathe' (1596, p. 42); the third has 'Sum of this whole Lath' (1656, p. 39).

[41] In short, he was in the same position as the compositor who set the 'third folio' edition (1663) of Shakespear.

assume that it was there for a reason and let it stand. If the final 'e' came and went, he should assume that it was there for decoration and ignore it.[42]

However that decision came to be made, it was certainly the right decision. From the 1650s onwards, by people who knew what they were talking about, LATH was invariably spelt 'lath'. In Kilburne's book (1659), the word occurs hundreds of times, and the spelling is perfectly consistent. When the word turns up sporadically elsewhere, that is how it is always spelt (Somner 1640, 1652, Philipott 1659, Somner 1693). The same spelling prevails in the eighteenth century (Lewis 1723, 1736, Jacob 1774); it never crossed Edward Hasted's mind to spell the word in any other way (Hasted 1778–99, 1797–1801). People who looked up the word in any edition of Johnson's *Dictionary* (first published 1755), or in any of the other dictionaries derived from that one, would have found many things to puzzle them (below, p. 273), but they would not have been left in any doubt about the spelling. People who looked up the word in Smart's *Pronouncing dictionary* (1836) would have learnt that it should rhyme with PATH.[43]

Rare instances of the spelling 'lathe' can certainly be found; and people who spelt the word like that were presumably mispronouncing it as well. In an eighteenth-century context, however, 'lathe' is an aberration. Sometimes it is just a sign of ignorance. Sometimes it means that the writer is copying too closely from Lambard.[44] And sometimes it means that the writer is looking at a map.

Cartographers, like lexicographers, were plagiarists most of the time. New maps were seldom genuinely new: they were copied from one or more old maps. A conscientious cartographer might aim to make some improvements of his own; a lazy one would copy the map as he found it. Beginning with the two earliest separate maps – an anonymous map of 1576–7, Philip Simonson's map of 1596 (see above) – it became traditional for maps of Kent to show the boundaries between one LATH and another. Those first two maps both use the spelling 'lathe', which was, of course, a perfectly acceptable spelling at the time. The next map in the sequence – a map drawn by John Norden for William Camden – is mostly a copy of Simonson's map, but opts for the spelling 'lath'. This change, it is clear, was made deliberately. Norden had decided, or Camden had decided, that 'lath' was to be preferred. It did no harm to write PART as 'Parte',[45] which could not be mispronounced; but it was better not to write LATH as 'lathe', which could. Unfortunately this was not the map which cartographers chose as their model. That honour went to another copy of Simonson's map (Speed 1611) in which the spelling 'lathe' was retained. As Speed's map was copied and recopied, this antique spelling persisted, regardless of the stricter rules which had been adopted meanwhile by printers. Eventually it even turned up in the maps which were made for later editions of Camden's book – the map drawn by Robert Morden (d. 1703) for Edmund Gibson's translation (1695, reprinted 1722, 1753, 1772), the map drawn by Edward Noble (d. 1784) for Richard Gough's translation (1789, reprinted 1806).

For the sort of people who bought maps, rather than making and selling them, for the sort of people who formed their first ideas about Kent by looking at a map, it thus became easy to fall into the trap of supposing that a lath was called a LATHE. For whatever reason, people did start falling into that trap; sooner or later the misunderstanding diffused itself into Kent. The Kent Archaeological Society, which collectively should have known better, deserves some share of the blame for letting this happen. The first article published in *Archaeologia Cantiana* which uses the word at all frequently is a piece by Cooper (1868),[46] and the spelling there is 'lathe'. (The editor who let this pass was T. G. Faussett.) That particular article has no importance; I cite it only because it shows which way the wind was blowing. As late as the 1880s, the Ashford-based historian Robert Furley was still resolutely speaking of 'laths' at every opportunity (e.g. Furley 1886, pp. 361, 369);[47] but by then he was in the minority – not quite, however, a minority of one – and within a few years he was dead.

What are we to learn from this? We can be sure, for a start, that LATH is the genuine word. I do not stipulate for any particular pronunciation – people's vowels are their own concern – but anyone who grew up (as I did) calling a bath a 'baahth' will presumably feel bound to enunciate this word in the same affected manner. (The plural has to be 'laahdhz', with 'th' voiced to 'dh', via the same rule which applies to PATH and words like it.)[48] LATHE, if it existed at all, would be the corresponding verb. It so happens that a verb TO LATHE, meaning 'to meet', is listed in the dictionary of Kentish dialect compiled by Parish and Shaw (1888); but they do not say where they had encountered the word, or in what sort of context they had heard

[42] By the same logic, I call the author 'Lambard'. (He was 'Lambard' on the title-page of the first edition, 'Lambarde' on that of the second.) From the mid seventeenth century onwards, this was the normal spelling (except that he was sometimes misnamed 'Lamberd' or 'Lambert'). His descendants used that spelling – until some time in the nineteenth century, when they decided (as they were entitled to do) that 'Lambarde' looked more genteel.

[43] Or indeed with LATH, 'a thin slip of wood'; but obviously not with LATHE, 'an engine by which any substance is cut and turned'.

[44] Thus Harris (1719) spelt the word 'lathe' when he was borrowing from Lambard, but 'lath' when he was borrowing from Kilburne.

[45] As in 'Parte of Midlesex', 'Parte of Essex'.

[46] Sussex-connected, London-based, William Durrant Cooper wrote about many things, but this paper was his only foray into Kent. It was read at the KAS's annual meeting, Ashford, 1866.

[47] The KAS made another visit to Ashford in 1883, and this paper of Furley's was read on that occasion. The volume in which it appeared was edited by the Rev. W. A. Scott Robertson, and he also spelt the word 'lath' (Robertson 1880, pp. 350–2). Furley died in 1887, Scott Robertson in 1897.

[48] Which explains, I suppose, why in the sixteenth century the 'e' occurs more consistently in the plural than in the singular (above, p. 270).

people use it. As a noun, LATHE is a monstrosity. There is no doubt about that: the question is what we do next. Have we become so addicted to this final 'e' that we cannot face the prospect of living without it? Or can we find the courage (little enough) needed to break the habit? Only time will tell.

(3) Laths in the rest of England?

It was not always obvious that laths were peculiar to Kent. Despite a great weight of evidence seeming to favour that conclusion, there was a time when historians were more inclined to think that laths had once existed everywhere, and that Kent was unique only in having held on to something which other counties had lost. Among historians, this perverse way of looking at things was first promoted by William Lambard (1536–1601).

Lambard was not from Kent. He was a Londoner by birth; by training he became a lawyer; Lincoln's Inn was the centre of his world. In 1568 he completed and saw through the press a collection of Anglo-Saxon laws which had been begun by his friend Laurence Nowell (b. 1530, last occ. 1569). One of the appendices included in that book, under the title *Leges Edouardi Regis*, was a (much interpolated version of a twelfth-century) Latin tract which tried to give some description of the English legal system, as it had existed before the conquest. There is (in this version of the text) a passing remark to the effect that 'some' shires were subdivided into 'leths', in the same sort of way that some northern counties (the ones which had wapentacs instead of hundreds) were subdivided into 'thridings'.[49] To Lambard, at the time, the word 'leth' meant nothing. Within the next few years, however, in the course of compiling his 'Topographical dictionary', he came across documentary evidence which proved that one late medieval county (viz. Kent) was organized into lasts – *lastus* in Latin, presumably 'last' in English – which did indeed bear some resemblance to the ridings of Yorkshire; and it occurred to him that a 'last' might be the same thing as a 'leth'.[50] After 1570, having married a young (very young) Kentish girl, he began spending part of his time at the house he had acquired in Kent; and fairly soon he came to understand that the medieval 'lasts' still had some sort of existence, and that in English they were actually called 'laths'.

Since before 1568, Lambard had been aware of a (fifteenth-century) chronicle from the abbey of Crowland in Lincolnshire, written by (someone impersonating) abbot Ingulf, who died in 1109. To Lambard, as to a depressingly long list of contemporary and later historians, this chronicle appeared to be a thoroughly reliable source. One of the stories that he found there goes like this. In the reign of king Alfred, England was constantly under attack by Danish pirates, and law and order began to break down, to the extent that some of the English, copying the Danes, started making raids on their own country. To restore order, Alfred divided his kingdom into shires, divided the shires into hundreds, divided the hundreds into tithings, and made it a law that every adult male should join one of these tithings, whose members were all to be answerable for one another's good behaviour. By about 1575, combining this story of Ingulf's with the passage from the *Leges Edouardi*, Lambard had come up with a theory of his own. The system of government created by king Alfred consisted, he thought, of four tiers, not just three. There were shires; there were laths or ridings (which Ingulf had forgotten to mention); there were hundreds or wapentacs; and finally there were tithings. (Perhaps we are expected to use our own discretion in deciding that laths would not have been needed except in counties with a large number of hundreds; but Lambard gives us no hint of this.)

When he came to write an introduction for his book about Kent, Lambard digressed into an explanation of his theory, paraphrasing Ingulf's story, but adding this new twist to it (Lambard 1576, pp. 20–1). He allows himself to make this digression, he says, so as not to have to keep repeating himself in the other books which he is intending to write.[51] In the event, none of those other books was ever published – as far as we know, not one of them was even started – and the series began and ended with the book about Kent. Nevertheless, this theory of Lambard's attracted some attention. Straight away, the whole passage was quoted word for word by William Harrison (1535–1593), in the introduction which he was writing for Raphael Holinshed's *Chronicles* (Harrison 1577, cols. 73vb–4rb);[52] and Lambard's ideas were thus given a level of circulation which otherwise they could not have expected.

In the longer run, they penetrated into the glossaries of medieval Latin. For a start, we find Sir Henry Spelman (1563/4–1641) swallowing the theory whole.[53] If we look

[49] *In quibusdam prouinciis anglice uocabatur 'leþ' quod isti dicunt 'trihinge'* (Lambard 1568, f. 134v). That passage will not be found in the latest edition of this tract (O'Brien 1999), which aims to present the text in something like the form intended by its original author.

[50] That is the sense of a note written by Lambard in the margin of a copy of his 1568 book, against the passage just quoted: *laþe opinor, quod nunc Last dicitur*, 'meaning a lath, I think, which is now called a last'. That copy, now in the Huntington Library, has been reproduced on microfilm, and is available through EEBO.

[51] 'Thus muche therefore I thought good, nowe at the first to open, the more at large, bicause it may serue generally for all Shyres, and shall hereafter deliuer me from often repetition of one thing. Where, by the way, (least I might seeme to haue forgotten the Shire that I haue presently in hand) it is to be noted, that that which in the west countrey was at that time, (and yet is) called, a Tithing, is in Kent termed a Borow' (Lambard 1576, p. 22).

[52] This essay was dedicated to Lord Cobham – lord lieutenant of Kent, lord warden of the Cinque Ports, constable of Dover castle – from whose patronage Harrison had benefited. In a revised form, it was reprinted in the second edition ten years later, and the quotation from Lambard occurs there too (Harrison 1587, cols. 153a–4a, ed. Edelen 1968, pp. 82–6).

[53] 'The whole of England, as I have said more than once, was divided up by King Alfred into counties', and so on. *Diximus non semel, Angliam totam ab Aluredo Rege in Comitatus distribui: Comitatus (pro locorum varietate) in Trithingas, Rapas, et Lathas: eas iterum in Hundreda, seu Wapentachia: atque ista denuo in Tithingas, quas et Decurias vocant et*

up the word *læstum*,[54] we are told that this is 'a relatively large portion of a county, containing three hundreds, or sometimes more than three',[55] and that lath is the current English name for these divisions. It would be possible to write a whole article deconstructing this paragraph of Spelman's;[56] but I am not intending to write it myself. From Spelman this definition was adopted (with modifications) by William Somner (1652);[57] not much later, crossing the sea, it was incorporated into the great glossary compiled by Charles du Fresne (1610–1688), sieur de Du Cange, first published at Paris in 1678. Du Cange's entry for LASTUM is a shortened version of Spelman's entry, with some adjustments derived from Somner's.

(4) Laths in Ireland?

Edmund Spenser (d. 1599) was one of the people who knew about Lambard's theory and assumed that it was literally true. How he first came to be aware of the theory is uncertain. It may be significant that he was briefly employed, in 1578–9, as secretary to a newly appointed bishop of Rochester;[58] if the bishop bought or was given a copy of Lambard's book, his secretary might have had a chance to read it. (Much of Spenser's life is a matter of 'ifs' and 'might haves'.) By the time that he came to write about it, many years later, he seems to have been trusting to memory, and his memory let him down in some respects. He thought that a lath was smaller than a hundred, not larger, and that a wapentac was coordinate with a lath.

In 1596, Spenser wrote an essay called 'A view of the state of Ireland'. It takes the form of a dialogue. Eudoxus is ignorant but willing to learn; he asks the questions. Irenaeus (like Spenser) has been living in Ireland for many years and knows it very well; he is the man with the answers. As the conversation goes on, Irenaeus keeps hinting that he has a big idea – a plan for transforming Ireland into a peaceful, law-abiding country – and finally Eudoxus demands to know what it is, 'that generall reformation which you spake of, ... by which you said all men should be contained in duty ever after'. Irenaeus's big idea turns out to be that the policy once applied in England by king Alfred should now be applied in Ireland. 'It is written', he explains (apparently Eudoxus is not aware of the fact), 'that King Alured, or Aldred, did divide the Realme into Shires, and the Shires into Hundreds, and the Hundreds into Lathes or Wapentackes, and the Wapentackes into Tythings'; and the head of each tithing, 'whom they called the Tythingman or Borsholder, that is, the eldest pledge', was required to arrest anyone who misbehaved, or seemed to be about to misbehave.

> And if all that Tything fayled, then all that Lathe was charged for that Tything, and if that Lathe fayled, then all that Hundred was demaunded for them; and if the Hundred, then the Shire, who joyning eftsoones together, would not rest till they had found out and delivered in that undutifull fellow, which was not amesnable to Law.

This was not by any means the only precedent: Moses had organized the Israelites, Romulus had organized the Romans, in a similar way. The important point was that Alfred's policy had succeeded in England, and would, if the experiment were made, succeed in Ireland too.

> By this ordinance, this King brought this Realme of England (which before was most troublesome) unto that quiet State, that no one bad person could stirre, but he was straight taken holde of by those of his owne Tything, and their Borsholder, who being his neighbor or next kinsman was privie to all his wayes, and looked narrowly into his life. The which institution (if it were observed in Ireland) would worke that effect which it did in England, and keep all men within the compasse of dutie and obedience.

Before this 'general reformation' could be brought about, it would be necessary for Ireland to be thoroughly pacified, and then, for some length of time, garrisoned with very large numbers of English troops; but these obstacles did not seem unsurmountable – at least they did not seem so to Irenaeus.

In October 1598 Spenser's home in county Cork was looted and burnt down by not-yet-pacified Irishmen. By December he was back in England; a few weeks later he died.

As a policy proposal, this essay of Spenser's led nowhere. There was never the slightest chance of Irenaeus's plan being put into effect. Even so, in the course of propounding it, Spenser had said many things, about Ireland and about English attitudes towards Ireland, which were, and still are, of interest. The essay circulated in manuscript; it was put into print in 1633;[59] from 1679 onwards it was included in editions of Spenser's collected works. If that had been the end of the story, I would not have thought it worth mentioning. It was not the end of the story.

When Samuel Johnson set about compiling his dictionary, Spenser was one of the authors whose works he read through line by line, looking for words and usages of words

Friborgas (Spelman 1626, p. 365). (It was Spelman's idea to mention the rapes of Sussex in this context.) As far as I know, the quasi-Latin word *latha* was his invention.

[54] That spelling was Lambard's invention: the manuscript he was copying from says *lestum* – and would say *lęstum*, if that were what it meant to say.

[55] *Est portio Comitatus maior, tres vel plures interdum Hundredos continens* (1626, p. 422). Spelman had also seen a Latin-plus-English edition of some ordinances relating to Romney Marsh (below, p. 274), where he found the word *lastum* and found it translated 'assembly'; but he thought that perhaps the translator had been guessing.

[56] Which is reproduced word for word in subsequent editions (1664, 1687).

[57] *Lastum, quandoque Læstum et Lestum, Anglis hodie 'Lath'.*

[58] John Young, bishop of Rochester 1578–1605, previously master of Pembroke College in Cambridge, where Spenser had been a student.

[59] It was edited by a Dublin antiquary, Sir James Ware (1594–1666), from a copy belonging to another Dubliner, James Ussher (1581–1656), archbishop of Armagh. The passages which I have quoted come from this edition (Ware 1633, pp. 100–1, Hadfield and Maley 1997, pp. 136–7), but I have made a few small corrections which seem to be required by the context.

which needed to be taken note of. This essay about Ireland yielded a good crop of words which Johnson had never (or hardly ever) come across before – and one of them was LATH. Checking with Du Cange, he discovered that there was some difference of opinion with regard to the meaning of the word; giving Du Cange the benefit of the doubt (a sensible choice), he defined a lath as 'a part of a county', not as 'a part of a hundred'; but then he quoted the passage he had found in Spenser:

If all that tything failed, then all that lath was charged for that tything; and if the lath failed, then all that hundred was demanded for them; and if the hundred, then the shire, who would not rest till they had found that undutiful fellow, who was not amesnable to law.

Through Johnson (1755), the word LATH entered the lexicographical tradition, trailing behind it this quotation from 'Spenser's *Ireland*'.[60] I leave it to the reader to guess what confusion resulted from that.

(5) Laths in Romney Marsh

The body responsible for supervising Romney Marsh – for making sure that the land was properly drained and yet also properly defended against the sea – was not formally incorporated until the fifteenth century but had existed long before that (Teichman Derville 1936). In the thirteenth century the twenty-four jurats of the Marsh were already claiming that ancient custom gave them the right to decide what work needed to be done, and to apportion the cost of it among everyone who owned a share of the land there. Because this was indeed the custom, and because it seemed expedient for the custom to be maintained, the king and his representatives were ready to back them up.

Meetings of this body were known by a special name. The earliest record of such a meeting that Teichman Derville could discover dates from 1263, and the word used there is *lestum* (or *lestus*): *in pleno lesto apud Snergate*, 'in plenary session at Snargate'.[61] The same word recurs sporadically after that; by the fourteenth century the spelling had shifted to *lastum*. In that form (definitely neuter) the word is used frequently in a set of new regulations drawn up on 12 July 1361, in the presence of three commissioners appointed by the king.[62] There is an annual meeting, *lastum principale*, held at Dymchurch, Newchurch, or some other suitable place, where the bailiff presents his accounts, and where a new bailiff and new jurats are elected when that becomes necessary; there are other meetings too, but we are not told much about them, except that they have sometimes been thinly attended. (In future any jurat who misses the annual meeting will have to pay twelve pence as a penalty; if he misses one of the other meetings, he will have to pay six pence.) A dictionary of medieval Latin, as it was used in England, should certainly include an entry or sub-entry for LASTUM: 'a meeting of the governing body of Romney Marsh'.[63]

William Dugdale, paraphrasing this document in English (1662, pp. 31–3),[64] translated *lastum* as 'last'. Apparently he did not think that any explanation was called for. Just as Lambard had done before in a different context, he took it for granted that anything called a *lastum* in Latin would be called a 'last' in English. Like Lambard, Dugdale was mistaken.[65]

In English, from the sixteenth century onwards, these meetings were called laths. (Normally they were held at Dymchurch, where a hall was built for the purpose.) The earliest surviving original records are the paymaster's accounts for the period 1537–45.[66] These accounts are in English; and the word they use is LATH. In the sixteenth century, as is to be expected, it was often written 'lathe'; but the standardized spelling was 'lath' (Kilburne 1659, p. 75; Hasted 1797–1801, vol. 8, p. 473), and that remained the accepted form of the word until the 1930s.[67] A dictionary of modern English, if it aims to be comprehensive, should certainly include an entry or sub-entry for LATH: 'a meeting of the governing body of Romney Marsh'.[68]

How can this be? If the word is LASTUM in Latin, why is it not LAST in English? If LATH in English, why not LATHUM in Latin? Of course it would not be surprising if a scribe had occasionally misheard or miscopied the word, but that is no answer here. As far as the evidence goes, it is consistent. In Latin records (for as long as records continued to be be written in Latin) the word was always LASTUM. In English records (once records began to be written in English) the word was always LATH.

[60] The only other instance cited by Johnson is a passing reference to 'lath silver' in an essay of Francis Bacon's. The passage can be found – where probably Johnson found it – in *The works of Francis Bacon*, 4 vols. (London, 1730), vol. 3, p. 549.

[61] Teichman Derville 1936, p. 22, from the fifteenth-century cartulary of Horton priory, BL Stowe 935. Another snippet from the same document, *per ballivum lesti marisci*, is quoted elsewhere (p. 11).

[62] Thomas de Lodelowe, Robert Belknap and Thomas Colepeper; their commission was dated 17 February 1361 (*Calendar of patent rolls 1358–61*, p. 585).

[63] Or of some similar body which took its constitution from that one.

[64] Dugdale was using two manuscript copies of the text; it had in fact already been printed twice, by Berthelet (1543b), and again (with an English translation) by Wolfe (1597). The latter edition is the one referred to by Spelman (above, note 55).

[65] As he could have discovered for himself by looking at Kilburne's book (1659, p. 75).

[66] With the other records listed by Teichman Derville (1936), this volume is now in the East Kent Archives Centre, S/Rm/FAe1. I am indebted to Alison Cable for her kindness in consulting the volume and answering my questions about it.

[67] It was Teichman Derville who decided to change it to 'lathe', persuaded (so it seems) by Gordon Ward that this would have been the authentic Old English name (1936, p. 22).

[68] Parish and Shaw (1888, p. 90) have 'LATH, the name of an annual court held at Dymchurch' (for which they cite a newspaper report of one such meeting in 1876). They also have 'LAST, an ancient court in Romney Marsh' (which, though they do not say so, can only have come from Dugdale).

There is, as far as I can judge (I am open to correction), no reason why we should not regard LATH as a continuation of Old English *læð*, predictably altered in form, but not altered in meaning. The noun *læð* means 'a formal meeting of some kind' (above, p. 5). By the twelfth century, we would expect it to have turned into 'leth'; by the fourteenth century, we would expect it to have turned into 'lath'; in the sixteenth century we would expect to find it spelt 'lath' or 'lathe', sometimes without but often with an ornamental 'e' at the end. For lack of evidence, only this last prediction makes contact with reality.

On that interpretation, the Latin word is the puzzle. If this meeting was properly called a lath, why did scribes writing in Latin insist on calling it a *lastum*? From the fact that they did this regularly, I think we can be sure that a lath was regularly called *last* by people who were speaking French – the sort of French, that is, which was used by English lawyers. (Thus, for example, the phrase quoted above, *in pleno lesto apud Snergate*, is only Latin on the surface: underneath it is French, *en plein lest a Snergate*.) But that only gives us a different view of the puzzle, and does not bring us any closer to solving it.

I can only suppose that the confusion between 'lest' and 'leth', as it affected the name of the divisions of the county (above, p. 7), had resulted in some unconscious rationalization. What was properly called a lest was already so generally called a leth (in English but not in French) that what was properly called a leth began to be called a lest (in French but not in English). By the thirteenth century, it seems, people had come round to assuming that 'leth' could only be an English word, that 'lest' could only be a French word, and that the two words, in every context, were exactly equivalent in meaning.

Appendix I
Lambeth Palace Library MS. 1212 and the lost cartulary of Christ Church, Canterbury*

Lambeth Palace Library 1212 is a large and very impressive register which originated in the archbishop's treasury at Canterbury (Du Boulay 1966, pp. 4–9). The bulk of it was written in the 1270s; but one portion of it is earlier than that, and there are numerous additions as well, some of them as late as the 1320s. As is proved by a note in this manuscript (fo. 64v), the treasury was housed in Saint Gregory's priory, outside the north gate of the city. It was the treasurer and his staff who had custody of the archbishop's archive, and the documents copied into this register were mostly kept there.

The book has a complicated history. Before it became a book, Lambeth 1212 was a collection of separate booklets, made up of separate quires. Some of the quires became transposed, while they remained unbound; but these rearrangements can very easily be reversed, thanks to the clerk who numbered the leaves (writing small arabic numerals at the top centre of each recto page) before they started happening. If the quires are put back into the sequence they were in at the moment when the leaves were numbered, the result will look something like Table 22.[1] Since that moment, one quire (*q*) has been moved; one quire (*c*) has been taken apart; and two quires (*1* and *r*) have each been inserted into a preceding quire (*1* into *k*, *r* into *p*). It also emerges that one whole quire (between *u* and *w*) has been lost. Essentially this was all worked out by Holtzmann (1930–1, pp. 197–9).

One of the booklets which came to be included in Lambeth 1212 is a portion of an earlier register (quires *k–1*), a rather elegant piece of work, obviously distinct from the rest. Perhaps this booklet originated in the treasury; at least it is clear that the scribe who compiled it was somebody who had access to the archbishop's archive. What it contains is a collection of charters dating from between the 1070s and the 1220s; but the script is thought to be appreciably later than that, perhaps *c.* 1240–50.[2] The booklet owes its survival to the fact that it was subsequently used (apparently on just one occasion) as a guide-book for a search of the archive. Against many of the entries a note has been added recording that the search was successful (*Hec inuenitur*, 'This is still there'); against one (fo. 105r), a note recording that it was not (*Hec deest*, 'This is missing'). In one of the other booklets, a paragraph added at the foot of the page (fo. 30v) ends with a note explaining that there is a problem with this document: the sealed original is not available, and the text has been copied instead from an 'old register'.[3] As Major (1950, p. 159) observed, that seems sure to be a reference to quires *k–l*, where the text in question is indeed to be found (fo. 104r).

Though I have not looked at the palaeographical evidence as closely as it deserves, it seems to me that in scanning through Lambeth 1212 one soon begins to recognize the work of four successive groups of scribes, associated (as the documents they copied prove) with four successive archbishops: Robert Kilwardby (1273–8), Johan Pecham (1279–92), Robert Winchelsey (1294–1313), Walter Reynolds (1313–27). Apparently this has to mean that the staff of the treasury (the clerical staff at least) was replaced whenever the archbishopric changed hands: the treasury clerks were appointed by the archbishop, and their tenure ended with the death (or resignation) of the archbishop who had made the appointment. The only official whose name had much chance of being recorded was the treasurer himself; and it does seem to be arguable – from the data collected by Du Boulay (1966, pp. 396–8) – that each new archbishop appointed a new treasurer.[4] The script differs, from one group of scribes to the next; so does the level of competence, as far as one can judge of it from the work that they did here. To put it briefly, Kilwardby's clerks were excellent; Pecham's were pretty bad; Winchelsey's were pretty good; Reynolds's were mediocre.

The bulk of Lambeth 1212 was obviously the work of a team of scribes working for archbishop Kilwardby. In

* This paper was written several years ago, and I had hoped that it would have been published long before now. Since it has not, I print a revised version of it here.

[1] In constructing this table I have had to depend on the collation reported by James (1932, pp. 828–9), which, in a few places, does not add up correctly; so a small amount of guesswork is involved. The modern foliation suffers from one hiccup: four numbers (151–4) were accidentally repeated.

[2] This is the date suggested by Major (1950, p. 158). For the rest of Lambeth 1212, the date she suggested was 'probably about 1260–70', but this estimate errs slightly on the early side, as the contents prove (Du Boulay 1966, p. 5).

[3] *Hec non habetur sigillata set transcripta est de regestro ueteri inter cartas Iohannis regis.* The original was later discovered to be in the bishop of Rochester's archive, and a note to this effect was added by a different hand: *Istud originale remanet penes episcopum Roffensem.*

[4] Kilwardby's treasurer was Thomas de Lindestede: a copy of a letter addressed to him occurs in Lambeth 1212 (fo. 206r).

quires	medieval foliation	17th-century pagination	modern foliation	booklets
a–b		1–12	1–6	
c	1–13	14–18, 25–48, 19–22	8–10, 14–26, 11–12	royal charters
d	14–25	49–74	27–39	
e	26–33	75–92	40–8	non-royal charters
f	34–41	93–108	49–56	
g	42–53	109–30	57–67	
h	54–64	131–54	68–79	agreements
i	65–74	155–74	80–90	
j	75–8	176–85	92–6	
k	79–86	186–93, 218–25	97–100, 113–16	'old register'
l	87–99	194–217	101–12	
m	100–3	226–33	117–20	
n	106–17	234–59	121–33	papal letters
o	118–26	260–77	134–42	
p	127–34	278–85, 294–301	143–6, 151–4	
q	135–49	376–409	188–204	'landbooks'
r	150–3	286–93	147–50	
s	154–65	304–27	152A–4A, 155–63	copy of 'old book'
t	166–77	328–51	164–75	
u	178–89	352–75	176–87	
[*v*]	[190–203]			
w	204–14	410–31	205–15	memoranda (cont.)

Table 22. Quires of Lambeth 1212 restored to the order determined by the medieval foliation.

booklet after booklet, the original text ends in the mid 1270s; all documents later than the 1270s are more or less obviously the work of different scribes. When Kilwardby's clerks took over the treasury, in 1273, they were appalled by the state that the archive was in at the time. (They may have been too polite to say so, but their actions express their sentiments plainly enough.) Nobody really knew what charters and other documents ought to exist, or where they were to be found. Over the next few years, Kilwardby's clerks brought order out of chaos. They tracked down the originals, classified them, numbered them, transcribed them, and finally deposited them in their proper place, within the storage system that they had devised.[5] As was first discovered by Collins (1948, p. 241), the few originals which still survive have numbers on their backs which resulted from this reorganization of the archive; but the principal product was Lambeth 1212 itself – or, to be more precise, the collection of booklets from which Lambeth 1212 was assembled later. This is where the treasury clerks made their copies of all important documents, so that in future they could consult them here, without having to handle the originals.

Kilwardby's clerks were the authors of Lambeth 1212. The idea, the design, the execution – all were due to them. How many hands were at work I cannot say. The stretch of text which I have looked at most closely (see below) was written, as far as I can tell, by just two scribes; but I am doubtful whether that is true for every booklet. By and large, the scribes involved were following a standard procedure. They used gatherings of twelve leaves each, ruled for roughly forty lines per page, with wide margins for any annotation which might be needed. In some places, where the nature of the text invited it, they used a columnar format;[6] but most of the time they wrote across the whole width of the page. Every document they chose to transcribe was transcribed in full. A short description of it was entered in a table of contents, keyed to a marginal number in the main text, and a note was added stating where the original was to be found. The classification imposed on the archive is reflected in the organization of Lambeth 1212. There is a separate booklet for each of four classes of formal documents: one for royal charters (*Carte regum*), one for non-royal charters (*Carte aliorum quam regum*), one for agreements (*Composiciones*), and one for papal letters (*Priuilegia et bulle*). Within each booklet the scribes brought the record up to date; in some of the booklets they started making additions,[7] as batches of incoming documents were delivered

[5] The new organization of the archive, so far as it can be reconstructed from marginal notes in Lambeth 1212, is described by Sayers (1966, pp. 98–9).

[6] One such page (fo. 170r) is reproduced by Hoyt (1962, pl. XIV).

[7] Sayers (1966) overlooked this point. Since some of the documents in question date from very near the end of Kilwardby's time in office, and since she was mistakenly regarding them as part of the original text, she thought it likely that Lambeth 1212 was compiled by the clerks who arrived with Kilwardby's successor.

to the treasury. The intention was for each separate booklet to continue expanding indefinitely in the future, new quires being added at the end whenever necessary. But that plan was brought to a sudden end, in spring 1278, when the news arrived of Kilwardby's transfer to Rome.[8]

All in all, the manuscript covers a lot of ground, and different parts of it will be of interest to different people. For anyone interested in the pre-conquest history of Christ Church, the most immediately relevant booklet is the one which forms most of quire *q* (fos. 191–204).[9] Originally this was a quire of 12 (fos. 192–203), and the final leaf (fo. 204) was the start of a second quire. (There is a catchword to prove it at the foot of fo. 203v.) Before the scribe had filled this leaf (before he had even started on the verso, in fact), a change of plan supervened and the booklet was discontinued. The unused sheets of the second quire were removed; the outermost sheet was kept, folded back to front, and wrapped around the first quire, so as to turn it into a quire of 14 (fos. 191–204). The blank leaf thus brought to the front was used for the table of contents (fo. 191v), and for adding one more document (fo. 191r). For the heading we have to look at what was initially the first page of the first quire (fo. 192r). It reads: *Transcripta de codicellis primariis siue cartis terrarum antiquitus dictis landboc*, 'Copies of original documents or land charters (which in English were) anciently called "land books" '. More than twenty documents follow,[10] all of them (so it appears) copied word for word directly from the originals in the Christ Church archive. In the majority of cases, the originals are still in existence; and Lambeth 1212's copies are then of no value, except as proof that such documents were thought to be of some interest at the time, and as a means of assessing the scribe's accuracy. For several charters, however, Lambeth 1212's copy is the only one, or the only one which gives the text in full.[11] As far as I have checked his work, the scribe appears to have been honest and accurate enough (except that he did not hesitate to modernize the spelling). He is, of course, not answerable for the authenticity of the documents he copied, only for his transcription.

The following booklet (quires *r–u*) is the one which I have looked at most closely. It consists of three quires of 12 leaves each (fos. 152A–4A, 155–87), prefaced by a quire of 4 for the table of contents (fos. 147–50). Quire *r* was transposed, after 1323 (see below), and the table thus became separated from the booklet to which it relates. The text is the work of two scribes, both of them highly competent. Scribe 1 wrote the whole of the main text (beginning on fo. 152Ar and ending on fo. 184v), with (so far as I have checked his transcription) very few mistakes; he left spaces for coloured initials, but these were never supplied.[12] Scribe 2 added much peripheral material – headings, marginal notes, and the whole of the table of contents (fos. 147r–8v). This second scribe was evidently very familiar with the material, and I would guess that he had supervised the project throughout, intervening personally towards the end to add these finishing touches.[13]

The contents fall into three sections. The first and largest (ending on fo. 177r) is (1) a copy of the Christ Church cartulary which I call C3, and which I propose to discuss in some detail below. That occupies the whole of the first two quires and overlaps into the beginning of the third. Leaving one page blank (which means, 'And now for something completely different'), the same scribe resumes by copying out (2) a series of documents relating to the financial affairs of Christ Church. The first of these (fos. 178r–80v) is the report of an investigation into the costs involved in maintaining the army of servants employed by the monks; that investigation took place, we are told, in 1276–7. To this is appended a batch of shorter memoranda (fos. 181r–2v) bearing on other aspects of the priory's cash-flow.[14] Leaving another page blank (which carries the same message as before), the scribe continues by entering (3) a list of the churches and other benefices in the archbishop's gift (fos. 183v–4v); a note at the foot of the first page tells us that this list reflects the situation existing in 1272–3, when Kilwardby first arrived.[15] A note added at the end of this list is a specimen of the work of Pecham's clerks (fo. 184v). The remaining pages (fos. 185r–7v), originally left blank, were filled up later with additions by Winchelsey's clerks; blank spaces in the preliminary quire were also made use of by them (fos. 148v–9r), and by Reynolds's clerks after that (fos. 149v–50v).

This addition by Reynolds's clerks – which consists of extracts from the proceedings of the Exchequer in September and October 1323 – is of some incidental interest, because it helps to explicate the sequence of events which turned the original collection of booklets into the existing book. The text continues from the last page of quire *r* (fo. 150v) onto an added leaf at the front of quire *s* (fo. 151A). It was not until after that, therefore, that quire *r* became transposed (in consequence of which a marginal note was added on

[8] Kilwardby resigned the archbishopric in June 1278, after being made cardinal bishop of Porto. (He died at Viterbo in September 1279.)

[9] The three preceding leaves (fos. 188–190) seem all to be singletons, technically part of this quire but not part of the booklet.

[10] In Sawyer's (1968, p. 58) list of the contents of Lambeth 1212, this booklet begins with no. 230 and ends at the end with no. 981. The added document on fo. 191r is Sawyer's no. 50.

[11] In Sawyer's list (see previous note), the items not marked with a dagger are mostly known from the copy in Lambeth 1212 alone.

[12] The missing letter is written in this space, in small script, as a cue for the rubricator. Perhaps the intention was for the coloured initials all to be inserted at once when the booklet had expanded to the point that it was ready to be bound.

[13] It is conceivable that scribe 2 was the treasurer himself, whose name is known (above, note 4). I do not press the point.

[14] The titles are listed by James (1932, p. 833).

[15] He was consecrated in February 1273, still 1272 by the thirteenth-century reckoning. Some entries in this list have been updated by later scribes – the entry relating to Wingham, for example, against which someone has scribbled the remark *Mutata in prepositturam et sex prebendas*, 'Changed into a provostship and six prebends' (fo. 183v). That plan originated with Kilwardby; Pecham brought it to fruition (Fowler 1926, p. 233).

fo. 150v referring to fo. 151A as 'the fifth following leaf'), and not until after that that Lambeth 1212 was bound.[16] Perhaps the binding was done by Reynolds's clerks, the last who made any significant additions to it; perhaps it was done by the clerks who arrived with the next archbishop, Simon Meopham. It happens to be a known fact that Meopham's clerks reorganized the archive again (Churchill 1929; Sayers 1966, pp. 99–101), and that might explain why they took no interest in Lambeth 1212 – no active interest, at least. Whoever made the decision, the upshot was that the existing quires in their existing order – quire *v* had gone astray, quires *k–l* had been included – were delivered to the binder, and the binder turned them into a book. Lambeth 1212 ceased to be a living record. Bound and shelved, it became a book of reference, more and more out of date as time passed by.[17]

It remained at Canterbury at least until the 1540s – somebody copying extracts from it then referred to it as 'the old white book' (Barnes 1959, p. 59) – but not long after that it became a collector's item. For a time it must have belonged to Lord Lumley (d. 1609), whose name is written at the foot of the first page; then it was acquired by Archbishop Bancroft (d. 1610) for the library which he was creating at Lambeth Palace. In 1648 that library was shut down, and its books were transferred to Cambridge; in 1664 they were returned to Lambeth Palace; by then, it seems, this particular book had gone missing. Since it turns up next in the library of Roydon Hall (in East Peckham, Kent), we have to infer that it was appropriated by Sir Roger Twysden (d. 1672).[18] In December 1681, without doubt, it belonged to Twysden's son Sir William Twysden (d. 1697): that is when Sir William's librarian numbered the pages (and wrote a note on a flyleaf saying that he had done so). Fifteen years after Sir William's death, the title, house and estate (as much as was left of it) were inherited by his younger son and namesake, Sir William Twysden (d. 1751). Soon after that, the Roydon Hall library was put up for sale; and by March 1715 it had been bought by Sir Thomas Saunders Sebright (1692–1736), of Beechwood (in Flamstead, Hertfordshire).[19] During Sir Thomas's time, the Twysden manuscripts were fairly easy to get at – Hearne (1719) and Wilkins (1721) both thank him for access to them – but after that they seem to have dropped out of sight. Finally, in April 1807, part of the Beechwood library was sold by auction (Leigh and Sotheby 1807), and that is when three of the Twysden manuscripts, including this one, were acquired for Lambeth Palace Library.[20] There it was re-accessioned as manuscript 1212.

The lost Christ Church cartulary

The medieval archive of Christ Church contained a very large number of pre-conquest charters. Many of these documents survive. Some are still in Canterbury; some were acquired by early modern collectors of medieval manuscripts. A few more are known to have existed in the seventeenth century and have only gone missing since then. Reassembled as far as it can be, this collection of documents forms the chief source of evidence for working out the early history of the church (Brooks 1969, 1984, 1995).[21]

As well as preserving the originals, the monks used them for compiling a cartulary, and this too is a significant text, in more than one respect. It is important, most obviously, because it includes edited versions of several documents which do not survive in any other form. But it is also important in itself, as an example of the sort of archival research which medieval monks might think of undertaking. It has generally been called a cartulary, and I see no objection to that name; but I think that it might better be described as a calendar, at least in its original form. In this form the text, whatever we call it, was meant to serve as a guide to the contents of the church's archive. By its nature it was a composite text, pieced together from many others; but it was also (originally) a single text, compiled on one occasion for one purpose. It needs to be treated as such, and evaluated as such, before being decompiled. Here I am echoing the opinion expressed by Fleming (1997, pp. 85–6), which seems to me exactly right.[22]

[16] A marginal note on the last page of quire *p* (fo. 154v) refers to the second leaf in quire *r* (fo. 148) as 'the second following leaf'. That note must have been made before quire *r* was transposed; but it cannot have been made till after quire *q* had been transposed, and that did not happen till after the leaves had been numbered. If the text which continues from the last page of quire *u* (fo. 187v) onto the first page of quire *q* (fo. 188r), is, as I suppose, the work of one of Winchelsey's clerks, it will follow that the foliation is earlier than 1313.

[17] In the early sixteenth century, somebody went to the trouble of making a copy of Lambeth 1212, reorganizing the contents to some extent; the resulting manuscript is Oxford, Bodleian Tanner 223 (which I have not seen). That this manuscript was copied directly from Lambeth 1212 is a well-established fact (Collins 1948, pp. 240–1; Major 1950, p. 158; Kreisler 1967, pp. iii–iv); so it has no textual value. The only question worth asking, it seems, is why the copy was made.

[18] Twysden was detained at Lambeth (where the palace had ceased to be a palace and become a prison) in 1643–5.

[19] News of the sale reached the Earl of Oxford's librarian, Humfrey Wanley. At first it was thought possible that only the printed books had been sold and that the Twysden manuscripts might still be available; but that hope was quickly dashed (Wright and Wright 1966, pp. 3–4).

[20] The three manuscripts in question are nos. 1211–13 (Todd 1812, p. 264): 1211 (a Qur'an obtained from Istanbul by Sir Paul Pindar as a present for Sir William Twysden, Roger's father) was lot 1149; 1212 was lot 1220; 1213 (James 1932, pp. 834–40) was lot 1192. I am grateful to Ms Emily Walhout of the Houghton Library at Harvard for a photocopy of the sale catalogue, and to the Lambeth Palace librarian, Dr Richard Palmer, for confirming these identifications.

[21] I am indebted to Professor N. P. Brooks for a copy of those sections of his thesis which relate to the Christ Church cartulary, and for his comments on a draft of the present paper.

[22] But I cannot speak at all favourably of her edition (Fleming 1997, pp. 109–52). For each paragraph, Fleming seems to have started with a transcript of T1, and then to have overwritten this with a transcript of C5, so far as C5 is legible. The justification for that procedure escapes me. In any case, though Fleming's text may be useful – if one ignores the editorial clutter – in forming a rough idea of the contents of C3/C5 (as far as the end of C3/A1), it is not to be relied on in detail. Neither the transcription nor the collation approaches the level of accuracy which ought to be aimed for, given all the technical advantages that a modern editor enjoys.

The original, which I call C3, was still in existence in the late thirteenth century, but has disappeared since then. It has to be reconstructed from three surviving copies:

A1 = Cambridge, Corpus Christi College 189, fos. 195–201 plus part of another leaf, 11 × 7.5 inches (Davis 1958, no. 163); from Saint Augustine's, later twelfth century. Printed in full by Twysden (1652, cols. 2207–26)

C5 = Canterbury Cathedral Archives, Reg. P, fos. 11–34, 7.5 × 5 inches (Davis 1958, no. 163A); from Christ Church, early thirteenth century

T1 = London, Lambeth Palace Library 1212, fos. 147–50, 152A–4A, 155–77, 12.5 × 9 inches (Davis 1958, no. 159); from the archbishop's treasury, circa 1275. Many paragraphs printed, in disconnected form, by Kemble (1848), Haddan and Stubbs (1871), Birch (1885–93), and others

As far as I can see, the textual evidence is consistent with the view that all three copies derive independently from C3. At least it is certain that C5 does not derive from A1, and that T1 does not derive from either A1 or C5.

The earliest manuscript, A1, consists of a single quire, bound up as part of a book which came, without any doubt, from Saint Augustine's.[23] At first sight it may seem surprising to find a copy of a Christ Church cartulary here, but I see no reason not to think that A1 was written by a scribe from Saint Augustine's, given access to the original. One detail tending to confirm this is the fact that in A1 (and A1 alone) Saint Augustine's name is written in capital letters, wherever it occurs. The manuscript dates from the second half of the twelfth century.[24] It is a neat piece of work, in the same hand throughout, and in good condition; its defect is that it gives only an abbreviated version of the text. Most paragraphs have been shortened, more or less drastically. It also turns out, from collation with the other manuscripts, that A1's text, even where it is unabridged, is not particularly accurate.

C5 is the worst copy in some respects, in others perhaps the best. With the rest of the register in which it was eventually bound, this booklet suffered damage around the edges in the Canterbury fire of 1670, and parts of the text were destroyed or rendered illegible. Even in an undamaged condition, C5 would not have inspired much admiration. The text, by a single scribe throughout, is very untidily written. Spelling mistakes and other small slips are numerous. On the other hand, there do not seem to be many large errors. For all his faults, the scribe does appear to have been capable of copying correctly, so far as the substance was concerned. The dating of C5 is uncertain; opinions vary between the late twelfth and the early thirteenth century.[25] I am inclined to think that C5 may be later than it looks. The scribe who wrote it was, I suspect, not accustomed to writing the formal sort of script that he uses here, and had to make a special effort. Now and then, his script begins to sprout curlicues which look as if they might date, say, from *c.* 1220–40; but then (so it seems) the scribe remembers his instructions and reverts to a laboured imitation of a plain twelfth-century script. For present purposes, the dating of C5 does not need to be exactly determined; but eventually it would be good to know, not just when, but also why and for whom this copy was being made.

T1 is the latest but in detail often the most reliable copy. Unlike A1 and C5, which can only be dated approximately, from the style of the script, T1 can be dated precisely. Together with most of the rest of Lambeth 1212, this booklet resulted from a burst of activity in the mid 1270s, while Robert Kilwardby was archbishop (see above). The locus for this activity was the archbishop's treasury in Canterbury, the staff of which had access to the Christ Church archive (the collection of documents of which the monks had custody) as well as to the separate archive for which they themselves were responsible. As has been said already, two scribes worked on this copy. Scribe 1 wrote the whole of the main text, numbering the paragraphs as he went along; scribe 2 added headings and notes, made corrections here and there, and wrote the table of contents. Among his other contributions, this second scribe supplied a title for the text, *Memoranda cartarum et conciliorum Arch' C' et ecc'e Cant'*, 'Memoranda of charters and councils of the archbishopric and church of Canterbury', and specified the exemplar from which it was taken, *Transcripta de veteri libro Cantuar'*, 'Copied from an old Canterbury book' (fo. 152Ar). This 'old book' was presumably C3 itself, made available to the archbishop's officials, perhaps released to them on loan.

As evidence for reconstructing C3, this third and last copy suffers from one major disadvantage, because here, with the best of intentions, the contents were quite extensively rearranged. In A1 and C5 the order of the paragraphs is identical; and by inference that was the order existing in C3. Plainly enough the intention had been for the documents to be arranged in chronological sequence, but in C3 that intention was only imperfectly realized. In T1 an effort was made to improve the order, where it was obviously wrong, but again the attempt was only partially successful. At the end of paragraph 48, there is a note added by scribe 2 saying that this entry ought to have been placed further on, *Istud debet esse infra Dccccxii* (fo. 161r); there is a matching note at the end of paragraph 65, *Hic debet esse quod est supra xlviii* (fo. 163r). These notes seem to prove that it was the scribes working on T1 who were responsible for re-

[23] This book contains the manuscript of Willelm Thorne's chronicle of Saint Augustine's, written in the 1390s. A section of Thorne's narrative (Twysden 1652, col. 1772) is derived from a text that occurs in A1 (Fleming 1997, pp. 114–15); apparently that is the reason why A1 got bound up here.

[24] Fleming (1997, p. 86), following Brooks (1969), dates A1 to the mid twelfth century, *c.* 1150. I am not well acquainted with manuscripts from Saint Augustine's (I do not know, for instance, when scribes there stopped writing *ę* and started invariably writing *e*, as the A1 scribe does), but on general grounds would prefer a rather later date, perhaps *c.* 1160–80.

[25] This booklet was dated to the later twelfth century by Urry (1967, p. 75), whose opinion is not lightly to be disregarded.

organizing the contents, and for numbering the paragraphs accordingly.[26]

As well as the abbreviation peculiar to A1 and the rearrangement peculiar to T1, a comparison between the three manuscripts elicits one other large fact. The text appears to have expanded over time. Every document appearing in A1 appears also in C5 and T1 (often in a longer form); every document appearing in C5 appears also in T1. On the other hand, there are several documents included in the later copies which do not appear in the earliest one, several more included in the latest copy which do not appear in the earlier ones.[27] I see no reason for resisting the obvious conclusion. If the original survived, it would, I suppose, display the same sort of appearance which is observable in Lambeth 1212, and in many other books of similar type, where documents were continually being added, singly or in batches, over some more or less protracted span of time. In the absence of the original, we catch only accidental glimpses of this process of accretion, as successive copies (A1, C5, T1) record successive moments in the evolution of the exemplar (C3/A1, C3/C5, C3/T1).[28] The contents of C3, in state C3/C5, are listed in Table 23. What happened to C3, after the 1270s, we have no means of knowing.

Of C3's format – the size of the pages, the arrangement of the text, the quantity of decoration – I have not been able to discover any definite hint. The only copy which may possibly have been meant to resemble the original in general appearance is C5. We might venture to suppose, in a tentative way, that C3 looked like a handsomer version of C5. In all three copies, space is left for a coloured initial at the start of each new paragraph; in all three copies, these spaces remain blank. On the assumption that anything true for every copy was true for the exemplar too, no doubt we shall think it safe to infer that C3 was meant to be adorned with coloured initials; whether we go so far as to infer that the initials were missing there too is a more delicate question.

[26] In two places a paragraph was overlooked, and had to be added (by scribe 1) in the margin. At the foot of fo. 164v is a paragraph (Sawyer no. 959) marked for insertion between paragraphs 76 and 77. At the foot of fo. 165v is an explanatory remark (Sawyer no. 1647) which ought to be attached, as it is in C5, to paragraph 83.

[27] To be precise, there are eight documents absent from A1 which are present in C5 and T1 (Table 24). Taking them one by one, we cannot hope to say for certain whether the document was omitted from A1, accidentally or on purpose, or whether it was added to C3 after A1 had been copied off. For methodological reasons, the latter view is the one that we ought to prefer (because it is more conservative): any document in this category is to be regarded as an interpolation or addition in C3/C5 unless somebody can show some good reason for thinking otherwise. (To make the case, a two-pronged argument is needed: it has to be shown that the document in question is rather unlikely to have been omitted from C3 but rather likely to have been omitted from A1. The arguments sketched out by Fleming (1997, pp. 89–90) seem inadequate to me.) The same considerations apply to those documents absent from A1 and C5 but present in T1 (Table 25).

[28] I use a simplified notation here, citing just the earliest copy for each state of the text. Written out in full, the notation would be C3/A1C5T1, C3/C5T1, C3/T1.

As far as the text is concerned, the earliest state which we can hope to visualize is C3/A1, the state existing when the earliest copy was made. But I think it is clear that C3/A1 was already some distance away from the original, say C3/0. It ends with two post-conquest documents – one charter of Henric I, one of archbishop Anselm – which seem so out of keeping with the compiler's purpose (so far as we can judge of it from the rest of the text) that they are fairly sure to have been added by somebody else.[29] Because we are working from copies, not from C3 itself, we cannot expect it to be easy to decide why and when C3 was first put together. One document included in C3/A1 – an uninspired piece of pseudo-historical narrative purporting to explain why the archbishops ceased being buried at Saint Augustine's and began being buried at Christ Church – is, if I read it correctly, unlikely to be earlier than the 1090s; but if anyone wished to suggest that this document was an interpolation in C3/A1, not properly part of C3/0, there would be no means of disproving that suggestion. Similarly, one recurrent feature of the C3/A1 text, the use of the formula 'primate of the whole of Britain', has been taken to imply that C3 cannot be earlier than the 1070s. For myself I do not doubt that. But if anyone wished to suggest that this formula is the leitmotiv of an interpolator (who, hypothetically, worked his way through C3/0 inserting the words *primas totius Britanniae* wherever he found a suitable context for them), again there would not be any means of disproving that suggestion.

It is not impossible that some early version of C3 was compiled in the time of archbishop Lanfranc (1070–1089), when a text like C3 would arguably have had some usefulness; and Fleming claims to have proved that this was the case. Her principal argument (Fleming 1997, p. 105) is that C3 must have been compiled before 1083 because, if he had been at work after that, the compiler would have included a paragraph mentioning the donations of queen Mathildis (who died in November that year). But this argument will only hold if we think it safe to disregard two other possibilities. First, the compiler may have been deliberately confining his attention to documents earlier than some cut-off date – 1066, 1070, or any other cut-off which would have excluded queen Mathildis. Second, he may have failed to complete his task. If we think it at all conceivable either that the compiler was not intending to cover the recent past, or that he was intending to do so but failed to reach his target, we are not going to be persuaded by Fleming's argument. The conclusion may perhaps be right, but this attempt to prove it falls short.[30]

[29] Professor Brooks suggests to me that the internal analysis of C3/A1 can be taken further than this, if one looks at the typology of the entries. I am inclined to agree; but I would prefer to see the text of C3 formally reconstructed before pursuing this line of investigation. As Fleming (1997, p. 103) points out, to understand the compiler's purpose one needs to understand not only why certain documents were included, but also why certain other documents, which presumably might have been, were not. That again is a question which I would prefer to postpone.

[30] Fleming (1997, pp. 100–1) has a second argument, more involved but no more convincing, which aims to prove that C3 was compiled before the

A1	C5	T1	number in T1	Birch	Sawyer	Fleming	
	11r	152Ar	1			1	Jaffé 1885–8, no. 1998
195r	11r	152Ar	2		1609	2	
195r	11r–v	152Ar	3		8	3	
195r	11v	152Ar–v	4		230	4	
195r	11v	152Av	5		1610	5	
195r	11v–12r	152Av	6		19	6	
195r–v	12r–13r	153Av–4Ar	9		22	7	
195v	13r	154Ar	10	161	1611	8	
195v–6r	13r–v	154Ar	11		90	9	
196r–v	13v–14v	154Av–5r	12			10	Twysden 1652, cols. 2209–11
196v	14v	155r	13	173	1612	11	
196v	14v	155r	15	243	38	12	
196v	14v–15r	155r	16	301	1613	13	
196v–7r	15r–v	155v–6r	19	290		14	
197r	15v	156v–7r	21	294	155	15	
197r	15v–16r	157r	22	320	1259	16	
197r	16r	157v	24		160	17	
197r	16r	155r	14	215	111	18	
197r–8r	16r–17r	158r–9r	33	385	1436	19	
198r	17r–v	157v	25	323	1615	20	
198r	17v	157v	26	329	1616	21	
198r	17v	157v	27	336	1617	22	
198r–v	17v–18r	158r	28	345	1618	23	
198v	18r	158r	29	347	175	24	
198v	18r	158r	30	367	1619	25	
198v	18r	158r	31	371	186	26	
198v	18r	158r	32	372	1620	27	
198v	18r	159r	34	374	187	28	
198v	18v	159r	35	382	1621	29	cf. Sawyer nos. 1266, 1264
198v	18v	159r	36	401	188	30	
198v–9r	18v–19r	159v	37	402	1414	31	
199r	19r–v	159v–60r	38	408	1623	32	
199r	19v	160r	40	422	1438	33	
199r	19v	160r	41	427	1625	34	
199r	19v	160r	42	420	286	35	
199r–v	19v	160r	43	446	1626	36	
199v	20r	160v	44	572	1627	37	
199v	20r	160v	45	578	1628	38	
199v	20r	160v	46	637	1629	39	
199v	20r	161r	50	733	1209	40	
199v	20v–1r	155v	18		132	41	
199v–200r	21r	155r–v	17	263	1614	42	
200r	21r	160v–1r	47		398	43	
200r	21r–v	161r	51	747	1210	44	
200r	21v	161v	54	861	537	45	
200r	21v	161v	55	881	546	46	
200r	21v	161v	56	176	31	47	
200r	21v–2r	161r–v	52	766	477	48	
200r–v	22r	161v–2r	57	1038	1632	49	
200v	22r	162r	58	1049	1633	50	
200v	22r–3r	162r–v	59	1065	1212	51	two paragraphs run together
200v	23r	162v	60	1065	1212	52	by Kemble (1848)
200v	23r	163r	63		1636	53	
200v	23r	163r	64		1503	54	
200v	23r–v	163r–v	67		1378	55	
200v	23v	163v	68		1638	56	
200v	23v	163v	69		905	57	
200v	23v	160r	39	414	1624	58	
200v	23v–4r	161r	48		1639	59	
200v	24r	161r	49	698	1630	60	
200v–1r	24r	162v	61	1102	1634	61	
201r	24r	162v–3r	62	1126	1635	62	
201r	24r	164v	72		1640	63	
	24r–v	164v	75		952	64	
201r	24v	164v	73		1641	65	
201r	24v	164v	74		950	66	
201r	24v	164v	76		1642	67	
201r	24v	164v–5r	77		1222	68	
201r	24v	165r	78		1221	69	
	24v–5v	163v–4r	70		914	70	
201r	25v	164r–v	71		1218	71	
201r	25v	163r	65		1637	72	

A1	C5	T1	number in T1	Birch	Sawyer	Fleming	
201r	25v–6r	163r	66		1646	73	
201r	26r	165r	80		1643	74	
201r–v	26r	165r–v	82		1089	75	
201v	26r–v	165v	83		1047	76–7	cf. Sawyer no. 1647
201v	26v	166r	86		1090	78	
201v	26v	165v	84		1645	79	
201v	26v–7r	165v–6r	85		1530	80	
201v	27r	161v	53	823	1631	81	
201v	27r	165r	79		1389	82	
201v	27r	165r	81		1644	83	
	27r–v	157r–v	23	311		84	
	27v–8r	156r–v	20	291	1258	85	
201v	28r–v	164v	[76 bis]		959	86	
	28v	167v–8r	99			87	*Hee sunt consuetudines . . .*
201v	28v	166v	94			88	Johnson and Cronne 1956, no. 756
201v	28v–9r	166v	95			89	Brett and Gribbin 2004, no. 16
	29r–v	170r	103				*De Derenta, ii sull'*
	29v–33r	170r–2r					Rex tenet Derteford

Table 23. Contents of C3 in its early thirteenth-century state (C3/C5).

It seems to me, however, that C3 is later than that. The argument which I propose to make depends on finding an answer to this question: when did it become the official theory that Christ Church had been – not just ought to have been but actually had been – served by monks throughout its history? This is a complicated question: to discuss it in full would mean discussing various annalistic texts and various forgeries, the dating of which is hardly any easier to settle than the dating of C3. But there is a short cut. We can get some way towards an answer by looking at Willelm of Malmesbury's *Gesta pontificum*, and at the alterations which Willelm made in his text between the 1120s and the 1140s. By a stroke of good luck, the autograph manuscript survives: we can see directly what erasures and additions were made. From the copies that were taken from this manuscript from time to time, we can restore the passages which Willelm decided later to suppress, and we can work out the sequence of the changes that he made.[31]

Writing in the 1120s, Willelm was unaware of the theory that Christ Church had always been, had never not been, inhabited by monks. On the contrary, his understanding was that the monks had been brought in by archbishop Ælfric (995–1005), the clerks who were there previously having been evicted to make way for them. He had only one sentence to say about archbishop Ælfric, and this was the substance of it.[32] As I read the evidence, that is the fact of the matter – the clerks were indeed thrown out, and Ælfric was indeed the man who did it – and Willelm had not yet been persuaded to see things differently. In the 1140s, however, this passage was extensively rewritten.[33] 'What some people say' about Ælfric, that he threw out the clerks and replaced them with monks (here Willelm is quoting himself), appears, he says now, 'unlikely to be true' (he does not positively say that it is false), because it is a known fact that there have been monks at Christ Church since the time of archbishop Laurence. As proof of this he refers his readers to the letter from pope Bonifacius to king Ethelbert which they will find quoted below (ed. Hamilton 1870, pp. 46–7), the same letter which forms the first paragraph in C3/C5. This is one of the batch of Christ Church forgeries which Willelm had obligingly included in the first edition of his book, back in the 1120s. Even if it were genuine, however, the letter would not prove the point. It would prove that king Ethelbert had intended to establish a community of monks, and that the pope had approved of his plan; but it would not prove that Ethelbert's intention was realized – still less that the community survived without interruption

foundation of Saint Gregory's church – earlier, therefore, than 1085, by which time Saint Gregory's is known to have been in existence. But the argument turns on a passage in the supposed 'foundation charter' (Brett and Gribbin 2004, no. 1), which is an obvious forgery.

[31] A new edition of the *Gesta pontificum* is said to be forthcoming; for the moment I continue to rely on Hamilton's (1870) edition. This was based on the autograph original, the manuscript which he called A (Oxford, Magdalen College 172). For the other four manuscripts collated by Hamilton, the textual relationships are (approximately) as follows: B and C reflect A's original state; E reflects a second state, not earlier than 1136; D reflects a third state, not earlier than 1140; a few alterations in A are later still. E was corrected, after 1158, to bring it into line with the latest state of A, but in its uncorrected form was earlier than D, not later. Only this last point was not quite grasped by Hamilton (1870, p. xxii), but the variants he quotes go to prove it. (Since this was written, the new edition has been published (Winterbottom and Thomson 2007).)

[32] *. . . sedit (annis xi) Wiltunensium ante episcopus Elfricus, qui clericis a Cantuaria proturbatis monachos induxit* (ed. Hamilton 1870, p. 32). The words *annis xi*, inserted in A, are absent from B and C but present in E and D; they were no doubt always intended to be part of the text. (It should be noted, by the way, that Willelm had muddled his list of archbishops, putting Ælfric in front of Sigeric, not behind him. He never corrected that error.)

[33] The passage was made to read: *sedit annis xi Wiltunensium prius episcopus Elfricus, qui et ante abbas Abbendoniensis fuerat. De quo quod quidam dicunt, eum in archiepiscopatu Cantuariensi monachos proturbatis clericis posuisse, uerisimile non uidetur: constat enim monachos in aecclesia Sancti Saluatoris fuisse a tempore Laurentii archiepiscopi, qui primus beatissimo Augustino successit, sicut ex epistola Bonefatii papae ad regem Ethelbertum quae inferius ponetur constabit.* The statement that Ælfric had been abbot of Abingdon is incorrect: in fact he was a monk of Abingdon who became abbot of Saint Alban's (Brooks 1984, p. 279, with references, including Ælfric's will).

for the next five hundred years. Nevertheless, with some reluctance, Willelm was now accepting the official theory.

By the 1140s, therefore, the Christ Church monks had decided to forget that their community owed its existence to archbishop Ælfric. They had constructed an imaginary past for themselves, and they had invested their future in it. But that had only happened within the previous twenty years. In the 1120s, whatever the monks may or may not have been saying among themselves, they had not shared their thoughts with outsiders. If even Willelm of Malmesbury – well-informed and favourably disposed towards Christ Church – was allowed to remain in ignorance, we are entitled to assume that ignorance prevailed quite generally. Either the theory had not been invented at all, or else it had not yet been put into circulation.

Here we intersect with one of the preoccupations of C3's compiler. Whatever the original documents might say or fail to say, the compiler was determined to create the impression that the monastic community had maintained a continuous existence from the very beginning. Over and over again, he includes a phrase – *ad opus monachorum ibidem deo seruientium*, or something similar – asserting that some donation to Christ Church was intended specifically to benefit the monks, the monks who were there at the time and their successors. In this aspect, the cartulary is a piece of pseudo-historical propaganda. Over and over again, moreover, the compiler includes a curse, sometimes borrowing it from the original that he has in front of him, but usually inventing his own form of words – a threat that anyone infringing the terms of the donation is sure to go to hell. By deliberately repeating himself in paragraph after paragraph, the compiler drives his message home: these donations were meant for the monks, and any person who disregards that fact is inviting his own damnation.

There was, during the 1120s, a period when the Christ Church monks were seriously afraid that they might be evicted from their church. After the death of archbishop Radulf in October 1122, it soon became clear that the next archbishop was not going to be a monk, and the monks got it into their heads that without a monk as archbishop their own future would be in jeopardy (Bethell 1969). Their fears proved to be groundless;[34] but for a while the sense of panic was strongly felt. The early 1120s were a difficult time for the Christ Church monks. The pope had turned against them; the archbishop of York was thumbing his nose at them; the monks of Saint Augustine's were ringing their bells whenever they pleased, without waiting for the Christ Church bells to ring first; and the new archbishop was a stranger, not even a monk, imposed on them against their will. It seems to me that C3 was compiled in about 1125–30, while the monks of Christ Church were still recovering from the shock of the election of archbishop Willelm.

In its earliest form, C3 invites comparison with a shorter text from Rochester, which also served as a calendar of the church's archive.[35] This text begins with an entry recording a donation made in 738 by Eadberht king of the Cantware (Campbell 1973, no. 3) and ends with an entry recording a donation by Willelm II (Davis 1913, no. 400). On the face of it, the list was drawn up after the death of Willelm II but before the death of Henric I, i.e. in the interval 1100×35. But the dating can be tightened up slightly, because the cartulary into which this text was copied is fairly sure to be earlier than 1130.[36] The entries here take this basic form: *Anno ab incarnatione domini ... ... rex ... dedit aecclesiae sancti Andreae ... et commendauit ... episcopo.* The date is sometimes omitted, but the name of the bishop to whom the land was 'commended' is consistently included. As in C3, the compiler is putting his own interpretation on the documents that he mentions; as in C3, he makes his point by repetition – specifically by repetition of the word *commendauit*. He is insisting on the distinction between the church, which exists forever, and the bishop, who is its trustee for the time being. As at Christ Church, that distinction became critical in the 1120s, when the Rochester monks found themselves cohabiting with a bishop who was not a monk, but I do not know that anyone would have thought that it needed to be emphasized before then.[37]

Over some uncertain length of time, a series of additions and interpolations made in C3 (Table 24) resulted in state C3/C5, the state existing when the next copy was made. Some of these additions are in keeping with the purpose originally intended for C3; some are not.[38] The two texts added right at the end, though both have been much misunderstood, are not really very hard to make sense of. One is the list printed from T1 by Hoyt (1962, pp. 199–202). In that manuscript it carries the title (supplied by scribe 2) *Sulinges maneriorum archiepiscopatus Cantuariensis in Cancia*, 'Sulungs of the manors of the archbishopric of Canterbury in Kent'; the only other known copy is

[34] Here again, Willelm of Malmesbury acted as a spokesman for the Christ Church monks. Writing soon after the event, he included some angry remarks about the conduct of the election, and about the character of the new archbishop (ed. Hamilton 1870, p. 146); but later he suppressed these remarks (the passage was erased from A and is missing from E and D).

[35] R1, fos. 215r–16r. There are later versions of this list, beginning with the one which appears in a quire inserted into the same cartulary in the late twelfth century (fos. 177r–8r).

[36] As I have argued elsewhere (Flight 1997a, p. 31), the cartulary dates from 1122×30, the later bound being based on negative evidence – the absence of any mention of Boxley church, given to Rochester in 1130.

[37] One other point of resemblance to C3 is striking. This Rochester text has marginal notes giving obits for Offa (fo. 215r, 12 August), and for three recent benefactors, Willelm I, Willelm II and Lanfranc (fo. 216r). In C3/C5, similarly, there is a solitary note (perhaps marginal in C3 itself) giving obits for king Eadbald and his mother Berta (Fleming 1997, p. 109). Of course it is true that a list like this does have a commemorative aspect, but I hardly think that one can press that point as far as Fleming (1997, pp. 102–6) proposes.

[38] The text interpolated near the end (beginning *Hee sunt consuetudines ...*) is an interesting account of the assets of Newington church. The gist of it was reported by Du Boulay (1966, pp. 176–7); the text itself was printed, very inaccurately, by Fleming (1997, pp. 151–2). I have thought it worth printing again (above, p. 216).

A1	C5	T1	number in T1	Birch	Sawyer	Fleming	
	11r	152Ar	1			1	Jaffé 1885–8, no. 1998
	24r–v	164v	75		952	64	
	24v–5v	163v–4r	70		914	70	
	27r–v	157r–v	23	311		84	
	27v–8r	156r–v	20	291	1258	85	
	28v	167v–8r	99			87	*Hee sunt consuetudines . . .*
	29r–v	170r	103				*De Derenta, ii sull' . . .*
	29v–33r	170r–2r					*Rex tenet Derteford . . .*

Table 24. Documents absent from A1 but present in C5 and T1.

the one in C5 (which has no title, only a blank line which may have been intended for one). Though Hoyt convinced himself otherwise, this list is obviously derived from DB-Ke chapters 2–4, i.e. the chapters describing the lands of the archbishopric; more immediately, it is derived from the marginal annotation that was added to a transcript of these chapters procured by the monks of Christ Church (above, pp. 92–4). The other text (beginning *Rex tenet Derteford*) is basically an epitome of DB-Ke (excluding chapters 2–4 and chapter 13) reorganized to take account of the fact that since 1088 the bishop of Bayeux has vanished from the scene. In T1 its title is *Item tocius Cancie sulinges ut uidetur*, 'Also, sulungs of the whole of Kent, so it seems'. As well as the copies in C5 and T1, there is a copy of this text in a very much earlier manuscript (C1, fos. 5vc–7ra). This text is of no great importance, but the reader who wishes to know more about it will find it printed and discussed in detail above (chapter 6).

A further series of additions and interpolations (Table 25) – so disparate that they must surely have been made by several different scribes, on several different occasions – resulted in state C3/T1, the state existing when the last copy was made (the latest state, therefore, that we can know about).[39] Only a few of these additions show any regard for C3's original purpose: by this time, C3 had become a general-purpose register, into which any sort of document might be copied, if it seemed sufficiently ancient, if it seemed sufficiently interesting.[40]

In the nature of the case, it is impossible to prove that documents occurring only in T1 were copied by T1 from C3; but there is a presumption in favour of that view, and I can see no indications to the contrary. Scribe 1 seems to keep copying without a break, as far as fo. 177r; when he reaches the end, he makes it clear that he has reached the end, by leaving a whole page blank. That is how he lets us know that he is about to start copying from a different exemplar.[41] Scribe 2, in the additions he made, seems also to be assuming that the text is continuous throughout. Most of the paragraphs peculiar to T1 are treated in the regular way (annotated in the margin, listed in the table of contents), with no hint that they are anything other than an integral part of the text. Towards the end, it is true, the treatment becomes irregular,[42] but I see no significance in this fact, except that the scribes were losing interest. Scribe 1 stopped numbering the paragraphs; scribe 2 wrote brief descriptions of the contents in the margins, guiding readers to the start of each new paragraph, but did not bother to make matching entries in the table of contents.

The final stretch of text in T1 (fos. 172v–7r),[43] all of which (titles included) I take to have been copied from C3/T1, consists of the following paragraphs:

Hee sunt consuetudines archiepiscopi in pascha de presbiteris et ecclesiis (fo. 172v)

Hec sunt que debentur de Sancto Augustino singulis annis Ecclesie Christi (fo. 172v)

Iste ecclesie pertinent ad Sanctum Martinum de Doforis . . . (fos. 172v–3r)

Hec est institucio antiqua ante aduentum domni Lanfranci archiepiscopi (fo. 173r)

Romscot de Eastkent (fo. 173r)

[39] The order in which the documents are listed is the order obtaining in T1: how far this differed from the order obtaining in C3 we cannot tell. (To the extent that they fall into batches, however, it is probably safe to assume that within each batch C3's order was maintained.)

[40] The items numbered 96–8 relate to the question whether it is right for monks to own parish churches: these documents tend to prove that it is not just right but a thoroughly good idea. The items numbered 101–2 are part of the Becket dossier: a version of the 'constitutions of Clarendon', copied from Herbert of Bosham, and a version of some orders issued by the king (Knowles, Duggan and Brooke 1972), largely the same as Willelm of Canterbury's version.

[41] The only point at which one might think of seeing some discontinuity is at fo. 169v, where the scribe, having finished a paragraph (no. 102), leaves the rest of the page (18 lines) blank. But his reason for doing this is clear enough, I think, because the next paragraph is laid out in three columns: the scribe, I take it, preferred to start a new page before starting a new format. This next paragraph (no. 103) is also present in C5 (it is the list printed by Hoyt); so in any case it is not to be thought that a change of exemplar occurred at this point.

[42] The last item in the table of contents is: *CIII. De sullingis maneriorum Archiepiscopatus Cant', et aliorum quorundam* (fo. 148v). The last three words, 'and of some other people', are a forlorn allusion to the epitome of DB-Ke, which scribe 2 found it hard to see the sense of.

[43] The penultimate paragraph is a schedule of the farms due from the monks' manors, the same document that was copied into C4 (above, p. 33).

A1	C5	T1	number in T1	Birch	Sawyer	Fleming	
		152v–3r	7				Jaffé 1885–8, no. 2133
		153r	8				Jaffé 1885–8, no. 2132
		166r	87		1087		
		166r	88				Bates 1998, no. 75
		166r	89				Bates 1998, no. 71
		166r	90				Bates 1998, no. 70
		166r–v	91				Bates 1998, no. 129
		166v	92				Bates 1998, no. 73
		166v	93				Bates 1998, no. 76
		167r	96				*Sunt nonnulli stulto …*
		167r–v	97				Jaffé 1885–8, no. 4761
		167v	98				*Episcopus missam …*
		168r–v	100				*Fulchestan de beneficio …*
		168v–9r	101				*De aduocacione …*
		169r–v	102				*Siquis inuentus fuerit …*
		172r–v					*Hee sunt firme monachorum …*
		172v–7r					*Hee sunt consuetudines …*

Table 25. Documents absent from A1 and C5 but present in T1.

Hec sunt maneria archiepiscopatus (fo. 173r), *Hec sunt maneria episcopi Roffensis* (fo. 173r), *Hec sunt maneria monachorum in Kent* (fo. 173v)

De maneriis archiepiscopatus (fos. 173v–4v), *Incipiunt maneria monachorum in Kent* (fos. 174v–6r), *Incipiunt terre episcopatus Roffensis* (fo. 176r–v)

Per totam ciuitatem Cant' habet rex sacam et socam … (fo. 176v)

Sturssete et Petham reddunt de firma … (fos. 176v–7r)

De militibus archiepiscopi (fo. 177r)

Without exception, the same items all occur in C1. Conversely, with just one exception (see below), all the texts copied into C1 by the main scribe (fos. 1ra–7ra) and by a second scribe (fo. 7rb–c) occur again in T1, in the same sequence.[44]

It does not need to be argued at length that T1 is derived from C1: that much is perfectly obvious. As far as we know, it was the main scribe of C1 who selected these documents (except the last one) and put them into this sequence; it was the second scribe who decided to append a list of the archbishop's knights. Decisions made by those two scribes are what gave the text its shape – the shape which it retains in T1. In detail too, features of the text which are more or less certain to have originated in C1 turn up again in T1. In C1 the entry relating to Ulcombe (the last entry in the section describing the archbishop's own lands) has two words added between the lines, by a later hand (fo. 3va). Somebody reading (perhaps transcribing) this entry came across a mention of king 'E', and decided that he ought to explain who this was, for the benefit of future readers less knowledgeable than himself; so (picking up his pen) in tiny script he inserted the words *s' Ædwardi* (where *s'* stands for *scilicet*, 'namely'). To all appearances, those words came into existence in C1 itself, through a spur-of-the-moment decision made by someone consulting that manuscript. When we find the same words in T1 – corrupted, however, into *sc'i Edmundi* (fo. 174v) – that fact by itself is virtual proof that T1 derives from C1.[45]

The only question, then, is whether T1 was copied from C1 itself, or (as I suppose) from a copy of C1. This is a matter of judgment, not of proof. We may think it unlikely that scribe 1 would have managed to misread *s' Ædwardi* as *sc'i Edmundi* if he had been copying directly from C1; but we cannot think it impossible.[46] All scribes, even the most competent, do silly things now and then. In the end, the best answer seems to be simply this. We know that T1 was being copied from C3, and there is nothing to suggest that the copyist switched to a different exemplar at the point where T1's contents begin to agree with C1's. Given that, the chances are that T1 is a second-hand copy – that this whole stretch of text was first copied from C1 into C3, and then afterwards copied from C3 into T1, along with the rest of C3's contents. It is, by the way, easier to believe that one of the monks might have been given access to C1, for the

[44] The documents added by a third scribe at the end of C1 (fos. 7va–8vb) do not appear in T1. Three explanations are possible: (i) that they were not (though they might have been) copied from C3 into T1, (ii) that they were not (though they might have been) copied from C1 into C3, or (iii) that they were not added to C1 till after C3 had been copied off. The last possibility is chronologically awkward, and I am inclined to rule it out; I see no way of deciding between (i) and (ii).

[45] This evidence was noted by Kreisler (1967, p. 228). Misread as it is in T1, the passage seems to be saying that a man named Ælfer held Ulcombe from the archbishop 'in the time of Saint Edmund'. Scribe 2 has added *Nota* in the margin. It might indeed be a notable fact, if it were not quite wrong.

[46] A similar instance, also noted by Kreisler (1967, p. 209), is a pair of place-names, *Wy, Tænham*, quite distinct in C1 (fo. 1vb), which in T1 have been fused to make *Pittenham* (fo. 173r).

purpose of copying it into the priory's cartulary, than that Kilwardby's clerks might have got their hands on it.

One final complication can be quite briefly disposed of. The single text which is present in C1 but absent from the corresponding section of T1 is the same epitome of DB-Ke (*Rex tenet Derteford* . . .) which T1 has copied once already (fos. 170r–2r), from a previous section of C3. As I understand it, what happened here was this. By the time that it came to be transcribed into T1, C3 contained two copies of this text. The earlier copy, seemingly taken from the original (definitely not from C1),[47] was among the additions made in C3/C5; from there, some time later, it was transcribed into C5. Later again, after C5 had been copied off, somebody decided to transcribe C1 into C3, and by doing so added a second copy of the same epitome. Some time after that, C3 was transcribed into T1. When he came to the first copy of this text, scribe 1 reproduced it as a matter of course. When he came to the second copy, some pages later, he recognized it as another copy of the same text, saw no point in writing it out again, and decided (or was given permission) to omit it. The copy which scribe 1 did make was edited by scribe 2; and it is clear, from some of the corrections inserted by him, that he was checking the text against a C1-like source – either C1 itself or a copy derived from C1.[48] Since we have already concluded that C1 (or most of it) was transcribed into C3, and that C3 (or most of it) was transcribed into T1, it is obvious what the simplest explanation will be: that these corrections came from the copy of C1 in C3. I can see no reason not to be content with that.

[47] The best indication of this is the entry relating to Repton (cf. DB-Ke-12rb46), where C5 and T1 have the correct reading, *Rapintune pro i iugo*, but C1 has *sull'* instead of *iugo* (fo. 6ra).

[48] That these corrections derive (directly or indirectly) from C1 was recognized by Kreisler (1967, pp. 203–6). In the Repton entry (see previous note), scribe 1 had *iugo*, correctly, but scribe 2 changed this to *sull'*; so T1 is affected by an error which occurs (and seems to have originated) in C1.

Appendix II
The Christ Church account of the trial on Penenden Heath

Two documents exist which tell us something about a meeting of the county court of Kent at which archbishop Lanfranc came into collision with the king's brother Odo, earl of Kent as well as bishop of Bayeux. The first is a factual record of the court's proceedings, neutral in tone, surviving as a contemporary copy written by a scribe who is known to have worked for Lanfranc (above, ???). The second is a piece of narrative, frankly partisan, composed at Christ Church long after the event, not demonstrably in existence before about 1120. Which of these documents sounds more likely to be reliable?

For anyone coming to the subject for the first time, it will seem amazing that this question has to be asked. Is the answer not utterly obvious? It *is* obvious; and anyone who wishes to look into the matter more closely should be sure to remember that, despite an edifice of historical scholarship built up over four hundred years which might almost have been designed to hide the fact. Until almost the last moment, I had been intending to ignore the second document. But the reader is entitled to know what all the fuss is about; so I print the text below.

In rather the same way that the search for so-called 'satellites' distracted attention from the primary records of the survey – giving historians the illusion that they were making progress when in fact they were just wandering further and further from the point – much effort has been wasted on derivative versions of this text, all of which are manifestly worthless. There is only one version which has even the shadow of a claim to possess some evidential value; and there is only one copy of this version which has any textual value. The rest is just confusion.

The manuscript in question is a glossed copy of the Epistles of Saint Paul (Manchester, John Rylands University Library, Latin 109) which certainly did once belong to the cathedral priory in Rochester and was probably written there. In 1735 it was owned by the Lincolnshire antiquary Maurice Johnson (1688–1755); after that its next recorded home is at Haigh Hall in Lancashire, in the library of the Earl of Crawford and Balcarres. In 1901 the manuscripts from Haigh Hall were bought for the John Rylands Library, and that is how this book arrived in Manchester. Together with the other Latin manuscripts, it was catalogued by James (1921, vol. 1, pp. 193–4).[1]

[1] I am indebted to Anne Marie Clarkson of the John Rylands University Library for information about the manuscript, and for letting me have excellent scans of the first five pages.

Before it left Rochester, at some uncertain date (apparently not till after an 'ex libris' inscription had been added at the foot of fo. 3r), two stray leaves were tucked in at the front of the book (fos. 1–2),[2] presumably to keep them safe.

These leaves have 27 lines to the page. Two scribes are represented.[3] The first scribe (1r1–2v15), using an early form of Christ Church script, wrote the copy of the text printed below, which begins at the top of the first page and ends halfway down the fourth. The second scribe (2v16–27), using a larger and more developed form of Christ Church script, wrote a copy of a charter of Henric I for archbishop Radulf and the monks of Christ Church (Johnson and Cronne 1956, no. 1055), which begins on the next line and is broken off at the foot of the page (with the words *exquirere deberent*).[4] It seems fairly certain that these two leaves are a fragment of a Christ Church manuscript; it seems probable that they were sent to Rochester in the 1120s, so that the first article – which was of interest to the monks there too – could be copied into the cartulary which was being compiled at that time (R1, fos. 168r–70v). Perhaps the two leaves ought to have been returned to Christ Church, once they had been transcribed; in the event they stayed in Rochester.

The manuscript is in good condition, the script is easy to read, and the text is in satisfactory shape. (It was printed, almost impeccably, by Le Patourel (1948, pp. 21–4); it was printed again, a little less accurately, by Bates (1998, pp. 319–21).) There is only one significant scribal error. In a sentence towards the end, where the context requires the single word *dimidiam*, this copy has the phrase *aut totam aut dimidiam* repeated from the previous sentence. I should have said that this was an obvious error, except that (to my knowledge) it has not been noted before.[5]

Another obvious fact (at least I should have thought it so) is that the text as we have it shows signs of having evolved through three versions, each with its own peroration. As the paragraphs are numbered below, the first version consisted

[2] Anne Clarkson tells me that the manuscript is so tightly bound that it is impossible to tell whether fos. 1–2 are conjoint or not.

[3] The comments which follow are mine, but Tessa Webber permits me to say that she is of a similar opinion. Neither hand is a hand that she recognizes from other Christ Church manuscripts.

[4] This page is reproduced by James (1921, vol. 2, pl. 143).

[5] But it was seen by Philipott (1659, p. 231), who paraphrases this passage correctly but does not make any comment.

of paras. 1–4, the second of paras. 1–6, the third of paras. 1–9. There is a crucial sentence in para. 3, the syntax of which reflects the evolution of the text. At first, I suppose, the sentence read like this:

Et quoniam multa placita de diratiocinationibus terrarum, inter archiepiscopum et praedictum baiocensem episcopum ibi surrexerunt, ...

Then a phrase was inserted which is the cue for paras. 5–6:

Et quoniam multa placita de diratiocinationibus terrarum, et uerba de consuetudinibus legum *inter archiepiscopum et praedictum baiocensem episcopum ibi surrexerunt, ...*

And then another phrase was inserted which is the cue for paras. 7–9.

Et quoniam multa placita de diratiocinationibus terrarum, et uerba de consuetudinibus legum inter archiepiscopum et praedictum baiocensem episcopum ibi surrexerunt, et etiam inter consuetudines regales et archiepiscopales ...

To put it differently, the text as we have it consists of three segments, only rather loosely connected; and each segment has to be evaluated by itself.

The first segment (paras. 1–4) is no more objectionable than one would expect it to be. It is biased, of course, but does not seek to disguise the fact. It is certainly not contemporary – the rude remarks about bishop Odo could not have been written till after he had fallen from power – but need not be very much later. The sentence in which Hugo de Montfort makes a surprise appearance reads like an interpolation, but most of the text could conceivably have been written as early as the 1080s.[6]

Anyone reading this version of the text is sure to ask the same question. Is that all? Two manors (Stoke and Denton) which actually belonged to the church of Rochester, two small manors (Detling and Preston) which were just limbs of the manor of Maidstone, and 'many other small pieces of land' which were not worth mentioning by name? Did Lanfranc accomplish nothing more than that?

Each in turn, the added segments were inspired by a sense that Lanfranc had failed to make the most of his opportunity (the same sentiment which later inspired the various derivative versions). Somebody thought that Lanfranc should have got the court to ratify his church's franchises (paras. 5–6). Somebody thought that Lanfranc should also have got the court to decide how far these franchises were transcended by the king's prerogative, and conversely what the archbishop's entitlements were on manors belonging to the king (paras. 7–9). Perhaps Lanfranc ought to have done these things; but belated attempts to persuade us that he did should rather be taken to imply that he did not. Both segments are manifestly unreliable.[7]

In printing the text, I have not transcribed it quite as tightly as Le Patourel. All through, I substitute 'et' for '&', 'ae' for 'ę', ',' for '.' in mid sentence. (I also use ':', not ';', to represent *punctus elevatus*.) The manuscript's word-division is not always satisfactory (*de esse* for *deesse*, *exprecepto* for *ex precepto*), and a scribe who writes 'indignities' when apparently he means 'in dignities' is not a guide whom we should think of following closely; in this respect I have allowed myself some latitude. I have also made two large changes, dividing the text into paragraphs and dissecting it into its three constituent segments.

Significant variants are cited from R1, but not from any other manuscript.[8] Errors in the previous editions are noted, in case the reader may wish to put them right; they are, as will be seen, all too small to affect the meaning.

The text

(1) Tempore magni regis Willelmi qui anglicum regnum armis conquisiuit, et suis ditionibus subiugauit: contigit Odonem baiocensem episcopum et eiusdem regis fratrem multo citius quam Lanfrancum archiepiscopum in angliam uenire, atque in comitatu de cænt cum magna potentia residere, ibique potestatem non modicam exercere. Et quia illis diebus in comitatu illo quisquam non erat qui tantae fortitudinis uiro resistere posset: propter magnam quam habuit potestatem terras complures de archiepiscopatu cantuarberiae et consuetudines nonnullas sibi arripuit, atque usurpans suae dominationi [a]ascripsit.

(2) Postea uero non multo tempore contigit praefatum Lanfrancum cadomensis aecclesiae abbatem iussu regis in angliam quoque uenire, atque in archiepiscopatu cantuarberiae deo disponente totius angliae regni primatem sullimatum esse. Ubi dum aliquandiu resideret, et antiquas aecclesiae suae terras multas sibi deesse inueniret, et suorum neglegentia antecessorum illas distributas atque distractas fuisse repperisset: diligenter inquisita et bene cognita ueritate, regem quam citius potuit et non pigre inde requisiuit.

(3) Precepit ergo rex comitatum totum absque mora considere, et homines comitatus omnes francigenas et pre-

[6] The opening words have been thought to imply that the king was already dead (Levison 1912, p. 718). A document from Rochester, which begins in a similar way, goes on to say explicitly that Willelm I has now been succeeded by his son: *Tempore uuillelmi regis anglorum magni patris uuillelmi regis eiusdem gentis, fuit quedam contentio inter Gundulfum hrofensem episcopum et Pichot uicecomitem de Grendebruge, ...* (R1, fo. 175v). Even so, I would think it possible that paras. 1–4 were written during the king's lifetime, by an author who was conscious of speaking to posterity.

[7] I leave it to the reader to compare paras. 7–8 with the parallel passages in the records of the survey. (Anyone who tries this will be following a path first trodden by William Lambard (1576, pp. 178–80), who discovered manuscript R1 in 1573, and wrote a note in it to say so. Evidently he reported his discovery to Archbishop Parker: the earliest published reference to R1, and to R1's copy of the text in question here, is a marginal note which appears in some copies of Parker's big book (1572–4) – those copies which have the altered setting of pages 95–8.)

[8] To all appearances, the version which appears in R3 was copied (with alterations) from R1 (it has the same title), and the version which appears in a register compiled for bishop Hamo de Hethe (Maidstone, Centre for Kentish Studies, DRb/Ar2) was copied (with alterations) from R3 (it has the same interpolated passages).

cipue anglos in antiquis legibus et consuetudinibus peritos in unum conuenire. Qui cum conuenerunt, apud pinendenam omnes pariter consederunt. Et quoniam multa placita de diratiocinationibus terrarum, et uerba de consuetudinibus legum inter archiepiscopum et praedictum baiocensem episcopum ibi surrexerunt, et etiam inter consuetudines regales et archiepiscopales quae prima die expediri non potuerunt: ea causa totus comitatus per tres dies fuit ibi detentus.

(4) In illis tribus diebus diratiocinauit ibi Lanfrancus archiepiscopus plures terras quas tunc tenuerunt homines ipsius episcopi, uidelicet herbertus filius iuonis, Turoldus de [b]rouecestra, Radulfus de curua spina, et alii plures de hominibus suis, cum omnibus consuetudinibus et rebus quae ad easdem terras pertinebant super ipsum baiocensem episcopum et super ipsos praedictos homines illius et alios, scilicet, Detlinges, Estoces, Prestetuna, danituna, et multas alias minutas terras. Et super hugonem de monte forti [c]diratiocinauit hrocinges, et broc, et super radulfum de curua spina lx solidatas de pastura in [d]grean. Et omnes illas terras et alias diratiocinauit ita liberas atque quietas, quod in illa die qua ipsum placitum finitum fuit, non remansit homo in toto regno angliae qui aliquid inde [e]calumniaretur, neque super ipsas terras etiam paruum quicquam [f]clamaret.

(5) Et in eodem placito non solum istas praenominatas et alias terras, sed et omnes libertates aecclesiae suae et omnes consuetudines suas renouauit, et renouatas ibi diratiocinauit, soca, saca, toll, team, [g]flymenafyrmthe, grithbrece, foresteal, haimfare, infangenne þeof, cum omnibus aliis consuetudinibus paribus istis uel minoribus istis, in terris, et [h]in aquis, in siluis, in uiis, et in pratis, et in omnibus aliis rebus, infra ciuitatem et extra, infra burgum et extra, et in omnibus aliis locis. Et ab omnibus illis probis et sapientibus hominibus qui affuerunt, fuit ibi diratiocinatum et etiam a toto comitatu concordatum atque iudicatum, quod sicut ipse rex tenet suas terras liberas et quietas in suo dominico: ita archiepiscopus cantuarberiae tenet suas terras omnino liberas et quietas in suo dominico.

(6) Huic placito interfuerunt Goisfridus episcopus constantiensis qui in loco regis fuit, et iustitiam illam tenuit, Lanfrancus archiepiscopus qui ut dictum est placitauit et totum diratiocinauit, Comes cantiae, uidelicet praedictus Odo baiocensis episcopus, Ernostus episcopus de [i]rouecestra, Ægelricus episcopus de cicestra, uir antiquissimus et legum terrae sapientissimus, qui ex precepto regis aduectus fuit ad ipsas antiquas legum consuetudines discutiendas et edocendas, in una quadriga, Ricardus de tunebrigge, Hugo de [j]monte forti, Willelmus de arces, Haimo uicecomes. Et alii multi barones regis et ipsius archiepiscopi, atque illorum episcoporum homines multi. Et alii aliorum comitatuum homines etiam cum toto isto comitatu, multae et magnae auctoritatis uiri francigenae scilicet et angli.

(7) In horum omnium praesentia multis et apertissimis rationibus demonstratum fuit, quod rex anglorum nullas consuetudines habet in omnibus terris cantuariensis aecclesiae, nisi solummodo tres. Et [k]illae tres quas habet consuetudines, hae sunt. Una, si quis homo archiepiscopi effodit illam regalem uiam [l]quae uadit de ciuitate in ciuitatem. Altera, si quis arborem incidit iuxta regalem uiam, et eam super ipsam uiam deiecerit. De istis duabus consuetudinibus qui culpabiles inuenti fuerint, atque detenti dum talia faciunt, siue [m]uademonium ab eis acceptum fuerit, siue non: tamen [n]in secutione ministri regis et per [o]uadimonium, emendabunt quae iuste emendanda sunt. Tertia consuetudo talis est. Si quis in ipsa regali uia sanguinem fuderit, aut homicidium, uel aliud aliquid fecerit quod nullatenus fieri licet, si dum hoc facit deprehensus atque detentus fuerit: regi emendabit. Si uero deprehensus ibi non fuerit, et inde absque uuade data semel abierit: rex ab eo nichil iuste exigere poterit.

(8) Similiter fuit ostensum in eodem placito, quod archiepiscopus cantuariensis aecclesiae in omnibus terris regis et comitis debet multas consuetudines iuste habere. Etenim ab illo die quo clauditur alleluia, usque ad octauas paschae, si quis sanguinem fuderit, archiepiscopo emendabit. Et in omni tempore tam extra quadragesimam quam infra quicunque illam culpam fecerit quae cilduuite uocatur, archiepiscopus aut totam aut dimidiam emendationis partem habebit. Infra quadragesimam quidem totam, et extra: [p]dimidiam emendationem. Habet etiam in eisdem terris omnibus, quaecunque ad curam et salutem animarum uidentur pertinere.

(9) Huius placiti multis testibus multisque rationibus determinatum finem postquam rex audiuit: laudauit, laudans cum consensu omnium principum suorum confirmauit, et ut deinceps incorruptus perseueraret firmiter precepit. Quod propterea scriptum est hic, ut et futurae in aeternum memoriae proficiat, et ipsi futuri eiusdem aecclesiae christi cantuarberiae successores sciant, quae et quanta [q]in dignitatibus ipsius aecclesiae a deo tenere, atque a regibus et principibus huius regni aeterno iure debeant exigere.

Manchester, John Rylands University Library, Latin 109, fos. 1r–2v, without title; R1, fos. 168r–70v, with title in red *De placito apud pinendenam inter lanfrancum archiepiscopum, et odonem baiocensem episcopum*; Le Patourel 1948, pp. 21–4; Bates 1998, pp. 319–21

[a] assc- *with the first* s *erased* : asc- *R1* [b] hr- *R1* [c] diracionauit *R1* [d] *glossed* insula est [e] -umpn- *with* p *erased* : -umn- *R1* [f] -mer- *bates* [g] *extending into the margin* [h] in *om. bates* [i] hr- *R1* [j] -e *om. bates* [k] -e *bates* [l] -e *bates* [m] -dim- *le patourel, bates* [n] ins- *perhaps rightly* [o] -dem- *le patourel* [p] aut totam aut *repeated by error before* dimidiam [q] ind- *wrongly*

Bibliography

Alecto Historical Editions 1986 Alecto Historical Editions (publ.), *Great Domesday* (London, 1986).

Baldwin 1993 R. Baldwin, 'Seasalter: a problem borough in Domesday Kent re-examined', *Archaeologia Cantiana*, 110 (1993 for 1992), 237–67.

Ballard 1920 A. Ballard (ed.), *An eleventh-century inquisition of St Augustine's, Canterbury* (British Academy, Records of the social and economic history of England and Wales IV-2, 1920).

Bandinel 1813 B. Bandinel (ed.), *Monasticon anglicanum*, new ed., parts I–III (London, 1813).

Barnes 1959 R. G. Barnes, 'Lambeth MS. 1212 and the White Book of Canterbury', *Bulletin of the Institute of Historical Research*, 32 (1959), 56–62.

Basire 1800 J. Basire (engr.), *Exemplar libri censualis vocati Domesday Book* (London, 1800).

Bates 1998 D. Bates (ed.), *Regesta regum Anglo-Normannorum: the acta of William I (1066–1087)* (Oxford, 1998).

Berthelet 1543a T. Berthelet (pr.), *Actes made in the session of this present parlyament* (London, 1543).

Berthelet 1543b T. Berthelet (pr.), *The grantes ordinances and lawes of Romeney marshe* (London, 1543).

Bethell 1969 D. Bethell, 'English black monks and episcopal elections in the 1120s', *English Historical Review*, 84 (1969), 673–98.

Birch 1885–93 W. de G. Birch, *Cartularium saxonicum*, 3 vols. (London, 1885–93).

Birch 1887 W. de G. Birch, *Domesday Book: a popular account of the Exchequer manuscript so called* (London, 1887).

Black 2001 S. B. Black, *A scholar and a gentleman: Edward Hasted, the historian of Kent* (Otford, 2001).

Book of fees *The book of fees, commonly called Testa de Nevill*, 3 vols. (HMSO for PRO, 1920–31).

Box 1926 E. G. Box, 'Lambarde's "Carde of this Shyre"', *Archaeologia Cantiana*, 38 (1926), 89–95.

Box 1927 E. G. Box, 'Lambarde's "Carde of this Shyre," third issue, with roads added', *Archaeologia Cantiana*, 39 (1927), 141–8.

Brett 1996 M. Brett, 'The church at Rochester, 604–1185', in N. Yates (ed.), *Faith and fabric: a history of Rochester Cathedral, 604–1994* (Woodbridge, 1996), 1–27.

Brett and Brooke 1981 M. Brett and C. N. L. Brooke (eds.), *Councils and synods, with other documents relating to the English church – volume I, part II – 1066–1284* (Oxford, 1981).

Brett and Gribbin 2004 M. Brett and J. A. Gribbin (eds.), *English episcopal acta – 28 – Canterbury 1070–1136* (Oxford, 2004).

Brooks 1969 N. P. Brooks, *The pre-conquest charters of Christ Church Canterbury* (DPhil thesis, Oxford University, 1969).

Brooks 1984 N. P. Brooks, *The early history of the church of Canterbury* (Leicester, 1984).

Brooks 1994 N. Brooks, 'An edition of the Rochester bridgework list', in N. Yates and J. M. Gibson (eds.), *Traffic and politics: the construction and management of Rochester Bridge, AD 43–1993* (Woodbridge, 1994), 362–9.

Brooks 1995 N. P. Brooks, 'The Anglo-Saxon cathedral community, 597–1070', in P. Collinson, N. L. Ramsay and M. J. Sparks (eds.), *A history of Canterbury Cathedral* (Oxford, 1995), 1–37.

Brooks and Kelly, to appear N. P. Brooks and S. E. Kelly (eds.) *Charters of Christ Church Canterbury* (Anglo-Saxon Charters, to appear).

Calendar of charter rolls *Calendar of the charter rolls preserved in the Public Record Office*, 6 vols. (HMSO for PRO, 1903–27).

Calendar of inquisitions post mortem *Calendar of inquisitions post mortem preserved in the Public Record Office*, 20 vols. (HMSO for PRO, 1904–95).

Calendar of patent rolls *Calendar of the patent rolls preserved in the Public Record Office*, 37 vols. (HMSO for PRO, 1891–1916). – I restrict this citation to the volumes covering the period from 1216 till 1399.

Caley and Ellis 1817–30 J. Caley and H. Ellis (eds.), *Monasticon anglicanum*, new ed., 6 vols. in 8 (London, 1817–30). – Three parts of volume 1 had already been published (Bandinel 1813) before Caley and Ellis took over.

Cam 1930 H. M. Cam, *The hundred and the hundred rolls: an outline of local government in medieval England* (London, 1930).

Cam 1933 H. M. Cam, 'Early groups of hundreds', in J. G. Edwards, V. H. Galbraith and E. F. Jacob (eds.), *Historical essays in honour of James Tait* (Manchester, 1933), 13–25.

Camden 1590 W. Camden, *Britannia*, 3rd ed. (London, 1590).

Camden 1594 W. Camden, *Britannia*, 4th ed. (London, 1594).

Campbell 1973 A. Campbell (ed.), *Charters of Rochester* (Anglo-Saxon Charters I, London, 1973).

Chaplais 1987 P. Chaplais, 'William of Saint-Calais and the Domesday Survey', in J. C. Holt (ed.), *Domesday studies* (Woodbridge, 1987), 65–77.

Cheney 1983 C. R. Cheney, 'Service-books and records: the case of the "Domesday monachorum"', *Bulletin of the Institute of Historical Research*, 56 (1983), 7–15.

Cheney and John 1986 C. R. Cheney and E. John (eds.), *English episcopal acta 3 – Canterbury 1193–1205* (London, 1986).

Cheney and Jones 1986 C. R. Cheney and B. E. A. Jones (eds.), *English episcopal acta 2 – Canterbury 1162–1190* (London, 1986).

Churchill 1929 I. J. Churchill, *Table of Canterbury archbishopric charters* (Camden Miscellany 15, 1929).

Clark 1992 C. Clark, 'Domesday Book – a great red-herring: thoughts on some late-eleventh-century orthographies', in C. Hicks (ed.), *England in the eleventh century: proceedings of the 1990 Harlaxton Symposium* (Stamford, 1992), 317–31.

Clark and Murfin 1995 P. Clark and L. Murfin, *The history of Maidstone: the making of a modern county town* (Stroud, 1995).

Clover and Gibson 1979 H. Clover and M. Gibson (eds.), *The letters of Lanfranc archbishop of Canterbury* (Oxford, 1979).

Collins 1948 A. J. Collins, 'Documents of the Great Charter', *Proceedings of the British Academy*, 34 (1948), 233–79.

Colvin 1964 H. M. Colvin, 'A list of the archbishop of Canterbury's tenants by knight-service in the reign of Henry II', in F. R. H. Du Boulay (ed.), *Documents illustrative of medieval Kentish society* (Kent Records 18, 1964).

Condon and Hallam 1984 M. M. Condon and E. M. Hallam, 'Government printing of the Public Records in the eighteenth century', *Journal of the Society of Archivists*, 7 (1982–5), 348–88.

Cooper 1868 W. D. Cooper, 'John Cade's followers in Kent', *Archaeologia Cantiana*, 7 (1868), 233–71.

Craster 1930 H. H. E. Craster, 'A contemporary record of the pontificate of Ranulf Flambard', *Archaeologia Aeliana* (4), 7 (1930), 33–56.

Cronne and Davis 1968 H. A. Cronne and R. H. C. Davis (eds.), *Regesta regis Stephani ac Mathildis imperatricis ac Gaufridi et Henrici ducum Normannorum 1135–154* (Regesta regum Anglo-Normannorum III, Oxford, 1968).

Crouch 1988 D. Crouch, 'Earl William of Gloucester and the end of the Anarchy: new evidence relating to the honor of Eudo Dapifer', *English Historical Review*, 103 (1988), 69–75.

Cullen, to appear P. Cullen, *The dictionary of Kent place-names* (English Place-Name Society, to appear).

Curia regis rolls *Curia regis rolls preserved in the Public Record Office*, 17 vols. (HMSO for PRO, 1922–91).

Darlington 1955 R. R. Darlington (ed.), 'Wiltshire Geld Rolls', in R. B. Pugh and E. Crittall (eds.), *The Victoria History of the Counties of England: a history of Wiltshire*, vol. 2 (London, 1955), 169–217.

Dart 1726 J. Dart, *The history and antiquities of the cathedral church of Canterbury, and the once-adjoining monastery* (London, 1726).

Davis 1934 B. F. Davis, 'An early alteration of the boundary between Kent and Surrey', *Archaeologia Cantiana*, 46 (1934), 152–5.

Davis 1958 G. R. C. Davis, *Medieval cartularies of Great Britain: a short catalogue* (London, 1958).

Davis 1913 H. W. C. Davis (ed.), *Regesta Willelmi conquestoris et Willelmi rufi 1066–1100* (Regesta regum Anglo-Normannorum I, Oxford, 1913).

Davis and Chibnall 1998 R. H. C. Davis and M. Chibnall (eds.), *The Gesta Guillelmi of William of Poitiers* (Oxford, 1998).

Dodwell 1954 C. R. Dodwell, *The Canterbury school of illumination 1066–1200* (Cambridge, 1954).

Domesday Book Domesday Book, 2 vols. (London, 1783). – The parliamentary edition, printed by John Nichols from a transcript by Abraham Farley.

Douglas 1933 D. C. Douglas, 'Odo, Lanfranc, and the Domesday Survey', in J. G. Edwards, V. H. Galbraith and E. F. Jacob (eds.), *Historical essays in honour of James Tait* (Manchester, 1933), 47–57.

Douglas 1936 D. C. Douglas, 'The Domesday Survey', *History*, 21 (1936), 249–57.

Douglas 1944 D. C. Douglas (ed.), *The Domesday Monachorum of Christ Church Canterbury* (London, 1944).

Du Boulay 1966 F. R. H. Du Boulay, *The lordship of Canterbury: an essay on medieval society* (London, 1966).

Du Cange 1678 Charles du Fresne, sieur de Du Cange, *Glossarium ad scriptores mediae et infimae Latinitatis*, 3 vols. (Paris, 1678). – The Frankfurt edition of 1710 is available on the web at www.uni-mannheim.de /mateo /camenaref/ducange.html.

Dugdale 1655 W. Dugdale, *Monasticon Anglicanum*, vol. 1 (London, 1655).

Dugdale 1662 W. Dugdale *The history of imbanking and drayning of divers fenns and marshes* (London, 1662).

Eales 1985 R. Eales, 'Local loyalties in Norman England: Kent in Stephen's reign', *Anglo-Norman Studies*, 8 (1985, 88–108.

Eales 1992 R. Eales, 'An introduction to the Kent Domesday', in A. Williams and G. H. Martin (eds.), *The Kent Domesday* (London, 1992), 1–49.

ECCO Eighteenth Century Collections Online, accessible (through a subscribing library) at galenet.galegroup .com/servlet/ECCO.

Edelen 1968 G. Edelen (ed.), *William Harrison – The description of England* (Ithaca, 1968). – Based on the second (1587) edition.

EEBO Early English Books Online, accessible (through a participating library) at eebo.chadwyck.com.

Egan 1993 M. Egan, 'Wricklemarsh revisited', *Archaeologia Cantiana*, 110 (1993), 161–76.

Erskine and Williams 2003 R. W. H. Erskine and A. Williams (eds.), *The story of Domesday Book* (Chichester, 2003).

Farrer 1925 W. Farrer, *Honors and knights' fees*, vol. 3 (Manchester, 1925).

Faussett 1862–72 T. G. Faussett, 'Charters of Cumbwell Priory', *Archaeologia Cantiana*, 5 (1862), 194–222, 6 (1866), 190–222, 8 (1872), 271–93. – Faussett adopted the surname 'Godfrey-Faussett' in about 1870.

Feet of fines I. J. Churchill (ed.), *Calendar of Kent feet of fines to the end of Henry III's reign* (Kent Records 15, 1939–56).

Feudal aids *Inquisitions and assessments relating to feudal aids*, 6 vols. (HMSO for PRO, 1899–1920).

Fleming 1997 R. Fleming, 'Christ Church Canterbury's Anglo-Norman cartulary', in C. Warren Hollister (ed.), *Anglo-Norman political culture and the twelfth-century renaissance* (Woodbridge, 1997), 83–155.

Flight 1997a C. Flight, *The bishops and monks of Rochester, 1076–1214* (Kent Archaeological Society Monograph Series VI, Maidstone, 1997).

Flight 1997b C. Flight, *The earliest recorded bridge at Rochester* (British Archaeological Reports, British Series 252, Oxford, 1997).

Flight 1998 C. Flight, 'The earldom of Kent from *c.* 1050 till 1189', *Archaeologia Cantiana*, 117 (1998), 69–82.

Flight 2000 C. Flight, 'Parish churches in the diocese of Rochester, *c.* 1320–*c.* 1520', *Archaeologia Cantiana*, 119 (2000), 285–310.

Flight 2005 C. Flight, 'A list of the holders of land in Kent, *c.* 1120', *Archaeologia Cantiana*, 125 (2005), 361–79.

Flight 2006 C. Flight, *The survey of the whole of England: studies of the documentation resulting from the survey conducted in 1086* (British Archaeological Reports, British Series 405, Oxford, 2006).

Flower and Smith 1941 R. Flower and H. Smith (eds.), *The Parker chronicle and laws (Corpus Christi College, Cambridge, MS 173): a facsimile* (London, 1941).

Fowler 1926 R. C. Fowler, 'The religious houses of Kent', in W. Page (ed.), *Victoria History of the county of Kent*, vol. 2 (London, 1926), 112–242.

Frampton 1915 T. S. Frampton, 'St Mary's, Westenhanger', *Archaeologia Cantiana*, 31 (1915), 82–91.

Franklin 1993 M. J. Franklin (ed.), *English episcopal acta 8 – Winchester 1070–1204* (Oxford, 1993).

Furley 1886 R. Furley, 'The early history of Ashford', *Archaeologia Cantiana*, 16 (1886), 161–78.

Gale 1691 T. Gale (ed.), *Historiae britannicae, saxonicae, anglo-danicae, scriptores XV*, 2 vols. (Oxford, 1691).

Gibson 1978 M. Gibson, *Lanfranc of Bec* (Oxford, 1978).

Gibson 1993 M. Gibson (ed.), 'Vita Lanfranci', in G. d'Onofrio (ed.), *Lanfranco di Pavia e l'Europa del secolo XI* (Rome, 1993), 661–715.

Giraud 1905 F. F. Giraud, 'Notes on an early Cinque Ports charter', *Archaeologia Cantiana*, 27 (1905), 37–43.

Glover 1976 J. Glover, *The place names of Kent* (London, 1976).

Gough 1992 H. Gough, 'Eadred's charter of AD 949 and the extent of the monastic estate of Reculver, Kent', in N. Ramsay, M. Sparks and T. Tatton-Brown (eds.), *St Dunstan: his life, times and cult* (Woodbridge, 1992), 89–102.

Gough 1780 R. Gough, *British topography*, 2 vols. (London, 1780).

Graham 1917–56 R. Graham (ed.), *Registrum Roberti Winchelsey Cantuariensis archiepiscopi*, 2 vols. (Canterbury and York Society 51–2, 1917–56).

Greenstreet 1876 J. Greenstreet, 'Assessments in Kent for the aid to knight the Black Prince, anno 20 Edward III', *Archaeologia Cantiana*, 10 (1876), 99–162.

Greenstreet 1877 J. Greenstreet, 'Fragment of the Kent portion of Kirkby's Inquest temp. Edward I', *Archaeologia Cantiana*, 11 (1877), 365–9.

Greenstreet 1877–83 J. Greenstreet, 'Abstracts of the Kent Fines (*Pedes Finium*), levied in the reign of Edward II', *Archaeologia Cantiana*, 11 (1877), 305–58, 12 (1878), 289–308, 13 (1880), 289–320, 14 (1882), 241–80, 15 (1883), 273–310.

Greenstreet 1878 J. Greenstreet, 'Holders of knight's fees in Kent at the knighting of the king's son, anno 38 Henry III (A.D. 1253–4)', *Archaeologia Cantiana*, 12 (1878), 197–237.

GREx The exchequer's annual accounts, the great rolls (E 372), duplicated by the chancellor's rolls (E 352), cited by year and by the page of the printed text. The earliest roll is an isolated survivor from the reign of Henric I; the main sequence begins with the second year of Henric II. (The 'Red Book' (E 164/2, ed. Hall 1896) contains some excerpts from the lost roll for 1155, but none from any earlier roll.) The rolls for 1130, 1156–8 and 1189 were edited by Hunter (1833, 1844a, 1844b); the rolls for 1159–88 and 1190–1225 have been published (1884–2008) by the Pipe Roll Society.

Grove 1985 A. Grove, 'The lost manor and church of Elnothington', *Archaeologia Cantiana*, 100 (1985), 153–6.

Gullick 1987 M. Gullick, 'The Great and Little Domesday manuscripts', in A. Williams and R. W. H. Erskine (eds.), *Domesday Book studies* (London, 1987), 93–112. – Reprinted in Erskine and Williams (2003).

Gullick and Pfaff 2001 M. Gullick and R. W. Pfaff, 'The Dublin pontifical (TCD 98 [B.3.6]): St Anselm's?', *Scriptorium*, 55 (2001), 284–94.

Haddan and Stubbs 1871 A. W. Haddan and W. Stubbs (eds.), *Councils and ecclesiastical documents relating to Great Britain and Ireland*, vol. 3 (Oxford, 1871).

Hadfield and Maley 1997 A. Hadfield and W. Maley (eds.), *Edmund Spenser – A view of the state of Ireland – from the first printed edition* (Oxford, 1997). – Based on a reprint (1809) of the edition by Ware (1633).

Haines 1930 C. R. Haines, *Dover priory: a history of the priory of St Mary the Virgin, and St Martin of the New Work* (Cambridge, 1930).

Hall 1896 H. Hall (ed.), *The Red Book of the Exchequer* (Rolls Series XCIX, 1896). – The original is E 164/2.

Hallam 1986 E. M. Hallam, *Domesday Book through nine centuries* (London, 1986).

Hallam 1987 E. M. Hallam, 'Annotations in Domesday Book since 1100', in A. Williams and R. W. H. Erskine (eds.), *Domesday Book studies* (London, 1987), 136–50. – Reprinted in Erskine and Williams (2003).

Hamilton 1870 N. E. S. A. Hamilton (ed.), *Willelmi Malmesbiriensis monachi de gestis pontificum Anglorum libri quinque* (Rolls Series 52, 1870). – Edited again by Winterbottom and Thomson (2007).

Hannen 1914 H. Hannen, 'An account of a map of Kent dated 1596', *Archaeologia Cantiana*, 30 (1914), 85–92.

Hannen 1915 H. Hannen, 'Further notes on Phil. Symonson', *Archaeologia Cantiana*, 31 (1915), 271–4.

Hannen 1927 H. Hannen, 'Philipott's Villare Cantianum. A bibliographical note', *Archaeologia Cantiana*, 39 (1927), 149–51.

Hardman 1933 F. W. Hardman, *The pronunciation of Kent place-names* (Walmer, 1933).

Hardwick 1858 C. Hardwick (ed.), *Historia monasterii S. Augustini Cantuariensis* (Rolls Series 8, 1858).

Harris 1719 J. Harris, *The history of Kent*, vol. 1 (London, 1719). – A second volume was projected but never published.

Harrison 1577 W. Harrison, 'An historicall description of the Islande of Britayne', in R. Holinshed, *The firste volume of the chronicles of England, Scotlande, and Irelande* (London, 1577). – Revised for the second edition (1587).

Harvey 1971 S. P. J. Harvey, 'Domesday Book and its predecessors', *English Historical Review*, 86 (1971), 753–73.

Harvey 1975 S. P. J. Harvey, 'Domesday Book and Anglo-Norman governance', *Transactions of the Royal Historical Society* (5), 25 (1975), 175–93.

Haskins 1918 C. H. Haskins, *Norman institutions* (Cambridge, Massachusetts, 1918).

Hasted 1778–99 E. Hasted, *The history and topographical survey of the county of Kent*, 4 vols. (Canterbury, 1778–99).

Hasted 1797–1801 E. Hasted, *The history and topographical survey of the county of Kent*, 2nd ed., 12 vols. (Canterbury, 1797–1801). – Page images accessible through ECCO; searchable text at www.british-history.ac.uk/subject.aspx?subject=5&gid=99. Citations which take the form 'Hasted 1:234' refer to this edition (as reprinted in 1972).

Hastings and Kimball 1979 M. Hastings and E. G. Kimball, 'Two distinguished medievalists – Nellie Neilson and Bertha Putnam', *Journal of British Studies*, 18 (1979), 142–59.

Hearne 1719 T. Hearne (ed.), *Guilielmi Neubrigensis historia, sive chronica rerum Anglicarum* (Oxford, 1719).

Hearne 1728 T. Hearne (ed.), *Liber niger scaccarii*, 2 vols. (Oxford, 1728). – Printed from a transcript of E 164/12, the 'Little Black Book'.

Henshall and Wilkinson 1799 S. Henshall and J. Wilkinson, *Domesday; or, an actual survey of South-Britain … completed in the year 1086* (London, 1799). – This part covers Kent, Suussex and Surrey; ten more parts were projected but never published.

Hershey 2004 A. H. Hershey (ed.), *The 1258–9 special eyre of Surrey and Kent* (Surrey Record Society 38, 2004).

Hildebrand 1884 F. Hildebrand, 'Über das französische Sprachelement im Liber Censualis Wilhelms I. von England', *Zeitschrift für romanische Philologie*, 8 (1884), 321–62.

Holtzmann 1930–1 W. Holtzmann (ed.), *Papsturkunden in England*, vol. 1 (Berlin, 1930–1).

Holtzmann 1935–6 W. Holtzmann (ed.), *Papsturkunden in England*, vol. 2 (Berlin, 1935–6).

Hoyt 1962 R. S. Hoyt, 'A pre-Domesday Kentish assessment list', in P. M. Barnes and C. F. Slade (eds.), *A medieval miscellany for Doris Mary Stenton* (Pipe Roll Society NS 36, 1962 for 1960), 189–202.

Hull 1955 F. Hull, 'The lathe in the early sixteenth century', *Archaeologia Cantiana*, 68 (1955), 97–100.

Hunter 1833 J. Hunter (ed.), *Magnus rotulus scaccarii, vel magnus rotulus pipae, de anno tricesimo-primo regni Henrici primi (ut videtur)* (London, 1833). – Reprinted with a list of addenda and corrigenda in 1929.

Hunter 1844a J. Hunter (ed.), *The great rolls of the pipe for the second, third, and fourth years of the reign of King Henry the Second* (London, 1844.). – Reprinted in 1930.

Hunter 1844b J. Hunter (ed.), *The great roll of the pipe for the first year of the reign of King Richard the First* (London, 1844).

Illingworth 1812 W. Illingworth (ed.), *Rotuli hundredorum*, vol. 1 (Record Commission, 1812).

Jackson 1625 R. Jackson (publ.), *The inrichment of the Weald of Kent* (London, 1625).

Jacob 1774 E. Jacob, *The history of the town and port of Faversham, in the county of Kent* (London, 1774).

Jaffé 1885–8 P. Jaffé (ed.), *Regesta pontificum Romanorum*, 2nd ed., 2 vols. (Leipzig, 1885–8).

James 1921 M. R. James, *A descriptive catalogue of the Latin manuscripts in the John Rylands Library at Manchester*, 2 vols. (Manchester, 1912). – Reprinted with corrections in 1980.

James 1932 M. R. James, *A descriptive catalogue of the manuscripts in the library of Lambeth Palace: mediaeval manuscripts* (Cambridge, 1932).

Johnson and Cronne 1956 C. Johnson and H. A. Cronne (eds.), *Regesta Henrici primi 1100–1135* (Regesta regum Anglo-Normannorum II, Oxford, 1956).

Johnson 1755 S. Johnson, *A dictionary of the English language*, 2 vols. (London, 1755).

Jolliffe 1929 J. E. A. Jolliffe, 'The hidation of Kent', *English Historical Review*, 44 (1929), 612–18.

Jolliffe 1933 J. E. A. Jolliffe, *Pre-feudal England: the Jutes* (London, 1933). – Reviewed by Gordon Ward in *Archaeologia Cantiana*, 45 (1933), 290–4. Ward's tone was condescending but mild: he did not foresee the harm this book would do.

Kelly 1995 S. E. Kelly, *Charters of St Augustine's Abbey Canterbury and Minster-in-Thanet* (Anglo-Saxon Charters IV, Oxford, 1995).

Kemble 1848 J. M. Kemble, *Codex diplomaticus aevi saxonici*, vol. 6 (London, 1848).

Kemp 1986–7 B. R. Kemp (ed.), *Reading Abbey cartularies* (Royal Historical Society, Camden Fourth Series 31, 33, 1986–7).

Ker 1957 N. R. Ker, *Catalogue of manuscripts containing Anglo-Saxon* (Oxford, 1957).
Ker 1960 N. R. Ker, *English manuscripts in the century after the Norman Conquest* (Oxford, 1960).
Kerling 1973 N. J. M. Kerling (ed.), *Cartulary of St Bartholomew's Hospital* (London, 1973).
Kilburne 1659 R. Kilburne, *A topographie, or survey of the county of Kent* (London, 1659).
Kirke 1932 E. M. Kirke, 'Index to the Kent Domesday and Domesday Monachorum', in W. Page (ed.), *The Victoria History of the County of Kent*, vol. 3 (London, 1932), 437–52.
Knapton 1978 A. Knapton, 'À la recherche de Marie de France', *Romance Notes*, 19 (1978), 248–53.
Knocker 1934 H. W. Knocker, [Review of Putnam 1933], *Archaeologia Cantiana*, 46 (1934), 217–19.
Knowles 2002 D. Knowles (ed.), *The monastic constitutions of Lanfranc*, rev. C. N. L. Brooke (Oxford, 2002).
Knowles, Duggan and Brooke 1972 M. D. Knowles, A. J. Duggan and C. N. L. Brooke, 'Henry II's supplement to the Constitutions of Clarendon', *English Historical Review*, 87 (1972), 757–71.
Kreisler 1967 F. F. Kreisler, *Domesday Monachorum reconsidered: studies in the genesis of Domesday Book and its relationship to sources and 'satellites'* (PhD thesis, Princeton University, 1967).
Lambard 1568 W. Lambard, *Archaionomia, siue de priscis Anglorum legibus libri* (London, 1568).
Lambard 1576 W. Lambard, *A perambulation of Kent* (London, 1576).
Lambard 1596 W. Lambard, *A perambulation of Kent*, 2nd ed. (London, 1596).
Lambard 1656 W. Lambard, *The perambulation of Kent*, 3rd ed. (London, 1656).
Lambard 1730 W. Lambard, *Dictionarium topographicum et historicum* (London, 1730). – Edited from the autograph manuscript.
Larking 1860 L. B. Larking (ed.), 'Inquisitiones post mortem', *Archaeologia Cantiana*, 3 (1860), 243–74.
Larking 1861 L. B. Larking, 'Notes from the chartulary of the abbey of St Bertin', *Archaeologia Cantiana*, 4 (1861), 203–19.
Larking 1868 L. B. Larking, 'On the heart-shrine in Leybourne church, and the family of de Leybourne', *Archaeologia Cantiana*, 7 (1868), 329–41.
Larking 1869 L. B. Larking (ed.), *The Domesday Book of Kent* (London, 1869).
Lawrence 1983 M. Lawrence, 'A Saxon royal manor, Burr's Oak Farm, East Peckham', *Archaeologia Cantiana*, 98 (1983), 253–5.
Lawson and Killingray 2004 T. Lawson and D. Killingray (eds.), *An historical atlas of Kent* (Chichester, 2004).
Leigh and Sotheby 1807 Leigh and Sotheby (publ.), *A catalogue of the duplicates and a considerable portion of the library of Sir John Sebright, bart. ... which will be sold by auction ... on Monday, April 6th, 1807, and six following days* (London, 1807).
Lemon 1856 R. Lemon (ed.), *Calendar of state papers, domestic series, of the reigns of Edward VI, Mary, Elizabeth 1547–80* (London, 1856).
Le Patourel 1948 J. Le Patourel, 'The reports of the trial on Penenden Heath', in R. W. Hunt, W. A. Pantin and R. W. Southern (eds.), *Studies in medieval history presented to Frederick Maurice Powicke* (Oxford, 1948), 15–26.
Levison 1912 W. Levison, 'A report on the Penenden trial', *English Historical Review*, 27 (1912), 717–20.
Lewis 1723 J. Lewis, *The history and antiquities ecclesiastical and civil of the Isle of Tenet in Kent* (London, 1723). – A second edition, 'with additions', appeared in 1736.
Livett 1938 G. M. Livett, 'Early Kent maps (sixteenth century)', *Archaeologia Cantiana*, 49 (1938), 247–77. – With a 'supplementary note' in the next volume.
Luard 1864–9 H. R. Luard (ed.), *Annales monastici*, 5 vols. (Rolls Series 36, 1864–9).
MacMichael 1963 N. H. MacMichael, 'Filston in Shoreham: a note on the place-name', *Archaeologia Cantiana*, 77 (1963 for 1962), 133–41.
Maitland 1887 sep F. W. Maitland (ed.), *Bracton's note book*, 3 vols. (London, 1887).
Major 1950 K. Major (ed.), *Acta Stephani Langton* (Canterbury and York Society, 1950).
Martin and Martin 2001 D. Martin and B. Martin, 'Westenhanger Castle – a revised interpretation', *Archaeologia Cantiana*, 121 (2001), 203–36.
Moore 1918 N. Moore, *The history of St Bartholomew's Hospital*, 2 vols. (London, 1918).
Morey and Brooke 1967 A. Morey and C. N. L. Brooke (eds.), *The letters and charters of Gilbert Foliot* (Cambridge, 1967).
Morgan 1983 P. Morgan (ed.), *Domesday Book – 1 – Kent* (Chichester, 1983).
Muhlfeld 1933 H. E. Muhlfeld (ed.), *A survey of the manor of Wye* (New York, 1933).
Neilson 1932a N. Neilson, 'Introduction to the Kent Domesday', in W. Page (ed.), *The Victoria History of the county of Kent*, vol. 3 (London, 1932), 177–200.
Neilson 1932b N. Neilson (ed.), 'The Domesday Monachorum', in W. Page (ed.), *The Victoria History of the county of Kent*, vol. 3 (London, 1932), 253–69.
Newton 1741 W. Newton, *The history and antiquities of Maidstone, the county-town of Kent* (London, 1741).
Nicolson 1696–7 W. Nicolson, *The English historical library*, 2 parts (London, 1696–7).
Norden 1605 J. Norden, *Cantium quod nunc Kent* (1605). – A map of Kent drawn by John Norden for the folio edition of Camden's *Britannia* (1607).
O'Brien 1999 B. R. O'Brien (ed.), *God's peace and king's peace: the laws of Edward the Confessor* (Philadelphia, 1999).
Pächt, Dodwell and Wormald 1960 O. Pächt, C. R. Dodwell and F. Wormald, *The St Albans psalter* (London, 1960).
Page 1932 W. Page (ed.), *The Victoria History of the county of Kent*, vol. 3 (London, 1932).
Palmer 1982 R. C. Palmer, *The county courts of medieval England 1150–1350* (Princeton, 1982).
Parish and Shaw 1888 W. D. Parish and W. F. Shaw, *A dictionary of the Kentish dialect* (Lewes, 1888).

Parker 1572–4 M. Parker, *De antiquitate Britannicae ecclesiae et priuilegiis ecclesiae Cantuariensis, cum archiepiscopis eiusdem 70* (London, 1572). – The title page is dated '1572', but alterations and additions continued being made for at least two years after that.

Patterson 1973 R. B. Patterson (ed.), *Earldom of Gloucester charters: the charters and scribes of the earls and countesses of Gloucester to A.D. 1217* (Oxford, 1973).

Pearson 2001 H. Pearson, 'The Alecto Domesday project', in E. Hallam and D. Bates (eds.), *Domesday Book* (Stroud, 2001), 151–8.

Philipot 1659 J. Philipot, 'The etymology, derivation, and definition, of all the hundreds and parishes mentioned in the map of Kent', in T. Philipott, *Villare Cantianum* (London, 1659), 393–401. – Written in an unaffected, conversational style, very different from the body of the book, by someone who knew, what Thomas Philipott did not know, how Queenborough got its name. I take it that this is the appendix 'collected by John Philipott Esq; father to the authour' which is mentioned on the title page (mistakenly described, however, as a list of the sheriffs of Kent).

Philipott 1659 T. Philipott, *Villare Cantianum: or Kent surveyed and illustrated* (London, 1659). – Written in 1657–8, published in 1659, reissued in 1664 with many alterations (Hannen 1927). The book includes an appendix credited to Philipott's father (Philipot 1659).

Phillimore & Co. 1975–86 Phillimore & Co. (publ.), *History from the sources – Domesday Book – a survey of the counties of England*, 34 vols. in 39 (Chichester, 1975–86). – One supplementary volume was issued in 1982; three volumes containing indexes appeared in 1992.

Philp 1968 B. J. Philp, *Excavations at Faversham, 1965: the royal abbey, Roman villa and Belgic farmstead* (Bromley, 1968).

Philp 2003 B. J. Philp, *The discovery and excavation of Anglo-Saxon Dover* (Dover, 2003).

Plumptre 1861 F. C. Plumptre, 'Some account of the remains of the priory of St Martin's, and the church of St Martin-le-Grand, at Dover', *Archaeologia Cantiana*, 4 (1861), 1–26.

Pollard and Strouts 2005 E. Pollard and H. Strouts, 'The dens of Benenden and a possible early lathe boundary', *Archaeologia Cantiana*, 125 (2005), 43–65.

Putnam 1933 B. H. Putnam (ed.), *Kent keepers of the peace, 1316–17* (Kent Records 13, 1933).

Pynson 1515 R. Pynson (pr.), *Anno Septimo – Henrici viii - Statuta* (London, 1515).

Ragg 1932 F. W. Ragg (transl.), 'Text of the Kent Domesday', rev. W. Page, in W. Page (ed.), *The Victoria History of the county of Kent*, vol. 3 (London, 1932), 203–52.

Rawlinson 1720 [R. Rawlinson], *The English topographer* (London, 1720).

Rees 1975 U. Rees (ed.), *The cartulary of Shrewsbury Abbey* (Aberystwyth, 1975).

Richardson and Sayles 1963 H. G. Richardson and G. O. Sayles, *The governance of medieval England* (Edinburgh, 1963).

Robertson 1956 A. J. Robertson (ed.), *Anglo-Saxon charters*, 2nd ed. (Cambridge, 1956).

Robertson 1880 W. A. Scott Robertson, 'Romney, Old and New', *Archaeologia Cantiana*, 13 (1880), 349–73.

Robertson 1893 W. A. Scott Robertson, 'The old church of St. Martin, at Dover', *Archaeologia Cantiana*, 20 (1893), 295–304.

Round 1899 J. H. Round (ed.), *Calendar of documents preserved in France, illustrative of the history of Great Britain and Ireland* (HMSO for PRO, 1899).

Round 1901 J. H. Round, 'The counts of Boulogne as English lords', *Studies in peerage and family history* (1901), 147–80.

Rule 1884 M. Rule (ed.), *Eadmeri Historia novorum in Anglia* (Rolls Series 81, 1884).

Saltman 1956 A. Saltman, *Theobald archbishop of Canterbury* (London, 1956).

Sanders 1963 I. J. Sanders, *English baronies* (Oxford, 1963). – First published in 1960, reprinted 'with corrections' in 1963.

Sawyer 1955 P. H. Sawyer, 'The "original returns" and Domesday Book', *English Historical Review*, 70 (1955), 177–97.

Sawyer 1962 P. H. Sawyer (ed,), *Textus Roffensis – Part II* (Early English Manuscripts in Facsimile XI, Copenhagen, 1962).

Sawyer 1968 P. H. Sawyer, *Anglo-Saxon charters: an annotated list and bibliography* (London, 1968). – A revised listing is available online through www.trin.cam.ac .uk/kemble.

Saxton 1575 C. Saxton, *Cantii, Southsexiae, Surriae, et Middelsexiae comitatuum … vera descriptio* (London, 1575). – A map of the four south-eastern counties, drawn by Christopher Saxton. (The portion covering Kent is reproduced by Livett (1938).) An anonymous map, *The Shyre of Kent, Diuided into the five Lathes therof* (reproduced by Box 1926 and Livett 1938), was copied from Saxton's map.

Sayers 1966 J. E. Sayers, 'The medieval care and custody of the archbishop of Canterbury's archives', *Bulletin of the Institute of Historical Research*, 39 (1966), 95–107.

Scargill-Bird 1887 S. R. Scargill-Bird (ed.), *Custumals of Battle Abbey* (Camden Society, 1887).

Sheppard 1881 J. B. Sheppard, 'Second report on historical MSS belonging to the Dean and Chapter of Canterbury', *Historical Manuscripts Commission: Appendix to Eighth Report* (London, 1881), 315–55.

Simonson 1596 P. Simonson, *A new description of Kent divided into the fyue Lathes therof: and subdivided into Baylywickes; and Hundredes …* (1596). – A half-inch map of Kent, surveyed and drawn by Philip Simonson (d. 1598).

Smart 1836 B. H. Smart, *A new critical pronouncing dictionary of the English language* (London, 1836).

Smith 1980 D. M. Smith (ed.), *English episcopal acta – 1 – Lincoln 1067–1185* (Oxford, 1980).

Somner 1640 W. Somner, *The antiquities of Canterbury* (London, 1640).
Somner 1652 W. Somner, 'Glossarium', in R. Twysden, *Historiae anglicanae scriptores X* (London, 1652), apparatus, sigs. X3–2D8.
Somner 1660 W. Somner, *A treatise of gavelkind, both name and thing* (London, 1660).
Somner 1693 W. Somner, *A treatise of the Roman ports and forts in Kent*, ed. J. Brome (Oxford, 1693).
Southouse 1671 T. Southouse, *Monasticon Favershamiense in agro Cantiano* (London, 1671). – Not yet available through EEBO, but I am told that it soon will be.
Speed 1611 J. Speed, *The theatre of the empire of Great Britaine* (London, 1611).
Spelman 1626 H. Spelman, *Archaeologus* (London, 1626).
Stapleton 1846 T. Stapleton, 'Observations upon the succession to the barony of William of Arques', *Archaeologia*, 31 (1846), 216–37.
Stenton 1964 D. M. Stenton, *English justice between the Norman Conquest and the Great Charter 1066–1215* (Philadelphia, 1964).
Stevens 1722–3 J. Stevens, *The history of the antient abbeys, monasteries, hospitals, cathedral and collegiate churches*, 2 vols. (London, 1722–3).
Stevenson 1907 W. H. Stevenson, 'A contemporary description of the Domesday Survey', *English Historical Review*, 22 (1907), 72–84.
Stubbs 1879–80 W. Stubbs (ed.), *The historical works of Gervase of Canterbury*, 2 vols. (Rolls Series 73, 1879–80).
Tatton-Brown 1997 T. Tatton-Brown, 'The Abbey precinct, liberty and estate', in R. Gem (ed.), *English Heritage book of St Augustine's Abbey Canterbury* (London, 1997), 123–42.
Teichman Derville 1936 M. Teichman Derville, *The level and the liberty of Romney Marsh* (Ashford, 1936).
Tester 1974 P. J. Tester, 'Excavations at Boxley Abbey', *Archaeologia Cantiana*, 88 (1974), 129–158.
Thomson 1926 G. S. Thomson (ed.), *The Twysden lieutenancy papers, 1583–1668* (Kent Records X, 1926).
Thorn and Thorn 2001 F. Thorn and C. Thorn, 'The writing of Great Domesday Book', in E. Hallam and D. Bates (eds.), *Domesday Book* (Stroud, 2001), 37–72, 200–3.
Thorpe 1865 B. Thorpe (ed.), *Diplomatarium anglicum aevi saxonici* (London, 1865).
Thorpe 1769 J. Thorpe, *Registrum Roffense* (London, 1769).
Thorpe 1788 J. Thorpe, *Custumale Roffense* (London, 1788).
Todd 1812 H. J. Todd, *Catalogue of the archiepiscopal manuscripts in the library at Lambeth Palace* (privately printed, 1812).
Toller 1898 T. Northcote Toller (ed.), *An Anglo-Saxon dictionary* (Oxford, 1898). – Available online through lexicon.ff.cuni.cz/etc/aa_texts.html.
Tottell 1556 R. Tottell (pr.), *Magna charta, cum statutis quae antiqua vocantur, ... quibus accesserunt nonnulla nunc primum typis edita* (London, 1556).
Turner and Salter 1915–24 G. J. Turner and H. E. Salter (eds.), *The register of St Augustine's Abbey Canterbury commonly called the Black Book* (London, 1915–24).
Twine 1590 J. Twine, *De rebus Albionicis, Britannicis atque Anglicis, commentariorum libri duo* (London, 1590).
Twysden 1652 R. Twysden (ed.), *Historiae anglicanae scriptores X ... nunc primum in lucem editi* (London, 1652).
Urry 1967 W. Urry, *Canterbury under the Angevin kings* (London, 1967).
Wallenberg 1934 J. K. Wallenberg, *The place-names of Kent* (Uppsala, 1934).
Ward 1932 G. Ward, 'The list of Saxon churches in the Textus Roffensis', *Archaeologia Cantiana*, 44 (1932), 39–59.
Ward 1933 G. Ward, 'The lists of Saxon churches in the Domesday Monachorum, and White Book of St Augustine', *Archaeologia Cantiana*, 45 (1933), 60–89.
Ward 1934 G. Ward, 'The lathe of Aylesford in 975', *Archaeologia Cantiana*, 46 (1934), 7–26.
Ward 1935 G. Ward, 'The Westenhanger charter of 1035', *Archaeologia Cantiana*, 47 (1935), 144–52.
Ward 1936 G. Ward, 'The Wilmington charter of A.D. 700', *Archaeologia Cantiana*, 48 (1936), 11–28.
Ware 1633 J. Ware (ed.), *A view of the state of Ireland, written ... by Edmund Spenser, Esq. in the yeare 1596* (Dublin, 1633).
Warner and Gilson 1921 G. F. Warner and J. P. Gilson, *Catalogue of western manuscripts in the Old Royal and King's collections*, 4 vols. (London, 1921).
Warnicke 1973 R. M. Warnicke, *William Lambarde, Elizabethan antiquary, 1536–1601* (Chichester, 1973).
Webb 1756 P. C. Webb, *A short account of some particulars concerning Domes-day Book, with a view to promote its being published* (London, 1756).
Webber 1995 T. Webber, 'Script and manuscript production at Christ Church, Canterbury, after the Norman Conquest', in R. Eales and R. Sharpe (eds.), *Canterbury and the Norman Conquest: churches, saints and scholars 1066–1109* (London, 1995), 145–58.
Wilkins 1721 D. Wilkins, *Leges Anglo-Saxonicae ecclesiasticae et civiles* (London, 1721).
Williams and Erskine 1987 A. Williams and R. W. H. Erskine (eds.), *Domesday Book studies* (London, 1987). – Reissued in a smaller format as Erskine and Williams 2003.
Williams and Martin 1992 A. Williams and G. H. Martin (eds.), *The Kent Domesday* (London, 1992).
Williams and Martin 2002 A. Williams and G. H. Martin (eds.), *Domesday Book: a complete translation* (London, 2002).
Winterbottom and Thomson 2007 M. Winterbottom and R. M. Thomson (eds.), *William of Malmesbury – Gesta pontificum Anglorum – The history of the English bishops*, 2 vols. (Oxford, 2007).
Witney 2000 K. Witney (ed.), *The survey of Archbishop Pecham's Kentish manors 1283–85* (Kent Records 28, 2000).

Wolfe 1597 J. Wolfe (publ.), *The charter of Romney Marsh* (London, 1597).
Woodcock 1956 A. M. Woodcock (ed.), *Cartulary of the priory of St. Gregory, Canterbury* (Royal Historical Society, Camden Third Series 88, 1956).
Woodruff 1911 C. E. Woodruff, *A catalogue of the manuscript books in the library of Christ Church Canterbury* (Canterbury, 1911).
Wright and Wright 1966 C. E. Wright and R. C. Wright (eds.), *The diary of Humfrey Wanley 1715–1726* (London, 1966).

Index

All places are in Kent, unless there is some indication to the contrary. Among places in Kent, parish names are distinguished by bold type: every parish church existing at the end of the thirteenth century is listed in this index, even if the place goes unmentioned in the body of the book.

This is not an index to the DB text for Kent. The reader who requires such an index will find one at the end of any of the previous editions of DB-Ke (Larking 1868, Kirke 1932, Morgan 1983, Williams and Martin 1992); the reader who would like to have a copy of the PDF file for chapter 4 has only to ask me for it.

www.ingramcontent.com/pod-product-compliance
Ingram Content Group UK Ltd.
Pitfield, Milton Keynes, MK11 3LW, UK
UKHW061845041026
15591UKWH00015B/915

9 781407 305417